FAWN M. BRODIE

No Man Knows My History

Mrs. Brodie was professor of history at the University of California, Los Angeles. She died in 1981, shortly after completing her last book, *Richard Nixon: The Shaping of His Character*.

Jim Jones
Geana
Poisoned cool
aid

330

Book of Abraham

No Man Knows My History

4 Bro. Hyrum
William leaves (false prophet
Joseph
Don Carlos
Samuel

Joseph
son died
twins died
son - Joseph

Lineola self
learn

282

Brian DAvid Mitchell

JOSEPH SMITH

From an oil painting by Majors, made in Nauvoo

FAWN M. BRODIE

No Man Knows My History

THE LIFE OF
Joseph Smith

THE MORMON PROPHET
Second Edition, Revised and Enlarged

VINTAGE BOOKS

A Division of Random House, Inc.   New York

*To the memory of my cousin
Lieutenant McKeen Eccles Brimhall
killed in France September 20, 1944*

338

Preface

I T was in a funeral sermon that the Mormon prophet flung a challenge to his future biographers. To an audience of ten thousand in his bewitching city of Nauvoo Joseph Smith said on April 7, 1844: *"You don't know me; you never knew my heart. No man knows my history. I cannot tell it; I shall never undertake it. I don't blame anyone for not believing my history. If I had not experienced what I have, I could not have believed it myself."*

Since that moment of candor at least three-score writers have taken up the gauntlet. Many have abused him; some have deified him; a few have tried their hands at clinical diagnosis. All have insisted, either directly or by implication, that they knew his story. But the results have been fantastically dissimilar.

In official Mormon biographies he has been made a prophet of greater stature than Moses. Nineteenth-century preachers made him a lecherous rogue; and twentieth-century chroniclers have been bemused with what they diagnosed as paranoiac delusions. The reason for these disparate opinions is by no means lack of biographical data, for Joseph Smith dared to found a new religion in the age of printing. When he said "Thus saith the Lord!" the words were copied down by secretaries and congealed forever into print.

There are few men, however, who have written so much and told so little about themselves. To search in his six-volume autobiography for the inner springs of his character is to come away baffled. The reason is partly that he dictated all of it to secretaries as the official history of his church. His story is the antithesis of a confession.

Legend has it that shortly before his death he put all his private records in a great copper pot and ordered William Huntington to bury them deeper than a plow's furrow in some obscure corner of Nauvoo. But even if these should miraculously come to light, it is doubtful if they would be any more self-searching than the records already published. For Joseph Smith, like most great natural leaders, seldom wrote or spoke except with an audience in mind. This fact is what makes it so difficult to evaluate his own account of his adolescent life, which was written two decades afterward at the height of his career. And the later years of his journal — in which he wrote repeated denials of polygamy — are no less troublesome, for after his death a dozen women proudly signed affidavits that he had taken them as wives.

Wherever Joseph Smith went he roused a storm, and from his earliest years country newspapers gave him liberal publicity. Copies of these newspapers, some of which antedate all the early Mormon histories, have fortunately been preserved. During his short, tumultuous career Joseph was haled into court more than a score of times, on charges varying from disturbing the peace to treason. Many of the court records are also extant. Thus, it is not that documents are lacking: it is rather that they are fiercely contradictory, and — even more important — that they are scattered from Vermont to California.

The task of assembling these documents — of sifting first-hand account from third-hand plagiarism, of fitting Mormon and non-Mormon narratives into a mosaic that makes credible history, absorbing all the while the long-forgotten realities of religion and politics between 1805 and 1844 — is not a dull one. It is exciting and enlightening to see a religion born. And Joseph Smith's was no mere dissenting sect. It was a real religious creation, one intended to be to Christianity as Christianity was to Judaism: that is, a reform and a consummation.

But the story of Joseph Smith is more than the story of a new religion. If one were unscrupulously selective in choosing details, one could make him out to be not only a prophet, but also a political menace — a dictator complete with army, propaganda ministry, and secret police who created an authoritarian dominion on the American frontier. It is easy to match his unscientific racial theories, his autocratic organization, and his boundless ambition with the theories, organizations, and ambitions of modern dictators. But to be content with drawing such parallels is to reject history for yellow journalism.

It is true that Joseph Smith bucked cherished American traditions — the rigid separation of church and state, the sanctity of private property, and the inviolability of the marriage code. And it was his destruction of an opposition printing press that precipitated his lynching. But it is also true that he was purely a Yankee product and that a great deal that was good in American folklore and thinking found its way into his writings and into his church. The cornerstone of his metaphysics was that virile concept which pervaded the whole American spirit and which was indeed the noblest ideal of Jesus and Buddha, that man is capable of eternal progress toward perfection.

But Joseph's conception of perfection was by no means exclusively spiritual. His kingdom of God upon earth was saturated with the Yankee enthusiasm for earthly blessings. No one more ingeniously than he combined Jewish and Christian mysticism with the goal of perpetual prosperity. "Adam fell that men might be," he wrote, "and men are that they might have joy." And for Joseph Smith joy came, not from melancholy contemplation, but from planning bigger and better cities, building bigger and nobler temples, and creating for himself the nucleus of an American empire.

The source of his power lay not in his doctrine but in his person, and the rare quality of his genius was due not to his reason but to his imagination. He was a mythmaker of prodigious talent. And after a hundred years the myths he created are still an energizing force in the lives of a million followers. The moving power of Mormonism was a fable — one that few converts stopped to question, for its meaning seemed profound and its inspiration was contagious.

Preface to the Second Edition

In the twenty-five years since the first printing of this biography others besides myself have done much digging in documents relative to Joseph Smith's life, and have published considerable material that adds measurably to my own research. These same years have seen also the continuing growth of a considerable clinical literature on human behavior, some of which is decidedly relevant to an understanding of the more baffling aspects of the Mormon prophet's character. However, there is as yet no competent appraisal of Joseph Smith by a psychologist, psychiatrist, or psychoanalyst. I have written a supplement for this edition that is intended to inform the reader of the nature of new historical discoveries, particularly in regard to Joseph Smith's "first vision," and his controversial Book of Abraham. The supplement also includes additional speculation on the nature of his evolution, but it is not intended to be a comprehensive clinical portrait, which would have to be the work of a professional based on much more intimate knowledge of the man than is presently possible.

The new discoveries do not necessitate important revisions in this biography. On the contrary, I believe that the new data tend on the whole to support my original speculations about Joseph Smith's character. The text of this edition contains certain significant additions, but they are not long, and have been woven into the original in a fashion that permits the pagination to remain unchanged. A few specific details shown to be inaccurate by new discoveries have been deleted. Because of the technical difficulties of massive insertion and deletion, I have elected to put the detailed account of new material into the supplement. It should be read as an addition to, and not as a corrective for, the text itself.

Considerable new material relating to the many wives of Joseph Smith has been published; one new listing by Jerald and Sandra Tanner, in their *Joseph Smith and Polygamy* (Salt Lake City, 1969), raises the putative number to eighty-four. Evidence for the additional marriages comes from records of temple "sealings" in Utah. What complicates the use of such evidence is the fact that over two hundred women, apparently at their own request, were sealed as wives to Joseph Smith after his death in special temple ceremonies. Moreover, a great many distinguished women in history, including several Catholic saints, were also sealed to Joseph Smith in Utah. I saw these astonishing lists in the Latter-day Saint Genealogical Archives in Salt Lake City in 1944. I rejected all such names except those like Nancy Hyde and Patty Sessions, where there was additional evidence of some kind of marriage in Nauvoo. I did not consider a Utah temple record by itself to be evidence enough.

So long as it is impossible to distinguish among those women who requested the sealing after Joseph Smith's death, and those who wanted an additional sealing in a Utah temple to further solemnize a ceremony of some sort that had taken place in Nauvoo, I will keep the number of wives tentatively at forty-eight. I cheerfully concede, however, that this list is incomplete and that it may well be expanded, perhaps greatly expanded, should additional new manuscript evidence become available.

In past years I have tried in successive printings to edit out small factual errors as they were pointed out to me. Hopefully, this edition will see the elimination of almost all of them. Of course, I have not changed everything declared to be an error by critics, because I count many of these criticisms subjective, interpretative, and often altogether inaccurate.

Research for this new edition has taken me into a morass of contradictory material I was not eager to step back into. But the experience has proved exhilarating rather than depressing. I have found impressive the indefatigability of many of the young historians of Mormonism, some of whom follow high standards of research. Important material that had been kept buried for generations has been released from the Mormon Church archives in Salt Lake City. The honesty and courage of the editors of the new Mormon journal *Dialogue*, which is uncensored by church leaders, has made possible the dissemination of valuable research that in earlier times would have found no outlet. The fear of church punishment for legitimate dissent seems largely to have disappeared, and I am happy to give specific thanks to several historians who have blossomed in the new climate of liberation.

FAWN M. BRODIE
Pacific Palisades
1970

Acknowledgments

SINCE RESEARCH IN Mormon history is primarily library research, I owe much to the patience and friendliness of librarians at the University of Chicago, the Utah State Historical Society, the Western Reserve Historical Society, the New York Public Library, the New York State Library, and the Library of Congress. The Huntington Library furnished me with a microfilm of early letters of Oliver Cowdery. The county clerks at Chardon, Ohio, and Woodstock, Vermont, went to much trouble to unearth for me early court records involving Joseph Smith and his father.

I am indebted to Dr. Frederick M. Smith, president of the Reorganized Church of Jesus Christ of Latter-day Saints, for permission to examine the letters of Emma Smith and other manuscript material in Independence, Missouri, and am grateful for the many courtesies of Mr. Israel A. Smith and Mr. S. A. Burgess.

Mr. Alvin Smith at the Latter-day Saints Church Historian's Office in Salt Lake City kindly permitted me to examine several early Mormon periodicals. Mrs. Vesta P. Crawford, Mrs. Claire Noall, Mr. Stanley Ivins, and Mrs. Juanita Brooks were notably generous in allowing me to examine the fruits of their own excellent research in early Mormon documents. Dr. Milo M. Quaife and Dr. Dean Brimhall read my manuscript and gave me the benefit of their extensive knowledge of Mormon history and psychology. The map "Mormon Country" was drawn by Mr. Jerome S. Kates.

I have been particularly fortunate in having the friendly assistance of Mr. Dale L. Morgan, whose indefatigable scholarship in Mormon history has been an added spur to my own. He not only shared freely with me his superb library and manuscript files, but also went through the manuscript with painstaking care. He has been an exacting historian and a penetrating critic.

Throughout a period of research and writing extending into seven years I have needed and received the constant encouragement of my husband, Dr. Bernard Brodie. His own special perspective on the Mormon society and his enthusiastic interest in my research were of immeasurable value. He read the manuscript many times, each time effecting some improvement in its literary qualities. But all this was secondary to a more intangible kind of assistance which came from his qualities of judgment and perception and which has affected my whole approach to the book.

F. M. B.

Contents

Illustrations

No Man Knows My History

CHAPTER I

The Gods Are among the People

An old New England gazetteer, singing the charms of Vermont's villages and the glories of her heroes, strikes a discordant note when it comes to Sharon: "This is the birthplace of that infamous impostor, the Mormon prophet Joseph Smith, a dubious honor Sharon would relinquish willingly to another town."

The shame that Sharon once felt has faded with time. The church that Joseph founded is eminently respectable, and the dreamy town in the White River Valley where he was born has long since abandoned hope of being noted for anything else. Near by, on one of the lovely hills of which New England is fashioned, stands a shrine that draws Mormon pilgrims from afar and stops many a passer-by.

Far to the west lie the geographical areas with which Mormonism is generally identified, but one cannot understand the story of its founder without knowing something of Vermont at the turn of the nineteenth century. Joseph Smith was not a mutation, spewed up out of nature's plenty without regard to ancestry or the provincial culture of his state; he was as much a product of New England as Jonathan Edwards. Much about him can be explained only by the sterile soil, the folk magic of the midwives and scryers, and the sober discipline of the schoolmasters.

His ancestors had been in New England for more than a century. Robert Smith had come to Massachusetts in 1638 and John Mack in 1669. But Joseph Smith was born not in Topsfield, Massachusetts, nor in Lyme, Connecticut — where the houses of imported brick and Lombardy poplars were already old, where the cemeteries were spacious and decently maintained — but among the wooded foothills of the Green Mountains. And the migration of his grandparents into Vermont is a story of disintegration not only of a family but of a whole culture.

For the century and a half in which the descendants of Robert Smith lived in Topsfield they were conservative, respectable, active in local politics, and moderately prosperous. Asael Smith, grandfather of the prophet, was the first to respond to the restlessness that followed in the wake of the Revolution. The older social and moral traditions in Massachusetts were cracking as the ideas that had broken the colonies loose from England seeped into the church.

Like many others of the time Asael was avowedly Christian but basically irreligious. "As to religion," he wrote to his children, "I would not wish to point any particular form to you; but first I would wish you to search the Scriptures and consult sound reason. . . . Any honest calling will honor you if you honor that. It is better to be a rich cobbler than a poor merchant; a rich farmer than a poor preacher." *

In middle age he left Massachusetts to clear a farm in the virgin forests of the Green Mountains. With him went his son Joseph (father of the Mormon prophet), a two-hundred-pound youth, six feet tall and handsome, who, Jacob-like, wrestled with only one man whom he could not throw. They chopped and burned, and like their migrant neighbors counted the harvest before the stumps were rotting, and heaped scorn upon the low valleys to the south.

In 1789 a Connecticut minister touring central Vermont wrote: "Words cannot describe the hardships I undergo. People nasty — poor — low-lived — indelicate — and miserable cooks. All sadly parsimonious — many profane — yet cheerful and much more contented than in Hartford — and the women more contented than the men — turned tawney by the smoke of the log huts — dress coarse, and mean, and nasty, and ragged . . . yet the women quiet — serene, peaceable — contented, loving their husbands — their home — wanting never to return — nor any dressy clothes; I think how strange! I ask myself are these women of the same species with our fine ladies? Tough they are, brawny their limbs — their young girls unpolished — and will bear work as well as mules." †

Not long after Perkins recorded his mixed admiration and distaste, Joseph Smith met and married a daughter of this breed.

---

* This letter was dated April 10, 1799. See *Topsfield Historical Society Collections*, Vol. VIII, pp. 92–4.

† Nathan Perkins: *Narrative of a Tour through the State of Vermont, 1789* (Tuttle, 1930), p. 18.

If she too was tawny, tough, and brawny-limbed we cannot know, for Lucy Mack Smith had no portrait made till she was toothless and withered. Pretty she must have been, for her sons were handsome and her daughters married young, but she had known neither luxury nor security. Her father, Solomon Mack, was a son of misfortune.

Although Solomon came from a line of Scotch clergymen, poverty had kept him from the seminary, and he had grown up on a farm without schooling or religion — to use his own words, "like a wild ass's colt." He had fought in the French and Indian War, and then in the Revolution with his two sons, Jason and Stephen. But when his daughter Lucy was married, Solomon was an impecunious and rheumatic old man who rode about the countryside on a side-saddle and talked about writing a memoir of his trials and misadventures.

The surprising thing about Joseph Smith's maternal grandfather is that he actually succeeded, when he was seventy-eight years old, in getting out his chapbook: *A Narrative of the Life of Solomon Mack, containing an account of the many severe accidents he met with during a long series of years, together with the extraordinary manner in which he was converted to the Christian Faith. To which is added a number of Hymns, composed on the death of several of his relations.** That the spelling was bad and the hymns unfortunate was quite overshadowed by the substantial accomplishment of the writing itself. It gave the family status. In later years Lucy could read the book successively to each of her nine children, pointing to it as proof that the Mack blood was something more than common stuff.

And it set a family precedent. The mantle of authorship was to rest not only upon Solomon, the grandfather, but upon Lucy, upon her son Joseph, and in fact upon his son and grandson — an unbroken tradition for five generations. Neither Solomon nor his daughter had much formal schooling, but the impulse to self-expression was strong within them, and the fact that both married schoolteachers compensated in part for the absence of slate and birchrod drilling.

Solomon Mack admitted in his *Narrative* that he had suffered from fits, and this has been pounced upon by biographers eager to explain the supposed aberrations of the grandson in terms of

* Windsor: Printed at the expense of the author, 1810.

a congenital instability. For a long time it was popularly believed that Joseph Smith had inherited a tendency to epilepsy. But the *Narrative* makes clear that the fits followed a head injury that Solomon received late in life when struck by a falling tree.

Actually the Mack family was marked neither by psychoses nor by literary talent, but rather by a certain nonconformity in thinking and action. As religious dissenters they believed more in the integrity of individual religious experience than in the tradition of any organized sect. Solomon in his old age fell into a kind of senile mysticism, with lights and voices haunting his sickbed. Jason Mack, Lucy's eldest brother, ran sharply counter to the religious and economic traditions of New England when he became a "Seeker" and set up in New Brunswick a quasi-communistic society of thirty indigent families whose economic and spiritual welfare he sought to direct.*

Jason, however, has not received the attention from Mormon historians that has been devoted to another of Lucy's brothers. When the stock from which the Mormon prophet sprang is called idle, thriftless, and degenerate, Stephen Mack is cited triumphantly to the contrary. He made a fortune in Detroit and left an estate worth fifty thousand dollars at his death. He had prospered even before he left Vermont, for he furnished Lucy with the dowry which the father could not provide. The thousand dollars he and his partner gave her just after her marriage made the girl — considering that this was Vermont in 1796 — a virtual heiress.

Joseph and Lucy united in their marriage the divergent heterodoxies of their parents, both of which were reactions from Jonathan Edwards's soul-searing Calvinism. "I spent much of my time," Lucy wrote in later years, "in reading the Bible and praying; but, notwithstanding my great anxiety to experience a change of heart, another matter would always interpose in all my meditations — If I remain a member of no church all religious people will say I am of the world; and if I join some one of the different denominations, all the rest will say I am in error. No church will admit that I am right, except the one with which I

* Lucy Smith: *Biographical Sketches of Joseph Smith the Prophet and His Progenitors for Many Generations* (Liverpool, England, 1853), pp. 21, 52.

am associated. This makes them witnesses against each other." *
This was the universal logic of dissent, a conviction shared by
thousands of New Englanders in this period. Lucy had a vigorous though unschooled mind, and her belief was simply the core
of Antinomianism — the inner life is a law unto itself; freedom and integrity of religious experience must at all costs be
preserved.†

Joseph and Lucy spent twenty years together in New England, yet neither joined a denomination or professed more than
a passing interest in any sect. The Methodist revivals in Vermont
in 1810 excited Lucy for a time, but only further convinced
Joseph "that there was no order or class of religionists that knew
any more concerning the kingdom of God than those of the
world."

He reflected that contempt for the established church which
had permeated the Revolution, which had made the federal government completely secular, and which was in the end to divorce the church from the government of every state. In the
New World's freedom the church had disintegrated, its ceremonies had changed, and its stature had declined. Joseph's
father, Asael, had frankly gloried in his freedom from ecclesiastical tyranny. The son remained aloof from any church until
the one organized by his own son, looking instead to his own
dreams—called "visions" by his wife—for spiritual guidance.

Lucy especially was devoted to the mysticism so often
found among those suddenly released from the domination
and discipline of a church. Like her father she accepted a highly
personalized God to whom she would talk as if He were a
member of the family circle. Her religion was intimate and
homely, with God a ubiquitous presence invading dreams, pro-
voking miracles, and blighting sinners' fields. Her children
probably never learned to fear Him.

Had Joseph and Lucy Smith remained in New England for
the second twenty years of their married life they might, like
their grandparents, have settled into respectable oblivion. But
the Revolution, which had uprooted their parents from a cen-

* *Biographical Sketches*, p. 37.
† See John M. Mecklin: *The Story of American Dissent* (New York, 1934), pp. 37,
123.

tury-old New England farm tradition, had wakened the whole Atlantic seaboard people, who stood up to peer over the Appalachians and see for the first time their vast, fruitful hinterland. The call of the Genesee country and the Finger Lakes was already stirring the blood of young New England men when this couple spoke their marriage vows. And events moved slowly but inexorably to push them into the tide that was spilling over into the West.

After six years of tilling a rocky farm in eastern Vermont, they set up a shop in Randolph. Here Joseph Smith, Senior, first heard of the fantastic profits pouring into the laps of speculators who exported the aromatic ginseng, the root of a plant that grew wild in the Green Mountains. New Englanders preferred sarsaparilla, Solomon's-seal, maidenhair, pleurisy root, and skunk cabbage, but ginseng in China was considered a remedy for everything from dizziness to pleurisy. Vermont farmers were selling it for export at two shillings a pound, and a root shaped like the body of a man was guaranteed to sell in China, where it was prized as a cure for declining virility, for two hundred to four hundred dollars.

Joseph invested all his money in a shipment of ginseng. Lucy wrote that the agent entrusted with the cargo returned from China with a chest of money but absconded to Canada, leaving them penniless.* Her husband had recently lost $2,000 in bad debts and owed $1,800 to Boston merchants. To satisfy his creditors he sold the farm for $800, and Lucy made up the difference with her dowry. The family now began its peregrinations, first to Royalton and thence to Sharon, where Joseph rented his father-in-law's farm and supplemented his meager earnings by teaching school in the winter.

Their new home was lonely and isolated, high in the hills above the White River, with wooded knolls rolling away toward the sunset in lush green disarray. Beauty was there, but little promise. The land agents had cruelly tricked their Yankee brothers when they sold them Vermont, for when the hillsides were cleared of timber the farmers discovered that all their toil

---

* This may have been the case, although historians of the time reported that the market at this date was glutted. See Samuel Williams: *Natural and Civil History of Vermont* (Burlington, 1809), Vol. I, pp. 85–6; and George V. Nash: "American Ginseng," *U. S. Dept. of Agriculture Bulletin* No. 16, 1898.

had uncovered only barren soil and boulders. The Smiths, like their neighbors, wearily rolled the great rocks off the fields and piled them up into walls that ran like causeways up, down, and around the hills.

Lucy meanwhile had borne two sons and a daughter, and on December 23, 1805 she gave birth to a third son. No comet appeared in the sky at his coming; no alarums startled the countryside. He was accepted that cold winter night probably with more resignation than delight, and was christened without undue ceremony Joseph Smith, after his father.

The child was born into an insecurity that in a lifetime of thirty-eight years he was never to escape. By his fifth year the family had moved three times, from Sharon back to Randolph, thence again to Royalton, and finally to Lebanon, across the border in New Hampshire. Depression hung over New England, for its commerce was ruined by Jefferson's embargo against England and France and later by the War of 1812, and only a thriving smuggling business around Lake Champlain remained of the formerly lucrative trade with Canada.

Counterfeiters infested the area, duping the unwary and fleeing over the border at the first whisper of pursuit. On the 1st of April 1807 Beniah Woodward passed on to the elder Joseph Smith a false ten-dollar bill, and a fortnight later Abner Hayes paid him thirty-seven dollars in worthless paper. When Joseph launched a complaint in the Woodstock court on April 14, Hayes skipped to Canada, but Woodward paid with thirty-nine stripes and two years at hard labor for this and other misdeeds. Many years later a relative of Woodward took a neat revenge by insinuating that Smith had himself been guilty of making bogus money, and his account was widely believed.*

When the family moved to Lebanon, New Hampshire, its fortunes brightened. Hyrum, the second son, was sent to Moore's Academy in Hanover. But he brought home from school a fever that was devastating the whole countryside in 1813. The popular

---

* See the article signed "Vermonter" in the *Historical Magazine*, November 1870, pp. 315–16. There it is said that Daniel Woodward stated that Smith had been "implicated with one Jack Downing in counterfeiting money, but turned State's evidence and escaped the penalty." I have examined the records of these trials in the Woodstock, Vermont, courthouse. The trial of George Downer, the only name corresponding with Downing, makes no mention of Joseph Smith, and the other trials at which Smith was a witness make it clear that he was a victim, not an accomplice.

remedy was a hot bath made of a decoction of hemlock boughs, but since tubs big enough to hold a man were rare in every village, a coffin-like tub of pine boards was carried from house to house. Small wonder that Vermont had a death toll of six thousand.*

One by one the children of Joseph and Lucy Smith fell ill. The eight-year-old Joseph seemed to recover well enough, though slowly, until one day Lucy was terrified to discover huge infections breaking out upon his shoulder and leg. Herb poultices were as unavailing as the usual prayers, and Lucy finally called in a physician. He bled the boy, plied him with purges, and probed his ugly sores. When the leg infection refused to heal, he talked of amputation, but Lucy fought against the saw and knife with a fury that annoyed but checked the barber-surgeon. He had to content himself with chiseling out a piece of bone below the child's knee.

When the savage operation began, Joseph would not let himself be tied to the bed, nor could the father force whiskey between his lips to stifle the pain. He screamed to his mother to leave the room, lest she should suffer more than he, and Lucy later spread the story of his heroism down the valley. It may have been this suffering that endeared Joseph to his mother above her other children. Great things were expected of the child whose mettle had been tested in so fearsome an ordeal.

When the boy's convalescence seemed tardy, he was sent to an uncle in Salem, where he got the first tang of salt air in his nostrils. Salem he always remembered, and the port city lured him back under singular circumstances twenty-five years later. Now he made a quick recovery and returned to Lebanon with only a barely perceptible limp, which, however, stayed with him for life.

Under the pressure of months of sickness the family's hopes of prosperity collapsed, and the Smiths moved back across the Connecticut River into Vermont. For three years they sowed seed in Norwich and hopefully waited for a harvest from a soil that had long since given up its best. The elder Smith listened ever more avidly to descriptions of the deep black loam and mild climate of Ohio. Finally in 1816, the historic year without a summer, he was rooted out.

* J. A. Gallup: *Epidemic Diseases in the State of Vermont* (Boston, 1815), pp. 72–5.

Snow fell in June; leaves froze on the trees, and the farmers had to replant. Then came in July what Lucy called an "untimely frost," and their crops were again wiped out. Disheartened farmers packed their wagons and moved along the muddy roads to the west. Emigration in this year, called in Vermont folklore "eighteen-hundred-and-froze-to-death," reached its peak for all time. In the train went Joseph Smith, leaving Lucy and eight children, the youngest only a few months old.

Weeks later, when his letter came bidding them pack the buckboard and follow him west, it was not from Ohio, where most Vermonters expected to find the promised land, but from Palmyra in western New York, two thirds the distance from Albany to the great falls of the Niagara. Young Joseph, at ten, was old enough to know that this was not a move to another village over the hills, but a tearing up at the roots. Few men who left Vermont for the West ever came back. Crossing the mountains had the same exciting and frightening finality as crossing the sea on an immigrant ship.

Joseph watched his mother fill the wagon and heard her argue with their creditors over the value of their meager household goods and farm. The land sharks knew the worth of a note from a man gone into the sunset and they hounded Lucy for debts till she was frantic lest she have too little left for food. Alvin was eighteen and Hyrum sixteen, but even they were no match for the men who snooped about the Norwich home offering pittances for the things they prized. The boys stood by in outraged helplessness, miserable and dumb, and ever more eager to see the good new land beyond the mountains where you could dig a six-foot grave and not chip your shovel on a single stone.

Biographers of Joseph Smith have commonly held that western New York was then a wilderness, where wolf packs still roamed and local libraries were rarer than Indian reservations.* But when the buckboard came to a stop in Palmyra, the weary brood looked out upon a town of almost four thousand citizens, twice the size of the village they had left. Canandaigua, twelve miles south, was even bigger, and boasted a twenty-year-old academy, two "respectable private female seminaries," five common schools, three libraries, thirty-nine stores, seventy-six shops,

---

* See especially I. Woodbridge Riley: *The Founder of Mormonism* (New York, 1902), p. 42.

three churches, and paved sidewalks. And Manchester village, on whose borders the Smiths eventually settled, had not only a school and a town library of six hundred volumes, but a woolen mill, a flour mill, a paper mill, and a blast furnace.

Palmyra was booming in 1817 as never before or since. De Witt Clinton had just forced through the New York Assembly a bill providing for the most stupendous engineering feat of his generation, the construction of the 363-mile Erie Canal to connect the Great Lakes with the port of New York. Palmyra was on the surveyed route. Although the canal was to be eight years in the building, farmers already were counting their profits, and land prices across the state were leaping upward. In 1790 unimproved land had sold for two to four shillings an acre; by 1800 it cost between $1.50 and $4. But by 1817 every landowner had become a speculator and was charging $6 an acre for unwanted uplands and $30 to $45 for improved land with a cabin.

In Ohio Joseph Smith, Senior, could have found equally good land for $1.25 an acre; in Manchester township he paid boom prices and began clearing a farm under a crushing burden of debt and the constant threat of foreclosure. He could not know that he had come at the peak of a speculative spiral, that Palmyra, instead of doubling its population in the next decade, would actually shrink by three hundred citizens and remain even a century later a town of little more than four thousand. Ontario County was not the frontier, but relatively settled country, with sixteen taverns on the sixteen-mile road between Canandaigua and Geneva. The Mormon prophet's father was not a Thomas Lincoln, who in that same year was hewing out a farm six hundred miles west in Indiana's isolation.

There were no squatter privileges in western New York, and Smith needed cash to pay the installments on his land. For more than two years he lived in Palmyra, where Lucy opened a small "cake and beer shop," selling gingerbread, boiled eggs, root beer, and oilcloth accessories which she designed and painted. After months of hiring out to farmers, Smith signed a note for a hundred acres of unimproved land two miles south of Palmyra. In one year they made a substantial initial payment, built a log house, and began the arduous task of clearing the forest.

Like their neighbors the Smiths tapped their sugar maples and boiled down the sap for syrup and sugar. They made seven thousand pounds in one season and won the fifty-dollar bounty for top production in the county. But, for all their toil, the making of a profitable farm was a slow and uncertain process. It took three men and a yoke of oxen five weeks to clear and sow a ten-acre field. When the wheat turned yellow between the stumps, the farmers dreamed of reaping forty bushels an acre. But the crude threshing devices — a flail or the bare hoofs of cattle — wasted the kernels, and when the winnowing was done there was no buyer for the product. In 1818 wheat brought only twenty-five cents a bushel in barter value, for in that decade it was seldom a cash crop unless one paid the prohibitive costs of overland transport to Albany.

Harvests were fair from 1817 to 1819 and then excellent until 1824. But debts piled up nevertheless, and one dispossessed settler after another moved on into Ohio, and from there to Indiana, where they bought the farms abandoned by the men whom Illinois had lured still farther west. The greatest migrations were in depression years, 1819 seeing the sale of over five million acres of public land.*

The vast resources of the hinterland stirred the most sluggish fancies, and an optimism that was to become basic in American thinking for a hundred years now swept the United States. A reflection of this optimism was the noisy campaign for public works in the 1820's, which reached its peak with the building of the Erie Canal. When the last load of dirt was hauled away and the last aqueduct finished in 1825, De Witt Clinton filled a bucket with salt water from the Atlantic Ocean and sailed in state, to the sound of guns by day and the light of bonfires by night, to pour it into the fresh waters of Lake Erie. All along the route the settlers drank and feasted and planned the spending of their profits.

In this atmosphere of unbridled anticipation Joseph Smith grew into manhood. Coupled with the optimism was a militant patriotism. The West believed that America was the greatest

* For a detailed picture of the economy and social life of western New York in this period see O. Turner: *History of the Pioneer Settlement of Phelps and Gorham's Purchase* (New York, 1851); William Darby: *A Tour from the City of New York to Detroit* (New York, 1819); Robert Munro: *A View of the Present Situation of the Western Parts of the State of New York* (Frederick-Town, 1804); John Fowler: *Journal of a Tour in the State of New York in the Year 1830* (London, 1831); *History of Ontario County, New York* (Philadelphia, 1876).

of nations because its democracy was based on the laws of nature, and that it would steadily become more perfect and its people more purified until the whole world would follow its example. General Lafayette's tour of the United States in 1825 was the signal for a patriotic orgy. In Joseph Smith's neighborhood, where he arrived in June, "bonfires blazed on hilltops; cannon thundered their salute; old soldiers rushed weeping to his arms; committees met and escorted him to their villages, and hundreds sought the honor of a grasp of his hand." *

Such spectacle and parade mitigated the drudgery that primitive farming methods imposed on the Smith family and their neighbors. But more enduring were the extravagant hopes for prosperity that buoyed up the countryside. The community was unstable, not only because of the lure of cheaper land in Ohio and the general fever of speculation, but also because of the character of the citizens themselves. Emigrants from New England were the adventurous, the discontented, the nonconformists. The old mores that they brought to the young communities were bound to be flexed and distorted by the new freedom.

Nowhere was lapse from the old codes more evident than in the churches, which were racked with schisms. The Methodists split four ways between 1814 and 1830. The Baptists split into Reformed Baptists, Hard-Shell Baptists, Free-Will Baptists, Seventh-Day Baptists, Footwashers, and other sects. Unfettered religious liberty began spawning a host of new religions.

Carried along in the migration had come the flotsam of the godly. There was Isaac Bullard, wearing nothing but a bearskin girdle and his beard, who gathered a following of "Pilgrims" in 1817 in Woodstock, Vermont, half a dozen hills away from the old Smith farm. Champion of free love and communism, he regarded washing as a sin and boasted that he had not changed his clothes for seven years. Forsaking Vermont for the promised land, the Pilgrims crossed the mountains into New York, followed the same long road across the state as had Joseph Smith, and drifted down the Ohio into Missouri.

There was Ann Lee, mother of the Shakers, who called herself the reincarnated Christ and who with her celibate communists had fled New England's wrath. In the religiosely fecund atmosphere of New York State her sect flourished and spread.

* *History of Ontario County,* p. 42.

In 1826 some Shakers built community halls in Sodus Bay, only thirty miles from Palmyra. The young Joseph Smith might have spent an evening at their shuffling processional dance, watching first one and then another break away and whirl dervish-like till they fell exhausted on the floor, uttering an incoherent gibberish generously referred to as "the gift of tongues." Wherever the Shakers settled, there circulated the usual obscene myths, one that they castrated their males; others that they stripped and danced naked in their meetings, indulged in promiscuous debauchery, and practiced infanticide.

For all their incongruity the Shakers had a certain dignity, which came from their cleanly habits and intense industry. Such was not true of the entourage of another female subdivinity ruling in Jerusalem, twenty-five miles from Joseph Smith's home. This was Jemima Wilkinson, the "Universal Friend," who thought herself to be the Christ. Unperturbed by the Palmyra newspaper which unsympathetically prefixed an "anti" and called her a consummate impostor, she governed her colony by revelations from heaven and swore that she would never die. She was a handsome woman with fine eyes and jet-black hair, which curled over the purple robe hanging from her shoulders. Gossip had it that although she could neither read nor write she could recite the whole Bible from its having been read to her. Jemima's chief aide, whom she called the Prophet Elijah, would tie a girdle tight about his waist, and when his belly swelled in protest, he would be filled with prophetic visions.

Two years after the Smiths arrived in Ontario County, rumors stirred the neighborhood that "the Friend" had died and that despite her followers' denials her body was moldering in a Jerusalem cellar. For nine years lawsuits over the disposition of her property troubled the Canandaigua courthouse and kept remembrance of her fresh.*

Eccentrics like Bullard, Ann Lee, and Jemima Wilkinson were only the more conspicuous personalities on the purple fringe of organized religion. The sober preacher trained in the dialectics of the seminary was rare west of the Appalachians.

* For accounts of Jemima Wilkinson, the Shakers in western New York, and Isaac Bullard, see David Hudson: *History of Jemima Wilkinson* (Geneva, New York, 1821); Richard McNemar: *The Kentucky Revival* (New York, 1846); Z. Thompson: *History of Vermont,* Part II, pp. 203–4; and the *Wayne Sentinel* (Palmyra, New York), May 26, 1826.

One found instead faith healers and circuit-rider evangelists, who stirred their audiences to paroxysms of religious frenzy. The Baptists boasted in 1817 that in New York State west of the Hudson there were only three preachers who had ever been to college. The settlers in the old Northwest Territory demanded personality rather than diplomas from the men who called them to God.

Palmyra was the center of what the circuit riders later called the "burnt over" district. One revival after another was sweeping through the area, leaving behind a people scattered and peeled, for religious enthusiasm was literally being burnt out of them. There are no detailed descriptions of the revivals in Palmyra and Manchester between 1824 and 1827, when they were at their wildest; and we cannot be certain that they matched in pathological intensity the famous revivals that had shaken Kentucky at the turn of the century.

Evangelists had swarmed over the hill country, preaching in great open-air camp meetings where silent, lonely frontiersmen gathered to sing and shout. Revivalists knew their hell intimately — geography, climate, and vital statistics — and painted the sinner's fate so hideously that shuddering crowds surged forward to the bushel-box altars to be born again. Hundreds fell to the ground senseless, the most elegantly dressed women in Kentucky lying in the mud alongside ragged trappers. Some were seized with the "jerks," their head and limbs snapping back and forth and their bodies grotesquely distorted. Those who caught the "barks" would crawl on all fours, growling and snapping like the camp dogs fighting over garbage heaps behind the tents.

One preacher wrote to another: "Thousands of tongues with the sound of hallelujah seemed to run through infinite space; while hundreds of people lay prostrate on the ground crying for mercy. Oh! my dear brother, had you been there to have seen the convulsed limbs, the apparently lifeless bodies, you would have been constrained to cry out as I was obliged to do, *the gods are among the people!*" *

Revival conversions were notoriously shortlived. The great evangelist Charles G. Finney noted with dismay that where

---

* See Catherine Cleveland: *The Great Revival in the West, 1797–1805* (Chicago, 1916), p. 93; and Richard McNemar: *The Kentucky Revival*, p. 26.

the excitement had been wildest it resulted in "a reaction so extensive and profound as to leave the impression on many minds that religion was a mere delusion." James Boyle wrote to Finney in 1834: "I have visited and revisited many of these fields, and groaned in spirit to see the sad, frigid, carnal and contentious state into which the churches had fallen . . . within three months after we left them." *

The revivals by their very excesses deadened a normal antipathy toward religious eccentricity. And these pentecostal years, which coincided with Joseph Smith's adolescence and early manhood, were the most fertile in America's history for the sprouting of prophets. In the same decade that young Joseph announced his mission, William Miller proclaimed that Jesus would visit the earth in March 1843 and usher in the millennium. Thousands flocked to his ranks, auctioned off their property, and bought ascension robes. John Humphrey Noyes was converted to the theory that the millennium had already begun, and laid plans for a community based on Bible communism, free love, and scientific propagation. Matthias strode about New York City brandishing a sword and a seven-foot ruler, shouting that he had come to redeem the world. And down in the south of Ohio, Dylks, the "Leatherwood God," proclaimed his divinity to a groveling congregation with shouts and snorts that shook the roof of his tabernacle.

Of these and other prophets only one was destined for real glory. Jemima Wilkinson was forgotten with the division of her property; the Noyes Oneida community degenerated from a social and religious experiment into a business enterprise; and Dylks was ridden out of the Leatherwood country astride a rail. William Miller, although his Adventists are still an aggressive minority sect, never regained face after 1845, when after two recalculations Jesus still failed to come. But Joseph Smith, a century after his death, had a million followers who held his name sacred and his mission divine.

* See Charles G. Finney: *Memoirs* (New York, 1876), p. 78; and *Literary and Theological Review*, March 1838, p. 66.

CHAPTER II
Treasures in the Earth

THE ROAD THAT led Joseph Smith into the career of "prophet, seer, and revelator" is overgrown with a tangle of legend and contradiction. Mormon and non-Mormon accounts seem to conflict at every turn. The earliest non-Mormon documents that mention him at all — an early court record and newspaper accounts — indicate that Joseph reflected the religious independence of his father. The haranguing of the revivalist preachers seems to have filled him only with contempt. But these documents contrast remarkably with Joseph's official biography, begun many years later when he was near the summit of his career. The latter tells the story of a visionary boy caught by revival hysteria and channeled into a life of mysticism and exhortation.

The evidence, however, leaves no doubt that, whatever Joseph's inner feelings, his reputation before he organized his church was not that of an adolescent mystic brooding over visions, but of a likable ne'er-do-well who was notorious for tall tales and necromantic arts and who spent his leisure leading a band of idlers in digging for buried treasure. This behavior is confirmed by the most coldly objective description of young Joseph that remains, which historians have hitherto overlooked or ignored. This description seems also to be the earliest public document that mentions him at all. The document, a court record dated March 1826, when Joseph was twenty-one, covers his trial in Bainbridge, New York, on a charge of being "a disorderly person and an impostor." On the basis of the testimony presented, including Joseph's own admissions of indulging in magic arts and organizing hunts for buried gold, the court ruled him guilty of disturbing the peace.

Four years after this trial Joseph's Book of Mormon appeared, whereupon the local editors in Palmyra, who had never previously considered him worthy of comment, began to explore the vagaries of his youth. The editor of the Palmyra *Reflector*,

[16]

Abner Cole, under the pseudonym Obadiah Dogberry, wrote during 1830 and 1831 a series of articles describing in exuberant detail Joseph's adolescent years.

Later, in 1833, when Joseph's church was rapidly gaining in notoriety and power, a disgruntled ex-Mormon named Hurlbut went about Palmyra and Manchester soliciting affidavits from more than a hundred persons who had known Joseph before he began his religious career. These sworn testimonies, which were published in 1834 by Eber D. Howe in a vitriolic anti-Mormon book called *Mormonism Unvailed,* may have been colored by the bias of the man who collected them, but they corroborated and supplemented the court record and Dogberry's editorials.* Since the story that they relate of Joseph Smith's adolescent years is further substantiated by certain admissions in his own autobiography and in the naïve biography dictated by his mother, it is possible to reconstruct Joseph's youth with a fair degree of accuracy.

Significantly, Joseph Smith's first sketch of his early years took the form of an apology for his youthful indiscretions. Shortly after *Mormonism Unvailed* appeared, he wrote a reply for his church newspaper:

At the age of ten my father's family removed to Palmyra, New York, where, and in the vicinity of which, I lived, or, made it my place of residence, until I was twenty-one; the latter part, in the town of Manchester. During this time, as is common to most or all youths, I fell into many vices and follies; but as my accusers are, and have been forward to accuse me of being guilty of gross and outrageous violations of the peace and good order of the community, I take the occasion to remark that, though, as I have said above, "as is common to most, or all youths, I fell into many vices and follies," I have not, neither can it be sustained, in truth, been guilty of wronging or injuring any man or society of men; and those imperfections to which I allude, and for which I have often had occasion to lament, were a light, and too often, vain mind, exhibiting a foolish and trifling conversation.†

* Since the books and newspapers in which these documents originally appeared are so rare as to be inaccessible to the general reader, the court record, the significant portions of Dogberry's editorials, and the most important affidavits are reproduced in Appendix A.

† *Latter-Day Saints Messenger and Advocate,* Vol. I (Kirtland, Ohio, November 6, 1834), p. 40.

Although fifty-one of Joseph's neighbors signed an affidavit accusing him of being "destitute of *moral character and addicted to vicious habits*," there is no evidence that viciousness was a part of his nature, and his apology can be accepted at full value. Actually he was a gregarious, cheerful, imaginative youth, born to leadership, but hampered by meager education and grinding poverty.

A landlord class was battening on his labor, driving westward helplessly ensnared families like his own. In the Palmyra newspaper he could read of their mortgage sales, six to ten every week on the front page. He lived far enough east to see opulence and parade and not far enough west to escape a crushing burden of debt. His family, having slipped downhill since those early years when his mother's dowry had been the envy of the neighborhood, had lost security and respectability.

But the need for deference was strong within him. Talented far beyond his brothers or friends, he was impatient with their modest hopes and humdrum fancies. Nimble-witted, ambitious, and gifted with a boundless imagination, he dreamed of escape into an illustrious and affluent future. For Joseph was not meant to be a plodding farmer, tied to the earth by habit or by love for the recurrent miracle of harvest. He detested the plow as only a farmer's son can, and looked with despair on the fearful mortgage that clouded their future.

There is, of course, a gold mine or a buried treasure on every mortgaged homestead. Whether the farmer ever digs for it or not, it is there, haunting his daydreams when the burden of debt is most unbearable. New England was full of treasure hunters — poor, desperate farmers who, having unwittingly purchased acres of rocks, looked to those same rocks to yield up golden recompense for their back-breaking toil. "We could name, if we pleased," said one Vermont weekly, "at least five hundred respectable men who do in the simplicity and sincerity of their hearts believe that immense treasures lie concealed upon our Green Mountains, many of whom have been for a number of years industriously and perseveringly engaged in digging it up." *

When these men migrated west, they brought with them the whole folklore of the money-digger, the spells and incantations,

---

* Reprinted in the *Wayne Sentinel* (Palmyra, New York), February 16, 1825.

the witch-hazel stick and mineral rod. But where the Green
Mountains yielded nothing but an occasional cache of counterfeit money, western New York and Ohio were rich in Indian
relics. Hundreds of burial mounds dotted the landscape, filled
with skeletons and artifacts of stone, copper, and sometimes
beaten silver. There were eight such tumuli within twelve miles
of the Smith farm.* It would have been a jaded curiosity indeed
that would have kept any of the boys in the family from spading
at least once into their pitted surfaces, and even the father suc-
cumbed to the local enthusiasm and tried his hand with a witch-
hazel stick. Young Joseph could not keep away from them.

Excitement over the possibilities of Indian treasure, and perhaps buried Spanish gold, reached its height in Palmyra with
the coming of what the editor of the Palmyra *Reflector* called
a "vagabond fortune-teller" named Walters, who so won the
confidence of several farmers that for some months they paid
him three dollars a day to hunt for buried money on their property. In addition to crystals, stuffed toads, and mineral rods, the
scryer's usual paraphernalia, Walters claimed to have found an
ancient Indian record that described the locations of their hidden treasure. This he would read aloud to his followers in what
seemed to be a strange and exotic tongue but was actually, the
newspaper editor declared, an old Latin version of Caesar's
[Cicero's?] *Orations*. The press accounts describing Walters's
activity, published in 1830–1, stated significantly that when he
left the neighborhood, his mantle fell upon young Joseph
Smith.†

Joseph's neighbors later poured out tales of seer stones, ghosts,
magic incantations, and nocturnal excavations. Joseph Capron
swore that young Joseph had told him a chest of gold watches
was buried on his property, and had given orders to his followers "to stick a parcel of large stakes in the ground, several rods
around, in a circular form," directly over the spot. One of the
group then marched around the circle with a drawn sword "to

* For descriptions and locations of the Indian tumuli in western New York see
E. G. Squier: *Antiquities of the State of New York* (Buffalo, 1851), pp. 31, 66, 97, 99;
O. Turner: *Pioneer History of the Settlement of Phelps and Gorham's Purchase* (1851),
p. 216; and *History of Ontario County* (1876), p. 101. The *Palmyra Herald* on August 14, 1822 and the *Palmyra Register* on May 26, 1819 reported discoveries of new
mounds.

† See Appendix A.

guard any assault which his Satanic majesty might be disposed
to make," and the others dug furiously, but futilely, for the
treasure.

Another neighbor, William Stafford, swore that Joseph told
him there was buried money on his property, but that it could
not be secured until a black sheep was taken to the spot, and
"led around a circle" bleeding, with its throat cut. This ritual
was necessary to appease the evil spirit guarding the treasure.
"To gratify my curiosity," Stafford admitted, "I let them have
a large fat sheep. They afterwards informed me that the sheep
was killed pursuant to commandment; but as there was some
mistake in the process, it did not have the desired effect. This, I
believe, is the only time they ever made money-digging a profitable business." *

Joseph's money-digging began in earnest with his discovery
of a "seer stone" when he was digging a well for Mason Chase.
Martin Harris stated that it came from twenty-four feet underground, and Joseph Capron testified that Joseph could see wondrous sights in it, "ghosts, infernal spirits, mountains of gold
and silver." Joseph's wife once described this stone as "not exactly black but rather dark in color," though she admitted to
none of the early uses to which it was put.†

In later years Joseph frankly admitted in his church newspaper and also in his journal that he had been a money-digger,
although, he wrote, it was not particularly profitable as he got

---

* See Appendix A for more complete extracts from these affidavits.

† Emma Smith's description was written in a letter to a Mrs. Pilgrim from Nauvoo,
Illinois, March 27, 1871. It is now in the library of the Reorganized Church in Independence, Missouri. Martin Harris's statement was published in *Tiffany's Monthly*,
1859, pp. 163–70. He said further: "There was a company there in that neighborhood,
who were digging for money supposed to have been hidden by the ancients. Of this
company were old Mr. Stowel — I think his name was Josiah — also old Mr. Beman,
also Samuel Lawrence, George Proper, Joseph Smith, jr., and his father, and his
brother Hiram Smith. They dug for money in Palmyra, Manchester, also in Pennsylvania and other places."

Joseph exhibited his seer stone as late as December 27, 1841. (See Brigham
Young's journal in the *Millennial Star*, Vol. XXVI, p. 119.) After his death it was
taken to Utah. According to Hosea Stout, Brigham Young exhibited to the regents of
the University of Deseret on February 26, 1856 "the Seer's stone with which The
Prophet Joseph discovered the plates of the Book of Mormon." Hosea Stout said it
was almost black, with light-colored stripes. (See the typewritten transcript of his
journal in the Utah State Historical Society Library, Vol. VI, pp. 117–18.)

"only fourteen dollars a month for it." * But that he indulged in all the hocus-pocus attributed to him by his neighbors he vigorously denied.

Crystal-gazing is an old profession and has been an honored one. Egyptians stared into a pool of ink, the Greeks into a mirror, the Aztecs into a quartz crystal, and Europeans into a sword blade or glass of sherry — any translucent surface that made the eyes blur with long gazing. When Joseph Smith first began to use his seer or "peep" stone, he employed the folklore familiar to rural America. The details of his rituals and incantations are unimportant because they were commonplace, and Joseph gave up money-digging when he was twenty-one for a profession far more exciting.

WHEN in later years Joseph Smith had become the revered prophet of thousands of Mormons, he began writing an official autobiography, in which his account of his adolescent years differed surprisingly from the brief sketch he had written in 1834 in answer to his critics. Here was no apology but the beginning of an epic.

When he was fourteen years old, he wrote, he was troubled by religious revivals in the neighborhood and went into the woods to seek guidance of the Lord.

It was the first time in my life that I had made such an attempt, for amidst all my anxieties I had never as yet made the attempt to pray vocally. . . . I kneeled down and began to offer up the desires of my heart to God. I had scarcely done so, when immediately I was seized upon by some power which entirely overcame me, and had such an astonishing influence over me as to bind my tongue so that I could not speak. Thick darkness gathered around me, and it seemed to me for a time as if I were doomed to sudden destruction. But, exerting all my powers to call upon God to deliver me out of the power of this enemy which had seized upon me, and at the very moment when I was ready to sink into despair and abandon myself to destruction — not to an imaginary ruin, but to the power of some actual being from the unseen world, who had such marvelous power as I had never

* *Elder's Journal*, Far West, Missouri, Vol. I (1838), p. 43; and Joseph Smith: *History of the Church*, Vol. III, p. 29. (This history, compiled chiefly from Smith's manuscript journals on the file in Salt Lake City, will hereafter be referred to simply as *History of the Church*.)

before felt in any being — just at this moment of great alarm, I saw a pillar of light exactly over my head, above the brightness of the sun, which descended gradually until it fell upon me.

It no sooner appeared than I found myself delivered from the enemy which held me bound. When the light rested upon me I saw two personages, whose brightness and glory defy all description, standing above me in the air. One of them spake unto me, calling me by name, and said — pointing to the other — *"This is my beloved Son, hear Him."*

My object in going to inquire of the Lord was to know which of all the sects was right, that I might know which to join. No sooner, therefore, did I get possession of myself, so as to be able to speak, than I asked the personages who stood above me in the light, which of all the sects was right — and which I should join. I was answered that I must join none of them, for they were all wrong, and the personage who addressed me said that all their creeds were an abomination in His sight: that those professors were all corrupt; that "they draw near to me with their lips, but their hearts are far from me; they teach for doctrines the commandments of men: having a form of godliness, but they deny the power thereof." He again forbade me to join with any of them: and many other things did he say unto me, which I cannot write at this time. When I came to myself again, I found myself lying on my back, looking up into heaven.*

Lesser visions than this were common in the folklore of the area. Elias Smith, Vermont's famous dissenting preacher, at the age of sixteen had had a strikingly similar experience in the woods near Woodstock, when he saw "the Lamb upon Mt. Sion," and a bright glory in the forest. John Samuel Thompson, who taught in the Palmyra Academy in 1825, had seen Christ descend from the firmament "in a glare of brightness exceeding tenfold the brilliancy of the meridian Sun," and had heard Him say: "I commission you to go and tell mankind that I am come; and bid every man to shout victory!" but Thompson had never described this as anything but a dream. Asa Wild of Amsterdam, New York, had talked with "the awful and glorious majesty of the Great Jehovah," and had learned "that every denomination of professing Christians had become extremely corrupt," that two thirds of the world's inhabitants were about to be destroyed and the remainder ushered into the millennium. "Much more the Lord revealed," Wild had said, "but forbids my re-

* *History of the Church,* Vol. I, pp. 5–7.

lating it in this way. I shall soon publish a cheap pamphlet, my religious experience and travel in the divine life."*

But his own vision, as described by Joseph Smith eighteen years after the event, clearly dwarfed all these experiences. One would naturally expect the local press to have given it considerable publicity at the time it allegedly occurred. And Joseph's autobiography would indeed lead one to believe that his vision of God the Father and His Son had created a neighborhood sensation:

I soon found, however, that my telling the story had excited a great deal of prejudice against me among professors of religion, and was the cause of great persecution, which continued to increase; and though I was an obscure boy, only between fourteen and fifteen years of age, and my circumstances in life such as to make a boy of no consequence in the world, yet men of high standing would take notice sufficient to excite the public mind against me, and create a bitter persecution; and this was common to all the sects — all united to persecute me.

Oddly, however, the Palmyra newspapers, which in later years gave him plenty of unpleasant publicity, took no notice of Joseph's vision at the time it was supposed to have occurred. In fact, Dogberry insisted in the Palmyra *Reflector* on February 1, 1831: "It however appears quite certain that the prophet himself never made any serious pretentions to religion until his late pretended revelation [the discovery of the Book of Mormon]." He noted on February 14 that Joseph's followers in Ohio were claiming he had "seen God frequently and personally," and that "commissions and papers were exhibited said to be *signed* by Christ himself." But he insisted on February 28: "It is well known that Joe Smith never pretended to have any communion with angels until a long period after the *pretended* finding of his book."†

* See the *Wayne Sentinel*, October 22, 1823, for Wild's account. The Elias Smith vision is described in *The Life, Conversion, Preaching . . . of Elias Smith*, written by himself (Portsmouth, New Hampshire, 1816), p. 58. He came originally from Lyme, Connecticut, the home town of Solomon Mack, and migrated to Vermont in the same period that Mack did. Thompson's dream is described in his *Christian Guide* (Utica, New York, 1826), p. 71.

† Palmyra *Reflector* files are in the New York Historical Society; other Palmyra papers are in the New York State Library at Albany. See Appendix A.

Joseph's first published autobiographical sketch of 1834, already noted, contained no whisper of an event that, if it had happened, would have been the most soul-shattering experience of his whole youth. But there are two manuscript versions of the vision between 1831 and the published account in Orson Pratt's *Remarkable Visions* in 1840 which indicate that it underwent a remarkable evolution in detail. In the earlier, which Joseph dictated in 1831 or 1832, he stated that "in the 16th year of my age ... the Lord opened the heavens upon me and I saw the Lord." By 1835 this had changed to a vision of two "personages" in "a pillar of fire" above his head, and "many angels." In the published version the personages had become God the Father and His son Jesus Christ, and the angels had vanished. Joseph's age had changed to fourteen.*

Although Joseph's final dating of the beginning of his mission was fixed at 1820, there is evidence that his mother and brothers, Hyrum and Samuel, apparently did not stop going to their Presbyterian church until September 1828.† Lucy Smith, when writing to her brother in 1831 the full details of the Book of Mormon and the founding of the new church, said nothing about the "first vision." The earliest published Mormon history, begun with Joseph's collaboration in 1834 by Oliver Cowdery, ignored it altogether, stating that the religious excitement in the Palmyra area occurred when he was seventeen (not fourteen). Cowdery described Joseph's visionary life as beginning in September 1823, with the vision of an angel called Moroni, who was said to have directed Joseph to the discovery of hidden golden plates. Significantly, in later years some of Joseph's close relatives confused the "first vision" with that of the angel Moroni.‡

---

* See *Times and Seasons* (Nauvoo, Illinois) March 15, 1842. For the three differing accounts of the vision dictated by Joseph Smith in 1831–2, 1835, and 1839, see Dean D. Jessee's "Early Accounts of Joseph Smith's First Vision," *Brigham Young University Studies*, Vol. IX, 1969, pp. 275–294. For details see the supplement.

† Records of the Presbyterian Church in Palmyra, as filmed in 1969 by Reverend Wesley P. Walters, describe the proceedings on March 3, 10, 24, and 29, 1830, when Lucy Smith and her sons Hyrum and Samuel were suspended from the church for "neglecting public worship and the sacrament of the Lord's supper for the last eighteen months."

‡ Lucy Smith to Solomon Mack, January 6, 1831, in Ben E. Rich: *Scrapbook of Mormon Literature* (Chicago, Illinois, 190?) Vol. I, p. 543. When Lucy wrote her biography of Joseph in 1845, with the collaboration of Martha Coray, she quoted directly from Joseph's published history of the first vision rather than describing

When Joseph began his autobiography, in 1838, he was writing not of his own life but of one who had already become the most celebrated prophet of the nineteenth century. And he was writing for his own people. Memories are always distorted by the wishes, thoughts, and, above all, the obligations of the moment.

If something happened that spring morning in 1820, it passed totally unnoticed in Joseph's home town, and apparently did not even fix itself in the minds of members of his own family. The awesome vision he described in later years was probably the elaboration of some half-remembered dream stimulated by the early revival excitement and reinforced by the rich folklore of visions circulating in his neighborhood. Or it may have been sheer invention, created some time after 1830 when the need arose for a magnificent tradition to cancel out the stories of his fortune-telling and money-digging. Dream images came easily to this youth, whose imagination was as untrammeled as the whole West.

A FEW discerning citizens in Joseph's neighborhood were more amused at his followers than alarmed at the moral implications of his money-digging. One native, in writing his impressions of the boy in later years, recognized certain positive talents: "Joseph had a little ambition, and some very laudable aspirations; the

---

any of it in her own words. For Cowdery's history see *Latter-Day Saints Messenger and Advocate* (Kirtland, Ohio, 1834–5), especially Letter IV, February 1835, p. 78. Joseph's brother William said in a sermon in Deloit, Iowa, June 8, 1884: "It will be remembered that just before the angel appeared to Joseph, there was an unusual revival in the neighborhood. . . . Joseph and myself did not join; I had not sown all my wild oats. . . . it was at the suggestion of the Rev. M——, that my brother asked of God. While he was engaged in prayer, he saw a pillar of fire descending. Saw it reach the top of the trees. He was overcome, became unconscious, did not know how long he remained in this condition, but when he came to himself, the great light was about him, and he was told by the personage whom he saw descend with the light, not to join any of the churches. That he should be instrumental in the hands of God in establishing the true church of Christ. That there was a record hidden in the hill Cumorah which contained the fulness of the Gospel. You should remember Joseph was but about eighteen years old at this time, too young to be a deceiver." (*Saints Herald*, Vol. XXXI, pp. 643–4).

Joseph's cousin George A. Smith made the same kind of error in two sermons in Salt Lake City. See *Journal of Discourses*, Vol. XII, p. 334, and Vol. XIII, p. 78. Edward Stevenson, in his *Reminiscences of Joseph the Prophet* (Salt Lake City, 1893), p. 4, stated that in Pontiac, Michigan, in 1834 he heard the prophet testify "with great power concerning the vision of the Father and the Son." But the manuscript autobiography upon which these reminiscences are based, written in 1891, when describing the same incident spoke only of the "vision of an Angel."

mother's intellect shone out in him feebly, especially when he used to help us solve some portentous questions of moral or political ethics in our juvenile debating club, which we moved down to the old red schoolhouse on Durfee street, to get rid of the critics that used to drop in upon us in the village. And subsequently, after catching a spark of Methodism in the camp meeting, away down in the woods, on the Vienna road, he was a very passable exhorter in the evening meetings."*

This is one of two non-Mormon accounts which indicate that Joseph Smith, for all his enthusiasm for necromancy, was not immune to the religious excitement that periodically swept through Palmyra. His mother wrote that from the first he flatly refused to attend the camp meetings, saying: "I can take my Bible, and go into the woods and learn more in two hours than you can learn at meeting in two years, if you should go all the time." † But it is clear that he was keenly alert to the theological differences dividing the sects and was genuinely interested in the controversies. Although contemptuous of sectarianism, he liked preaching because it gave him an audience. And this was as essential to Joseph as food.

Daniel Hendrix, who helped set type for the Book of Mormon, once wrote that Joseph had "a jovial, easy, don't-care way about him that made him a lot of warm friends. He was a good talker, and would have made a fine stump speaker if he had had the training. He was known among the young men I associated with as a romancer of the first water. I never knew so ignorant a man as Joe was to have such a fertile imagination. He could never tell a common occurrence in his daily life without embellishing the story with his imagination; yet I remember that he was grieved one day when old Parson Reed told Joe that he was going to hell for his lying habits." ‡

Joseph himself spoke frequently of his "native cheery temperament," and it is evident that from an early age he was a friendly, entertaining youth who delighted in performing before his friends. At seventeen he was lank and powerful, six feet tall and moderately handsome. His hair, turning from tow

---

* O. Turner: *History of the Pioneer Settlement of Phelps and Gorham's Purchase,* p. 214.

† *Biographical Sketches,* p. 101.

‡ Letter of Hendrix dated February 2, 1897, published in the *St. Louis Globe Democrat,* as cited in William A. Linn: *The Story of the Mormons* (New York, 1902), p. 13.

color to light brown, swept back luxuriantly from his forehead. Even at this age there was something compelling in his bearing, and older men listened to his stories half-doubting, half-respectful. He never lacked a following.

His imagination spilled over like a spring freshet. When he stared into his crystal and saw gold in every odd-shaped hill, he was escaping from the drudgery of farm labor into a glorious opulence. Had he been able to continue his schooling, subjecting his plastic fancy and tremendous dramatic talent to discipline and molding, his life might never have taken the exotic turn it did. His mind was agile and eager, and disciplined study might have caused his creative talents to turn in a more conventionally profitable direction.

Stephen A. Douglas, also a great natural leader, was in these same years attending the Canandaigua Academy, some nine miles south, and it was there that he took the measure of his own vigorous talents and proceeded to put them to use. The two probably did not meet in their youth, but when their paths crossed years later in Illinois the two men had become, each in his own fashion, the most celebrated figures on the Mississippi frontier.

But whether Joseph's ebullient spirits could ever have been canalized by any discipline is an open question. He had only limited formal schooling after leaving New England. And since he never gained a true perspective of his own gifts, he probably was inclined to regard them as more abnormal — or supernatural — than they actually were. What was really an extraordinary capacity for fantasy, which with proper training might even have turned him to novel-writing, was looked upon by himself and his followers as genuine second sight and by the more pious townspeople as outrageous lying.

WHEN Joseph was eighteen his eldest brother Alvin died in sudden and dreadful agony from what his mother described as an overdose of calomel prescribed by a physician to cure a stomach disorder. Lucy Smith in her narrative mentioned the death briefly and almost philosophically, for twenty years had passed to mitigate her sorrow, but she omitted altogether its curious sequel.

Alvin had been no churchgoer, and the minister who preached his funeral sermon "intimated very strongly that he had gone to hell."* The family's rage against the parson had barely cooled when they heard a rumor that Alvin's body had been exhumed and dissected. Fearing it to be true, the elder Smith uncovered the grave on September 25, 1824 and inspected the corpse. On September 29, and for one week succeeding, he published the following paid advertisement in the *Wayne Sentinel:*

TO THE PUBLIC:

Whereas reports have been industriously put in circulation that my son, Alvin, has been removed from the place of his interment and dissected; which reports every person possessed of human sensibility must know are peculiarly calculated to harrow up the mind of a parent and deeply wound the feelings of relations, I, with some of my neighbors this morning repaired to the grave, and removing the earth, found the body, which had not been disturbed. This method is taken for the purpose of satisfying the minds of those who have put it in circulation, that it is earnestly requested that they would desist therefrom; and that it is believed by some that they have been stimulated more by desire to injure the reputation of certain persons than by a philanthropy for the peace and welfare of myself and friends.

(Signed)   Joseph Smith
Palmyra, September 25, 1824

It is difficult to explain this cruel practical joke as other than someone's attempt to ridicule the digging activities of the Smith family, which had never seriously been interrupted. In fact, by the time he was nineteen young Joseph was beginning to acquire a reputation for being a necromancer of exceptional talent who numbered even his father and brother Hyrum among his followers. His mother wrote that Josiah Stowel (or Stoal) came all the way from Pennsylvania to see her son "on account of having heard that he possessed certain keys by which he could discern things invisible to the natural eye." †

Stowel, an elderly farmer from South Bainbridge (now Afton), New York, had come north to visit relatives and had met Joseph in Palmyra. Simpson Stowel begged him to display his magic talents before the old man, and Joseph, being Simpson's friend, obliged by describing in detail the Stowel "house

---

* Statement of William Smith, young brother of Joseph, in an interview with E. C. Briggs and J. W. Peterson, published in the *Deseret News* (Salt Lake City, Utah), January 20, 1894.

† *Biographical Sketches,* pp. 91–2.

and outhouses" in South Bainbridge. Stowel was so impressed that he begged the youth to go south with him and look for a lost silver mine said to have been worked by the Spaniards in the Susquehanna Valley. He would pay him, he said, fourteen dollars a month and board him free.*

Harvest was over, and the prospect of seeing new country probably attracted Joseph as much as the cash salary. Always loyal to his family, he insisted that his father be included in the arrangement, and they set forth with Stowel for the south. They stopped in the Allegheny foothills, staying for a time in Harmony, Pennsylvania, on the banks of the romantic Susquehanna. Here they boarded with a big, bearish Vermonter named Isaac Hale.

Their host, a famous hunter, spent most of his time in the forests, leaving his wife and daughters to look after the gardens and cows. Joseph was at once attracted to the twenty-one-year-old Emma, a dark, serious-faced girl with great luminous hazel eyes. She was quiet almost to taciturnity, with an unapproachable air to which Joseph, who at twenty was already accounted "a great favorite with the ladies," responded with more than casual attentiveness.

In the beginning Isaac Hale helped subsidize Stowel's expeditions into the mountains, but with the first failures he was quickly disillusioned and shortly became contemptuous. Nine years later he wrote of Joseph, who had by then become his son-in-law: "His appearance at this time, was that of a careless young man — not very well educated, and very saucy and insolent to his father. . . . Young Smith gave the 'money-diggers' great encouragement, at first, but when they arrived in digging to near the place where he had stated an immense treasure would be found — he said the enchantment was so powerful that he could not see. They then became discouraged, and soon after dispersed. This took place about the 17th of November, 1825." †

Eventually Joseph's father went back to Palmyra, but the youth remained on the farm of Josiah Stowel, who seems never to have lost faith in the supernatural talents of his protégé. Joseph worked on the farm, attended school in the winter, and

---

* For Stowel's statement see his testimony in the Bainbridge court trial of 1826, reprinted in Appendix A. See also *History of the Church,* Vol. III, p. 29.

† For Hale's affidavit see Appendix A.

spent his leisure hunting for treasure and riding into Pennsylvania to see Emma Hale.

In March 1826 Joseph's magic arts for the first time brought him into serious trouble. One of Stowel's neighbors, Peter Bridgman, swore out a warrant for the youth's arrest on the charge of being a disorderly person and an impostor. On the witness stand Joseph denied that he spent all his time looking for mines and insisted that for the most part he worked on Stowel's farm or went to school. He admitted, however, that "he had a certain stone, which he had occasionally looked at to determine where hidden treasures in the bowels of the earth were; that he professed to tell in this manner where gold-mines were a distance under ground, and had looked for Mr. Stowel several times, and informed him where he could find those treasures, and Mr. Stowel had been engaged in digging for them; that at Palmyra he pretended to tell, by looking at this stone, where coined money was buried in Pennsylvania, and while at Palmyra he had frequently ascertained in that way where lost property was, of various kinds; that he had occasionally been in the habit of looking through this stone to find lost property for three years, but of late had pretty much given it up on account its injuring his health, especially his eyes — made them sore; that he did not solicit business of this kind, and had always rather declined having anything to do with this business." *

Stowel defended Joseph with great vigor, insisting that he "positively knew" the latter could see valuable treasures through the stone. Once the youth had told him to dig at the roots of an old stump, promising that he would find a chest of money and a tail-feather. At a depth of five feet he had uncovered the tail-feather, only to discover that the money had "moved down."

His testimony, however well-intentioned, did the prisoner more harm than good. Stowel's relatives attacked Joseph bitterly, and the court pronounced him guilty, though what sentence was finally passed the record does not say. Oliver Cowdery's history, the only Mormon account that ever mentioned this trial, denied that Joseph had been found guilty. ". . . some very officious person," Cowdery wrote, "complained of him as a disorderly person, and brought him before the authorities of the

---

* For the complete text of the court record of this trial see Appendix A.

county; but there being no cause for action he was honorably acquitted." *

It would seem that this trial, the first in a long series of crises in his life, shocked Joseph into a sense of the futility of his avocation, for he now gave up his money-digging altogether, although he retained his peepstone and some of the psychological artifices of the rural diviner.

It may be that this renunciation came in part from disillusionment with his own magic. Most bucolic scryers are ignorant, superstitious folk who believe profoundly in their mineral rods and rabbits' feet. Professional magicians, on the other hand, are not naïve. The great anthropologist Sir James Frazer sagely pointed out that in primitive tribes the intelligent novitiate studying to be a medicine man is likely to see through the fallacies that impress duller wits. The sorcerer who believes in his own extravagant pretensions is much more likely to be cut short in his career than the deliberate impostor, and the ablest are those who plan and practice their trickery. Where the honest wizard is taken aback when his charms fail conspicuously, the deliberate deceiver always has an excuse. Certainly Joseph's mentor, the conjurer Walters, belonged to the latter class.

It is clear that Joseph had no desire to make a life profession of emulating Walters. Perhaps he gave up the trickery and artifice just when their hollowness became most evident to him; perhaps his renunciation was due entirely to Emma Hale. But he could not cast off his unbridled fancy and love of theatricalism, which had attracted him to necromancy in the first place.

After the trial he remained for some months with Stowel, for he was now very much in love and reluctant to return to Palmyra without taking with him Emma as his wife. But Isaac Hale, holding Joseph to be a cheap impostor, thundered a refusal when asked for her hand and drove him out of the house. Joseph now made clandestine visits whenever Hale went hunting, and begged the girl to run away with him.

Skeptical, unsure of him, and concerned over their future, she hesitated. But there were only about two hundred people in

* *Latter-Day Saints Messenger and Advocate* (Kirtland, Ohio), October 1835. Cowdery states that this trial took place before 1827. It should therefore not be confused with two later trials in the same area, where Joseph actually was acquitted.

Harmony, and she scorned the scattering of eligible men in the village. Now approaching twenty-three, she may have felt herself threatened with spinsterhood. Moreover, Joseph had all the ardor of a youth of twenty-one, but none of the usual inarticulateness. She was wildly in love with him.

He was big, powerful, and by ordinary standards very handsome, except for his nose, which was aquiline and prominent. His large blue eyes were fringed by fantastically long lashes which made his gaze seem veiled and slightly mysterious. Emma was probably quick to notice what many of his followers later believed had a supernatural cause, that when he was speaking with intense feeling the blood drained from his face, leaving a frightening, almost luminous pallor. However she may have disapproved of his money-digging, she must have had faith in his insight into mysteries that common folk could not fathom; she needed no one to tell her that here was no ordinary man.

Stowel, who was fond of the couple and anxious to further their marriage, arranged for Emma to visit Joseph at his home in South Bainbridge. On January 18, 1827 they were secretly married at the home of Squire Tarbell. After the ceremony they departed for Manchester to live with Joseph's parents.

Eight months later they returned to Harmony to brave the wrath of Isaac Hale and to secure some furniture and livestock that Emma owned in her own name. Since Joseph had no wagon, he hired Peter Ingersoll to drive them the distance, and it is to him that we are indebted for a description of the meeting.*

Hale met the couple in a flood of tears. "You have stolen my daughter and married her," he cried. "I had much rather have followed her to her grave. You spend your time in digging for money — pretend to see in a stone, and thus try to deceive people."

"Joseph wept," Ingersoll said, "and acknowledged he could not see in a stone now, nor never could; and that his former pretensions in that respect, were all false. He then promised to give up his old habits of digging for money and looking into stones." Somewhat conciliated, Hale told Joseph that if he would move to Pennsylvania and work for a living, he would help him get into business, and to this Joseph agreed.

* For Ingersoll's statement see Appendix A.

But there was a great impatience in this youth which made grubbing in the soil a hateful labor. In truth he was through with money-digging. But if he had become disillusioned with the profession, he had retained a superb faith in himself. In the next five years Joseph climbed up out of the world of magic into the world of religion. He was transformed from a lowly necromancer into a prophet, surrounded no longer merely by a clientele but by an enthusiastic following with common purposes and ideals.

CHAPTER III
Red Sons of Israel

WESTERN NEW YORK regarded its Indian mounds with a curiosity that made an amateur antiquarian of almost everyone in the area. What had caused the giant heaps of skeletons nobody seemed to know, but nobody lacked a theory. The Palmyra newspapers showed a continuing interest in the mystery, one editor writing in 1818 that the luckless inhabitants were "doubtless killed in battle and hastily buried," and another saying more humbly in 1823 that "what wonderful catastrophe destroyed the first inhabitants is beyond the researches of the best scholar and greatest antiquarian." *

It was a common legend that western New York and Ohio had once been the site of a terrible slaughter and that the mounds were the cemeteries of an entire race. New York's famous governor, De Witt Clinton, fascinated by the antiquities of his state, had stopped by Canandaigua in 1811 to examine three mounds and after counting the rings of the trees growing on their surfaces had estimated their age at more than a thousand years. The Moundbuilders, he said, were unquestionably a lost race, which had once been vast in number and greatly superior in civilization to the Iroquois.†

There was universal admiration for the palisaded, geometrical forts, the ruins of which were silhouetted against the sky atop the conelike drumlins that dotted the landscape. Since the pottery and copper ornaments buried in the mounds were frequently beautiful in design and skillfully wrought, few believed they were the handiwork of the despised red man. The *Palmyra Register* in January 1818 pointed out that the Moundbuilders "had made much greater advances in the arts of civilized life" than any Indians, and the *Palmyra Herald* in February 1823

---

* *Palmyra Register*, January 21, 1818, and *Palmyra Herald*, February 19, 1823.

† De Witt Clinton: "Discourse," *New York Historical Society Publications*, Vol. II (1811), p. 93. See also E. G. Squier: *Antiquities of the State of New York*, p. 213.

insisted that the antiquities "clearly prove them to be the work of some other people."

The theory persisted for half a century that the Moundbuilders were a race of peaceful farmers and metalworkers who had been invaded and utterly exterminated by a bloodthirsty race that was ancestor to the modern Indian. William Henry Harrison, shortly before his election to the Presidency, wrote that the last great battle took place on the banks of the Ohio, where "a feeble band was collected, remnant of mighty battles fought in vain, to make a last effort for the country of their birth, the ashes of their ancestors and the altars of their gods." *

The mystery of the Moundbuilders attracted no one more than Joseph Smith. According to his mother, he was spinning theories about them before he was twenty: "During our evening conversations, Joseph would occasionally give us some of the most amusing recitals that could be imagined. He would describe the ancient inhabitants of this continent, their dress, mode of travelling, and the animals upon which they rode; their cities, their buildings, with every particular; their mode of warfare; and also their religious worship. This he would do with as much ease, seemingly, as if he had spent his whole life with them." †

Some time between 1820 and 1827 it occurred to the youth that he might try to write a history of the Moundbuilders, a book that would answer the questions of every farmer with a mound in his pasture. He would not be content with the cheap trickery of the conjurer Walters, with his fake record of Indian treasure, although he might perhaps pretend to have found an ancient document or metal engraving in his digging expeditions. Somewhere he had heard that a history of the Indians had been found in Canada at the base of a hollow tree. And a Palmyra paper in 1821 had reported that diggers on the Erie Canal had unearthed "several brass plates" along with skeletons and fragments of pottery.‡

* "Discourse on the Aborigines of the Ohio Valley," *Ohio Historical and Philosophical Society Transactions*, 1839, p. 11.

† Lucy Smith: *Biographical Sketches*, p. 85. This occurred before Alvin's death in November 1823.

‡ Peter Ingersoll stated that in 1827 he heard Joseph mention the Indian history found in Canada. See Appendix A. The discovery of the brass plates was reported in the *Western Farmer* (Palmyra, New York), September 19, 1821.

Perhaps Joseph speculated that since his own family took such pleasure in his stories a greater public might do the same. The dream of somehow recouping the family fortune must have been with him since childhood, and his marriage had doubtless doubled his ambition. Alert to the intellectual currents of his period, though only the backwash swirled through his community, he saw in all the antiquarian speculation an unparalleled opportunity.

The plan of Joseph's book was to come directly out of popular theory concerning the Moundbuilders. His "Book of Mormon" was basically the history of two warring races, one "a fair and delightsome people," farmers, stock-raisers, temple-builders, and workers in copper, iron, and steel; the other a "wild and ferocious, and a bloodthirsty people; full of idolatry and filthiness; feeding upon beasts of prey, dwelling in tents, and wandering about in the wilderness, with a short skin girded about their loins, and their heads shaven; and their skill . . . in the bow, and the cimeter and the axe." *

Actually the Moundbuilders had been not a lost race, but the direct ancestors of certain of the upper Mississippi Indian tribes. But at that time only a few antiquarians knew that the Indians had made a practice of exhuming, collecting together, and reburying in mounds all the bones of the recently dead. Even after the coming of the white man this ceremony, known as the Festival of the Dead, had been celebrated in the Mississippi Valley. The Indian forts, on the other hand, were the fairly recent handiwork of the Iroquois.†

The quiet research of genuine scholars lay of course in a different world from Joseph's. He therefore accepted the popular theory of a lost race in all its details, including the last great battle of extermination, which he decided might very well have been in his own neighborhood. There was a hill near his father's farm that looked as if it might have been an immense Indian

---

* The Book of Mormon (Palmyra, 1830), pp. 72, 144–5. The spelling is that of the original.

† Many of the mounds were simply crematories, where the bodies were elaborately entombed and then burned, one on top of another. See E. G. Squier: *Antiquities of the State of New York*, p. 79, and Henry C. Shetrone: *The Moundbuilders; a reconstruction of the life of a prehistoric American race, through exploration and interpretation of their earth mounds* (New York, 1930).

mound, rising alone and mysterious out of the gently rolling
landscape. From its summit he could see for miles in every direction, and it may have struck him as an admirable site for a
gigantic defensive battle. What better place to discover a record
of the lost people?

About a year after Joseph's marriage, rumor spread through Palmyra that he had unearthed an extraordinary treasure from the
big hill on the turnpike just outside Manchester. No two of
Joseph's neighbors had the same version of the story. Peter
Ingersoll, who claimed to be Joseph's confidant, had a savagely
cynical account. One day Joseph had taken home some fine
white sand tied up in his frock, and his family, seated around
the dinner table, asked him what he was carrying. "At that moment," he is said to have told Ingersoll, "I happened to think
of what I had heard about a history found in Canada, called
the golden Bible; so I very gravely told them it was the golden
Bible. To my surprise, they were credulous enough to believe
what I said. Accordingly I told them that I had received a commandment to let no one see it, for, says I, no man can see it
with the naked eye and live. However, I offered to take out the
book and show it to them, but they refused to see it, and left
the room. Now," he concluded, "I have got the damned fools
fixed, and will carry out the fun."

One thing, however, puzzled Ingersoll. "Notwithstanding, he
told me he had no such book, and believed there never was any
such book, yet, he told me that he actually went to Willard
Chase, to get him to make a chest, in which he might deposit his
golden Bible. But, as Chase would not do it, he made a box
himself, of clap-boards, and put it into a pillow case, and allowed
people only to lift it, and feel of it through the case."

Chase told a different tale. In June 1827, he said, the elder
Smith told him that a spirit had informed young Joseph that a
record engraved on golden plates lay buried near his home. But
when he tried to get the plates, he found a toad guarding them,
which changed into a man and struck him on the head. This,
Chase said, had happened several years before. In September
1827 Joseph had confided in him that at last he was to be allowed
to dig up the plates and translate their contents; but he needed

a chest to house them and promised Chase a share in the book if he would build it.

Suspicious of the whole story, Chase refused: "A few days afterwards, he told one of my neighbors that he had not got any such book, nor never had such an one; but that he had told the story to deceive the d—d fool, (meaning me,) to get him to make a chest."

Very few friends realized that the discovery had religious significance. Joseph Capron said that Joseph's father gave him "no intimation, at that time that the book was to be of a religious character, or that it had anything to do with revelation. He declared it to be a speculation. . . ." And as early as February 1831 the editor of the Palmyra *Reflector* insisted that when Joseph first claimed to have found the plates "no *divine* interposition had been *dreamed* of." *

To Joseph's family and a few intimates like Martin Harris, however, the finding of the golden plates had world-shattering significance. Harris was a prosperous farmer who had followed an erratic trail of religious enthusiasms, having been successively a Quaker, a Universalist, and a Restorationist. In describing Joseph's discovery to a local preacher he declared that "an important epoch had arrived — that a great flood of light was about to burst upon the world, and that the scene of divine manifestation was to be immediately around us." The Golden Bible, he said, would "contain such disclosures as would settle all religious controversies and speedily bring on the glorious millennium." Harris told the editor of the Rochester *Gem* that Joseph Smith "had been visited by the spirit of the Almighty in a dream, and informed that in a certain hill in that town [Manchester] was deposited a Golden Bible, containing an ancient record of divine origin." †

For a long time Joseph was extremely reluctant to talk about the plates. When his brother Hyrum begged him to tell the story of their discovery before a church council in 1831, he replied "that it was not intended to tell all the particulars of the coming forth of the Book of Mormon; and also said that it was not

* For texts of these accounts see Appendix A.

† See John A. Clark: *Gleanings by the Way* (Philadelphia, 1842), pp. 224–5, for an account of Clark's interview with Harris. For complete text of the Rochester *Gem* article, published September 5, 1829, see Francis W. Kirkham: *A New Witness for Christ in America* (Independence, Missouri, 1942), pp. 151–2.

expedient for him to relate these things." * But when in 1838 he set about writing the official history of the beginnings of his church, he was generous with details.

On the night of September 21, 1823, he wrote, he was kneeling by his bed asking forgiveness for his sins when a light filled his shabby room and a personage appeared at his side standing in the air.

He had on a loose robe of most exquisite whiteness. . . . His hands were naked and his arms also, a little above the wrist, so, also were his feet naked, as were his legs, a little above the ankles. His head and neck were also bare. . . . his whole person was glorious beyond description, and his countenance truly like lightning.

. . . He called me by name, and said unto me that he was a messenger sent from the presence of God to me and that his name was Moroni; that God had a work for me to do; and that my name should be had for good and evil among all nations, kindreds, and tongues, or that it should be both good and evil spoken of among all people. He said there was a book deposited, written upon gold plates, giving an account of the former inhabitants of this continent, and the sources from whence they sprang. He also said that the fullness of the everlasting Gospel was contained in it, as delivered by the Savior to the ancient inhabitants; also that there were two stones in silver bows — and these stones, fastened to a breastplate, constituted what is called the Urim and Thummim — deposited with the plates; and the possession and use of these stones were what constituted "Seers" in ancient or former times; and that God had prepared them for the purpose of translating the book.

Three times that night the spirit appeared, as angels are wont to do, for, to be authentic, celestial truth must be thrice repeated. The next day Joseph went to work in the fields with his father, but, feeling faint, started home before the day was spent. He fell unconscious on the ground, when the angel once more appeared to him and told him to relate his visions to his father. This he said he did, and the elder Smith assured him that they were truly of God.

Joseph related that he found the plates in a stone box along with a sword and breastplate, to which were fastened the magic Urim and Thummim. The plates were thin, he said, about eight inches square, bound together with three huge rings, and

* From the unpublished *Far West Record,* as reprinted in *History of the Church,* Vol. I, p. 220n.

covered with engraved characters. Greed so filled his heart when he first saw them that the angel forbade him to touch them until he should become sufficiently purified and instructed in the things of the kingdom. Once each year for four years he returned to the spot, and finally, on September 21, 1827, he was permitted to carry the plates home.

Of the four-year period between 1823 and 1827 Joseph wrote nothing in his autobiography, though it can scarcely be said to have been a time of penance and purification, since it coincided with his most intensive money-digging activities. Exactly how he described the discovery of the golden plates to his family one cannot be sure, but it is clear that much of the story that he later wrote in his autobiography was known to his family and friends as early as 1827. Although confusion persisted over certain details, the main outlines were the same in that year as a decade later. In 1831 Lucy Smith wrote to her brother a full description of the coming of the angel and the unearthing and translation of the record, concluding soberly: "I want you to think seriously of these things, for they are the truths of the living God." *

ALTHOUGH Joseph divulged almost no details about the golden plates other than the visions, Lucy Smith bubbled over with gossip. Her story is a mine of rich anecdote, garrulous and amusing, and adds to the confusion and contradiction already manifested in other documents. Emma and Joseph, she wrote, brought home the plates on September 22, 1827. Joseph showed her the magic spectacles, which she described as "two smooth three-cornered diamonds set in glass and the glasses set in silver bows." † With them was a breastplate, which he kept wrapped in a muslin handkerchief. "It was concave on one side and convex on the other, and extended from the neck downwards as far as the center of the stomach of a man of extraordinary size. . . . The whole plate was worth at least five hundred dollars." ‡

---

* Published in Ben E. Rich: *Scrapbook of Mormon Literature*, Vol. I, p. 543.

† Martin Harris, however, said they were "white, like polished marble, with a few grey streaks," and David Whitmer described them still differently as "two small stones of a chocolate color, nearly egg shape, and perfectly smooth, but not transparent." See *Tiffany's Monthly*, 1859, p. 166, and *Kansas City Journal*, June 5, 1881.

‡ Joseph may have found a copper breastplate, for such objects were frequently discovered in the mounds. The Ohio State Museum has an impressive collection.

Lucy never saw the golden plates, for Joseph warned his family that it meant instant death to look at them and frequently changed their hiding-place; but she lived in a constant state of alarm lest they be stolen. Willard Chase hired a conjurer from sixty miles away to divine their whereabouts, and Joseph at once transferred them from under the family hearthstone to a place beneath the floor of a cooper's shop across the street. Chase's sister, who apparently was more accomplished than the conjurer, divined this hiding-place by means of a green stone, and that night the shop was raided, the floor ripped up, and the chest demolished. But Joseph calmly informed his family that he had taken out the record the evening before, renailed the empty box, and replaced it beneath the floor. The plates were safe beneath a pile of flax in the shop.

To Lucy's naïve anecdotes Joseph's converts added in later years stories of their own, and the many legends embellishing the discovery of the golden plates became as real to the Mormons as Joseph's own account of the angel. By 1856 Heber C. Kimball was describing before congregations in Great Salt Lake City a vast cave in the hill "Cumorah," where Joseph and others saw a vision of "more records than ten men could carry. There were books piled upon tables, book upon book." *

Perhaps in the beginning Joseph never intended his stories of the golden plates to be taken so seriously, but once the masquerade had begun, there was no point at which he could call a halt. Since his own family believed him (with the possible exception of his cynical younger brother William), why should not the world? Martin Harris, who not only accepted but freely elaborated upon the story, was talking openly of financing the publication of the translation and had promised to pay Joseph's debts. His sublime faith in the existence of a record he had never seen augured well for the success of the book, which Joseph was now fully determined to write.

But writing in his father's home was impossible because of the persistent inquisitiveness of his family and neighbors. So he decided to return to Harmony, Pennsylvania. Martin Harris agreed to pay his debts and finance the journey, promising to follow him later and help with the translation by acting as secretary.

* *Journal of Discourses*, Vol. IV, p. 105.

Joseph's going may have been at Emma's insistence, for if one of their neighbors is to be believed, she was miserably unhappy in Manchester. Lorenzo Saunders, then a sixteen-year-old youth, wrote of her long after: "Joseph's wife was a pretty woman, just as pretty a woman as I ever saw. When she came to the Smiths she was disappointed and used to come down to our house and sit down and cry. Said she was deceived and got into a hard place." *

Perhaps her tears were only for their poverty and the inevitable petty troubles that sprang from living in a house not her own. But Emma was not so credulous that she could refrain from wondering about plates that were too sacred to be seen but not to be stolen.

JOSEPH and Emma moved into a house in Harmony that belonged to Isaac Hale, who was gratified to hear Joseph say "that he had given up what he called 'glass-looking,' and that he expected to work hard for a living, and was willing to do so." Hale soon discovered, however, that instead of getting down to serious farming his son-in-law was busy translating characters from a mysterious set of plates he had brought from New York.

"I was shown a box," he said, "in which it is said they were contained, which had to all appearances been used as a glass box of the common window glass. I was allowed to feel the weight of the box, and they gave me to understand, that the book of plates was then in the box — into which, however, I was not allowed to look. I inquired of Joseph Smith, Jr., who was to be the first who would be allowed to see the Book of Plates? He said it was a young child. After this, I became dissatisfied, and informed him that if there was anything in my house of that description, which I could not be allowed to see, he must take it away; if he did not, I was determined to see it. After that, the Plates were said to be hid in the woods." †

Emma was Joseph's first scribe. She never saw the plates, although they often lay on the table wrapped in a small linen tablecloth. Despite her skepticism and bewilderment Joseph ap-

* Unpublished affidavit of Lorenzo Saunders made in Reading, Michigan, September 20, 1884, now in the library of the Reorganized Church.

† For Hale's complete statement see Appendix A.

EMMA SMITH

CHARACTERS SAID TO HAVE BEEN COPIED FROM THE GOLDEN PLATES

parently had so frightened her about the consequences of examining them that she dared finger them under their covering only when she moved them to dust the table. "They seemed to be pliable like thick paper," she later said, "and would rustle with a metallic sound when the edges were moved by the thumb as one does sometimes thumb the edges of a book." *
Mystified by his ability to translate the characters without even unwrapping the plates, merely by staring into his stone — or stones (for she said later that he used the Urim and Thummim for the first 116 pages and the little dark seer stone for the remainder †) — she began to take down his dictation.

Although the prose had the familiar ring of the King James Bible, the story was like nothing she had ever read or dreamed. "I, Nephi," the book began, "having been born of goodly parents, therefore I was taught somewhat in all the learning of my father; and having seen many afflictions in the course of my days — nevertheless, having been highly favored of the Lord in all my days; yea, having had a great knowledge of the goodness and the mysteries of God, therefore I make a record of my proceedings in my days." ‡

Joseph explained that the record was a history of the Indians from the earliest times. Like the Bible, it was written by prophets and divided into books. The first prophet, Nephi, was a young Hebrew who had left Jerusalem 600 B.C. and had sailed to America with his father, Lehi, and a few followers to avoid the destruction of the city. Lehi actually was an obscure Biblical name, but Emma probably knew it better as the name of a river, the Lehigh, which ran not far south of Harmony.

Like Joseph himself, Nephi had two elder brothers, Laman and Lemuel, and three younger, Sam, Jacob, and Joseph. Laman and Lemuel were evil-tempered, sinful youths who so incurred the wrath of God that He cursed them and all their descendants with a red skin.§ Nephi and his pious younger brothers begat white children, who were favored by the Lord. And thus it hap-

---

* *Saints Herald,* Vol. XXVI (October 1, 1879), p. 289.

† Letter to Mrs. Pilgrim, now in the library of the Reorganized Church.

‡ This at least was the first sentence in the final draft, though an earlier draft of this portion was lost.

§ Lemuel is a Biblical name, but it happened also to be that of a neighbor, Lemuel Durfee, who signed an affidavit in 1833 charging Joseph Smith with an immoral character and vicious habits. See Howe: *Mormonism Unvailed,* pp. 261–2.

pened that two races grew up in America — the Nephites, peace-loving and domestic, and the Lamanites, bloodthirsty and idolatrous.

The two races fought intermittently for a thousand years. To defend themselves against the Lamanites, the Nephites finally erected "small forts, or places of resort; throwing up banks of earth round about" with "timbers built up to the height of a man, round about the cities . . . a frame of pickets built upon the timbers." This kind of description must have sounded familiar to Emma, for western New York was famous for its palisaded Indian forts, one chain running fifty miles from Cattaragus Creek to the Pennsylvania border.

After each battle the dead were "heaped up upon the face of the earth, and they were covered with a shallow covering." This, it was to be obvious to everyone who read the book, was the explanation of the Indian mounds, the biggest mounds of all marking the site of the last great battle, which had wiped out the white Nephite race.*

Whatever initial misgivings may have troubled Emma vanished before the substantial stream of prose that flowed from her husband's lips. She could fathom neither the sources of his ideas nor his marvelously fecund imagination. It is probable that the reality of the golden plates no longer troubled her half so much as Joseph's apparent lack of confidence in her. His refusal to show her the plates became the first serious barrier between them. Never again would she or anyone else share his inner secrets. For Joseph played out his role of "translator" with such consistency and skill that she could not doubt him.

Martin Harris came to Harmony in February 1828, eager to know of the book's progress. When he learned in detail what the plates contained he was overwhelmed; for the book solved the knotty problem of the origin of the red man, which had been a puzzle ever since 1500. Had Harris been a learned man, he would have known that various writers had designated as

* The Book of Mormon (1830), pp. 358, 363, 267. Compare these forts with descriptions by O. Turner in *Pioneer History of the Holland Purchase*, p. 38. It was then a common belief that Indian tribes exterminated one another. The *Palmyra Register* on January 28, 1818 quoted from the *Western Gazetteer* the story of a fight between the Wabash and the Mississippi Indians, a thousand on each side, which ended with but seven left on one side and five on the other. The mounds where the dead were buried could still be seen in Indiana, the article concluded.

the ancestral home of the American Indian not only Jerusalem, but also Iceland, Wales, Rome, Phœnicia, Carthage, Egypt, and China. But he was satisfied to know that they were descendants of the Hebrews, for of all the theories then current the most popular among clergymen in Europe as well as America was that the red men were a remnant of the Lost Ten Tribes of Israel.

America's most distinguished preachers — William Penn, Roger Williams, Cotton Mather, Jonathan Edwards — had all espoused the theory. Edwards had even written a tract pointing out what he thought were likenesses between the Muhhekaneew Indian tongue and Hebrew. The historian H. H. Bancroft later wrote: "The theory that the Americans are of Jewish origin has been discussed more minutely and at greater length than any other. Its advocates, or at least those of them who have made original researches, are comparatively few, but the extent of their investigations and the multitude of the parallelisms they adduce in support of their hypothesis exceed by far anything we have yet encountered." * Josiah Priest wrote in 1833 in his *American Antiquities:* "The opinion that the American Indians are descendants of the Lost Ten Tribes is now a popular one and generally believed."

Fantastic parallels were drawn between Hebraic and Indian customs, such as feasts of first fruits, sacrifices of the first-born in the flock, cities of refuge, ceremonies of purification, and division into tribes. The Indian "language" (which actually consisted of countless distinct languages derived from numerous linguistic stocks) was said to be chiefly Hebrew. The Indian belief in the Great Spirit (which originally had been implanted by French and Spanish missionaries) was said to be derived in a direct line from Jewish monotheism. One writer even held that syphilis, the Indian's gift to Europe, was an altered form of Biblical leprosy.

* *Native Races,* Vol. V, pp. 77–8. Among the early books discussing the subject are James Adair: *The History of the American Indians* (London, 1775); Charles Crawford: *Essay upon the Propagation of the Gospel, in which there are facts to prove that many of the Indians in America are descended from the Ten Tribes* (Philadelphia, 1799); Elias Boudinot: *A Star in the West; or, a Humble Attempt to Discover the Long Lost Tribes of Israel* (Trenton, 1816); Ethan Smith: *View of the Hebrews; or the Ten Tribes of Israel in America* (Poultney, Vermont, 1823); Josiah Priest: *The Wonders of Nature and Providence Displayed* (Albany, 1825); Israel Worsley: *A View of the American Indians, pointing out their origin* (London, 1828).

Joseph Smith had every opportunity to become familiar with such parallelisms. A Jewish rabbi, M. M. Noah, editor of the *New York Enquirer,* had summarized them in a long speech that had been republished in full in Joseph's home-town paper on October 11, 1825. "If the tribes could be brought together," Noah had concluded, "could be made sensible of their origin, could be civilized, and restored to their long lost brethren, what joy to our people!" Joseph unquestionably had access to the *Wayne Sentinel,* for on August 11, 1826 his father was listed among the delinquent subscribers as owing $5.60.

Joseph's familiarity with the theory of the Hebraic origin of the Indians seems, however, to have come chiefly from a popular book by Ethan Smith, pastor of a church in Poultney, Vermont. This book, *View of the Hebrews; or the Ten Tribes of Israel in America,* was published in 1823, a second edition in 1825. Ethan Smith had managed to collect all the items of three generations of specious scholarship and piecemeal observation on this subject, and had added to them Caleb Atwater's accurate descriptions of the Ohio mounds and Alexander von Humboldt's glowing account of the architectural ruins of Central America.

Ethan Smith's theory of the origin of the Indian mounds was exactly the same as that which formed the heart of the Book of Mormon story: "Israel brought into this new continent a considerable degree of civilization; and the better part of them long laboured to maintain it. But others fell into the hunting and consequently savage state; whose barbarous hordes invaded their more civilized brethren, and eventually annihilated most of them, and all in these northern regions!" *

It may, in fact, have been *View of the Hebrews* that gave Joseph Smith the idea of writing an Indian history in the first place. "If the Indians are of the tribes of Israel," Ethan Smith said pointedly, "some decisive evidence of the fact will ere long be exhibited." And he described in great excitement the discovery of an ancient Hebrew phylactery bound in leather, which had allegedly been unearthed in Pittsfield, Massachusetts. He reported also a provocative legend, said to have come from an Indian chief, that the red men "had not long since a book which they had *for a long time preserved.* But having lost the knowl-

* *View of the Hebrews* (1825), p. 184.

edge of reading it, they concluded it would be of no further use
to them; and they buried it with an Indian chief." *

Joseph Smith knew this legend, for he quoted it in his church
newspaper in later years as evidence of the historical accuracy of
the Book of Mormon, although he was careful to use as a source
Josiah Priest's *American Antiquities,* which had reprinted
Ethan Smith's account in 1833, three years after the Book of
Mormon was published. It may never be proved that Joseph saw
View of the Hebrews before writing the Book of Mormon, but
the striking parallelisms between the two books hardly leave a
case for mere coincidence.†

Both books opened with frequent references to the destruction of Jerusalem; both told of inspired prophets among the
ancient Americans; both quoted copiously and almost exclusively from Isaiah; and both delineated the ancient Americans
as a highly civilized people. Both held that it was the mission of
the American nation in the last days to gather these remnants
of the house of Israel and bring them to Christianity, thereby
hastening the day of the glorious millennium. *View of the Hebrews* made much of the legend that the "stick of Joseph" and
the "stick of Ephraim" — symbolizing the Jews and the lost
tribes — would one day be united; and Joseph Smith's first advertising circulars blazoned the Book of Mormon as "the stick
of Joseph taken from the hand of Ephraim."

Ethan Smith had excitedly described copper breastplates,
taken from the mounds, which had two white buckhorn buttons fastened to the outside of each plate, "in resemblance of
the Urim and Thummim," the ancient magic lots that miraculously blazed on the ephod of the high priest of ancient Israel.
And this reference Joseph elaborated into the fabulous magic
spectacles with which he translated the golden plates.

* Ibid., p. 223.
† Joseph published the story of the long-buried book in the *Times and Seasons,*
Nauvoo, Illinois, Vol. III (June 1, 1842), pp. 813–14. He was then editor. Ethan
Smith is listed as the original source, although Priest is listed as the author of the
entire article. In the issue of June 15, 1842 Joseph quoted a long extract from Alex-
ander von Humboldt, which had been reprinted in Boudinot's *A Star in the West.*
Such extracts indicate that he was very familiar with the literature supporting the
hypothesis of the Hebraic origin of the Indians. The scholarly Mormon historian B. H.
Roberts once made a careful and impressive list of parallels between *View of the
Hebrews* and the Book of Mormon, but for obvious reasons it was never published.
After his death copies were made which circulated among a limited circle in Utah.

View of the Hebrews, however, was only a basic source book for the Book of Mormon. The themes that Joseph borrowed he elaborated with a lavish fancy. This can be seen particularly in the story of Quetzalcoatl, whom Ethan Smith described as "the most mysterious being of the whole Mexican mythology," the white, bearded Aztec god who taught his people their prized peaceful arts and for whose return the Aztecs were hoping when Cortes appeared. Ethan Smith described Quetzalcoatl as "a type of Christ," but Joseph saw in the legend evidence that Christ Himself had come to the New World.* The occasional crucifixes found in the mounds gave further weight to this theory, since it was not until years later that scholars proved them to be French and Spanish in origin.

Jesus said: "Other sheep I have, which are not of this fold; them also I must bring, and they shall hear my voice." These other sheep, Joseph said in his Book of Mormon, were the Lamanites and the Nephites, whom Jesus had visited some time in the early weeks following his final ascension. Christ's coming to America, he wrote, had been preceded by cataclysmic destruction which annihilated great portions of the population, and by three days of darkness, which brought the remainder to their knees in anguished repentance. The dramatic appearance of Jesus then made such an impact upon the devastated people that the red and white tribes accepted his gospel and lived together as brothers for several generations, before Satan's wiles began again to split them asunder.

Thus, where *View of the Hebrews* was just bad scholarship, the Book of Mormon was highly original and imaginative fiction.

Thirty-five years after the Book of Mormon was published, an old antiquarian in Ohio who had spent years in trying to prove that the Indians were descended from the Hebrews pretended to have discovered in a mound several stone plates with the Ten Commandments inscribed in Hebrew. After his death investigators discovered that he had laboriously chipped the stone himself, copying the characters from a Hebrew Bible which he had

* Modern paleographers have fixed the date of Quetzalcoatl's death at A.D. 1208. See *The American Aborigines, Their Origin and Antiquity,* ed. D. Jenness (Fifth Pacific Science Congress, Toronto, 1933), p. 239.

neglected to destroy.* Between this pathetic petty deception and the Book of Mormon lies the difference between a painfully cramped imagination and an audacious and original mind. Joseph Smith took the whole Western Hemisphere as the setting for his book and a thousand years of history for his plot. Never having written a line of fiction, he laid out for himself a task that would have given the most experienced novelist pause. But possibly because of this very inexperience he plunged into the story.

Sagacious enough to realize that he could not possibly write a history of the Lost Ten Tribes, he chose instead to describe only the peregrinations of two Hebrew families, headed by Lehi and Ishmael, who became the founders of the American race. He began the book by focusing upon a single hero, Nephi, who like himself was peculiarly gifted of the Lord. This device launched him smoothly into his narrative and saved him from having bitten off more than he could chew.

* This story is told by E. O. Randall in "The Mound Builders and the Lost Tribes: the 'Holy Stones of Newark,' " *Ohio Archeological and Historical Society Publications,* Vol. XVII (April 1908). Modern Mormons have used the discovery of this Decalogue as evidence of the truth of the Book of Mormon, apparently unaware that it was pure fakery. See "Decalogue Uncovered in Ohio Mound," *Deseret News,* Church Section, Salt Lake City, November 8, 1941, p. 2.

CHAPTER IV
A Marvelous Work and a Wonder

MARTIN HARRIS was a round-faced, slightly bearded man whose sad, empty eyes betrayed something of his credulous nature. His wife thought him a fool and nagged at him incessantly about the money he was throwing away on the Golden Bible. Although he supported Joseph stubbornly, her barbs made him hesitate about financing publication of the book until he had examined the plates for himself. He had lifted them many times in their clapboard chest, estimating their weight at forty or fifty pounds, but this had only whetted his curiosity.

When Joseph maintained his refusal to open the chest, Harris insisted on seeing at least a copy of the engraved characters. He would take them to New York City, he said, to the most learned men in the land. If he could get their testimonials that the characters were truly Hebrew, it would create a great sensation.

But the characters were not Hebrew, Joseph explained. They were an altered or "reformed" Egyptian. Since engraving was a tedious process, the Nephite prophet Mormon had chosen this language rather than Hebrew because it required less space.

The choice of Egyptian for the language of the plates was clearly the fruit of Joseph's reading. Ethan Smith had described the Indian inscriptions as "hieroglyphical records and paintings," and the *Wayne Sentinel* on June 1, 1827 had published an account of a discovery of a Mexican manuscript in hieroglyphics, which was considered proof that originally the Mexicans and Egyptians "had intercourse with each other, and . . . had the same system of mythology."

At this time the Egyptian language was popularly believed to be indecipherable, for it was not until 1837 that the grammar worked out from the Rosetta stone by the French scholar Champollion was first published in England. Joseph was not likely, therefore, to be held accountable by any scholar for the accuracy of his Egyptian characters, particularly since they were "re-

formed." Eventually he gave in to the entreaties of his secretary
and furnished him with a sheet of characters.

The first scholar whom Harris visited was Samuel L. Mitchell,
vice-president of Rutgers Medical College and known the country over as a living encyclopedia. If Harris hoped to impress
anyone with documentary proof that the Indians were brother
to the Jews, he could scarcely have selected a less sympathetic
scholar. For Mitchell was one of the few antiquarians of his day
who believed the now established theory that the Indians had
originated in eastern Asia.* This theory already had a bulky
though recondite literature supporting it. But even in the nineteenth century, Mongolian civilization was too remote to most
Americans for the idea to be widely accepted. The Yankee knew
only the stereotyped Chinese mandarin, almond-eyed, yellow-
skinned, and dressed in embroidered silks, a figure bearing no
resemblance to the copper-colored Indian, buckskin-clad and
dirty, who menaced the outposts along the frontier.

Although Mitchell gave Harris no satisfaction, he directed
him to Charles Anthon, professor of Greek and Latin at Columbia College. Exactly what took place at this interview is
one of the minor conundrums facing a student of Mormon
documents. Anthon wrote later that the paper "consisted of all
kinds of crooked characters disposed in columns, and had evidently been prepared by some person who had before him at the
time a book containing various alphabets. Greek and Hebrew
letters, crosses and flourishes, Roman letters inverted or placed
sideways, were arranged in perpendicular columns, and the
whole ended in a rude delineation of a circle divided into various compartments, decked with various strange marks, and evidently copied after the Mexican calendar by Humboldt, but
copied in such a way as not to betray the source whence it was
derived." But the only paper — or portion of it — that Martin
Harris preserved does not fit this description. (See cut.)

When Harris returned, word went about that Anthon had declared the characters to be ancient shorthand Egyptian. Eventually the scholar learned that his name was being used to advertise the Book of Mormon and he wrote a violent denial. "The

* See his article "The Original Inhabitants of America Shown to Be of the Same
Family with Those of Asia," *American Antiquarian Society Transactions*, Vol. I (1820).
See also *The American Aborigines*, ed. D. Jenness (1933).

whole story about my having pronounced the Mormonite inscription to be 'reformed Egyptian hieroglyphics' is perfectly
false." He had been convinced in the interview, he said, that
the whole story of the Golden Bible was either "a hoax upon the
learned" or "a scheme to cheat the farmer of his money." *

Nevertheless, Harris came home willing to risk his ten-thousand-dollar farm in financing the Book of Mormon, and his
account of the interview suggests why. He told Joseph that
Anthon had pronounced the characters Egyptian, Chaldaic,
Assyriac, and Arabic, and had given this opinion in writing.
Then becoming curious about the paper, he had asked Harris
for full details. After hearing the story of the angel and the
golden plates, he had torn up his own statement in disgust. But
as they were about to part, the scholar had suggested that the
plates be brought to him for translation. This was forbidden,
Harris had told him, and added that part of the record was
sealed. To which Anthon had answered shortly: "I cannot read
a sealed book."

When Joseph had heard Harris to the end, he thumbed
through the Old Testament to the 29th chapter of Isaiah and
read him the eleventh and twelfth verses: "And the vision of
all is become unto you as the words of a book that is sealed,
which men deliver to one that is learned, saying, Read this, I
pray thee: and he saith, I cannot; for it is sealed: And the book
is delivered to him that is not learned, saying, Read this, I pray
thee: and he saith, I am not learned." Harris was overwhelmed;
he had fulfilled a prophecy!

Joseph apparently felt that his reformed Egyptian characters
were a success, since he allowed them to be used later in a bold
little circular advertising the Book of Mormon.† And Martin
became the perfect believer. "He said he had no more doubt of
Smith's commission than of the divine commission of the apostles," wrote J. A. Clark, who knew him in these years. "The very
fact that Smith was an obscure and illiterate man showed that
he must be acting under divine impulse: 'God had chosen the
foolish things of the world to confound the wise, and the weak

---

* See Anthon's letter to E. D. Howe, February 17, 1834. *Mormonism Unvailed,*
pp. 270–2.

† At least one copy is still extant, in the possession of the church historian in Salt
Lake City.

things to confound the mighty' . . . he was determined that the book should be published though it consumed all his worldly substance." * Henceforth he was Joseph's champion, and his liberal purse became the cornerstone of a new religion.

IN April 1828 Harris moved to Harmony expecting to relieve Emma of the task of taking Joseph's dictation. Mrs. Harris, frantic now lest her husband give away his modest fortune altogether, insisted on going with him. She stated flatly, according to Joseph's mother, that "her object in coming was to see the plates, and that she would never leave until she had accomplished it."

Joseph was desperately poor, Emma was pregnant, and the coming of the grim, determined woman whom they could ill afford to offend must have made hideous the fortnight she remained. For she ransacked every corner and cupboard in the house, badgered relatives and neighbors, and even searched the woods for signs of freshly dug soil. With mingled cajolery and cursing Harris finally persuaded her to return home, and then, taking up where Emma left off, he began to write down the story of the Book of Mormon.

A blanket flung across a rope divided the room where they worked. On one side sat Joseph staring into his stones, and on the other was Harris writing at a table. Joseph warned his scribe that God's wrath would strike him down should he dare to examine the plates or look at him while he was translating. Harris never betrayed his trust, though he once admitted that he tried to trick Joseph by substituting an ordinary stone for the seer stone.†

They worked together for two months. Progress was painfully slow, less than two pages a day, for during this period only 116 pages of foolscap were completed, including what Emma had written during the winter. For all his facility in the local debating society, Joseph had yet to learn how to write. Moreover, his sentences had to be compounded correctly, for Harris believed that the translation was automatic, and revision was therefore unthinkable.

But none of Joseph's secretaries knew the rudiments of punc-

* *Gleanings by the Way* (Philadelphia, 1842), p. 230.

† See the summary of Harris's sermon in Salt Lake City, September 4, 1870, *Historical Record*, Vol. VI, p. 216.

tuation, and when the manuscript finally went to press there
was scarcely a capital letter, comma, or period in the whole. The
typesetters broke up the clauses as they saw fit, with the result
that of the first two hundred sentences one hundred and forty
began with "And."

By mid-June Harris was tired of taking dictation and begged
to take the first 116 pages of the manuscript back to Palmyra to
show his wife. This at first Joseph flatly forbade. But as Emma's
confinement approached, he became less adamant, and finally
gave in. It was a grave strategic blunder, for Lucy Harris
promptly stole the manuscript from her husband, and neither
pleas nor blows could make her divulge its hiding-place.

For some weeks Joseph was too preoccupied to wonder why
Harris did not return. Emma's son died at birth, and for a fortnight thereafter Joseph was frantic lest he lose his wife as well.
With her recovery, however, he began to be uneasy over Martin's long delay. Emma, who by now had come to accept the
Book of Mormon in full faith and was eager to see it published,
begged him to go back to Manchester to recover the precious
document.

Lucy Smith wrote that when Joseph confronted his scribe,
Martin Harris confessed his folly, crying out in bitter remorse:
"I have lost my soul; I have lost my soul!"

"Oh, my God," Joseph cried. "All is lost! What shall I do?"
He wept and groaned, and walked the floor continually, and
after a while told Harris to go back and search once more.

"No," he replied, "it is all in vain; for I have ripped open
beds and pillows; and I know it is not there."

"Then must I return to my wife with such a tale as this,"
Joseph cried. "I dare not do it, lest I should kill her at once.
And how shall I appear before the Lord? Of what rebuke am
I not worthy from the angel of the Most High?"

Despairingly he realized that it was impossible for him to re-
produce the story exactly, and that to redictate it would be to
invite devastating comparisons. Harris's wife taunted him: "If
this be a divine communication, the same being who revealed
it to you can easily replace it." *

Apparently she had actually destroyed the manuscript, for it

* See Lucy Smith: *Biographical Sketches*, pp. 121 ff., and J. A. Clark: *Gleanings
by the Way*, p. 247.

has never reappeared. But for weeks Joseph writhed in self-reproach for his folly. To admit that the whole story of the golden plates was a mere figment of his dreaming would be to destroy Emma's faith in him forever. It would mean the end of Harris's patronage and the undying contempt of his father-in-law, upon whom he would probably have to depend for a livelihood. His father's family was counting on sales of the Book of Mormon to prevent foreclosure on their farm, since they had no money for the final payment. A retreat from the fantasy that he had created was impossible.

Some time in July he saw the solution. Like Jemima Wilkinson, he would simply inquire of the Lord for a "revelation" to clear him of his difficulty. Whereupon he looked into the Urim and Thummim and received two long communications, which said in part: "The works, and the designs, and the purposes of God cannot be frustrated, neither can they come to nought. For God doth not walk in crooked paths. . . . Remember, remember, that it is not the work of God that is frustrated but the work of men. . . . Behold, thou art Joseph, and thou wast chosen to do the work of the Lord, but because of transgression, if thou art not aware thou wilt fall. . . . Nevertheless, my work shall go forth."

The revelations then forbade Joseph to retranslate the first part of the plates because the devil was out to thwart the publication of the book and would see to it that the stolen version was published in altered form. In His boundless wisdom, however, the Lord had foreseen this contingency and had provided a set of small plates, called the plates of Nephi, which covered exactly the same period in Indian history as the lost manuscript. This record was primarily religious history, in contrast with the first version, which had been largely political. Once he had translated it, he could go back to the old plates and carry on, presumably from page 117.*

Although he may not have sensed their significance, these, Joseph's first revelations, marked a turning-point in his life. For they changed the Book of Mormon from what might have been merely an ingenious speculation into a genuinely religious book.

---

* The revelations were first published in the *Book of Commandments* (Independence, Missouri, 1833). Later editions, with the title *Doctrine and Covenants,* were not arranged chronologically and did not place these revelations first.

Martin Harris, who had never ceased to look upon the golden record as "a marvelous work and a wonder," accepted the revelations, and his faith may well have made Joseph realize what he had but dimly sensed before, that he had at his fingertips the beginnings of a church. Henceforth God was inextricably bound up with the book, and by the time it was finished, eleven months later, plans for the organization of this church were already crystallizing in Joseph's mind. His bold preface, used only in the first edition, was designed to thwart any attempt on the part of Lucy Harris to use the stolen manuscript. It showed that by the summer of 1829 his partnership with the Lord was already definitive:

TO THE READER —

As many false reports have been circulated respecting the following work, and also many unlawful measures taken by evil designing persons to destroy me, and also the work, I would inform you that I translated, by the gift and power of God, and caused to be written, one hundred and sixteen pages, the which I took from the Book of Lehi, which was an account abridged from the plates of Lehi, by the hand of Mormon; which said account, some person or persons have stolen and kept from me, notwithstanding my utmost exertions to recover it again — and being commanded of the Lord that I should not translate the same over again, for Satan had put it into their hearts to tempt the Lord their God, by altering the words, that they did read contrary from that which I translated and caused to be written; and if I should bring forth the same words again, or, in other words, if I should translate the same over again, they would publish that which they had stolen, and Satan would stir up the hearts of this generation, that they might not receive this work: but behold, the Lord said unto me, I will not suffer that Satan shall accomplish his evil design in this thing: therefore thou shalt translate from the plates of Nephi, until ye come to that which ye have translated, which ye have retained; and behold ye shall publish it as the record of Nephi; and thus I will confound those who have altered my words. I will not suffer that they shall destroy my work; yea, I will shew unto them that my wisdom is greater than the cunning of the Devil. Wherefore, to be obedient unto the commandments of God, I have, through his grace and mercy, accomplished that which he hath commanded me respecting this thing. I would also inform you that the plates of which hath been spoken, were found in the township of Manchester, Ontario county, New-York.

THE AUTHOR

When Joseph's father paid him a visit in February 1829, the youth gave forth a revelation on his behalf with all the confidence of an Old Testament prophet:

Now behold, a marvelous work is about to come forth among the children of men. Therefore, O ye that embark in the service of God, see that ye serve him with all your heart, might, mind and strength, that ye may stand blameless before God at the last day; Therefore, if ye have desires to serve God, ye are called to the work, For behold the field is white already to harvest, and lo, he that thrusteth in his sickle with his might, the same layeth up in store that he perisheth not, but bringeth salvation to his soul; And faith, hope, charity and love, with an eye single to the glory of God, qualify him for the work. Remember faith, virtue, knowledge, temperance, patience, brotherly kindness, godliness, charity, humility, diligence. Ask, and ye shall receive, knock and it shall be opened unto you. Amen.

This mosaic of extracts from Isaiah, St. John, Revelations, and St. Matthew had the ring of divinity.* The father believed that God in truth was speaking through his son, and Joseph Smith had won another convert, the first who would remain true to the church for life. Thereafter Joseph received revelations freely for his brothers, secretaries, and friends. The revelation for Martin Harris scored his arrogance and never ending demands to see the plates, but significantly promised him that if he humbled himself he would later be allowed to see the golden record along with two other witnesses.

In later years Joseph described the spirit of revelation as "pure intelligence" flowing into him. "It may give you sudden strokes of ideas," he said "so that by noticing it, you may find it fulfilled the same day or soon; (i.e.) those things that were presented unto your minds by the Spirit of God, will come to pass." † Such an unspectacular process must have disappointed his questioners, for what he was describing was simply his own alert, intuitive understanding and creative spirit.

EXACTLY when Martin Harris returned to Harmony to begin writing the translation of the "plates of Nephi" is not known, but it was some time during the winter of 1828-9. Joseph now plunged into the story with ease, for he had behind him not

---

* Cf. Isaiah xxix:14, John iv:35, Revelation xiv:15, Matthew vii:7.
† *History of the Church*, Vol. III, p. 381.

only the earlier practice in dictating but also a fruitful period of reflection. It was now more than a year since he first asserted he had unearthed the plates, and he probably had the plan of the book worked out in his mind in considerable detail. Nevertheless, in writing the early portion of the book his literary reservoir frequently ran dry. When this happened he simply arranged for his Nephite prophets to quote from the Bible. Thus about twenty-five thousand words in the Book of Mormon consisted of passages from the Old Testament — chiefly those chapters from Isaiah mentioned in Ethan Smith's *View of the Hebrews* — and about two thousand more words were taken from the New Testament.

Joseph made minor changes in these Biblical extracts, for it seems to have occurred to him that readers would wonder how an ancient American prophet could use the exact text of the King James Bible. But he was careful to modify chiefly the italicized interpolations inserted for euphony and clarity by the scholars of King James; the unitalicized holy text he usually left intact.

In his first chapters Joseph borrowed from his own family traditions. His mother for many years had cherished the details of several of her husband's dreams, and one of these the youth incorporated wholesale into his narrative. Lehi, father of the hero Nephi, was made to have a vision that paralleled the dream of Joseph's father in minute detail.*

* *The Vision of Lehi* (Book of Mormon (1830), pp. 18–20.)	*Dream of Joseph Smith, Sr.* (Lucy Smith: *Biographical Sketches,* pp. 58–9.)
. . . me thought I saw a dark and dreary wilderness. . . .	I thought I was thus traveling in an open and desolate field, which appeared very barren. . . .
I beheld a tree, whose fruit was desirable, to make one happy . . . most sweet, above all that I ever had before tasted. . . . I began to be desirous that my family should partake of it also. . . .	. . . a tree, such as I had never seen before. . . . I found it delicious beyond description. As I was eating, I said in my heart, "I cannot eat this alone, I must bring my wife and children.". . .
And I beheld a rod of iron; and it extended along the bank of the river, and led to the tree. . . .	I beheld a beautiful stream of water, which ran from the east to the west. . . . I could see a rope running along the bank of it. . . .
. . . a great and spacious building . . . filled with people, both old and young, both male and female; and their manner	I beheld a spacious building . . . filled with people, who were very finely dressed. When these people observed us in the low

Early in the writing Joseph vigorously attacked the Catholic Church. The prophet Nephi was made to have a vision in which he foretold the state of America in the last days. Then, he said, the scourge of the land would be "that great and abominable church . . . the whore of all the earth . . . whose foundation is the devil." Nephi derided the Catholic version of the Bible as one having many "plain and precious things" deleted, and accused the priests of desiring "gold, and silver, and the silks, and the scarlets, and the fine-twined linen, and the precious clothing, and the harlots."

This attack must have pleased Martin Harris, for the first anti-Catholic feeling was beginning to surge in western New York. Before 1816 there had been no Catholics in this area; but the Erie Canal had brought a tremendous influx of Irish labor. Landing penniless in New York City, the "foreigners" had sailed up the Hudson by hundreds to work on the big ditch. Their priests had followed after, and Catholic church spires had risen successively westward — Albany, Geneva, Rochester, Buffalo.

It was to be some years before the nativistic frenzy that led to the burning of nunneries in New York and Boston would reach its peak, but as early as 1828 Josiah Priest, publishing in Albany, was calling the Catholic Church "Babylon the Great." Rochester, next door to Palmyra, blistered the Roman Church at every opportunity, the *Rochester Observer* calling it "the Beast" and "the mother of abominations." When Catholic stagecoach-owners refused to abolish Sunday mails at the request of Protestant owners, the *Rochester Album* published on February 29, 1828 an obviously counterfeit letter bearing the signature of Pope Leo XII:

To the elect elders of Rochester:
You must take the public conveyances into your hands. You must not deal at all with unbelievers; and if they murmur at your doings,

---

of dress was exceeding fine, and they were in the attitude of mocking and pointing their fingers towards those which had come at, and were partaking of the fruit.

valley, under the tree, they pointed the finger of scorn at us.

(A reverse borrowing is unlikely, since this was but one of six dreams that Lucy remembered in detail and had probably told and retold throughout the years.)

send in their names to us, and we will use our holy rack, our thumb screws, our Iron Bed, and many other such arguments, by which we shall no doubt convince them of their damnable heresies. . . .*

Martin Harris had paid his first visit to Harmony a fortnight after this uproar and may have brought news of it to Joseph Smith, for the diction of the anti-Catholicism in the Book of Mormon had the same flavor as the pseudo-encyclical: "And it came to pass," said Nephi, "that I saw among the nations of the Gentiles, the foundation of a great church. And the angel said unto me, Behold the foundation of a church, which is most abominable above all other churches, which slayeth the Saints of God, yea, and tortureth them and bindeth them down, and yoketh them with a yoke of iron, and bringeth them down into captivity."

In April 1829 Martin Harris was replaced by a new secretary. This was Oliver Cowdery, a young schoolmaster from Palmyra who had been boarding with the Smith family. He came down to Harmony with Joseph's younger brother Samuel, who bore the melancholy tidings that Joseph, Senior, and Lucy Smith had been evicted from their house and farm and forced to move in with Hyrum. The news stung Joseph to a fury of impatience. He knew that he must finish the Book of Mormon as fast as possible.

Cowdery had been attracted by the warm friendliness of the Smith family, and Lucy's richly dramatic stories about the Golden Bible had already made him a convert. Joseph at once saw his superiority to Martin Harris. The schoolteacher, a gentle, humorless youth having little education but possessing a certain talent for writing, was twenty-two, a year younger than Joseph. He was so carried away by Joseph's engaging confidence and the stupendous implications of his golden record that he began taking dictation at once.

"These days were never to be forgotten," Cowdery later wrote. "To sit under the sound of a voice dictated by the inspiration of heaven awakened the utmost gratitude of this bosom." But he admitted on another occasion that he sometimes "had sea-

* F. J. Zwierlein: *Life and Letters of Bishop McQuaid, prefaced with a History of Catholic Rochester* (Louvain, 1925), p. 27. Cf. Book of Mormon, pp. 28, 32. See also Josiah Priest: *A View of the Expected Christian Millennium* (Albany 1828).

sons of skepticism, in which I did seriously wonder whether
the prophet and I were men in our sober senses when we would
be translating from plates through 'the Urim and Thummim'
and the plates not be in sight at all." *

David Whitmer, a young farmer from Fayette, New York,
and a friend of Cowdery, paid them a visit and watched the
process of translation with great wonder. "Joseph Smith," he
said, "would put the seer stone into a hat, and put his face in the
hat, drawing it closely around his face to exclude the light; and
in the darkness the spiritual light would shine. A piece of something resembling parchment would appear, and on that appeared the writing. One character at a time would appear, and
under it was the interpretation in English. Brother Joseph
would read off the English to Oliver Cowdery who was his
principal scribe, and when it was written down and repeated
to Brother Joseph to see if it was correct, then it would disap-
pear, and another character with the interpretation would appear. Thus the Book of Mormon was translated by the gift and
power of God, and not by any power of man."

For all the magic appliances at Joseph's disposal, the work
progressed as unevenly as with the ordinary novelist. "At
times," David Whitmer wrote, "when Brother Joseph would attempt to translate, he would look into the hat in which the
stone was placed, he found he was spiritually blind and could
not translate. He told us that his mind dwelt too much on
earthly things, and various causes would make him incapable
of proceeding with the translation. When in this condition he
would go out and pray; and when he became sufficiently humble before God, he could then proceed with the translation."
Martin Harris stated that when Joseph became weary of translating he went out and exercised by throwing stones out on the
river.†

Compared with the snail's pace at which the lost 116 pages
had been written, the speed with which Joseph now dictated
to Cowdery was phenomenal. They began working together
on April 7, 1829, and the 275,000-word manuscript was finished

---

* See *Latter-Day Saints Messenger and Advocate,* October 1834, and *Defense in
a Rehearsal of My Grounds for Separating Myself from the Latter-Day Saints* (Norton,
Ohio, 1839). The latter was written after Cowdery's excommunication in 1838.

† See David Whitmer: *Address to All Believers in Christ* (Richmond, Missouri,
1887), pp. 12, 30; and *Historical Record,* Vol. VI, p. 216.

by the first week in July. Mormons have maintained that the
volume was written in seventy-five working days. This would
mean an average of 3,700 words a day, if one includes the
27,000 words he quoted directly from the Bible. This accomplishment, it has been said, "was far beyond his natural ability
to achieve." *

It is clear, however, that Martin Harris wrote part of the new
version before Cowdery replaced him, since in March 1829 Joseph had a revelation for Harris which said in part: ". . . when
thou hast translated a few more pages, thou shalt stop for a season. . . ." Harris may have been taking dictation for as much
as four months, and he claimed in later years that he had been
scribe for nearly a third of the published Book of Mormon.†
The fact that early pages of both manuscripts are in Cowdery's
hand may simply indicate that he copied Harris's text.‡

There is no doubt, however, that Joseph had developed a remarkable facility for dictation. The speed was not "far beyond
his natural ability"; it was evidence of his ability. To belittle
his creative talent is to do him as great an injustice as to say
that he had no learning — a favorite Mormon thesis designed
to prove the authenticity of the book.

His talent, it is true, was not exceptional, for his book lacked
subtlety, wit, and style. He was chiefly a tale-teller and preacher.
His characters were pale, humorless stereotypes; the prophets
were always holy, and in three thousand years of history not a
single harlot was made to speak. But he began the book with
a first-class murder, added assassinations, and piled up battles by
the score. There was plenty of bloodshed and slaughter to make
up for the lack of gaiety and the stuff of humanity.

Many stories he borrowed from the Bible. The daughter of
Jared, like Salome, danced before a king and a decapitation

* See Francis W. Kirkham: "The Writing of the Book of Mormon," *Improvement
Era,* June 1941, pp. 341 ff.

† See *Doctrine and Covenants* (Salt Lake City, 1921), Section 5, verse 30; and a
letter from Simon Smith to Joseph Smith, son of the prophet, dated Bristol, England,
December 29, 1880. Simon Smith reported an interview with Harris in Utah. This
letter is in the Reorganized Church library.

‡ There were originally two manuscripts of the Book of Mormon, the second
copied by Cowdery from the first. One was placed in the cornerstone of the Nauvoo
House and destroyed by seeping water, except for a few pages, some of which are
in the church library in Salt Lake City. The other copy was preserved intact by Oliver
Cowdery and David Whitmer and is now in possession of the Reorganized Church.

followed. Aminadi, like Daniel, deciphered handwriting on a wall, and Alma was converted after the exact fashion of St. Paul. The daughters of the Lamanites were abducted like the dancing daughters of Shiloh; and Ammon, the American counterpart of David, for want of a Goliath slew six sheep-rustlers with his sling.

The book improved in tempo as it was written; there were fewer sermons and more adventures. But the prose style was unfortunate. Joseph's sentences were loose-jointed, like an earthworm hacked into segments that crawl away alive and whole. Innumerable repetitions bogging down the narrative were chiefly responsible for Mark Twain's ejaculation that the book was "chloroform in print." The phrase "and it came to pass" appeared at least two thousand times.

The last half of the book, however, possessed a dramatic intensity utterly lacking in the first half. Whereas the early portion had no political flavor except for casual references to America as "the land of liberty" and descriptions of democratic elections among the Nephites, the remainder was charged with a crusading spirit that stemmed directly from the greatest murder mystery that ever stirred New York State.

In 1827 there were no monarchists or dictators threatening American democracy, and no invaders on the border. Yet the country was seized by a swiftly spreading fear that the Republic was in danger. The terror began in western New York in September 1826, when the Book of Mormon had barely been conceived, and it swelled to cover eight states before the book reached the press late in 1829.

In Batavia, on the road to Buffalo, a printing press was burned and its owner beaten by a group of masked men. In the press office were fresh proofs of a new book, an exposé of the secret rites and oaths of Freemasonry. The author, William Morgan, was abducted some days later and carried to Canandaigua, nine miles from Joseph Smith's home, for a mock trial. He was then taken secretly to Fort Niagara on the Canadian border, where he disappeared.

Five prominent Masons in Canandaigua were tried for his murder in January 1827. The whole countryside moved in to hear the proceedings. When three were acquitted and the other two received sentences of less than a year, the public felt cheated.

Further trials were held in February, and anti-Masonry spread with each acquittal. Morgan and the Masons became the standing theme of conversation in field and tavern. Ancient suicides, long buried and forgotten by everyone save the coroners who had sat upon them, were raked up in all their lurid details and the Masons were found to have murdered them all. The skulls, it was said, served as tankards in the lodges.

Churches dismissed pastors who would not renounce Masonry, and deacons who would not resign their membership were forbidden the sacrament. Anti-Jackson politicians saw in the rising fever the makings of a political party. Although the Palmyra newspapers maintained a measure of objectivity for a time, this eventually broke down and the local lodge was forced to disband.

In October 1827 a bloated corpse was washed up on the shore of Lake Ontario. The turf had scarcely been planted on the grave when someone suggested that the corpse was Morgan's. "The whole country therefore," wrote an observer, "rang with the exclamation, 'Morgan is found!' " * Mrs. Morgan had not a particle of doubt of the identity of the body, fully believing it to be that of her husband. Only one difficulty remained and that was a mere trifle: there was not a single article of the clothes found upon the deceased that belonged to Morgan. Since an election was approaching, the funeral show was delayed until shortly before the voting. Then hundreds of thousands of people poured into Batavia to join in the obsequies of the great Masonic martyr.

The Masons now found evidence in Canada that the corpse was not Morgan's but that of Timothy Monroe, who had been drowned some weeks earlier. For the second time the body was disinterred, and Mrs. Monroe positively identified it.†

New trials continued in 1828. The sheriffs who chose the juries, and the judges who pronounced sentence, were accused of being Masons. Newspapers that refused to denounce Masonry were attacked for prostituting the God-given right of free

---

* See William L. Stone: *Letters on Masonry and Anti-Masonry* (New York, 1832), pp. 228, 287–8; *Proceedings of the U. S. Anti-Masonic Convention,* held at Philadelphia, September 11, 1830; and the files of the *Wayne Sentinel,* 1827–30.

† Is it possible that Joseph Smith combined the first syllables of Morgan and Monroe to coin the name "Mormon"? For Joseph's own definition of "Mormon" in later years see below, p. 276.

speech. Mountebank anti-Masonic professors of Masonry traveled about the country giving exhibitions of Masonic ceremonials, working their audiences into a delirious hatred.

The Democrats were appalled to count nineteen anti-Masonic conventions within twelve months and began to wonder if they might lose the election because their beloved Andrew Jackson was a Mason of high rank. Masonry was being denounced everywhere as a threat to free government, a secret cabal insidiously working into the key positions of state in order to regulate the whole machinery of the Republic.

So it happened that Joseph Smith was writing the Book of Mormon in the thick of a political crusade that gave backwoods New York, hitherto politically stagnant and socially déclassé, a certain prestige and glory. And he quickly introduced into the book the theme of the Gadianton band, a secret society whose oaths for fraternal protection were bald parallels of Masonic oaths, and whose avowed aim was the overthrow of the democratic Nephite government.

"And it came to pass that they did have their signs," he wrote, "yea, their secret signs, and their secret words; and this that they might distinguish a brother who had entered into the covenant, that whatsoever wickedness his brother should do, he should not be injured by his brother, nor by those who did belong to his band, who had taken this covenant; and thus they might murder, and plunder, and steal, and commit whoredoms, and all manner of wickedness, contrary to the laws of their country, and also the laws of their God. . . ."

Like the Masons the Gadiantons claimed to derive their secrets from Tubal Cain. Boring from within, they became powerful enough to bring about the murder at different times of four chief judges, democratic rulers of the Nephite people. Strengthened by dissenters from the Nephite church, they lived in anarchy among the mountains, descending in periodic raids until the government itself was overthrown and the land of liberty ruled by tyranny. In the end Gadianton Masonry became so powerful that it precipitated the war of extermination fought near the hill Cumorah.

Before burying the golden plates, Moroni, last of the Nephites, engraved a solemn warning to the gentiles of 1830: ". . . and whatsoever nation shall uphold such secret combinations, to get power and gain, until they shall be spread over the nation, behold, they shall be destroyed, for the Lord will not suffer that the blood of his saints, which shall be shed by them, shall always cry unto him from the ground for vengeance upon them, and yet he avengeth them not; wherefore, O ye Gentiles, it is wisdom in God that these things should be shewn unto you, that thereby ye may repent of your sins and suffer not that these murderous combinations shall get above you." *

* The Book of Mormon (1830), pp. 424, 554. There is good evidence that Joseph Smith was familiar with Masonic literature even before the murder of William Morgan. Professor J. H. Adamson of the University of Utah has analyzed in detail Smith's use of the Masonic legends of Enoch and Hiram Abiff, widely popularized in New York State with the publication in 1802 of Thomas S. Webb's *Free Mason's Monitor,* and spread further as Masonic lodges multiplied. The Masons had adopted the ancient Cabbalistic figure of Enoch son of Jared, who was said to have had a vision on the Hill Moriah of a cavern which contained an engraved golden plate, and a pillar of brass holding a metal ball with magical qualities. The secret of the treasure is discovered by Master Masons excavating for the foundation for Solomon's temple. Hiram Abiff, "the widow's son," dies rather than reveal the secret to men of evil. The loyal Masons pursue Abiff's murderers, and slay one of them with a sword in his sleep. They are rewarded by King Solomon, who puts the treasures into the temple, along with brass records and the sacred Urim and Thummim. Joseph Smith's adaptation of these myths will be obvious to any student of the *Book of Mormon* and the history of its writing. Engraved golden plates, brass plates, a magical ball called "the Liahona," the Urim and Thummim, and the treasure cave in the hill, were all incorporated into his story and into his book. I am indebted to Mrs. Adamson for a copy of her late husband's carefully documented study, still in manuscript.

CHAPTER V
Witnesses for God

THE BOOK OF MORMON was a mutation in the evolution of American literature, a curious sport, at once sterile and potent. Although it bred no imitators outside Mormonism and was ignored by literary critics, it brought several hundred thousand immigrants to America in the nineteenth century. The twentieth century sees the distribution of thousands of copies each year. For more than a hundred years missionaries have heralded it throughout the world as religious history second only to the Bible.

Scholars of American literary history have remained persistently uninterested in the Book of Mormon. Their indifference is the more surprising since the book is one of the earliest examples of frontier fiction, the first long Yankee narrative that owes nothing to English literary fashions. Except for the borrowings from the King James Bible, its sources are absolutely American. No sociologist has troubled to draw parallels between the Book of Mormon and other sacred books, like the Koran and *Science and Health,* though all are ostensibly divinely inspired and all are an obscure compound of folklore, moral platitude, mysticism, and millennialism.

Every creed perhaps must have its sacred books. And among such books the Mormon Bible is one of the most remarkable for sheer pretension. It is easy enough to deride its style, and painstaking research can uncover the sources of all its ideas. But nothing can detract from the fact that many people have found it convincing history. Henry A. Wallace recognized this when he said in 1937: "Of all the American religious books of the nineteenth century, it seems probable that the Book of Mormon was the most powerful. It reached perhaps only one per cent of the people of the United States, but it affected this one per cent so powerfully and lastingly that all the people of the United States

No Man Knows My History

have been affected, especially by its contribution to opening up one of our great frontiers." *

Unwilling to credit Joseph Smith with either learning or talent, detractors of the Mormons within a few years declared that the Book of Mormon must have been written by someone else, and eventually laid the mantle of authorship upon one of Joseph's converts, Sidney Rigdon, a Campbellite preacher from Ohio. The theory ran as follows: The Book of Mormon was a plagiarism of an old manuscript by one Solomon Spaulding, which Sidney Rigdon had somehow secured from a printing house in Pittsburgh. After adding much religious matter to the story, Rigdon determined to publish it as a newly discovered history of the American Indian. Hearing of the young necromancer Joseph Smith, three hundred miles away in New York State, he visited him secretly and persuaded him to enact a fraudulent representation of its discovery. Then nine months after the book's publication Smith's missionaries went to Ohio and the pastor pretended to be converted to the new church.

An apostate, Philastus Hurlbut, claimed to have uncovered this deceit in 1833 when he heard old neighbors of Spaulding say that parts of the Book of Mormon were the same as the manuscript they had heard read to them twenty years before. But the only Spaulding manuscript Hurlbut could find was a fabulous Indian romance, stuffed with florid sentiment a world away from the simple, monotonous prose and forthright narrative of the Mormon Bible.

Through the years the "Spaulding theory" collected supporting affidavits as a ship does barnacles, until it became so laden with evidence that the casual reader was overwhelmed by the sheer magnitude of the accumulation. The theory requires a careful analysis because it has been so widely accepted. The documentary evidence on both sides is so burdensome, however, that I have relegated it to an appendix.†

Recent critics who insist that Joseph Smith suffered from delusions have ignored in the Book of Mormon contrary evidence difficult to override. Its very coherence belies their claims. Bernard DeVoto called the book "a yeasty fermentation, form-

* Address before the New York Times National Book Fair, *New York Times,* November 5, 1937.
† See Appendix B.

less, aimless, and inconceivably absurd — at once a parody of all American religious thought and something more than a parody, a disintegration. The œstrus of a paranoiac projected it into a new Bible." *

Far from being the fruit of an obsession, the Book of Mormon is a useful key to Joseph's complex and frequently baffling character. For it clearly reveals in him what both orthodox Mormon histories and unfriendly testimony deny him: a measure of learning and a fecund imagination. The Mormon Church has exaggerated the ignorance of its prophet, since the more meager his learning, the more divine must be his book. Non-Mormons attempting psychiatric analyses have been content to pin a label upon the youth and have ignored his greatest creative achievement because they found it dull. Dull it is, in truth, but not formless, aimless, or absurd. Its structure shows elaborate design, its narrative is spun coherently, and it demonstrates throughout a unity of purpose. Its matter is drawn directly from the American frontier, from the impassioned revivalist sermons, the popular fallacies about Indian origin, and the current political crusades.

Any theory of the origin of the Book of Mormon that spotlights the prophet and blacks out the stage on which he performed is certain to be a distortion. For the book can best be explained, not by Joseph's ignorance nor by his delusions, but by his responsiveness to the provincial opinions of his time. He had neither the diligence nor the constancy to master reality, but his mind was open to all intellectual influences, from whatever province they might blow. If his book is monotonous today, it is because the frontier fires are long since dead and the burning questions that the book answered are ashes.

This is particularly true of the religious matter. In the speeches of the Nephite prophets one may find the religious conflicts that were splitting the churches in the 1820's. Alexander Campbell, founder of the Disciples of Christ, wrote in the first able review of the Book of Mormon: "This prophet Smith, through his stone spectacles, wrote on the plates of Nephi, in his Book of Mormon, every error and almost every truth discussed in New York for the last ten years. He decided all the great controversies: — infant baptism, ordination, the trinity, regenera-

* "The Centennial of Mormonism," *American Mercury*, Vol. XIX (1930), p. 5.

tion, repentance, justification, the fall of man, the atonement, transubstantiation, fasting, penance, church government, religious experience, the call to the ministry, the general resurrection, eternal punishment, who may baptize, and even the question of free masonry, republican government and the rights of man. . . . But he is better skilled in the controversies in New York than in the geography or history of Judea. He makes John baptize in the village of Bethabara and says Jesus was born in Jerusalem." *

If one has the curiosity to read through the sermons in the book, one will be impressed with Joseph Smith's ability to argue with equal facility on both sides of a theological debate. Calvinism and Arminianism had equal status, depending upon which prophet was espousing the cause, and even universalism received a hearing. The great atheist Korihor was struck dumb for his blasphemy, yet he stated his case with more eloquence than the prophet who called down upon him the wrath of heaven.

The facility with which profound theological arguments were handled is evidence of the unusual plasticity of Joseph's mind. But this facility was entirely verbal. The essence of the great spiritual and moral truths with which he dealt so agilely did not penetrate into his consciousness. Had it done so, there would have been no book. He knew these truths as intimately as a bright child knows his catechism, but his use of them was utterly opportunistic. The theology of the Book of Mormon, like its anthropology, was only a potpourri.

As his history drew near its close and he began seriously to think of publication, Joseph became more and more dissatisfied with the Indian narrative as it stood. He had written a record of a thousand years — 600 B.C. to A.D. 400. But apparently he was troubled by rather widespread speculation that the Indians had been in America almost since the days of the Flood. Many thought they had emigrated at the time of the building of the tower of Babel and the great dispersion of tongues, and Joseph seems to have realized that if this theory were to gain in popularity the claims of his book might be scorned.

Writers argued variously that the emigrants had sailed in

* *Millennial Harbinger*, Vol. II (February 1831), p. 85.

boats, or crossed Bering Strait on the ice, or traversed the sunken continent that was said to have joined the Old World with the New. Caleb Atwater, when examining the Ohio ruins in 1820, wrote that the mounds marked "the progress of population in the first ages after the dispersion, rising wherever the posterity of Noah came." *

Joseph may have received a sketchy introduction to the literature supporting this theory in Ethan Smith's *View of the Hebrews,* which quoted several Indian legends vaguely similar to the story of the great Flood. At any rate he was impressed with the probability of the "dispersionist" thesis, for in the last weeks of writing he dictated a terse little history of a people called the Jaredites, which he appended to the Nephite record. This history, he said, had been recorded on a separate set of twenty-four gold plates. It told the story of Jared, who with some followers had fled the tower of Babel and sailed to America about 2500 B.C. They crossed the sea in eight watertight barges, so constructed that they would sail any side up, with windows placed in both the top and the bottom.

Joseph's preoccupation with magic stones crept into the narrative here as elsewhere. The Jaredites had sixteen stones for lighting their barges; God had touched each one with His finger and made it forever luminous. He had given the Nephites, on the other hand, two crystals with spindles inside which directed the sailing of their ships.

Like Noah's ark, the Jaredite barges contained everything which the settlers might need on the new continent: "their flocks which they had gathered together, male and female of every kind . . . fowls of the air . . . fish of the waters . . . swarms of bees . . . seed of every kind." This little detail regarding cargo, flung casually into the story, partly settled the question of how animals had come to America, a problem men had puzzled over for three centuries. Some believed that angels had carried them, others that God had created two Adams and two Edens. One historian, in speculating on whether or not the animals had been brought in boats, was mystified by the presence of cougars and wolves in the New World. "If we suppose those first peoples so foolish as to carry such pernicious animals

---

* "Description of the Antiquities Discovered in the State of Ohio," *American Antiquarian Society Transactions,* Vol. I (1820), p. 202.

to new countries to hunt them, we cannot still think them to have been so mad as to take also many species of serpents for the pleasure of killing them afterward." *

Joseph did not trouble to explain the presence of wild animals in America, and he was careless in his choice of domestic beasts. He had the Jaredites bring horses, swine, sheep, cattle, and asses, when it was known even in his own day that Columbus had found the land devoid of these species.† He blundered similarly in having the Nephites produce wheat and barley rather than the indigenous maize and potatoes.

Always an eclectic, Joseph never exhausted any theory he had appropriated. He seized a fragment here and another there and of the odd assortment built his history. As we have seen, he left unused the one hypothesis that might have helped to save the book from being made so grotesque by twentieth-century archæological and anthropological research. This neglect was probably a result of his reading *View of the Hebrews,* which had scorned the theory expounding the Asiatic origin of the Indian.

Since the ancient Hebrew was far more real than the contemporary Mongolian to the rural folk of western New York, where the Old Testament was meat and drink and the gathering of Israel marvelously imminent, Joseph's instinct in ignoring the Asiatic theory was sound. Cathay was a barren field for religious enterprise. The old Northwest Territory desired its antiquities to prove the validity of Biblical history. It was not ripe for the archæology and ethnology of another century, which would reconstruct the varied civilizations of pre-Columbian America with infinite labor and painstaking care.

The lengths to which Joseph went to make his book historically plausible showed considerable ingenuity. He took pains to make the narrative chronologically accurate and filled it with predictions of events that had already taken place, stated as if they were yet to happen. He even inserted a prophecy of his

* Francisco Javier Clavijero: *History of Mexico* (American edition, Richmond, Virginia, 1806), p. 111.

† Mormons have never satisfactorily excused these inclusions, though they point to discoveries of small prehistoric horses in the New World as evidence of the truth of the Book of Mormon, and ignore the fact that these animals became extinct long before the supposed Jaredite migration.

own coming, calling himself "a choice seer" and predicting that his name would be called Joseph, "after the name of his father."

Of the 350 names in the book he took more than a hundred directly from the Bible. Over a hundred others were Biblical names with slight changes in spelling or additions of syllables. But since in the Old Testament no names began with the letters F, Q, W, X, or Y, he was careful not to include any in his manuscript.

Despite these artifices he was conscious that the book had many obvious defects. To explain them away he put an excuse in the mouth of Moroni: "And if our plates had been sufficiently large we should have written in Hebrew; but the Hebrew hath been altered by us also, and if we could have written in Hebrew, ye would have had none imperfection in our record." Even this did not satisfy him, for he felt compelled to apologize on the title-page: "Now if there be fault, it be the mistake of men." This he repeated near the end of the book with a guarded warning: ". . . and if there be faults, they be the faults of a man. But behold, we know no fault. Nevertheless, God knoweth all things; therefore he that condemneth, let him be aware lest he shall be in danger of hell fire."

A CAREFUL scrutiny of the Book of Mormon and the legendary paraphernalia obscuring its origin discloses not only Joseph's inventive and eclectic nature but also his magnetic influence over his friends. Secretaries usually have no illusions about the men from whom they take dictation, but Oliver Cowdery and Martin Harris were caught in the spell of one of the most enigmatic characters of the century.

Since the first-hand accounts describing Joseph are either scurrilous or blindly adoring, it is difficult to call back the essence of what Cowdery in later years described as Joseph's "mysterious power, which even now I fail to fathom." * His natural talent as a leader included first of all an intuitive understanding of his followers, which led them to believe he was genuinely clairvoyant. Soon after his coming to Harmony, Cowdery had written back to David Whitmer that Joseph told him "his secret

* *Defense in a Rehearsal of My Grounds for Separating Myself from the Latter-Day Saints* (Norton, Ohio, 1839).

thoughts, and all he had meditated about going to see him, which no man on earth knew, as he supposed, but himself." *

But Joseph had more than "second sight," which is common-place among professional magicians. At an early age he had what only the most gifted revivalist preachers could boast of — the talent for making men see visions. This was an aptitude un-suspected in himself until the spring of 1829, when the Book of Mormon was nearly complete.

For some time Joseph had been anxious to organize a church. This was the logical outgrowth of the planning of the Book of Mormon and stemmed from the same obscure hunger for power and deference that had stimulated his earliest fantasies. And since Joseph was an organizer as well as a dreamer, the building of a church was inevitable. Cowdery, however, who had none of Joseph's audacity, was disturbed because his leader was not even an ordained preacher. They argued the matter of authority and ordination at length, and finally decided to fast for many hours and then go to the woods and pray.

No one can walk in the woods in May without an exaltation of spirit, and when the two men knelt in prayer Cowdery was overcome with a vision of heaven. "The voice of the Redeemer spake peace to us," he said, "while the veil was parted and the angel of God came down clothed with glory, and delivered the anxiously looked for message, and the keys of the Gospel of re-pentance . . . as we heard we rejoiced, while his love enkin-dled our souls, and we were rapt in the vision of the Almighty! Where was room for doubt? Nowhere; uncertainty had fled, doubt had sunk, no more to rise, while fiction and deception had fled forever." †

Joseph also described this vision, but without hyperbole. He wrote simply that the angel was John the Baptist, who had con-ferred upon them the true Hebraic priesthood of Aaron and had ordered them to baptize each other. Ten years later Cow-dery left Joseph Smith in disillusionment, yet he wrote of this season as hallowed and said of the vision: ". . . the angel was John the Baptist, which I doubt not and deny not." ‡

* As reported by David Whitmer to Orson Pratt in 1878. *Millennial Star,* Vol. XL, p. 772.

† *Latter-Day Saints Messenger and Advocate* (Kirtland, Ohio), October 1834.

‡ *Defense in a Rehearsal of My Grounds for Separating Myself from the Latter-Day Saints.*

HYRUM SMITH

Oliver Cowdery

THE THREE WITNESSES TO THE BOOK OF MORMON

Martin Harris

David Whitmer

Thus began the era of miracles among the followers of Joseph Smith. Supernatural phenomena followed hard upon one another as the contagion spread. A rivalry sprang up among Joseph's patrons. Joseph Knight brought a wagonload of provisions thirty miles to aid in the Lord's work and returned with a revelation in his pocket. David Whitmer's father, not to be outdone, promised free board and lodging if Joseph would finish the translation of the plates back in Fayette, New York.

When David brought his wagon to Harmony to move the couple north to his father's home, he had a minor miracle to tell. Seven acres of his twenty-acre field had been miraculously plowed during the night. Lucy Smith later wrote that three mysterious strangers further hastened his journey by spreading one of his fields with fertilizer. David was eager to see that the plates were carefully packed, but Joseph soberly informed him that they were to be carried by a special messenger. And when along the road they saw a bearded man with a bulging knapsack on his back, he told David that it was the angel messenger in disguise.

Mrs. Whitmer, already burdened with many children, was the only person who resented Joseph's coming. As the days went by she grew more weary and more bewildered. Then one morning she came in from the milking trembling with excitement. On her way to the barn in the mist of the early dawn she had been confronted by an old man with a white beard. "You have been faithful and diligent in your labors," he had said, "but you are tired because of the increase in your toil; it is proper therefore that you should receive a witness that your faith might be strengthened." Whereupon he had showed her the golden plates.*

It is probable that no one was more surprised at this than Joseph Smith. The tractable Cowdery had seen a vision after long fasting and intense prayer, but Mother Whitmer had had a vision on his behalf quite by herself, and Joseph doubtless pondered this miracle in his heart with wonder. Moved by the hospitality showered upon him, he repaid it with the only

---

* The Whitmer family miracles were described by David Whitmer in an interview with Orson Pratt in 1878, and also by Lucy Smith. See *Biographical Sketches*, pp. 136-7, and the *Millennial Star*, Vol. XL, pp. 772-3. Joseph made no mention of them in his own journals.

wealth he had, personal revelations carrying the blessings of heaven.

Martin Harris hung about the Whitmer home like a begging spaniel, continually reminding Joseph of his promise that three men were to see the plates. Finally the witnesses were chosen: Harris, Cowdery, and David Whitmer. Joseph instructed them carefully in the Lord's name: "Behold, I say unto you, that you must rely upon my word, which if you do with full purpose of heart, you shall have a view of the plates, and also the breast-plate, the sword of Laban, the Urim and Thummim. . . . And it is by your faith that you shall obtain a view of them. . . . And ye shall testify that you have seen them. . . . And if you do these last commandments of mine, which I have given you, the gates of hell shall not prevail against you." *

The four men walked into the woods and knelt in prayer. Joseph led the entreaty, and the others followed in solemn succession. Then they waited silently for a miracle. The summer breeze stirred the leaves above them, and a bird chirped loudly, but nothing happened. The ensuing stillness became oppressive. Then Harris, whose heart was stabbed with doubt, rose shame-faced and wretched. Blaming their failure upon his presence, he asked to go and pray alone.

"He accordingly withdrew from us," Joseph said, "and we knelt down again, and had not been many minutes engaged in prayer, when presently we beheld a light above us in the air, of exceeding brightness; and behold, an angel stood before us. In his hands he held the plates which we had been praying for these to have a view of. He turned over the leaves one by one, so that we could see them, and discern the engravings thereon distinctly. He then addressed himself to David Whitmer, and said, 'David, blessed is the Lord, and he that keeps His commandments;' when, immediately afterwards, we heard a voice from out of the bright light above us, saying, 'These plates have been revealed by the power of God, and they have been translated by the power of God. The translation of them which you have seen is correct, and I command you to bear record of what you now see and hear.'"

Joseph now went in pursuit of Harris, whom he found on his knees near by. Together they prayed, and the prophet said

* *Doctrine and Covenants*, Section 17.

that the same vision came again. Harris sprang to his feet shouting: " 'Tis enough; 'tis enough; mine eyes have beheld; mine eyes have beheld; Hosanna, Hosanna, blessed be the Lord." *

Following the command of the revelation, the three men signed a statement drawn up by Joseph which was printed at the end of the Book of Mormon:

THE TESTIMONY OF THREE WITNESSES

Be it known unto all nations, kindreds, tongues, and people, unto whom this work shall come, that we, through the grace of God the Father, and our Lord Jesus Christ, have seen the plates which contain this record, which is a record of the people of Nephi, and also of the Lamanites, his brethren, and also of the people of Jared, which came from the tower of which hath been spoken; and we also know that they have been translated by the gift and power of God, for his voice hath declared it unto us; wherefore we know of a surety, that the work is true. And we also testify that we have seen the engravings which are upon the plates; and they have been shewn unto us by the power of God, and not of man. And we declare with words of soberness, that an Angel of God came down from heaven, and he brought and laid before our eyes, that we beheld and saw the plates, and the engravings thereon; and we know that it is by the grace of God the Father, and our Lord Jesus Christ, that we beheld and bear record that these things are true. And it is marvellous in our eyes: Nevertheless, the voice of the Lord commanded us that we should bear record of it; wherefore, to be obedient unto the commandments of God, we bear testimony of these things. — And we know that if we are faithful in Christ, we shall rid our garments of the blood of all men, and be found spotless before the judgement seat of Christ, and shall dwell with him eternally in the heavens. And the honor be to the Father, and to the Son, and to the Holy Ghost, which is one God. Amen.

OLIVER COWDERY
DAVID WHITMER
MARTIN HARRIS

According to the local press of the time, the three witnesses all told different versions of their experience,† a fact that makes it all the more likely that the men were not conspirators but victims of Joseph's unconscious but positive talent at hypnosis.

* *History of the Church*, Vol. I, pp. 54–5.
† Palmyra *Reflector*, March 19, 1831.

Martin Harris was questioned by a Palmyra lawyer, who asked him pointedly: "Did you see the plates and the engravings upon them with your bodily eyes?" To which he replied: "I did not see them as I do that pencil-case, yet I saw them with the eye of faith; I saw them just as distinctly as I see anything around me — though at the time they were covered with a cloth." *
However, when Harris was a very old man he told one interviewer that he "saw the angel turn the golden leaves over and over" and heard him say: "The book translated from those plates is true and translated correctly." †

David Whitmer told the editor of the *Reflector* that Joseph had led him to an open field, where they found the plates lying on the ground. But in later years Whitmer's story too was richly embellished. "We saw not only the plates of the Book of Mormon," he said, "but also the brass plates, the plates of the book of Ether, the plates containing the records of the wickedness and secret combinations of the people of the world. . . . there appeared as it were a table with many records or plates upon it, besides the plates of the Book of Mormon, also the Sword of Laban, the directors — i.e., the ball which Lehi had, and the Interpreters." ‡

All three witnesses eventually quarreled with Joseph and left his church. At their going he heaped abuse upon them, but none ever denied the reality of his vision, and Cowdery and Harris eventually were rebaptized. Joseph had no fear in vilifying them; he neither expected nor received reprisals. For he had conjured up a vision they would never forget.

Not content with the testimony of the three witnesses, Joseph drew up a second statement:

AND ALSO THE TESTIMONY OF EIGHT WITNESSES

Be it known unto all nations, kindreds, tongues, and people, unto whom this work shall come, that Joseph Smith, Jr. the Author and Proprietor of this work, has shewn unto us the plates of which hath

* As related to J. A. Clark, who was then in Palmyra. See *Gleanings by the Way*, pp. 256–7.

† Interview with Ole Jensen in Clarkston, Utah, published in J. M. Sjodahl: *Introduction to the Study of the Book of Mormon*, pp. 58–60.

‡ See the Palmyra *Reflector*, March 19, 1831, and David Whitmer's interview with Orson Pratt forty-nine years afterward, published in the *Millennial Star*, Vol. XL, pp. 771–2.

been spoken, which have the appearance of gold; and as many of the leaves as the said Smith has translated, we did handle with our hands; and we also saw the engravings thereon, all of which has the appearance of ancient work, and of curious workmanship. And this we bear record, with words of soberness, that the said Smith has shewn unto us, for we have seen and hefted, and know of a surety, that the said Smith has got the plates of which we have spoken. And we give our names unto the world, to witness unto the world that which we have seen: and we lie not, God bearing witness of it.

CHRISTIAN WHITMER	HIRAM PAGE
JACOB WHITMER	JOSEPH SMITH, SEN.
PETER WHITMER, JR.	HYRUM SMITH
JOHN WHITMER	SAMUEL H. SMITH

It will be seen that four witnesses were Whitmers and three were members of Joseph's own family. The eighth witness, Hiram Page, had married a Whitmer daughter. Mark Twain was later to observe: "I could not feel more satisfied and at rest if the entire Whitmer family had testified."

In later editions the words "Author and Proprietor," which may merely have followed the copyright form, were changed to "translator." The same change was made on the book's title-page, which in the first edition was signed "Joseph Smith, Author and Proprietor."

One of the most plausible descriptions of the manner in which Joseph Smith obtained these eight signatures was written by Thomas Ford, Governor of Illinois, who knew intimately several of Joseph's key men after they became disaffected and left the church. They told Ford that the witnesses were "set to continual prayer, and other spiritual exercises." Then at last "he assembled them in a room, and produced a box, which he said contained the precious treasure. The lid was opened; the witnesses peeped into it, but making no discovery, for the box was empty, they said, 'Brother Joseph, we do not see the plates.' The prophet answered them, 'O ye of little faith! how long will God bear with this wicked and perverse generation? Down on your knees, brethren, every one of you, and pray God for the forgiveness of your sins, and for a holy and living faith which cometh down from heaven.' The disciples dropped to their knees, and began to pray in the fervency of their spirit, supplicating God for more than two hours with fanatical earnestness; at the end of which time, looking again into the box, they were now persuaded that they saw the plates." *

Yet it is difficult to reconcile this explanation with the fact that these witnesses, and later Emma and William Smith, emphasized the size, weight, and metallic texture of the plates.† Perhaps Joseph built some kind of makeshift deception. If so, it disappeared with his announcement that the same angel that had revealed to him the sacred record had now carried it back into heaven.

Exactly how Joseph Smith persuaded so many of the reality of the golden plates is neither so important nor so baffling as the effect of this success on Joseph himself. It could have made of him a precocious and hard-boiled cynic, as a little experimentation with the new art of "mesmerism" made of the famous preacher LaRoy Sunderland some years later. But there is no evidence of cynicism even in Joseph's most intimate diary entries. The miracles and visions among his followers apparently served only to heighten his growing consciousness of supernatural power. He had a sublime faith in his star, plus the enthusiasm of a man constantly preoccupied with a single subject, and he was rapidly acquiring the language and even the accent of sincere faith.

THE BOOK OF MORMON was printed by Egbert B. Grandin, printer of the local *Wayne Sentinel,* after Joseph had failed to secure a contract from Thurlow Weed, editor of the Rochester *Anti-Masonic Inquirer.* Martin Harris guaranteed $3,000 for the printing of 5,000 copies, agreeing to mortgage his farm if necessary in order to make up the sum. By this time he had left his wife, having satisfied her with a settlement of eighty acres and a house.

Before the printing was finished, however, the professionally righteous citizens of Palmyra formed a citizens' committee and organized a boycott of the Book of Mormon. When they presented a long list of names to the printer he took fright, stopped

* *History of Illinois* (Chicago, 1854), p. 257.

† William Smith's description, given in a sermon in Deloit, Iowa, June 8, 1884, was published in the *Saints Herald,* Vol. XXXI, p. 644.

the printing, and refused to resume it until he had been paid in full.*

Harris had not yet mortgaged his farm and there was no money available. Hyrum Smith, who disliked Harris and suspected that he wanted all the profits from the book sales,† suggested that they try to sell the copyright for enough money to ensure publication. Joseph then looked into the Urim and Thummim and received a revelation directing Cowdery and Hiram Page to go to Toronto, where they would find a man anxious to buy it.

"We did not find him," Cowdery later wrote, "and had to return surprised and disappointed. . . . I well remember how hard I strove to drive away the foreboding which seized me, that the First Elder had made tools of us, where we thought in the simplicity of our hearts that we were divinely commanded." ‡

This was the first time that a revelation had gone awry. With disarming candor Joseph explained: "Some revelations are of God: some revelations are of man: and some revelations are of the devil. . . . When a man enquires of the Lord concerning a matter, if he is deceived by his own carnal desires, and is in error, he will receive an answer according to his erring heart, but it will not be a revelation from the Lord." §

Joseph now had only one resource. Martin Harris had been an embarrassingly zealous proselyter who advertised his own visionary experiences as freely as those of Joseph. He had seen Jesus in the shape of a deer, he said, and had walked with Him two or three miles, talking with Him as familiarly as one man talks with another. The devil, he said, resembled a jackass, with very short, smooth hair similar to that of a mouse. He prophesied that Palmyra would be destroyed by 1836, and that by 1838 Joseph's church would be so large that there would be no need for a president of the United States. Publicly Harris met with

---

* See Lucy Smith: *Biographical Sketches*, p. 150.

† This was David Whitmer's opinion. See *Address to All Believers in Christ*, p. 31.

‡ *Defense in a Rehearsal of My Grounds for Separating Myself from the Latter-Day Saints.*

§ This story was told by David Whitmer. "I could tell you other false revelations that came through Brother Joseph as mouthpiece. Many of Brother Joseph's revelations were never printed. The revelation to go to Canada was written down on paper, but was never printed." *Address to All Believers in Christ*, p. 31.

amused tolerance and only occasional bitter scorn. Privately Palmyra gossiped about his scandalous conduct with his neighbor Haggard's wife.*

In desperation Joseph lashed at Harris with the Lord's word:

I command you to repent — repent, lest I smite you by the rod of my mouth, and by my wrath, and by mine anger, and your sufferings be sore.

How sore you know not!

How exquisite you know not!

Yea, how hard to bear you know not!!

. . . And I command you that you preach nought but repentance, and show not these things unto the world until it is wisdom in me. . . .

And again, I command thee that thou shalt not covet thy neighbor's wife; nor seek thy neighbor's life.

And again, I command thee that thou shalt not covet thine own property, but impart it freely to the printing of the Book of Mormon. . . .

And misery thou shalt receive if thou wilt slight these counsels; yea, even the destruction of thyself and property. . . .

Pay the printer's debt! Release thyself from bondage.†

Thoroughly scared, Harris hastily sold his farm. Grandin was paid in full, and by March 26, 1830 the Book of Mormon was put on sale in the Palmyra bookstore. On April 2 the Rochester *Daily Advertiser* published the first review:

BLASPHEMY — BOOK OF MORMON, ALIAS THE GOLDEN BIBLE

The Book of Mormon has been placed in our hands. A viler imposition was never practiced. It is an evidence of fraud, blasphemy, and credulity, shocking both to Christians and moralists. The author and proprietor is Joseph Smith, Jr., a fellow who by some hocus pocus acquired such influence over a wealthy farmer of Wayne county that the latter mortgaged his farm for $3,000, which he paid for printing and binding five thousand copies of the blasphemous work.

* See J. A. Clark: *Gleanings by the Way,* pp. 258, 348; and the statement of Lucy Harris in E. D. Howe: *Mormonism Unvailed,* pp. 14, 256.

† *Book of Commandments,* Chapter xvi, pp. 40–1.

CHAPTER VI
The Prophet of Palmyra

THE BOOK OF MORMON was the catapult that flung Joseph Smith to a place in the sun. But it could not be responsible for his survival there. The book lives today because of the prophet, not he because of the book. For Joseph, writing was always the means to an end, never the end in itself, and the moment he had felt the brief warm glow of satisfaction at seeing his words in print, he turned to the serious business of organizing his church.

In the beginning the book was clearly the moving power. It was not only a magnet attracting followers, but also a significant force in Joseph's own behavior. What had been originally conceived as a mere money-making history of the Indians had been transformed at some point early in the writing, or possibly even before the book was begun, into a religious saga. The end result was a document of quasi-Biblical authority. It was something that he could offer to his followers as sober proof of the authenticity of his own prophetic mission.

While rival prophets like Isaac Bullard, Jemima Wilkinson, and Joseph Dylks suffered from no compulsion whatever to prove their pretensions, Joseph Smith, whether for lack of self-confidence or the greater reasonableness of his nature, seems to have felt urgently the need for preparation and for confirming testimony. The Book of Mormon itself was not enough; he needed first three, then eight witnesses to its authenticity, and in later years he continued to exploit facts or legends that would tend to support the book's historical accuracy.

An apocryphal story about Jemima Wilkinson relates that one day she led her colony to the shore of Seneca Lake and told them that she was about to walk upon the water. First, however, she tried the surface gingerly, and when her toes broke through, she turned back unabashed to shore, saying coolly that her followers' faith was already of such prodigious strength that no miracle was necessary.

There is a similar, and equally apocryphal story about Joseph Smith, which holds that he too boasted he would walk upon the water, but that he secretly built a plank bridge underneath the surface of the pond. The public demonstration was a note-worthy success until he reached the middle, when, thanks to mischievous boys, instead of planks he trod on water and barely escaped drowning.* Baseless though this story may be, it is none the less symbolic.

A fortnight after the publication of the Book of Mormon Joseph Smith announced to his following his official title as "Seer, a Translator, a Prophet, an Apostle of Jesus Christ, and Elder of the Church through the will of God the Father, and the grace of your Lord Jesus Christ." It is not easy to trace the steps by which Joseph assumed this role. Apparently he slipped into it with ease, without the inner turmoil that preceded the spiritual fervor of so many of the great religious figures of the past.

Within two years of his first revelation, which had sprung out of the mundane crisis of the lost manuscript, he had established the true "Church of Christ," bulwarked by the ancient priesthood of Israel and claiming to be, not another fragment of Protestantism, but the restored religion of Jesus Himself. But since the history of this period is based on documents written many years later, one cannot see the stumblings and hesitations that must have attended Joseph's transformation. The casual reader will be shocked by his deceptions — sometimes clumsy, but even more shocking when they were deft — because Joseph was practicing in the field of religion, where honesty and integrity presumably should count for something.

It should not be forgotten, however, that for Joseph's vigorous and completely undisciplined imagination the line between truth and fiction was always blurred. "Behold," said Lehi in the Book of Mormon, "I have dreamed a dream; or, in other words, I have seen a vision." And for Joseph what was a dream one day could become a vision the next, and a reality the day after that. It is doubtful if he ever escaped the memory of the conscious artifice that went into the Book of Mormon, but its phe-

* This story was first denied in the *Evening and Morning Star* (Kirtland, Ohio), April 1834, pp. 300-1, and again in the *Latter-Day Saints Messenger and Advocate,* December 1835, pp. 230-1.

nomenal success must have stifled any troublesome qualms. And at an early period he seems to have reached an inner equilibrium that permitted him to pursue his career with a highly compensated but nevertheless very real sincerity. Certainly a persisting consciousness of guilt over the cunning and deception with which his prophetic career was launched would eventually have destroyed him.

Joseph's great dramatic talent found its first outlet in the cabalistic ritual of rural wizardry, then in the hocus-pocus of the Gold Bible mystery, and finally in the exacting and apparently immensely satisfying role of prophet of God. His talent, like that of many dramatic artists, was emotional rather than intellectual, and it was free from the tempering influence that a more critical audience would have exercised upon it.

How uncritical his following was may be seen from an account of one of his early cottage meetings, which was attended by thirteen-year-old Mary Elizabeth Rollins. "I sat with the others," she wrote many years later in her autobiography, "on a plank that had been provided, the ends resting on boxes. After prayer and singing, Joseph began talking. Suddenly he stopped and seemed almost transfixed, he was looking ahead and his face outshone the candle which was on a shelf just behind him. I thought I could almost see the cheek bones, he looked as though a searchlight was inside his face and shining through every pore. I could not take my eyes from his face. After a short time he looked at us very solemnly and said: 'Brothers and Sisters do you know who has been in your midst this night?' One of the Smith family said, 'An angel of the Lord.' Joseph did not answer.

"Martin Harris was sitting at the Prophet's feet on a box, he slid to his knees, clasped his arms around the Prophet's knees and said: 'I know, it was our Lord and Saviour, Jesus Christ.' Joseph put his hand on Martin's head and answered: 'Martin, God revealed that to you. Brothers and Sisters, the Saviour has been in your midst. I want you to remember it. He cast a veil over your eyes for you could not endure to look upon Him, you must be fed with milk and honey, not meat. I want you to remember this as if it were the last thing that escapes my lips. He has given you all to me and commanded me to seal you up to everlasting Life that where he is you may also be, and if you are tempted of Satan say "Get thee behind me Satan." ' These words and his looks are photographed on my brain. Then he knelt and prayed. I have never heard anything like it since. I felt he was talking to the Lord. . . ." *

Although Joseph exerted what some of his contemporaries described as a "magnetic" sway over his people, there was an equally significant reverse influence. The young prophet was himself molded by the insistent demands of his audience. Among his first converts was Newel Knight, the son of one of his earliest patrons. Young Knight had suffered for years from an undiagnosed sickness and had become obsessed with a fear for his salvation. When Joseph requested him to pray in a public meeting, he was overcome by shyness and refused. Joseph's insistence only added to his dismay, and he begged to be allowed to wait until he could go to the woods and pray alone. Agonized praying in the forest stillness, however, served only to increase his conviction of sin. When he returned home, his wife was frightened at his contorted face and ran to find Joseph Smith.

When he arrived he found Knight rolling on the floor in a fit, his features distorted and his limbs twisted horribly. A dozen people were crowding into the room, eager to see a devil wrestling with a man's soul. They turned to stare at the youth who called himself a prophet, and Joseph must have realized with a sense of panic that he was expected to perform a miracle. When the convulsions became unbearable to watch, he reached out and seized Knight's hand.

"Almost immediately he spoke to me," Joseph wrote in his autobiography, "and with great earnestness requested me to cast the devil out of him, saying that he knew he was in him, and that he also knew that I could cast him out."

"If you know that I can, it shall be done," Joseph replied, and in the conventional exorcist's fashion commanded the devil in the name of Christ to release the man's soul. Immediately Knight cried out that he saw the devil leave him and vanish from sight. His convulsions ceased and he fell upon the bed unconscious, awakening later to testify that he had glimpsed eternity.

Joseph must have been overwhelmed by this miracle, for he had no idea how common were such occurrences. He was as

* Autobiography of Mary E. Rollins Lightner, MS.

unsophisticated as the rest of the village about mental therapy. If he had been troubled by a sense of inadequacy for the great role into which he had stumbled, more by accident than by design, this may well have dissolved it forever.

The Church of Christ was formally established on Tuesday, April 6, 1830, with six members. Within a month the number had jumped to forty. Most of the converts, like Joseph Knight and his son Newel, came from southern New York, not Palmyra, where Joseph was denied even the use of the town meeting hall. In Colesville and Bainbridge he had found men and women who were won to him not only by the fabulous story of the golden plates but also by his first hesitating sermons.

But for every person he baptized, there were a dozen who remembered his early trial for money-digging and believed him now to be not only a fraud but also a callous blasphemer. Some of them tore out a dam that his followers had built across a stream to make a pool deep enough for baptisms. After it was defiantly rebuilt and the ceremonies performed, about fifty men surrounded the house where Joseph and his converts took refuge. All day the mob milled around the house. That night a constable appeared at the door with a warrant for Joseph's arrest on the old charge of disorderly conduct.

Joseph had been in court before, and it held no terrors for him, but he was afraid of the men who jeered at him from the darkness and whose obscene epithets carried into the parlor. He talked earnestly with the constable, pleading his innocence with such eloquence that the officer confessed his warrant had been a mere subterfuge to get him into the hands of the mob, and he promised to save him from a tar-and-feather party. Accordingly, when their wagon was waylaid on a lonely road, the constable whipped up his horses and galloped all the way to South Bainbridge.

Here Joseph was brought to trial. Joseph Knight, angered at this affront to religious liberty, hired two able lawyers for the youth's defense. As in the first trial, Stowel and Jonathan Thompson supported him as best they could. Stowel's daughters, called to testify for the prosecution, said nothing but good on his behalf, and the court after an all-day session sent in a verdict of acquittal.

But at the very moment he secured his freedom another constable served a warrant upon him and hurried him off to the next county for trial. Here, according to Joseph's lawyer, the prosecution sent out runners who "ransacked the hills and vales, grog shops and ditches, and gathered together a company that looked as if they had come from hell and been whipped by the soot boy thereof." *

Until two o'clock in the morning these men told all the gossip of the hill country about the money-digger and his golden plates, the fortune-teller turned baptizer. Newel Knight, forced to testify of his encounter with the devil, rebuffed the prosecution with a stout and witty defense. "There was not one particle of testimony against the prisoner," said his lawyer. "No, sir, he came out like the three children from the fiery furnace, without the smell of fire upon his garments."

Despite a second acquittal resentment against him increased. "You would have thought, sir," his lawyer related, "that Gog and Magog were let loose on the young man. . . . The cry of 'False prophet! false prophet!' was sounded from village to village, and every foul epithet that malice and wicked ingenuity could invent was heaped upon him."

Very early the young prophet learned to use persecution as a means of identifying himself with the great martyrs. In writing of his ill-treatment in his history he said: "They spit upon me, pointed their fingers at me, saying, 'Prophesy, prophesy!' And thus did they imitate those who crucified the Savior of mankind, not knowing what they did." The insults magnified the significance of his mission, else they would have been unbearable.

Meanwhile an avalanche of misfortune descended upon the whole Smith family. Creditors swarmed down upon Hyrum's household with warrants for his own and his father's arrest on charges of debt. Hyrum fled the village, but Joseph senior was taken into custody because he could not pay a fourteen-dollar note. Lucy wrote that the Quaker creditor offered to tear up the note if her husband would burn his copies of the Book of Mormon, but that he preferred martyrdom to a denial of the truth and was unceremoniously hauled off to jail.

* Speech of John Reid (not a convert) at Nauvoo, published in the *Times and Seasons*, Vol. V (June 1, 1844), pp. 549–52.

Faced with the bankruptcy of his family and the growing hostility in southern New York, Joseph returned to his farm in Pennsylvania, where he planted his crops and hopefully awaited the return of his brother Samuel, who had gone south to sell copies of the Book of Mormon. Tedious and solitary field labor he had always detested, and he chafed under it now like a newly broken ox.

Impatient at his absence, Oliver Cowdery paid him a visit and urged him to be about the business of his church. Very shortly Joseph announced a new revelation, which said in part: "Magnify thine office, and after thou hast sowed thy fields and secured them, go speedily unto the church which is in Colesville, Fayette and Manchester, and they shall support thee; and I will bless them both spiritually and temporally; but if they receive thee not, I will send them a cursing instead of a blessing. . . . And in temporal labors thou shalt not have strength, for this is not thy calling." *

This revelation was meant, not for Cowdery, but for Emma Smith. Racked anew with doubt, chagrined over their poverty, and frightened by the rancor that greeted her husband's preaching, she had been the first to urge him to go back to the soil. She had seen no plates and heard no voices. She had held out six weeks after the church was organized before she was baptized, and now it was mid-July and she had not been "confirmed" an official member. Her parents' contempt, her neighbors' derision, and even the death of her child she had borne with fortitude. But the prospect of living off the dubious and intermittent charity of Joseph's followers was more than this proud girl could stomach. The Lord's command to leave their farm, the only security their marriage offered, to return to Colesville, where Joseph was in constant danger of being mobbed, or to Manchester, where her father-in-law lay in jail, or to Fayette to live by the generosity of Mrs. Whitmer, filled her with fury.

In desperation Joseph called upon the Lord to speak to her, and the resulting revelation is the clearest mirror we have that reflects what was then in Emma's heart: "Hearken unto the voice of the Lord your God, while I speak unto you, Emma Smith, my daughter . . . thou art an elect lady whom I have called. Murmur not because of the things which thou hast not

* *Book of Commandments,* Chapter xxv, verse 14.

seen. . . . And the office of thy calling shall be for a comfort unto my servant, Joseph Smith, Jun., thy husband, in his afflictions with thy consoling words, in the spirit of meekness. . . . And thou needest not fear, for thy husband shall support thee from the Church. . . . cleave unto the covenants thou hast made. Continue in the spirit of meekness and beware of pride. Let thy soul delight in thy husband. . . . And except thou do this, where I am you cannot come." *

A whole month passed, however, before Emma consented to the confirmation ceremony, and the occasion of her acquiescence apparently made a vivid impression on Joseph, for he described the evening in detail in his history almost ten years later: ". . . we prepared some wine of our own making, and held our meeting, consisting only of five, viz., Newel Knight and his wife, myself and my wife, and John Whitmer. We partook together of the Sacrament, after which we confirmed these two sisters into the Church, and spent the evening in a glorious manner. The Spirit of the Lord was poured out upon us, we praised the Lord God, and rejoiced exceedingly." †

Shortly afterward the couple left Harmony and moved back to Fayette, New York, to the home of Peter Whitmer. Emma never saw her parents again. With every new success of his son-in-law, Isaac Hale's tongue grew more acid, for he never lost his conviction that the youth was a barefaced impostor. But Joseph seems to have shrugged off this contempt with a light heart, since no malice against the old man crept into his journal. Emma believed in him, and nothing else mattered. He was done with the soil forever.

THE MOMENT was auspicious in American history for the rise of a prophet of real stature. Although the authority and tradition of the Christian religion were decomposing in the New World's freedom, there was a counter-desire to escape from disorder and chaos. The broken unity of Christianity was laboring at its own

* *Book of Commandments,* Chapter xxvi, pp. 58–9. When this revelation was revised for the second edition, the line "thy husband shall support thee *from* the Church," was changed to "support thee *in* the Church." See *Doctrine and Covenants,* Section 25. Ann Lee, founder of the Shakers, had also been called the "elect lady," the reference originating in the New Testament, II John, verse 1.

† *History of the Church,* Vol. I, p. 108.

reconstruction. William Ellery Channing in the East and Alexander Campbell in the West were symbols of this need for synthesis. Each fought for a universal morality and abhorred the sectarianism that finally enmeshed them both.

Channing preached a sophisticated heresy akin to deism, and Campbell, at the other extreme, tried to reconstruct the primitive Christian church, with all its naïve realism, oversimplified ethics, and antiquated theology. But America was ripe for a religious leader wearing the mantle of authority and speaking God's word as one ordained in heaven to that purpose. His mission should be to those who found religious liberty a burden, who needed determinate ideas and familiar dogmas, and who fled from the solitude of independent thinking.

Joseph Smith, attempting to fill this role, was not unconscious of its exactions. He bulwarked his new and precarious position by using rich old symbols, familiar, sure-fire, and eminently safe. Like Alexander Campbell he went to the New Testament for titles — apostle, elder, priest, deacon, teacher, and patriarch — and generously conferred them upon his male converts. With an insight rare among the prophets of his own generation, he did not make a complete break with the past. He continued the story, he did not present a new cosmology.

In the beginning there was nothing original in Joseph's ethics, but nothing in universal morals was omitted from it. He grafted only two things on New Testament Christianity, himself and his book. Out of the fusion came a new growth, drawing its strength from the great moral code of the old church, and its novelty and flavor from the man.

Very quickly he discarded the last remnants of his youthful necromancy, giving up the mineral rod even before the Book of Mormon was completed. Later he stopped using the stones, except in rare instances, realizing finally that by drawing the attention of his followers they robbed him of his own authority. David Whitmer wrote that "Joseph gave the stone to Oliver Cowdery, and told me as well as the rest that he was through with it, and he did not use the stone any more. . . . He told us that we would all have to depend on the Holy Ghost hereafter to be guided into truth and obtain the will of the Lord. The revelations after this came through Joseph as 'mouthpiece';

that is, he would enquire of the Lord, pray and ask concerning a matter, and speak out the revelation." *

Very shortly Joseph met what every new leader must face sooner or later, the problem of defining his own power. Cowdery believed in a general sharing of the apostolic gifts, tried his own hand at writing revelations, and even demanded that Joseph amend some of his own. Joseph met this challenge with a paralyzing dignity: "By what authority do you command me to alter or erase, to add to or diminish from, a revelation or commandment from Almighty God?"

Cowdery at once retreated, but secretly he encouraged Hiram Page, who was also trying to get revelations through a little black seer stone with two holes drilled through it. Seeing at once that Page was only Cowdery's tool, Joseph struck at his secretary with the Lord's word and ordered him to stop his rival's mouth: "Behold, I say unto thee, Oliver . . . no one shall be appointed to receive commandments and revelations in this Church, excepting my servant Joseph Smith, Jun., for he receiveth them even as Moses. . . . But thou shalt not write by way of commandment, but by wisdom: And thou shalt not command him who is at thy head, and at the head of the Church. . . . And again, thou shalt take thy brother, Hiram Page, between him and thee alone, and tell him that those things which he hath written from that stone, are not of me, and that Satan deceiveth him. . . ." †

Page publicly renounced the stone in the first general church conference in September 1830, and it was generally understood that the spiritual gifts shared in common by the early disciples of Jesus were now concentrated in the person of the "First Elder." For Joseph this was a salient victory. To have given either disciple free rein would have meant quick chaos, but so to deprive them of the privileges he himself enjoyed was the first step toward authoritarianism in his church. The pattern was set.

As Joseph gained in power and confidence there was a measurable improvement in the quality of his revelations. Instead of

* *Address to All Believers in Christ*, p. 32.
† *Doctrine and Covenants*, Section 28. See also *History of the Church*, Vol. I, p. 105. Page's stone, which seems originally to have been an Indian relic, is now in the library of the Reorganized Church.

brief, hesitating orders on temporal and often frankly financial matters, he began to preach sermons in the name of the Lord. At times he appropriated the lyrical style of the Bible so expertly that the instrument sounded under his touch with astonishing brilliancy and purity of tone. Liberally paraphrasing Isaiah and the Revelation of St. John, he seized upon the most provocative of religious symbols — the chosen people, the gathering of Israel, the end of the world, eternal damnation, the second coming of Christ, the resurrection — and exploited all the rich and moving irrationalism inherent in them.

For centuries these symbols had been threaded into the patterns of Christian thinking. They were the stock in trade of every frontier preacher. But Joseph used them as no one had before him. Instead of retelling the legends of the ancient chosen people, he created a new chosen people. Instead of arguing about the ambiguities of St. John, he transformed the apocalypse into terse, naïve prophecy and dispatched the most sophisticated metaphysical problems with dexterous oversimplifications.

While his sectarian rivals were preaching spiritedly, but obscurely, about the coming millennium, he began to lay concrete plans for the building of the New Jerusalem. Less than five months after the official organization of his church he said in a revelation: ". . . no man knoweth where the city of Zion shall be built, but it shall be given hereafter. Behold, I say unto you that it shall be on the borders by the Lamanites." And he ordered Oliver Cowdery, who had been trying without success to sell copies of the Book of Mormon in the East, to go west to preach among the Indians and keep an eye out for a likely spot on which to build the city of God.

Joseph had written the book with an eye to red as well as white converts and had always hoped that the red man might be persuaded that it was the history of his ancestors. He had even inserted a prophecy in the book saying that in the last days the record would be shown to the red man by the gentiles. "And then shall they rejoice . . . and many generations shall not pass away among them, save they shall be a white and delightsome people."

Here Joseph was offering the red man, not restoration, but assimilation, not the return of his continent, but the loss of his identity. The promise of a white skin to the convert did not seem a genetic absurdity to a people who were being told in sober history books that the pigment of the red man in New England who had adopted the white man's way of life had actually become lighter than that of his savage brothers.*

Three men were appointed to accompany Cowdery on his Indian mission. One was impetuous twenty-three-year-old Parley Pratt, who had been a convert only three weeks. He was a former Campbellite who had come from Ohio to New York State to preach to his relatives and had fallen under the persuasive influence of Hyrum Smith. Impatient now to convert his Campbellite friends, he steered the party to Mentor, Ohio, where lived the preacher who had converted Pratt to Campbellism.

This was Sidney Rigdon, a dignified and rather handsome man, who welcomed them cordially, examined the Book of Mormon with interest but some suspicion, and promised to read it. Rigdon was a close associate of Alexander Campbell and one of the most famous orators in northern Ohio.

Although Pratt did not know it, his coming could not have been more opportune. For several years past, Rigdon had been the most successful revivalist on the Western Reserve. He was "gifted with very fine powers of mind," wrote a fellow preacher, "an imagination at once fertile, glowing and wild to extravagance, with temperament tinged with sadness and bordering on credulity." He was emotional and humorless, and subject to fits of melancholy and "nervous spasms and swoonings" that he attributed to the Holy Ghost.

Three months before Pratt's coming he had quarreled with Campbell over the question of re-establishing the ancient communism of the primitive Christian church. Clearly the most fanatical and literal-minded of the Disciples of Christ, Rigdon had so zealously espoused the principle of holding things in common that he had set up a small communistic colony in Kirtland, a thriving town next door to Cleveland. But Campbell had fought Rigdon bitterly on the subject. After an open break in the conference of August 1830, Rigdon left "chafed

---

* See Samuel Williams: "A Dissertation on the Colors of Men, Particularly on That of the Indians of America," *Natural and Civil History of Vermont* (Burlington, 1809), Vol. I, p. 502.

and chagrined" and never met with the Disciples in a general meeting afterward.

Rigdon was nursing his grievance when the Mormon missionaries arrived. For years he had believed fervently in the gathering of Israel and the imminence of the millennium, and he saw in the Book of Mormon concrete evidence that the gathering was about to begin, that a new prophet had arisen who was really rebuilding the primitive church of Jesus. Campbell later wrote that Rigdon fasted and prayed for days, until when "one of his fits of swooning and sighing came upon him, he saw an angel and was converted." *

In less than three weeks after the Mormons arrived not only Rigdon but the whole of his communistic colony in Kirtland had been baptized. Rigdon set forth at once for New York State, taking with him the prosperous Kirtland hatter Edward Partridge. Joseph Smith was not quite twenty-five years old; Rigdon was thirty-seven. But Joseph quickly took the measure of the older man. To the pious, sweet-tempered Partridge he gave only the brief revelation bestowed like a prayer upon most newcomers, but for Rigdon he prepared a glowing welcome: "Behold verily, verily I say unto my servant Sidney, I have looked upon thee and thy works. I have heard thy prayers, and prepared thee for a greater work. Thou art blessed, for thou shalt do great things. . . ."

"Brother Joseph rejoiced," David Whitmer later wrote, "believing that the Lord had sent to him this great and mighty man, Sidney Rigdon, to help him in the work." Joseph apparently was overwhelmed that a learned and influential man had come to him, in faith and without greed. Though conscious of his lack of schooling, and fearful lest his ignorance lose him the man, Joseph made no attempt to hide his small learning and explained in the revelation that the Lord preferred "the weak things of the world, those who are unlearned and despised, to thrash the nations."

It was inevitable that Rigdon should hear snatches of gossip about the young prophet's colorful past, and Joseph boldly suggested that he go south to interview the magistrates at Coles-

* *Millennial Harbinger*, Vol. II (1831), p. 100. For a first-hand account of Rigdon's character and his quarrel with Campbell see A. S. Hayden: *Early History of the Disciples in the Western Reserve* (1876), pp. 191-2, 209, 299.

ville and South Bainbridge who had recently acquitted him.
When Rigdon returned with a transcript from the dockets of
the two judges affirming his innocence, Joseph had a new revelation awaiting him.

Some months earlier he had experimented with the idea of
"revealing" a lost book of the Bible and had dictated to Cowdery a fragment said to have come from a parchment buried by
St. John. Then without benefit of either plates or parchment
he had revealed a conversation between God and Moses that, he
said, had been omitted from the Old Testament because of the
wickedness of the Hebrews. Now he revealed a third lost book,
the history of Enoch, whom according to the Bible God had
"translated" into heaven without his ever having died.*

Elaborating upon the brief Biblical reference, Joseph wrote
one of the longest and most remarkable revelations of his career.
Enoch, he said, had founded Zion, the City of Holiness, which
was such a model of civic goodness that the Lord had transported it intact to heaven to be his personal dwelling-place forever. And now in the last days, after the Lord had sent truth
forth "out of the earth" (a deft reference to the Book of Mormon), He would gather His elect to build the New Jerusalem,
to which the city of Enoch would one day descend from heaven
in millennial greeting.

When Rigdon read the Book of Enoch, the scholar in him
fled and the evangelist stepped into the place of second in command of the millennial church. He could not rest until he had
persuaded Joseph to accompany him to Ohio, and within a
fortnight the prophet announced a new revelation which ordered the uprooting of the whole church: "And again, a commandment I give unto the church, that it is expedient in me
that they should assemble together at the Ohio, until the time
that my servant Oliver Cowdery shall return unto them." †

This terse edict roused a storm. Many converts felt that the
Ohio preacher was leading their seer around by the nose. David
Whitmer wrote that Rigdon "soon worked himself deep into
Brother Joseph's affections, and had more influence over him

* The parchment of John at first consisted of only three verses published as Section 6 in the *Book of Commandments*. It was considerably elaborated in the revised
Doctrine and Covenants, as Section 7. The Book of Moses and the Book of Enoch
were published separately in 1851 in a pamphlet called *The Pearl of Great Price*.
† *Doctrine and Covenants*, Section 37.

than any other man living. He was Brother Joseph's private
counsellor and his most intimate friend and brother for some
time after they met."

For several weeks Joseph patiently argued with his sixty followers, telling them that Kirtland was the eastern boundary of
the promised land, which extended from there to the Pacific
Ocean.* Finally, sensing a coming crisis, he gave forth as a
revelation a skillful political document: "But the day soon
cometh that ye shall see me. . . . the angels are waiting the
great command to reap down the earth, to gather the tares that
they may be burned. . . ." There followed an enticing picture of
the promised land, "a land flowing with milk and honey, upon
which there shall be no curse when the Lord cometh. And I
will give it unto you for the land of your inheritance, if you
seek it with all your hearts." Then, as if in afterthought: "And
they that have farms that cannot be sold, let them be left or
rented as seemeth them good." †

John Whitmer wrote that when the revelation was read in a
general conference, "the solemnities of eternity rested on the
congregation," but added shortly that some fought it, believing
"that Joseph had invented it himself to deceive the people that
in the end he might get gain." ‡

But once the majority had accepted it, Joseph prepared to
move. With him went Emma, tight-lipped and weary, but more
hopeful than she had been for many weeks. In four years of
marriage she had lived in seven different towns, usually upon
the charity of friends. She had buried her first child; she had
seen her family estranged and bitter, her father-in-law in jail,
and her husband twice on trial. Now she was pregnant again,
and the promise of a ready-made church in Ohio, almost three
hundred miles west of the scenes of her sorrows and humilia-
tions, must have seemed to her heaven-sent. In January 1831
they set forth in a sleigh with Rigdon and Edward Partridge,
to carry the gospel to the West.

* Letter from Joseph Smith to the Kirtland converts, carried by John Whitmer,
and quoted in Howe: *Mormonism Unvailed*, p. 111.

† *Doctrine and Covenants*, Section 38.

‡ John Whitmer: "History of the Church," MS., Chapter i. The manuscript of
this history is in the library of the Reorganized Church. When it was published in
the *Journal of History*, Vol. I, the significant last portion — part of Chapter xix and
all of Chapters xx and xxi — written after Whitmer had left the church, was omitted.

CHAPTER VII
The Perfect Society and the Promised Land

O HIO HAD SEEN prophets before. In 1812 Abel Sargent, who talked with angels and received revelations, toured the state with his twelve women apostles pretending to raise the dead and preaching the odd doctrine that if one were sufficiently holy one could live without food. The sect suffered eclipse in Marietta, when a convert put the belief to the test, went nine days without eating, and died.

Of fresher memory was Joseph Dylks, who announced in Salesville in 1828 that he was the true Messiah come to usher in the millennium in 1832. The whole community went over to him. "I am God," he cried, "and there is none else! In me Father, Son, and Holy Ghost are met. All who put their trust in me shall never taste death!" To which his followers shouted: "We shall never die!" and groveled at his feet crying: "Behold our God!" According to a historian of the time, about thirty of his disciples near Bakersfield "assembled on the Sabbath and rolled naked on the floor, men and women together, as part of their worship, and committed sins too revolting to mention." *

But the Mormon prophet was of a different breed. It was late in January 1831 when his sleigh ran down the valley formed by a branch of the Chagrin River to the town of Kirtland. Rigdon stopped the horses in front of the Gilbert and Whitney general store. Joseph at once alighted, sprang up the steps, and walked into the store, where the junior partner was standing.

"Newel K. Whitney! Thou art the man!" he exclaimed extending his hand.

"You have the advantage of me," replied the young merchant. "I could not call you by name as you have me."

"I am Joseph the Prophet," he said, smiling. "You've prayed me here, now what do you want of me?"

* J. B. Turner: *Mormonism in All Ages* (New York, 1842), p. 98. See also R. H. Taneyhill: "The Leatherwood God," *Ohio Valley Historical Series,* No. 7, 1871.

This bold introduction wholly disarmed Whitney. He gave the prophet his home for a temporary residence and his loyalty for life.

There were now about one hundred and fifty converts in Kirtland, more than twice the number that had followed him from New York State. But Joseph was disturbed by the fanaticism that possessed this people. Prayer meetings were punctuated by fits and trances. Converts would roll along the floor to the church door and out upon the frozen ground in a masochistic frenzy. Some would mount stumps to preach to imaginary congregations in unknown tongues; others, making apish grimaces, would speed across the fields, returning with revelations that they swore they had copied from pieces of parchment hanging in the night sky.

Unlike the usual evangelist, who saw the spirit of the Lord in such corybantism and mass hysteria, Joseph Smith recognized a menace to his church. He had seen enough of this kind of revivalism in Palmyra to know that in the end it brought only cynicism and disintegration, and his first important revelation in Kirtland denounced the false spirits.*

Basically Joseph's was not a revivalist sect. Although he followed some of the revivalist patterns, he appealed as much to reason as to emotion, challenging his critics to examine the evidences of his divine authority — the Book of Mormon, the lost books of Moses and Enoch, the sworn statements of his witnesses, and numerous Bible-like revelations. The importance of this appeal cannot be overestimated, for it drew into the Mormon ranks many able men who had turned in disgust from the excesses of the local cults. The intellectual appeal of Mormonism, which eventually became its greatest weakness as the historical and "scientific" aspects of Mormon dogma were cruelly disemboweled by twentieth-century scholarship, was in the beginning its greatest strength.

The revivalist sects were inherently democratic since they subsisted on the spontaneous enthusiasm of masses of the people, which the exhorters inflamed but never controlled. But the structure of the Mormon Church was autocratic from the

---

* *Doctrine and Covenants,* Section 50. For descriptions of the hysteria see John Whitmer: "History of the Church," MS., Chapter vi; Parley P. Pratt: *Autobiography* (Chicago, 1888), p. 65; E. D. Howe: *Mormonism Unvailed,* pp. 105–7.

beginning. Shortly after Joseph's coming to Kirtland a woman convert named Hubble began to preach in the streets, calling herself a prophetess and ingratiating herself with many elders. According to Ezra Booth, even Sidney Rigdon "gave her the right hand of fellowship and literally saluted her with what they called the kiss of charity." But Joseph declared her to be of the devil. Finally he forbade the preaching of Mormonism by anyone except elders "regularly ordained by the heads of the Church." *

But the authoritarian nature of Joseph's rule was very different from the imperious dictatorship of Jemima Wilkinson, whose rule by revelation extended to the most petty details of her colony. By ordaining every male convert a member of his priesthood he used the popular and democratic sentiment that all who felt the impulse had the right to preach. Any man could proclaim the gospel provided that he subjected himself to the ultimate authority of the prophet.

Joseph's clergy was thus entirely composed of laymen; moreover, of practically all the laymen in his church. The result was a pyramidal church structure resting on the broadest possible base and possessing astonishing strength. By giving each man a share in the priesthood Joseph quickened a sense of kinship and oneness with the church. There was a feeling of common ownership and responsibility which was immensely satisfying to men for whom religion had hitherto been a wholly passive experience.

The common frontier sentiments against priestcraft, elaborate clerical dress and ritual, and ostentatious display of any kind in relation to worship were all served by the Mormon system of priesthood. Simplicity and informality were among the earliest Mormon ideals, and they were personified in the prophet, with his homely speech and impromptu manner. What Joseph had created was essentially an evangelical socialism, which made up in moral strength what it lacked in grandeur.

Nearly every man had a New Testament title — deacon, teacher, priest, elder, "seventy," or bishop. Each title carried a certain rank, progression from lower to higher being dependent upon a man's faith, his zeal for the church, and the good-

* See *Doctrine and Covenants*, Section 42, and Ezra Booth: "Letter No. 8," republished in Howe: *Mormonism Unvailed*, p. 216.

will of his superiors in the hierarchy. Each convert had not only the dignity of a title but the duties attending it. He was expected to work strenuously for the church, and he did. His only recompense, and it was ample, was a conviction that he was furthering the work of the Lord in the last days.

In no other period in American history were "the last days" felt to be so imminent as in that between 1820 and 1845. William Leany, an early Mormon convert, wrote in his memoirs that he was "glad to hear the best men of our time discuss the approach of the Millennium, as they would say, at the end of 2000 years came the flood and at the end of 4000 years came Jesus and His Apostles and at the end of 6000 years we must look for something stupendous." *

According to calculations then current, the earth would be six thousand years old some time during the nineteenth century. Since a thousand years was as a single day to God, the seventh was expected to be the day of rest and peace. "All evil passions, covetousness, cruelty, luxury, ambition, pride, vanity, wrath, self-will, haughtiness, treachery, conceitedness, hatred, malice, envy — these shall not exist," wrote Josiah Priest in 1828. "There shall be no crying, no sighing, nor death." † William Miller believed that Christ would probably descend in 1843; Captain Saunders in England and Joseph Wolff in Palestine were certain that the date was in 1847.

Many Mormon converts had been caught by the contagion of millennialism and saw in the rise of the new prophet, with his private and mysterious illumination, final evidence of the impending arrival of Christ. Many sprang to Joseph's cause hoping to stand at his right hand at the Judgment Day. And since Joseph himself was infected with the millennial spirit, he encouraged this sentiment.

When he selected twelve of his ablest men as apostles to supervise his rapidly developing proselyting system, he showered them with blessings that confirmed their belief in the imminence of stupendous events. He promised Lyman E. Johnson that he should "see the Saviour come and stand upon the earth with power and great glory." Joseph's younger brother William

---

* "Leany Family History as Written from Memory by William Leany," MS. A typewritten transcript is in the Utah State Historical Society Library.

† *A View of the Expected Christian Millennium*, p. 14.

and Orson Hyde were told that they would "stand on earth and bring souls till Christ comes." And although Joseph never officially forecast the exact year of the Second Advent, he once ventured to suggest that "even fifty-six years should wind up the scene." *

CROWDS began to pour into Kirtland. "Many travelled fifty and a hundred miles to the throne of the prophet," wrote the editor of the *Painesville Telegraph,* "to hear from his own mouth the certainty of his excavating a bible and spectacles. Many, even in the New England states, after hearing the frantic story of some of these 'elders,' would forthwith place their *all* into a wagon, and wend their way to the 'promised land,' in order, as they supposed, to escape the judgments of Heaven which were soon to be poured out upon the land." †

Among the visitors was Ezra Booth, a popular Methodist preacher. In his party was a woman with a paralyzed arm. During their interview with Joseph Smith the conversation veered to the subject of healing, and one said: "Here is Mrs. Johnson with a lame arm; has God given any power to men now on earth to cure her?"

Joseph sat silent, but some moments later, when the question had been almost forgotten, he rose and strode across the room. Taking her useless hand in his he said solemnly: "Woman, in the name of the Lord Jesus Christ, I command thee to be whole!" and immediately left the room.

A Campbellite preacher in describing what followed wrote that "the company were awe-stricken at the infinite presumption of the man, and the calm assurance with which he spoke. The sudden mental and moral shock — I know not how better to explain the well-attested fact — electrified the rheumatic arm — Mrs. Johnson at once lifted it up with ease." ‡

The miracle at once converted Booth and the whole Johnson family. Then a lesser miracle brought into the Mormon

---

* See *History of the Church,* Vol. II, p. 182. The apostolic blessings were published in full in the *Millennial Star,* Vol. XV, pp. 206–7, and in the *History of the Church,* Vol. II, pp. 189–91, but were omitted from the official history of the Reorganized Church of Jesus Christ of Latter-Day Saints.

† E. D. Howe: *Mormonism Unvailed,* pp. 115–16.

‡ Quotation from a sermon of A. Hinsdale, August 3, 1870, published in A. S. Hayden: *Early History of the Disciples,* pp. 250–1.

Church Symonds Ryder, a Campbellite evangelist whose fame was almost as great as Rigdon's. When he read about the great Peking earthquake of 1831, he remembered that a Mormon girl had predicted the event some weeks before. These two conversions left the established preachers in the vicinity thunderstruck. The China earthquake was burlesqued in the local press as "Mormonism in China," and Thomas and Alexander Campbell rushed to northern Ohio to preach frantically against the new religion.

Eber D. Howe, editor of the *Painesville Telegraph,* furious when his own wife and daughter joined the Mormons, offered his press to the Campbells, and published on March 8 and 15 the first searching analysis of the Book of Mormon, Alexander Campbell's "Delusions," which had appeared in the *Millennial Harbinger.*

Undismayed by this opposition, Joseph, at Rigdon's suggestion, set to work "translating" the New Testament. Rigdon hoped further to pique Alexander Campbell, who had published a revised version of his own in 1827. Besides this translation Joseph was pouring forth revelations delineating his new gospel. And his successes, which must have seemed phenomenal to him, matured his language and emboldened his tongue.

He had always been at ease before an audience, but now he was developing into a preacher of uncommon talent. His eloquence, wrote Parley Pratt, was "not polished — not studied — not smoothed and softened by education and refined by art. . . . He interested and edified, while, at the same time, he amused and entertained his audience; and none listened to him that were ever weary with his discourse. I have even known him to retain a congregation of willing and anxious listeners for many hours together, in the midst of cold or sunshine, rain or wind, while they were laughing at one moment and weeping the next." Even the acid-tongued Eber Howe admitted that his address was "easy, rather fascinating and winning." He did not always speak grammatically, and his metaphors were homely and picturesque rather than poetic. But his voice was powerful and carried a conviction that held his listeners transfixed.

With his success came a dignity that always nonplused scoffers. A female preacher traveling through Ohio in 1831 blundered into the local excitement. "Can you," she asked Joseph bluntly, "in the presence of Almighty God, give your word by oath — that an angel from heaven showed you the place of those plates — and that you took the things contained in that book from those plates?"

He replied softly: "I will not swear at all."

Whereupon she turned on him in fury. "Are you not ashamed of such pretensions? You, who are no more than an ignorant ploughboy of our land! Oh! blush at such abominations! and let shame forever cover your face!"

He answered only by saying: "The gift has returned back again, as in former times, to illiterate fishermen." *

His new dignity and sense of the responsibility of his office did not stifle his sense of humor, however. "He was a right jolly prophet," said one of his converts, "used to laugh from the crown of his head to the soles of his feet — shook every bit of flesh in him." His bent for occasional comedy disconcerted those who expected a patriarchal solemnity, but it endeared him to many others.

One day he was explaining his creed and book to the Campbellite preacher Hayden. "Oh this is not the evidence I want," Hayden said, "the evidence that I wish to have is a notable miracle . . . if you perform such a one then I will believe with all my heart and soul."

"Well," said Joseph, "what will you have done? Will you be struck blind or dumb? Will you be paralyzed, or will you have one hand withered? Take your choice, choose what you please, and in the name of the Lord Jesus Christ it shall be done."

"That is not the kind of miracle I want," Hayden protested.

"Then sir," said Joseph, "I can perform none; I am not going to bring trouble upon anyone else, sir, to convince you." †

ACCORDING to the Acts of the Apostles, the disciples of Christ "had all things common; and sold their possessions and goods, and parted them to all men as every man had need." Never in American history was this scriptural passage so influential as in the second quarter of the nineteenth century. Scores of commu-

* *Vicissitudes Illustrated in the Experience of Nancy Towle, in Europe and America, Written by Herself* (Portsmouth, 1833), 2nd ed., pp. 156–7.

† As related by George A. Smith on June 24, 1855 in Salt Lake City. *Journal of Discourses*, Vol. II, p. 326.

nal societies sprang up over the country, religious, non-religious, celibate, and free-love. The Shakers were communists, as were the followers of Jemima Wilkinson. When Joseph Smith first rode into the Susquehanna Valley to find the silver mine for Josiah Stowel, he went into the province where Coleridge, Southey, and Wordsworth had planned to found Pantisocracy and where the German Harmonists, led by George Rapp, were building Economy on the banks of the Ohio.

If it had ever occurred to Joseph Smith to turn his church into a communistic society, he betrayed no such intention until after meeting Rigdon. The latter had not only studied the New Testament; he had also absorbed much of the recent national excitement over Robert Owen's New Harmony.

The famous English philanthropist had been offered a fortune, ironically enough by the Grand Duke Nicholas, to start his socialistic enterprise in Russia, but Owen preferred America as a field for social reform. In 1825 he bought Harmony, Indiana, from George Rapp for $100,000, and with tremendous fanfare organized New Harmony with 900 members, 30,000 acres, and $150,000 capital. Owen-inspired communities immediately mushroomed all over the country.

Owen was permitted to preach communism before a joint session of Congress, with the President and the Supreme Court in attendance. He toured the nation making speeches, and in April 1829 Sidney Rigdon heard him in a fortnight-long debate with Alexander Campbell in Cincinnati. By this date, however, New Harmony was dismally disintegrating. Owen had lost four fifths of his fortune — but none of his magnificent enthusiasm, for he was blithely negotiating with the Mexican government for an immense area in Chihuahua or Texas.

In one respect only Owen's venture was a notable success. He made America community-minded. The same generation which believed so fervently in the perfectibility of man, which tossed out Calvinism and embraced in its stead Unitarianism, millennialism, and total abstinence, was ripe, ideologically at least, for communism as well. In 1840 Emerson wrote to Carlyle: "Not a reading man but has a draft of a new community in his waistcoat pocket."

But quite overwhelming the enthusiasm for perfection in a socialist society were the tremendous forces of industrial and agricultural expansion, which rewarded capitalism with fabulous dividends, removed the italics from the French word *millionaire,* and made "Good land!" a national ejaculation.

Joseph Smith set up an economic order in his church which followed with a certain fidelity the life history of the typical communistic society of his time. When he first arrived in Kirtland, he found Rigdon's tiny "community" in chaos. "The disciples had all things in common," wrote John Whitmer, "and were going to destruction very fast as to temporal things; for they considered from reading the Scriptures that what belonged to a brother belonged to any of the brethren; therefore, they would take each other's clothes and other property and use it without leave, which brought on confusion and disappointment. . . ." *

Before long Joseph issued a revelation setting up the United Order of Enoch. "Behold," said the Lord, "thou shalt consecrate all thy properties, that which thou hast unto me, with a covenant and a deed which cannot be broken, and they shall be laid before the bishop of my church." † Private property became church property, and private profit a community spoil.

Production was kept on an individual basis. Each convert, after "consecrating" his all to the church, was given back certain property "sufficient for himself and family," over which he acted as a foreman or "steward." The system was thus more akin to farm tenancy than to the true communal agriculture practiced by the Shakers and New Harmonists. Upon the death or disaffection of the steward, the land reverted to the church, which permanently held the title.

Whatever surplus the steward exacted from the land, or whatever profit the mechanic derived from his shop, was contributed to the church storehouse and treasury, the convert keeping only what was "needful for the support and comfort" of himself and family. The spirit of true Marxian communism — "from each according to his ability, to each according to his need" — was implicit in the whole system.

Joseph had tasted the degradation of poverty and through-

* "History of the Church," MS., Chapter ii.
† *Book of Commandments,* Chapter xliv, verse 26. This should not be confused with the revised version of this revelation published later in the *Doctrine and Covenants.*

out his life was quick to champion the poor. But a hard core of common sense tempered his humanitarianism. "There are three kinds of poor," he was fond of saying, "the Lord's poor, the devil's poor, and the poor devils." * This same shrewd understanding illumined the revelations that set up the framework of the United Order. They urbanely prescribed legal forms that a court of law could be certain to uphold should a convert apostatize, and that incidentally made it possible to threaten malcontents with the loss of their property should they want to leave the church. "He that sinneth and repenteth not," said the Lord, "shall be cast out, and shall not receive again that which he has consecrated unto me." †

Although every man was free to till his own earth and patch his own roof, the stimulus to conscientious endeavor lay solely in the convert's love for the church. All profit was absorbed by the storehouse, and the industrious member was expected to accept the distribution of his surplus as the church authorities saw fit.

If a man wished to improve his property or enlarge his capital, he was subject to the discretion and patronage of the bishop. This was the honest and industrious Edward Partridge, who was given unlimited secular authority. He not only judged the "needs" of each convert in allocating land, but also determined the accuracy of the "surplus" handed in at harvest. He had the prodigious task of supplying stewardships for those who came into the church without money, like the prophet and innumerable other dispossessed farmers, and of relieving distress wherever property failed to yield sufficient income to support its steward. In addition he was directed to purchase land, establish new enterprises, care for the aged, and build churches and schools.

The structure of the United Order as developed in Joseph's revelations is sketchy and ambiguous, and the details of how it was actually worked out in Kirtland are simply not recoverable. It is clear, however, that Joseph did not immediately thrust

---

* According to John D. Lee. See *Mormonism Unveiled, including the life and confessions of the late Mormon Bishop John D. Lee* (St. Louis, 1877), p. 183.

† *Book of Commandments,* Chapter xliv, verse 31. See in particular the deeds for the consecration of the property of Titus Billings, *History of the Church,* Vol. I, pp. 365–7n. Billings released his rights and interests "forever," and the church leased the property back to him for the duration of his life or membership in the church.

the new economy upon the Kirtland converts, who were new to him and relatively settled financially. He wisely experimented first with the New York Mormons who had followed him west, since they possessed a greater social homogeneity and a more liquid capital. These converts he settled in Thompson, an adjoining village, under the leadership of Newel Knight. When a revelation commanded the Ohio converts to "impart of their lands" to their Eastern brethren, Ezra Thayer and Leman Copley volunteered a thousand-acre tract for half its value, and the experiment was quickly launched.*

JOSEPH's enthusiasm for the United Order was always tempered by the fact that it was Rigdon's conception. It is doubtful if he realized in the beginning how much added power such a system automatically thrust into his own hands, although he quickly learned to consider it his right to supervise the temporal as well as the spiritual affairs of his people. At first he left the management of the Order largely in the hands of subordinates, for he was far more interested in his plans for building a New Jerusalem.

"And with one heart and with one mind," he wrote in the Lord's name, "gather up your riches that ye may purchase an inheritance which shall hereafter be appointed unto you. And it shall be called the New Jerusalem, a land of peace, a city of refuge, a place of safety for the Saints of the Most High God. . . . And there shall be gathered unto it out of every other nation under heaven; and it shall be the only people that shall not be at war one with another." †

He had not yet selected the site for the holy city. Pratt had returned from the Lamanite mission with glowing descriptions of Jackson County, near the Indian border in upper Missouri, and Cowdery, who had remained there proselyting, was certain that in Independence, about two hundred and fifty miles up the Missouri River from St. Louis, he had found the ideal place for Zion. Here all roads ended and only a deep black trail stretched out toward Santa Fe, eight hundred miles southwest.

---

* *History of the Church*, Vol. I, p. 180n., and Ezra Booth: "Letter No. 7," in Howe: *Mormonism Unvailed*, p. 201.

† *Doctrine and Covenants*, Section 45.

Although less than four years old, Independence was already the boom town of the frontier. It had for a market the emigrant Indians — Sacs, Foxes, and Kickapoos, who were pouring through to take up new homes on the Great Plains — as well as the half-starved Kansas Indians who lived directly west. It furnished supplies for Cantonment (later Fort) Leavenworth, which an Italian traveler described in 1837 as "some wretched barracks and a second-rate blockhouse" with "a regiment of dragoons and artillery to keep the savages respectful."

The soldiers had partly checked the Comanche and Pawnee raids on the Santa Fe caravans, the annual value of which in ten years had jumped from $3,000 to $270,000. Ox and mule teams traveled from May to October carrying cotton, woolens, super blues, stroudings, bombazettes, light cutlery, and mirrors, and returning with bullion, Mexican dollars, fine gold, beaver, mules, and asses. These caravans were outfitted in Independence with provisions enough to last to the buffalo country, and when they returned, coming into port from a sea of prairie, destitute of food and clothing, the traders spent their money so freely that the whole of Missouri used Mexican dollars as a medium of exchange.

Independence had no bank, no printing press, and no church, but it boasted one Yankee shopkeeper who had sold sixty thousand dollars' worth of goods in three years. Steamboats sailed up the river as far as Council Bluffs. The Missouri General Assembly that very December had thrown open most of the highly prized 46,000 acres of seminary lands in Jackson County for sale at two dollars an acre, and public lands farther west were selling at a dollar and a quarter an acre in eighty-acre lots. An 1837 gazetteer reported that "a rage for that quarter pervaded the whole emigrating world." *

History has vindicated Cowdery's enthusiasm for Independence, since Kansas City sprang from its environs. But there were too many land agents in Missouri in the 1830's to permit so succulent a speculation to fall into the hands of any sect.

* Alphonse Wetmore: *Gazetteer of the State of Missouri* (St. Louis, 1837), p. 92. See also Charles J. Latrobe: *The Rambler in North America* (London, 1832-3), Vol. I, p. 128; Count Francesco Arese: *A Trip to the Prairies and the Interior of North America,* 1837-38 (New York, 1934), p. 65; and the Wetmore diary in *Southwest on the Turquoise Trail* (ed. by A. B. Hulbert, 1933), pp. 176 ff.

Joseph hesitated at first about Independence, for he was troubled by the fact that the mission to the Indians had been a flat failure. Pratt blamed the Indian agents and jealous sectarian priests, who had become alarmed, he said, at his and Cowdery's initial success among the Delawares and had ordered them out of Indian territory. But Cowdery was having no more success among the whites. His letter of May 7, 1831 had concluded: "We are well, bless the Lord; and preach the Gospel we will, if earth and hell oppose our way — for we dwell in the midst of scorpions — and in Jesus we trust."

To his converts who were reluctant to purchase land until the exact site for Zion had been chosen, Joseph procrastinated as best he could in a new revelation: "And inasmuch as ye have not lands, let them buy for the present time in those regions round about, as seemeth them good. . . . The place is not yet to be revealed. . . ." * As late as May he had no intimation that within a month a twin disaster would precipitate an exodus to Missouri.

ALTHOUGH Joseph attempted to stamp out the religious pathology that permeated the Kirtland colony, a residue remained which he made no effort to dispel. Ezra Booth declared that "an expectation universally pervaded the church that the time was not far distant when the deaf, the dumb, the maimed, the blind, etc., would become the subjects of the miraculous power of God, so that every defect in their systems would be entirely removed." Many believed that if they had sufficient faith they would never taste death, and scorned the services of doctors.

Joseph was probably troubled, as many faith healers had been before him, by the seemingly fitful and capricious manner in which God performed miracles. It must have been humbling to discover that although he could successfully command the Lord to heal a paralyzed arm and cast out a devil, he was powerless to assist Emma in her heartbreaking suffering with childbirth. In her second confinement she bore twins, but both died, and he was as helpless to comfort her as he had been to relieve her pain.

Another pair of twins had been born in Kirtland at the same

* *Doctrine and Covenants*, Section 48.

time. When their mother died, they were given to the prophet and his wife to rear. Emma took them joyfully and humbly and soon learned to love them as her own.

By the time plans were completed for Joseph's first general conference in Kirtland his sorrow at the loss of his own children was largely dissipated, and also, apparently, his sense of helplessness before the specter of death. Optimistic and exuberant, he became careless with prophecy. Ezra Booth, who described the conference in detail shortly after he left the church, wrote that on the day before the meetings began Joseph promised that "not three days should pass away before some should see the Savior face to face." *

The prophet set the keynote for the first assembly by unriddling the mystery of the Lost Ten Tribes, revealing that they lived in a land "contiguous to the north pole, separated from the rest of the world by impassable mountains of ice and snow." The high point of the conference, however, was his announcement that God had restored to earth the Melchizedek or higher priesthood — the Holy Order of the Son of God. This was different from the priesthood of Aaron enjoyed by the Jews and restored to the Mormon people by John the Baptist. Throughout history only Melchizedek and Christ had been endowed with its prerogatives, but now it was to be the privilege of every true believer in the gospel.†

Joseph now selected several of his key men and began to ordain them as high priests. While the solemn prayers were going forward, the fierce-looking, fanatical Lyman Wight, who had been one of Rigdon's most zealous communists, jumped upon a bench. Booth wrote that his arms were outstretched, his hands cramped back, and his whole system agitated as he cried: "If you want to see a sign look at me!" and shouted that he saw the heavens opened and the Son of Man sitting on the right

* Booth's detailed account of the conference and the story of his own disillusionment were written in a series of letters to Edward Partridge and published in 1831-2 in the *Ohio Star* at Ravenna. They were reprinted in E. D. Howe: *Mormonism Unvailed*. For further details of the conference see John Whitmer: "History of the Church," MS., Chapter vii; and *History of the Church,* Vol. I, p. 176n.

† It seems likely that Joseph's concept of dual priesthood came directly from James Gray's *Dissertation on the Coincidence between the Priesthoods of Jesus Christ and Melchisedec* (Philadelphia, 1810). Joseph was familiar with Gray's works. His own signed copy of Gray's *Mediatorial Reign of the Son of God* (Baltimore, 1821) may be seen in the library of the Reorganized Church.

hand of the Father. One man was suddenly stricken deaf and dumb. Joseph strode over to him and commanded the devil to flee, and immediately the lost senses returned. The whole congregation was electrified.

But at this point, if Booth's account is to be relied upon, it would seem that Joseph was so excited by the return of his gift for miracle-making that he lost all discretion. Seizing a convert's hand which had been crippled by an accident, he cried: "Brother Murdock, I command you in the name of Jesus Christ to straighten your hand!" and tugged at the stiffly curled fingers. Again he demanded it, but the fingers merely returned to their old distortion.

Quickly he turned to an old man lame in one leg and ordered him to rise and walk. The man took a step or two and then his faith failed. Now a father brought in a dead child, whom he had refused to bury until after the conference. The most earnest and frantic prayers left the tiny gray body motionless. Joseph found it impossible to reproach the parents for lack of faith, since they were the last to be convinced that the child could not be made to breathe again. Finally, numb and desolate, they turned on the elders and reproached them bitterly for having advised against medical aid. A chill spread over the whole conference.

On the second day when without explanation Rigdon dismissed the congregation abruptly before the time was half spent, Joseph must have realized that he was facing the first major failure of his life. A few denounced him in scorn, and the silent looked at him with cold eyes.

It was in this hour that Newel Knight brought him word of the second misfortune, which threatened to topple the economic structure of the church before it was half built. Leman Copley and Ezra Thayer had renounced their generous offering of land in Thompson and were invoking Ohio state law to rid themselves of the New York "trespassers." *

Joseph was beginning to feel the pressure of the vexations that had racked the Shakers and precipitated the ruin of New Harmony. Analyzing in 1870 the collapse of American communistic experiments, John Humphrey Noyes laid it to "general

* See John Whitmer: "History of the Church," MS., Chapter viii, and Newel Knight's journal, published in *Scraps of Biography*, p. 70.

depravity"; Joseph struggled four years with lawsuits and poverty to discover this for himself.

Now, however, with the swift energy that never seemed to fail him in a crisis, he found in a single night the solution that would solve the plight of the New York colony and at the same time divert attention from the disastrous conference. Zion would save him. Like Robert Owen, whose failure at New Harmony had turned him to Chihuahua, Joseph sought the frontier, where men had sunk no deep roots and necessity would enforce co-operation. A new revelation commanded thirty men, including himself and Rigdon, to leave at once for Missouri.*

To those converts, now thoroughly alarmed, who had deeded him their property and consecrated their money, he promised land in abundance in Missouri. Quickly the word spread about that miracles could not be performed in Ohio because it was not consecrated ground, that only in the promised land could the blind be made to see, the lame to walk, and the dead be quickened. The next conference would be held in Independence, where a glorious temple would be built in honor of the Lord. There the children of God would worship in riches and abundance.

When some of the men demurred at starting off posthaste for the Indian border, another revelation lashed at them: "Wo unto you rich men, that will not give your substance to the poor, for your riches will canker your souls. . . . Wo unto you poor men, whose hearts are not broken, whose spirits are not contrite, and whose bellies are not satisfied, and whose hands are not stayed from laying hold upon other men's goods, whose eyes are full of greediness, and who will not labor with your own hands! But blessed are the poor who are pure in heart, whose hearts are broken, and whose spirits are contrite, for they shall see the kingdom of God coming in power and great glory unto their deliverance; for the fatness of the earth shall be theirs." †

* *Doctrine and Covenants*, Section 52.

† *Doctrine and Covenants*, Section 56. See also Ezra Booth: "Letter No. 5," in Howe: *Mormonism Unvailed*, p. 194.

CHAPTER VIII
Temple-Builder

It was two hundred and fifty miles to Independence from St. Louis, where Joseph left the luxury of the steamboat and began to walk. As the settlements grew scarcer and the hills flattened out into prairies baking under the July sun, the weary Mormon elders must have been dismayed by the remoteness of the promised land. At the beginning of the journey they were buoyed up by extravagant hopes, some predicting mass conversions of the Indians through the gift of tongues and all chanting the refrain: "We shall winter in Ohio but one winter more." In a burst of oratory Joseph told his men that he had seen a vision of several hundred converts awaiting them in Zion.

Independence, however, proved to be the crudest kind of frontier village, with little more than a dozen log houses, three stores, a schoolhouse, and a brick courthouse. The Mormon colony consisted of three or four females. Joseph was dismayed by Cowdery's ineptness as a missionary, but failed at first to sense the shock and bewilderment that swept over his men. Few of them saw anything but the rawness and frankly commercial atmosphere of Independence, although Joseph was himself astute enough to see why it was the key town along the whole frontier.

But even Joseph had some misgivings until he climbed to the top of the highest hill west of the town. Though it was covered with woods, he could see from its summit the valley of the Blue River and to the westward a prairie so vast and so flat that it left him wordless with wonder. He was standing, it seemed, on the last big hill between the Indian border and the peaks of the Rocky Mountains hundreds of miles west. Here in the center of the continent he would build a temple to the Lord unto which red men and white would flow in a great stream, uniting at last in the brotherhood of the gospel.

When the recently dispossessed New York colony arrived, he settled them on the low land between Independence and the

Indian border, the first cabin rising in what is now the heart of Kansas City. The temple site was dedicated in a simple but moving ceremony, with the cornerstone laid at the foot of a sapling whose vigor and promise symbolized the future of the church.

Now, however, the disillusionment of many elders began to show itself. Edward Partridge, who had been given control of the United Order in the new Zion, complained about the quality of the land selected for purchase. When Joseph replied with some heat that Heaven had selected the land, Partridge replied pointedly: "I wish you not to tell us any more that you know these things by the spirit when you do not; you told us that Oliver had raised up a large church here, and there is no such thing."

"I see it, and it will be so," Joseph affirmed calmly, but Ezra Booth thereafter watched him with suspicion and on his return to Ohio published in the *Ohio Star* a detailed and sardonic description of the journey.

According to Booth, Rigdon was particularly annoyed with Joseph, telling him bluntly that his vision "was a bad thing," and urging an immediate return to Ohio. For all his visionary propensities, Rigdon had no real foresight. He was appalled by the remote, unfriendly settlement and refused to sever his ties with Kirtland. Joseph was therefore torn between his two key men. Since Rigdon's prestige was indispensable to the growth of the church, Cowdery lost out and Joseph agreed to return to Ohio. The Mormons were thus split in two, the Missouri colony becoming a haven for the disinherited and the Kirtland church retaining the prestige of the prophet's presence.

Eight hundred miles of bad roads separated the two groups. Communication by letter was slow and uncertain, but a remarkable liaison system was nevertheless maintained. A printing press was set up in Independence to publish the *Evening and Morning Star,* westernmost newspaper in the United States. W. W. Phelps, poet and anti-Masonic journalist from New York State, was made editor. The *Star* printed many of Joseph's revelations and all his letters to the church.

Co-operation between the two United Orders, however, proved impossible. The Missouri Order, more genuinely communal, took root quickly, the contents of the storehouse swelling under the conscientious direction of Edward Partridge. But Kirtland was an unfortunate mixture of new and landless converts, old settlers reluctant to deed their farms to the church, and a penniless hierarchy that had no steady income.

In late October 1831 the machinery of the Kirtland Order finally began to move, primed by a $10,000 loan from Charles Holmes.* Newel K. Whitney was made bishop, and his store became the storehouse and commissary. A new revelation suggested that if debts accumulated, the account was to be "handed over to the Bishop of Zion, who shall pay the debt out of that which the Lord shall put into his hands." † The unfortunate Partridge thus became responsible for the debts of the whole church.

At the urging of his chief men, who subscribed to the pervasive Yankee tradition that preachers should leave civil affairs alone, Joseph relinquished most of the management of the United Orders to the bishops and spent the winter of 1831 revising the Bible and collecting and editing his revelations for publication in book form. He had moved to Hiram, about forty miles southeast of Kirtland, accepting the hospitality of John Johnson, whose wife had been spectacularly healed the previous summer.

The Bible revision was tedious, but the discipline had an enduring effect upon Joseph's thinking and style. Here was no careless spinning of loose-jointed sentences. It was meticulous emendation, which taught him for the first time the value of the word. He modernized many sentences and made occasional changes in doctrine. But the most interesting parts of Joseph's Bible were the interpolations concerning himself and the Mormon Zion.

He could not resist the temptation to insert in the Book of Genesis a prophecy of his own coming. Joseph, son of Jacob, was made to say: "Thus saith the Lord God of my fathers unto

* The record of this loan is in the Chardon, Ohio, courthouse (Vol. V, p. 63). Along with several others Joseph Smith signed two notes on October 5, 1831, each for $5,000, the first payable on May 1, 1837 and the second on September 1, 1837. On October 15, 1831 he borrowed $200 more from Holmes. In April 1838 Holmes sued Joseph Smith for $15,000 to recover the notes. Apparently they were never paid, for Smith lost the case by default. By that date he had left Kirtland forever.

† *Doctrine and Covenants* (1921), Section 72, verse 13.

me, A choice seer will I raise up out of the fruit of thy loins, and he shall be esteemed highly among the fruit of thy loins. . . . and his name shall be called Joseph, and it shall be after the name of his father. . . ."

Then he elaborated that prophecy of Isaiah concerning the learned man and the sealed book which had so impressed Martin Harris after his return from the visit to Charles Anthon, enlarging it with such fidelity to the details of the New York episode that it must have astonished even Harris. The prophecy of Isaiah was also made to include references to the Book of Mormon witnesses and the return of the golden plates to the Lord.* Perhaps Joseph was still troubled by a sense of inadequacy. He had not yet learned to reject such petty devices and to stand squarely on his own feet.

The painstaking study of the Bible served, however, to stimulate some of his best revelations. In this single year, 1831, he wrote three times as many as in the last ten years of his life. Many were commonplace orders to missionaries, and others were attempts to solve the difficulties that kept cropping up in the United Order. But some were pure theology.

Paul's First Epistle to the Corinthians contained three verses that caught his interest: "There are also celestial bodies, and bodies terrestrial: but the glory of the celestial is one, and the glory of the terrestrial is another. There is one glory of the sun, and another glory of the moon, and another glory of the stars: for one star differeth from another star in glory. So also is the resurrection of the dead."

Upon reading these lines, he said, there came to him and Rigdon a vision of the resurrection in which they saw the three great kingdoms to which all men would be assigned at the Judgment Day. The celestial kingdom, whose glory was that of the sun, would be the inheritance of members of the true church; the terrestrial, whose glory was that of the moon, would be the dwelling-place of those who had never known the gos-

---

* See Genesis 1 and Isaiah xxix. For a detailed analysis of the changes in the whole Bible see George B. Arbaugh's *Revelation in Mormonism* (Chicago, 1932), pp. 75–85. The revision of the Bible was not printed in Joseph's lifetime. Emma retained the manuscript, and the Reorganized Church printed it at Plano, Illinois, in 1867. The Utah Mormons prefer the King James version, on the grounds that Joseph never completed his final revision.

pel. Then he coined the word "telestial" for a third kingdom, whose glory was that of the stars, to be peopled with those who had refused the law of God.

This trinity of kingdoms comprised a very different resurrection scene from the one he had described in the Book of Mormon, where the "lake of fire and brimstone" figured prominently in the sermons of the Indian prophets. Joseph had taken a long step toward Universalism, for even the "liars, sorcerers, adulterers, and whoremongers" were guaranteed telestial glory, and only a handful of unregenerates called the Sons of Perdition were to be eternally damned.

The *Evening and Morning Star* published the long revelation describing this vision in December 1833, and added that when the two men emerged from the office "one of the brethren reported that Joseph appeared as strong as a lion but Sidney seemed weak as water; and Joseph, noticing his partner's condition, smiled and said, 'Brother Sidney is not as used to it as I am!'"

Years later, when the prophet was writing his history, he had the revelation of the three glories copied into the record and commented on it with the enthusiasm of an author who has stumbled upon a bit of his early writing and marvels at its brilliance or stylistic beauty: "Every law, every commandment, every promise, every truth . . . witnesses the fact that that document is a transcript from the records of the eternal world. The sublimity of the ideas; the purity of the language; the scope for action . . . are so much beyond the narrow-mindedness of men, that every honest man is constrained to exclaim: '*It came from God.*'"*

DESPITE the rich outpouring of revelations during the time Joseph lived with the Johnson family, several of Johnson's sons became disaffected and left the church. Hiram was rapidly becoming an unfriendly town. Symonds Ryder left the church because a special revelation on his behalf misspelled his name. Ezra Booth had been out of the church for some months, disillusioned by what he called Joseph's "habitual proneness to jesting and joking," and convinced by the trip to Missouri that all of Joseph's revelations sprang out of mundane crises rather

* *History of the Church*, Vol. I, pp. 252–3.

than from the promptings of the Lord. Booth's letters in the *Ohio Star* caused widespread indignation against the prophet.

To plague Joseph further, the twin babies he had adopted contracted measles. Their illness in another man's house was not easy to bear. At this point word came from the Missouri colony that a rebellion was brewing, and Joseph realized that only a personal visit to Independence would prevent serious apostasy. When news of his going spread through the town, a gang of Mormon-baiters led by Symonds Ryder determined to hasten his departure in characteristic frontier fashion. Fortified by a barrel of whisky, they smashed their way into the Johnson home on the night of March 24, 1832 and dragged Joseph from the trundle bed where he had fallen asleep while watching one of the twins. They stripped him, scratched and beat him with savage pleasure, and smeared his bleeding body with tar from head to foot. Ripping a pillow into shreds, they plastered him with feathers. It is said that Eli Johnson demanded that the prophet be castrated, for he suspected Joseph of being too intimate with his sister, Nancy Marinda. But the doctor who had been persuaded to join the mob declined the responsibility at the last moment, and Johnson had to be content with seeing the prophet beaten senseless.* Rigdon likewise was beaten and dragged into unconsciousness over the frozen ground.

After a time Joseph sat up and began to tear at the tar which filled his mouth. His lips were bleeding from a glass vial that he had crushed between his teeth when someone tried to force it down his throat. He made his way back to the house stiff with cold and pain. Emma opened the door. In the half light the great blotches of tar on his naked body looked to her like blood and she fainted on the doorstep.

Throughout the night Emma and her friends patiently scraped at the tar. The next day was the Sabbath, and Joseph had been expected to preach. Into the Mormon congregation came several of the assailants, taking their seats with cynical expectancy. To their astonishment the prophet walked into the assembly at the appointed hour, fresh scars and bruises showing

---

* See Brigham Young's sermon of November 15, 1864, *Journal of Discourses*, Vol. XI, pp. 3–4, and Clark Braden: *Public Discussion of the Issues between the Reorganized Church . . . and the Church of Christ, Disciples* (St. Louis, 1884), p. 202. Nancy Johnson — later Mrs. Orson Hyde — eventually became one of Joseph's plural wives. See Appendix C.

on his face and hands. With a true instinct for the occasion, he thundered no denunciations, but preached as usual, and the quiet dignity of his sermon added to the aura of heroism fast beginning to surround him. This was the first and the last act of violence against the Mormons in Ohio.

Five days later one of the twins died, leaving only the little girl, Julia Murdock, to the sorrowing pair. The Smiths now left Hiram for good, Emma going back to Kirtland, and Joseph starting with Rigdon for Independence.

THE MISSOURI MORMONS had never quite forgiven their prophet for returning to undedicated and unconsecrated Ohio and feared that his allegiance would be diverted permanently from the promised land by Rigdon. Moreover, they were jealous of the Kirtland converts, who had won all the key positions in the church government. Oliver Cowdery was mere assistant printer; David Whitmer and Martin Harris held no office whatever. Sensitive to violations of the spirit of democracy, even in religion, the Missouri members were incensed because administrative decisions were made without their vote. They had not questioned the revelations, however, until they received the one commanding Zion to pay Kirtland's debts.

On his arrival, Joseph swiftly relieved the major tensions. To satisfy each convert's hunger for some small share in the church government, he held what became the characteristic Mormon election, in which he was unanimously voted president of the church by open ballot. He co-ordinated the two branches of the United Order, appointing a nine-man board, which included Cowdery and Harris. The board members were ordered to pool their holdings in Kirtland and Independence in one immense stewardship. The two commissaries were amalgamated and the bishops ordered to negotiate a $15,000 loan. Rigdon succeeded in allaying the antagonism that had developed against him; and the visit, successful beyond their hopes, marked the beginning of a year of phenomenal growth for the church in Jackson County — a growth, however, which began to stimulate in the old settlers an open and increasingly ugly hostility.

When Joseph returned to Ohio in May 1832, he left three hundred converts in Missouri. This number doubled in a single year. The colony was poor and provisions were scarce. "Our food," wrote Parley Pratt in his autobiography, "consisted of beef and a little bread made of corn, which had been grated into coarse meal by rubbing the ears on a tin grater." But such privation heightened the sense of kinship and oneness with God. "There was a spirit of peace and union and love and goodwill manifested in this little Church in the wilderness, the memory of which will be ever dear to my heart," Pratt said.

Missouri was now acutely conscious of the Indians at her western border. The federal government, slowly purchasing land in Ohio, Kentucky, and Illinois, was moving thousands of them out upon the great treeless plains. Through Independence trekked Shawnees, Kickapoos, and Pottawattamies, pitching their tents outside the village for a night before crossing the border. The old settlers counted the Indian guns and listened uneasily to their lamentation and despair, but the Mormons watched the migration with a kind of ecstasy. They knew that Andrew Jackson was an unwitting tool in the hands of God, for this was the beginning of the gathering of Israel.

Confident that these "remnants of Jacob" would soon swell the ranks of the church, Phelps hailed each tribe triumphantly in the *Evening and Morning Star*. The world for him was blazing with signs of Christ's coming, which he ventured to predict was less than nine years away. Revolution stirred in a dozen countries in the early thirties; South Carolina, thirty years before the Civil War, threatened to split the United States by secession; a plague of "fiery serpents" ravaged India; thirty thousand natives starved in the Cape Verde Islands; Asiatic cholera began to devastate the Atlantic seaboard; a handful of Polish Jews migrated to Palestine to prepare for the Messiah — all these events were recorded on the little press in Independence in 1832 as unmistakable signs of the times.

Unfortunately for the United Order in Missouri, only about half of the incoming converts could be persuaded to join — invariably the poorer half. The deeds of consecration made out to Titus Billings, which apparently are the only ones extant, revealed him to be without capital, and his furniture, wagons, and animals to be worth little more than three hundred dollars. When the mixture of communists and non-communists became too troublesome, Joseph sent word to Missouri that unless a man joined the Order he should be denied membership in the church.*

When the Order was harassed by slackers, Phelps struck at them in the *Star:* "He that will not work is no disciple of the Lord." And when the more enterprising preferred hiring out to gentiles to laboring for the Order, he elaborated upon the 24th Psalm in condemning them: "One cannot be above another in wealth, nor below another for want of means, for the earth is the Lord's and the fulness thereof. Neither shall men labor for the Lord for wages. . . . But the laborer in Zion shall labor for Zion; and if they labor for money, they shall perish." †

Nothing was so dangerous to the Order in Missouri as apostasy, for when a man left the church and was refused the return of his property he promptly went to the courts. The Shakers had been singularly favored by the law in such actions, but the Missouri judges scorned the Mormon deeds and awarded judgment to the dissenter.‡

Resentment in Zion against Joseph's absence never completely died, for his partiality to Kirtland remained too obvious. Phelp's pleas for a permanent removal to Missouri became such a nuisance that Joseph silenced him with the Lord's word: ". . . say unto your brethren in Zion, in love greeting, that I have called you also to preside over Zion in mine own due time. Therefore, let them cease wearying me concerning this matter." §

Despite the fact that Missouri was draining off his most zealous millenarians, Joseph was now determined to keep Kirtland the center of the church. There fortune was smiling on him. On November 6, 1832 Emma had borne him a son, who did not die in the first hazardous days as had his first-born and the twins. The whole church shared in his joy, lavishing gifts and homage upon the baby, whom he christened Joseph.

Just before the child was born the prophet had made a trip to New York City, where he successfully negotiated some loans

---

* See *History of the Church,* Vol. I, pp. 365–7n., 298; also *Evening and Morning Star,* Vol. I (January 1833), p. 121.

† *Evening and Morning Star,* Vol. I (December 1832), p. 108.

‡ Ibid., Vol. I (July 1833), p. 219.

§ *Doctrine and Covenants,* Section 90. See also *History of the Church,* Vol. I, p. 316.

in the name of the Kirtland United Order. His letter to Emma written after his first tour around Manhattan Island betrayed not only his astonishment at the city's grandeur but also something of his anxiety to reckon with the vast metropolis in his own scheme of things:

October 13, 1832

My dear wife,

This day I have been walking through the most splendid part of the city of New York. The buildings are truly great and wonderful to the astonishing of every beholder, and the language of my heart is like this. Can the great God of all the earth maker of all things magnificent and splendid be displeased with man for all these great inventions sought out by them. My answer is no it can not be, seeing these great works are calculated to make men comfortable wise and happy, therefore not for these works can the Lord be displeased. Only against man is the anger of the Lord kindled because they give him not the Glory. Therefore their iniquities shall be visited upon their heads and their works shall be burned up with unquenchable fire. . . .

Oh how long, O Lord, shall this order of things exist and darkness cover the Earth and gross darkness cover the people. After beholding all that I had any desire to behold I returned to my room to meditate and calm my mind and behold the thoughtful home of Emma and Julia rushes upon my mind like a flood and I could wish for a moment to be with them. My breast so fills with all the feelings and tenderness of a parent and husband, and could I be with you I would tell you many things. Yet when I set foot upon this great city like Ninevah . . . my bowels is filled with compassion towards them. . . .

I prefer reading and praying and holding communion with the holy Spirit and writing to you than walking the streets and beholding the distractions of men. . . .

your affectionate husband until Death

JOSEPH SMITH JUNIOR *

It will be seen that Joseph was now taking himself very seriously as a prophet of the Lord and did not relax from his role even before his wife — perhaps especially before his wife.

Joseph's trip to New York kindled in him an interest in national affairs that he never thereafter lost. But he could not

---

* The original of this letter is in the library of the Reorganized Church. It is one of the few undictated letters extant and reveals in Joseph at this early date all the rich talent that went into the creation of his revelations.

look at a national crisis except in terms of himself, his church, and the millennium. While he was in New York there was much concern over the first serious threat of South Carolina to split the Union. Shortly after his return the legislature of the southern state nullified the obnoxious tariff act of 1832 and threatened to secede if enforcement was attempted.

Andrew Jackson thundered against the rebellious state, prayed to God to prevent civil war, and called out the federal troops. News of the crisis flooded Ohio papers, and on December 25, 1832 Joseph began to prophesy:

Verily, thus saith the Lord, concerning the wars that will shortly come to pass, beginning at the rebellion of South Carolina, which will eventually terminate in the death and misery of many souls; And the time will come that war will be poured out upon all nations, beginning at this place. For behold, the Southern States shall be divided against the Northern States, and the Southern States will call on other nations, even the nation of Great Britain, as it is called, and they shall also call upon other nations, in order to defend themselves against other nations; and then war shall be poured out upon all nations.

And it shall come to pass, after many days, slaves shall rise up against their masters, who shall be marshalled and disciplined for war. . . . And thus, with the sword and by bloodshed the inhabitants of the earth shall mourn; and with famine, and plague, and earthquake, and the thunder of heaven, and the fierce and vivid lightning also, shall the inhabitants of the earth be made to feel the wrath, and indignation, and chastening hand of an Almighty God, until the consumption decreed hath made a full end of all nations. . . .

President Jackson remained ignorant of the edict of the Almighty and acted instead as if the Lord were on the side of peace. And peace continued for twenty-eight years. The prophecy was quietly abandoned and excluded from early collections of Joseph's revelations. It was not exhumed from his private papers until nineteen years later, when Brigham Young, seeing the whirlwind hour darkening, ordered its publication. After the Civil War it became the most celebrated of all of Joseph's predictions.

Converts streamed into Kirtland in 1832 and 1833 as the prophet's vigorous missionary campaign began to bear fruit.

Inevitably the newcomers were impressed upon meeting the young Mormon leader. No longer lean and gangling, he had developed into a tall, powerful, and altogether striking figure. "There was something in his manner and appearance that was bewitching and winning," John D. Lee recalled a few years later; "his countenance was that of a plain, honest man, full of benevolence and philanthropy and void of deceit or hypocrisy."

Joseph's four brothers were also tall, well-formed men, all six feet or over, and together with their father they formed an arresting picture as they walked about Kirtland streets. Bound to each other by extraordinary fraternal loyalty as well as by a sense of power derived from their unity, they furnished enormous material and psychological support to the prophet. William alone chafed under his leadership, but did not for some years break into open rebellion.

Joseph was still so young, so full of zest for living and of rich humor, that he found it difficult to maintain constantly before his friends the sober mien and dignified language expected of a holy man. One couple arriving in Kirtland found him playing with some children and forthwith turned their wagons back to New England. Others were appalled at his unashamed pride in his prowess at wrestling. But usually new converts were won by his humanness and informality.

George A. Smith delighted in the story of the Canadian convert who was asked to pray one night and "hallooed so loud he alarmed the whole village." Joseph came running to the house. "What is the matter? I thought by the noise that the heavens and earth were coming together." Learning the cause of the disturbance, he told the Canadian bluntly: "You should not give way to such an enthusiastic spirit and bray so much like a jackass." The man apostatized for the remark, but the chuckling brethren agreed they were well rid of him.*

By this time Joseph had secured a house and a beautiful 140-acre farm. The editor of the *Painesville Telegraph* wrote with his customary malice that the prophet had secured deeds to this farm and to two Kirtland lots in his own name. "Thus it is that these self-made prophets and high priests are acquiring

* See Smith's sermon of March 18, 1855, *Journal of Discourses*, Vol. V, p. 214.

possessions of real estate in a rich and flourishing country, while their dupes are packed off to the wilds of Missouri." *

But his own people did not begrudge him the best. They swore that his fields produced twice as much as before and that every cow presented to him doubled its output of milk. They noted with pleasure that Joseph could build more rods of good fence in one day than most men could in two, that his fence was always clear of underbrush, that his logs were neatly piled and his yard clean and orderly.

One afternoon in November 1832 Joseph was chopping wood in the forest behind his home when his friends brought a new convert, whom they introduced as Brigham Young. A Vermonter by birth like the prophet, he had caught the same restless contagion that drove the Smith family west. He was older than Joseph and shorter, but stocky and powerful, with hands that were made to work with tools. He had been a painter and glazier, he said, and had tried a variety of jobs and a variety of religions, but there had been no purpose in his life until he read the Book of Mormon.

There was a hard strength in this man that Joseph must immediately have sensed, for Young radiated an air of robust vitality. They spent the rest of the day together and at night went to a cottage meeting. There Joseph asked him to pray. He responded surprisingly with an exhibition of the "gift of tongues," one of the phenomena that Joseph had been gently trying to suppress. Perhaps he fell into this idiom, which was so foreign to his hard-headed nature, in his anxiety to impress the prophet. At any rate, Joseph seems to have been reluctant to offend a man with so much promise and surprised the audience by saying approvingly: "Brother Brigham was speaking the true Adamic language."

The gift of tongues thus acquired status in the church, and though Joseph repeatedly cautioned against its misuse, it continued as one of the most popular "gifts of the spirit" enjoyed by his people. It provided the most inarticulate convert with a spontaneous, mysterious, and immensely satisfying form of self-expression.

The best evidence of the magnetism of the Mormon religion was that it could attract men with the quality of Brigham

* E. D. Howe: *Mormonism Unvailed*, p. 227.

Young, whose tremendous energy and shrewd intelligence were not easily directed by any influence outside himself. His conversion had been intellectual rather than emotional, since it was the Book of Mormon that had attracted him to the church. But the prophet at once kindled in him an astonishing religious ardor. Joseph had a creative imagination and verbal facility the like of which Young had never seen. Blunt of speech himself and cautious in his planning, he was drawn to the prophet irresistibly. Here was a man who could make him see visions — not of misty angel presences, but of the kingdom of God upon earth. "I wanted to thunder and roar out the Gospel to the nations," Young later said. "It burned in my bones like fire pent up . . . nothing would satisfy me but to cry abroad in the world, what the Lord was doing in the latter-days." *

Since a preacher without a chapel was no better than a common circuit rider, Joseph began in the spring of 1833 an active campaign for the building of a temple in Kirtland. A revelation setting the dimensions at fifty-five by sixty-five feet and calling for three stories promised a somewhat more imposing structure than the usual frontier church. In the beginning he dared not call it a temple, because he had already dedicated the land for the temple in Zion. But he could kindle little enthusiasm for a "house and school" despite three provocative revelations on the subject.† It required the promise of a great and mysterious "endowment" to induce the subscription of enough money even to lay the foundation.

As the walls began to rise, the general apathy changed to eagerness. Sidney Rigdon, always melodramatic, walked upon the masonry at night crying aloud to heaven and washing the fresh mortar with his tears. Joseph worked frequently with the masons, calling down the blessings of heaven as he hoisted the heavy stones.

The prophet was losing the pettiness that had stamped much of his early scheming. He was growing to fit his calling. His ambition, which enlarged in direct proportion to his success, was not wholly personal, since his plans were for his church and thus only incidentally for himself.

* *Journal of Discourses,* Vol. I (1854), p. 313.
† See *Doctrine and Covenants,* Sections 88 (verse 119), 94, 95.

No sooner had the foundation of his temple been built than he began to design a city of twelve temples. He blocked out the city in squares of uniform size, divided by phenomenally wide streets, with schools and temples placed at regular intervals. This city, he said, should contain between 15,000 and 20,000 citizens, with each man living in his own brick or stone house, set back from the street in a handsome garden. Barns and stables were to be kept outside the city on surrounding farms. Although drawn with an eye to mathematical precision rather than beauty, this ideal city was a remarkable piece of urban planning, and Brigham Young used the plans fourteen years later in laying out the spacious squares and wide streets of Salt Lake City.

Grandiose as the plan may have seemed in 1833, it was really a symbol of Joseph's swiftly widening vision. He was beginning to grasp something of the tremendous potentiality of his power. Although Kirtland had even fewer converts than Zion, where the number had reached about 1,200, and although the whole church economy was based on borrowed money, the city of twelve temples was no idle dream.

The prophet had a clear view of the horizon, but a fog lay at his feet. He had no prescience of the suffering and destruction that were to mock his dreams. Kirtland was not his city of twelve temples, nor even Independence. Every Zion that he planted was rooted up before it flowered. And Zion in Independence was doomed even now.

A week after the laying of the cornerstone for the Kirtland temple he ordered the building of the temple in Zion. A revelation on August 2, 1833 commanded his people there to give a tithe of all their property to start the temple fund, the Lord promising that if this was done Zion would become "very glorious, very great, and very terrible," with the nations of the earth honoring her. "But if she observe not," the revelation continued, ". . . I will visit her according to all her works, with sore affliction, with pestilence, with plague, with sword, with vengeance, with devouring fire. Nevertheless, let it be read this once to her ears, that I, the Lord, have accepted of her offering; and if she sin no more none of these things shall come upon her. . . ." *

* Ibid., Section 97.

No other of all Joseph Smith's revelations was so badly timed. For Zion had already been struck "with sword, with vengeance, with devouring fire." Exactly a fortnight earlier a mob had stormed into Independence, burned the printing house, smashed the press, carried off the newly printed collections of revelations, tarred and feathered Bishop Partridge, and ordered the whole colony to leave the county.

CHAPTER IX
Expulsion from Eden

Few episodes in American religious history parallel the barbarism of the anti-Mormon persecutions. That the town in which these began should bear the name of Independence only accentuates the tragic irony of the case. Intermittently for thirteen years burnings and pillaging hounded the Mormons wherever they tried to settle in the Mississippi Valley, until it seemed there was something inevitable in the terrorism that bloodied their trail.

The tenuous, shifting area known as the frontier attracted men who though brave and adventurous were often also illiterate, thriftless, and antisocial. Preferring hunting to farming, they packed their wagons and moved on west as soon as neighbors came within gunshot distance. Western Missouri, according to a traveling preacher of the time, had "a semi-barbarian population constantly pressing on the heels of the retreating savages."

In ordinary times this class would have sold out to the Mormons and moved on west, but now a barrier hemmed them in. Andrew Jackson in 1830 had fixed the Indian frontier by law, thereby temporarily forbidding them the space for roaming to which they were accustomed, and the vast plains to the west, barren of timber and short of water, did not invite the careless encroachment on Indian territory that had been so common in the central Mississippi Valley.

The Missourians were irritated by reports of Mormon sermons like those of Oliver Cowdery, who told the Delawares that they "should be restored to all their rights and privileges; should cease to fight and kill one another; should become one people; cultivate the earth in peace, in common with the pale faces. . . ." To any frontiersman this was political imbecility.

Moreover, the Mormons were not luckhunters, eager to move on if new territory opened up or a crop was blistered by frost. They had come to stay till the millennium, buying and building with a kind of desperate haste lest the day of the Lord's coming find their lamps untrimmed. Their very industry counted against them. Professional gamblers, real-estate speculators, and tradesmen, who lived by their wits and swallowed the political emoluments of the county, watched with a dour resentment Mormon cabins springing up and Mormon crops showing green among the tree stumps.

Even the more literate of the lot — the editors, lawyers, and clergymen — were agitated over the political implications of the Mormon emigration. "The day is not far distant . . ." they complained, "when the sheriff, the justices, and the county judges will be Mormons, or persons wishing to court their favor from motives of interest or ambition. What would be the fate of our lives and property, in the hands of jurors and witnesses, who do not blush to declare, and would not upon occasion hesitate to swear, that they have wrought miracles, and have been the subjects of miraculous supernatural cures, have conversed with God and His angels, and possess and exercise the gifts of divination and of unknown tongues, and fired with the prospect of obtaining inheritances without money and without price — may better be imagined than described."

The Mormon settlers were no more tactful than most religious zealots, and their very enthusiasm was an irritation. "We are daily told," the old settlers said, "and not by the ignorant alone, but by all classes of them, that we, (the Gentiles,) of this county are to be cut off, and our lands appropriated by them for inheritances. Whether this is to be accomplished by the hand of the destroying angel, the judgments of God, or the arm of power, they are not fully agreed among themselves." *

Worst crime of all, the Mormons were Northerners who owned no slaves. Previous to their arrival the bulk of the immigrants had come from Kentucky and Tennessee, many with a retinue of Negroes. The population of Missouri in 1830 was over one-fifth slave. Early in 1832 the old settlers accused the Mormons of "endeavoring to sow dissensions and raise seditions" among their slaves, and the church elders promised to curb the offenders.

In the following year a handful of free Negroes who had been

* These quotations are from a summary of the grievances of the old settlers published in the *Western Monitor* (Fayette, Missouri), August 2, 1833.

converted to the church tried to emigrate to Independence. Phelps discovered that a Missouri law forbade their entry without a certificate of citizenship from another state, and published a reprint of the statute in the *Evening and Morning Star,* in order, he said, "To prevent any misunderstanding among the churches abroad, respecting free people of color, who may think of coming to the western boundaries of Missouri, as members of the Church."

He added in what he believed was a cautious vein, since he knew he was handling dynamite: "So long as we have no special rule in the Church, as to people of color, let prudence guide, and while they, as well as we, are in the hands of a merciful God, we say: Shun every appearance of evil." Later in the same issue he wrote: "As to slaves, we have nothing to say; in connection with the wonderful events of this age much is doing toward abolishing slavery, and colonizing the blacks in Africa." *

Phelps was completely unprepared for the explosion that followed. The old settlers, who believed it to be a direct invitation to free Negroes to emigrate to Missouri, with explicit instructions for evading the law designed to exclude them, immediately called a mass meeting. Here they drew up a manifesto demanding the expulsion of the Mormons. "We believed them deluded fanatics," they wrote, "or weak and designing knaves, and that they and their pretensions would soon pass away; but in this we were deceived." Denouncing Phelps's articles, they insisted that the coming of free Negroes would corrupt their blacks and instigate them to bloodshed. "We, therefore, agree," the manifesto concluded, "that after timely warning, and receiving an adequate compensation for what little property they cannot take with them, if they refuse to leave us in peace, as they found us — we agree to use such means as may be sufficient to remove them, and to that end we each pledge to each other our bodily powers, our lives, fortunes and sacred honors." †
Among the hundreds of signatures to this declaration were the names of all the county officers elected to administer justice — the judge of the court, the county clerk, the constable, his deputy, and the jailer.

* *Evening and Morning Star,* Vol. II (July 1833), pp. 218–19, 221.
† Ibid., pp. 226–31.

Phelps somersaulted backwards to undo the mischief. Know-ing that another mass meeting was scheduled for July 20, he rushed the publication of a *Star* extra, which said in part: "Hav-ing learned with extreme regret that an article entitled 'Free People of Color' in the last number of the *Star,* has been mis-understood, we feel in duty bound to state, in this *Extra,* that our intention was not only to stop free people of color from emigrating to this state, but to prevent them from being ad-mitted as members of the Church." *

Ignoring this recantation, five hundred settlers met in Inde-pendence and drew up five demands: first, that no Mormon settle in Jackson County in the future; second, that those al-ready settled promise to sell their lands and leave; third, that the Mormon press, storehouse, and shops close immediately; and fourth, that the leaders stop all immigration from Ohio. The fifth demand was a not too cryptic direction that "those who fail to comply with these requisitions, be referred to those of their brethren who have the gifts of divination, and of un-known tongues, to inform them of the lot that awaits them." †

The mass meeting shortly turned into a mob. When the de-mands were read aloud, the men gave a great shout and headed for the Mormon community, west of the town. Partridge was given exactly fifteen minutes to capitulate. When he pleaded for more time, the men marched to the *Star* office, where they wrecked the press, smashed the furniture, and then razed the two-story brick building. All copies they could find of the *Book of Commandments,* the compilation of Joseph's revela-tions, were carried off or destroyed. Not content with destruc-tion of property, the mob thirsted for the sport of mauling men, and Edward Partridge and Charles Allen fell victim to that ever popular diversion, the tar-and-feather party.

When night fell, the women and children who had fled to the woods and cornfields crept back to Independence and gath-ered timidly to stare at the ruin that had been the press office. Many crowded into the home of Edward Partridge, whose friends were scraping at the tar on his body to keep the acid that had been mixed with it from eating into his flesh. Despite his

* Mormon historians have pointed out that this reversal expressed only Phelps's opinion and was not church policy. *History of the Church,* Vol. I, pp. 378–9n.
† *Western Monitor,* August 2, 1833.

pain, the bishop maintained a stoic dignity, saying quietly that he bore the mob no malice and was proud to have been persecuted for the truth's sake. His frightened people were raised to a kind of solemn ecstasy by the joy he took in his suffering, feeling themselves kin to the ancient disciples of Jesus who had bled and died for the gospel.

Three days later the mob reassembled and charged into the Mormon settlement brandishing dirks and rifles, threatening the church leaders with a hundred lashes — the equivalent of a death sentence — and swearing that unless the whole colony left Jackson County their slaves would fire the Mormon crops and cabins. Under this pressure the nine leading Mormon men promised that they would leave the county with half the colony by January 1, the remainder to follow before spring.

JOSEPH was appalled when Oliver Cowdery brought him this news. Until now opposition had been directed chiefly against his own person, and he had long since learned to meet ridicule and threats with indifference. Always affable, and rapidly growing in political wisdom, he had scorned reprisals. Now he cautioned his people in Independence to do likewise. An immediate revelation ordered them to renounce war and proclaim peace, and to bear all indignities with patience.*

Joseph's only direct action was to delegate two men to petition the Governor of Missouri for justice. Unofficially he suggested that Zion had brought down the calamity upon herself. "I am not at all astonished," he wrote on September 4 to Vienna Jacques, "at what has happened to you, neither to what has happened to Zion, and I could tell you the whys and wherefores of all these calamities. But alas, it is vain to warn and give precepts, for all men are naturally disposed to walk in their own paths as they are pointed out by their own fingers, and are not willing to consider and walk in the path which is pointed out by another . . . although he should be an unerring director, and the Lord his God sent him."

Few of the Missouri Mormons had a better right to an explanation for Zion's misfortunes than Vienna Jacques. A bachelor woman with a modest capital of fourteen hundred dollars, she had been ordered to Zion by a personal revelation from Jo-

* *Doctrine and Covenants*, Section 98.

seph, which had commanded her to take only enough money
for expenses and to consecrate the remainder to the Lord. In
return for her faithfulness she had been promised an inheritance
in Independence.* To comfort her now Joseph concluded his
letter with a prayer and a promise:

> . . . O Lord, let Zion be comforted, let her waste places be built
> up and established an hundred fold . . . let Thy handmaid live till
> her soul shall be satisfied in beholding the glory of Zion; for not-
> withstanding her present affliction, she shall yet arise and put on her
> beautiful garments, and be the joy and glory of the whole earth.
> Therefore let your heart be comforted. . . . I will assure you that
> the Lord has respect unto the offering you made.†

Early in October 1833 Joseph and Sidney Rigdon left Kirtland on a preaching tour through Canada and the East. Joseph
could do nothing for Zion and knew it. To go there himself
would only further inflame the old settlers, and to remain in
Kirtland meant facing the remonstrances of his people, who
could not understand his inaction. He suggested that those in
Missouri who were in greatest danger leave Jackson County,
but advised the remainder to wait until the animosity had died
down before taking any action. Cowdery he sent off to New
York to buy a new printing press, promising that if he set it
up in Kirtland he should be the editor of the *Star*.

Upon his return from Canada Joseph was more noncommittal about Zion than before. "We are informed, however," he
wrote to Moses Nickerson on November 19, "that those persons
[the mob] are very violent, and threaten immediate extermination upon all those who profess our doctrine. How far they will
be suffered to execute their threats, we know not, but we trust
in the Lord, and leave the event with Him to govern in His
own wise providence." ‡

FOLLOWING their prophet's counsel, the Missouri converts
turned the other cheek. Their only action in self-defense was
a vigorous petition to the Governor requesting sufficient troops

* Ibid., Section 90.
   † *History of the Church*, Vol. I, p. 408. It is said that Vienna Jacques later be-
came one of Joseph's plural wives. See Appendix C.
   ‡ *History of the Church*, Vol. I, p. 442.

to maintain order while they brought suit for property damages. Replying late in October, Governor Dunklin expressed warm sympathy, but postponed action by advising the Mormons to appeal first of all to the local judges. The church leaders in Independence then sought out four lawyers — Wood, Reese, Doniphan, and Atchison — who agreed to take their case.

The following night, October 31, 1833, fifty men attacked an outlying Mormon colony west of the Big Blue River, unroofed and partly demolished ten cabins, whipped and stoned the men, and drove the women and children shrieking into the woods. When this was repeated on subsequent nights, the Mormons began to organize for defense.

Learning late one afternoon that the storehouse was being sacked, one hastily armed group rushed to the spot. Only a single culprit, who had stayed to hurl a final brickbat through the door, was caught. When he was taken before a justice of the peace, the justice not only refused to swear out a warrant for his arrest but actually arrested and jailed the captors on the prisoner's cry of false arrest. John Corrill in his history commented wryly on this incident: "Although we could not obtain a warrant against him for breaking open the store, yet he had gotten one for us by catching him at it."

Organizing and arming as best they could, the Mormons tried patrolling their own settlements. One band, led by David Whitmer, clashed with some marauders on November 4. In the exchange of fire two non-Mormons and one Mormon were killed. Magnified reports of this affray spread terror through the county. The infuriated old settlers threatened to murder the Mormons they had already jailed and at the same time screamed for the militia lest the Mormons, in revenge for their own dead, massacre the citizens of Independence. "It is possible," wrote Isaac M'Coy in an inflammatory letter to the *Missouri Intelligencer,* "that they designed to kill or drive out all the inhabitants and to destroy the village." *

The Lieutenant Governor of the state, Lilburn Boggs, who was living in Independence at the time, called out the militia to restore order. But he placed at its head Colonel Thomas Pitcher, who had been one of the signers of the manifesto

* *Missouri Intelligencer and Boon's Lick Advertiser,* December 21, 1833.

ordering the Mormons to leave the county. Boggs himself was one of the biggest landowners in western Missouri, his holdings stretching along the river from Livingston to Independence. No one more than he feared the influx of a sizable voting bloc of non-slaveholders.

Hearing that their imprisoned brethren were about to be shot, the Mormons gathered in force just west of Independence. Here they were approached by Colonel Pitcher, who demanded the surrender of their arms and insisted that several men give themselves up to be tried for the murder of the two recently slain Missourians. Ostensibly friendly, Boggs personally urged the Mormons to obey, promising blandly that he would order Pitcher to disarm the mob as well. Despite their misgivings, the church leaders capitulated.

The news that the Mormons were disarmed overspread the county in a single afternoon. When Boggs sardonically suggested that the old settlers also be disarmed, Pitcher grinned in his beard. That night the mob systematically sacked every Mormon community, beat and whipped the men, and drove the women and children out like cattle. Before morning twelve hundred people had been herded forth in the teeth of a November gale. A few fled to Clay County, where they were received with sympathy; the majority huddled for days among the cottonwoods lining the Missouri River, hungry, weaponless, and leaderless, praying passionately for a miracle.

The brutality of the Jackson County mob won for the Mormons their first champions outside the church. The Missouri press almost universally deplored the outrage, and newspapers throughout the nation reprinted the details with indignant editorial comment.* The lawyers retained by the Mormons now threw caution aside and fought honestly for their clients' rights. Led by the courageous Doniphan, they roused Governor Dunklin to promise a military escort to return the Mormons to their homes. Dunklin gave them for the first time permission to organize into militia groups and to apply for public arms. He frankly said, however, that he had no constitutional power to maintain a constant guard once they had been reinstated; and without such protection the Mormons were afraid to return lest

---

* See the *Missouri Intelligencer*, November 16, 1833, *Niles Register*, September 14, 1833, and the *Salt River Journal* and *Liberty Enquirer* for this period.

the whole bloody affair be repeated. They knew it was hazardous even to send witnesses to a court of inquiry, and begged
that it be postponed until trustworthy militiamen could be sent
into the county.

Although some of the exiles now moved on into surrounding counties, the bulk of the Mormons remained bivouacked on
the Missouri bottoms, waiting hopefully for word from their
prophet.

On the night of November 13 a cry of astonishment resounded through the camp: "In God's name look to the heavens! The stars are falling out of the sky!" The shivering people
crawled out of their bark shelters and peered upward through
the gaunt trees. Hundreds of brilliant meteors were shooting
across the firmament, leaving in their wake long trains of light.
It was one of the greatest meteoric showers in the century, and
all over the States people watched it awed and frightened. But
nowhere else as among these outcasts did men greet it with
such rapture: "God be praised, it is a sign of the end of the
world!"

IT took exactly one month for news of the banishment to reach
the prophet. He received letters from Phelps and Hyde that
were fairly accurate, but on the same day a courier brought him
a fantastic story of a battle in which the Mormons had killed
more than twenty Missourians.

However ambitious he may have been for his people, Joseph
had never counted on bloodshed to help his cause. He began
dimly to realize the explosive possibilities of the theocracy he
was building. From the first appearance of trouble he had forbidden reprisals, but now in some inexorable fashion there had
come shooting, bleeding, and dying for his sake.

Had Joseph's certainty of the divinity of his mission been
more substantial he would no doubt have cursed the Missouri
settlers into hell for obstructing the work of the Lord. This, in
fact, he finally did, but not until a decade later when he was
writing the history of his church from a more secure position in
Nauvoo, Illinois. Now he seems to have been racked with a
sense of impotence and irresolution, for he replied to his
wretched people in a half-suspicious vein that tripled their despair:

Kirtland, December 5, 1833.

Dear Brethren: —

We have just received a letter from Brother Phelps, dated 6th and 7th November, at Liberty, which gives us the painful intelligence of the rage of the enemy, and your present unsettled situation. But I must inform you that there is a great dubiety resting upon our minds, with regard to the true state of affairs of Zion; for there seems to be some difference in the statements of Elder Phelps' letter and that of Elder Hyde's communication. . . . It appears, brethren, that the above statements were made mostly from reports, and there is no certainty of their being correct; therefore, it is difficult for us to advise, and we can only say, that the destinies of all people are in the hands of a just God, and He will do no injustice to anyone; and this one thing is sure, that they who live godly in Christ Jesus, shall suffer persecution. . . .

It is your privilege to use every lawful means in your power to seek redress for your grievances from your enemies, and prosecute them to the extent of the law; but it will be impossible for us to render you any temporal assistance, as our means are already exhausted, and we are deeply in debt, and know of no means whereby we shall be able to extricate ourselves. . . .*

Eleven days later, on December 16, a new revelation officially explained the curse that had descended over Zion: "I, the Lord, have suffered the affliction to come upon them, wherewith they have been afflicted, in consequence of their transgressions. . . . Behold, I say unto you, there were jarrings, and contentions, and envyings, and strifes, and lustful and covetous desires among them; therefore by these things they polluted their inheritances." †

Phelps had been aware of this attitude in the prophet even before he saw the revelation, for he had written on December 15 a despairing letter that reflected the bewilderment of every devout man who has seen the innocent suffer along with the godless. "I know it was right that we should be driven out of the land of Zion, that the rebellious might be sent away. But, brethren, if the Lord will, I should like to know what the honest in heart shall do? Our clothes are worn out; we want the necessaries of life, and shall we lease, buy, or otherwise obtain land where we are, to till, that we may raise enough to eat? Such is

* *History of the Church*, Vol. I, pp. 449–50.
† *Doctrine and Covenants*, Section 101.

the common language of the honest, for they want to do the will of God." *

Most of the Mormons by now had settled in Clay County, where the citizens had agreed to give them temporary shelter. Pending a settlement, Joseph ordered the whole colony to remain as near Jackson County as possible, and emphatically forbade them to sell their property.

He took this stand first of all because he did not yet realize the gravity and inevitability of the conflict between his own land-hungry, communistic millenarians and the frontier flotsam. Secondly, he had a stubborn faith in the law and a conviction that if not in the local courts, then in Jefferson City or in Washington his people would be accorded justice. Phelps wrote to him: "Our people fare very well, and when they are discreet, little or no persecution is felt." Such observations helped to confirm his faith that a lasting peace might yet be established.

He had his Missouri leaders prepare a petition to Andrew Jackson, and took pains to write an eloquent plea of his own. When it was finished, he mailed with it a copy of his latest revelation, in which the Lord had commanded the children of Zion to importune first at the feet of the judges, then at the feet of the Governor, and finally at the feet of the President. "And if the president heed them not," it said, "then will the Lord arise and come forth out of his hiding place, and in his fury vex the nation. . . ." †

Even had this threat reached Jackson's desk, it probably would have gone unnoticed among the three thousand words of the revelation. But secretaries snared the document and politely informed the prophet that his proper recourse was to apply to the authorities of Missouri. Yet the gesture was not wasted on the Mormon people, who were comforted by the thought of Old Hickory quaking in his shoes.

Little by little Joseph came to understand how basic were the animosities between his people and the old settlers, and he showed himself willing to compromise even on fundamental issues. Missouri had particularly resented the communistic nature of the Mormon settlement. With the closing of the store-

---

* *History of the Church*, Vol. I, p. 457.
† *Doctrine and Covenants*, Section 101.

house the Order in Independence had collapsed. A reaction upon the heavily mortgaged Kirtland Order could not be avoided, and its decline set in swiftly. In the Missouri debacle Joseph now saw a chance to erase the whole economic experiment — which in Kirtland had never yielded anything but trouble — and at the same moment make a concession to the gentile world. Not even Rigdon's lofty protests could surmount the argument that to abolish communism would ease the tension in Zion.

On April 10, 1834 the Kirtland council dissolved the Order. Dividing the community property was a thorny business. Tired of quibbling and recrimination, Joseph finally resorted to a revelation to parcel out the real estate, deeding himself the temple lot, Rigdon the tannery, Cowdery the printing shop, and most of the other leaders the lots on which they were then living. In 1835, when the time came to print this curious document in the *Doctrine and Covenants,* he substituted fictitious names to avoid any unpleasantness — Ahashdah for Whitney, Olihah for Cowdery, Pelagoram for Rigdon, Mahemson for Harris, and Gazelam for himself. He even used code names for the industries — Laneshine house for the printing shop and Ozondah for the store.* Except for a few leaders who knew better, the Mormons believed these to be the names of people living in the days of Enoch.†

From this moment Joseph began to efface the communistic rubric in his young theology. Since most copies of the *Book of Commandments* had been burned, it was easy for him to revise drastically the revelation on the United Order when it was republished in the enlarged *Doctrine and Covenants* in 1835. The Lord no longer demanded consecration of a man's total property, but only a donation of his "surplus" over and above living expenses. In reprinting the first twelve issues of the *Evening and Morning Star,* Joseph revised most, though not all, of the descriptions of the original Order and commanded his missionaries to destroy the notion abroad that the church had ever been a common-stock concern.

---

* Ibid., Section 104.

† So William West was informed in 1836. See his *A Few Interesting Facts Respecting the Rise, Progress and Pretensions of the Mormons* (Warren, Ohio, [?] 1837) pp. 13–14.

Although Rigdon repeatedly urged a restoration, Joseph made only one effort to revive the Order after 1834. This was a greatly revised consecration program that he launched in Missouri in 1838. It collapsed at the end of the year when the Mormons were driven out of the state altogether. Thereafter the prophet was content to let the United Order be translated to the plane of abstract ideals, where it was destined to remain. Years after his death, experiments with communal living were tried in the desert isolation of the Great Basin, but these also disintegrated because, it was said, the Mormons proved as yet unworthy to live the higher law of God.

During Joseph's lifetime, however, there was never a return to complete freedom of enterprise. The church remained a force in the financial and economic affairs of its members, and the prophet never lost the conviction that it was his right to be mentor to his people in matters of property and finance as well as matters of the spirit. Joseph's kingdom, unlike that of Jesus, was unmistakably of this world.

CHAPTER X
The Army of the Lord

THE PAST that Joseph had hoped to bury in New York now returned to plague him. He had made a vindictive enemy of Philastus Hurlbut, a handsome, ambitious convert whom he had excommunicated in June 1833 for "unchristian conduct with the ladies." In vengeful mood, Hurlbut began an investigation of the beginnings of the Mormon Church.

In Conneaut, about fifty miles east of Kirtland, he heard a rumor that one John Spaulding had seen a resemblance between Joseph's Book of Mormon and an old manuscript written many years earlier by his brother, Solomon Spaulding. Electrified by the idea that the Book of Mormon might be proved a forgery, Hurlbut ransacked Conneaut for evidence. Solomon had died seventeen years before, and his wife had remarried and moved away; but John Spaulding and his wife Martha, together with several neighbors, remembered dimly that Solomon's old historical novel had been about a lost people who were ancestors of the Indians. That it was not a religious history they were all agreed; but under Hurlbut's excited prodding they managed to recall an astonishing number of details that coincided exactly with those in the Book of Mormon — astonishing because it had been twenty years since the single occasion on which they had heard Solomon read his manuscript aloud.

Hurlbut wrote down their affidavits, collected their signatures, and went off triumphantly to Palmyra, where he expected to find additional evidence. Though he discovered there nothing to bolster his theory, he ran headlong into the whole folklore of Joseph's money-digging. He spent two months in Palmyra in the autumn of 1833, assiduously collecting affidavits from more than a hundred of Joseph's acquaintances. The substance of their stories was devastating, and he knew it.

Only one thing remained to complete his case: rediscovery of Solomon Spaulding's manuscript. After finding Spaulding's widow in Massachusetts, he was directed by her back to eastern New York, where he located the manuscript in a trunk in the attic of an old farmhouse. Now to his bitter chagrin he found that the long chase had been vain; for while the romance did concern the ancestors of the Indians, its resemblance to the Book of Mormon ended there. None of the names found in one could be identified in the other; the many battles which each described showed not the slightest similarity with those of the other, and Spaulding's prose style, which aped the eighteenth-century British sentimental novelists, differed from the style of the Mormon Bible as much as *Pamela, or Virtue Rewarded* differed from the New Testament.*

Hurlbut knew, however, that he had a keg of powder even without the manuscript. He boldly exhibited his affidavits in Kirtland, lectured in the surrounding towns, and arranged to publish the documents in book form with the assistance of Eber D. Howe. The lectures caused a furor. Orson Hyde wrote to Missouri that they had "fired the minds of the people with much indignation against Joseph and the Church," and Heber Kimball reported in his journal that enemies "were raging and threatening destruction upon us, and we had to guard ourselves night after night, and for weeks were not permitted to take off our clothes." †

But what Joseph dreaded more than gentile savagery was the effect of Hurlbut's lectures on his own people. Apprehensive converts were besieging Oliver Cowdery and Martin Harris with questions about the golden plates, and Harris was expanding an already Hydra-headed legend. He was indiscreet enough to tell a friend confidentially that the prophet had drunk too much liquor while translating the Book of Mormon. Brought to trial by the High Council for his heresy, he amended the statement to say that the drunkenness had occurred previous to the translation.‡

Realizing that the unchecked rumor-mongering might destroy him, Joseph began an immediate counter-offensive. He

* The manuscript Hurlbut found was published first by the Reorganized Church in Lamoni, Iowa, in 1885 under the title *The Manuscript Found, or the Manuscript Story of the late Rev. Solomon Spaulding*. For a detailed discussion of the Spaulding theory see Appendix B.

† *History of the Church*, Vol. I, p. 475, and *Times and Seasons*, Vol. VI, p. 771.

‡ *Times and Seasons*, Vol. VI, p. 992.

collected copies of every affidavit, read them aloud to his followers, and proceeded to demolish them as fabrications of the
devil. The variety and cunning of the attacks against him was
proof, he said, that Satan was out to wreck the true church, but
his machinations were certain to come to naught. "I will stand
like the sun in the firmament when my enemies and the gain-
sayers of my testimony shall be put down and cut off, and their
names blotted out from among men."

Rigdon, meanwhile, with an obscenity incongruous in a minister, smeared Hurlbut with personal scandal.* Apoplectic with
rage, Hurlbut began publicly to threaten the life of the prophet.
This gave Joseph an opportunity for which he had scarcely
dared to hope. Early in January 1834 he issued a complaint and
Hurlbut was brought to trial on April 1. Hurlbut lost the
case and was held in two-hundred-dollar bond to keep the peace
for six months.

The adverse decision shattered his influence. He sold his manuscript for five hundred dollars to Howe, who printed the book
Mormonism Unvailed under his own name. Although troubled
over this publication, Joseph was confident that after weather-
ing Hurlbut's lectures he could meet this storm too. And he was
right.

For most Mormons it was enough that the prophet branded
the book a pack of lies. It was his word against Hurlbut's. It
was the Book of Mormon and the *Book of Commandments*
against a volume of what they considered perjured testimony.
The scales were heavily weighted in Joseph's favor. Those who
knew at first hand the truth of many of Hurlbut's accusations
had long since dismissed it as Joseph's juvenile folly. Many in
the church shared the attitude of Brigham Young, who had a
healthy understanding of human frailty: "If he acts like a devil,
he has brought forth a doctrine that will save us, if we abide
by it. He may get drunk every day of his life, sleep with his

---

* His charges were later printed in the *Latter-Day Saints Messenger and Advocate*,
December 1835, p. 227, and in a letter to the *Boston Journal* dated May 27, 1839,
republished in Henry Mayhew: *History of the Mormons* (Auburn, 1853), pp. 45–8.
Eva L. Pancoast has convincingly cleared Hurlbut of most of Rigdon's charges. See
her "Mormons in Kirtland" (M.A. thesis, Western Reserve University, Cleveland,
1929). Her contention, however, that Hurlbut joined the church purposely to expose
it is based on an error in dates. Hurlbut announced his intention of exposing Joseph
Smith in the *Chardon Spectator*, January 18, 1834, not January 18, 1833, as Miss
Pancoast says.

146]   *No Man Knows My History*

neighbor's wife every night, run horses and gamble. . . . But the doctrine he has produced will save you and me and the whole world." *

ONE thing, however, none of Joseph's followers could understand or forgive: his seeming lethargy about the fate of Zion. He was waiting for the tedious processes of the law, but his people expected him to call down armies of angels.

Late in February 1834 Parley Pratt and Lyman Wight arrived from Missouri storming for action. Wight was a boisterous, bellicose convert who had seen the glory of the Lord and was hell-bent to fight for Him. His zeal and Pratt's flamboyant eloquence stirred up the whole Kirtland colony. The men had brought with them the good news that Governor Dunklin had arrested Colonel Pitcher and was investigating the unlawful seizure of the Mormon arms. He had called out the militia to be ready to escort the Mormons back to Jackson County after a special court of inquiry, and had once more advised the church members to apply for public arms.

There remained the unpleasant fact that even if all the Mormons in Jackson County had muskets they were still outnumbered by the old settlers. To remedy this, Wight and Pratt had a plan. They would raise an army which would march to Missouri in time to be there at the reinstatement. Ostensibly the army would go as a group of settlers; actually it would be a trained military force, which would maintain a constant and vigilant patrol until the church was wealthy enough to buy out the property of the mob's leaders.

The enthusiasm that greeted this plan stiffened Joseph to a decision. Quick-springing visions of an army of liberation marching triumphantly into the promised land betrayed his sounder judgment. "Behold I say unto you," said a new revelation, "the redemption of Zion must needs come by power; Therefore, I will raise up unto my people a man, who shall lead them like as Moses led the children of Israel. For ye are the children of Israel, and of the seed of Abraham, and ye must needs be let out of bondage by power, and with a stretched-out arm." †

---

* Young stated on November 9, 1856 that he told this to a priest shortly after his own conversion, and before meeting Joseph Smith. *Journal of Discourses,* Vol. IV, p. 78.

† *Doctrine and Covenants,* Section 103.

His leading elders Joseph dispatched on a whirlwind recruiting tour. Kirtland became the scene of feverish preparation, which the *Painesville Telegraph* editor described with somewhat less than his usual malice:

Old muskets, rifles, pistols, rusty swords and butcher knives, were soon put in a state of repair and scoured up. Some were borrowed, and some were bought on credit if possible, and others were manufactured by their own mechanics. . . . Old men, invalids, and females, who could not endure the toils and hardships of a pedestrian excursion of 1,000 miles, felt it to be a great privilege to contribute liberally in the way of funds and the materiel of war. Poor fanatical females, who could save no more than a shilling per day, by their exertions, threw in all they could raise, for the purpose of helping on with the expedition, and, as they supposed, thereby securing the smiles and blessings of the Lord.*

Joseph had hoped for an army of five hundred, but two months of vigorous recruiting yielded fewer than two hundred volunteers. By the end of April scarcely more than a hundred dollars had been raised in Kirtland, although the elders brought back two hundred and fifty dollars from converts in the East. Finally a revelation gave the prophet permission to mortgage the property that had formerly belonged to the Order.†

During this period reports from Missouri were depressing. Then word came that mob rule had become law in Independence, that every Mormon caught venturing into the county was clubbed unmercifully, and that the court of inquiry had broken up in disorder. Although Joseph was greatly disturbed by this news, it served only to whet the eagerness of "Zion's Camp" to be off to the rescue.

On Sunday, May 4, 1834, the army met in Kirtland to hear an address by Rigdon. With a full and measured eloquence he urged them to deeds of valor and promised them the glory of the Christian martyrs and the victories of the ancient Hebrew legions. At this time he announced also that the prophet and the High Council had agreed to his suggestion that the name of the church be changed from Church of Christ to Church of Latterday Saints. By this measure they hoped to avoid the hated nick-

* E. D. Howe: *Mormonism Unvailed*, pp. 155–6.
† *Doctrine and Covenants*, Section 104, verses 84–5.

names Mormon and Mormonite, since something more specific than "Christian" was needed for identification.

Joseph had divided his army into companies of twelve, allowing each one to elect its own captain. Every man was assigned a specific duty — that of cook, fireman, waterman, wagoner, horseman, or commissary. A soldier in the forefront of the group carried a white flag with the word *Peace* lettered across it in red.

On May 5 they started out in good order, strictly observing Joseph's injunction to evade all questions and keep their destination secret. Whenever they reached a sizable town, they dispersed and passed through it on different streets. Sentinels were posted at night with orders to look upon every questioner as a spy or horse-thief.

During a three-day rest at Salt Creek, Illinois, the troops cleaned and polished their guns and drilled in simple maneuvers. With surprise and pleasure many learned for the first time that Joseph was an expert shot and a superb horseman. They knew that his slight lameness had kept him out of the militia and were therefore astonished at his apparent command of military language and tactics. The younger men drilled with slavish devotion.

Actually Joseph had always been fascinated by military lore — which perhaps accounted for the innumerable battles in the Book of Mormon. He carried a rifle, an elegant brace of pistols, and the best sword in the army. Yet despite his love of military pageantry and display, he had little stomach for battle. The carnage of war was abhorrent to him, and he had no ambition to be a famous warrior.

Some of his men found it difficult to reconcile his enthusiasm for parade and drill with his cautious efforts to conceal his own identity. Frequently he changed his position in the party and adopted the pseudonym Captain Cook. He kept with him always a large, savage bulldog, which the men soon learned to detest. After crossing the Mississippi he took the further precaution of selecting a personal bodyguard of twenty men. Most of Zion's Camp, however, looked upon such measures with approval. Their prophet was no ordinary general whose role could be filled by the next in rank.

Permeating the military atmosphere was the stern discipline

of the gospel. Every night before retiring Joseph blew a blast upon a sacred ram's horn, and his men knelt in prayer for succor and guidance. Minor miracles were a daily occurrence. Parley Pratt, who was frequently separated from the army on recruiting trips, said that an angel awakened him one morning when oversleeping would have meant disaster. Martin Harris offered his naked toe to a five-foot black snake in the road, and when it refused to bite him proclaimed an apostolic victory over the serpent. When he repeated the experiment with another snake and got a severe bite on the ankle, the company jeered uproariously at his lack of faith, and Joseph publicly upbraided him for making a mockery of the Lord's gifts.

Joseph himself, however, added to the supernatural occurrences. Stopping near an Indian mound on the Illinois River, he excavated a skeleton from near its surface and said to his companions: "This man in mortal life was a white Lamanite, a large, thick-set man, and a man of God. His name was Zelf. He was a warrior and chieftain under the great prophet Onandagus, who was known from the eastern sea to the Rocky Mountains. The curse of the red skin was taken from him, or, at least in part." Lifting the thigh bone, which had been broken, and pointing to an arrowhead still lodged between two ribs, he described in vivid detail the great battle in which Zelf had been killed. Brigham Young eagerly seized the arrowhead, and others carried off the leg and thigh bones for souvenirs.*

After a fortnight of marching, high spirits gave way to bickering. Every company ran short of bread except that of Brigham Young, who had noted the dangerously low supply of meal and had sent two men forward to purchase some for his own dozen soldiers. To the undercurrent of complaints Young listened in silence. Since the failure of the United Order Joseph had had the reputation of being a poor financier, and many of the Camp privately regretted that he was treasurer for the army. His integrity they did not doubt, but everyone knew that money melted too fast in Joseph's fingers. Generous to a fault, he was the wrong man to plan a thousand-mile journey for two hundred men.

The heat became intense. Unused to marching, the soldiers

---

* *History of the Church,* Vol. II, pp. 79–80; and "Elder Kimball's Journal," *Times and Seasons,* Vol. VI, p. 788.

suffered from blistered, bleeding feet. When it rained, the roads became quagmires. Wagons were stuck in every mudhole and frequently broke down altogether. Food shortages persisted until the army was reduced to living on johnnycake and corn dodger. The men stifled any open protest until one day Joseph purchased a dozen cured hams that were partly spoiled on the outside. Six of these were flung down outside his tent with the acid complaint: "We don't eat stinking meat!"

The loudest grumbler was the petulant and humorless Sylvester Smith. One day he violated a sacred camp rule by refusing to share his bread with Parley Pratt. The two men wrangled bitterly until Joseph burst upon them threatening both with a scourging from the Lord. The following morning horrified guards rushed to Joseph with news that all the horses were badly foundered. "It is a witness that God has His eyes upon us," the prophet said. "His hand is in this misfortune. But those brethren who will humble themselves shall find their horses restored to health." All morning the men watched their animals with apprehension, praying for the Lord's favor. Only one horse died — that of Sylvester Smith. The bickering ceased abruptly, and the army looked at the prophet with new wonder.

For several hundred miles Sylvester maintained a frightened but resentful silence. Just after crossing the Mississippi River he narrowly escaped being bitten by the prophet's bulldog. Publicly he showered Joseph with abuse. "If that dog bites me," he finished wildly, "I'll kill him!"

"If you do, I will whip you," cried Joseph hotly.

Sylvester advanced shrieking, his fists clenched. "And if you do, I'll defend myself the best way I can."

This was one of the rare occasions when Joseph's urbane temper vanished completely. "I'll whip you," he shouted, "in the name of the Lord! And if you continue in the same spirit and don't repent, that dog will eat the flesh off your bones and you shall not have the power to resist!"

Sylvester turned pale, for Joseph's curses were not to be lightly regarded. But now several onlookers jumped to his defense. The dog was a nuisance, they declared, and generally hated throughout the camp. Moreover, they did not approve of whipping "in the name of the Lord," and bluntly told the prophet so.

Joseph retreated hastily before their disapproval, which he

knew to be just. "A spirit of dissension pervades the whole camp," he said defensively. "I descended to it purposely to show you how base and ignoble your attitude has become. It was the spirit of a dog, and men ought never to place themselves on a level with beasts. Are you not ashamed of such a spirit? I am." *

What passed through Brigham Young's mind as his prophet backed down, one can only guess. His years of leadership lay ahead, stretching over endless wagon trails and across dusty plains. The man who was to bring thousands of wretched outcasts to the inhospitable mountains of the West and build a homeland there would not have yielded to a mutinous upstart. This lame retreat of Joseph's was weakness, boding no good for the company's discipline in the dangerous days ahead. Nevertheless, there was something in Joseph that made Brigham content to acknowledge himself the lesser man.

THE DISPUTE was suddenly forgotten when Orson Hyde and Parley Pratt returned from a special mission to Governor Dunklin. They brought bitter news. Until the coming of Zion's Camp the Governor had been working cautiously on the Mormon side. In confidence he had informed the Mormons of his negotiations with the War Office to secure a federal arsenal, which he planned to have built in Jackson County. This would have made permanently available a unit of the federal army to guard the Mormons against further molestation. Moreover, the Governor had seriously considered dividing Jackson County between the opposing groups.

He had sent an order on May 2 to Colonel Lucas requiring him to restore the Mormon arms that had been unlawfully seized the preceding November. But before Lucas received the order, news of the coming of Zion's Camp leaked out. The old settlers stormed the Independence jail and seized the Mormon arms sequestered there. Then they methodically ravaged all the remaining Mormon property. Between April 24 and 30 they burned one hundred and fifty houses.

---

* The story of Joseph's quarrels with Sylvester Smith was told in detail in the minutes of the Kirtland council meeting of August 27, 1834, when Sylvester was brought to trial for his misconduct. See *History of the Church*, Vol. II, pp. 150–60. For additional details see Howe: *Mormonism Unvailed*, p. 161.

The coming of Zion's Camp and the complete desolation of the Mormon settlements melted Dunklin's resolution. He told Joseph's emissaries that to restore their property to the Mormons at this particular time was completely impracticable.

Zion's Camp was not a band of colonists, arriving in cumbrous wagons piled high with bedding and new seed. It was an army, however ill-trained and badly armed. It was almost exclusively male, militarily organized, and secretive in its intentions. All along the route men had stared at it in curiosity and fear. "There go the Mormons," they whispered, "on their way to kill the Missourians and get back their land." Runners carried the word to every settlement in upper Missouri. "The Mormons are coming! They are crossing the river! They will murder our women and children!" * Without waiting to be summoned, militiamen from four counties formed into companies to meet the "invasion."

Fearing a massacre themselves, the Mormons in Clay County had established a homemade arsenal, where the women molded bullets and the men manufactured crude swords, dirks, and pistols in a desperate effort to make up for their lost weapons. Civil war was certain to break out the moment Zion's Camp crossed the Missouri River.

Joseph was now in a hopeless quandary. There could be no turning back; his men were spoiling for a fight and confidently expected angels to join them in battle. But he must have known that battle with the gentiles meant a one-sided slaughter, for scouts kept him informed of the forces rising against him.

The little band advanced slowly along the north bank of the Missouri. Shortly after crossing the Wakenda River the prophet learned that an armed band on the other side of the Missouri was planning an attack that night. He had to choose between spending the night some distance out on the prairie, where his men would be safe from ambush but without fuel and water, or in the woods near the river, where they would have convenience but little security.

Joseph favored the prairie, but Lyman Wight, who was second in command and accorded the rank of general, insisted on staying in the woods. Sylvester Smith, ever more eager to bait

* As described by John Corrill in a letter to W. W. Phelps dated June 14, 1834. *History of the Church*, Vol. II, p. 92n.

the prophet, warmly defended Wight's stand. After some arguing Joseph exclaimed impatiently: "Thus saith the Lord God — march on!" Wight defiantly drew aside and prepared to camp, while Sylvester took up a stand in the center of the road, turning back all he could and crying: "Are you following your general or some other man?" The majority followed the prophet and camped eight miles out on the prairie, where they drank stinking water and went meatless to bed. Neither group was molested.

The next morning instead of punishing Wight and Smith as any military commander would have done, Joseph chose to defend his own stand as if he were himself on trial. By the spirit of God, he said, "he knew exactly when to pray, when to sing, when to talk, and when to laugh." Wight was contrite and swore strict obedience, but Sylvester Smith raged: "You have stamped out liberty of speech! You prophesy lies in the name of the Lord! You've got a heart corrupt as hell!"

Joseph seized the horn with which he called his men to prayer and flung it at his accuser with all his might. Missing him, it smashed upon the ground. To the troubled, silent onlookers this seemed an omen of evil.*

Three days later Joseph camped on Fishing River, which bordered Clay County. He dared not cross it without more information. Many of his soldiers were impatient; others were apprehensive. But no one realized how terrifying a foe had on that very day begun its attack. Three of the men were down with cholera.

MEANWHILE several influential citizens in Jackson County had been working feverishly for a peace settlement. Judge Ryland had secured from the old settlers a list of proposals, which were read publicly before a gathering of Mormons and non-Mormons in Clay County. The Jackson County citizens proposed to buy all the land held by the Mormons at double the appraised value, that value to be determined by three disinterested arbitrators chosen and agreed to by both parties. Twelve Mormons were to be allowed to assist the arbitrators in their appraisal. Once the price was fixed, the Missourians would pay the sum

* For first-hand descriptions of this episode see *History of the Church*, Vol. II, pp. 100, 101, 154, 159, and Howe: *Mormonism Unvailed*, p. 161.

within thirty days. In return the Mormons were to promise never to settle in the county again. The settlers offered further to sell their own lands to the Mormons under the same terms.

This peace offer the Mormons could not bring themselves to accept. To buy out the gentiles, whose holdings were far greater, was absolutely impossible. The Mormons were impoverished, and Zion's Camp was bringing only men, not money. But to sell their lands was to deny their God and forgo the building of a temple on His appointed site. It meant selling their birthright like Esau, their own and that of their posterity, and the thought was hateful. Moreover, the generosity of the offer was superficial and deceptive, for most of the Mormon property was ashes.

Under the leadership of W. W. Phelps the Mormons in Clay County rejected the proposals but promised to submit a counterplan, guaranteeing that Zion's Camp should not cross Fishing River until an agreement was reached.

Disturbing the negotiations more than anything else was a faction among the old settlers who openly scoffed at arbitration and thirsted for the blood of the prophet. James Campbell, leader of this group, vowed he would intercept Joseph before he reached any of his colonists. "The eagles and turkey buzzards shall eat my flesh," he swore, "if I do not fix Joe Smith and his army so that their skins will not hold shucks before two days are past."

Choosing eleven lieutenants, he started after dusk on June 17 across the treacherous Missouri River to ambush the prophet. Halfway across, the boat capsized. Joseph noted in his journal that one man floated downstream to an island from which "he swam off naked about daylight, borrowed a mantle to hide his shame, and slipped home rather shy of the vengeance of God." The majority were not so lucky. Joseph stated that seven of the twelve men drowned, including Campbell, whose body floated downstream and lodged upon a pile of driftwood. There it was found three weeks later, the flesh picked clean. God had seen to it, Joseph told his men, that Campbell had fulfilled his oath with his own flesh.*

Learning that Zion's Camp planned to stay at Fishing River,

* Judge Josiah Thorpe, however, stated that only two men drowned, Campbell and Everett, the owner of the ferry. *Early Days in Missouri*, letter 16.

about two hundred men gathered at Williams Ferry on June 19 and prepared to cross the Missouri for an attack. The first scow-load of forty men had scarcely left the landing when a squall broke upon the river. "Wind and rain, hail and thunder met them in great wrath," Joseph later wrote, "and soon softened their direful courage and frustrated all their designs. . . . It seemed as if the mandate of vengeance had gone forth from the God of battles to protect His servants from the destruction of their enemies."

Yet the crossing was successfully accomplished and the occupants of the boat opened fire while they were still some distance from the Mormon camp. However, the rain soaked their ammunition and vicious hail drove them to shanties and hollow trees for shelter. The men left behind gave up their forty comrades for lost and crawled under their wagons to escape the storm.

Zion's Camp, meanwhile, had found shelter in a Baptist church. Joseph was in and out repeatedly, checking reports from his scouts, for the shots had warned him of coming trouble. Satisfied finally that there was no danger for the remainder of the night, he came in to rest. Shaking the water from his hat and clothes, he declared soberly: "Boys, there is some meaning to this. God is in this storm." *

The rain dampened the ardor as well as the ammunition of the attackers. The forty who had crossed the river rowed back the next morning and the whole group returned to Independence.

Two days after this incident Cornelius Gilliam, sheriff of Clay County, came to Zion's Camp. Gilliam, who had campaigned for sheriff with the slogan that he had shot more wolves than any other man in Missouri, minced no words. To enter Jackson County with arms would be an act of insurrection. The Governor had said explicitly that it would bring the state militia down upon the heads of the invaders. To remain camped near the border was to invite bloodshed. The Mormons had only two alternatives — to sell their lands, disperse their army, and return to Kirtland, or to purchase the land of the old settlers at double its value.

* This story was told by Wilford Woodruff. See *History of the Church*, Vol. II, p. 104n.

Joseph heard the sheriff through. Taking stock of his circumstances, he found them bad. Zion's Camp had started from Ohio with the law on its side, but somehow that same law was now stubbornly opposing him. The prophet had been four times in court and on three occasions had bested his opponents. His profound respect for the law made difficult his recognition of the fact that it could be twisted to suit the passion of a people.

Joseph lacked one useful capacity of the natural leader; he was unable to gauge the repercussions of his policies upon the opposition. Strategically, the whole concept of Zion's Camp had been a mistake. Had it been executed with complete secrecy, had the men traveled in pairs rather than as a group, the infiltration into Clay County might have been accomplished. The impression of an invasion, at least, would have been avoided. Yet entering a hornets' nest is bound to provoke trouble no matter how clever the mode of entry.

Joseph finally promised Gilliam that Zion's Camp would not cross the Missouri into Jackson County. Then he proposed a peace plan of his own. The Mormons would purchase all the property of the settlers in Jackson County who were Mormon-baiters, the price to be set by twelve disinterested men and the payment made in one year. He insisted, however, that the damages already sustained by his people must be deducted from the value of the property. This plan was pure face-saving. He knew full well that his cause was lost, and the knowledge was the more bitter to him because it was a cause he had championed only under pressure.

Some hours after Gilliam's departure Joseph called his men together and read a new revelation commanding them to "wait for a little season for the redemption of Zion. . . . For behold, I do not require at their hands to fight the battles of Zion. . . . I will fight your battles. Behold, the destroyer I have sent forth to destroy and lay waste mine enemies; and not many years hence they shall not be left to pollute mine heritage. . . . For it is my will that these lands should be purchased. . . . sue for peace not only to the people that have smitten you, but also to all people." *

The revelation went on to say that the men of the army had been brought to Missouri for "a trial of their faith." Now they

* *Doctrine and Covenants*, Section 105.

were to return to Kirtland and receive their reward, a great blessing or "endowment," which would be bestowed in the Kirtland temple. Zion could not be redeemed until all her leading elders had been so blessed.

Few of Joseph's men had realized the gravity of their position, and they were completely unprepared for this capitulation. Lyman Wight shouted for action and was pacified only by a personal perusal of the revelation. The prophet tried to soften his men's disappointment by an unofficial promise that "within three years they should march to Jackson County and there should not be a dog to open his mouth against them." * Very shortly he set the official date for the redemption of Zion as September 11, 1836.†

Such pledges did not at the time seem improbable, for cholera was rapidly decimating the population of the state. In St. Louis alone seven thousand people perished in five weeks. But with its customary indiscrimination the plague struck down the godly as well as the godless. Sixty-eight members of Zion's Camp were attacked within a fortnight. Fourteen of these men died.

The only remedy the frontier knew was to drench the victim in cold water and feed him whisky thickened with flour. With the prophet among them, however, the Mormons had confidently expected a more potent therapy. When the epidemic first appeared, Joseph had tried the sacred ritual of the laying on of hands. "But I quickly learned," he said, "by painful experience, that when Jehovah decrees destruction upon any people, and makes known His determination, man must not attempt to stay His hand. The moment I attempted to rebuke the disease I was attacked, and had I not desisted in my attempt to save the life of a brother, I would have sacrificed my own."

During the epidemic Joseph and his men cautiously entered Clay County and joined their brethren. The prophet comforted them with pledges that he would return to Ohio and raise enough money to buy out the whole of Jackson County. He

* According to Reed Peck, a member of the army. The original of the Reed Peck manuscript, dated Quincy, Illinois, September 18, 1839, and published by L. B. Cake in 1899, is now in my possession. It was furnished me by Peck's granddaughters, Mabel Peck Myer and Hazel Peck Cass, of Bainbridge, New York.

† Letter from Joseph Smith to the High Council of Zion, dated August 16, 1834. *History of the Church*, Vol. II, p. 145.

ordered Zion's leaders to accompany him back to Kirtland to receive the temple endowment.

As he had expected, his own proposal for a peace settlement was turned down. The editor of the *Liberty Enquirer,* who had always been friendly to the Mormon cause, in noting this rejection added: "We have no doubt but the citizens of Jackson are determined to dispute every inch of ground, burn every blade of grass, and suffer their bones to bleach on the hills, rather than the Mormons should return to Jackson County."

On July 9 the prophet started for Kirtland, leaving instructions for his people to hold no public meetings and to refrain from voting in the coming state elections. After his departure the *Liberty Enquirer* observed: "The excitement which existed in this country about the time the Mormons from Ohio arrived, has entirely subsided. Many of them have returned to the East and the rest are scattered throughout the country and are actively engaged in assisting the citizens in saving their crops of wheat, etc. We rather think the WAR is over!"

CHAPTER XI
Patronage and Punishment

Zion's Camp was Joseph Smith's second major failure. Yet it was of much profit to him. First-hand acquaintance with the ferocity of anti-Mormonism shocked him into a policy of prudence and conciliation, which won him several years of peace. This period he utilized to advantage in welding his priesthood into a phalanx strong enough to withstand the terrific onslaughts of apostasy and civil strife that came later.

Zion's Camp seems also to have heightened his sense of accountability toward his own people. When the terrified Heber Kimball watched his friends seized with cholera convulsions in Missouri, he vowed secretly that he would never sin again. And though Joseph's journal contained no such ingenuous resolution, it is clear that he too was overwhelmed with anguish and humility. Houses had been burned; men had been beaten and stoned; women and men had died from exposure and disease — all in his name. Missouri hate had been spent, not against himself, but against his people and the gospel to which they clung with such selfless devotion.

The gospel was now a force outside himself, a force that he might help guide but could never again wholly control. He now sensed that he must no longer give out revelations for the incidental occasion. "Thus saith the Lord" was a trumpet call not to be weakened by too ready use. During the next ten years, therefore, he dictated scarcely more than a dozen revelations, although in the previous five-year period he had given out more than a hundred.* Just as his stature as a religious leader had been enhanced by his discarding the seer stones in

* The Reorganized Church in its compilation lists only five revelations after July 1834. The Utah Church lists thirteen, of which several are but a sentence in length and trivial in content. Both churches include additional sections in their respective editions of the *Doctrine and Covenants* which are extracts from letters and sermons, but not specific revelations. And a few revelations that are not included in the *Doctrine and Covenants* of either branch of the church are printed in the *History of the Church*. Certain foreign-language editions contain still other revelations.

favor of the revelation, so now it was further increased by his reliance upon the authority of his own teachings rather than upon the ubiquitous and uncompromising direction of God.

Upon his return from Missouri Joseph faced an acute crisis. Far from being a second Moses, he had left the exiled colony still outside the promised land and had returned with little except consoling words for the families of the fourteen dead. Kirtland met him with a hostility that exceeded his worst fears, for Sylvester Smith had rushed back with a dismal story of defeat without honor. "I was met," Joseph wrote in his journal, ". . . with a catalogue of charges as black as the author of lies himself; and the cry was Tyrant — Pope — King — Usurper — Abuser of men — Angel — False Prophet — Prophesying lies in the name of the Lord — Taking consecrated monies — and every other lie to fill up and complete the catalogue." *

He faced the charges in a council meeting, arguing without respite hour after hour until his mild voice was hoarse and his face was lined with weariness. Innuendoes concerning the mishandling of funds he met by calling for reports from several commissaries, who defended him earnestly. Then he retold the story of his quarrels with Sylvester Smith, deftly turning the man's heated accusations till they seared Sylvester more than they had ever burned himself. Finally after six hours the man began to stammer an apology, and Joseph relaxed, victorious and spent.†

Once this crisis was passed, Joseph set about assuaging the feeling of frustration that followed the failure of Zion's Camp. He had promised his men a great endowment in the temple and now bent his tremendous energy and enthusiasm toward completion of that structure. Before long the temple became a symbol of hope and anticipation almost displacing the symbol of Zion. Those who had property mortgaged it to buy lumber and plaster; the poor gave of their own sweat.

All converts who stopped in Kirtland on the way to Missouri were reminded that Zion would remain in bondage until the Kirtland temple was finished. When John Tanner, who had

---

* *History of the Church*, Vol. II, p. 144.

† The story of this trial is told in *History of the Church*, Vol. II, pp. 142–4, 160. Sylvester Smith's apology, dated October 28, 1834, was published in the *Latter-Day Saints Messenger and Advocate*, Vol. I, p. 2.

just sold two farms and 2,200 acres of timber, visited Kirtland
in January 1835 and learned that the temple mortgage was
about to be foreclosed, he canceled his plans to go to Missouri,
loaned the temple committee $13,000, signed a note with the
prophet for $30,000 worth of goods, and gave Joseph an addi-
tional personal loan of $2,000.

Nine years later Tanner handed the prophet the personal
note. "What would you have me do with it?" Joseph asked
him, and Tanner replied: "Brother Joseph, you are welcome
to it." *

Such open-handedness Joseph loyally repaid with positions in
his ever expanding hierarchy. He wrote quite frankly in his
journal that George Boosinger was ordained to the high priesthood "in consequence of his having administered unto us in
temporal things in our distress." † There were no men, however, to whom he felt so indebted as the members of Zion's
Camp. These were tested Saints, deserving of rank. In the spring
of 1835, when he enlarged his priesthood to include twelve
apostles and a special quorum of seventy men, nine of the
apostles and all of the "seventies" were members of his army.

Zion's Camp had taught Joseph something of the mistrust of
autocratic power that pervaded Yankee thinking. He had already taken care to change his own title from "First Elder" to
"President of the High Priesthood." "President" was not a New
Testament word, as were all other ranks in his priesthood; but
in the early bloom of this Republic it had tremendous prestige,
plus a connotation of responsibility to the people.

The church was now governed by five councils — the presidency, the apostles, the seventies, and the two high councils of
Kirtland and Missouri. A revelation gave them all equal authority. Noting this, the discerning John Corrill wrote with satisfaction: "I saw that there were several different bodies that had
equal power; I thought, therefore, they would serve as a check
upon each other, and I concluded there was no danger when
the full power and authority was reserved to the people." ‡

Soon, however, a rivalry sprang up among the five bodies.

* *Scraps of Biography,* Faith Promoting Series, Vol. X (Salt Lake City, 1883),
pp. 12, 16.
† *History of the Church,* Vol. II, p. 429.
‡ See *Doctrine and Covenants,* Section 107, and John Corrill: *A Brief History of
the Church of the Latter-Day Saints* (1839), p. 25.

The apostles, who were Joseph's favorite and ablest men, quickly garnered so much power that the Kirtland High Council protested that they were setting themselves up as "an independent council, subject to no authority of the Church, a kind of outlaws!" * The Twelve, however, listened to no one but their prophet. They were virile men, with the tough and arrogant strength of youth. None was over thirty-six; four were only twenty-four. Joseph himself was still under thirty.

The poet-journalist W. W. Phelps coined in one idle hour a sobriquet for each of the Twelve. Brigham Young he styled appropriately "The Lion of the Lord." The studious Orson Pratt he called "The Gauge of Philosophy," and his great proselyting brother Parley "The Archer of Paradise." Lyman Wight, rampageous general of Zion's Camp, became "The Wild Ram of the Mountains." These happy epithets stuck to the men for life.

The constant jockeying for power among the councils soon made it clear to Joseph that equality was impossible. "The duty of the President," he finally decreed, "is to preside over the whole church, and to be like unto Moses." † Once more his word was the law of God, against which there could be no appeal. Soon it was officially announced that an insult to Joseph would be considered "an insult to the whole body," and the High Council saw to it that this rule was respected. Once when Joseph requested a donation of twelve dollars to pay for a record book and Henry Green said privately that he thought the prophet was extorting more than the cost of the book, he was cut off from the church for the remark.‡

Basically, therefore, the church organization remained autocratic; only the trappings were democratic. The membership voted on the church officers twice a year. But there was only one slate of candidates, and it was selected by the first presidency, comprised of Joseph himself and his two counselors. Approval or disapproval was indicated by a standing vote in the general conference. Dissenting votes quickly became so rare that the elections came to be called — and the irony was unconscious — the "sustaining of the authorities."

* *History of the Church*, Vol. II, p. 240.
† *Doctrine and Covenants*, Section 107, verse 91.
‡ *History of the Church*, Vol. II, p. 275.

Joseph was particularly generous with positions to members
of his own family. His father was made patriarch of the church.
Hyrum early replaced F. G. Williams as the third man in the
presidency, along with Joseph and Rigdon. Don Carlos Smith,
although only nineteen, was appointed president of the high
priests, and Samuel Smith became general agent for the "literary firm," which supervised all the church publications.

The church accepted the prophet's nepotism without resentment until he made his brother William an apostle. Hyrum
was a gentle, self-effacing person whose loyalty to Joseph already was proverbial. Samuel and Don Carlos were silent and
industrious. But William, a gaunt, raw-boned, cadaverous-
looking youth, possessed none of his brothers' gracious qualities. He was lusty, hot-tempered, and always in debt. Oliver
Cowdery pronounced the apostolic blessing over his head with
great misgivings: "We pray that he may be purified in heart
. . . that he may be equal with his brethren."

Soon William brought a complaint against a father for beating his fifteen-year-old daughter, and Joseph, suspecting William's concern to be more amatory than humanitarian, sided
with the parents. William in a towering rage resigned his apostleship and went up and down the Kirtland streets exclaiming
against his brother. The Saints were mortified, and the gentiles
grinned to hear him.

The other apostles, who would have been pleased to see him
excommunicated altogether, were bitterly opposed to his reinstatement in the quorum. But William had now poisoned Samuel's mind, and Joseph could ill afford two apostate brothers.
Finally he was forced to resort to a revelation to convince the
angry apostles that his brother must be forgiven: "As for my
servant William, let the Eleven humble themselves in prayer
and in faith, and wait on me in patience, and my servant William shall return, and I will yet make him a polished shaft in
my quiver, in bringing down the wickedness and abominations
of men; and there shall be none mightier than he, in his day
and generation. . . ." *

Using the whip upon the apostles rather than upon his brother

---

* Ibid., Vol. II, p. 300. This revelation was never included in the *Doctrine and
Covenants*. More complete details of Joseph's troubles with William in Kirtland may
be found in his history, Vol. II, pp. 297–343.

was a mistake, for William came back into office more impertinent than before. He organized a debating society, which soon became notorious for malicious and carping criticism. Joseph walked into a meeting of the society one night at William's home and reproached him for the tenor of the discussion. William replied with a stream of abuse. The elder Smith, who lived in the same house, listened to the quarrel in shocked silence until William called Joseph a tyrant and impostor. Then he intervened, thundering for an end to the scene. Joseph bowed in assent and made for the door, but William was not so easily stopped.

"I'll say what I please in my own house," he shouted.

Joseph whirled back, remembering well the credit and charity he had doled out whenever William pleaded need. "Then I will speak too," he cried, "for I built this house and it is as much mine as yours."

At this William lunged at him. Joseph flung off his coat to free his arms for defense. But William was too quick, caught him off guard, and sent him crashing to the floor. There he pommeled him mercilessly until Hyrum succeeded in dragging him off.

The fight shocked the church. The faithful shook their heads in despair that Joseph should be so cursed in his own family, and mournfully revived the gossip about another battle which had occurred earlier that same summer. Calvin Stoddard, Joseph's brother-in-law, had accused Joseph of depriving him of some water rights. In the ensuing quarrel Stoddard had called him a "damned false prophet," and Joseph had promptly knocked him down. Stoddard brought suit for assault, but by the time the case came to court he had mellowed sufficiently to forgive the prophet publicly, and the judge duly handed down a verdict of acquittal.*

What most troubled the converts about these family quarrels was that both Stoddard and William Smith had called Joseph a false prophet. This was both heresy and a gross offense against decorum. If they honestly doubted Joseph, theirs should

* The court record may be found in the Court of Common Pleas, County of Geauga, Ohio, under the date of June 16, 1835. The *Painesville Telegraph,* in response to a request from Joseph Smith that the notice of the acquittal be made public, published in full the testimony given at the trial, most of which was of an amusing and not too flattering character. See June 26, 1835.

be the decency at least to keep silent and not gratify the gentiles. The faithful said unhappily: "A prophet is not without honor save in his own family."

No one in Kirtland was more incensed at William than his fellow apostles, who now forced his resignation. This Joseph fought. William's thrashing had crippled him for several days and was a stinging slap at his pride, for he was vain of his wrestling prowess. But the unity of his family was one of the cornerstones upon which he had built his career, and except for William it was a rugged stone. The thought of its cracking caused all hurt of injured dignity to vanish.

"I freely forgive you," he wrote to William in a letter that was shortly made public, "and you know my unshaken and unchangeable disposition; I know in whom I trust; I stand upon the rock; the floods cannot, no, they shall not overthrow me. You know the doctrine I teach is true, you know that God has blessed me. I brought salvation to my father's house, as an instrument in the hands of God, when they were in a miserable situation. . . .

"And if at any time you should consider me to be an impostor, for heaven's sake leave me in the hands of God, and think not to take vengeance on me yourself. Tyranny, usurpation, and to take men's rights, ever has been and ever shall be banished from my heart. David sought not to kill Saul, although he was guilty of crimes that never entered my heart. . . ." *

William finally made a public confession before the High Council and congregation and thus escaped an ecclesiastical trial. Joseph usually tried to conciliate his foes rather than bludgeon them out of his church. His only whip was the public confession, a stinging weapon in its own right, but one designed to have the opposite effect of an excommunication. The mere threat of such a confession was usually sufficient to curb delinquents. But with William the pain of confession was transient; he never ceased being a thorn.

AT no time in Joseph Smith's career was he more at peace with the world than in the three years following the march of Zion's Camp. There was nothing for his people to argue about except theology, and nothing to oppose except indiscretions in the man-

* *History of the Church*, Vol. II, p. 343.

ners and morals of the young. The official history of the church in these years consists largely of a series of ecclesiastical trials — for sexual misbehavior, whiskey-drinking, and heresy.

The High Council was bent on banishing liquor more than anything else — more even than adultery. Ohio now was engulfed in the rising tide of temperance agitation. In 1834 there were five thousand temperance societies in the United States, with a membership of over a million. Ninety per cent of these lived north of the Mason-Dixon line, and the majority were concentrated in New York and Ohio. After 1836, when the American Temperance Society adopted total abstinence in its platform, there was scarcely a Protestant preacher on the Western Reserve who had not taken the pledge.

The lesser stimulants were likewise abused. Tobacco was called a "nerve-prostrating, soul-paralyzing drug, a fleshly, ungodly lust." Coffee was deplored as an excitant to amorousness, and tea-drinking was thought to be as bad as toddy-guzzling. Food fads and alcoholic cures periodically swept the nation. The popular *Journal of Health,* published from 1829 to 1835, held that sparing use of meat was responsible for the robustness of the Irish, and recommended a vegetarian diet. Self-denial was nowhere more fashionable than among the minor sects.*

In 1833 Joseph dictated a revelation called "The Word of Wisdom," which today is the best known of all he ever wrote. It suggested that church members abstain from tobacco, alcohol, and hot drinks, that they use wine only at communion and meat only in winter. Joseph made it clear, however, that the revelation was given "not by commandment or constraint," but merely as good counsel. He was only deferring to the pressure of the times, for he was too fond of earthly pleasures to become a temperance crusader.

The exact circumstances that stimulated this revelation were later described by Brigham Young. Joseph's leading men met regularly, he said, in a room above the prophet's kitchen. Emma complained bitterly after each gathering about having to clean

---

* See M. Wilford Poulson: "An Interesting Old Volume" (Background of Mormon Word of Wisdom), *The Scratch* (Brigham Young University, March 1930); John A. Krout: *The Origins of Prohibition* (New York, 1925); and Douglas Branch: *The Sentimental Years, 1836–1860* (New York, 1934).

so filthy a floor, for "the first thing they did was to light their pipes, and, while smoking, talk about the great things of the kingdom, and spit all over the room." This "made the Prophet think upon the matter, and he inquired of the Lord relating to the conduct of the Elders in using tobacco, and the revelation known as the Word of Wisdom was the result of his inquiry." *

For some years, in fact, Joseph did not take his "Word of Wisdom" seriously. After a double wedding in January 1836 he wrote in his journal: "We then partook of some refreshments, and our hearts were made glad with the fruit of the vine. This is according to the pattern set by our Savior Himself, and we feel disposed to patronize all the institutions of heaven." A fortnight later at the marriage of his apostle John Boynton he was presented with "three servers of glasses filled with wine" to bless. "And it fell to my lot to attend this duty," he said, "which I cheerfully discharged. . . . our hearts were made glad while partaking of the bounty of the earth which was presented, until we had taken our fill; and joy filled every bosom. . . ."

When the High Council took it upon itself to enforce the "Word of Wisdom," going so far in February 1834 as to rule that disobedience was sufficient grounds for depriving a man of his office, the prophet's cavalier behavior was a grave embarrassment. Almon Babbitt, brought to trial for drinking, defended himself by saying that he knew it was wrong but he was only following the example of President Joseph Smith.†

By the end of the year, however, the pressure had become too much for Joseph. Rigdon, a fanatical temperance enthusiast, on December 4, 1836 forced through a vote for total abstinence; ‡ Joseph bowed to public opinion, replaced wine with water in the communion, and let the High Council do its worst. The revelation eventually evolved into a great moral issue, the use of tea, coffee, tobacco, and alcoholic liquors becoming to every good Mormon the badge of the heretic and the unrighteous.

* *Journal of Discourses*, Vol. XII, p. 158.

† For accounts of Joseph's own wine-drinking following the pronouncement of the "Word of Wisdom" see *History of the Church*, Vol. II, pp. 252, 369, 378, 447.

‡ According to Wilford Woodruff's Journal, as quoted by Matthias F. Cowley in *Wilford Woodruff* (Salt Lake, 1909), p. 65.

CHAPTER XII
Master of Languages

THERE IS NO BETTER indication of Joseph's developing maturity following the debacle of Zion's Camp than the subtle change in his public attitude toward learning. His own lack of formal schooling he had always felt as a frustration, since the New England reverence for education permeated every village in which he had lived. Perhaps it was partly in compensation for his sense of inferiority in this regard that he had endowed himself with mystic powers to which no one else could aspire. His clarion call had been an apt defense from the Bible: "The wisdom of the wise shall perish and the understanding of the prudent shall be hid."

He had not only exulted in his lack of learning but also much exaggerated it, a familiar kind of overcompensation. So carefully had he fostered the myth of his illiteracy that his followers had come to take pride in their own lack of schooling. "My source of learning," W. W. Phelps had written in the *Messenger and Advocate,* "and my manner of life, from my youth up, will exclude me from the fashionable pleasure of staining my communications, with the fancy colors of a freshman of Dartmouth, a sophomore of Harvard, or even a graduate of Yale; nothing but the clear stream of truth will answer the purpose of the men of God." *

"Spring water tastes best right from the fountain," Joseph's people were fond of saying, and looked to him as the source of all wisdom. In March 1833 he had organized a "School of the Prophets" for the instruction of his elders, but it was in no sense an academy; the only course was the study of Joseph's revelations. Parley Pratt, who taught a similar school in Missouri related in his autobiography that they "prayed, prophesied, and exercised themselves "in the gifts of the spirit."

Joseph, however, at heart always had been tremendously impressed by book learning, particularly when it was accom-

* *Latter-Day Saints Messenger and Advocate,* October 1834, p. 22.

panied by facility with language. Hidden under the guise of mysticism was an insatiable curiosity and hunger for knowledge. From the very beginning of his church he had encouraged schooling for the children of his followers. In Missouri his people had built schoolhouses before cabins and granaries.

After Zion's Camp, perhaps partly in revulsion from Missouri barbarism, perhaps partly as an answer to a long-felt personal need, Joseph began to make learning a Mormon ideal. He enlarged the School of the Prophets to include classes in Greek and Hebrew, hiring as instructor a Jewish rabbi, Joshua Seixas, originally from Andover Academy. All the leading Mormon dignitaries attended, untroubled by the paradox that they should struggle with Hebrew grammar on weekdays and speak fluently in tongues on Sunday. The common school in Kirtland was expanded to include adult classes in mathematics, geography, and English grammar.

Flinging aside his cloak of omniscience, Joseph himself began with enormous zest to study Hebrew and English grammar. His English teacher, C. G. Webb, when asked many years later about the diligence of his famous pupil, replied: "Joseph was the calf that sucked three cows. He acquired knowledge very rapidly . . . while Heber C. Kimball never came to understand the difference between noun and verb." *

Joseph's delight in working with languages soon crept into his journal: "It seems as if the Lord opens our minds in a marvelous manner," he wrote, "to understand His word in the original language; and my prayer is that God will speedily endow us with a knowledge of all languages and all tongues."

Here was a transformation! Seven years before, he was writing the Book of Mormon with the aid of the Urim and Thummim, miraculous shortcut to "reformed Egyptian." Later he had amended the Bible with no guide but the Holy Spirit. Now he was at last pursuing knowledge the hard way, and with an enthusiasm so infectious that John Corrill said it inspired the whole church "with an extravagant thirst after knowledge."

"My soul delights in reading the word of God in the original," Joseph wrote "and I am determined to pursue the study of languages until I shall become master of them."

* W. Wyl: *Mormon Portraits* (Salt Lake City, 1886), p. 25. See Louis C. Zucker: "Joseph Smith as a Student of Hebrew," *Dialogue,* II: 41ff., 1968.

A DRAMATIC but over-rigorous test of Joseph's new scholarship came in the summer of 1835 when he received as visitor one Michael Chandler, who had been touring the country exhibiting four Egyptian mummies along with several papyri. Chandler said that he had heard of Joseph Smith's reputation as a translator and had come to Kirtland to see if he could get the papyri deciphered. Linguists in New York and Philadelphia had pronounced them authentic Egyptian, but could only guess at the meaning.

This was a period of unlicensed looting of the Egyptian tombs. A good many sarcophagi had found their way to America and had aroused widespread curiosity. Almost no one knew that the hieroglyphs could be deciphered.* With the whole of Kirtland's male population interested in the study of ancient languages, it was inevitable that Chandler's mummies should fall into the hands of the church. Joseph told Josiah Quincy in 1844 that his mother purchased them "with her own money at a cost of six thousand dollars," although he wrote in his journal that they had been bought by "some of the Saints" in Kirtland.†

After a preliminary examination the prophet pronounced one papyrus to be the writings of Abraham and another the writings of Joseph of Egypt. All Kirtland marveled at the chain of odd accidents that had brought the precious documents to their prophet, and saw in the coincidences the finger of the Lord.

Instead of proceeding with the translation by inspiration as in the past, however, Joseph set about laboriously formulating an Egyptian alphabet and grammar. But his naïve and heartwarming faith in his new language tools was shortlived. Like all the other amateur Egyptologists of his day, he soon gave up in despair, certain that the papyri would not give up their secrets even to the serious scholar. To Joseph's followers, however, it was unthinkable that the papyri be left a mystery, especially since he had deduced their authorship. Eventually he

---

* By now Champollion had worked out the entire system from the Rosetta stone, but his scholarship was not made available to the British public until 1837, with the publication of John G. Wilkinson's *Manners and Customs of the Ancient Egyptians* (1837).

† Josiah Quincy: *Figures of the Past* (Boston, 1883), p. 386. Cf. *History of the Church*, Vol. II, p. 236.

TIMES AND SEASONS.

"Truth will prevail."

Vol. III. No. 9.]   CITY OF NAUVOO, ILL. MARCH, 1, 1842.   [Whole No. 45.

A FAC-SIMILE FROM THE BOOK OF ABRAHAM.

NO. 1.

EXPLANATION OF THE ABOVE CUT.

Fig. 1,—The Angel of the Lord.

2. Abraham, fastened upon an Altar.

3. The Idolatrous Priest of Elkenah attempting to offer up Abraham as a sacrifice.

4. The Altar for sacrifice, by the Idolatrous Priests, standing before the Gods of Elkenah, Libnah, Mahmachrah, Korash, and Pharaoh.

5. The Idolatrous God of Elkenah.

6. The " " " Libnah.

7. The " " " Mahmachrah.

8. The " " " Korash.

9. The " " " Pharaoh.

10. Abraham in Egypt.

11. Designed to represent the pillars of Heaven, as understood by the Egyptians.

12. Raukeeyang, signifying expanse, or the firmament, over our heads; but in this case, in relation to this subject, the Egyptians meant it to signify Shamau, to be high, or the heavens: answering to the Hebrew word, Shaumahyeem.

FACSIMILE FROM THE BOOK OF ABRAHAM

EXPLANATION OF THE ABOVE CUT.

Fig. 1. Kolob, signifying the first creation, nearest to the celestial, or the residence of God. First in government, the last pertaining to the measurement of time. The measurement according to celestial time; which, celestial time, signifies one day to a cubit. One day, in Kolob, is equal to a thousand years, according to the measurement of this earth, which is called by the Egyptians Jah-oh-eh.

Fig. 2. Stands next to Kolob, called by the Egyptians Oliblish, which is the next grand governing creation, near to the celestial or the place where God resides; holding the key of power also, pertaining to other planets; as revealed from God to Abraham, as he offered sacrifice upon an altar, which he had built unto the Lord.

Fig. 3. Is made to represent God, sitting upon his throne, clothed with power and authority; with a crown of eternal light upon his head; representing, also, the grand Key words of the Holy Priesthood, as revealed to Adam in the Garden of Eden, as also to Seth, Noah, Melchisedek, Abraham and all to whom the Priesthood was revealed.

Fig. 4. Answers to the hebrew word Raukeeyang, signifying expanse, or the firmament of the heavens; also, a numerical figure, in Egyptian, signifying one thousand; answering to the measuring of the time of Oliblish, which is equal with Kolob in its revolution and in its measuring of time.

Fig. 5. Is called in Egyptian Enish-go-on-dosh; that is one of the governing planets also; and is said by the Egyptians to be the Sun, and to borrow its light from Kolob through the medium of Kae-e-vanrash, which is the grand Key, or in other words, the governing power, which governs fifteen other fixed planets or stars, as also Floeese or the Moon, the earth and the Sun in their annual revolutions. This planet receives its power through the medium of Kli-flos-is-es, or Hah-ko kau-beam, the stars represented by numbers 22, and 23, receiving light from the revolutions of Kolob.

Fig. 6. Represents this earth in its four quarters.

Fig. 7. Represents God sitting upon his throne, revealing, through the heavens, the grand Key words of the Priesthood; as, also, the sign of the Holy Ghost unto Abraham, in the form of a dove.

Fig. 8. Contains writing that cannot be revealed unto the world; but is to be had in the Holy Temple of God.

Fig. 9. Ought not to be revealed at the present time.

Fig. 10. Also.

Fig. 11. Also.—If the world can find out these numbers. So let it be. Amen.

Figures 12, 13, 14, 15, 16, 17, 18, 19, and 21, will be given in the own due time of the Lord.

The above translation is given as far as we have any right to give, at the present time.

FACSIMILE FROM THE BOOK OF ABRAHAM

slid into accustomed paths and dictated a translation by direct inspiration from heaven.*

The prophet never deciphered that papyrus which told the story of Joseph in Egypt, contenting himself with a translation of the writings of Abraham. The resulting narrative, which remained unpublished until 1842, was a brief account of the creation of the earth and the beginnings of Israelite history, the story for the most part paralleling the first two chapters of Genesis. Joseph had worked with Genesis twice before, once in writing the lost book of Moses and again in amending the Old Testament. But his eclectic habits would permit no stale repetition, and Abraham's account has a freshness and originality all its own.

Instead of saying: "God created the earth," he wrote: "The Gods organized the earth." This change, which represented a significant step in Joseph's slowly evolving metaphysical system, had its roots in his new learning. The idea of the plurality of God he had picked up from his classes in Hebrew, where he had learned that *Elohim,* one of the Hebrew words for God, is plural, and had therefore concluded that the Bible had been carelessly translated.†

Joseph's new concept that the earth had been "organized" out of already existing matter rather than created out of nothing had a less obvious but no less definite root in his new scholarship. He had recently been reading Thomas Dick's *Philosophy of a Future State,* a long-winded dissertation on astronomy and metaphysics.‡ Dick's elucidation of the thesis that matter is eternal and indestructible Joseph had found convincing, and he had logically concluded that God must have made the heavens and the earth out of materials He had on hand.

Dick's whole work made a lasting impression on Joseph, whose open-mindedness, stemming no doubt from the insubstantial character of his religious credo, was unique among

---

* "I have set by his side," wrote his secretary Warren Parrish, "and penned down the Egyptian hieroglyphicks as he claimed to receive it by direct inspiration from Heaven." See Parrish's letter in the *Painesville Republican,* February 5, 1838, reprinted in *Zion's Watchman,* March 24, 1838.

† So Parley Pratt pointed out in the *Millennial Star,* Vol. III (Liverpool, England, August 1842), p. 71.

‡ Sidney Rigdon quoted openly from Dick in an article called "The Saints and the World," *Latter-Day Saints Messenger and Advocate,* November 1836, pp. 422–3.

ministers of the gospel. This book was his first introduction to the mathematics of the heavens — the millions of stars, the immeasurable distances — and he had to come to grips with the infinitude of the universe in his own consciousness. The facts of astronomy must somehow be welded to his own special structure of Jewish and Christian mysticism. He was groping for a new metaphysics that would somehow take account of the new world of science. In his own primitive and egocentric fashion he was trying to resolve the most troublesome philosophic problem of the nineteenth century.

His solution was the Book of Abraham. Like the philosophic novelist who creates a character greater than himself to voice the distillate of his own speculations, Joseph created Abraham an eminent astronomer who penetrates all the mysteries of the universe. Abraham relates that there is one star, Kolob, lying near the throne of God, which is greater than all the rest. One revolution of Kolob takes a thousand years, and from this revolution God Himself reckons time. Kolob and countless lesser stars are peopled by spirits that are eternal as matter itself. These spirits are not cast in the same mold, but differ among themselves in quality of intelligence as the stars differ in magnitude.

These concepts, which developed peculiar ramifications in Joseph's later teachings, came directly from Dick, who had speculated that the stars were peopled by "various orders of intelligences," and that these intelligences were *"progressive beings"* in various stages of evolution toward perfection.*

The Book of Abraham expressed not only the germ of Joseph's metaphysical system, but also more of his theorizing on the subject of race, which was fast becoming the most dangerous political and moral question in the Republic. As the Book of Mormon had solved the question of the origin of the red man, so the Book of Abraham dispatched the problem of the origin of the Negro.

Joseph as a youth had read in his geography book the common tradition that all races of men are descended from the three

---

* Compare the Book of Abraham with Dick: *Philosophy of a Future State* (Brookfield, Massachusetts, 2nd ed., 1830), pp. 101, 230, 241, 249. Dick held that in all probability "the systems of the universe revolve around a common centre . . . the throne of God."

sons of Noah: Ham, Shem, and Japheth.* Noah had cursed his son Ham, decreeing that Ham's son, Canaan, should be a "servant of servants" unto his brethren. This story, which all the Southern preachers used to justify slavery, Joseph now amplified in his characteristic fashion.

Pharaoh, first ruler of Egypt, he said, was the son of Egyptus, daughter of Ham. All Egyptians therefore inherited the curse of the black skin. With this curse went a denial of the right of priesthood. In practical language this meant that in Joseph's church no Negro could be ordained even into the lowly rank of deacon.

The Book of Abraham in effect crystallized Joseph's hitherto vacillating position on the Negro problem. Soon he published a statement in his church newspaper attacking the abolitionist position as one "calculated to lay waste the fair states of the South, and let loose upon the world a community of people, who might, peradventure, overrun our society, and violate the most sacred principles of human society, chastity and virtue." ". . . we have no right," he concluded, "to interfere with slaves, contrary to the mind and will of their masters."

Perhaps this attitude was merely a concession to Missouri. "In one respect," Joseph continued in the same article, "I am prompted to this course in consequence of many Elders having gone into the Southern States, besides there being now many in that country who have already embraced the fulness of the Gospel." † Moreover, abolitionists were unpopular at this time among the majority of the Northerners, and Joseph was not prompted to espouse a cause pronounced devilish on both sides of the Mason-Dixon line. His attitude reflected simply the prevailing opinion of the time.

To silence the few abolitionists in his own ranks, who urged that all slave-holding Mormons be deprived of fellowship, he permitted himself to be led into a complicated justification of slavery that went even further than the curse of Ham. He expanded the old story, ennobled by Milton, of the war in heaven between the followers of Lucifer and Jehovah. And he taught

---

* See Thomas T. Smiley: *Sacred Geography* (Philadelphia, 1824). The copy owned by Joseph Smith may be seen in the library of the Reorganized Church in Independence, Missouri.

† *Latter-Day Saints Messenger and Advocate*, April 1836, pp. 290 ff.

that there had been, not two, but three divisions in heaven, and
that one third of the spirits had been neutral, choosing neither
side, but waiting to join the victors. Orson Hyde, expounding
this doctrine in 1845, stated that the neutral spirits "rather lent
an influence to the devil, thinking he had a little the best way
to govern, but did not take a very active part, anyway were required to come into the world and take bodies in the accursed
lineage of Canaan; and hence the negro or African race." *

All of Joseph's teaching on the subject of race revolved around
the doctrine that held that the Latter-day Saints were the children of Israel. Nor was this merely a figurative relationship.
Joseph taught that many of his converts, as well as his own family, were direct descendants of Jacob through the blood of his
son Ephraim, and that those less favored who were of gentile
blood could become children of Israel by obedience to the
church. Joseph preached that "the effect of the Holy Ghost upon
a Gentile, is to purge out the old blood, and make him actually
the seed of Abraham." †

From the standpoint of the church which survived him, the
Book of Abraham was the most unfortunate thing Joseph ever
wrote. By outliving the Civil War, which forever banished
slavery as an issue between Mormon and gentile, its racial doctrine preserved the discrimination that is the ugliest thesis in
existing Mormon theology.

Moreover, the book laid Joseph open to the ridicule of future
scholars, for his papyri were almost certain to be examined at
some later date by experts in the Egyptian language. Unlike
the golden plates, which had been whisked back into heaven,
the mummies and papyri were kept on exhibit in both Kirtland
and Nauvoo. The actual papyri escaped scholarly examination
for many years. After Joseph's death they were sold by a friend
of William Smith to the Wood museum and were thought to
have burned in the great Chicago fire.‡ Such a disaster might
have ended all chance of exposing Joseph's mistake had he not

* "Speech before the High Priests," Nauvoo, April 27, 1845; printed in pamphlet
form by the *Millennial Star* office, July 1845. See p. 27.
† *History of the Church,* Vol. III, p. 380.
‡ This was their fate according to official Mormon histories. However, the *San
Francisco Daily Evening Bulletin,* September 25, 1857, stated that two of the four
mummies were sold to a Mr. Wyman of the Philadelphia Museum. Unfortunately this
museum was closed shortly after and its exhibits scattered.

preserved three facsimiles of the papyri, which he published in 1842 with elaborate interpretations.

These interpretations were first challenged in 1860, when a French traveler, Jules Remy, who had become interested in the Mormons, called them to the attention of the Coptic student Theodule Deveria in the Louvre. Remy arranged the two strikingly divergent interpretations in parallel columns and published them in 1861 in his *A Journey to Great Salt-Lake City.*

Later the half-dozen leading Egyptologists who were asked to examine the facsimiles agreed that they were ordinary funeral documents such as can be found on thousands of Egyptian graves.* The discovery in 1967 that eleven fragments of the papyri had found their way to the New York Metropolitan Museum of Art led to fresh interpretations by scholars which confirmed the earlier appraisals.† Joseph, however met no such competition during his life time. And even if he had, it would have mattered little to his people. It would have been the word of a mere schoolman against the word of God.

JOSEPH's temple was his particular delight. It was a massive three-story stone building, a not unhappy mixture of Gothic, colonial, and Greek revival, which dominated the landscape for miles around. The interior, which Joseph had himself designed, was in some respects unique among churches in America. Two auditoriums, one above the other, occupied the first and second

* See F. S. Spalding, *Joseph Smith Jr. as a Translator* (Salt Lake City, 1912). Dr. A. H. Sayce of Oxford stated that facsimile No. 2 was an "ordinary hypocephalus," and No. 3 "a representation of the goddess Maat leading Pharaoh before Osiris behind whom stands the goddess Isis." Arthur Mace of the Metropolitan Museum of Art called Joseph's interpretation "a farrago of nonsense from beginning to end." Dr. W. M. Flinders Petrie of London University wrote: "It may safely be said that there is not a single word that is true in these explanations." Dr. J. H. Breasted of the University of Chicago wrote that "Joseph Smith represents as portions of a unique revelation through Abraham things which were commonplaces and to be found by many thousands in the everyday life of the Egyptians."

† The museum returned the papyri to the Utah Mormons. New scholarly translations were published in *Dialogue, a Journal of Mormon Thought,* Vol. III, Summer 1968. For a summary see the supplement at the end of this volume. A filmed copy of "Joseph Smith's Egyptian Alphabet and Grammar," formerly unknown save to Mormon archivists, was reproduced in 1969 by Jerald Tanner of the Modern Microfilm Company in Salt Lake City. It further illustrated Joseph Smith's extraordinary capacity for linguistic fantasy.

stories, and the third floor was given over to classrooms for the School of the Prophets. Each auditorium had twelve pulpits at either end, symbolic of the number of apostles. These pulpits were elevated and terraced, highly ornamented with excellent carving, and hung with rich velvet. Each bore three gold letters, designating the rank of the man who was to occupy it.

Over the arched window behind the pulpits for the members of the higher, or Melchizedek, priesthood, was the text that Aaron had worn in a golden plaque across his forehead: *Holiness unto the Lord*. The two auditoriums could be halved or quartered by working a series of pulleys that lowered canvas curtains or "veils." The curtains could be lowered even between the rows of pulpits, thereby ensuring privacy for discussion among the various council heads. Except for the unique pulpit system and veils, the temple interior was much like that of other Yankee meeting houses and was much less intricate than those of some of the temples constructed later.

As the time for the dedication approached, Joseph became more and more concerned over his promise to Zion's Camp that a great endowment would descend upon the Saints with the temple's completion. There must somehow be a cleansing of his people, a purging of iniquity and corruption, in preparation for an outpouring of the Holy Spirit that they would never forget.

In his leisure he pored over the New Testament, searching for ceremonials used in the primitive church that he had not yet incorporated into his own. He noted that among the early Christians, as well as the Jews, footwashing, anointing with oil, and even bathing had been religious rituals. The footwashing ceremonial he had incorporated about three years before, when he had girded himself with a towel after the fashion of Jesus and had washed the feet of the members of his council. Although he had delicately varied the New Testament ritual by requesting each councilman to wash his own feet first, the ceremony attained a measure of dignity and emotional value.*

Footwashing was practiced regularly on the Western Reserve by many of the smaller Baptist sects — the Original Free-Will Baptists, Six-Principles Baptists, Seventh-Day Baptists, United

* *History of the Church*, Vol. I, p. 323.

Baptists, and Dunkers. Joseph, however, used it sparingly, for it could too easily tumble into the ludicrous. Ohio was chuckling over the story of some pious woolen-factory workers who, after working all day in blue wool, had been caught unexpectedly in a Newlight footwashing ceremony. The sober elders, towels girded about their waists, had stared in astonishment at the array of blue feet presented to them, and the tale had gathered added color as it was retold across the state.*

Joseph sensed intuitively what most revivalist preachers learned from successive failures — that any religious ritual to be successful must be performed with artistry, and artistry requires meticulous preparation and rehearsal. When, therefore, he decided to include washings and anointings in the temple ceremonials, he knew that they could not be introduced casually.

Several days before the official dedication on March 27, 1836, he taught the new rites to his leading elders. He gathered them in a circle with his father seated in the center. Holding a bottle of oil in his left hand, he raised his right hand to heaven and bade the men do the same. Earnestly he blessed the oil and then poured a few drops on the old man's head. The circle of elders now crowded together, piling their hands on the head of the elder Smith, while Joseph blessed him in words that had a certain measured eloquence and beauty:

"The heavens are opened to me," he said softly, his face white in the candlelight, "and I behold the celestial kingdom of God, and the glory thereof, whether in the body or out I cannot tell. I see the transcendent beauty of the gate through which the heirs of that kingdom will enter, which is like unto circling flames of fire; also the blazing throne of God, whereon is seated the Father and the Son."

Each man thus blessed in turn felt in the pressure of the hands piled on his head the solemn weight of eternity. Soon all the elders began to glimpse the heavens. "Angels ministered unto them," Joseph wrote in his journal, "as well as to myself, and the power of the Highest rested upon us, the house was filled with the glory of God, and we shouted Hosanna to God and the Lamb." On successive nights he repeated the ceremony

* William C. Howell: *Recollections of Life in Ohio from 1813 to 1840* (Cincinnati, 1895), p. 106.

until all of his hierarchy had been anointed. The washing ritual itself Joseph may have considered too delicate a matter to describe in his journal.

As the time for the temple dedication drew nearer, he introduced a "sealing" ceremony, in which all the blessings called down upon his men were to be sealed in heaven. When his quorums were gathered in the attic story of the temple, he went back and forth from one room to another, coaching each group in the prescribed order of the evening: first, a solemn prayer; second, a united shout: "Hosanna to God and the Lamb, with an Amen, Amen and Amen"; third, a silent prayer from every man's heart to heaven. Before long the men confided to one another that the Holy Ghost was like fire in their bones; visions and prophesying were punctuated by shouts of Hosanna and Amen that shook the new-laid rafters.

Five years before, it will be remembered, when Joseph arrived in Kirtland, he had found a spontaneous orgiastic revival in full progress and had ruthlessly stamped it out. Now he was intoxicating his followers with the same frenzy he had once so vigorously denounced. For the first time his church was indulging in the theatricalism and delirium of the camp meeting.

The preliminary ceremonies roused the Saints to such a pitch of excitement that when the day of dedication arrived a thousand people crowded into the lower auditorium and another thousand stood outside, hoping to catch echoes of the Lord's mysteries. The morning services, during which Joseph read the dedicatory prayer, were quiet and unspectacular; but in the evening, when only men were allowed in the temple, the emotional flood fed by a fortnight of exhortation and ecstasy broke loose.

"Do not fear to prophesy good concerning the Saints," Joseph urged them with consummate evangelistic skill, "for if you prophesy the falling of these hills and the rising of the valleys, the downfall of the enemies of Zion and the rising of the kingdom of God, it shall come to pass. Do not quench the Spirit, for the first one that opens his mouth shall receive the spirit of prophecy."

George A. Smith now leapt to his feet and began to tell wondrous things about the future. Then, Joseph wrote in his journal, a noise like the sound of a rushing mighty wind filled the temple. "All the congregation simultaneously arose, being moved upon by an invisible power; many began to speak in tongues and prophesy; others saw glorious visions; and I beheld the Temple was filled with angels, which fact I declared to the congregation. The people of the neighborhood came running together (hearing an unusual sound within, and seeing a bright light like a pillar of fire resting upon the Temple), and were astonished at what was taking place."

For two days and two nights the men stayed in the temple, fasting and praying, washing and anointing, prophesying and giving glory to God. Finally someone took up a collection for the purchase of bread and wine, "sufficient," Joseph wrote, "to make our hearts glad." Then the brethren continued "exhorting, prophesying, and speaking in tongues until five o'clock in the morning. The Savior made His appearance to some, while angels ministered to others, and it was a Pentecost and an endowment indeed, long to be remembered."*

"A report went abroad," wrote John Corrill, who was in charge of the temple, "that some of them got drunk; as to that every man must answer for himself." And he pointedly added: "A similar report, so the reader will recollect, went out concerning the disciples at Jerusalem, on the day of the Pentecost." †

But all the ecstasy that had been flaming for a fortnight paled before the dramatic effulgence of the final services. The temple was filled and overflowing. Joseph and Oliver Cowdery climbed to their pulpits and motioned for the veils to be lowered about them. The audience sat enrapt while the two men, completely screened from view, prayed wordlessly. Oliver was exultant at having been chosen above Hyrum Smith and Rigdon for this holy moment. He was once again Second Elder, a rank for which he had long hungered and fought. All the jealous dissatisfaction that had gnawed him since Rigdon's ascendancy vanished as he knelt beside his prophet in the tiny white-curtained room.

When the veils rolled backward again, they were standing to-

---

* For a complete description of the temple ceremonies see *History of the Church*, Vol. II, pp. 379–83, 420–36. All quotations, except where noted, are drawn from this source.

† John Corrill: *Brief History of the Church*, p. 23.

gether looking heavenward. Oliver was deathly pale. "We have seen the Lord," intoned the prophet. "He was standing upon the breastwork of the pulpit, before us, and under His feet was a paved work of pure gold in color like amber. His eyes were as a flame of fire, the hair of His head was white like the pure snow. His countenance shone above the brightness of the sun, and His voice was as the sound of the rushing of great waters, even the voice of Jehovah, saying —

" 'I am the first and the last, I am He who liveth, I am He who was slain, I am your advocate with the Father. Behold, your sins are forgiven you, you are clean before me, therefore lift up your heads and rejoice. Let the hearts of your brethren rejoice. . . . For behold, I have accepted this house, and my name shall be here. . . .'"

But this was not all. "Moses appeared before us," Joseph continued, "and committed unto us the keys of the gathering of Israel from the four parts of the earth, and the leading of the Ten Tribes from the land of the north." After this, Elias appeared to them, and then Elijah, who proclaimed: "Therefore the keys of this dispensation are committed into your hands, and by this ye may know that the great and dreadful day of the Lord is near, even at the doors."

Never again in Mormon history was there to be a period of spiritual transport like this. With rare insight Joseph never made an effort to recapture the magic and mystery of these days. No one who participated in the dedication ceremonies ever forgot them. For weeks afterward the Saints spent all their time going from house to house, feasting, prophesying, and pronouncing blessings on one another. "One would have supposed," wrote John Corrill, "that the last days had truly come."

CHAPTER XIII
My Kingdom is of this World

JOSEPH SMITH just missed being a very handsome man. His nose, peaked and protuberant, was not too attractive in profile. But visitors and converts alike described his eyes as astonishingly beautiful and his smile as ingratiating and infectious. Although the paleness of his face seemed to belie his youth and health, the effect was startling rather than unpleasant.

He had remarkable presence, his size and bearing dominating every gathering into which he walked. Added to this was a cordiality that disarmed all but his bitterest foes. "Joseph shook hands with all the world," said one convert. "The people fairly adored him."

It was inevitable that a man with so much physical charm should become a target of the gossips. As we have seen, his name was linked with Nancy Marinda Johnson's as early as 1832. Then some time in 1835 it began to be whispered about that he had seduced a seventeen-year-old orphan girl whom Emma had taken into the family. This was Fannie Alger, whom Benjamin Johnson described in later years as "a very nice and comely young woman about my own age, toward whom not only myself, but everyone, seemed partial for the amiability of her character." It was whispered even then, Johnson said, that Joseph loved her.*

The prophet's grammar teacher, C. G. Webb, told one writer that this girl was "unable to conceal the consequences of her celestial relation with the prophet," and that Emma drove her out of the house. Whether or not Fannie Alger bore Joseph a child, it is clear that the breath of scandal was hot upon his neck. Warren Parrish, who for a time was Joseph's secretary, told young Benjamin Johnson that he and Oliver Cowdery knew the report of an illicit affair between the girl and the

* For complete documentation on Fannie Alger and all the other women Joseph Smith is said to have married see Appendix C.

prophet to be true, for they "were spied upon and found to-gether."

Cowdery made no secret of his indignation, and Joseph finally called him in and accused him of perpetuating the scandal. ". . . We had some conversation," Cowdery wrote to his brother, "in which in every instance I did not fail to affirm that what I had said was strictly true. A dirty, nasty, filthy affair of his and Fanny Alger's was talked over in which I strictly declared that I had never deserted from the truth in the matter, and as I supposed was admitted by himself." The most that Joseph could wring from Oliver was an admission that he had never heard the prophet acknowledge his guilt. And Joseph had to be content with publishing in the *Elders' Journal* of July 1838 the sworn statements from three witnesses that Cowdery had made this admission. Cowdery himself stoutly refused to exonerate the prophet, and eventually was excommunicated from the church for several misdemeanors, among them "insinuating that the prophet had been guilty of adultery." *

Fannie moved on into Indiana, where she married, and reared a large family. When in later years polygamy had become an accepted pattern in Mormon life, Joseph's leading elders looked back to the Kirtland days and concluded that Fannie Alger had been the prophet's first plural wife. But when they questioned her about her relation with Joseph, she replied: "That is all a matter of my own, and I have nothing to communicate."

In 1835, however, it seemed to those who knew of it to be an unfortunate infatuation. The scandal was insufferable to Emma, who was passionately fond and jealous of her husband. She had, moreover, a keen sense of the propriety and dignity of his office and must have been humiliated for the church itself, which was beginning to attain stature and some degree of stability.

There is no record of her anger except in the dubious gossip of neighbors that crept into print after half a century. Joseph almost never mentioned Emma in his journals and apparently at this time did not confide his domestic troubles to his friends. But in November 1835 he made a public statement, part of which by its strange emphasis would seem to indicate that his domestic life was far from tranquil: "Wives, submit yourselves unto your own husbands, as unto the Lord, for the husband is the head of

* *History of the Church,* Vol. III, p. 16.

the wife, even as Christ is the head of the Church. . . . Wives, submit yourselves unto your own husbands, as it is fit in the Lord." *

There were other reasons, less provocative perhaps than the winsome servant girl, why Joseph was beginning to reflect seriously — and therefore imaginatively — upon the whole institution of marriage. The Geauga county court had forbidden Mormon elders to perform the marriage ceremony on the ground that they were not regularly ordained ministers. Rigdon had retained the right, but only by proving in court that he was still registered as a minister of the Disciples of Christ.† The restriction was an intolerable insult to Joseph, who was thereby denied a right exercised by the lowliest circuit rider.

Moreover, Kirtland was full of converts who had left behind them spouses who could not be persuaded to join the church. Since divorce was always difficult and often impossible to obtain, a critical social problem developed. Martin Harris had been brought to trial for adultery as early as 1832.‡ But such trials clearly were not the remedy for the growing evil. One convert, who had left a vixenish spouse in New York State, told Ezra Booth on the first trip to Missouri that Joseph had given him leave "to take a wife from among the Lamanites." § But marriage with the Indians was hardly a satisfactory solution in any case, and was scarcely to be suggested to women who had left their husbands for the cause of the prophet.

There was Lydia Goldthwait Baily, a convert of great charm, whose husband refused either to follow her to Kirtland or to grant her a divorce. Newel Knight, now a widower, fell in love with her, and there were few men for whom Joseph had so deep an affection. Newel, a trusted friend, gentle and generous, became so despairing over the hopelessness of his lot that Joseph was sorely tempted to defy the law in his favor. Finally, on November 23, 1835, he married them in a simple ceremony in the Knight home.

In his manuscript journal Knight related how Joseph told his congregation that "he had married Brother Newel Knight

* *Latter-Day Saints Messenger and Advocate,* November 1835.

† *Chardon Spectator and Geauga Gazette* (Chardon, Ohio), October 30, 1835; and *History of the Church,* Vol. II, p. 408.

‡ *Evening and Morning Star* (Independence, Missouri), July 1832, p. 31.

§ Booth letter No. IX, in Howe: *Mormonism Unvailed,* p. 220.

to Lydia Baily (or Goldthwait) properly although the laws of
Ohio had not yet granted him the right to marry. But, said he, I
have done it by the authority of the holy Priesthood and the Gentile law has no power to call me to account for it. It is my religious privilege, and even the Congress of the United States has
no power to make a law that would abridge the rights of my
religion."

Joseph's preoccupation with the marital difficulties prevalent
in Kirtland — including his own — coincided in time with his
writing of the Book of Abraham. And he obviously emerged
from his intensive study of Genesis with considerable detachment concerning the holiness of monogamy. Newel Knight confided in his journal that at his wedding feast Joseph "said
many things relative to marriages anciently, which were yet to
be revealed."

And before long, in that mysterious fashion by which extra-
marital relations become known and chronicled in the unwrit-
ten history of a small town, Kirtland began to be associated with
the word "polygamy."

It is hardly likely that this charge could have had its basis in
an occasional extralegal marriage ceremony like that of Newel
Knight. Several men, Orson Pratt among them, insisted in later
years that Joseph was actually teaching the principle of polygamy at this early date.* But their statements were made about
half a century later. There were many contemporaneous inti-
mations of matrimonial informalities in Kirtland but no mention of a revelation on the subject. John Whitmer wrote that in
1836 the church leaders "lusted after the forbidden things of

* Joseph F. Smith, Jr., the present historian of the Utah Church, asserted to me
in 1943 that a revelation foreshadowing polygamy had been written in 1831, but that
it had never been published. In conformity with the church policy, however, he
would not permit the manuscript, which he acknowledged to be in possession of the
church library, to be examined. Orson Pratt's statement was made in a speech at
Plano, Illinois, September 12, 1878, where he reported that the apostle Lyman Johnson had told him that "Joseph had made known to him as early as 1831 that plural
marriage was a correct principle." See *Historical Record*, Vol. VI, p. 230. The prophet's nephew, Joseph F. Smith, stated in a letter to his son: ". . . the revelation was
given as far back as 1834, and was first reduced to writing in 1843." See Joseph F.
Smith, Jr.: *Blood Atonement and the Origin of Plural Marriage* (1905), p. 58. The
Reorganized Church in Missouri, founded by the prophet's son, stoutly insists that
Joseph Smith never practiced or taught polygamy, but the evidence against this stand
is overwhelming. See Appendix C in particular.

God, such as covetousness, and in secret combinations, spiritual-wife doctrine, that is, plurality of wives. . . ." Oliver Olney held that "an unlawful intercourse amongst the two sexes existed, of which testimony plainly spoke, and said further that it was whispered about that the same marriage system practiced in the days of Solomon and David would eventually prevail again.*

In August 1835 the church issued the first of a series of official denials of the charge of polygamy. This was a resolution adopted at the church conference: "Inasmuch as this Church has been reproached with the crime of fornication and polygamy, we declare that we believe that one man should have one wife, and one woman but one husband, except in case of death, when either is at liberty to marry again." †

Since Joseph was in Michigan when this resolution was adopted by the church, and since it was written in Cowdery's hand and introduced by him to the conference, there is a possibility that Joseph would not have approved it. However, it may be observed that the wording of the resolution was such that it did not strictly forbid a man's having more wives than one. The construction "one woman *but* one husband" was not paralleled in "one man should have one wife."

When an anonymous article advocating polygamy as a means of ending prostitution and spinsterhood appeared on February 4, 1837 in the *Cleveland Liberalist,* a paper widely read in Kirtland, the gossips buzzed again, and the priesthood was stirred to new action. The Quorum of the Seventies passed a resolution denying fellowship to any member guilty of polygamy, and the Elders' Quorum brought to trial at least one member, Solomon Freeman, for "living with another woman" though he had a wife in Massachusetts. Freeman nonplused the elders by vowing he would not "cross the room" to get a writ of divorce from his first wife.‡

Distortion of the marriage code and experimentation with sex-

* See John Whitmer: "History of the Church," MS., Chapter xx; and Oliver Olney: *Absurdities of Mormonism Portrayed* (Hancock County, Illinois, 1843), p. 5. Olney was president of the Teachers' Quorum in Kirtland at this time. He was excommunicated in 1842 for having revelations of his own.

† *History of the Church*, Vol. II, p. 247.

‡ The Seventies resolution was published in the *Latter-Day Saints Messenger and Advocate,* May 1837, p. 511. The trial of Freeman was recorded in the Elders Quorum Record, MS., under the date of November 23, 1837. This record is in the library of the Reorganized Church.

ual relationships was common in these years among minor religious sects. On the one extreme were the Shakers, the Harmonists, and the followers of Jemima Wilkinson, who practiced celibacy. On the other were the Perfectionist societies led by Simon Lovett and John Humphrey Noyes, which indulged in free love. Lovett began preaching the doctrine of Spiritual Wifehood in New England in 1835, the same year that heard the first whispers of polygamy among the Mormons.

Noyes, who later founded the famous free-love community at Oneida, New York, wrote to a friend in 1836: "The marriage supper of the Lamb is a feast at which every dish is free to every guest. In a holy community there is no more reason why sexual intercourse should be restrained by law, than why eating and drinking should be. . . . The guests of the marriage supper may each have his favorite dish, each a dish of his own procuring, and that without the jealousy of exclusiveness. I call a certain woman my wife; she is yours; she is Christ's; and in Him she is the bride of all saints. She is dear in the hands of a stranger, and according to my promise to her I rejoice." When the scandal-hungry editor of the Philadelphia *Battle-Axe* published this, the whole nation shuddered with pleasurable horror.*

Rumors of polygamy among the Mormons were not loud, but they were persistent. While there is no irrefutable evidence that it was actually practiced at this time — despite some highly irregular marriages and the Fannie Alger scandal — there was talk of it, talk that increased with the passing years.† And it can hardly have been baseless, since the Mormon Church was soon to avow and to become notorious for this aberration, so extraordinary in the milieu of Puritan America.

Whatever breach had opened up between Joseph and Emma was apparently quickly closed. No hint of it crept into his journal. But this absence may suggest freedom from frustration as much as a sense of decorum. A man of Joseph's physical charm scarcely needed to retire to his journal to relieve vague longings; nor indeed did he need to suffer them. Kirtland was overflowing with women who idolized him. Eliza Snow, gifted

* See W. Hepworth Dixon: *Spiritual Wives* (Philadelphia, 1868), pp. 237, 262 ff.

† In July 1838 the *Elders' Journal* in Far West, Missouri, published replies to the questions most often asked about the Mormons. One read: "Do the Mormons believe in having more wives than one?" The answer was: "No, not at the same time. But they believe that if their companion dies, they have a right to marry again."

poetess and daughter of one of the wealthiest men in Mantua, had joined the Mormons and become mistress of a school in Kirtland. She boarded at the prophet's home, and it soon became common gossip among the non-Mormons that she was "infatuated with Smith." *

Back in February 1831 Joseph had written a revelation that said: "Thou shalt love thy wife with all thy heart, and shalt cleave unto her and none else." † If in 1835, after eight years of marriage to a woman somewhat his senior, Joseph began to yearn for variety and adventure, he must soon have realized that for a prophet it is easier to change marriage laws than to contravene them. Since the wrong was but a wrong in the world, and the world lay in his hand, he might easily make it right.

THE PARADISE of the prophet had much of the earth in it. Joseph had the poor man's awe of gold, and it crept into his concept of heaven. When God would descend to the holy city, he said, paraphrasing Isaiah, "for brass, He will bring gold; and for iron He will bring silver; and for wood brass; and for stones iron; and . . . the feast of fat things will be given to the just." ‡ And when the lost tribes of Israel streamed forth at last from the north countries to join the Saints, they too would be laden with jewels and gold.

"It passes for a current fact," wrote Ezra Booth late in 1831, "that there are immense treasures in the earth, especially in those places in the State of New York from whence many of the Mormonites emigrated last spring; and when they become sufficiently purified, these treasures are to be poured into the lap of their church; to use their own language, they are to be the richest people in the world." §

Mormon theology was never burdened with otherworldliness. There was a fine robustness about it that smelled of the frontier and that rejected an asceticism that was never endemic to America. The poverty, sacrifice, and suffering that dogged the

* Christopher G. Crary: *Pioneer and Personal Reminiscences* (Marshalltown, Iowa, 1893), p. 45. Crary lived in Kirtland during the whole Mormon period.

† *Doctrine and Covenants*, Section 42, verse 22.

‡ *History of the Church*, Vol. I, p. 198.

§ Letter No. 3, Howe: *Mormonism Unvailed*, p. 187. This is a noteworthy remnant of the money-digging enthusiasm of the prophet's youth.

Saints resulted largely from clashes with their neighbors over social and economic issues. Though they may have gloried in their adversity, they certainly did not invite it. Wealth and power they considered basic among the blessings both of earth and of heaven, and if they were to be denied them in this life, then they must assuredly enjoy them in the next.

It seemed for a time during the late thirties that heaven was practically at Kirtland's gates. The city, according to the Mormon press, was "all activity, all animation — the noise and bustle of the teams with lumber, brick, stone, lime or merchandise, were heard from the early dawn of morning till the grey twilight of evening. The sound of the mechanic's hammer saluted the ear of the sluggard before the rising sun had fairly dispelled the sable shades of night, and the starting up, as if by magic, of buildings in every direction around us, were evidence to us of buoyant hope, lively anticipation, and a firm confidence that our days of pinching adversity had passed by, and that the set time of the Lord to favor Zion had come. . . ." *

Kirtland actually was in the throes of the maddest speculative craze in the nation's history. Land prices all over the West were spiraling at a fantastic rate. Lots bought in Buffalo at $500 an acre in 1835 were in 1836 being sold and resold in parcels until they were going at $40 a foot, or $10,000 an acre. Land prices over the whole of Ohio were higher than they were to be for another seventy years. Along the south shore of Lake Erie, from Buffalo past Kirtland to Cleveland, cities were platted at every indentation of the coast, the speculators predicting one solid city along the whole two-hundred-mile distance.

The great influx of immigration into Ohio — which caused her population to leap 62 per cent in the thirties as compared with a national rise of 32 per cent — particularly aggravated the land boom in that state. Credit was easy. Land banks were flooded with paper money, shortly to prove worthless.†

Within Kirtland itself lots jumped from $50 to $2,000, and surrounding farms from $10 and $15 an acre to $150. "Real es-

* *Latter-Day Saints Messenger and Advocate,* June 1837, p. 520. A retrospect written after financial panic had struck the city.

† See Guy H. Salisbury: "The Speculative Craze of '36," *Buffalo Historical Society Publications,* Vol. IV (1896), p. 331; Rowland H. Rerick: *State Centennial History of Ohio,* Vol. I (1902), p. 264.

tate rose from one to 800 per cent, and in many case more," said the editor of the *Messenger and Advocate*. "Men who were not thought worth fifty or an hundred dollars became purchasers to the amount of thousands. Notes, (some cash) deeds, and mortgages passed and repassed, till all, or nearly all, vainly supposed they had become wealthy. . . ." *

No less than his Saints, the prophet was infected with the virus of speculation. He began buying and selling land with the extravagant abandon that infused the whole West. His grammar teacher reported that he frequently played auctioneer. "And a very good auctioneer he was. The Saints were full of enthusiasm and lots went up from a hundred dollars to three and four thousand." † Such activity did not seem indecorous either to Joseph or to his people, who by now had come to accept his eager participation in secular affairs as well as tutelage in things of the spirit. The whole church identified prosperity with the goodness of God.

Occasionally Joseph met opposition to his real-estate transactions. When he tried to purchase the farm of Isaac McWithy for three thousand dollars, suggesting a down payment of "four or five hundred dollars to take him to Zion, and settle him there, and an obligation for the remainder, with good security and interest," McWithy, who had little taste for the Missouri wilderness, refused the offer and was brought to trial before the High Council for his insolence.‡ But such cases were rare.

Joseph's credit was good. His imposing temple, which had cost between $60,000 and $70,000, was deemed excellent security, despite the $13,000 debt hanging over it; and a big steam mill in which he had invested thousands of dollars was expected soon to begin making money. He borrowed everywhere — in sums ranging from a $350 loan from the Painesville bank to a six-month credit for goods in Cleveland and Buffalo amounting to $30,000.§

* *Latter-Day Saints Messenger and Advocate*, June 1837, p. 521.
† Interview with W. Wyl, *Mormon Portraits*, p. 36.
‡ *History of the Church*, Vol. II, p. 446.
§ The small loan is noted in *History of the Church*, Vol. II, p. 324. The $30,000 credit is mentioned by Cyrus Smalling, secretary for a time to Joseph Smith in Kirtland, in a letter dated Kirtland, March 10, 1841. This was first published in E. G. Lee: *The Mormons, or Knavery Exposed* (Philadelphia, 1841), pp. 12–15.

On July 11, 1836 Andrew Jackson issued his specie circular, for-bidding agents to accept anything but gold and silver for the sale of public land. Its purpose was merely to dam the flood of depreciated bank paper that was pouring into the United States Treasury, but the deflationary trend that it started moved swiftly into the great panic of 1837.

The Mormons for a time survived the impact of the specie circular in Kirtland, but in Missouri it spelled trouble. The sale of public land on the whole frontier dropped from $25,-000,000 in 1836 to less than $7,000,000 in 1837. The Mormons in Missouri, like everyone else on the border, had been buying public land on credit. Credit now was denied them.

To make matters worse, the old settlers in Clay County, with whom the Saints had taken temporary refuge after being ex-pelled from Jackson County, were becoming impatient for them to move on. The sinister mutterings that the Mormons had come to dread in Jackson County now began to spread through Clay as one by one the anti-Mormon accusations were revived.

Joseph seriously considered moving the whole colony to Wis-consin, where the troubles that invariably overtook the Mormons would not be aggravated by the slavery question, but he finally decided that it was easier to settle them in the still uninhabited prairie counties of upper Missouri. He ordered W. W. Phelps to explore the area, and in March 1836 sent Partridge, Morley, and Corrill to Missouri with $1,450 to purchase new sites.

Since most of upper Missouri was government land, these men were caught by the specie circular before they could use much of the currency entrusted to them. The Missouri Saints themselves were desperately poor. Phelps wrote back to Kirt-land a description of northern Missouri which reflected his melancholy:

Here sickness comes, and where does it not? The ague and fever; the chill fever, a kind of cold plague, and other diseases, prey upon emigrants till they are thoroughly seasoned to the climate. Here death puts an end to life, and so it does all over the globe. Here the poor have to labor to procure a living, and so they do anywhere else. Here the saints suffer trials and tribulations, while the wicked enjoy the world and rejoice, and so it has been since Cain built a city for

the ungodly to revel in. But it is all right, and I thank God that it is
so. The wicked enjoy this world and the saints the next.*

The pressure from the Clay County settlers became more and
more insistent. At a general meeting on June 29, 1836 they publicly invited the sect to move. "We therefore, in a spirit of frank
and friendly kindness," read the resolution in part, "do advise
them to seek a home where they may obtain large and separate
bodies of land, and have a community of their own. . . . we
request them to leave us, when their crops are gathered, their
business settled, and they have made every suitable preparation
to move."

A new appeal from the Mormon leaders to Governor Dunklin met with a frigid reception. "The time was," Dunklin wrote,
"when the people (except those in Jackson county) were divided, and the major part in your favor; that does not now seem
to be the case. . . . Your neighbors accuse your people of holding illicit communication with the Indians, and of being opposed to slavery. You deny. Whether the charge or the denial
is true I cannot tell. The fact exists and your neighbors seem to
believe it is true; and whether true or false, the consequences
will be the same (if your opponents are not merely gasconad-
ing), unless you can, by your conduct and arguments, convince
them of your innocence. If you cannot do this, all I can say to
you is that in this Republic, the *vox populi* is the *vox dei*." †

The Missouri Saints were now in a dismal predicament. Bewildered and bitter, they remembered that their prophet had
appointed September 11, 1836 as the date for the redemption of
Zion.‡ But as the day approached they saw before them not a
triumphal entry into the New Jerusalem, but a miserable northward trek to the dreaded prairies, where there was said to be
neither timber nor water in sufficient quantity. Most of them
accepted their lot without protest, however, confident that the
millennium could not be far distant. *"Then,"* they said, "the
righteous will feed themselves on the finest of wheat. . . .
Then, for brass the Lord will bring gold, and for iron silver, and

* Letter dated Liberty, Missouri, October 20, 1834, published in the *Latter-Day
Saints Messenger and Advocate,* Vol. I, p. 22.
† This letter was received in Liberty, Missouri, July 28, 1836. See *History of the
Church,* Vol. II, pp. 461–2, for complete text.
‡ Ibid., Vol. II, p. 145.

for wood brass . . . and *then* the land will be worth possessing
and the world fit to live in." *

Joseph felt keenly the plight of his Missouri colony. Specie
must somehow be collected and sent to them in quantities sufficient for down payments on new land. But he was also in desperate need of money to settle many Kirtland debts. In September he would have to pay Charles Holmes the $10,000 he had
borrowed in 1831 to set the ill-fated United Order in motion.
The $30,000 credit he had obtained in the spring must be met
in November. And along with a host of lesser debts, there was
the sum of $13,000 still owing on the temple.

The desire for money in gold and silver became almost an
obsession with him. With the need so critical, he began to lend
a serious ear to a story that had appeared in the *Painesville Telegraph* concerning a vast treasure buried beneath an old house
in Salem, Massachusetts. Salem was the magic city of Joseph's
childhood, the place where he had first tasted the exciting world
outside his spare Vermont village. The lure of the old port
swept over him now and helped to crystallize his impulse to
try his luck at finding the buried gold. A convert named Burgess claimed to know the exact location of the house and offered to lead Joseph to the spot.†

It was a child's dream. For all his acumen, there was something very simple in Joseph's approach to his complicated difficulties. He clung to the daydreams of his youth, seeking their
fulfillment with such singleness of purpose and childlike faith
that he was bound on occasion to be spectacularly successful.
Although it had been almost ten years since he had looked for
buried gold, the old eager optimism now came back with an
irresistible force.

He could not, however, help sensing the unseemliness of a
treasure hunt on the part of the Lord's anointed, and while this
feeling did not deter him, it did serve to make him secretive of
his intentions. When he went east with Rigdon, Cowdery, and
Hyrum Smith, it was ostensibly on a missionary tour.

When they arrived in Salem early in August 1836, he was

---

* *Latter-Day Saints Messenger and Advocate*, Vol. I (1834), p. 22.

† This whole story is told in detail by Ebenezer Robinson in the *Return*, Vol. I
(Davis City, Iowa, July 1889), p. 105. Robinson was a convert in Kirtland at the
time. After Joseph Smith's death he followed the faction led by Rigdon. Ultimately he
became an adherent of David Whitmer.

faced with the awkward task of explaining his true objective. Rarely in these years did he speak in the Lord's name, but this was an occasion that required it. "I, the Lord your God," said the message, "am not displeased with your coming on this journey, notwithstanding your follies. I have much treasure in this city for you, for the benefit of Zion. . . . I will give this city into your hands, that you shall have power over it, insomuch that they shall not discover your secret parts; and its wealth pertaining to gold and silver shall be yours. Concern not yourselves about your debts, for I will give you power to pay them. . . . And inquire diligently concerning the more ancient inhabitants and founders of this city. For there are more treasures than one for you in this city. Therefore, be ye wise as serpents and yet without sin. . . ." *

For more than a month he made surreptitious inquiries and tracked down clues. Some time in September he returned to Kirtland, as barren of treasure as he had ever been. The true nature of the trip could no longer be kept secret, and his followers shook their heads in sorrow and disbelief. "We speak of these things with regret," wrote Ebenezer Robinson in 1889 in describing the episode.

Joseph made no apology for this indiscretion. In his history he described the trip to Salem as an ordinary missionary tour, and the incident eventually was forgotten. Probably none of his followers was aware that a chapter in Joseph's life had been brought, somewhat belatedly, to a close.

* *Doctrine and Covenants,* Section 111.

CHAPTER XIV
Disaster in Kirtland

ALTHOUGH JOSEPH had returned from Salem without a chest of money, he was not exactly empty-handed. On behalf of the Kirtland mercantile firms he had succeeded in New York City in borrowing $5,600 from Halstead Haines and Company. Later, Hyrum Smith and Oliver Cowdery succeeded in obtaining credit in the East for about $60,000 worth of goods. These windfalls made it easy for him to borrow further on a smaller scale in the Kirtland area. Timothy Martindale loaned him $5,000, Winthrop Eaton $1,150, and the Bank of Geauga $3,000.*

But Joseph understood perfectly that continued borrowing only postponed the day of reckoning. While new loans meant a temporary respite, they added weight to an already frightening burden of debt. For two months he planned with his brethren how best to bring about its liquidation. The result of these deliberations was the Kirtland Safety Society Bank Company, organized in November 1836 with a capital stock of "not less than four million dollars," and directed by Sidney Rigdon as president, and Joseph as cashier.† The bank was expected to solve the problem of debts by the beguilingly simple expedient of stamping out new notes. Whenever possible, these notes were to be exchanged for hard money.

At any time other than the mid-thirties such a plan would have been mad. The frontier had always favored the expansion of currency and any law designed to relieve the debtor class. Now, because of the frenetic land speculation, there was an

---

* The loan from Halstead Haines had not been paid by 1841, when it amounted with interest to $7,000. See p. 201 for list of debts compiled by Joseph Smith in 1841. The $60,000 loan was noted by John Corrill in *Brief History of the Church*, pp. 26–7, and by Cyrus Smalling, one of Joseph's clerks, in a letter published in E. G. Lee: *The Mormons, or Knavery Exposed*, p. 14. The smaller loans are still on record in the Chardon, Ohio, courthouse, where suit was brought to recover the money. See Vol. U, pp. 106, 277.

† *History of the Church*, Vol. II, p. 471.

enormous demand for money and a need for new banking facil-
ities. All that was required to start a bank in the West was an
unlimited amount of nerve and the necessary capital to pay the
engraver and printer for making the notes.

One bank in Ohio was chartered as an Orphan's Institute;
another was founded on the charter of a moribund library association, its total assets a remnant of dog-eared books. The number of authorized banks operating in the state had jumped from
eleven in 1830 to thirty-three in 1836. Besides these there were
nine unauthorized institutions also issuing money. Bank-note
circulation in 1836 was seventy per cent greater than in 1835.
There were at least three hundred different kinds of authorized
notes, to say nothing of the illegal bills and counterfeits, variously styled yellow dog, smooth monkey, blue pup, and sick
Indian.*

To the chaos of Ohio's banking system was now added Joseph's Safety Society. Subscriptions to the capital stock ranged
from $1,000 to $500,000, most of the subscribers paying in Kirtland boom-town lots at five and six times normal value. According to the *Painesville Telegraph,* Joseph estimated his own land
in Kirtland at $300,000, and stated that the whole capital stock
of the bank was comprised in land lying within two square
miles.†

The bank was said to have been established by a revelation
from God, and rumor skipped through the town that the
prophet had predicted that like Aaron's rod it would swallow
up all other banks "and grow and flourish, and spread from the
rivers to the ends of the earth, and survive when all others
should be laid in ruins." ‡

The *Messenger and Advocate* announced the organization of
the bank in January 1837 and published an appeal which said
in part: ". . . we invite the brethren from abroad, to call on us,

* See R. H. Rerick: *State Centennial History of Ohio,* p. 272; C. C. Huntington:
"A History of Banking and Currency in Ohio before the Civil War," *Ohio Archeo-
logical and Historical Publications,* Vol. XXIV (1915), pp. 358, 377; A. B. Coover:
"Ohio Banking Institutions 1803–1866," ibid., Vol. XXI (1912), p. 296.

† *Painesville Telegraph,* January 27, 1837. See also Oliver Olney: *The Absurdities of Mormonism Portrayed,* p. 4.

‡ According to Warren Parrish, who succeeded Joseph as cashier of the bank,
in a letter dated March 6, 1838, published March 24, 1838 in *Zion's Watchman.* This
letter was certified to be a statement of fact by Luke Johnson and John F. Boynton
(former apostles) and Sylvester Smith and Leonard Rich (former seventies).

and take stock in our Safety Society; and we would remind
them also of the sayings of Isaiah . . . 'Surely the isles shall
wait for me, and the ships of Tarshish first, to bring thy sons
from far, their silver and their gold (not their bank notes) with
them, unto the name of the Lord thy God.' " *

On January 1, 1837, the same day that the printed bank notes
arrived in Kirtland, there came the disconcerting news that the
Ohio legislature had refused to incorporate the bank. Its operation thus became illegal in the same week that the publicity
campaign was launched. Joseph explained to his people that
"because we were Mormons, the legislature raised some friv-
olous excuse on which they refused to grant us those banking
privileges they so freely granted to others." Actually only one
new bank was allowed incorporation in this legislative session.
The hard-money wing of the Democratic Party — known as the
"no bank" party or Locofocos — had gained control and was
determined to stop the increase of wildcat banks.†

Joseph, however, was too resourceful to be stopped by a formality. On January 2 the Kirtland Safety Society Bank became
the Kirtland Safety Society Anti-Banking Company. The already engraved bank notes were stamped with the prefix *anti*
before and the suffix *ing* after the word "bank." By this device
Joseph expected to circumvent what he considered the preju-
diced decision of the legislature and perhaps at the same time
appeal to the fast rising anti-banking sentiment.

Now began the most exuberantly prosperous fortnight in
Kirtland's history. Everyone's pockets bulged with bills. Local
debts were paid off at once, and Joseph sent couriers east to pay
the huge obligations of the Kirtland mercantile firms. With a
good deal of fanfare he announced further that a union had
been formed with the Monroe bank of Michigan Territory,
Oliver Cowdery becoming the vice-president.

None of the men who remained faithful to Joseph ever publicly discussed the true financial situation of the Kirtland bank.
But several apostates at different times related an identical anecdote which suggests something of the quality of the bank's assets. Lining the shelves of the bank vault, they said, were many

---

* The parenthetical expression is a part of the original text. Reprinted in *History
of the Church,* Vol. II, p. 473.

† E. H. Roseboom: *A History of Ohio* (New York, 1934), p. 160.

boxes, each marked $1,000. Actually these boxes were filled with "sand, lead, old iron, stone, and combustibles," but each had a top layer of bright fifty-cent silver coins. Anyone suspicious of the bank's stability was allowed to lift and count the boxes. "The effect of those boxes was like magic;" said C. G. Webb. "They created general confidence in the solidity of the bank and that beautiful paper money went like hot cakes. For about a month it was the best money in the country." *

Joseph's secretary, Warren Parrish, who was cashier for a short time, wrote in 1838: "I have been astonished to hear him declare that we had $60,000 in specie in our vaults and $600,000 at our command, when we had not to exceed $6,000 and could not command any more; also that we had but about ten thousand dollars of our bills in circulation when he, as cashier of that institution, knew that there was at least $150,000." †

The *Painesville Republican,* a paper generally friendly to the Mormons, remarked dryly on January 19, 1837: "With respect to the ability of the Kirtland Society to redeem their notes we know nothing farther than what report says. It is said they have a large amount in specie on hand and have the means of obtaining much more, if necessary. If these facts be so, its circulation in some shape would be beneficial to the community."

Cleveland merchants, alarmed by the newspaper insinuations, began to refuse the notes, though not before about $36,000 worth had been passed in the city.‡ Merchants in Buffalo and New York scorned them from the beginning, and no bank anywhere would touch them. Soon the bills were streaming back into Kirtland. Joseph redeemed a good number before he realized that the run on the bank was about to ruin him. On January 27, less than a month after the bank's opening, the *Painesville Telegraph* reported that he had "shut up shop . . . saying he would not redeem another dollar except with land."

Everyone possessing Kirtland bank bills now tried desperately to get rid of them. By February 1 they were selling for

* As related in an interview with W. Wyl. See *Mormon Portraits*, p. 36; also Oliver Olney: *Absurdities of Mormonism Portrayed*, p. 4, and the letter of Cyrus Smalling in E. G. Lee: *The Mormons, or Knavery Exposed*, p. 14.

† Letter to *Zion's Watchman*, published March 24, 1838. Cyrus Smalling also wrote that Joseph had collected only $6,000 in specie. See E. G. Lee: *The Mormons, or Knavery Exposed*, p. 14.

‡ See *Ohio City Argus*, January 19, 1837.

twelve and one half cents on the dollar.* Smith and Rigdon resigned, and F. G. Williams and Warren Parrish took over the offices of president and cashier in a final effort to salvage something from the wreckage.

From its beginning the bank had been operating illegally. A state law fixed the penalty for such an offense at a thousand dollars and guaranteed informers a share of the fine. It was inevitable that one of the prophet's enemies should set the law upon him, and on February 8 a writ was sworn out by Samuel D. Rounds. When the court convened on March 24, Joseph's lawyers tried to prove that the statute had not been in force at the time of the bank's organization, but they lost the case and Joseph was ordered to pay the thousand-dollar penalty and costs.†

If the bank needed a final blow to shatter what little prestige it still held among the faithful, it received it when Warren Parrish resigned as cashier, left the church, and began openly to describe the banking methods of the prophet. Parrish was later accused of absconding with $25,000,‡ but if he took the sum it must have been in worthless bank notes, since that amount of specie in the vaults would have saved the bank, at least during Joseph's term as cashier.

May brought disaster to the whole country. Within a single month 800 banks containing $120,000,000 in deposits suspended operations. The panic of 1837 had arrived, and a nation gone loco over land settled down to its day of retribution.

The Kirtland bank, which had collapsed four months before the panic began, actually continued issuing notes until June. Then on June 29 Rigdon was brought to court "for making spurious money," § and the practice was finally stopped. It was not until August, however, that Joseph formally renounced the bank in the *Messenger and Advocate* and warned his people against accepting the bank notes.

Oliver Cowdery's Bank of Monroe teetered on the brink of disaster until the last week in March, when, with only $1,026

---

* According to Cyrus Smalling. See E. G. Lee: *The Mormons, or Knavery Exposed*, p. 14. See also William Harris: *Mormonism Portrayed* (Warsaw, Illinois, 1841), p. 30.

† The record of this trial may be seen in the Chardon, Ohio, courthouse, Vol. U, p. 362.

‡ *Elders' Journal*, August 1838, p. 56.

§ According to an entry in Willard Richards's diary under this date.

left in specie, it suspended payment "for sixty days." The *Monroe Times,* which published the financial statement, concluded manfully: "It is only necessary to caution the holders of the bills not to throw them away, but be assured *the Bank will not go down!"* *

The rise and fall of the bank brought very little actual change to Kirtland's economy. The disaster was as much an illusion as the prosperity had been. Warren Parrish recognized this when he wrote on March 8, 1838: "Knowing their extreme poverty when they commenced in this Mormon speculation, I have been not a little surprised to hear them assert they were worth from three to four hundred thousand dollars each, and in less than ninety days after become insolvent, without any change in their business affairs." †

Some of the Saints lost very real though modest fortunes. But eventually they washed the slate clean of grievances and refused to sully their journals with complaints. Joseph's grammar teacher, who became disaffected many years later, told W. Wyl that he had lost $2,500. "I got for my money the blessing of the Lord," he said, "and the assurance that bye and bye the notes of that bank would be the best money in the country!" ‡

The legend of Joseph's prophecy that some day the bank notes would be as good as gold never died down. Years later Brigham Young collected some of the gold dust that was coming into Salt Lake City from the gold fields of California, manufactured a supply of coins, and ordered that the pack of Kirtland bills he had carried west with him be issued on a par with the gold. Joseph thus found at least one man who could make his prophecies come true.

The toppling of the Kirtland bank loosed a hornets' nest. Creditors swarmed in upon Joseph armed with threats and warrants. He was terribly in debt. There is no way of knowing exactly how much he and his leading elders had borrowed, since the loyal Mormons left no itemized account of their own claims. But the local non-Mormon creditors whom he could not repay

---

* Reprinted in the *Painesville Republican,* March 23, 1837. The financial statement was signed by B. J. Hathaway, cashier, and Oliver Cowdery, vice-president.

† Letter to *Zion's Watchman,* published March 24, 1838.

‡ *Mormon Portraits,* p. 35.

	DATE BORROWED	DATE DUE	AMOUNT DUE	AMOUNT OF SUIT	PLAINTIFF	DATE OF ARREST	AMOUNT OF BAIL	DECISION
1.	Oct. 5, 1831	May 1, 1837	$9,840.00	$15,000.00	Charles Holmes			Defendants defaulted
2.	June 17, 1836	Dec. 17, 1836	295.00	400.00	John A. Newbold			Settled out of court
3.	Oct. 11, 1836		1,150.00	2,000.00	Winthrop Eaton	June 9, 1837		Damages awarded
4.	Oct. 11, 1836	Jan. 1, 1837	5,037.00		Timothy Martindale	Feb. 22, 1837	$10,000.00	Settled out of court
5.	Nov. 15, 1836	Jan. 1, 1837	280.30	500.00	Ezra Holmes	Mar. 28, 1837		Settled out of court
6.	Dec. 1836		2,014.00	3,000.00	Hezekiah Kelley	Mar. 25, 1837	12,000.00	Damages awarded
7.	Dec. 14, 1836	Jan. 14, 1837	603.91	1,000.00	George Patterson John Patterson			Defendants defaulted
8.	Jan. 2, 1837	Feb. 15, 1837	3,018.00	4,000.00	Bank of Geauga	Mar. 24, 1837	16,000.00	Settled out of court
9.	Feb. 10, 1837		150.00	500.00	Seymour Griffith	July 27, 1837		Settled out of court
10.	Apr. 13, 1837		825.00	1,200.00	Nathaniel Bailey			Defendants defaulted
11.	Apr. 13, 1837		881.00	1,200.00	Ray Boynton Harry Clyde			Defendants defaulted
12.	June 1837	June 1837	(for labor and services)	2,000.00	T. Underwood R. Bald A. Spencer S. Hufy			Damages awarded
13.			214.34	1,000.00	William Backer	July 27, 1837	428.00	Plaintiff discontinues suit

brought a series of suits against the prophet which the Geauga county court duly recorded. These records tell a story of trouble that would have demolished the prestige and broken the spirit of a lesser man.*

Thirteen suits were brought against him between June 1837 and April 1839, to collect sums totaling nearly $25,000. The damages asked amounted to almost $35,000. He was arrested seven times in four months, and his followers managed heroically to raise the $38,428 required for bail. Of the thirteen suits only six were settled out of court — about $12,000 out of the $25,000. In the other seven the creditors either were awarded damages or won them by default.

Joseph had many additional debts that never resulted in court action. Some years later he compiled a list of still outstanding Kirtland loans, which amounted to more than $33,000.† If one adds to these the two great loans of $30,000 and $60,000 borrowed in New York and Buffalo in 1836, it would seem that

* See accompanying chart. This does not include the suit of Samuel D. Rounds to collect the $1,000 fine for operating the bank without a charter.

† Schedule setting forth a list of petitioners, creditors, their residence, and the amount due each:

To Keeler, McNeil and Co., New York	$8,000.00
To Halstead Haines and Co., New York	7,000.00
To Davenport and Boynton, New York	1,100.00
To Levitt Lloyd and Co., New York	600.00
To S. F. Scribner, Buffalo	1,500.00
To M. H. Bingo, Buffalo	1,334.79
To Keeler and Hempstead, Buffalo	1,567.59
To John A. Newbold, Buffalo	669.97
To Gardner and Patterson, Buffalo	280.94
To James Robison, Buffalo	98.00
To D. O. Ketchum, Buffalo	246.96
To W. B. Jones, Buffalo	848.75
To John Ayres, Buffalo	1,000.00
To Mead and Betts, Buffalo	3,670.64
To Holbrook and Finne	900.00
To Bailey, Keeler and Rensen, New York	1,804.94
To George Bosinger, Allen, Illinois	500.00
To W. B. Jones, Buffalo	821.06
To D. C. Coit, Buffalo	1,474.44
Total	$33,418.08

This list includes only those debts incurred before 1838, where Oliver Cowdery is a cosigner on the note. The original and complete list, which includes debts incurred later, may be found in the library of the Reorganized Church in Independence. The later debts are listed here on p. 266.

the Mormon leaders owed to non-Mormon individuals and firms well over $150,000.

This indebtedness hung over the prophet's head when he faced his church in a conference in April 1837. "Large contracts have been entered into for lands on all sides," he said, "where our enemies have signed away their rights. We are indebted to them, but our brethren abroad have only to come with their money, take these contracts, relieve their brethren from the pecuniary embarrassments under which they now labor, and procure for themselves a peaceable place of rest among us." He closed with what the church newspaper described as a prophecy: "This place must be built up, and will be built up, and every brother that will take hold and help secure and discharge these contracts shall be rich." *

It was a vain appeal and an unhappy promise. One by one the weak in faith left the ranks. Sylvester Smith, one of the first to apostatize, spread the poison of his disillusionment everywhere. At least six of the twelve apostles were in open rebellion, and Parley Pratt, whose rhapsodic eloquence had brought hundreds into the church, was even threatening to bring suit against the prophet. Pratt wrote a letter to Joseph on May 23, 1837 which said in part:

And now dear brother, if you are still determined to pursue this wicked course, until yourself and the church shall sink down to hell, I beseech you at least, to have mercy on me and my family, and others who are bound with me for those three lots (of land) which you sold to me at the extortionary price of 2,000 dollars, which never cost you 100 dollars. For if it stands against me it will ruin me and my helpless family, as well as those bound with me; for yesterday, President Rigdon came to me and informed me, that you had drawn the money from the bank, on the obligations which you held against me, and that you had left it to the mercy of the bank and could not help whatever course they might take to collect it; notwithstanding the most sacred promises on your part, that I should not be injured by those writings. I offered him the three lots for the writings; but he wanted my house and home also.

Now, dear brother, will you take those lots and give me up the writings, and pay me the 75 dollars, which I paid you on the same? Or will you take the advantage of your neighbor because he is in your power. . . . If not I shall be under the painful necessity of pre-

* *Latter-Day Saints Messenger and Advocate,* April 1837, p. 488.

FACSIMILE OF MORMON MONEY

LOWER AUDITORIUM, KIRTLAND TEMPLE

ferring charges against you for extortion, covetousness, and taking
advantage of your brother by an undue religious influence. . . .
Such as saying it was the will of God that lands should bear with
such a price; and many other prophesyings, preachings, and statements of a like nature.*

Joseph threatened to excommunicate any Saint who brought
suit against a brother in the church, and ordered Pratt to trial
before the High Council on May 29. But the council itself was
racked with schism, and the meeting broke up in disorder.†

Meanwhile, Grandison Newell, the most bellicose anti-Mormon in Ohio, who had gleefully watched the church's financial
structure collapse, determined to smash Joseph's personal prestige forever. He wrote open letters to the *Painesville Telegraph*
on May 16 and 26 accusing the prophet of inciting two Mormons, named Denton and Davis, to kill him so that he would
not proceed against the bank. Desperately shaken by this climax
to four months of continuing calamity, Joseph wrote in his journal: "It seemed as though the powers of earth and hell were
combining their influence in an especial manner to overthrow
the Church at once, and make a final end." Heber Kimball was
probably not exaggerating much when he said that at this time
"there were not twenty persons on earth that would declare that
Joseph Smith was a prophet of God." ‡

Since Grandison Newell was known publicly as "the Mormon Persecutor," many suspected that his suit against the
prophet was concocted out of pure malice. When the court
convened early in June, it was clear that he had no case, and few
were surprised when the judge dismissed the suit for want of
evidence.§

The Newell attack served to win Joseph a good deal of sympathy from his own people. Apostles T. B. Marsh and Orson
Hyde, who had been sharply critical of the banking failure, confessed their sins and begged forgiveness. Even Pratt was recon-

* This letter was taken from Joseph's files by his secretary, Warren Parrish, who
sent it to *Zion's Watchman*, where it was published on March 24, 1838. Pratt made
a statement in the *Elders' Journal* of August 1838 insisting that the letter was not
an exact copy of the original, but admitting that he had written a letter "in great
severity and harshness."

† *History of the Church*, Vol. II, p. 486.

‡ In a sermon delivered September 28, 1856. *Journal of Discourses*, Vol. IV, p. 105.

§ For a complete history of this case see the *Painesville Telegraph*, May 19, 26,
and June 9, 16, 30, 1837; also the *Painesville Republican*, July 6, 1837.

ciled, though he refused to stay in Kirtland, where the air was
still fetid with the breath of slander, and asked to be sent east
where he could clear his blood of acrimony by preaching to the
godless.

Joseph now realized that Kirtland must somehow be cleared
of his best elders until the banking fiasco could be forgotten and
the debts discharged or deferred. The best way to ensure the
loyalty of his men was to send them on missions, where they
could lose their petty grievances in preaching the purity of
the gospel. He decided, therefore, to establish a mission in England.

This was a plan he had contemplated ever since seeing the
phenomenal success of the Canadian mission. Many converts in
the Toronto area were urging that men be sent to England to
preach to their relatives. On June 1, 1837 Joseph appointed the
big, sloping-shouldered Heber Kimball to head a missionary
group. With him went the repentant Hyde and able young
Willard Richards. The English mission was thus born of disaster, and not even in his most extravagant daydreams could the
prophet have envisioned its success.

As the summer advanced, bringing the full measure of the panic
to the West, Joseph began to win back more of the ground he
had lost. Many who had been ready to apostatize when the Kirtland bank failed reconsidered when banks shut their doors
everywhere. With the whole financial structure of the nation
collapsing, Joseph's speculation now looked more like an indiscretion than grand larceny.

Many a Saint came to accept the dignified apology offered in
July by the *Messenger and Advocate:* "We believe that banking
or financiering is as much a regular science, trade or business,
as those of law, physic, or divinity, and that a man may be an
eminent civilian, and know nothing of consequence of the principle of medicine. He may be a celebrated divine, and be no
mechanic and no financier, and be as liable to fail in the management of a bank as he would in constructing a balloon or the
mechanism of a watch. . . . We are not prepared in our feelings to censure any man."

In mid-July Joseph left on a five-week missionary tour to
Canada, hoping that in his absence the enmity against him

would be still further dissipated. But he returned, refreshed and invigorated, to find that the church had split in two. The faction opposing him had rallied around a young girl who claimed to be a seeress by virtue of a black stone in which she read the future. David Whitmer, Martin Harris, and Oliver Cowdery, whose faith in seer stones had not diminished when Joseph stopped using them, pledged her their loyalty, and F. G. Williams, formerly Joseph's First Counselor, became her scribe. Patterning herself after the Shakers, the new prophetess would dance herself into a state of exhaustion before her followers, fall upon the floor, and burst forth with revelations.*

It was disheartening to Joseph to see his prized three "Book of Mormon witnesses" apparently ready to witness still another dispensation. But before long he effectively silenced the dancing seeress. Cowdery and Whitmer came back into the fold half-contrite, half-suspicious, and shortly thereafter went off to Missouri. Only Martin Harris, whose wagging tongue had become unbearable, was cut off from the church.† Joseph now felt free to test the loyalty of his Saints in a conference, and was once more sustained as President of the church by unanimous vote.

This triumph was illusory and shortlived. With the mercantile firms bankrupt, the steam mill silent, and land values sinking to an appalling low, Kirtland was fast disintegrating. Those Saints who had means were moving to Missouri, not only because it spelled Zion, but also because it was west, in which direction hope in America was always bent.

Joseph, in company with Sidney Rigdon, left for a visit to Missouri shortly after his return from Canada. His departure was doubtless hastened by the fact that six suits against him asking damages totaling $6,100 were pending in Chardon, and court was due to convene on October 24. It was impossible for him to meet these debts. He had sent out men in groups of eight from Kirtland to gather money to save the church, but he could not count upon their return for another three months.

During Joseph's two-month absence in Missouri the church in Kirtland went completely to pieces. After brawling in the

* See Lucy Smith: *Biographical Sketches,* pp. 211–13.

† According to one Kirtland settler, Harris's mind, "always unbalanced on the subject of Mormonism, had become so demented that he thought himself a bigger man than Smith, or even Christ." See C. G. Crary: *Pioneer and Personal Reminiscences,* p. 44. In his old age Harris rejoined the Mormons and went to Utah.

temple with members still loyal to the prophet, the dissenters set up a church of their own. They deluged the faithful with lawsuits, forcing many elders, including Brigham Young, to flee to Missouri to escape arrest. After the fracas in the temple Joseph Smith's father and sixteen others were arrested on a charge of riot, but the judge dismissed the case on the ground that there was no cause for action.* Next the dissenters tried to secure the printing press, with its eight hundred copies of the Book of Mormon, which had fallen into the hands of Grandison Newell.

At this stage of affairs Joseph returned from Missouri. He called for a public trial in the temple, determined that the sores that had so long been festering on the body of the church must be hacked out without mercy. The dissenters arrived in force. L. E. Miller, who was present, related afterward that Joseph came into the gathering "with a resolution and courage that the situation seemed to demand, and carried himself as one who felt that his soul and being had found themselves set firmly on the rock, while all else was but the shifting of sand or the swaying of reeds in the summer wind." † He made a resolute, determined battle.

Then Rigdon took the stand. He was half-sick and had to be supported to the pulpit. But it was a sickness born partly of hatred and despair, and once he began his denunciation he found unexpected reserves of energy and vitriol. For seven years he had watched the church gathering power, drawing much of its strength from the Baptists and Campbellites, whose leaders in the past had chosen to scorn him. He looked upon the glory of the church as a peculiarly personal triumph. Mormonism, he had written, "has puked the Campbellites effectually, no emetic could do half so well." ‡

Having little social vision and being completely incapable of understanding the economic forces that contributed to Kirtland's financial chaos, he had become a witch-hunter and now accused the dissenters of a long catalogue of crimes, which in-

* For descriptions of the temple riot and the resulting lawsuits see Eliza R. Snow Smith: *Biography and Family Record of Lorenzo Snow* (Salt Lake City, 1884), pp. 21–3, and Lucy Smith: *Biographical Sketches*, p. 211.

† As told to James H. Kennedy. See his *Early Days of Mormonism* (New York, 1888), pp. 166–7.

‡ *Latter-Day Saints Messenger and Advocate*, January 1837, p. 438.

cluded lying, stealing, adultery, counterfeiting, and swindling. His savage attack rose in a crescendo of violent epithets that stunned the Saints.* Finally, when his energy was spent, he let himself be helped down the long aisle to the entrance, and the congregation sat in silence while the temple doors closed behind him.

There followed a bitter· fight, as charges and counter-charges were hurled back and forth. Joseph completely lost control. Shouting above the din, he called for an end to debate and a vote on the excommunications. "Yes," yelled a dissenter, "you would cut a man's head off and hear him afterward!" † The meeting finally broke up, and Joseph left the temple conscious that he had lost, probably forever, what had been seven years in building.

Shortly after, when word came that Grandison Newell had secured a warrant for his arrest on a charge of banking fraud, Joseph knew that this was the finish and fled in the night with Rigdon, his horse turned toward Zion.

After their prophet's disappearance the dissenters seized the temple, and within the walls that had so recently resounded with hymns to his glory they passed resolutions proclaiming his depravity.

On the night of January 15–16, three days after Joseph's flight, the building housing the printing press caught fire and burned to the ground. Warren Parrish accused Joseph of being responsible for the incendiarism, saying that he had done it to prevent its printing matter against him, and also to fulfill a prophecy that God would destroy Kirtland by fire for its wickedness. Parrish by this time had come to believe the worst of Joseph and Rigdon, whom he had once looked to as gods. "I believe them to be confirmed infidels," he wrote, "who have not the fear of God before their eyes. . . . They lie by revelation, run away by revelation, and if they do not mend their ways, I fear they will at last be damned by revelation." ‡

* Rigdon published later a savagely obscene attack upon these men, and also Oliver Cowdery and David Whitmer in the *Elders' Journal*, August 1838, pp. 56–9.

† As told by L. E. Miller in Kennedy: *Early Days of Mormonism*, p. 168.

‡ Letter published in *Zion's Watchman*, March 24, 1838.

CHAPTER XV
The Valley of God

Poverty Joseph had borne before; tarring and beating he had turned to advantage. But to be exiled by his own disciples and driven from the temple in which he had been intoxicated with visions and glory killed much of his tenderness and naïve exuberance. In flight from Kirtland, Joseph reflected sorrowfully that at last he had the measure of his men's devotion, and it went no deeper than their pockets.

But there was a more fundamental cause of the hostility that had banished him to the wilderness. Distrust of clergymen who stepped outside their profession was one of the most deeply rooted mores of the Republic. Tocqueville had marveled at the pride that Americans took in their uncompromising separation of church and state and had noted that most ministers made it a point of honor to abstain from politics. The constitutions of almost every state in the Mississippi Valley expressly interdicted clergymen from taking any office of profit or trust as a gift of the people.

From the inauguration of the United Order to the collapse of the Kirtland Safety Society Bank, Joseph had been groping for control of the temporal as well as the spiritual life of his people. He had even dabbled hesitantly in politics by introducing a slate of Mormon candidates in the local Kirtland election of 1835 — a move that roused a storm in the *Painesville Telegraph.**

Cowdery accused him of attempting "to set up a kind of petty government, controlled and dictated by ecclesiastical influence, in the midst of this national and state government." † But to Joseph such a reproach was incomprehensible. Cowdery had seen visions that were more real to him than meat and drink, and Joseph could not understand why a man who had seen the glory of Jehovah in the Kirtland temple should afterward scorn

* See the issue of April 17, 1835.
† *History of the Church*, Vol. III, p. 18n.

a revelation because it dealt with the cost of a city lot instead of a celestial crown.

Kirtland's collapse might have shocked him into awareness of the social pressure he was opposing. But Joseph, like all true adventurers, could not see himself as part of the world; he was always astride it. The Kirtland debacle became a persecution symbol which heightened rather than humbled his sense of destiny. So swift a downfall could be explained only in terms of enemy conspiracy and the machinations of the devil. Hence there was no self-searching and but few regrets.

By the time he had covered the eight hundred miles to upper Missouri, much of his old buoyancy had returned. And his reception in Far West banished all traces of his gloom. The whole town turned out to meet him, singing and cheering. His oldest converts, who had been in Missouri since 1831, looked upon his flight from Kirtland as an answer to prayer. The bank failure, they said, was simply God's device for bringing the prophet to Zion to stay. It had been a net "to cull the Saints out from that region to the blessed and consecrated land." *

Joseph and his family lived at the home of George W. Harris, whose attractive wife, Lucinda, was famous as the widow of the great anti-Masonic martyr, William Morgan.† At this home, two months after her arrival, Emma bore another son. When the child lived through the first dreaded days of weakness and grew and fattened in Missouri sunshine, the whole church looked upon it as an omen of good fortune. Joseph now had three sons, Joseph, Frederick, and Alexander Hale.

Far West had enjoyed an extraordinary growth. Without goods and almost without money, the exiles in a single year had built a city out of naked energy and millennial hope. There were fifteen hundred Saints in the new Mormon county. Far West had been laid out on the plan of Joseph's ideal city, divided neatly into squares separated by streets wide enough for half a dozen wagons to pass abreast. A section of the prairie had been sold at auction for five thousand dollars, the proceeds going into a fund for building schools, and one schoolhouse had

---

* As said by Lyman Wight according to William Swartzell. See his *Mormonism Exposed, being a journal of a residence in Missouri from 28th of May to 20th of August 1838* (Pekin, Ohio, 1840), p. 17.

† Lucinda Harris was later listed by Mormon historians as one of Joseph Smith's plural wives. See Appendix C.

already been erected. Not long before Joseph's arrival the whole
male population of the county had turned out to excavate the
cavernous basement for a new temple.

In Far West Joseph could see at first hand the might of his
priesthood. Here were no scattered lonely cabins where every
man was jealous of his five-mile privacy; this was a kind of
frontier socialism, energized by millennial zeal and oiled by the
spirit of the brotherhood of man. It had speeded up tenfold
the usual painful process of individual adjustment to new land.

Quickly the prophet transferred all his enthusiasm to the
new country and began to speak of the Kirtland era with contempt as "seven long years of servitude, persecution, and affliction in the hands of our enemies." *

Meanwhile the good news came from Kirtland that many dissenting Saints, disgusted by the rantings of the apostates in the
temple, had rejoined the faithful and were planning to come to
Zion. Joseph's going had left a void that they had found intolerable. With each passing week they remembered less of their
prophet's financial ineptitude and more of his genial warmth
and his magnetic presence in the pulpit.

Six hundred Saints finally pooled their resources and started
for Zion in the longest wagon train that Kirtland had ever
seen. The gentiles shook their heads in wonder. "It was marvelous," wrote Christopher Crary, "to see with what tenacity
they held to their faith in the prophet, when they knew they
had been robbed, abused and insulted." † The departure of this
group reduced Kirtland to the sleepy village it had been when
Joseph arrived in 1831. Near-by Cleveland eventually became a
vast metropolis, its suburbs reaching out across the hills almost
to the temple doors, but the Mormon city, bereft of the virile
spirit of its leader, withered into a museum piece.

Far West was surrounded by thousands of unplowed acres
stretching west, north, and east. With characteristic energy Joseph set about surveying and laying claim to enormous tracts
of territory. Although the Missouri legislature had hoped that
the Mormons would be content with Caldwell County, which
had been set off specifically for them, they quickly spread into

* *History of the Church*, Vol. III, p. 11.
† *Pioneer and Personal Reminiscences*, p. 45.

Daviess, Carroll and Ray counties as well, where scattered hand-fuls of old settlers watched them with suspicion.

Shortly after his arrival Joseph rowed up the Grand River to Lyman Wight's ferry to explore land on the north bank in Daviess County. On a high bluff overlooking the river someone in the party discovered the ruins of what seemed to be an altar and excitedly led the prophet to it. After examining it Joseph stood silent, his eyes sweeping over the prairie that rolled away beneath him. In every season the prairie was a garden, its colors changing as the wild flowers bloomed and died. Now it was spring, and the whole landscape glowed with the color of peach blow.

The glory of the scene made Joseph heady as with new wine. "This is the valley of God in which Adam blessed his children," he said, "and upon this very altar Adam himself offered up sacrifices to Jehovah. This place is Tower Hill, and at its feet we will lay out a city which shall be called Adam-ondi-Ahman. Here Adam, the Ancient of Days, shall come to visit his people. He shall sit on a throne of fiery flame, as predicted by Daniel the prophet, 'with thousand thousands ministering unto him and ten thousand times ten thousand standing before him.' "

The Saints had long believed that Independence, in Jackson County, was the original site of the Garden of Eden. Now Joseph told them that Adam-ondi-Ahman was the land where Adam dwelt after his expulsion from Eden, and that Far West was probably the exact spot where Cain killed Abel.*

Joseph was quick to lay his fingers upon the pulse of his new country. Carefully he probed the sentiments of the nearest non-Mormons, listened for signs of disunity among his own people, and studied the political alignments dividing the state. Never before had he lived in a place where force was so triumphant and moral values at such a discount. Slowly something of the ruthlessness and cynicism of the frontier began to seep into his own thinking, and in fact to infect his whole people.

Here for the first time the Mormons were living in relative isolation with what seemed unlimited room for expansion. Certain that the last days were approaching, converts were immigrat-

---

* *History of the Church*, Vol. III, p. 35; *Doctrine and Covenants*, Section 117, verse 8; and John Corrill: *Brief History of the Church*, p. 28.

ing at a rate that astounded even Joseph, and from the English mission came word of phenomenal conversions among the poverty-ridden English workers. With such dynamic forces at his fingertips it is small wonder that the prophet began to dream of empire.

LIKE all the other border states, Missouri was pathologically sensitive on the slavery issue. Lynching was the common fate of colored criminals, and white men had been threatened with death by flogging for teaching Negroes to read.* Three years before Joseph's arrival a lynching party had seized a Negro murderer and burned him to death. When the leaders were brought to trial, the judge, whose name fittingly enough was Lawless, defined the duty of the jury in the following remarkable statement: "If the destruction of the murderer . . . was not the act of numerable and ascertainable malefactors; but of congregated thousands, seized upon and impelled by that mysterious, metaphysical, and almost electric frenzy which in all ages and nations has hurried on the infuriated multitude to deeds of death and destruction — then, I say, act not at all in the matter; the case transcends your jurisdiction — it is beyond the reach of human law!" †

Only one Missouri editor, Elijah Lovejoy, had the courage to protest this judicial sanction of mob rule, and for his indignant editorials in the *St. Louis Observer* he was hounded out of the state. Crossing the Mississippi into Illinois, he boldly founded a newspaper advocating freedom for the slaves. Late in 1837 a mob riddled him with bullets, and overnight abolitionism brought about a national emergency.

Lovejoy's martyrdom Joseph Smith did not savor. He knew all the details first-hand, having crossed the Mississippi not far north of Alton but two months after the murder. He realized now that despite his own cautious justification of slavery the Missourians could not forget the fact that the majority of his fast-growing colony were Yankees who abominated it. The whole Lovejoy tragedy made it clear that non-slaveholders in Missouri could expect no justice in the courts. Against the mob

* Harriet Martineau: *Retrospect of Western Travel* (New York, 1838), p. 32.
  † J. C. and Owen Lovejoy: *Memoir of the Rev. Elijah Lovejoy* (New York, 1838), p. 175.

spirit which was bound eventually to be kindled against his people, there seemed but one defense, an armed force.

From the bottom of his heart Joseph hated violence, but his people were demanding something more than meekness and compromise. It was common gossip among the old settlers that the Mormons would never fight; and Joseph came to realize that in a country where a man's gun spoke faster than his wits, to be known as a pacifist was to invite plundering.

For the first time he began to judge his men with an eye to their physical courage and quickness with a gun. He made Lyman Wight, whose foolhardy valor he had hitherto mistrusted, president of the new "stake in the tent of Zion" at Adam-ondi-Ahman. And he listened with interest to Sampson Avard, who claimed to know something about soldiering and who had a secret plan for the defense of the Saints.

Avard, who was cunning, resourceful, and extremely ambitious, suggested the formation of a military body, to be organized in companies of tens and fifties, each presided over by a captain. These men were to swear fraternal oaths binding them to everlasting secrecy. In times of danger they would communicate with one another by secret signs and passwords. They would not only defend the Saints against aggression from the old settlers, but also act as a bodyguard for the presidency and as a secret police for ferreting out dissenters.

Rigdon was immensely attracted to Avard's scheme. He did not greatly fear trouble with the Missourians, for he lacked Joseph's political acumen, but his hatred of heretics within the church had become an obsession. Many of the faction that had turned against Joseph when the bank failed in Kirtland — including Cowdery and David Whitmer — had filtered into Far West, half-forgiving, half-mistrustful, but unable to break completely with the prophet they had revered, and loved. Most of them blamed Rigdon for all the church's ills, and they found a willing ear among the old-time Missouri Mormons, who had always been jealous of his hold on the prophet. To Rigdon's old dislike of Missouri there was added, therefore, this new and intolerable feeling of insecurity. He hoped in Avard's band to set up a force that would stamp out malicious gossip against himself.

By mid-June 1838 there was whispered talk in Far West about

a secret society variously called the Brothers of Gideon (after the first "Captain General" Jared Carter, who had a brother named Gideon), the Daughters of Zion, the sons of Dan, and the Danites. The prophet and Rigdon were careful not to be associated too intimately with the band, leaving Avard to his own devices. And since he was at heart as rapacious and cruel as the worst border ruffian, those devices were not pretty.

John Corrill, who attended two early Danite meetings, came away convinced of Avard's villainy. He communicated his shocked protest to Rigdon, only to be advised to stay away from future meetings. A good many other Mormons who became Danites later described Avard's machinery. Their stories of oaths, passwords, and secret signs are fragmentary, but consistent.*

* David Whitmer and Oliver Cowdery held Rigdon chiefly responsible for the Danites. See *Address to All Believers in Christ*, p. 27, and *Defense in a Rehearsal of My Grounds for Separating Myself from the Latter Day Saints*. Most of the details of Danite activities come from apostates, but there are occasional allusions in the unpublished diaries and autobiographies of Danites who never left the church. Among them there is complete agreement that the Danites were a brotherhood organized for the defense of the Saints. See the typewritten transcripts of the "Biographical Sketch of Luman Andros Shurtliff," p. 32; the "Journal of Allen J. Stout," p. 9; and the "Diary of Oliver Boardman Huntington," Vol. I, p. 36. These are on file in the Utah State Historical Society Library. See also E. Robinson's account in *The Return* (Davis City, Iowa, October 1889), Vol. I, pp. 145–7.

The Mormons who apostatized on the Danite issue left a huge legacy of testimony about the aims and occasional depredations of the society. Orson Hyde, W. W. Phelps, and Thomas B. Marsh were among these, but they later returned to the church, and Hyde was even restored to full favor as an apostle. Their statements, therefore, are worth noting, and they fully corroborate the evidence furnished by the others. They were published in full in what is now a very rare document: *Correspondence, Orders, etc. in Relation to the Disturbances with the Mormons; and the evidence given before the Hon. Austin A. King, judge of the Fifth Judicial Circuit of the State of Missouri, at the Court-house in Richmond, in a criminal court of inquiry, begun November 12, 1838, on the trial of Joseph Smith. Jr., and others, for high treason and other crimes against the state* (Published by order of the General Assembly, Fayette, Missouri, 1841).

In addition to the testimonies of Hyde, Marsh, and Phelps, see the statements of Sampson Avard, John Corrill, John Cleminson, Reed Peck, and John Sapp, all of whom turned state's evidence. John Whitmer, John Corrill, and Reed Peck all wrote histories of this period which included details of the Danite organization. Whitmer's account has never been published, having been omitted from his "History of the Church" when it was published by the Reorganized Church in the *Journal of History*, Vol. I. The complete manuscript is in the church library at Independence. Corrill's *Brief History of the Church* was published in 1839 and is now very rare. Peck's manuscript [dated 1839], the original of which is now in my possession, was published by L. B. Cake in 1899 under the title: *Peepstone Joe Exposed*. For additional intimate details of the Danites see John D. Lee: *Mormonism Unveiled* (St. Louis,

But the most significant account came from the pen of the prophet himself, who described Avard's secret instructions to his captains in part as follows:

Know ye not, brethren, that it will soon be your privilege to take your respective companies and go out on a scout on the borders of the settlements, and take to yourselves spoils of the goods of the ungodly Gentiles? for it is written, the riches of the Gentiles shall be consecrated to my people, the house of Israel; and thus you will waste away the Gentiles by robbing and plundering them of their property; and in this way we will build up the kingdom of God, and roll forth the little stone that Daniel saw cut out of the mountain without hands, and roll forth until it filled the whole earth. For this is the very way that God destines to build up His kingdom in the last days. If any of us should be recognized, who can harm us? for we will stand by each other and defend one another in all things. . . . I would swear a lie to clear any of you; and if this would not do, I would put them or him under the sand as Moses did the Egyptian; and in this way we will consecrate much unto the Lord. . . . And if one of this Danite society reveals any of these things, I will put him where the dogs *cannot bite him.**

Joseph wrote in his history that he repudiated Avard and had him excommunicated as soon as he discovered these machinations. He stated further that he himself organized a military body made up of companies of tens and fifties which was completely distinct from Avard's. But it is clear that these were more of the prophet's characteristic efforts to write his own history as he wished it had been lived and not as it really happened. For Avard actually was not excommunicated until March 17, 1839, four months after he had turned traitor and left the church.† Between June and November 1838 he ruled the Danites with a free hand and was one of the most powerful men in the church.

Joseph shortly before his death inadvertently made a confused and damaging admission of his own relationship to the Danite organization: "The Danite system . . . never had any

1877), pp. 57 ff.; Oliver Olney: *The Absurdities of Mormonism Portrayed* (Hancock County, Illinois, 1843), p. 8; William Swartzell: *Mormonism Exposed, being a journal of a residence in Missouri from the 28th day of May to 20th of August 1838* (Pekin, Ohio, 1840), pp. 17–20.

  * *History of the Church,* Vol. III, pp. 180–1.
  † Ibid., Vol. III, p. 284.

existence. It was a term made use of by some of the brethren
in Far West, and grew out of an expression I made use of when
the brethren were preparing to defend themselves from the
Missouri mob, in reference to the stealing of Macaiah's images
(Judges: 18) — If the enemy comes, the Danites will be after
them, meaning the brethren in self-defense." *

Rigdon stated frankly and publicly that the Danite band was
organized "for mutual protection" against the depredations of
the Missourians, and denied only that he and the prophet had
been members.†

Although Joseph did not regularly attend the Danite meetings, there is no doubt that Avard had his sanction, for he formally addressed the Danites at least once and pronounced a
blessing upon Avard's head. "The time has come," he said in
his speech, "when the Lord has willed for us to take up arms
in our own defense. We wish to do nothing unlawful. If the
people of the world will but let us alone, we will preach the
gospel and live in peace. All we ask is that you place your trust
in the presidency — in Brother Sidney, Brother Hyrum and
myself — and I will give you a pledge that if we lead you into
any difficulty I will give you my head for a foot-ball to be kicked
about in Missouri dust." ‡

Avard was shrewd enough to make heresy against the presidency the most heinous crime in the church. This won him
complete freedom of action and blinded the prophet to the more
barbarous implications of his scheming. Avard told his men that
they "should support the presidency in all their designs, right
or wrong." He did not mince words. "If I meet one damning
and cursing the presidency, I can curse them too, and if he will
drink I can get him a bowl of brandy and after a while take him
by the arm, and get him one side in the brush when I will into
his guts in a minute and put him under the sod." §

* Minutes of a Nauvoo City Council Meeting, January 3, 1844, *History of the Church*, Vol. VI, p. 165.

† *Nauvoo Neighbor*, Vol. I (July 26, 1843), p. 2, republished in *History of the Church*, Vol. III, p. 453.

‡ As reported by John Cleminson and Reed Peck, who attended this meeting. See Peck's manuscript, p. 46, and the testimonies of both Cleminson and Peck in *Correspondence, Orders, etc. in relation to the disturbances with the Mormons*, pp. 114–20.

§ See Peck's manuscript, pp. 49–50, and his testimony in *Correspondence, Orders, etc.*, pp. 116–20.

IT was frightening to thoughtful men like Reed Peck and John Corrill to see the effect of Missouri upon Sidney Rigdon. Like Joseph he too was dreaming of empire. But where Joseph planned in terms of stately temples and ordered cities, Rigdon looked to a kingdom of men without sin. And since to Rigdon almost all the good things in life were evil, he intended to use his power in the kingdom to banish gaiety, good living, and independent thinking. He had always been unstable and fanatical, but no one could challenge his fierce loyalty to the prophet, even though it found expression chiefly in denunciation of real or imagined foes. Now he was translating his savage invectives into action.

From the moment of his arrival in Missouri he did not rest until he had seen Oliver Cowdery and John and David Whitmer cut off from the church. Their expulsion left him with no rivals of any stature. Of the eleven witnesses to the Book of Mormon only Joseph's father and brothers were left in the church.* Many of the apostles were away on missions, and Brigham Young, the only one capable of challenging Rigdon, had not yet been given a chance to show his strength.

Still Rigdon was not content. The dissenters, though living in ignominy and isolation, had chosen to remain in Far West, and their presence was a thorn in his flesh. They claimed a good deal of property in and about the town, to which the title had never been clear, and soon threatened to involve the church leaders in a series of lawsuits. At this time Rigdon and the prophet were planning to inaugurate a new economic experiment that would integrate the church into a self-sustaining unit capable of withstanding any assault. But until they gained a title to the disputed property, they could not hope to launch the new order without embarrassment. Rigdon was infuriated when Cowdery decided to carry the suits to the Missouri courts, which were almost certain to hand down a decision against the church presidency.

In a public speech on June 17 Rigdon poured out his spleen. He took as his text: "Ye are the salt of the earth, but if the salt hath lost its savor, wherewith shall the earth be salted? It is henceforth good for nothing but to be cast out and trodden

---

* Peter and Christian Whitmer were dead. Six had either left voluntarily or been cut off from the church. See David Whitmer: *Address to All Believers in Christ*, p. 28.

under foot of men." For an hour he harangued against the dissenters, becoming more and more infuriated. "If the county cannot be freed of these men in any other way," he finally shouted, "I will assist to trample them down or erect a gallows on the square of Far West and hang them up as they did the gamblers at Vicksburgh, and it would be an act at which the angels would smile with approbation."

Rigdon's passion struck fire, and angry murmurs spread through the crowd. Joseph rose to advise against lawlessness and stem the mounting ire. But he added a significant warning: "I don't want the brethren to act unlawfully but will tell them one thing. Judas was a traitor and instead of hanging himself was hung by Peter." *

This led John Corrill to believe that Rigdon's "salt sermon" was a signal to the Danites, and he secretly warned the dissenters to flee Far West.† This, however, they stubbornly refused to do. John Whitmer later testified that he went to the prophet and asked him frankly what he could do to mitigate the feeling roused against him by Rigdon's sermon. "The excitement is very high," Joseph agreed coldly, "and I don't know what can be done to allay it. But I will give you a frank opinion — if you will put your property into the hands of the bishop and high council and let it be disposed of according to the laws of the church, perhaps after a little while the church might have confidence in you."

"I wish to control my own property," Whitmer argued. "I want to be governed by the laws of the land and not the law of the church."

"Now you wish to pin *me* down to the law," Joseph replied, and abruptly terminated the discussion.‡

Soon the dissenters received a long letter written in Rigdon's characteristic bombastic style and laden with his venom. It was signed by eighty-three leading Mormons, including Hyrum Smith and several members of the High Council, and said in part:

* Rigdon's sermon and Joseph's comment were thus described by Reed Peck in his manuscript; see pp. 25–6.
† See Corrill's testimony in *Correspondence, Orders, etc.*, pp. 110–13.
‡ Testimony of John Whitmer, in *Correspondence, Orders, etc.*, pp. 138–9.

. . . Whereas the citizens of Caldwell county have borne with the abuse received from you at different times, and on different occasions, until it is no longer to be endured . . . out of the county you shall go, and no power shall save you. And you shall have three days after you receive this communication, including twenty-four hours in each day, for you to depart with your families peaceable; which you may do undisturbed by any person; but in that time, if you do not depart, we will use the means in our power to cause you to depart, for go you shall. . . .

You set up a nasty, dirty pettifogger's office, pretending to be judges of the law, when it is a notorious fact that you are profoundly ignorant of it. . . . You have also been threatening continually to enter into a general system of prosecuting, determined, as you said, to pick a flaw in the titles of those who have bought city lots and built upon them. . . .

We have evidence of a very strong character that you are at this very time engaged with a gang of counterfeiters, coiners and blacklegs . . . you have had the audacity to threaten us that if we offered to disturb you, you would get up a mob from Clay and Ray counties. For the insult, if nothing else, and your threatening to shoot us if we offered to molest you, we will put you from the county of Caldwell.*

Upon receiving this ultimatum the two Whitmers, with Oliver Cowdery and Lyman Johnson, set out for Clay County to hire a gentile lawyer. When they returned from Liberty, they met their families on the road, bearing a tale of Danite persecution that the men could not believe possible as coming from their former brethren. The Danites had surrounded their homes, ordered their wives to pack their blankets and leave the county immediately, and threatened death to anyone who returned to Far West. They had been robbed, according to John Whitmer, of all their goods save bedding and clothes.†

Missouri was teaching the Mormons much. This first act of violence was as much a release of their pent-up hatred against the whole state and the intermittent robberies, floggings, and

* *Correspondence, Orders, etc.*, pp. 103–6.

† "History of the Church," MS., Chapter xxii. John Whitmer never rejoined the Mormons. Oliver Cowdery returned to practice law in Kirtland. In Tiffin, Ohio, in 1843 he joined the Methodist Church. In 1848 he was rebaptized into the Mormon Church, but before his plans to go west could be carried out, he died of consumption in Missouri, in March 1850. See Stanley R. Gunn: "Oliver Cowdery, Second Elder of the Church . . ." MS. thesis, Brigham Young University, 1942.

burnings as against the handful of dissenters. For five years the Saints had choked back their resentment and swallowed meekly all the insults and calumny heaped upon them. They were weary of wearing the mantle of martyrdom and eager to unsheathe their swords. But attacking these few scapegoats did not purge the venom that had been storing up ever since 1833. Macbeth-like, the Danites looked about for new enemies when ridding themselves of one group had merely augmented their suspicion and brought a deep sense of guilt.

SHORTLY after the expulsion of the dissenters the prophet announced the revival, in modified form, of the old United Order. On July 8, 1838 he read to the Saints in Far West several revelations calling upon them to deed all their property to the church and promising in return that every man would receive a tract of land for his "everlasting inheritance," the number of acres being determined by the size of his family. The "surplus property" was to remain in the hands of the bishop, to be used for building the temple, supporting the church presidency, and "laying the foundation of Zion." Once the inheritances had been settled upon, every Saint was expected to give one tenth of his annual interest to the church.*

Rigdon followed the prophet's exposition with a heated warning that all who failed to consecrate their property to the Lord would eventually lose it to gentile marauders. Those who refused to comply were to be delivered over to the brothers of Gideon. With this threat ringing in their ears, and the fate of the dissenters a reminder that Rigdon's warnings could not be lightly dismissed, the Saints voted unanimously to consecrate their property to the Lord.

The new order was extremely unpopular. The majority, ac-

---

* Of the five revelations read in Far West on July 8 only three have been preserved, one of which is known as the "law of tithing." See *Doctrine and Covenants,* Sections 119, 120, and *History of the Church,* Vol. III, p. 44n. John D. Lee gives the most complete account of the substance of what must have been one of the missing revelations (*Mormonism Unveiled,* pp. 60–1). Lee's account is confirmed by William Swartzell's diary entry for July 22, 1838, where he reported Lyman Wight as preaching that "after brethren had bought lots to suit themselves they should consecrate all their money and property to the church so that church can purchase lands within twelve miles from the center of the stake in every direction" (*Mormonism Exposed,* p. 23). See also John Corrill: *Brief History of the Church,* p. 46, and the Reed Peck manuscript, p. 34.

cording to John D. Lee, "felt like Ananias and Sapphira — they dared not trust all to God and His Prophet. They felt that their money was as safe in their own possessions as it was when held by Church authorities." And it quickly became clear that the Saints had voted to please the priesthood, and then acted to suit themselves.

When he saw that the consecration plan was certain to fail, Joseph was quick to modify it. Instead of asking an outright transfer of title, he ordered the Saints to lease their property to the church "without consideration or interest" from ten to ninety-nine years. The whole church was then to be divided into four huge "corporations" — farmers, mechanics, shop-keepers, and laborers — which would utilize the land, machinery, and skills of the church members for the common good.

Very little is known about the operation of these co-opera-tives, since the Mormons were expelled from Missouri even be-fore the organization was complete. One convert, "Brother Winchester," wrote to his relatives in the early fall with great enthusiasm: "All kinds of necessary articles will soon be manu-factured by these firms that we may be under no necessity of purchasing of our enemies. The firms furnish constant employ for all who join them and pay $1.00 per day for a man's work. Any surplus that may remain after paying the demands of the firm is to be divided according to the needs and wants (Not ac-cording to the property invested) to each family, annually or oftener if needed. . . . The operations of these firms enables a man to get a comfortable house in a very few days when he gets about it. 1st by working for the firm 70 or 80 days then the firm turn out stone cutters, teams, carpenters, masons, &c., to complete the house and nearly every thing (save the land) is paid for by a man's own labor day for day." *

Apparently the agricultural corporation was the only one completely organized. This consisted of several co-operatives called the "Big Field United Firms," each of which supervised the communal farming of a seven-thousand-acre tract. Over-seers directed the allotment of work and the management of

* See the letter of "Brother Winchester," composed serially between September 6 and November 19, 1838 and copied into the Journal History in Salt Lake City under the date November 19, 1838. See also William Swartzell: *Mormonism Exposed*, p. 24, and the Reed Peck manuscript, p. 52.

horses and machinery. "Arrangements will soon be made," Winchester wrote, "that a person can get every necessary to eat, drink, live in, on & to wear, at the store house of the firms, and the best part of it all is that they want no better pay than labor. Arrangements are making that no person shall have the excuse for not laboring, nothing to do, nor shall the idle eat the bread of industry."

Reed Peck wrote in 1839 that many had been "violently opposed to this new church order but after much *argument, preaching, teaching,* and *explaining* by S. Avard the excitement was allayed and all but a few consented to give up their property. . . ." But Peck's implication that the Saints joined the firms out of fear of the Danites is hardly plausible. Most converts were willing to join as long as they retained title to their land. They accepted the plan for what it was — a serious attempt to wipe out poverty, to make the most of every man's labor, and to establish the church as a self-sufficient economic island in a turbulent gentile sea.

ON June 24, 1838 William Swartzell made a troubled entry in his diary: "I cannot listen with ease to the preaching of Lyman Wight — his exhorting a war upon the peaceful citizens of Missouri. . . . In one of his sermons he denounced them because they would not embrace the Mormon faith as 'hypocrites, long-faced dupes, devils, infernal hob-goblins, and ghosts, and that they ought to be damned and sent to hell where they properly belonged.' " *

No Saint was ever quite so eager to spread Mormonism by the sword as Lyman Wight. But his fulminations reflected a sentiment that was growing stronger. The Danites, bored with drilling and maneuvers, were thirsting for action and listened to reports of fresh gentile insults with their fingers on their guns.

On the Fourth of July several thousand Mormons gathered in Far West for a great celebration. Joseph had chosen the day for laying the cornerstone of the temple, and he planned to make it an occasion of pomp and splendor. The parade he had organized seven years earlier to celebrate the laying of the temple cornerstone in Independence had been thin, ragged, and a

* *Mormonism Exposed,* p. 12.

little ludicrous. But of this parade he made a spectacle that amazed and frightened the old settlers who had poured in to watch the ceremony. Every Mormon marched to the temple site, the "infantry" coming first, followed by the church leaders and civilians, and an impressive display of cavalry bringing up the rear. Here was the might of Zion for all to see.

Rigdon began the oration of the day with an ominous text: "Better, far better, to sleep with the dead than be oppressed among the living." Most of his speech was mild and patriotic, but when he reached the peroration he broke into a frenzy that chilled the hearts of thoughtful Mormons and turned the gentiles hot with rage:

Our cheeks have been given to the smiters, and our heads to those who have plucked off the hair. We have not only, when smitten on one cheek, turned the other, but we have done it again, and again, until we are wearied of being smitten, and tired of being trampled upon. . . . But from this day and hour, we will suffer it no more. . . .

And that mob that comes on us to disturb us, it shall be between us and them a war of extermination; for we will follow them till the last drop of their blood is spilled, or else they will have to exterminate us; for we will carry the seat of war to their own houses and their own families, and one party or the other shall be utterly destroyed. Remember it then, all men! We will never be the aggressors; we will infringe on the rights of no people, but shall stand for our own until death. . . . We this day then proclaim ourselves free, with a purpose and a determination that never can be broken — No never! no never!! no never!!!

The crowd broke into wild cheering and then shouted in unison with a thunder that carried over the prairies: "Hosanna, hosanna to God and the Lamb!" The gentiles, hands on their guns, slipped away silently. Joseph imprudently allowed the speech to be published in the Liberty press and had copies distributed in pamphlet form.* The Missouri newspapers replied with tirades of abuse.

Three days after the speech a violent electric storm swept across Far West. The Saints fled to their cabins in terror, for the Lord seemed bent on hurling His thunderbolts directly at the sacred city. One bolt shook the earth, and white-faced

---

* A copy may be seen in the Chicago Historical Society Library. The speech was reprinted in *Church History* (Lamoni, Iowa), Vol. II, pp. 157–65.

women eyed one another mutely, wondering which cabin had been singled out for justice. When the storm passed, they walked down the rain-drenched roads and collected in a crowd on the square. There the liberty pole around which they had paraded with such pride on the Fourth of July lay splintered on the ground. Uneasily they sensed an evil omen, and Luman Shurtliff cried out: "Farewell to our liberties in Missouri!"

CHAPTER XVI
The Alcoran or the Sword

Augusт 6, 1838 was election day in Missouri, and the Mormons for the first time in five years were choosing to vote. John D. Lee lay sprawled upon the grass in the public square at Gallatin, the county seat of Daviess County, where the vote between the Mormons and the old settlers was expected to be close. He listened in silence while one of the candidates, William Peniston, harangued against the Saints:

"They are a set of horse thieves, liars, and counterfeiters. They'll swear a false oath on any occasion to save another Mormon. They are thieves and knaves and dupes in the bargain, and no property is safe in Daviess County if they continue to pour into this area. If you suffer the Mormons to vote in this election, it will mean the end of your suffrage."

When the first Mormon stepped out of the group and walked silently over to the polls, a grinning settler barred his path. "Daviess County don't allow Mormons to vote no more than niggers," he said. When the man began to argue, the Missourian knocked him down. Immediately a fight broke out.

The Mormons, about thirty in number against over two hundred, were standing conveniently near a pile of oak hearts, each one four feet long and weighing about seven pounds. "They made," said Lee, "a very dangerous yet handy weapon." Lee jumped into the melee when he saw John L. Butler give the Danite signal for assistance. "I was an entire stranger to all who were engaged in the affray," he wrote, ". . . but I had seen the sign, and, like Samson when leaning against the pillar, I felt the power of God nerve my arm for the fray."

Butler was signaled out for especial attack, but he knocked a man down with every blow of his club. "When I called out for the Danites," he wrote later, "there was a power rested upon me such as one I never felt before. . . . I never struck a man the second time, and while knocking them down, I really felt that they would soon embrace the gospel." The riot was short, for the Missourians fled before the billets, but not before nine men were stretched on the ground and a score of others were crawling away fearfully bruised.

Butler then climbed to the top of the pile of lumber and said quietly: "My ancestors served in the War of the Revolution to establish a free and independent government — a government where all men have equal rights. I aim to have my rights as a free-born citizen, even if I have to fight for them. As for my religion, that's a matter between my God and me, and no man's business but my own. This day I'm going to have my vote, and I'll die fighting before I'm driven from these polls without it." The little knot of Mormons, still gripping their oak hearts, proceeded to the polls unmolested, and every man voted.*

This incident smashed the fragile peace that had prevailed in upper Missouri. Actually no one was killed in the fray, but the runner who brought news of it to Far West said that two Mormons had been slain and that Adam Black, who was justice of the peace in Gallatin, was uniting the gentiles in an army to expel the whole colony of Adam-ondi-Ahman from Daviess County.

Avard at once called out the Mormon troops in Far West, and Rigdon spurred them to deeds of valor. "Now we as the people of God do declare and decree," he shouted, brandishing his sword, "by the Great Jehovah, the eternal and omnipotent God, that sits upon his vast and everlasting throne, beyond that ethereal blue, we will bathe our swords in the vital blood of the Missourians or die in the attempt!" †

Joseph accompanied the little army to Adam-ondi-Ahman, where he learned that the election riot had been much exaggerated. Instead of returning to Far West, however, he made the mistake of marching his men to visit the justice of the peace, Adam Black. He entered Black's cabin with Avard and several others and demanded that he sign an agreement of peace.‡

---

* Butler's own account of this fight was copied into the unpublished Journal History in the church library in Salt Lake City, under the date August 6, 1838. See also John D. Lee: *Mormonism Unveiled*, pp. 58–60.

† As reported by William Swartzell, *Mormonism Exposed*, p. 29.

‡ Compare Joseph's account of this interview in his *History of the Church*, Vol. III, p. 59, with the sworn statement of Adam Black, published in *Correspondence, Orders, etc.*, pp. 55–7.

After some argument Black wrote out a statement promising to support the Constitution, and the Mormons retired.

As soon as the rabid Mormon-baiter Peniston learned of this visit, he magnified it into a story of intimidation and threatened murder, advertising the incident clear to Jefferson City. The judge of the circuit court, Austin A. King, who had hated the Mormons ever since his brother-in-law had been killed in a Mormon-gentile riot in Jackson County, immediately issued a warrant for Joseph's arrest.

Knowing that a trial in Gallatin was an invitation to a lynching, Joseph refused to give himself up unless he could be tried in his own county. When Lilburn Boggs, now Governor, heard of this, he ordered out six companies of militia to enforce King's warrant. Joseph capitulated, but through the intervention of his lawyers and old friends, Doniphan and Atchison, he won the concession that he be tried, not at Gallatin, but half a mile inside the Daviess County border. The prophet then stationed his own army along the county line and went to trial secure from the threat of an impromptu hanging. He was bound over on a five-hundred-dollar bond to keep the peace.

The trial did nothing to mitigate the hatred intensifying against the Saints. Millers refused to grind Mormon grain at any price, and flour in Far West soon disappeared altogether. The women tried to boil the unmilled wheat, and grated their corn on crudely perforated tin pails. The corn proved edible when baked with pumpkin, but the wheat was sodden and indigestible. Hundreds of newly arrived immigrants, living in covered wagons or bark tents, looked at the fast-approaching winter with panic.

Armed bands of Missourians prowled about, firing haystacks and granaries, stealing horses and cattle, and whipping Mormon farmers. Daily it became clearer that in every county save Caldwell the gentiles were hell-bent to drive the Mormons out. Soon the two big Mormon settlements of DeWitt and Adam-ondi-Ahman were in a state of siege, the women and children herded behind hastily improvised stockades, living off cornmeal and freshly killed cattle. When these provisions were gone and the Mormon men were worn out with watching, the land agents who had originally sold them their property sent word that they were willing to buy back the pre-emption rights whenever the sect agreed to leave. This extortion turned the Mormons sick.

By this time the prophet had expanded the Danite band into the "Armies of Israel," which included nearly every able-bodied Mormon. One convert, after describing in a letter the duties of the various companies — guarding, spying, foraging, arms-manufacturing, and so on — wrote frankly: "Those companies are called Israel's Army because the Prophet Daniel has said they shall take the kingdom and possess it forever." *

Despite the extensive organization and drilling of this army, it was still purely defensive. Joseph forbade any retaliation for the depredations of the old settlers and worked desperately with his lawyers to effect a peace. For a time it seemed as if his prudence would bear fruit. Doniphan came very near wiping out the Daviess County trouble by persuading the old settlers to sell out to the Mormons at a good price. But before this plan could be worked out, the old settlers in Carroll County formally demanded that the Mormons leave DeWitt, the Mormon river port. They set the deadline at October 1. Joseph replied coldly to this ultimatum by reinforcing the town with two hundred newly arrived Canadian converts, whereupon the Missourians laid siege to DeWitt in earnest, firing on everyone who approached.

When General Lucas, who commanded the militia in this area, heard of the skirmishes, he wrote to Governor Boggs: "If a fight has actually taken place, of which I have no doubt, it will create excitement in the whole of upper Missouri, and those base and degraded beings will be exterminated from the face of the earth." †

Under cover of darkness Joseph made his way to the beleaguered town. He found his people desperate for food and fuel and pathetically eager for miracles. The Missourians had caught some of the men out foraging and had beaten them into unconsciousness with hickory withes. The prophet looked at their backs ribboned with welts, and the rage that was so slow to mount in him surged into his throat. But he could not call down thunderbolts, and that is what it would have taken to

---

* "Brother Winchester" letter, copied into the Journal History under the date November 19, 1838.

† *Correspondence, Orders, etc.*, pp. 34–5.

aid these Saints, outnumbered as they were by ten to one. "Come back to Far West," he told them dully, and sent out a flag of truce.

When the wagons filed into Far West, a sullen, hopeless anger swept over the people. One woman, weak from childbirth, had died on the way, and when they learned of it the oldest converts began to count again the toll of martyrs to the gospel. But the younger men were cold to memories and eager for revenge. Nothing was gained by surrender, they said, nothing but death. And when Doniphan brought word that negotiations with the settlers in Daviess County had broken down and a mob of eight hundred men was threatening to devastate Adam-ondi-Ahman, it seemed a confirmation of their worst fears.

"If Carroll County can root the Mormons out, why not Daviess?" the old settlers were arguing. "To hell with compromise! To hell with Doniphan's peace settlement! The land sales are coming on, and if we drive the Mormons out we can get all the lands open to pre-emption. We can get all our land back again as well as all the pay we've got so far!"

Joseph called every able-bodied Mormon in Caldwell County to the Far West public square. There on October 14 he broke his long public silence.* "We are an injured people," he began. "From county to county we have been driven by unscrupulous mobs eager to seize the land we have cleared and improved with such love and toil. We have appealed to magistrates, judges, the Governor, and even to the President of the United States, but there has been no redress for us. The latest reply of Boggs to our petitions is to tell us to fight our own battles. And that, brethren, is exactly what we intend to do."

The crowd cheered his sober words as they had never cheered Rigdon's most truculent outbursts. "I have a great reverence for the Constitution," he went on, "but for the laws of this state I have no regard whatsoever, for they were made by a parcel of

* Except where noted, all the details of this chapter are taken from the *History of the Church*. This speech, however, was not recorded there, and the report given here is based upon the accounts of seven men. See the affidavits of T. B. Marsh, Orson Hyde, George M. Hinkle, John Corrill, W. W. Phelps, Sampson Avard, and Reed Peck in *Correspondence, Orders, etc.*, pp. 57–9, 97–129. The Marsh and Hyde account, which was made on October 24, is particularly important. Part of it was reproduced in *History of the Church*, Vol. III, p. 167. See also the Peck manuscript, p. 80. Joseph himself barely mentioned the speech in his history; see Vol. III, p. 162.

blacklegs. General Doniphan has authorized this body to act
as a regiment of the state militia under the command of Colonel
Hinkle. We are therefore acting within the law. All who are
with me will meet tomorrow to march to the defense of Adam-
ondi-Ahman with the words of the Savior ringing in our ears:
'Greater love hath no man than this, that he lay down his life
for his brethren.' "

He looked over the crowd as if searching for a familiar face.
"Some of the brethren aren't here today," he said. "Some of
those that Brother Sidney likes to call 'Oh, don't! men.' In time
of war we have no need for such. A man must declare himself
friend or enemy. I move a resolution that the property of all
'Oh, don't! men' be taken over to maintain the war."

As the crowd laughed and applauded, Rigdon started up, his
eyes blazing. "And I move," he shouted, "that the blood of the
backward be spilled in the streets of Far West!" But Joseph
silenced him.

"No, I move a better resolution. We'll take them along with
us to Daviess County, and if it comes to a battle, we'll sit them
on their horses with bayonets and pitchforks and make them
ride in front!" The men cheered, and the tension relaxed a
little.

Joseph went on to tell an anecdote. "An army captain was
stationed in a village with his regiment, which badly needed
food. The captain found a Dutchman with a rich harvest of
potatoes, but the man refused to sell. Explaining the matter to
his men, the captain thrice warned them not to let him catch
them touching the potatoes. But the next morning" — he paused
— "there was not a potato in the whole patch."

The men grinned. Their families were hungry and wretched.
They had lost horses, cattle, blankets, and wheat to their neighbors and needed no bolder hint.

As Joseph neared the end of his speech, all the pent-up hatred
that he had so long suppressed broke forth with unexpected
violence. "If the people will let us alone," he cried, "we will
preach the gospel in peace. But if they come on us to molest us,
we will establish our religion by the sword. We will trample
down our enemies and make it one gore of blood from the
Rocky Mountains to the Atlantic Ocean. I will be to this generation a second Mohammed, whose motto in treating for peace

was 'the Alcoran or the Sword.' So shall it eventually be with us — 'Joseph Smith or the Sword!' ' "

ONE hundred Mormons marched into Adam-ondi-Ahman the next day to reinforce the two hundred and fifty men assembled under Lyman Wight. After a conference with the prophet, Wight addressed his men. He stood by a fine brown horse with his famous bearskin flung over the saddle. A red handkerchief was bound about his head Indian fashion, with the knot in front, and his collar stood open showing his naked, hairy breast. "The sword has now been drawn," he shouted, flourishing an enormous cutlass, "and shall not be sheathed until we have won back everything the mobs have wrenched from us. Our cause is just; the Lord is on our side; and it makes no difference if our enemies number fifty or fifty thousand!" *

Wight's fierce aspect and bravado caught the men up in the wildest enthusiasm. John D. Lee said that he felt himself bullet-proof: "I thought that one Danite would chase a thousand Gentiles and two could put ten thousand to flight." The gentile spies who heard the speech rushed away to spread the news that the Wild Ram of the Mountains had fifteen thousand men under arms, ready to descend upon mob and militia alike.

News that the Mormons were on the offensive was a terrific shock to the gentiles in Daviess County. They scattered into the wind. When David Patten charged into Gallatin with a mounted company, he found it almost deserted. The men promptly looted Jacob Stollings's store and then set fire to it along with several cabins.

Young Oliver Huntington, who had already joined the Danites, but had been forbidden to go on the expedition to Gallatin because of his tender years, climbed Tower Hill and stood on Adam's altar to see what he could of the expected fight. "I saw the smoke rising toward Heaven, which filled me with ambition. . . ." he related. "In tears I looked far over the trees, and wished and sighed and wished again that I was there. . . . The next day I went to Bishop Knight's and saw the plunder . . . and heard them tell in what order they took the place." †

* As related by George Hinkle and James B. Turner, in *Correspondence and Orders, etc.*, pp. 125–9, 139–40, and by John D. Lee: *Mormonism Unveiled*, pp. 73–4.

† Unpublished diary of Oliver Boardman Huntington. See typewritten transcript in

While Patten was raiding Gallatin, Wight with another company attacked Millport, and Seymour Brunson attacked Grindstone Fork. They rounded up all the horses, cattle, and hogs they could find and drove them back to Adam-ondi-Ahman, but did not burn the cabins.

Back in Far West Rigdon spread news of victories and applauded when the first wagons piled high with "consecrated property" pulled into the square. But he was quick to see that the plunder was a horror to many Saints. One by one the disapproving and the faint of heart stole away with their families in the night. News of every fresh defection made Rigdon wild with anxiety. When Thomas B. Marsh, president of the apostles, and Orson Hyde, also an apostle, joined this exodus, he mounted his stand in the schoolhouse and blistered them with his hate:

"The last man has run away from Far West that is going to. The next man who starts shall be pursued and brought back, dead or alive. I move a resolution that if any man attempts to move out of this county or even packs his things for that purpose, then any man in this house who sees it shall, without saying anything to any other person, kill him and haul him aside into the brush. All the burial he shall have will be in a turkey buzzard's guts, and nothing will be left of him but his bones! Yesterday," he finished significantly, "one man in Far West slipped his wind and was dragged into a hazel bush for the buzzards to pick at. But the man who lisps it shall die!" *

By this time the gentiles had learned of the Mormon depreda-

the Utah State Historical Society Library, Vol. I, pp. 31–4. In his history Joseph Smith denied all stories of burning and pillaging, insisting that the mobs had fired their own cabins to cast blame upon the Mormons. But in a correspondence with Jacob Stollings, who was trying to discover if his account books had been burned along with his store, Joseph virtually admitted that the Mormons had been responsible. See *History of the Church,* Vol. III, pp. 316, 378. John Whitmer, in the last chapter of his manuscript "History of the Church," wrote that the Saints "began to rob and burn houses . . . took honey which they called sweet oil, and hogs which they called bear, and cattle which they called buffalo." See also *The Return,* Vol. I (December 1889), p. 189; and the testimonies of the eyewitnesses to the Mormon depredations: John Raglin, George W. Worthington, Porter Yates, Patrick Lynch, and William Morgan, in *Correspondence, Orders, etc.* Adam Black and William Peniston swore that their own houses had been destroyed. Thomas B. Marsh and Orson Hyde confirmed these stories; ibid., pp. 57–9.

   * This speech was reported in detail by W. W. Phelps and confirmed by Burr Riggs and Benjamin Slade. See *Correspondence, Orders, etc.,* pp. 120–5, 134–6, 143. Hyde returned to the church in 1839, Phelps in 1841, and Marsh in 1857.

tions. Within a week every isolated Mormon cabin was a pile of ashes. The old settlers blandly sent their intentions to the press: "We believe in less than six days Far West will be burnt and her fugitives driven from the borders of the state." * When Joseph ordered everyone into either Far West or Adam-ondi-Ahman for protection, gentile spies spread the report that an immense Mormon army was gathering which would lay waste the whole upper portion of the state.

Two of the worst gentile incendiarists sent an express to Governor Boggs on October 24 reporting that the Mormons had massacred a whole militia company of fifty men. Richmond, they said, was to be attacked at any moment. "We know not the hour and minute we will be laid in ashes — our country ruined — for God's sake give us assistance as quick as possible." †

The letter was a fantastic fabrication. The militia company in question, led by a Methodist minister, Captain Bogart, had been ordered to patrol the border of Caldwell County, and on the day of the supposed massacre it had done nothing more exciting than to enter the county illegally and capture three Mormons. This capture, however, had tragic repercussions, for the Mormon scout who brought news of it to the prophet was certain that the three men were to be shot at sunrise. Joseph at once dispatched sixty men under Captain David Patten to effect a rescue.

Bogart's men were strategically entrenched behind a slough bank in a scattering of oak timber on Crooked River. A thick grove of hickories on the nearest ridge made it impossible for anyone approaching from the east to discover the militiamen until practically upon them. The sixty Mormons came up over the ridge at dawn, their bodies silhouetted against the brightening sky. The guards took careful aim and fired, killing one Mormon outright, and then fled to give the alarm. Patten at once ordered a charge down the hill, and the men rushed down in a fast trot, shouting: "God and Liberty!" Patten led the charge, his white coat gleaming in the early light.

The Mormons made perfect targets, and three or four fell at

* Letter signed Accidentalist, dated October 22, 1838, and published in the *Missouri Argus*, St. Louis, November 1, 1838.

† Letter from Sashiel Woods and Joseph Dickson, *Correspondence, Orders, etc.*, p. 60.

the first volley. But the men rushed on into the oak grove with drawn swords and charged over the slough bank. All of Bogart's men fled but one, who hid behind a tree long enough to take careful aim at Patten's white coat. Struck in the abdomen, "Captain Fearnought" dropped to the ground. He died that night in terrible agony three miles outside Far West.

The fight was over and won and the prisoners released, but instead of exultation the Mormons were overwhelmed with gloom. Patten, a man of great strength and courage, had been the most beloved of all the apostles. "Alas," wrote John D. Lee, "my dream of security was over. One of our mighty had fallen, and by Gentile hands."

The Battle of Crooked River was reported to Governor Boggs as a massacre by the Mormons, although Bogart had actually lost but one man and the Mormons three. "The women and children are flying from Richmond in every direction," Judge Ryland wrote on October 25, "and the city is expected to be sacked and burned by the Mormon banditti tonight. We have sent since one o'clock this evening about one hundred well-armed and daring men . . . with the full determination to exterminate or expel them from the state *en masse.*"

On the same day that this deluge of rumor and falsehood reached him, Governor Boggs received the sworn statements of the two Mormon apostles, T. B. Marsh and Orson Hyde, exposing the Danites, admitting the burning and pillaging of Gallatin, and giving a detailed account of the prophet's "Mohammed" speech. They reported that the Danites planned to burn Richmond and Liberty and to poison the wells and food of the old settlers in an effort to start a pestilence. Even General Atchison, who until now had believed that the Mormons were entirely blameless, wrote angrily to Boggs: "From the late outrages committed by the Mormons, civil war is inevitable. They have set the laws of the country at defiance and are in open rebellion."

Boggs had never lifted a finger to stop the five-year-long depredations of the old settlers against the Mormons, but this news of the first Mormon resistance galvanized him into action. He wrote to General Clark on October 27 a command that was even more shocking than his past lethargy: "Your orders are to hasten your operations and endeavor to reach Richmond, in Ray

County, with all possible speed. The Mormons must be treated as enemies and must be exterminated or driven from the state, if necessary for the public good. Their outrages are beyond all description." *

THE PROPHET meanwhile was energetically preparing Far West for a siege. His men tore down cabins to build breastworks to prevent the cavalry from charging into the town, and hastily gathered in supplies of food. Blacksmiths hammered out crude swords and pikes from every available piece of steel. The women packed their bags and prepared to flee with the children northward into the scanty woods.

Joseph walked about the town, directing the measures for defense and calling out encouragement to every gloomy face. Coming upon a group of disconsolate guards shivering over a few firebrands, he caught first one and then another by the shoulders, shaking them roughly. "Get out of here, and wrestle, run, jump, do anything but mope around; warm yourselves up," he cried. "This inactivity will not do for soldiers!"

Forming them into a ring, he stepped inside and challenged them to wrestle. Catching his spirit, the men one by one stepped into the ring to try their strength, while the others shouted and applauded. Not one could throw Joseph, and finally, laughing and sweating, he left the ring to make way for a lesser man. As the sport went on, the crowd grew boisterous. Suddenly Sidney Rigdon broke into the ring, sword in hand, crying testily: "You are breaking the Sabbath, and I'll not suffer it."

For a moment the men were abashed and silent. Then one bolder than the rest called to the prophet, who had been watching Rigdon with a curious expression. "Brother Joseph, we want you to clear us from blame, for we formed the ring by your request. You told us to wrestle, and now Brother Rigdon is bringing us to account for it."

"Brother Sidney," Joseph answered deliberately, walking into the ring, "you had better get out of here and let the boys alone; they are amusing themselves according to my orders. You are an old man. You go and get ready for meeting and let the boys alone." Then catching Rigdon off guard, he knocked the sword

* Ryland's letter, the statements of Marsh and Hyde, Atchison's letter, and Boggs's "exterminating order" were all printed in *Correspondence, Orders, etc.,* pp. 57–62, 76.

from his hand and caught him by the shoulder. "Now old man, you must go out, or I will throw you down."

John D. Lee, who was watching the spectacle, said that "the prospect of a tussle between the Prophet and the mouthpiece of the Prophet was fun for all but Rigdon, who pulled back like a crawfish." Joseph knocked off his hat, dragged him bodily out of the ring, and with one jerk of his wrist ripped his fine pulpit coat from the collar to the waist. Then turning to the men he said: "Go in boys, and have your fun. You shall never have it to say that I got you into any trouble that I did not get you out of."

When Rigdon began whimpering about the loss of his coat, Joseph said: "You were out of your place. Always keep your place and you will not suffer. You have no one to blame but yourself."

"After that," said Lee, "Rigdon never countermanded the orders of the prophet, to my knowledge; he knew who was boss."

By October 29 all the outlying Mormon settlements had been evacuated except one. On a creek several miles from Far West Jacob Haun had just finished building a flour mill, which he swore he would not desert to a gentile arsonist. "You had better lose your property than your lives," the prophet told him, but Haun was unconvinced. When he departed, Joseph turned to Lyman Wight and John D. Lee, gravely troubled: "I wish they were here for their own safety. I am confident they will be butchered in the most fearful manner."

On October 30 the Mormon scouts and picket guards were driven into Far West by the approach of a large body of militia. Colonel Hinkle, who was in command of the Mormon troops, had been out with the scouts, one of whom noted that when they were most hotly pursued by the militia, Hinkle had turned his coat inside out. This act was reported to Joseph with a warning: "He's a fairweather Saint, and you'd best watch him close." John D. Lee heard the prophet thank the scout for the information and warn him to keep it secret. "It's a bad time," he said, "to ventilate an act like that."

The Mormon force guarding Far West was about eight hundred strong. It was badly armed, many of the men having no muskets, being armed only with single-shot pistols or home-made swords. But there was considerable ammunition, and the morale of the men was high. "Now, Father," wrote one Mormon in a letter on October 28, "come to Zion and fight for the religion of Jesus. Many a hoary head is engaged here, the Prophet goes out to the battle as in days of old. He has the sword that Nephi took from Laban. Is not this marvellous?" *

The militia halted just outside range of the Mormon guns, and the two forces watched each other warily. During this time a messenger from General Doniphan slipped into Far West with a message for the prophet. It was a copy of Boggs's "exterminating order." The note said further that the dreaded Samuel Lucas, armed with this order, was on his way to Far West with General Clark and six thousand men.

That night a wounded man stumbled into Far West with news that froze the blood of every Saint. The settlement at Haun's Mill had been attacked by two hundred militiamen. The Mormons had fled into the blacksmith shop, which they thought would make an admirable fort, but it had proved instead to be a slaughterhouse. Great cracks yawned between the logs of the shop, and the Missourians, hiding behind trees, picked off the Mormons at their leisure as if they had been killing cattle in a pen. When the women fled toward the brush, the men shot at them in derision. Old Thomas McBride fell wounded and surrendered his gun, whereupon one of the mob coolly hacked him to pieces with a corn-cutter.

After shooting down every Mormon they could see, the mob entered the blacksmith shop to finish off the wounded. They found nine-year-old Sardius Smith hiding under the bellows. His younger brother, shot through the hip, and pretending to be dead, heard the men drag Sardius out from his hiding-place. "Don't shoot," said one militiaman, "it's just a boy."

"It's best to hive them when we can. Nits will make lice," a man replied, and placing his rifle near the boy's head, blew out his brains.

When darkness came, the women crept back to the scene of carnage. Of the thirty-eight men and boys in the camp, seventeen had been slain and fifteen wounded. Fearful that the mob

* "Brother Winchester" letter, written serially between September 6 and November 19, 1838. Copied into the Journal History under the date November 19.

would return, the women lowered the dead into an unfinished well, hid the wounded in the woods, and then, stunned and desolate, made their way toward Far West.

As news of the massacre spread among the Saints, the men cursed as they had not cursed since they joined the church. But everywhere there was a deep conviction that the Haun's Mill colony would have been spared had Haun heeded the prophet.

There was no sleep for Joseph that night. He could not help feeling answerable for the horror. And in Far West he could see on the morrow a Haun's Mill massacre repeated a hundred times. His scouts were hourly bringing him reports. The militia was doubling — trebling. Already the Saints were outnumbered five to one in fighting men, and within two days ten thousand men would surround the town.

Joseph knew his own men well. He could list the lily-livered on his fingers and call the "Oh, don't! men" by their first names. Sending secretly for John Corrill and Reed Peck, dissenters whom Doniphan knew and respected, he said to them: "Find General Doniphan, and beg like a dog for peace." *

But knowing that his overtures might be spurned and that any hint of capitulation would demoralize his men and bring the militia whooping into the town, he played out his role of magnificent resistance to the end. When his men gathered before him the next morning, he met them with resolution and complete self-assurance:

I care not a fig for the coming of the troops. We've tried long enough to please the Gentiles. If we live together they don't like it; if we scatter they massacre us for it. The only law they know here is that might makes right. They are a damned set, and God will blast them into hell!

If they try to attack us we will play hell with their applecarts. Before now, men, you've fought like devils. But now I want you to fight like angels, for angels can whip devils. And for every one we lack in number to match the mob, the Lord will send an angel to fight alongside.†

* Reed Peck manuscript, p. 103.

† As reported by George Hinkle, James C. Owens, Samuel Kinnibel, and Sampson Avard, in *Correspondence, Orders, etc.* Their accounts were confirmed by E. Robinson in *The Return*, Vol. II (January 1890), p. 206.

Before the day was over, Corrill and Peck returned with word that Major-General Lucas, who was in command, was willing to meet the leading elders of Far West under a flag of truce between the lines. Shortly afterward a delegation of militiamen approached with a white flag, and Joseph sent to meet it Colonel Hinkle, Corrill, Peck, W. W. Phelps, and John Cleminson, all of whom he suspected of turning against him. "A compromise must be made on some terms," he said, "honorable or dishonorable." *

Lucas's terms were harsh. He demanded, first, the surrender of the Mormon leaders to be tried for treason; second, the confiscation of all Mormon property to liquidate Mormon debts and to indemnify the old settlers whose property had been damaged; third, the immediate mass migration of all Mormons from the state; and fourth, the surrender of their arms. The alternative to these terms was annihilation.

Hinkle requested a twelve-hour delay, but Lucas insisted on having Joseph Smith, Sidney Rigdon, Lyman Wight, Parley Pratt, and George Robinson as hostages. If by morning the Mormons still wanted to fight, he said, he would guarantee the prisoners' release.

When Joseph heard the terms, he called in his leading men who were in most imminent peril, chiefly those who had figured in the battle with Bogart's men, and bade them flee northward out of the state. He ordered all the plunder taken from the gentiles gathered together in one house, lest every man who was found with a saddle or a blanket not his own be hanged for stealing.† Then he called his troops together and addressed them sorrowfully:

You are good and brave men, but there are 10,000 men approaching Far West, and unless you were angels themselves you could not withstand so formidable a host. You have stood by me to the last; you have been willing to die for me for the sake of the Kingdom of Heaven, and that is offering enough in the sight of God. The blood-thirsty Lucas has demanded my surrender, and I shall offer myself

---

* See the Reed Peck manuscript, pp. 108–9, and a letter from George Hinkle to W. W. Phelps dated August 14, 1844, published in the *Messenger and Advocate*, Pittsburgh, August 1, 1845.

† Oliver B. Huntington diary (manuscript), Vol. I, p. 34.

up as a sacrifice to save your lives and to save the Church. Be of good cheer, my brethren. Pray earnestly to the Lord to deliver your leaders from their enemies. I bless you all in the name of Christ.*

General Lucas, impatient at the delay and suspicious of treachery, meanwhile ordered his troops to march on the city. When they were within six hundred yards of the breastworks, the Mormon hostages came forward. Upon sighting the white flag, the militia sent up a yell of triumph. "If the vision of the infernal regions could come suddenly to mind," wrote Parley Pratt in his autobiography, "with thousands of malicious fiends, all clamoring, exulting, deriding, blaspheming, mocking, railing, raging and foaming like a troubled sea, then could some idea be formed of the hell which we had entered."

The prisoners lay that night on the open ground, sodden and disconsolate, taunted by the guards and pelted by the rain. About midnight General Lucas appeared out of the darkness and called Lyman Wight aside. "I regret to tell you your die is cast, your doom is fixed, you are sentenced to be shot tomorrow morning on the public square in Far West at eight o'clock."

Wight spat contemptuously. "Shoot and be damned!"

Lucas looked at him with mingled admiration and regret. "We were in hopes you would come out against Joe Smith, but as you have not, you will have to share his fate."

"You may thank Joe Smith," Wight retorted, "that you are not in hell this night, for had it not been for him, by God I would have put you there!"

* As reported by John D. Lee, *Mormonism Unveiled*, p. 82.

CHAPTER XVII
Ordeal in Liberty Jail

A**T DAWN** the prisoners heard the rattle of arms and watched General Doniphan form his brigade. No Missourian had befriended the Mormons with such singleness of purpose and peculiar constancy. It was he whom Lucas had ordered to carry out the execution. When the line was formed, Doniphan walked over to the prisoners, his massive head and lean figure outlined in the growing light. "By God," he said without preamble, "you have been sentenced by the court-martial to be shot this morning; but I will be damned if I will have any of the honor of it, or any of the disgrace of it. I have ordered my brigade to take up the line of march, and to leave the camp, for I consider it to be cold-blooded murder!" With a gesture of farewell, he strode away and marched his men off briskly.

This insubordination threw the whole camp into confusion. Lucas called a second court-martial and read to the other generals Doniphan's defiant message: "It is cold-blooded murder. I will not obey your order. My brigade shall march for Liberty tomorrow morning at eight o'clock; and if you execute these men, I will hold you responsible before an earthly tribunal, so help me God."

After some debate Lucas suggested holding the execution in Independence. Doniphan's threat had given him pause, and he needed time to think. But he was determined at least to parade the captive prophet before his Saints, and marched back to Far West in an arrogant gesture of triumph.

This was the bitterest day Far West would ever see. Before the surrender there had been terror, but terror matched by courage and a steadfast resolve to die for the prophet's sake. Now there was only despair. The men slowly stacked their arms in the public square and stood in line to sign away their property to pay for a war that had been none of their making. The women crowded about the prison wagon, watching in silence the anguished leave-taking of the prisoners and their wives. Joseph's mother pushed her way through the crowd as the prison wagon was about to leave, reached through the canvas, and caught her son by the hand. He did not speak. "Joseph," she cried out at last, "I cannot bear to go until I hear your voice."

"God bless you, mother," he answered thickly, as the driver whipped up his horses and galloped them out of the city.

Then the militia went wild. According to Mormon accounts, six thousand men visited Far West in one week. They left nothing. Hogs and cattle they shot for sport, reducing the Mormons, who had been forbidden to leave the city, to a diet of parched corn. The leading elders whom Joseph had warned to flee were hunted down like prairie wolves, and those who resisted capture were shot. Rape went hand in hand with plunder; several girls were bound to the benches in the schoolhouse and violated by a score of men.

After six days of this sport General Clark ordered all the Mormon men into the public square. Fifty-six who were under arrest he ordered off to Richmond for trial. What he said to the remainder the Mormons never forgot:

. . . The character of this state has suffered almost beyond redemption, from the character, conduct, and influence that you have exerted, and we deem it an act of justice to restore her character to its former standing among the states, by every proper means. The orders of the governor to me were, that you should be exterminated, and not allowed to remain in the state, and had your leaders not been given up, and the terms of the treaty complied with, before this, you and your families would have been destroyed. . . .

I do not say that you shall go now, but you must not think of staying here another season, or of putting in crops, for the moment you do this the citizens will be upon you. . . . As for your leaders . . . their doom is sealed. . . . You have always been the aggressors — you have brought upon yourselves these difficulties by being disaffected and not being subject to rule — and my advice is, that you become as other citizens, lest by a recurrence of these events you bring upon yourselves irretrievable ruin.*

On the way to Independence, Joseph began to hope that he and his friends might escape execution altogether. "Be of good cheer, brethren," he encouraged them. "The word of the Lord

* Reprinted in *History of Caldwell and Livingston Counties* (St. Louis, 1886), p. 140.

THE KIRTLAND TEMPLE

LIBERTY JAIL

came to me last night that our lives should be given us." But the threat of death was still so perilously close that when he wrote to Emma just before reaching Independence, he could not mask his foreboding: "Oh Emma for God's sake do not forsake me nor the truth but remember me, if I do not meet you again in this life may God grant that we may meet in heaven. I cannot express my feelings, my heart is full. Farewell, oh my kind and affectionate Emma, I am yours forever your husband and true friend." *

Joseph was exhibited for a day in Independence like some rare animal. There he learned that he was to be sent back to Richmond to stand trial in a civil court for "treason, murder, arson, burglary, robbery, larceny, and perjury." Generals Lucas and Clark had finally been made to see that executing a civilian illegally would have unpleasant consequences.

In the Richmond jail the prisoners were chained together on the floor of a bare cell. Rigdon had contracted a fever from exposure, and the acute tension under which he was suffering brought back his old nervous spasms and fainting. The guards mocked at his delirium, and baited the others with tales of the looting, murder, and raping they had done at Far West.

Parley Pratt was lying next to the prophet late one night when these stories became so foul that he could not close his ears to them. Suddenly, he said, Joseph rose and spoke in a voice of thunder: "Silence, ye fiends of the infernal pit! In the name of Jesus Christ I rebuke you, and command you to be still; I will not live another minute and hear such language. Cease such talk, or you or I die this instant!"

The guards turned away abashed and half-scared. Pratt was overwhelmed. "I have seen ministers of justice," he wrote later in his autobiography, "clothed in magisterial robes, and criminals arraigned before them while life was suspended on a breath . . . but dignity and majesty have I seen but once, as it stood in chains at midnight in a dungeon in an obscure village in Missouri."

After five days the men were unshackled and taken into court. There Joseph was chilled at what he saw. His judge was Austin A. King, who but a week before had demonstrated his

* This letter is in the library of the Reorganized Church, Independence, Missouri.

impartiality by publishing a letter in the *Missouri Argus* accusing the Mormons of arson and murder.* Almost every man
who might have testified in his favor had been arrested and was
on trial. Joseph found missing among them the wily Brigham
Young, the gentle Edward Partridge, and the clowning Heber
Kimball; they alone had escaped the dragnet.

His eyes settled finally on the witnesses for the state. Among
them were the men who had arranged the truce, Corrill, Hinkle, Phelps, and Peck. John Whitmer had joined them. But the
greatest shock was the sight of Sampson Avard, arrogant as
ever, sitting in the witness box, the star performer for the prosecution.

Avard showed himself for what he was, an opportunist and
a coward. He told everything — the founding of the Danites,
the expulsion of the dissenters, the looting of Gallatin and Millport — whitewashing himself as best he could and heaping
blame upon Rigdon and the prophet. As a final triumphant
gesture he produced a document that he said was the Danite
constitution, complete with a list of Danite offices, which included a Secretary of War. This the lawyers pounced upon as
evidence of treason against the state.

The prophet Daniel had once spoken of a stone that rolled
down a mountain smashing everything in its path, a symbol of
God's kingdom, which would one day demolish all earthly governments. Avard, Corrill, and John Whitmer all testified that
the Mormon Church had been likened to this stone. Avard
swore that Lyman Wight had prophesied that the stone would
destroy first the dissenters, then Missouri, then the United
States, whose core was rotten.†

As Joseph listened he realized that Judge King was trying to
draw out evidence that the Mormons had set up a kingdom.
Until this could be established, the charge of treason was ridiculous. But though the apostates agreed in most details about
the Danites and the Mormon plundering, they could offer nothing but rumors about the temporal nature of Joseph's kingdom
of God upon earth.

---

* This letter, dated Richmond, October 24, 1838, was published November 8.

† The complete court record of this trial was published in *Correspondence, Orders,
etc.*, and was also printed as *United States Senate Document 189*, 26th Congress, 2nd
Session, February 15, 1841. Marsh and Hyde had sworn earlier that Joseph intended
to take the United States and "ultimately the whole world." Ibid., pp. 57–9.

Soon militiamen were called to the stand, the majority of whom were so illiterate they could not sign their own testimonies. They complained chiefly of petty thievery and burned cabins, bickering a good deal over identification of the Mormons who had done the raiding. No one remembered seeing the prophet on any raid.

Doniphan, who was lawyer for the Mormons, tried desperately to get his own witnesses on the stand. But it soon became common knowledge that the moment a Mormon witness was named, Captain Bogart hunted him down and arrested him. The defense could muster only six, three of them women, and these were stifled by the judge almost as soon as they began to talk. Doniphan finally gave up. "If a cohort of angels were to come down and declare you innocent," he said to Joseph, "it would make no difference, for King is determined to see you in prison."

King was sitting only as a committing magistrate and made no effort to decide on the prisoners' guilt. He released or admitted to bail all the Mormons but ten. Four were kept in Richmond jail; the other six, including Rigdon and the prophet, were sent to Liberty jail, in Clay County. All were denied writs of habeas corpus, and none was permitted to give bail.

Joseph entered the cramped stone cell of Liberty jail on November 30, 1838. Four months passed before his trial. He bore his imprisonment stoically, almost cheerfully, for there was a serenity in his nature that enabled him to accept trouble along with glory. For the first time in years he had ample leisure for meditation, and the sobering and maturing influence of his enforced idleness can clearly be seen in the series of remarkable letters he dictated to his people and various friends.

In his first letter he denounced Colonel Hinkle as a traitor who had decoyed him unaware, "as the Savior was led, into the camp of His enemies, as a lamb prepared for the slaughter, as a sheep dumb before his shearers." This was the beginning of the legend of the great betrayal, which made the name of Hinkle synonymous with Judas among the Mormons.

Then Joseph took up the charges leveled against him by the old settlers, answering them with skill and tact. For he knew himself to be on trial before his own people. Brigham Young had brought word that many Saints believed him a fallen prophet; Isaac Russell had already set up a little reform church, and Young had had to defend the prophet before the High Council.* Hardest of all for Young to silence had been William Smith, and Brigham winced every time he remembered the hot-headed youth saying that he hoped Joseph would never get out of the hands of his enemies alive. "If I had the disposing of my brother," William had shouted, "I would have hung him years ago!" †

Joseph now wrote to his people a defense and an apology. He did not deny responsibility for the Danites, but blamed Avard for teaching "many false and pernicious things," of which he had been "ignorant as well as innocent." Then, oddly, he chose to deny the ubiquitous rumor of polygamy — though it had not been mentioned in the Richmond trial. Finally he answered the accusation that he was a fallen prophet: "The keys of the kingdom have not been taken away from us, for verily thus saith the Lord, 'Be of good cheer, for the keys that I gave unto you are yet with you. . . . Zion shall yet live, though she seem to be dead.' " ‡

MEANWHILE the torpid Missouri conscience was beginning to stir. When a liberal St. Louis newspaper, the *Missouri Republican Daily,* published details of the Haun's Mill massacre, shocked legislators from that area clamored for an investigation. Letters appeared in the *Republican* demanding an appropriation for the Mormons' rehabilitation as their desperate plight finally won publicity.

The *Republican* exposed also the shameful story of the Daviess County land sales. With the evacuation of Adam-ondi-Ahman, the old settlers had organized a public auction. The town was real loot, for it had an admirable site, and everywhere half-built cabins and granaries bespoke once high hopes and incredible industry. The whole Mormon acreage, with fences, buildings, and improvements, had sold for $1.25 per acre. It would seem, said the editor flatly, that the Mormon oppressors

* *History of the Church,* Vol. III, pp. 224–6.
† See Young's statement in the *Millennial Star,* Vol. XXVII (October 21, 1865), p. 658.
‡ *History of the Church,* Vol. III, pp. 226–33.

"got up this crusade in order to obtain possession of the houses and lands of their victims." *

The Missouri legislature seethed and stuttered. After some pressure, Boggs presented the documents concerning the "Mormon War," which were referred to the Turner Committee for study with a view to their publication. This was the beginning of one of the most egregious whitewashings in the history of American state politics.

The Turner Committee saw at once that it was handling dynamite. The evidence attempting to prove the Mormon leaders guilty of treason was flimsy. The testimonies given at the Richmond trial established the fact of the Danite organization, but for all its tyranny it scarcely had the odor of a revolutionary conspiracy. Even the much-touted Danite constitution turned out to be relatively innocuous. The burnings and pillaging indulged in by the Mormons paled into nothingness beside the hideous story of Haun's Mill. And the Governor's exterminating order stank to heaven.

It was common knowledge that one member of the legislature had participated in the Haun's Mill massacre, and the *Republican* now accused him "of wanting all the facts suppressed." † But no member of the Turner Committee needed pressure to convince him that Missouri's honor was at stake. The decision was unanimous against publication of the documents.

On the day following Turner's report John Corrill read to the assembly a petition from the Mormon people. It was a melancholy catalogue of abuses, ending with a heart-rending plea for justice. Although Corrill was denouncing the Mormon leaders, he had chosen to champion the cause of the Saints themselves, and the legislators listened with respect. Then followed an acrimonious debate which continued intermittently for weeks, until the editor of the *Republican* wrote in exasperation on February 4, 1839: "The very members who first cried loudest for investigation . . . have solemnly declared that they will have no investigation."

The exterminating order was not rescinded. In late Decem-

* See *Missouri Republican Daily*, December 12, 13, 1838.
† Ibid., November 12, 1838.

ber, to aid the Mormons in their departure, the assembly appropriated $2,000. The niggardliness of this sum was thrown into bold relief not long after when the legislature voted $200,000 to pay the militia for the expenses of the Mormon war.

FAR WEST by this time had found a new leader. It was the one piece of luck in a whole avalanche of misfortune that Brigham Young had managed to keep out of jail. More than anything else the Mormons needed a man who looked at their exodus in terms of the supply problem. Young went to work with vigor that swept apathy and despair before it like a tidy broom. At his insistence two hundred of the best-equipped families pooled all their food and equipment to be used for the common good. He dispatched emissaries ahead to make deposits of corn along the route and to negotiate contracts for ferriage. In mid-February he was forced to flee to Illinois to escape arrest, but his foresight was already bearing fruit.

The Saints endured much suffering in the exodus, but luckily the season was stormless and the frozen roads were relatively passable. "The word *impossible* has become *obsolete* with us," Eliza Snow wrote to a friend late in February. "It astonishes our enemies that our people suffer no more while passing through . . . they say that the Mormons are so d—d sure of going to heaven they had as lief die as not." Estimates of the total number of Mormons expelled from Missouri varied all the way from the 8,000 of Eliza Snow to the exaggerated claim of 50,000 made in a rash moment by the prophet.*

Most of the Mormons stopped at Quincy, across the Mississippi River in Illinois, where the citizens extended charity and sympathy. There was a chronic border friction between Missouri and Illinois, and the "Suckers" welcomed the chance to demonstrate a nobility of character foreign to the despised "Pukes." More important, a presidential election was in the offing, and the Democratic Association, which controlled the votes in the Quincy area, was eager to make friends with this huge new voting bloc. Fearful lest the Mormons turn Whig in

---

* See the letter of Eliza Snow to Esqr. Streator, dated February 22, 1839, now in the Western Reserve Historical Society Library, Cleveland. Joseph's estimate was made in a letter to Isaac Galland written from Liberty jail and published in *Times and Seasons*, Vol. I, p. 52. Although Mormon historians generally estimate the number at 12,000 to 15,000 they insist that no more than 800 men were under arms at Far West.

bitterness against the Democratic government in Missouri they solicited funds for relieving the Mormons' distress and did their best to provide housing.

Despite this hospitality, it was clear to everyone that Quincy could absorb but a fraction of the destitute people. The Mormons were faced with the choice of either scattering widely or purchasing as a group several thousand acres of land on credit. The whole frontier tradition encouraged the former. But Joseph's priesthood had become a cohesive power that could not be dissolved by a word. Moreover, suffering had made these people kin.

Real-estate speculators in Illinois looked upon the Mormons as the fairest game that had ever come into the state. Long before all the fugitives had crossed the river, proposals were pouring in. Isaac Galland offered a twenty-thousand-acre tract lying between the Mississippi and Des Moines rivers in the Iowa Territory at two dollars an acre, the sum to be paid in twenty annual installments without interest. This was a part of the Half-Breed Tract, which had been set aside by the federal government for the offspring of the mixed "marriages" common in that area. The half-breeds, with a calculating insouciance, had sold and resold their claims for guns and horses, frequently selling the same claim to a half-dozen different bidders by using forged deeds. The worth of Galland's title to any part of the tract was extremely dubious.*

But the Mormons were as ignorant of this as of Galland's checkered past. His home county in Illinois, Hancock, knew him as a horse-thief and counterfeiter. When he had campaigned for the legislature in 1834, he had openly admitted his association with the notorious Massac criminals, and many voters had been so amused by his honest admission of his dishonest past that they had come very near electing him.†

Posing now as a sympathizer and probable convert, Galland wrote to the prophet in Liberty jail. Impressed, as always, by a facile tongue, Joseph replied with enthusiasm to Galland's commiseration and unctuous praise, and expressed his interest in the tract.‡ Thus it came about that in the first weeks of their arrival

---

* *History of Lee Co., Iowa* (1879), pp. 164–5.
† Thomas Ford: *History of Illinois* (Chicago, 1854), p. 406.
‡ See his letter to Galland, *Times and Seasons*, Vol. I (1840), p. 52.

in Illinois the Mormons began not only to be entangled in a net of fraudulent land deals but also to be sucked into the maelstrom of local politics.

Joseph's lonely months in Liberty jail were punctuated by occasional moments of pleasure and excitement. In the beginning he had visitors. Brigham Young came as often as he dared. Young Porter Rockwell, who had tagged the prophet ever since his early conversion in New York State, appointed himself a guardian and hung about the jail like a shaggy and dangerous watchdog, occasionally bringing the prisoners food and keeping them informed of local happenings. Rockwell, who had the face of a mastiff and the strength of a bear, was a jocose and amiable companion, who lightened the hours with his gossip and earthy humor. The guards good-humoredly tolerated him, unaware of his fabulous skill with a gun and the fierceness of his love for Joseph.

Emma visited the jail twice before leaving the state, bringing the six-year-old Joseph with her. These visits were happy, tender hours, marred only by the swiftness of their passing. When Joseph bade his wife and son a final farewell, he pronounced a blessing upon young Joseph's head with a sad solemnity which the boy never forgot.*

Their departure for Illinois left Joseph with a melancholia which he could not shake off. As the weeks dragged by and it seemed increasingly clear that Joseph and his fellow prisoners were not going to be brought to trial, he lost all faith in Doniphan and the other lawyers — to whom he had guaranteed fees now amounting to sixteen thousand dollars † — who met all his pleas with postponements. There seemed no hope save in an attempted break.

The men planned one night to overpower the jailer when he brought their supper, but by a coincidence six friends arrived for a visit that same evening, and the jailer brought extra guards. Hyrum rushed the jailer as he was admitting the visitors, but in the resulting confusion the friends, who were ignorant of the

* "Memoirs of President Joseph Smith, 1832–1914," *Saints Herald,* Vol. LXXXI (November 6, 1934), p. 1414.

† According to George A. Smith: *Journal of Discourses,* Vol. XIII (October 1868), p. 109.

plans, proved more hindrance than aid, and one guard escaped and slammed the heavy door shut.

The visitors, who were promptly arrested, now looked help-lessly to Joseph for advice. He advised each man to plead his own case. And when one protested: "But I don't understand the law," Joseph said wryly: "Well, go and plead for justice as hard as you can, and quote Blackstone now and then, and they will take it all for law." *

After some weeks the prisoners made a second attempt to win their freedom, this time by loosening the stones and timber in the prison wall. They used smuggled augers for tools, but the timber was tough and the auger handles gave way before the last stone was pried loose. When Rockwell tried to supply them with new tools, the guards became suspicious and discovered the hole. "It was a fine breach," Joseph wrote afterward with satis-faction, "and cost the county a round sum."

To the dirty food, unsanitary and crowded quarters, and the fear of lynching was added a new horror when someone smug-gled poison into the tea and coffee. McRae, who drank neither beverage, escaped, but all who drank them, he said, "were sorely afflicted, some being blind two or three days, and it was only by much faith and prayer that the effect was overcome."

The prison discomforts were borne with fortitude by all the men except Rigdon. His frequent fits were followed by periods of whining that wore on the nerves of the younger men. When on February 25 Doniphan finally succeeded in getting him re-leased on a writ of habeas corpus, the others watched his de-parture with relief. Joseph, whose disillusionment with the older man was now complete, wrote in his journal with con-tempt: "He said that the sufferings of Jesus Christ were a fool to his."

Glad as he was to be rid of him as a prison companion, the prophet was disquieted by thoughts of what Rigdon would do with the Saints in Illinois, and took immediate steps to curb his authority. Beware of "a fanciful and flowery and heated imagination," he wrote to his brethren, and ordered that the af-fairs of the church be transacted by a general conference rather than a single man. Fearful lest Rigdon try to revive the United

* As related by one of the prisoners, Alexander McRae, in the *Deseret News*, October 9, November 1, 1854.

Order and the Danites, he forbade the "organization of large
bodies upon common stock principles, in property, or of large
companies of firms," and warned against "the impropriety of
the organization of bands or companies, by covenants or oaths,
by penalties or secrecies." *

Although Joseph for the first time had the leisure to take
stock of his past errors, he wasted little time in self-reproach
and began spinning the pattern of an even more complicated
metaphysics. "Whether there be one God or many Gods, they
shall be manifest," he wrote to his brethren, suggesting the
richness of revelations to come, "all thrones and dominions,
principalities and powers, shall be revealed . . . also if there
be bounds set to the heavens, or to the seas; or to the dry land,
or to the sun, moon or stars . . . all their glories, laws, and set
times, shall be revealed."

But this time, he decided, there should be no casting of pearls
before swine. Only those men who had proved their loyalty in
the crucible of suffering should be privileged to hear the great
mysteries of the kingdom. This would be particularly true of his
new "patriarchal order of marriage," vulgarly referred to by his
enemies as a "community of wives."

It is doubtful if Joseph was yet clear in his own mind about
just what the ideal marriage order should be. But his long absence from Emma, and his vivid memory of the charming girls
who idolized him from a respectful distance — Eliza Snow,
who wrote long poems in his glory; Louisa Beaman, full-
breasted and disturbingly beautiful; the fiery Nancy Rigdon,
who had testified in his favor with such girlish vehemence at
the Richmond trial — served now to intensify his certainty that
there was a celestial marriage law specially designed for the
glory of his brethren.

Perhaps he remembered his months in Far West at the home
of Lucinda Morgan Harris — who told a friend in later years
that she had been the prophet's mistress — and concluded that
married women as well as virgins must be privileged to join his
own circle of spiritual wives. Queenly young Prescindia Huntington Buell, whose husband had turned against the church,
paid him a visit in jail in February. When she came a second

* *History of the Church*, Vol. III, pp. 295, 301, 303.

time in March and was turned away by the jailer, he wrote her a cryptic and tender letter in which he hinted of a great plan that he would soon unfold to his most faithful followers.*

Joseph's dreams of empire and indulgence were a natural consequence of brooding over his people's suffering and the injustice of his own imprisonment. But there was an intensity in his imagination that transformed the baseless fabric of his reverie into magnificent conviction:

"How long can rolling water remain impure?" he wrote. "What power shall stay the heavens? As well might man stretch forth his puny arm to stop the Missouri river in its decreed course, or to turn it up stream as to hinder the Almighty from pouring down knowledge from heaven, upon the heads of the Latter-day-Saints. What is Boggs or his murderous party, but wimbling willows upon the shore to catch the flood-wood? As well might we argue that water is not water, because the mountain torrents send down mire and roil the crystal stream . . . as to say that our cause is down because renegados, liars, priests, thieves, and murderers, who are all alike tenacious of their crafts and creeds, have poured down, from their spiritual wickedness in high places, and from their strongholds of the devil, a flood of dirt and mire and filthiness and vomit upon our heads.

"No! God forbid. Hell may pour forth its rage like the burning lava of Mount Vesuvius, or of Etna, or of the most terrible of the burning mountains; and yet shall 'Mormonism' stand. Water, fire, truth and God are all realities. Truth is 'Mormonism.' God is the author of it." †

As the days wore on and the frenzied hatred of the old settlers died down, the prisoners became more and more of an embarrassment to the local officials, who were reluctant to bring them to trial lest they be forced to acquit them. Finally, on April 6, 1839, Joseph and his men were taken from Liberty jail and hur-

---

* Letter to Mrs. Norman Bull (*sic*), *History of the Church*, Vol. III, pp. 285–6. Lucinda Harris and Prescindia Buell are both listed by Mormon historians as plural wives of Joseph. See Appendix C.

† These extracts are from a letter written March 25, 1839. See *History of the Church*, Vol. III, pp. 289–305.

ried off to Daviess County, the seat of their alleged crimes. Fearing a rescue party, the guard made a wide detour to avoid Far West, and finally deposited the prisoners in the Gallatin schoolhouse.

Six months earlier Joseph's presence would have been an invitation to hanging, but since the exodus of the Mormons the old settlers had returned to their careless and amiable ways. Having won the war and expropriated the Mormon property, they no longer were concerned over a handful of lives. By day the schoolhouse was full of visitors, curious and not unfriendly. Joseph's lawyer, Peter Burnett, noted that Lyman Wight, whose fierceness had become legendary, was a great favorite. He drank freely with his guards and discussed the recent battles with complete good nature and frankness. "There you rather whipped us," he would admit with a roar of laughter, "but here we licked you fair!" *

The prophet and Wight talked incessantly, Burnett said, and did not sleep at all for several nights. It was not because they had no cots or because the floor they were expected to sleep on was thick with mud — for Liberty jail had been no luxury palace — but rather that the breath of freedom was in their nostrils. Though lean and emaciated from their long idleness and foul food, they had watched the clouds from a horse's saddle instead of through a rusty grate and were infused with a wild new strength.

Burnett reported that almost everyone at the trial was drunk except Joseph, who, though he passed around as much liquor as anyone, kept sober the whole time. Joseph's counsel argued for a change of venue to another county, since it was impossible to get a panel of twelve men in Daviess County who had not been implicated in the Mormon war. The lawyers won their point, and with it Joseph's freedom.

For he knew he could never again return to prison and listen to the tortuous creaking of the machinery of Missouri justice. His lieutenants in the brush were eager to waylay the guard. "If you take a change of venue," Alanson Ripley had written to him, "let me know what county you will come to, and when,

---

* *Recollections and Opinions of an Old Pioneer* (New York, 1880), p. 65. Burnett later went west and became the first Governor of the state of California.

as near as possible, and what road you will come; for I shall be an adder in the path." *

As it turned out, Joseph did not need a rescue party. On the way to Boone County, Hyrum bought a jug of whisky sweetened with honey. To this propitiatory offering Joseph added a bribe of $800.† It was enough. The sheriff obligingly sold them several of the horses, and about twenty-five miles from Adamondi-Ahman — obviously close to Far West — the guard got drunk and went conveniently to sleep. Joseph mounted a fine dark chestnut stallion and with the other prisoners close behind him pounded up the road toward his old settlement, where he joined the last remnant of the Mormons who were headed for the Mississippi.

* *History of the Church*, Vol. III, p. 313. "Adder in the path" is part of the Biblical passage from which the name "Danites" evolved.

† "Memoirs of President Joseph Smith," *Saints Herald*, Vol. LXXXI (November 13, 1934), p. 1454. "Young Joseph" remembered the sheriff coming to collect the $800 from his father. For the vicinity of the escape see Hyrum Smith's account. *History of the Church*, Vol. III, p. 321n.

CHAPTER XVIII
Nauvoo

THERE ARE MORE bends in the Mississippi than even a river rat can remember, with every spring flood erasing some of the old and creating a score of new. But the bend that the Mormons made famous is likely to be as permanent a landmark as any on this fabulous river's course. It lies halfway down the state of Illinois, not far north of and across the river from Keokuk in Iowa. The river bank rises gently here to a point so high that one standing on its summit can see the river cutting a great silver semicircle at one's feet.

When Joseph Smith stood on this hill after his escape from Missouri in 1839, the spot was wooded and trackless and swamps covered the lowlands behind him. But he could see the glistening river with its islands lying to the north like lush garden places, and the green Iowa hills beyond. "It is a beautiful site," he said fervently, "and it shall be called Nauvoo, which means in Hebrew a beautiful plantation."* "Nauvoo" had the melancholy music of a mourning dove's call and somehow matched the magic of the site.

The city saw a growth even more spectacular than had Far West. It was laid out in neat squares, like a checkerboard shaped to fit a hill, with the square on the summit set aside for a temple. Almost at one breath it swallowed up the handful of near-by cabins known as Commerce, whose streets were resurveyed and widened to conform to Joseph's ideal city plan. Within a year after the prophet's coming, Nauvoo boasted two hundred and fifty houses, with scores more building. The timber had been felled, the swamps drained, and the cornerstones laid for an immense temple. Neatly fenced farms fanned out from the city across what had been scrub woods and marsh.

The year took a grievous toll of life. Weakened by a winter

* Professor Louis C. Zucker of the University of Utah has carefully documented Joseph Smith's indebtedness to his Hebrew teacher, Joshua Seixas. See his unpublished "Mormon and Jew; a Meeting on the American Frontier."

of hunger and exposure, the Saints fell easy victim to an epidemic of ague — perhaps typhoid or malaria — and died like flies in the frost. Joseph and Emma gave up their house to the sick and lived in a tent. Emma, who had considerable fame as an herb doctor, went among the stricken administering Sappington's pills, Dover's powders, and various of her own medicines, although she had not yet fully recovered from the birth of a new son, Don Carlos.

Cries for Joseph's prayers were so insistent that at the height of the epidemic he spent most of his days making the rounds of the sick. Usually his mere presence was enough to bring some relief, and occasionally he made spectacular healings. Parley Pratt walked with him one day to the home of Elijah Fordham, who lay swathed in poultices and almost unconscious. "His eyes were sunk in their sockets," Pratt wrote in his autobiography, "his flesh was gone, and the paleness of death was upon him."

"Do you have faith enough to be healed?" Joseph asked him.

"I fear it is too late," Fordham replied weakly. "If you had come sooner, I think I would have been healed."

Taking him by the hand, the prophet cried out in a voice that shook the house: "In the name of Jesus Christ arise and walk!"

Whereupon, said Pratt, "the man leaped from his bed, shook off the poultices and bandages from his feet, put on his clothes so quick that none got a chance to assist him, and taking a cup of tea and a little refreshment, he walked with us from house to house visiting other sick beds."

Joseph described no healings in his journal. For every success there were too many failures, and he could not reproach his people with lack of faith. Eventually the pestilence spent itself, and with the passing of years the stories of Joseph's healings multiplied. It was said that when he was worn out with praying for the sick, he gave his handkerchief to Wilford Woodruff and told him to wipe the faces of the stricken children, who were thereby saved in scores.

Before another year had passed, sickness made its first inroads upon the Smith family. First Joseph's father died, then his younger brother Don Carlos, and finally his newest son, who had been named Don Carlos after his uncle. Despite these sorrows Joseph was planning with undiminished vigor. There was an urgency in his exhortations which had a deeper cause than mere release from the stifling inactivity of Liberty jail. Joseph had come too close to death ever again to live in easy security. He knew now that persecution was as inevitable as the sunrise, and that to it the only answer was power. He intended to make of his church a political force that would command deference and a military force that would maintain peace.

Since he could have neither political nor military power without numbers, he pushed the missionary campaign with a strenuousness that dismayed the sick and poverty-ridden. The twelve apostles had been ordered off to Europe in the summer of 1839, though their cabins were unfinished and several were ill with ague. Brigham Young, gaunt and suffering, had taken leave of his destitute family and started off without strength or money. No one but Joseph could have persuaded him to leave under such wretched circumstances. With prodigious exertion he had brought the Saints out of Missouri and had labored the whole winter to keep them from starving. They had learned to run to him for counsel and had obeyed him implicitly even after Rigdon's arrival. Although Brigham Young was born to command men, he had not tasted the sweetness of such power before and was loath to relinquish it.

Joseph, however, had been eager to recover the prestige and authority that was his in Far West's palmy days. He had seized the reins and held them. Rigdon, feeble and emaciated from his months in jail and prey to every chill and fever that swept through Nauvoo, had been no rival.

The prophet predicted that Nauvoo would soon become the biggest city west of the Appalachians. Although it was above some river rapids which prevented the largest steamers from going north of Warsaw, he planned to remedy this by building a wing dam in the Mississippi, which would also make an ideal harbor and furnish water power for Nauvoo industry. Until it could be built he decided to have a Mormon port in Warren, just south of Warsaw, which could easily be connected with Nauvoo by rail.

Warsaw was jealous of the phenomenal Mormon city, fearful lest the new sect snatch all the political offices of Hancock County and rob her of her trade. Mormon occupation of Warren was a grave threat to Warsaw's prosperity, since the Warsaw

THE NAUVOO TEMPLE

LIEUTENANT-GENERAL JOSEPH SMITH

From an early portrait published in John C. Bennett's History of the Saints
(1842)

harbor was filling up with sandbars, and Warren provided the nearest landing-place. When the editor of the Warsaw newspaper learned of Mormon purchases in the vicinity, he wrote: "We sincerely hope this *curse* will be spared us."

The Warsaw paper, however, was the only unfriendly one in Illinois. The press all over the country was sympathizing with the Saints, for Joseph, resolving to make Missouri a byword for oppression and Boggs a synonym for tyranny, saw to it that the sufferings of his people received national publicity. The new Mormon paper, *Times and Seasons,* published eyewitness stories of the Haun's Mill massacre and exhaustive accounts of the expulsion, and copies were sent to all the leading American newspapers.

Noting the success of this publicity, the editor of the *Chicago Democrat* wrote sagely: "We will not go so far as to call the Mormons martyr-mongers, but we believe they are men of sufficient sagacity to profit by anything in the shape of persecution. . . . The Mormons have greatly profited by their persecution in Missouri. . . . let Illinois repeat the bloody tragedies of Missouri and one or two other states follow, and the Mormon religion will not only be known throughout our land, but will be very extensively embraced." *

Determined to secure justice, Joseph started for Washington in November 1839, armed with hundreds of affidavits and petitions. "It will be a long and lonesome time during my absence from you," he wrote back to Emma, "but shall I see so many perish and not seek redress? So I will try this once in the name of the Lord." †

In Washington he ran headlong into the most delicate and dangerous of all problems perplexing the American government, the issue of states' rights, which eventually he came to call "a stink in the nostrils of the Almighty." The Southern states were pathologically jealous of their sovereignty, and the balance between slave state and free hung by so fragile a thread that the boldest statesman dared not tamper with it. When Joseph called on President Van Buren, he was met with complete candor on this point: "I can do nothing for you. If I do

---

* March 25, 1840.

† The original of this letter, dated Springfield, Illinois, November 9, 1839, is on file in the library of the Reorganized Church.

anything, I shall come in contact with the whole state of Missouri." *

Van Buren expressed sympathy, however, as did the members of Congress whom the prophet interviewed, and promised to consider his case. But it soon became evident that with a presidential election in the offing few politicians — and particularly few Democrats — wanted to antagonize Missouri. Joseph wrote back bitterly to Nauvoo that the ruling principles in Washington were personal aggrandizement and popular clamor. Pending the decision of the Senate Judiciary Committee, to whom the Mormon petitions were given, he went to Philadelphia to consult with Parley Pratt, leaving the details in the hands of his able lawyer, Elias Higbee.

Meanwhile the Congressmen from Missouri, alarmed by Mormon demands for two million dollars in damages, began feverishly talking in their own behalf. Boggs sent to Washington a transcript of the damaging testimony given at Joseph's trial in Richmond.† This provided sufficient excuse for the Judiciary Committee to forget Boggs's exterminating order and the Haun's Mill massacre. Eventually Higbee was informed that redress must be sought in Missouri courts.

Henry Clay and John T. Stuart, Whig Senator from Illinois, tried to win a hearing for the Mormon petitions on the floor of Congress, but were voted down. When Joseph returned to Washington and once more appealed to Van Buren, the President replied with a phrase that typified the attitude of every American president from Van Buren to Lincoln when faced with an injustice that touched on slavery: "Sir, your cause is just, but I can do nothing for you."

Isaac Galland had set out to milk the Mormons dry. After getting properly baptized he wormed his way into Joseph's confidence and became his chief land agent. Joseph had already purchased from him $18,000 worth of land in and about Nauvoo, giving him Mormon-owned Missouri land in payment. He had also exchanged Missouri land for $80,000 worth of Gal-

---

* *History of the Church*, Vol. IV, p. 40.

† This was printed as *U.S. Senate Document 189*, 26th Congress, 2nd Session, February 1841. See Higbee's letters to Joseph Smith, *History of the Church*, Vol. IV, pp. 81-8.

land's Half-Breed lands in Iowa.* Galland's title to the Nauvoo tract was genuine, but his deeds to the Iowa territory were all forged.

Months passed before Galland's perfidy came to light. During this time he negotiated the purchase of two farms from Hugh and William White, costing $9,000, and an expensive 500-acre tract from the Hotchkiss syndicate costing $53,000. Notes for this property were signed by Joseph, Hyrum, and Sidney Rigdon.

Joseph was in absolute control of all land sales to his people. The High Council voted him treasurer of the church, and then bestowed the title of "Trustee-in-Trust" with power "to receive, acquire, manage, or convey property, real, personal, or mixed, for the sole use and benefit of said Church." Eventually he also became registrar of deeds, from which position he could lay his thumb on any clandestine sales.†

He fixed the average price of the Nauvoo city lot at five hundred dollars. To those who had been invalided from wounds received in Missouri he gave lots free. The attractive Sarah Cleveland, who with her husband had befriended him on his trip from Missouri to Illinois, was given a lot on the river directly across the street from his own, which fronted on the Mississippi at its most picturesque point.‡

To pay for the vast acreages he had contracted to buy, the prophet devised an ingenious system of land exchange. New converts in the East were advised to turn over their property to the church through his agents, Isaac Galland and William Smith (who had once more been forgiven and reinstated as an apostle). These agents in return gave orders on land in and about Nauvoo. The Eastern property was then either sold outright or transferred to the Hotchkiss syndicate in payment on the $53,000 debt.

The system had a bad defect in the high interest rate on the loans, which on the Hotchkiss purchase amounted to $6,000 in two years. To meet the interest Joseph had to make considerable profit on the land he sold to his own people. As a result the

---

* See Galland's letter to S. Swasey, July 22, 1839, now on file in Independence, Missouri, and *History of the Church*, Vol. IV, p. 270.

† *History of the Church*, Vol. IV, pp. 286–7, 543.

‡ Ibid., Vol. IV, p. 17; Vol. III, p. 362. Mrs. Cleveland was later listed by Mormon historians as one of Joseph's plural wives. See Appendix C.

rumor that he was "enriching himself on the spoils of the brethren" gained such proportions that it had to be officially denied in a church conference.*

When Galland went east to pay the interest to Hotchkiss and arrange for deeding Eastern lands to cover the whole debt, he absconded with the money. Joseph revoked his agency and sent out agents to catch up with him, writing to Hotchkiss in despair: "Why he has not done according to my instructions God only knows!" Eventually the man came back to Nauvoo and made some kind of restitution, but the damage inflicted on the land-exchange system was irreparable.

The full measure of Galland's double-dealing was not felt, however, until late in 1841, when the whole tangled litigation concerning the Half-Breed Tract was finally straightened out and his deeds proved worthless in the courts. Men who had escaped from Missouri and gone to Iowa with some little means were now reduced to beggary. A year's labor had been lost, and most of the two hundred and fifty families that had settled across the river came back penniless to Nauvoo.†

Joseph continually urged the industrialization of his city. Newcomers from the East and from England were told to put their capital into mills instead of land, and Joseph set up the Nauvoo Agricultural and Manufacturing Association, with a capital stock of $100,000, to co-ordinate all Mormon economic activity. Within two years the city had two big steam sawmills, a steam flour mill, a tool factory, and a foundry. Plans were laid for a chinaware factory, to be manned by English converts from the Staffordshire potteries.

Farmer converts who had no money for land were allowed to raise crops on a huge community farm just outside Nauvoo. Laborers and skilled craftsmen who lacked employment worked on the temple. Although their pay was uncertain and consisted of donated food and clothing, work on the huge structure was always a labor of love. All Nauvoo men were expected to spend each tenth day working there or else to give the equiv-

---

* *History of the Church,* Vol. IV, pp. 391, 437. The apostate William Harris said that ". . . lots that scarcely cost him a dollar are frequently sold for a thousand," *Mormonism Portrayed* (Warsaw, Illinois, 1841), p. 35. (Harris' book actually was written by Thomas Sharp, in part on information provided by Harris. See the *Warsaw Signal,* September 11, 1844.)

† *Hawk-Eye and Patriot* (Montrose, Iowa), October 7, 1841.

alent in goods or money. One group was sent up the Mississippi to the Wisconsin pineries, where they spent several winters cutting timber for the Lord's house.

Joseph's autarchic control was not, however, taken completely for granted. A city ordinance forbidding anyone to set up a business in Nauvoo without a license from the city council — which the prophet dominated — aroused so much resentment that it was repealed in May 1842. But Joseph himself felt that in matters of business as well as the spirit he was answerable to no one.

In January 1841 he presented to the church a revelation from God ordering the Saints to build a hotel. The extraordinarily mundane details of this commandment seem not to have troubled his people: ". . . And they shall not receive less than fifty dollars for a share of stock in that house, and they shall be permitted to receive fifteen thousand dollars from any one man for stock in that house. But they shall not be permitted to receive over fifteen thousand dollars from any one man. . . . And if they do appropriate any portion of that stock anywhere else, only in that house, without the consent of the stockholder, and do not repay fourfold for the stock which they appropriate anywhere else, only in that house, they shall be accursed, and shall be moved out of their place, saith the Lord God; for I, the Lord, am God, and cannot be mocked in any of these things." * The revelation then went on guilelessly to grant Joseph a suite of rooms in the hotel for himself and his posterity "from generation to generation, for ever and ever."

Joseph had somehow succeeded in welding two antithetical principles — he had come to identify the goodness of God with the making of money — and had succeeded in making the union palatable to his Saints.

Embedded in Joseph's character was the commonplace Yankee mixture of piety and avarice. But this seed he developed to a special flowering. The true mystic is preoccupied with things of the spirit, and in so far as he concerns himself with worldly affairs he denies his calling. But in Joseph's revelations lessons on the nature of God and guidance for the operation of a boarding house sit side by side — like Hyperion and the satyr — enthroned in equal majesty.

* *Doctrine and Covenants*, Section 124.

THE MORMON apostles who went to England had seen America's worst panic, and thought they knew something about the poverty attendant upon economic depression. But in England they found in addition to financial chaos and unemployment the appalling housing of the urban slums and a fearful burden of taxes weighing on the thin shoulders of the poor. The hated Corn Laws were still in force, stifling trade and doubling the cost of bread. Thousands of workers were crowded into squat tenements, built without water or sewers, and almost without windows. Sporadic strikes were suppressed with vicious cruelty, and the reform movement known as Chartism was looked upon as the dread specter of revolution. George A. Smith wrote back to Nauvoo: "I have seen more beggars here in one day than I saw in all my life in America." *

Shocked by what they found, the Mormon elders began to preach the glory of America along with the glory of the gospel. Brigham Young was convinced that emigration was the only solution for Europe's "overpopulation" and made this the theme of many of his sermons. Soon the missionaries were publishing in Liverpool a little journal called the *Millennial Star,* which frequently had the ring of a real-estate agency propaganda pamphlet:

Living [in America] is about one-eighth of what it costs in this country . . . millions on millions of acres of land lie before them unoccupied, with a soil as rich as Eden, and a surface as smooth, clear and ready for the plough as the park scenery of England. Instead of a lonely swamp or dense forest filled with savages, wild beasts and serpents, large cities and villages are springing up in their midst, with schools, colleges, and temples . . . there being abundant room for more than a hundred millions of inhabitants.†

Before long the apostles were converting Englishmen in thousands. Their success loosed a deluge of anti-Mormon pamphlets. Even the sophisticated London *Athenæum* took note of the new sect. "Mormonism is making rapid progress," it pointed out on April 3, 1841, "particularly in the manufacturing districts, and it is also spreading in Wales. Furthermore, its converts are not made from the lowest ranks; those sought and obtained by the Mormonite apostles are mechanics and trades-

---

* *Times and Seasons,* Vol. I (November 15, 1840), p. 223.
† *Millennial Star,* February 1, 1842.

men who have saved a little money, who are remarkable for their moral character, but who are exposed to the delusion from having, as Archbishop Sharpe expressed it, 'studied the Bible with an ill-balanced mind.' "

Only London was deaf to the call to Zion. Heber Kimball worked there for weeks before he washed its dust from his heels and consigned it to the devil. "We found the whole city given to covetousness," he wrote home, ". . . and all doors closed against us. We did not hesitate to stand in the midst of the streets and, Jonah-like, cry repentance unto the inhabitants . . . who are ripening in iniquity and preparing for the wrath of God, and like the ox going to the slaughter, know not the day of their visitation."

Two hundred converts left England for Nauvoo in 1840. In 1841 the number jumped to 1,200 and the following year to 1,600. "They had rather be slaves in America than starve in this country," wrote Parley Pratt. "I cannot keep them back." By 1844 there were at least 8,000 more clamoring to leave.*

Few apostles remained in Britain more than a year. But before they left their work in the hands of lesser men, they had organized an emigration system which became so well known for its honesty and efficiency that it was cited in the House of Commons as a model for other companies to follow. The Mormons set up an office, chartered their own ships, organized the emigrants so that there would be ample food and water, and charged less than four pounds for the journey all the way to New Orleans.

Much of the credit for the success of the emigration system was due Brigham Young, whose business head was one of the soundest in the church. He had been one of the first apostles to return to Nauvoo, and it was from there that he directed the missionary enterprise. And within a month after his return he had persuaded the prophet to shift all the business affairs of the church from the High Council over to the apostles. Joseph, however, still retained the ultimate authority in financial matters.

* See the emigration statistics compiled by James Linforth in *Route from Liverpool to Great Salt Lake Valley* (1855), pp. 14–15; George J. Adams: *A Few Plain Facts,* etc. (Bedford, England, 1841), p. 15; Joseph F. Smith, Jr.: *The Origin of the Reorganized Church* (Salt Lake City, 1907), p. 8.

It was a long time before Young succeeded in straightening out Nauvoo's chaotic finances, for Joseph's investments too often returned nothing. Although many rich converts trusted the prophet with their fortunes,* still he remained in debt. In the spring of 1841 he catalogued a list of his outstanding liabilities and found them to total over $70,000, in addition to another $33,000 carried over from Kirtland days.† It is not surprising, therefore, that he looked with interest upon the bankruptcy law that Congress passed in 1841 to relieve the straits of the debtor class.

No one in Washington, apparently, had any foresight as to the fabulous popularity of this bankruptcy law. In the brief period of its operation four hundred and forty millions of liabilities were wiped out for forty-four millions of assets. When Congress went back into session, it repealed the law in haste. But in the meantime the Mormon prophet, together with his brothers Hyrum and Samuel, and a host of leading Mormon dignitaries, had joined the stampede.‡

It was an evil day in the summer of 1840, some months after his return from Washington, that Joseph baptized into the church Dr. John Cook Bennett. He had been an instructor in "midwifery" in an obscure Ohio college, and was now secretary of the Illinois Medical Society and quartermaster general of the Illinois militia. He was thirty-five — the same age as the prophet

---

* Upon his arrival in Nauvoo Edward Hunter, third bishop of the church, unhesitatingly handed over to Joseph $7,000 in cash and $4,000 in merchandise. *Improvement Era*, Vol. XLIV (August 1941), p. 493.

† To the United States of America, September 10, 1840	$ 4,866.38
To Horace R. Hotchkiss and Co., Fair Haven, Conn.	50,000.00
To John Wilkie, Nauvoo	2,700.00
To Wm. Backenstos and Jacob Backenstos, Carthage	1,000.00
To John ? (name illegible)	1,100.00
To Truman Blodget	100.00
To William F. Cahoon, Nauvoo	500.00
To Edward Partridge's estate, Nauvoo	10,000.00
To Amos Davis, Nauvoo	2,800.00
	$73,066.38

These debts were copied from a "Schedule setting forth a list of petitioners, creditors, their residence and the amount due each," which is in the library of the Reorganized Church. The Kirtland debts have already been listed on page 201.

‡ See the notice of Joseph's bankruptcy proceedings in the *Wasp* (Nauvoo, Illinois), May 7, 1842. See also *History of the Church*, Vol. IV, pp. 594, 600; Vol. V, pp. 6–7, 200.

—but his short, dapper figure and dark complexion were in striking contrast with Joseph's blond and careless magnificence. Emma distrusted Bennett's easy, vivacious manner and facile tongue from the beginning, whereas Joseph was immediately attracted.

Before coming to Nauvoo, Bennett had written the prophet a barrage of letters proclaiming his own special virtues with the kind of extravagant rhetoric that most easily blinded Joseph to a man's true character. The prophet had drawn up a series of charters incorporating the city of Nauvoo, providing for a university, and calling for the organization of a militia body to be called the Nauvoo Legion. The city charter gave the Nauvoo city council power to "make, ordain, establish and execute all such ordinances not repugnant to the Constitution of the United States or of this State," an ingenious wording which Joseph later interpreted in the widest possible sense. The Nauvoo Legion was to be technically a part of the state militia, but actually an autonomous military body whose commander would be answerable only to the Governor. Bennett vowed he could push these charters through the Illinois legislature.

The Mormons at the moment were in a strategic position for bargaining for legislative favor. Soured on the Democratic Party by Van Buren's indifference, they had voted the straight Whig ticket in the election of November 1840, except for one candidate. In order to give their votes to a Democrat, James H. Ralston, who had done the prophet some favors, they scratched the name which happened to be last on the Whig list. The spurned candidate was an obscure young politician named Abraham Lincoln.*

Despite this demonstration of Whig preference, Joseph Smith made it clear that his people would join neither party, but would hold themselves free to vote according to services rendered. As a result, the legislative session of 1840–1 saw each party stumbling over the other in its frantic efforts to win the Mormon vote, which by now counted heavily in the balance of Illinois politics.

Bennett introduced himself to the leaders of both parties, and cozened them equally with promises of Mormon favor. The charters were rushed through both houses and passed by a voice

* *History of the Church*, Vol. IV, p. 248.

vote without ever being read, except by title. Bennett wrote back exultingly to the prophet: "Every power we asked has been granted, every request gratified, every desire fulfilled." Even Lincoln, he said, "had the magnanimity to vote for our act, and came forward, after the final vote to the bar of the house, and cordially congratulated me on its passage." *

The winning of the Nauvoo charters was Joseph's first great political victory, and it made him feel immeasurably obligated to Bennett. It is therefore not surprising that when ugly rumors of the man's debauchery and profligacy caught up with him in Nauvoo Joseph hastily dismissed them. When Hyrum learned on a trip east that Bennett had deserted a wife and two children and had been expelled from the Masonic lodge for unprincipled conduct, he wrote of it to Joseph,† but the prophet filed the letter in his drawer.

Less than one year after his coming to Nauvoo, Bennett had become "assistant president" of the church. Rigdon had never been deposed as First Counselor, but he had been practically bedridden since his release from jail, and Bennett assumed all his duties. In addition, Bennett became mayor of the city, chancellor of the University of Nauvoo, and brigadier-general of the Nauvoo Legion, second in command to Joseph. In a revelation the Lord had pronounced him blessed: "I have seen the work which he hath done, which I accept if he continue, and will crown him with blessings and great glory." ‡

Bennett was Joseph's most intimate friend and counselor for a year and a half. Although during this period Nauvoo was fast becoming the most notorious city in Illinois, outwardly it was a model of propriety. There was not a saloon in the city, and if a man wanted to drink he had to buy his whiskey from a shop specially licensed by the mayor and take it home with him. "If you want to retire from the noise of the Bacchanalian's song," said the *Times and Seasons,* "the midnight broils, and the scenes of drunkenness which disgrace so many of our cities and villages, come to Nauvoo — No such proceedings are allowed." §

For a time the city did have a brothel, which stood but a

* Letter from Springfield, December 16, 1840. *History of the Church*, Vol. IV, p. 248. See also Thomas Ford: *History of Illinois*, p. 263.
† *History of the Church*, Vol. V, p. 37.
‡ Ibid., Vol. IV, p. 341, and *Doctrine and Covenants*, Section 124, verse 17.
§ *Times and Seasons*, Vol. II (Aug. 2, 1841), p. 496.

square away from the temple, using a grocery store as a front. But when urchins scrawled witticisms over its rough boards and an unfriendly editor in Montrose, Iowa, slyly accused the prophet of abetting the "lonely wreck of folly," the Nauvoo city council pronounced it a nuisance — over the protests, it was said, of the worldly John C. Bennett — and a deputation of the Legion tipped it backwards over the edge of a gully, where it went crashing to the bottom.*

Nauvoo's self-righteous holiness did not endear her to her sister cities. They resented the pious-speaking city council, which would pass an ordinance threatening vagrants, idle persons, and those who could not "give a good account of themselves" with a five-hundred-dollar fine and a six-months jail sentence merely for indulgence in "profane or indecent language." † Did a sect have the right to impose its own standards on the casual visitor? they asked. Or was not this ordinance a device to keep non-Mormons out of the city? What were these "Saints" so anxious to hide?

The epithet "community of wives" came more and more to be applied to the holy city. So prominent an organ as the *New York Herald* on May 16, 1842 reported the rumor that in Nauvoo men and women "connected in promiscuous intercourse without regard to the holy bonds of matrimony." The lone Presbyterian minister in Hancock County wrote to a fellow pastor on May 3, 1842: "I presume Nauvoo is as perfect a sink of debauchery and every species of abomination as ever were Sodom or Nineveh." ‡

Stories of thievery, from whatever source, were pinned upon the Mormons by the outlying communities, and it became common gossip that Joseph himself sanctioned "milking the gentiles." The latter rumor the prophet combated strenuously. Hancock County had always been a hide-out for river pirates, and a few of these doubtful citizens joined the Mormons, expecting to find shelter from the law in the church's bosom. Joseph excommunicated as many as he could catch and denounced the use of his name as a shield for their infamy.

* Ibid., Vol. III (November 15, 1841), p. 599, and the *Wasp*, Vol. I, No. 26 (October 15, 1842).

† *Times and Seasons*, Vol. III (December 1, 1841), p. 622.

‡ Letter from the Reverend W. M. King to Absolom Peters, published in the *Illinois State Historical Society Journal*, Vol. XXXII, No. 2 (June 1939).

Few thoughtful persons believed that Nauvoo was either a den of debauchery or a hide-out for Mississippi outlaws. James Gordon Bennett, the urbane editor of the *New York Herald*, though not shy about printing salacious insinuations concerning the city, was always careful to print Mormon denials alongside, and in his editorials usually sided with the Mormon point of view. This Bennett took a peculiar interest in Joseph Smith and gave him extraordinarily good publicity. Said one editorial on January 19, 1842:

Here is a new prophet, starting into existence in the green valleys and lovely little hills of the town of Manchester, in Ontario County, New York — leaving New York as Moses left Egypt — wandering over the wild prairies of the west, as the great Jewish lawgiver wandered over the wilderness of Zion — and ultimately establishing a holy city and a new religious empire on the Mississippi, that numbers 10,000 persons in the city and 30,000 beyond its limits — with a splendid temple for public worship — and a military organization of 1500 "pretty well" disciplined troops.

This presents a germ of religious civilization, novel, affecting, inviting, wonderful, and extraordinary. . . . all the priests and philosophers of the day may take a lesson from Joe Smith, who seems to have hit the nail exactly on the head, by uniting faith and practice — fancy and fact — religion and philosophy — heaven and earth, so as to form the germ of a new religious civilization, bound together in love and temperance — in industry and energy — that may revolutionize the whole earth one of these days. Joe Smith is evidently no fool — he knows what he is about. Go ahead, old boy.

Few visitors to Nauvoo had either the New York editor's perception or his imagination, or had any idea of the potentialities of the Mormon movement. But many of them were troubled by the unmistakable military atmosphere that pervaded the city. Every village in the state had its militia group, which paraded on muster days in a carelessly impromptu fashion and made a beeline for the tavern when the dusty marching was over. The Nauvoo Legion, however, looked upon itself as the army of the Lord, drilled regularly and strenuously, and boasted smartly uniformed officers. Every able-bodied man between eighteen and forty-five was compelled to join, and heavy fines were imposed for failure to appear at parade. By January 1842 the Legion had a complement of 2,000 men.

John Cook Bennett used his position as quartermaster general of the Illinois militia to secure three pieces of cannon and about two hundred and fifty stand of small arms, which alarmed gentile rumor increased to thirty pieces of cannon and some five or six thousand muskets. Bennett took care to organize the Legion as a corps of riflemen, whereas the older units in the state were armed chiefly with swords and muskets.* Fancying himself a peerless strategist, he was never so pleased as when he was likened to Napoleon.

Joseph requested — and received — from Governor Carlin the commission of lieutenant-general and thereafter frequently jested about his outranking every military officer in the United States. He came to prefer the title "General" even to "President" and used it in much of his correspondence. His uniform was smartly designed: a blue coat with a plentiful supply of gold braid, buff trousers, high military boots, and a handsome chapeau topped with ostrich feathers. On his hip he carried a sword and two big horse-pistols. Delighting in the pomp and splendor of parades, he called out the Legion on every possible occasion, marching at the head on his magnificent black stallion, Charlie.

The military spirit infected all the boys in Nauvoo, and Joseph, with his eye ever on the future, soon had them organized into a military corps of their own. Between four and six hundred paraded and drilled with as much zest as their fathers.

Joseph's eldest son, who was a member of the boys' army, took part on the memorable occasion when they decided to invade Nauvoo. The Legion, prepared to give the boys a good scare, lined up to meet them. The men did not know that the youthful corps had raided their mothers' kitchens for every available pot and pan in the city, and when the boys charged out of the woods, beating on the kettles and shrieking, the Legion horses went into a panic and refused to charge. Finally the prophet, who was watching the scene mounted on the imperturbable Charlie, spurred the big stallion forward, squarely into the oncoming boys. They scattered nimbly, the invasion repelled, and the prophet became the hero of the day.†

* See Thomas Ford: *History of Illinois*, p. 267, and *Times and Seasons*, Vol. II, p. 419.
  † "Memoirs of President Joseph Smith," *Saints Herald*, January 1, 1935, p. 16.

The Legion was no mere toy to gratify Joseph's love of pageantry. It was first of all a bulwark against Missouri, for legally the prophet was still a fugitive from justice and could expect writs to be served on him without warning. As time wore on and rumors of the coming of Missouri sheriffs trickled persistently into Nauvoo, Joseph came to fear extradition more than anything else in the world.

In mid-September 1840 the first sheriff materialized, bearing a writ for Joseph from Governor Reynolds of Missouri, reinforced by a demand from the Illinois Governor, Thomas Carlin. When Joseph learned of the sheriff's approach, he immediately went into hiding. The sheriff returned the writ to Carlin and made no further effort to catch his prey.

Thereafter Joseph appointed a bodyguard of twelve men, his toughest fighters and most devoted friends. Among them were Porter Rockwell, William Hickman, Hosea Stout, Jonathan Holmes, and John D. Lee. The bodyguard, dressed in white uniforms, made a pretty sight marching and wheeling about the uniformed figure of their chief in Legion parades. Apparently this group was the sole remnant of the Danite band, though not all of the bodyguard had been Danites in Missouri. Lee, who called himself the Seventh Danite, was appointed to guard Joseph's home. "It was my duty to do as I was ordered," he wrote in his autobiography, "and not ask questions."

Eight months after the coming of the first sheriff from Missouri, a second one appeared, supported by a posse. They intercepted Joseph when he was returning unescorted to Nauvoo after a visit with Governor Carlin, who apparently knew and approved the plan in advance. The seizure was a virtual kidnaping. Not until he was carried into Quincy, the last town between him and a Missouri dungeon, was he able to obtain a writ of habeas corpus.

This respite was enough to save him. Stephen A. Douglas, judge of the Illinois Supreme Court, who happened to be in Quincy, offered to test the validity of the Missouri writ in near-by Monmouth. Then three prominent Whig lawyers — who suspected Douglas's motive to be largely political, since he was nominal head of the Illinois Democratic Party — rushed to Monmouth for the privilege of defending the prophet. With both political parties behind him, Joseph had little to fear.

Douglas freed him on a technicality, decreeing that the writ was dead since it had been returned to the Governor in September 1840. He refused to judge the case on its merits, there being no precedent to guide him on the issue of extradition, which involved, he said, "great and important considerations relative to the future conduct of the different states."

Joseph was free, but he was still a fugitive and could never be certain that the whole process would not one day be repeated, with the judge deciding against him. To meet this day, he planned to have an army in reserve.

John C. Bennett, however, looked upon the Legion with a much more aggressive imagination. In *Times and Seasons* he published a series of articles under the pseudonym "Joab, General in Israel," which made it clear that the Mormon Church was now a power capable of avenging the wrongs inflicted upon it — by the sword if need be.

At first Bennett's column was largely allegory and bombast. But it evolved into a hard-knuckled challenge to Missouri for restitution of Mormon property: "The blood of murdered Mormons cries aloud for help, and the restoration of the inheritances of the saints; and God has heard the cry — and if the *moral* battle *must* be fought, and the victory won, he who answers by fire will cause *sword and flame* to do their office, and again make the Constitution and Laws paramount to every other consideration — and I swear by the Lord God of Israel, that the sword shall not depart from my thigh, nor the buckler from my arm, until the trust is consummated, and the hydra-headed, fiery dragon slain." *

Bennett's columns enraged the gentiles and gave substance to the spreading idea that the Mormons intended to recapture their lost property by the sword. By accident or design, a United States artillery officer witnessed a full-dress parade of the Legion in Nauvoo on May 7, 1842. To the *New York Herald,* which published his article on June 17, he wrote excitedly:

What does all this mean? Why this exact discipline of the Mormon corps? Do they intend to conquer Missouri, Illinois, Mexico? It is true they are a part of the militia of the State of Illinois, by the charter of their Legion, but then there are no troops in the States like

* *Times and Seasons,* Vol. III (March 15, 1842), p. 724.

them in point of enthusiasm and warlike aspect, yea warlike character. Before many years this Legion will be twenty, and perhaps fifty
thousand strong, and still augmenting. A fearful host, filled with religious enthusiasm, and led on by ambitious and talented officers,
what may not be effected by them? Perhaps the subversion of the
constitution of the United States, and if this should be considered
too great a task, foreign conquest will certainly follow. Mexico will
fall into their hands, even if Texas should first take it. . . .

I have seen his [Bennett's] plans for the fortification of Nauvoo,
which are equal to any of Vauban's. . . . The time will come when
this gathering host of religious fanatics will make this country shake
to its centre. A western empire is certain!

CHAPTER XIX
Mysteries of the Kingdom

A MAN's MEMORY is bound to be a distortion of his past in accordance with his present interests, and the most faithful autobiography is likely to mirror less what a man was than what he has become. Joseph Smith always dictated his journal with an intense consciousness of his audience, and in the 1840's, when he began in earnest to write the official history of his church for the edification of posterity, he reconstructed his past as only a celebrated prophet of the nineteenth century would have lived it. It was all of one color, a succession of miracles and revelations, and in no sense an evolution. It became, in fact, an almost impenetrable hiding-place, where he concealed himself behind a perpetual flow of words.

He began the story of his life with the fabulous vision of the Father and the Son, which in 1842, when the account was first published, dated back twenty-two years.* Whether this was an elaboration upon a vivid childhood dream or a fantasy woven out of half-remembered miracle tales does not matter. Dream images came easily to him and with such intense color and luxuriant detail that the matter of accuracy or chronology was of no importance. When he described the vision in a letter to John Wentworth, editor of the *Chicago Democrat,* who had requested the story of his life, it was a thing of substance in his memory.

As his fame increased, Joseph became more and more preoccupied with the record of his life. Everything in his past was interpreted to enhance the glory of the present. "The history must continue and not be disturbed," he wrote, "as there are but few subjects that I have felt a greater anxiety about." †

The Book of Mormon must have been a source of secret worry. Later editions had corrected many of the errors in gram-

* It was first printed in *Times and Seasons,* Vol. III, March 1, 1842, though a short account by Orson Pratt was published in *Remarkable Visions* in 1840.
† *History of the Church,* Vol. VI, p. 66.

mar and spelling, but the book was still being challenged by critical readers. As editor of *Times and Seasons* Joseph published extracts from Ethan Smith, Josiah Priest, and Alexander von Humboldt and urged his people to read Stephens's *Incidents of Travel in Central America,* all of which seemed to corroborate the Book of Mormon story.*

All of the golden plate "witnesses" save his two brothers, Samuel and Hyrum, had either died or left the church. Oliver Cowdery had carried off one copy of the manuscript when he apostatized, leaving the other as the only tangible reminder of the book's origin. This manuscript Joseph decided to bury in the cornerstone of the Nauvoo House, along with a few other relics, and interrupted the ceremony of laying the stone in order to bring the manuscript from his home. Ebenezer Robinson was shocked to hear him say as he flipped through the pages to make sure it was complete: "I have had trouble enough with this thing." †

Joseph never apologized for the Book of Mormon. He called it bluntly "the most correct of any book on earth, and the keystone of our religion." There is no doubt, however, that he could be stung by barbs aimed at it. Eber D. Howe had once pointed out that the name Mormon came from a Greek word meaning "monster" and in modern usage referred to a particularly hideous baboon. Throughout the years this bit of philological research had been repeated over and again by anti-Mormon writers, until finally Joseph countered it with a little research — and imagination — of his own:

It has been stated that this word was derived from the Greek word *mormo.* This is not the case. There was no Greek or Latin upon the plates from which I, through the grace of God, translated the Book of Mormon. . . . We say from the Saxon, *good;* the Dane, *god;* the Goth, *goda;* the German, *gut;* the Dutch, *goed;* the Latin, *bonus;* the Greek, *kalos;* the Hebrew, *tob;* and the Egyptian, *mon.* Hence, with the addition of *more,* or the contraction *mor,* we have the word Mormon; which means, literally, *more good.*‡

* See *Times and Seasons,* June 15, July 15, and August 15, 1842.

† *The Return,* Vol. II (August 1890), p. 315.

‡ *Times and Seasons,* Vol. IV (May 15, 1843), p. 194. The bulk of this essay was omitted from the *History of the Church.* See Vol. V, p. 400.

The careful review of his own astonishing career entailed in writing his history filled Joseph with a sense of wonder. Although it seldom crept into the narrative, he could not repress it in his sermons and letters. "As for the perils which I am called to pass through," he said, "they seem but a small thing to me, as the envy and wrath of man have been my common lot all the days of my life; and for what cause it seems mysterious, unless I was ordained from before the foundation of the world, for some good end, or bad. . . . But, nevertheless, deep water is what I am wont to swim in; it has all become second nature to me." *

During the Nauvoo years, filled though they were with lawsuits, arrests, and intrigues among his own people, Joseph found time not only to write the history of his church, but also to bring Mormon theology to its full flowering. His teachings were now rarely presented as revelations; they were either introduced in sermons or imparted secretly.

Only two revelations of significance appeared in the four Nauvoo years; yet there was no more fruitful period in Joseph's thinking. Since the great amorphous mass of revelations flung together in the *Doctrine and Covenants* was unwieldy as a guide for his people, he spent considerable time working out a simplified and lucid creed. This took the form of thirteen "articles of faith," which became the functional basis of Mormon doctrine:

We believe in God the eternal Father, and in His Son Jesus Christ, and in the Holy Ghost.

We believe that men will be punished for their own sins, and not for Adam's transgression.

We believe that through the atonement of Christ all mankind may be saved by obedience to the laws and ordinances of the Gospel.

We believe that the first principles and ordinances of the Gospel are: (1) Faith in the Lord Jesus Christ; (2) Repentance; (3) Baptism by immersion for the remission of sins: (4) Laying on of hands for the gift of the Holy Ghost.

We believe that a man must be called of God by prophecy and by the laying on of hands, by those who are in authority, to preach the Gospel and administer in the ordinances thereof.

* Letter to the Saints, written September 1, 1842. *History of the Church,* Vol. V, p. 143.

We believe in the same organization that existed in the primitive Church; viz; apostles, prophets, pastors, teachers, evangelists, etc.

We believe in the gift of tongues, prophecy, revelation, visions, healing, interpretation of tongues, etc.

We believe the Bible to be the word of God, as far as it is translated correctly; we also believe the Book of Mormon to be the word of God.

We believe all that God has revealed, all that He does now reveal, and we believe that He will yet reveal many great and important things pertaining to the kingdom of God.

We believe in the literal gathering of Israel and in the restoration of the Ten Tribes; that Zion will be built upon this [the American] continent; that Christ will reign personally upon the earth; and that the earth will be renewed and receive its paradisiacal glory.

We claim the privilege of worshipping Almighty God according to the dictates of our own conscience, and allow all men the same privilege, let them worship how, where, or what they may.

We believe in being subject to kings, presidents, rulers, and magistrates, in obeying, honoring, and sustaining the law.

We believe in being honest, true, chaste, benevolent, virtuous, and in doing good to *all men;* indeed we may say that we follow the admonition of Paul, "We believe all things, we hope all things, we have endured many things, and hope to be able to endure all things. If there is anything virtuous, lovely, or of good report, or praiseworthy, we seek after these things."

Except for the reference to the Book of Mormon and the doctrine of continuous revelation, there was very little in this creed to which a Bible-reading Christian could object, but simply because there was so little in it that was at all new. Actually it was only the first rung in the ladder of Mormon theology. It ignored the Order of Enoch, which had figured so prominently in the church's early history, because Joseph was done with it forever.* It did not mention the doctrine of plurality of gods, which was one of the pillars of the new philosophy. And it did not even hint at the new and rapidly developing temple ritual.

In the spring of 1842 the simple rites of washing and anointing that had been performed in the Kirtland temple were trans-

* Joseph wrote in his journal on September 24, 1843: "I preached on the stand about one hour on the 2nd Chapter of Acts, designing to show the folly of common stock. In Nauvoo everyone is steward over his own." *History of the Church,* Vol. VI, p. 37.

formed into a complicated and mysterious ceremonial, which for a time was kept as secret as polygamy. In the beginning only men were permitted initiation, but by the spring of 1844 women were granted the same privilege.*

The succession of apostates who exposed the temple mysteries usually hinted of a great sexual orgy. Actually there was nothing gross or disgusting in the ceremony. Each initiate was washed and anointed by a member of his own sex and then dressed in a special undergarment covered with a modest, flowing robe. The purification ritual was as follows:

Brother, having authority, I wash you that you may be clean from the blood and sins of this generation. I wash your head that your brain may work clearly and be quick of discernment; your eyes that you may see clearly and discern the things of God; your ears that they may hear the word of the Lord; your mouth and lips that they speak no guile; your arms that they may be strong to wield the sword in defense of truth and virtue; your breast and vitals that their functions may be strengthened; your loins and reins that you may be fruitful in the propagating of a goodly seed; your legs and feet that you may run and not be weary, walk and not faint.†

The close affinity of religious and phallic rites is a commonplace in social history, and Mormon ritual doubtless had its roots in the same unconscious drives that led the prophet into polygamy. The endowment ceremony was essentially fertility worship, but its basic nature was so camouflaged that only the skeptical felt a sense of outrage.

A good deal of the ceremony performed after the rituals of washing and anointing was borrowed from the Freemasons. From his earliest youth in Palmyra Joseph had known the old Masonic legend that Masonry dated back to the time of Solomon's temple.‡ Although he had peppered the Book of Mor-

---

* Heber C. Kimball in his journal, pp. 14–15, noted that his wife, Vilate, had been washed, anointed, and sealed by Emma Smith. This is quoted by his daughter, Helen Mar Whitney, in *Plural Marriage as Taught by the Prophet Joseph* (Salt Lake City, 1882).

† W. M. Paden: *Temple Mormonism, Its Evolution, Ritual and Meaning* (New York, 1931), pp. 14–15. For the earliest description of the endowment ceremonies see I. M. Van Dusen: *The Sublime and Ridiculous Blended* (New York, 1848).

‡ The *Palmyra Register* on January 10, 1821 quoted the *Masonic Register* as follows: "Solomon was endowed with wisdom from on high to designate the plan; he called the craft together, and the temple of our God was begun and finished solely

mon with anti-Masonic strictures stemming from the Morgan hysteria, he had long since lost his hostility to the craft. Masonry was now as respectable as before 1827, and when Judge James Adams, Deputy Grand Master of the Illinois Masonic Order, urged him to set up a lodge in Nauvoo, he complied at once.

The lodge was formally installed on March 15, 1842, with headquarters in the big room over Joseph's store. John C. Bennett was secretary.* Joseph became a first-degree Mason on the night of the installation, and the next night rose to the sublime degree. His interest in Masonry became so infectious that many Mormon elders hastened to follow his lead, and within six months the lodge had 286 candidates. This accretion left the non-Mormon lodges thunderstruck, for in 1842 the total membership in all of Illinois was only 227. They saw in this growth not only a degeneration of the theory of selective membership but also a threat to control the Grand Lodge in Springfield.†

There is no doubt that Joseph's primary interest in Masonry lay in its ritual. Like Solomon he was a temple-builder. Whatever had come down through the ages that was of value he meant to incorporate into his church. Six weeks after the installation of the lodge he called seven of his leading men — Masonic Grand Master James Adams among them — and instructed them "in the principles and order of the Priesthood, attending to washings, anointings, endowments and the communication of keys." In this council, he said, "was instituted the ancient order of things for the first time in these last days." ‡ This order was an elaborate ritual designed for performance in the Nauvoo Temple. The ceremony, which for a time was kept completely secret, was reserved for the faithful, who believed it to be the summation of all spiritual blessings.

The men were stripped, washed, anointed, and then, as in the Masonic ceremony, dressed in a special "garment" which was held together with strings or bone buttons, metal being forbidden. According to John C. Bennett, this garment at first was a

---

by Masonic hands." Actually Masonry dates from about the thirteenth century. It originated in Britain as a trade guild, though it incorporated some symbols that date back to various mystery cults in antiquity.

  * See the *Wasp*, April 30, 1842, and *History of the Church*, Vol. IV, pp. 550–2.

  † John C. Reynolds: *History of the M. W. Grand Lodge of Illinois, Ancient, Free, and Accepted Masons* (Springfield, 1869), p. 166.

  ‡ *History of the Church*, Vol. V, p. 2.

kind of shirt, which was worn only during the ceremony and then hidden away as a kind of security against Destroying Angels. But it was shortly changed into an unlovely and utilitarian long suit of underwear, which the novice was instructed to wear always as a protection against evil.

The Masonic square and compass were cut into the garment on the breast and a slash was made across the knee. In the beginning the cut across the knee was apparently deep enough to penetrate the flesh and leave a scar, but this practice was eventually abandoned as a result of protests from the Mormon women. There was also a slash in the garment across the abdomen, symbolic of the disemboweling that would be the fate of anyone who revealed the sacred secrets.

After swearing to an oath of secrecy the initiate was dressed in white robes and permitted to witness a long allegorical drama depicting the creation of the earth and the fall of Adam. Joseph, it is said, took the role of God, Hyrum Smith that of Christ, and Bishop George Miller that of the Holy Ghost. The drama followed the language of Genesis, with God pretending to create Eve from the sleeping Adam, with Eve plucking raisins from a tiny tree symbolizing the tree of knowledge, and with W. W. Phelps as the devil crawling about serpent-like on his stomach.*

After being expelled from the Garden of Eden, the actors representing Adam and Eve donned tiny white aprons which were exactly like the Masonic aprons except that they were painted with green fig leaves. Then followed instruction in certain grips, passwords, and "keys." Each man was given a secret name by which he was to be known in the kingdom of heaven.

It may seem surprising that Joseph should have incorporated so much Masonry into the endowment ceremony in the very weeks when all his leading men were being inducted into the Masonic lodge. They would have been blind indeed not to see the parallelism between the costuming, grips, passwords, keys, and oaths. Joseph made free use of other Masonic symbols — the beehive, the all-seeing eye, the two clasped hands, and the point within the circle. The miracle play performed in the Mor-

---

* According to John C. Bennett: *History of the Saints* (Boston, 1842), p. 277. Succeeding years saw minor changes in this drama, but it is clear that the present Mormon ritual is essentially the same. The "second anointing," reserved for leading church officials has never been described in print.

mon ceremony differed only in subject matter from the Masonic drama of Hiram Abiff, and both used many of the same sonorous phrases from the Old Testament. Joseph taught his men simply that the Masonic ritual was a corruption of the ancient ritual of Solomon, and that his own was a restoration of the true Hebraic endowment.*

The elaboration of the temple endowment transformed the Mormon Church into a mystery cult. The secrecy, pageantry, and veiled phallicism appealed to very basic human instincts, and the fact that they seemed to be rooted in Old Testament tradition gave them an authenticity demanded by this Bible-reading people.

The temple mysteries were closely bound up with Joseph's new theories about the nature of heaven and hell. After death, he said, all souls went to the world of spirits — similar to the purgatory of Catholic theology — where they remained in a not unpleasant imprisonment until the Judgment Day. Only those who had joined the true church could clamber immediately up the road to godhood.

Those who had missed the chance to hear the gospel on earth could be freed from the world of spirits by the good offices of any Mormon. To liberate a dead relative or friend one simply acted as proxy in the ordinances of baptism and "sealing." In this manner not only relatives but also all the heroic figures of the past could be released from spiritual bondage, and every Mormon was granted the opportunity of going through the oddly exciting temple ritual not once but hundreds of times.

Paul's First Epistle to the Corinthians had made an ambiguous reference to baptism for the dead, and at least one German sect had practiced this ritual in Pennsylvania. Joseph taught it openly.† At first the Mormons were baptized in the Mississippi and later in an elaborate font standing upon the backs of twelve white wooden oxen in the temple basement.

It is doubtful whether Joseph sensed the truly staggering im-

* The most comprehensive analysis of the relation between Masonry and the Mormon temple ritual has been made by S. H. Goodwin. See his *Mormonism and Masonry* (Salt Lake City, 7th printing, 1938), and *Additional Studies in Mormonism and Masonry* (Salt Lake City, 1932). Wilford Woodruff once frankly admitted that some temple ordinances were first performed in the Masonic Temple in Nauvoo. *Temple Lot Case*, p. 299.

† *History of the Church*, Vol. IV, pp. 568–9; *Times and Seasons*, April 15, 1842.

plications of his endowment system. Upon his church now rested the burden of freeing the billions of spirits who had never heard the law of the Lord. Nauvoo had become the center not only of the world, but also of the universe. But Joseph laid no great emphasis on the temple ordinances. The costuming, pageantry, and general abracadabra had attracted him to the Masonic ritual in the first place, just as the theatricalism of the conjurer's art had lured him to the money-digging of his youth. And though he gave an ingenious theological significance to his own adaptation and development of the Masonic drama, it was always secondary to the pomp and spectacle. This was why Joseph could derive enormous satisfaction from playing the role of God in the temple allegory and yet, without any sense of impropriety, leave the lodge room to transact the sale of a city lot.

CHAPTER XX

In the Quiver of the Almighty

IT WOULD HAVE TAKEN a more phlegmatic person than Joseph to withstand the barrage of favorable newspaper publicity that he received in the spring of 1842. The *New York Herald, New York Tatler,* and *Boston Bee* all wrote lavish encomiums, spiced with enough mockery to please the gentile public. "There is some good in every sect of religion," wrote Bennett of the *Herald* in a whimsical mood, "and we give fair support to all, from the Pope of Rome to Joe Smith. All we ask in return for our reports is a good cool seat, bench, or location when the end of the world comes and the everlasting bonfire begins." *

Joseph ignored the mockery and republished Bennett's columns, carefully expurgated, in *Times and Seasons.* He was not one to quibble over details when he could reprint a paragraph like the following: "This Joe Smith is undoubtedly one of the greatest characters of the age. He indicates as much talent, originality, and moral courage as Mahomet, Odin, or any of the great spirits that have hitherto produced the revolutions of past ages. . . . While modern philosophy, which believes in nothing, but what you can touch, is overspreading the Atlantic States, Joe Smith is creating a spiritual system, combined also with morals and industry, that may change the destiny of the race." †

The prophet repaid James Gordon Bennett with an honorary LL.D. from the University of Nauvoo, with a brigadier-generalship in the Nauvoo Legion, and with the keys to the city. This was no mere gracious gesture acknowledging an unsolicited favor; it was a bid for Bennett's permanent support. For Joseph took the acclaim seriously. Here was the first editor of national prominence to describe the personage Joseph believed himself to be.

Thirteen years' adoration from his people had crystallized his

* *New York Herald,* November 7, 1842.
† Ibid., April 3, 1842.

abiding sense of destiny. Assault, apostasy, bankruptcy, and imprisonment he had weathered imperturbably, for each trouble had been transformed into a symbol of his special calling. Disaster had been a springboard from which he leaped to new successes. It was now easy for him to believe the simplest and most gratifying explanation for his success — that God had willed it. Without that belief he could not have spoken so exuberantly in His name.

Joseph accepted the newspaper effusions exultingly. They helped sharpen his self-consciousness, giving him a perspective on his position in the American scene that he had long sensed but never clearly formulated. He began to speculate on the role of the prophet in human society and evolved a theory of government suited to the empire he proposed to build.

"The great and wise of ancient days have failed in all their attempts to promote eternal power, peace, and happiness," he wrote. "Their nations have crumbled to pieces; their thrones have been cast down in their turn, and their cities, and their mightiest works of art have been annihilated; or their dilapidated towers, of time-worn monuments have left us but feeble traces of their former magnificence and ancient grandeur. They proclaim as with a voice of thunder, those imperishable truths — that man's strength is weakness, his wisdom is folly, his glory is his shame.

"Monarchial, aristocratical, and republican governments of their various kinds and grades, have, in their turn, been raised to dignity, and prostrated in the dust. . . . History records their puerile plans, their shortlived glory, their feeble intellect and their ignoble deeds. Have we increased in knowledge and intelligence? Where is there a man that can step forth and alter the destiny of nations and promote the happiness of the world?"

The answer, he said, was clear to every man who hungered after righteousness. The ideal government was a theocracy, a government by a prophet specially chosen to administer the laws of God. This government, he wrote, "is the only thing that can bring about the restitution of all things spoken of by all the holy Prophets. . . . The world has had a fair trial for six thousand years; the Lord will try the seventh thousand Himself." *

* *History of the Church*, Vol. V, pp. 61–6.

This was no mere word-spinning; it is clear that Joseph was coming to look upon himself as the key figure in the setting up of a great religious kingdom which would free the earth from oppression, tyranny, and bloodshed.

How much the glowing newspaper accounts contributed to this thinking cannot easily be measured. But there is no doubt that they betrayed Joseph into rashness. The fact that the Eastern editors talked openly of a Mormon empire obscured his view of the prodigious obstacles to any such enterprise. Actually he was far less secure than he knew, and his public displays of power did more to undermine than to sustain him. The Legion paraded too openly and too often for the good of the Saints.

"If he would take friendly advice," the editor of the *Sangamo Journal* in Springfield wrote curtly on January 21, 1842, "we would say, let some Joshua, the son of Nun, lead the armies, and let him stick to interpretation and prophecy — for we do assure him upon an honest belief, that his situation in Illinois is far more dangerous than ever it was in Missouri if he undertakes to take Mahomet's part."

The Legion was not the only irritation. Joseph now began playing politics in earnest. His people had voted the Whig ticket in 1840 and again in 1841, but he had made it clear from the beginning that this vote could be swung on a moment's notice. When the Democrats selected as candidates for governor and lieutenant-governor in the election of 1842 Adam W. Snyder and John Moore, both of whom had been active in getting the Mormon charters through the legislature, the prophet decided to shift the Mormon vote back to the Democratic party. He bared this intention with a proclamation that set both parties back on their heels:

To my friends in Illinois — the Gubernatorial Convention of the State of Illinois have nominated Colonel Adam W. Snyder for Governor, and Colonel John Moore for Lieutenant-Governor of the State of Illinois, election to take place in August next. . . . General Bennett informs us that no men were more efficient in assisting him to procure our great chartered privileges, than were Colonel Snyder, and Colonel Moore. They are sterling men, and friends of equal rights, *opposed to the oppressor's grasp, and the tyrant's rod*. With such men at the head of our State, Government will have nothing to fear.

In the next canvass we shall be influenced by *no party* consideration . . . *we care not* a FIG for WHIG *or* DEMOCRAT; they are both alike to us, but we shall go for our friends, our tried friends, and the cause of human liberty, which is the cause of God. We are aware that 'divide and conquer' is the watchword with many, but with us it cannot be done — we love liberty too well — we have suffered too much to be easily duped — we have no catspaws amongst us. . . .

Douglass [Stephen A. Douglas] *is a master spirit,* and his friends are our friends. . . . Snyder and Moore are his friends — they are *ours.* . . . We *will never be justly charged with* THE SIN OF *INGRATITUDE* — they have served us, and we will serve them.

> Joseph Smith,
> Lieutenant-General of the Nauvoo Legion.*

The Democrats, although happy to get the Mormon vote, were frankly embarrassed by this proclamation. This open sell-out so early in the campaign simply handed the Whigs a weapon. They were quick to use it.

The *Alton Telegraph* said on June 4: "This issuing a proclamation on the part of Joe Smith as *'Lieutenant General'* of the Nauvoo Legion, *commanding* his followers to vote for this or that candidate, is too bold a stride towards despotism ever to be long countenanced by a free and intelligent people." Joseph Duncan, the Whig candidate for governor, made repeal of the Mormon charters a basic plank in his platform and took the stump against the "foreigners" who were pouring into Nauvoo.

The *Sangamo Journal,* chief organ of the Whig Party, noting the publicity accorded Joseph in the columns of the *New York Herald,* republished appropriate sections with cryptic warnings. One of James Gordon Bennett's editorials the Whigs found particularly humiliating:

May not this wonderful Mormon movement be the signal for a new religious revolution? Is not Joe Smith its master spirit and General Bennett its military spirit? . . . In Illinois they have already shown how to acquire power and influence, by holding the balance of power between both great parties. *They can already dictate to the state of Illinois,* and if they pursue the same policy in other states, *will they not soon dictate to Congress and decide the Presidency?* †

* *Times and Seasons,* January 1, 1842.
† *New York Herald,* June 17, 1842, reprinted in the *Sangamo Journal,* July 8, 1842.

Nowhere did the fires of political resentment burn more furiously than in Warsaw, biggest non-Mormon town in Hancock County. Normally Democratic, the citizens here were not content with a switch to the Whigs, but endeavored to start an anti-Mormon party, which would draw its strength from the Democrats as well. The editors of the Warsaw paper, Thomas Sharp and Thomas Gregg, carried on a gusty feud with William Smith, who edited the new secular newspaper in Nauvoo, called the *Wasp*.

William set the pace in the first number of the *Wasp* by calling Thomas Sharp a "contemptible demagogue" and a "complete Jackass of an editor." To which Sharp replied in choice frontier diction: "We have received the first number of a new six by nine, recently started at Nauvoo, yclept 'The Wasp.' Of the 'varmint' itself we have nothing to say, further than that the title is a perfect *misnomer*. If it had been called *Pole Cat,* its name would then have corresponded perfectly with the character of its contents. It is needless to inform our readers that we don't fight with such animals — nature having given them a decided advantage."

This article William reprinted in the *Wasp* with a squib beneath: *"Well done Thom — ASS."* *

JOSEPH had little of William's crudeness, but both men had a certain earthiness and rough vigor that none of the other brothers seems to have possessed. "Josiah Butterfield came to my house," Joseph wrote in his journal one day, "and insulted me so outrageously that I kicked him out of the house, across the yard, and into the street." † Here was a prophet who could hold his own with any man on the frontier. Tough, hard-headed leaders like Brigham Young and Heber C. Kimball, who abominated sanctimonious humbug, never found Joseph guilty of it.

Much of the asceticism of the Kirtland era disappeared in Nauvoo. There were many days when the prophet gave himself over completely to the pleasures of the average man — attending the tent theaters that came to the city, frequenting band concerts and lectures on phrenology (only mesmerists and magicians were denied an audience in Nauvoo), and giving

* The *Wasp,* April 16, 23, 1842.
† *History of the Church,* Vol. V, p. 316.

cotillion parties in his big new hotel home, the Nauvoo Mansion.

Although Joseph controlled the dispensing of liquor and preached against grog shops, he nevertheless permitted the construction of a brewery and allowed it to advertise its beer and ale in the *Nauvoo Neighbor*. The ardent temperance crusaders in the city must have been discouraged by the prophet's unwillingness to co-operate with them. "It was reported to me," he wrote in his journal one day, "that some of the brethren had been drinking whisky that day in violation of the Word of Wisdom. I called the brethren in and investigated the case, and was satisfied that no evil had been done, *and gave them a couple of dollars with directions to replenish the bottle to stimulate them in the fatigues of their sleepless journey.*" *

When Jenetta Richards presented him with a bottle of wine made by her mother in England, he drank it with relish and noted the incident in his journal without apology.† For every convert who was shocked by such indulgence there were a score who were further endeared to the prophet by it. His good-humored tolerance of human frailty lost him no strong men.

An anecdote in the unpublished diary of Oliver Huntington drolly reflects Joseph's attitude toward temperance. "Robert Thompson was a faithful, just clerk for Joseph Smith the Prophet in Nauvoo," he wrote, "and had been in his office steady near or quite two years. Joseph said to brother Thompson one day, 'Robert I want you to go and get on a bust, go and get drunk and have a good spree. If you don't you will die.' "

"Robert did not do it," Huntington concluded soberly. "He was a very pious exemplary man and never guilty of such an impropriety as he thought that to be. In less than two weeks he was dead and buried." ‡

Joseph was friendly and hospitable to the hundreds of tourists who were attracted to Nauvoo. Steamboats plying up and down the river stopped regularly to discharge visitors, who were ceremoniously conducted on a tour of the city, including visits

---

* As printed in the *Millennial Star*, Vol. XXI, p. 283. The words I have italicized were omitted when this passage was reprinted in the *History of the Church*, Vol. V, p. 450.

† *History of the Church*, Vol. V, p. 380.

‡ See Vol. III, p. 166, of the typewritten transcript in the Utah State Historical Society Library.

to see the mummies, the baptismal font, and the temple, which was fast becoming an imposing monument. The prophet had few illusions about the tourists who wanted a personal interview. When one preacher admitted frankly: "I have no particular business . . . but I have taken the liberty to call on you," Joseph replied with wry humor: "A good many call on me that way, to satisfy their curiosity; and go away and say, 'Well, I've seen Joe Smith. Some of them say he is a pretty good looking, smart fellow. He looks as though he knew something, as if he was not the fool and knave he has been called.' But others go away and say, 'Well, I've seen Joe Smith — he is a great blubber-mouthed fellow, a knave, a drunkard, a mean, ignorant fellow.' " *

One visitor, Henry Caswall, an Episcopalian preacher from a St. Louis college, armed himself with an ancient manuscript psalter written in Greek and, pretending to be ignorant of its contents, offered it to Joseph for his scrutiny. Under the prophet's questioning he finally admitted that he believed the language to be Greek, but this Joseph contradicted. Caswall, exaggerating the imperfections of Joseph's grammar, later related the story as follows:

"No, it ain't Greek at all," Joseph said, "except perhaps a few words. What ain't Greek is Egyptian; and what ain't Egyptian is Greek. This book is very valuable. It is a dictionary of Egyptian hieroglyphics." Pointing to the capital letters at the commencement of each verse, he went on: "Them figures is Egyptian hieroglyphics, written in reformed Egyptian. Them characters is like the letters that was engraved on the golden plates."

When the prophet left the room, Caswall turned triumphantly to the men present and exposed the trick. "They appeared confounded for a while," he wrote, "but at length the Mormon doctor said: 'Sometimes Mr. Smith speaks as a prophet, and sometimes as a mere man. If he gave a wrong opinion respecting the book, he spoke as a mere man.' " †

This defense Joseph would readily have subscribed to himself. Weary of the restrictions imposed by the dignity of his office,

---

* W. S. B.: "A Visit to Nauvoo," *Universalist Union*, April 27, May 4, 1844.

† *The City of the Mormons, or Three Days at Nauvoo* (London, 1842), pp. 35, 43.

annoyed by tales of converts who apostatized when they saw him playing with his children or wrestling with his friends, Joseph often said impatiently: "A prophet is a prophet only when he is acting as such." *

Perhaps the most deliberate hoax ever played on Joseph Smith was contrived by three men in the near-by town of Kinderhook. One of them, Bridge Whitton, cut six copper sheets into the shape of a bell, and the other two, Robert Wiley and Wilbur Fugate, covered them with fanciful writing by a simple etching process. They smeared acid over the plates to corrode them, bound them together with a piece of rusted hoop iron, and carefully buried them along with some Indian bones in an Indian mound near by that had been an object of much curiosity and desultory digging. Wiley spread the story that he had dreamed of buried treasure three nights in succession, and invited assistance in hunting for it.

Two Mormons were present when the plates were found. Although they had suspected a hoax, the sight of the corroded plates banished their mistrust. Shouting for joy, they begged to take them to the prophet for deciphering. But before giving them up, Wiley was careful to clean them with sulphuric acid so that the "hieroglyphics" could easily be read.

The whole of Nauvoo soon buzzed with the discovery. The *Times and Seasons* published full reproductions as further proof of the authenticity of the Book of Mormon, and the printing office sold facsimiles at one dollar a dozen. Joseph stated in his journal that he "translated a portion" and discovered it to be a history of the person whose bones lay in the mound, "a descendant of Ham, through the loins of Pharaoh, king of Egypt."

If the Kinderhook conspirators expected to see another Book of Abraham result from their deception, they were disappointed. Perhaps Joseph had been made cautious by the Greek psalter trick, which Caswall had described in a nasty anti-Mormon tract; perhaps he had noted in the *New York Herald*, which he read regularly, that the Egyptian language had finally been deciphered and a grammar published in England.† At any rate, he never published the partial translation, and apparently did

* *History of the Church*, Vol. V, p. 265.
† *New York Herald*, December 28, 1842.

not even venture to suggest that the language was reformed Egyptian. The plates were sold to a St. Louis museum, and Fugate did not publicly admit the fraud until thirty-six years afterward.*

Although Joseph was done with translations, he never ceased delighting in exhibiting his linguistic talents. Occasionally in his letters and printed appeals for national support he made proud displays which so embarrassed later historians of his church that they were quietly deleted from the official histories. The most notorious example was his "Appeal to the Freemen of the State of Vermont, the 'Brave Green Mountain Boys,' and Honest Men," in which, with a blithe disregard for accuracy, he quoted from seventeen foreign languages:

Were I a Chaldean I would exclaim: Keed'nauh ta-meroon le-hoam elauhayauh dey-ahemayaua veh aur'kau lau gnaubadoo, yaba-doo ma-ar'gnau comeen tehoat sheamyauh allah. (Thus shall ye say unto them: The gods that have not made the heavens and the earth, they shall perish from the earth, and from these heavens.)

An Egyptian, Su-e-eh-ni. (What other persons are those?) A Grecian, Diabolos bssileuei. (The Devil reigns.) A Frenchman, Messieurs sans Dieu. (Gentlemen without God.) A Turk, Ain shems. (The fountain of light.) A German, sie sind unferstandig! (What consummate ignorance!) A Syrian, Zaubok! (Sacrifice!) A Spaniard, Il sabio muda conscio, il nescio no. (A wise man reflects, a fool does not.) A Samaritan: Saunau! (O stranger!) An Italian: Oh tempa! oh diffidanza! (O the times! O the diffidence!) A Hebrew: Ahtau ail rauey. (Thou God seest me.) A Dane: Hvad tidende! (What tidings!) A Saxon, Hwaet riht! (What right!) A Swede: Hvad skilia! (What skill!) A Polander: Nay-yen-shoo bah pon na Jesu Christus. (Blessed be the name of Jesus Christ.) A western Indian: She-mo-kah she-mo-keh teh ough-ne-gah. (The white man. O the white man, he very uncertain.) A Roman: Procul, O procul este profani! (Be off, be off ye profane!) But as I am I will only add; when the wicked rule the people mourn.†

* See the letter from Wilbur Fugate to James T. Cobb, dated Mound Station, Illinois, June 30, 1879, published in W. Wyl: *Mormon Portraits*, p. 207, and later in W. A. Linn: *The Story of the Mormons*, p. 87. See also *History of the Church*, Vol. V, p. 372; *Times and Seasons*, Vol. IV (May 1, 1843), pp. 185–7; *Nauvoo Neighbor*, February 7, 1844, p. 4.

† *The Voice of Truth* (1844), pp. 16–17. See also his letter to James Arlington Bennett, *Nauvoo Neighbor*, December 6, 1843, and his "Views on the Powers and Policy of the United States Government," *Times and Seasons*, Vol. VI (May 15,

WHEN Josiah Quincy and Charles Francis Adams visited the prophet, he conducted them personally on a tour about Nauvoo. Quincy wrote in his journal a detailed account of their conversation. As they passed the entrance to the temple, he said, Joseph stopped before a workman who was chiseling an immense face into the rock of a capstone. "General Smith," queried the man, looking up from his task, "is this like the face you saw in the vision?"

"Very near it," answered the prophet, "except — [and this, Quincy said, was added with an air of careful connoisseurship that was quite overpowering] except that the nose is just a thought too broad."

As they entered the Nauvoo Museum, Joseph introduced Lucy Smith: "This is my mother, gentlemen. The curiosities we shall see belong to her. They were purchased with her own money at a cost of six thousand dollars." Opening pine presses along the wall, he disclosed four black, shrunken bodies. "These are mummies," he said. "I want you to look at that little runt of a fellow over there. He was a great man in his day. Why that was Pharaoh Necho, King of Egypt!" He pointed to various hieroglyphs on the papyri, which were preserved under glass. "That is the handwriting of Abraham, the Father of the Faithful; this is the autograph of Moses, and these lines were written by his brother Aaron. Here we have the earliest accounts of the Creation, from which Moses composed the first Book of Genesis."

When Quincy questioned him about a drawing of a serpent walking about on a pair of legs, he expanded heartily: "Why that's as plain as a pikestaff. Before the Fall snakes always went about on legs, just like chickens. They were deprived of them in punishment for their agency in the ruin of man."

Although Quincy looked upon this exhibitionism as unexampled absurdity, he was not thereby blinded to the prophet's positive talents. His first impression had been favorable. "A *fine-looking man* is what the passer-by would instinctively have murmured upon meeting the remarkable individual," he wrote. And after conversing several hours, listening to one of his sermons, and making a tour of the "orderly city, magnificently laid

---

1844), p. 531. The linguistic essays were deleted when these were reprinted in the *History of the Church*. See Vol. VI, pp. 75, 197–209.

out, and teeming with activity and enterprise," he was ready to acknowledge that this man, more than almost any other he had ever met, was "best endowed with that kingly faculty which directs, as by intrinsic right, the feeble or confused souls who are looking for guidance."

Quincy's account is the most sagacious of all the commentaries written by travelers to Nauvoo. "If the reader does not know just what to make of Joseph Smith," he concluded, "I cannot help him out of the difficulty. I myself stand helpless before the puzzle." *

What had overpowered Josiah Quincy, as indeed it did most of the prophet's visitors, was Joseph's magnificent self-assurance. Increased success had served to intensify his boldness and exuberance. The zest for living that he radiated never failed to inspire his own people with a sense of the richness of life. They followed him slavishly and devotedly if only to warm themselves in the glow of his presence.

They built for him, preached for him, and made unbelievable sacrifices to carry out his orders, not only because they were convinced he was God's prophet, but also because they loved him as a man. They were as elated when he won a wrestling match as they were awed when he dictated a new revelation. They retold tales of his generosity and tenderness, marveling that he fed so many of the poor in Nauvoo at his table without stint, and that he entertained friend and enemy alike. He was a genial host, warmhearted and friendly to all comers, and fiercely loyal to his friends.

Joseph was no hair-shirt prophet. He believed in the good life, with moderate self-indulgence in food and drink, occasional sport, and good entertainment. And that he succeeded in enjoying himself to the hilt detracted not at all from the semi-deification with which his own people enshrouded him. Any protests of impropriety dissolved before his personal charm. "Man is that he might have joy" had been one of his first significant pronouncements in the Book of Mormon, and from that belief he had never deviated. He was gregarious, expansive, and genuinely fond of people. And it is no accident that his theology in the end discarded all traces of Calvinism and became an ingenuous blend of supernaturalism and materialism, which

* *Figures of the Past, from the Leaves of Old Journals* (Boston, 1883), pp. 377–400.

promised in heaven a continuation of all earthly pleasures —
work, wealth, sex, and power.

Since Joseph was himself the personification of the church,
its hero and ideal, whatever he did became a pattern for imita-
tion. Because he took Christian theology and ethics and mixed
them with business, politics, and empire-building, his people
came to do the same. The result was that Mormonism became
not only a belief but also a way of life. It had never pretended
to be a mystical sanctification or even a new ethical code. As a
religion it was as raw-boned and pragmatic as Joseph himself,
and as dynamic.

Although the prophet was the prime mover in all Mormon
thinking and activity, he was himself tremendously affected by
the powerful social unit he had created. As thousands of converts poured in from the East and Canada and the British Isles,
the increasing pressure of administrative duties — of settling
and housing these people and getting work for them — diverted
his energy more and more into secular affairs. But there was an
equally insistent pressure upon his inner character. These thousands looked to him to usher in the millennium. They clamored
for spiritual enlightenment and demanded to know the laws of
the kingdom of God. Joseph gave them the best that was in
him, without affidavits, witnesses, or apology. And to one who
reads through his sermons and journal for this period, it must
seem that the role of prophet had finally swallowed up the man.

But he had moods of uncertainty and doubt and could occasionally step out of himself and look with humor at what he
had become. When Josiah Quincy said to him: "It seems to me,
General, that you have too much power to be safely trusted to
one man," he replied: "In your hands or that of any other man,
so much power would, no doubt, be dangerous. I am the only
man in the world whom it would be safe to trust it with. Remember, I am a prophet!" But these last five words, Quincy
said, were spoken in "a rich, comical aside, as if in hearty recognition of the ridiculous sound they might have in the ears of a
Gentile."

Now and then he startled his own people with an expression
of detachment and irony. Once when introducing the Whig
politician Cyrus Walker to his people, he turned to him and said
with a little smile: "These are the greatest dupes, as a body of

people, that ever lived, or I am not so big a rogue as I am reported to be." *

On another occasion he confessed with simple candor: "I do not think there have been many good men on earth since the days of Adam; but there was one good man and his name was Jesus. . . . I love that man better who swears a stream as long as my arm yet deals justice to his neighbors and mercifully deals his substance to the poor, than the long, smooth-faced hypocrite. I do not want you to think I am very righteous, for I am not. God judges men according to the use they make of the light which He gives them." †

But such moods were momentary. He went on in this same sermon with a vivid self-characterization that more genuinely represented what Joseph had come to believe himself to be: "I am like a huge, rough stone rolling down from a high mountain; and the only polishing I get is when some corner gets rubbed off by coming in contact with something else, striking with accelerated force against religious bigotry, priestcraft, lawyer-craft, doctor-craft, lying editors, suborned judges and jurors, and the authority of perjured executives, backed by mobs, blasphemers, licentious and corrupt men and women — all hell knocking off a corner here and a corner there. Thus will I become a smooth and polished shaft in the quiver of the Almighty, who will give me dominion over all and every one of them, when their refuge of lies shall fail, and their hiding place shall be destroyed."

* *History of the Church*, Vol. V, p. 472.
† Ibid., p. 401.

CHAPTER XXI
If a Man Entice a Maid

I<small>T WAS IN</small> K<small>IRTLAND</small>, as we have seen, that Joseph began to tamper delicately with one of the most basic mores in Occidental society. He looked upon that society with the singular detachment that can come only to a man satisfied with his own ultimate authority and possessed by a longing to remold the world closer to his heart's desire. Nothing was so sacred that it could not be recast into a new utility or a new beauty.

Monogamy seemed to him — as it has seemed to many men who have not ceased to love their wives, but who have grown weary of connubial exclusiveness — an intolerably circumscribed way of life. "Whenever I see a pretty woman," he once said to a friend, "I have to pray for grace." * But Joseph was no careless libertine who could be content with clandestine mistresses. There was too much of the Puritan in him, and he could not rest until he had redefined the nature of sin and erected a stupendous theological edifice to support his new theories on marriage.

By the spring of 1840 this edifice was almost complete and had become so integral a part of his metaphysical system that he probably completely lost sight of the fact that it had not figured at all in the original design. Joseph was not given to self-searching or he might have been troubled by the intensity of his preoccupation with the nature of adultery. But when he described the new patriarchal order of marriage to Parley Pratt during their weeks together in Philadelphia in 1840, it was with the freshness and enthusiasm of a man who had stumbled quite by chance upon an ancient treasure.

"He taught me many great and glorious principles concerning God and the heavenly order of eternity," Pratt said. "It was at this time that I received from him the first idea of eternal family organization, and the eternal union of the sexes in those inexpressible endearing relationships which none but the highly

* As reported to W. Wyl by J. W. C., *Mormon Portraits*, p. 55.

intellectual, the refined and pure in heart know how to prize, and which are the foundation of everything worthy to be called happiness." *

Pratt had buried his first wife, with whom he had been very much in love, and had since remarried. Joseph now promised him that he would have both wives in heaven, provided that he was sealed to them in the temple under the new and everlasting covenant. And since heaven would bless his union with both wives in the hereafter, it could not logically frown on his having more than one wife on earth.

There was plenty of precedent for plural marriages in the Old Testament, beginning with Father Abraham. But it was Jacob's polygamous marriages that particularly interested Joseph Smith, and he frequently referred to the new marriage principle as the blessing of Jacob. He was fond of pointing to the commandment in Exodus: "And if a man entice a maid that is not betrothed, and lie with her, he shall surely endow her to be his wife." The sin of adultery lay not in the act itself but in the subsequent desertion. It was the abandonment of the humbled maid that led to the unspeakable evils of prostitution and infanticide.

Joseph taught none of this openly, for he feared that polygamy would bring down the wrath of the gentiles. Until the day it could be publicly proclaimed, any whisper of the doctrine of plural wives must be vehemently denied, and any man caught preaching it without his own personal sanction must be summarily cut off from the church. Eventually all the Saints would be taken into his confidence and welded into a force that could oppose any gentile threat, but until then the little lie must be voiced to protect the great truth.

To break the ground before sowing broadcast the seeds of his new doctrine, Joseph's press published a pamphlet in defense of polygamy by one Udney H. Jacob. Jacob produced a document of astonishing sophistication, advocating polygamy not only in the light of Old Testament precedent, but also as a solution for marital incompatibility. "What, although a woman is not known to be an adulteress," he wrote, "yet she may be a perfect devil to her husband, train him in the most imperious manner,

* *Autobiography*, p. 329. George A. Smith often testified that Joseph Smith taught him the principle of polygamy in 1839.

LUCY MACK SMITH IN NAUVOO

CAPSTONE OF THE NAUVOO TEMPLE

Now at the Quincy Historical Society

David Smith

Alexander Smith

Major Bidamon

Frederick Smith

Joseph Smith III

THE FOUR SONS OF JOSEPH SMITH

With Major Lewis Bidamon, second husband of Emma Smith

OLIVER BUELL

Who may have been a son of Joseph Smith by his plural wife Prescindia Huntington Buell. From Esshom's Pioneers and Prominent Men of Utah

despise him in her heart, abuse him before his children, drive him like a menial slave where she pleases; and he must tamely submit to the ungodly law of his wife, must hug the serpent to his bosom, and love her as he does his own body! Impossible, and degrading to the nature of man."

Such a wife must not be divorced, he said, for "a divorced man is not known in the whole canon of scriptures." But for her to continue performing the rituals of the marriage bed without any love for her husband — which he labeled "fornication in the wife" — was a gross sin. "In ancient times under the law of God," he concluded, "the permission of a plurality of wives had a direct tendency to prevent the possibility of fornication in the wife."

Whether Jacob was describing his own married state, or Joseph's, or simply that of any poor bedeviled male, one cannot know. But there is no doubt that Jacob looked upon woman as the inferior species. "The idea of a woman taking a man to be her husband is not found in the Word of God. But the man marries the woman; and the woman is given in marriage. But the husband is not the property of the wife in any sense of the word. . . . There is no positive law of God against a man's marrying Leah and Rachel both. . . . To God only are men accountable in this matter, and not to their wives." *

This pamphlet was published in 1842 in Nauvoo under the prophet's auspices (the title-page lists J. Smith as printer), although he was quickly forced to denounce it. But it must be considered a mere fragment of his elaborate framework of justification for plural marriage.

Paul had said that in heaven there would be no marriage or giving in marriage, but Joseph taught that this would not apply to his Saints. That which he and his elders sealed on earth would be binding also in heaven. There a man would have not only his wives and children, but also the prerogative of procreating more, until, as he expressed it to Parley Pratt, "the result of our endless union would be offspring as numerous as

* Udney Hay Jacob: *An Israelite, and a Shepherd of Israel. An Extract from a Manuscript entitled The Peacemaker, or the Doctrines of the Millennium, being a treatise on religion and jurisprudence, or a new system of religion and politicks* (Nauvoo, Illinois, 1842), pp. 15, 16, 29, 31.

the stars of heaven, or the sands of the seashore." This was the road to godhood.*

A man's glory in the next world would be determined by the knowledge he had gained and the excellence of his works upon earth. He who entered heaven with "ten talents" would have tenfold the glory of a man with one, and his rate of progress toward godhood would be ten times as rapid as that of the man who had been blind to the truth upon earth. Similarly, if a man went to heaven with ten wives, he would have more than tenfold the blessings of a mere monogamist, for all the children begotten through these wives would enhance his kingdom. The man with only one wife, on the other hand, would be denied even her and forced to spend eternity as a ministering angel rather than a god.

Joseph taught that "God himself was once as we are now, and is an exalted man." He had increased in skill and wisdom until He had come to govern myriads of worlds peopled by spirits of His own procreation. Ahead of every man there stretched this same boundless opportunity for progression throughout eternity. The rate of his spiritual growth would accelerate in direct proportion to the speed with which he accepted God's laws and performed God's rituals. Lorenzo Snow caught the essence of this philosophy in a terse and provocative line: "As man is, God once was; and as God is, man may become." It was the most challenging concept that Joseph Smith ever produced, and in a sense the most original.

It will be seen that the Mormon heaven was as changing, tumultuous, and infinitely varied as earth itself. Converts reared on a diet of harps and angels found this heaven exciting. To those infected with the prodigious optimism and enthusiasm of America, it seemed only reasonable that there need be no end to the explorations of the human spirit. To men who loved their wives, it was pleasant to hear that death was no separation, and to men who did not, it was gratifying to hear that there could be no sin in taking another. To every man in love with life — with the tantalizing richness of learning, the sweaty satisfaction of hard work, the luxury of sensual pleasure — Joseph's heaven had profound meaning.

* See Pratt's *Autobiography*, p. 329; *History of the Church*, Vol. V, pp. 391–2; and *Doctrine and Covenants*, Section 132.

ALTHOUGH many of the leading Mormon officials converted their first wives to polygamy before taking a second, Joseph did not take Emma into his confidence. Neither did he confide in his friends; there was disagreement among them in later years even over the identity of his first plural wife. Some, like Benjamin Johnson, were certain that it had been Fannie Alger, who after being expelled from Joseph's home in Kirtland had gone to Indiana, where she married and raised a large family. But others held that plural marriage was not officially inaugurated until April 5, 1841, the eve of the eleventh anniversary of the founding of the church, when he married the attractive twenty-six-year-old Louisa Beaman.

But it is doubtful if Louisa was even second on the list. The most famous woman in the church was William Morgan's widow, Lucinda, now married to George W. Harris, one of Joseph's key men, and incidentally a Mason of high rank. Although now almost forty, the small, bright-blue-eyed Lucinda had lost little of her blond beauty. It happened that she and Sarah Pratt were good friends, and she is said to have admitted to Mrs. Pratt in 1842 that she had been the prophet's mistress "since four years." *

Mormon historians, although listing Mrs. Harris as one of Joseph's plural wives, have been reluctant to admit the authenticity of Sarah Pratt's statement, since its implications are embarrassing. But they supply no date of the marriage ceremony, and it would appear that if indeed any ceremony was performed at all, it took place in Far West in 1838, when the prophet was living in the Harris home.

The extreme informality attending Joseph's earliest marriages (at least as it appears in the available records) is even more evident in the story of the prophet's relationship with Prescindia Huntington Buell. During the Missouri troubles of 1838-9 her husband, Norman Buell, temporarily left the church. About this time Prescindia bore a son. She admitted later that she did not know whether Norman Buell or the prophet was the father. But the physiognomy revealed in a rare photograph of Oliver Buell seems to weight the balance overwhelmingly on the side of Joseph's paternity. And there is evidence in the diary of the boy's uncle, Oliver Huntington, that young Buell was

* For documentation on the details of Joseph's plural wives see Appendix C.

later officially "sealed or adopted" to the prophet in the Mormon temple in Salt Lake City.

However, Prescindia seems not to have been married to Joseph Smith officially until December 11, 1841, some time after this child was born. She remained nominally Mrs. Buell, and lived with Norman Buell in Lima, Illinois, until a year and a half after Joseph's death, when she left Buell permanently and became a plural wife of Heber C. Kimball.

Before the expulsion of John C. Bennett in June 1842, Joseph had been married or "sealed" to an imposing list of women, almost all of them already married. In addition to Louisa Beaman, Mrs. Harris, and Mrs. Buell, there were Mrs. Zina Huntington Jacobs, Mrs. Mary Rollins Lightner, Mrs. Patty Sessions, possibly Mrs. Clarissa Hancock and Mrs. Sally Gulley, and probably Mrs. Nancy Hyde, with a doubtful Mrs. Durfee at the bottom of the list. There were undoubtedly others, for John C. Bennett, who knew of several of these marriages, hinted at others which cannot be identified from the available documents.*

Most attractive of all these women was the vivacious twenty-year-old Zina Huntington Jacobs, whom Joseph had taken into his home for a time during the great plague of 1840. Zina had been married to Henry B. Jacobs on March 7, 1841, and at the time of her sealing to Joseph, on October 27, 1841, she was seven months pregnant with Jacobs's child. Jacobs then apparently knew nothing of this special ceremony, for when he toured southern Illinois with John D. Lee in the winter of 1842, he talked constantly of his wife's loveliness and fidelity.

Zina's marriage with Jacobs proved unhappy, although she did not leave him until 1846, shortly before the birth of her second son, when she became one of the already numerous wives of Brigham Young.†

Only one of these married women described Joseph's court-

* Bennett listed Miss L***** B*****, who was married to Joseph Smith by Joseph Bates Noble. This is clearly Louisa Beaman. His Mrs. B**** is doubtless Mrs. Buell; and his Mrs. S******* is Mrs. Sessions. Mrs. D***** is probably Mrs. Durfee, and Mrs. G**** is possibly Mrs. Sally Gatty. But Mrs. A**** S****, said to have been married to Joseph by Brigham Young, and Miss B***** remain mysterious. (Stanley Ivins has uncovered evidence that this may be a Miss Sarah Bapson.)

† In January of that year, eighteen months after Joseph's death, her marriage to the prophet was again solemnized, this time in the newly completed Nauvoo temple. She was sealed to Joseph "for eternity," and to Brigham Young "for time." Jacobs stood humbly by as a witness. See the Nauvoo Temple Record, 1846, also Appendix C.

ship. This was Mary Elizabeth Rollins, who had adored Joseph from the time of her adolescent conversion in New York State and who was now married to the friendly but non-Mormon Adam Lightner. Although not married to Joseph Smith until February 1842, Mrs. Lightner reported that Joseph told her he had been commanded to take her for a wife as early as 1834. "I was [then] a thousand miles from him," she wrote. "He got afraid. The angel came to him three times, the last time with a drawn sword and threatened his life."

When Joseph told her about the angel in 1842, she refused to believe him. "If God told him so, why did he not come and tell me? The angel told him I should have a witness. An angel came to me — it went through me like lightning — I was afraid. . . . Joseph said I was his before I came here and he said all the Devils in Hell should never get me from him. I was sealed to him in the Masonic Hall, over the old brick store by Brigham Young in February 1842." *

THE MEN who were taken into the system at this early period — Hyrum Smith, Brigham Young, Heber Kimball, William Clayton, Willard Richards, and Benjamin F. Johnson — after an initial period of shock and spiritual torment, were won over with very little argument. Joseph's brother Don Carlos fought polygamy before his death in 1841. "Any man," he said to Ebenezer Robinson in June of that year, "who will preach and practice spiritual wifery will go to hell, no matter if it is my brother Joseph." †

But William Smith was an eager convert. His first plural wife was Mary Ann Sheffield, who had left a husband in England. "I never met William Smith but once before I married him," she related. "I met him coming from Keokuk. I think that was in April, 1843. . . . I do not know if I lived with him two weeks; cannot tell whether I lived with him one week or not."

* For Mrs. Lightner's complete statement see Appendix C. The story of the drawn sword appears frequently in the testimonies of the early polygamists. Joseph told Lorenzo Snow that he had "hesitated and deferred from time to time, until an angel of God stood by him with a drawn sword and told him that, unless he moved forward and established plural marriage, his Priesthood would be taken from him and he should be destroyed!" Eliza R. Snow Smith: *Biography of Lorenzo Snow*, pp. 69–70. See also the Benjamin F. Johnson manuscript.

† Robinson was co-editor of *Times and Seasons* with Don Carlos. See his reminiscences in *The Return*, Vol. III (February 1891), p. 28.

Before the death of his first wife in 1845, William took at least four other plural wives.*

But the true measure of the magnetism of plural marriage can be seen best in the attitude of the Mormon women. They required very little more persuasion than the men, though the reasons are not so obvious. Nauvoo was a severe town, puritanical and acutely self-righteous. But it was a town full of "church widows," whose husbands were out proselyting, spreading the gospel, in the East, in the South, in Canada, and in England. Several were making ready to go to the South Sea Islands. Orson Hyde, on the way to Palestine to dedicate that land to the restoration of the Jews, was exploring the possibilities of missions in Germany and Russia. Whether Nancy Hyde became a polygamous wife of Joseph Smith when Orson Hyde was on this mission, or earlier, is not clear. But her circumstances were typical of those of many women who found polyandry to their liking.

Moreover, Nauvoo was troubled by the old problem of the separated but undivorced female convert. Divorce was usually impossible, and so many women were pouring into Nauvoo eager to marry again that it was difficult for the church to maintain the discipline that would have been normal in a settled community. Marriage standards were extremely flexible all along the frontier.

It was easy, therefore, for many of the penniless and lonely women converts to slip into polygamy. But for every woman who entered the system for reasons of security — and a fragile security at that — there were a dozen for whom this necessity did not arise. There was no need whatever for the attractive virgin to become a second, third, or thirteenth wife, since frontier areas always had a surplus of men. And what of the married women who gladly signed themselves and their children over to the prophet's keeping and glory for eternity, leaving their unwitting husbands to be wifeless and childless in the celestial kingdom? Was this a melancholy commentary on their own marriage state or a tribute to Joseph's charm? Or was it

---

* Their names were Mary Jones, Priscilla Morgridge, Sarah Libby, and Hannah Libby. See the testimonies of several of these women published in the *Temple Lot Case,* pp. 380, 364; also J. F. Smith, Jr.: *Blood Atonement and the Origin of Plural Marriage,* p. 49.

perhaps a smothered yearning for new experiences, released now by opportunity masquerading as religious duty?

IT should have been obvious to Joseph that polygamous marriages could not long be kept secret. And soon the first fruits of "spiritual wifery" began to appear. Up to this time Joseph had taken care that almost all of his own plural wives were married women, but his leading elders could not easily follow his example.

No one in the whole of Nauvoo had a more strategic vantage point from which to discover exactly what was going on than the famous midwife Patty Sessions. A slim, wiry woman with hands admirably small for her work, she delivered babies for fees ranging from fifty cents to three dollars and was more esteemed than any doctor in the city. In the spring of 1842 Joseph added her to his circle of wives. Her daughter, Sylvia, who stood as witness at the marriage of her mother, also became his wife, but this, apparently, Patty never knew. She recorded her own marriage proudly in her secret journal, and from that moment forward knew her duty to the new order.

Joseph H. Jackson, who claimed to have been in the prophet's confidence for a time, stated that Mrs. Sessions, Mrs. Durfee, and a Mrs. Taylor were called "Mothers in Israel," and their duty was to instruct the younger women in the mysteries of polygamy. Whether Mrs. Taylor became a wife of the prophet is not known.*

After the expulsion of John C. Bennett the blame for the fatherless children arriving in the city was laid at his door.† But while he was still in power, suspicion fell on every man who was seen out after curfew. The number of first wives who knew the truth about polygamy was then extremely small, and the remainder were seething with suspicion and furiously angry at what seemed to be the appalling moral laxity in Nauvoo.

The Female Relief Society, which Joseph had organized in mid-March 1842 with Emma as president, was quickly diverted from charitable offices to the purging of iniquity. With a passion that probably came less from her exalted standards of moral

---

* *A Narrative of the Adventures and Experiences of Joseph H. Jackson* (Warsaw, Illinois, 1844), p. 14.

† Oliver Olney: *The Absurdities of Mormonism Portrayed*, p. 19.

behavior than from an unuttered dread of what she might discover, Emma probed and questioned every woman who came
into the organization.

Assisting her in the leadership of the society were some of the
ablest women in the church: Mrs. Elizabeth Ann Whitney, Mrs.
Sarah M. Cleveland, Elvira Cowles, and the poetess Eliza R.
Snow. Joseph publicly commended them for their zeal in making "a select society of the virtuous," but warned them that
"they must be extremely careful in their examinations, or the
consequences would be serious." * Eventually every one of these
women became his plural wife with the exception of Mrs. Whitney, who granted him instead the privilege of marrying her
seventeen-year-old daughter Sarah.

The practice of enlarging the circle of wives in order to win
the loyalty of influential Nauvoo women was effective up to a
point, after which it became highly dangerous. Sooner or later
some woman would be sufficiently revolted by polygamy to tell
the whole world about what was going on in Nauvoo. Mrs.
Sarah M. Kimball, whom Joseph approached in 1842, told him
to teach the concept to someone else, but she kept silent.† Mrs.
Orson Pratt, who also refused the prophet, confided in a few
friends, but did not discuss polygamy publicly until she was
an embittered and lonely old woman.

But a self-possessed eighteen-year-old English girl, Martha
Brotherton, chose to speak her mind. Brigham Young, who had
not been lax in following his prophet's lead, had set his heart
on the high-spirited English lass. He took her to the famous
rendezvous over Joseph's store, locked the door, and proceeded
with the curious, bobtailed, hortatory courtship that was becoming so common in the city:

"Brother Joseph has had a revelation from God that it is lawful and right for a man to have two wives. . . . If you will
accept of me I will take you straight to the celestial kingdom,
and if you will have me in this world, I will have you in that
which is to come, and brother Joseph will marry us here today,

* *History of the Church*, Vol. IV, p. 570.

† Sarah M. Granger Kimball, wife of Hiram S. Kimball, later swore to an affidavit
saying: "Early in 1842 Joseph taught me the principle of marriage for eternity, and
the doctrine of plural marriage. . . . I asked him to teach it to someone else. He
looked at me reprovingly . . . [saying] 'I will not cease to pray for you.' " *Historical Record*, Vol. VI, p. 232.

and you can go home this evening, and your parents will not know anything about it."

When the girl demurred and begged for time, Brigham called in Joseph, who also urged her to make an immediate decision. "Just go ahead, and do as Brigham wants you to," he said, and added with a laugh: "He is the best man in the world, except me." Then he went on more seriously: "If you will accept of Brigham, you shall be blessed — God shall bless you, and my blessing shall rest upon you . . . and if you do not like it in a month or two, come to me, and I will make you free again; and if he turns you off, I will take you on."

"Sir, it will be too late to think in a month or two after," Martha answered wryly. "I want time to think first."

To this the prophet replied: "But the old proverb is, 'Nothing ventured, nothing gained.' "

Finally and reluctantly they let her go home, where she promised to pray in secret for guidance. The moment she arrived, however, she wrote down the whole episode while it was still fresh in her memory, and showed it to her parents. The Brothertons in high dudgeon took a steamboat to St. Louis, but not before they had given Martha's recital enough circulation so that everyone in Nauvoo knew it within a week. Eventually Martha published her account in a St. Louis paper.* But even before it appeared, Joseph had taken measures to kill the rumors her departure had set in motion.

Hyrum at the April conference contradicted the report "that a sister had been shut in a room for several days, and that they endeavored to induce her to believe in having two wives." The twelve apostles all testified that Joseph's principles were strictly virtuous, and Joseph himself took the stand in a blistering sermon against all adulterers and fornicators who were making use of his name to sanction their corruption.

---

* See the *St. Louis Bulletin,* July 15, 1842, p. 2. This was reprinted in many Eastern and Illinois papers, and also in Bennett's *History of the Saints.* The prophet never replied directly to her charges, but Heber Kimball and Brigham Young called her story a base falsehood, and Martha's two sisters and brother-in-law, who had remained true to the church, were persuaded to swear that she was not only a liar but also a harlot. See *Affidavits and Certificates Disproving the Statements and Affidavits Contained in John C. Bennett's Letters,* a pamphlet published by the church leaders on August 31, 1842. Elizabeth Brotherton, who signed one of these statements against Martha, became the plural wife of Parley Pratt on July 24, 1843. See *Utah Genealogical and Historical Magazine,* Vol. XXVII (1936), pp. 108–9.

"We have among us," he said in part, "thieves, adulterers, liars, hypocrites. If God should speak from heaven, he would command you not to steal, not to commit adultery, not to covet nor deceive, but be faithful over a few things. As far as we degenerate from God, we descend to the devil and lose knowledge, and without knowledge we cannot be saved. . . . The Church must be cleansed, and I proclaim against all iniquity. A man is saved no faster than he gets knowledge." *

Joseph could with a certain honesty inveigh against adultery in the same week that he slept with another man's wife, or indeed several men's wives, because he had interposed a very special marriage ceremony. And who was to say him nay, since in the gentile world the simple pronouncement of a few time-worn phrases by any justice of peace was all that was necessary to transform fornication into blessed matrimony. The spoken word stood between him and his own guilt. And with Joseph the word was God.

* See *History of the Church*, Vol. IV, pp. 585–8, for a complete report of the minutes of this conference.

CHAPTER XXII

The Bennett Explosion

I T IS ONE of the odd coincidences of Mormon history that the three men who most astutely judged the potentialities of the Mormon movement all bore the name Bennett. James Gordon Bennett, editor of the *New York Herald,* though fascinated by the Mormon phenomenon, was content to watch it from a distance. James Arlington Bennett, a prominent New York lawyer and textbook writer, wrote admiring and imaginative letters which much influenced Joseph Smith, but he delayed going to Nauvoo until after the prophet's death. But John Cook Bennett, sensing the dynamism in the church, and no doubt attracted by the rumors of polygamy, wasted no time in entrenching himself.

For a year and a half he was Joseph's most intimate friend, showered with favors that older converts, who had sacrificed fortune and health to the gospel, would have given much to share. Only those close to the prophet knew of the stormy sessions that marred this friendship. For Bennett was too ambitious and too wayward to stay in favor. Callous, profligate, and too wise in his profession as physician and instructor of midwifery, he was eager to exploit polygamy.

After the two men broke completely, Joseph said in a guarded public statement that he had caught Bennett preaching promiscuous intercourse as early as December 1840 and had let him off with a severe rebuke. Then in mid-July 1841 he had again discovered that Bennett was seducing innocent women, this time in the name of the prophet and with the promise of marriage. Joseph said that when he confronted Bennett with the evidence and also with letters showing him to be a wife-deserter, Bennett in despair took poison — not enough to kill himself (though he was physician enough to be able to measure the correct dose), but enough to convince everyone that his repentance was sincere.*

* *History of the Church,* Vol. V, pp. 37, 42.

Actually Bennett may have been taking spiritual wives with Joseph's complete sanction, as were Brigham Young and Heber C. Kimball early in 1842. But it is clear from the innuendoes in Joseph's statement that Bennett looked upon the whole celestial-marriage paraphernalia as mere show and dispensed with it whenever he pleased. Unlike Joseph, he had never been troubled by the necessity of rationalizing his own impulses or of squaring himself with God.

By the spring of 1842 Joseph realized that he was nurturing a volatile and dangerous rival. He suspected Bennett of plotting to have him "accidentally" shot at the Legion target practice. But the actual spark that set off the explosion of his expulsion seems to have been ignited by a rivalry for the affections of nineteen-year-old Nancy Rigdon, daughter of Sidney.

Since Joseph's courtship of Nancy was described by her brother John and her brother-in-law George W. Robinson as well as by Bennett, there is no reason for doubting the story. Joseph arranged for a private interview with Nancy at the home of Mrs. Orson Hyde. But Nancy had been forewarned by Bennett, and met his exhortations with tears and abuse, finally threatening to scream until the whole town came running unless he let her go home. The next day Joseph made the mistake of dictating a letter to her:

Happiness is the object and design of our existence; and will be the end thereof, if we pursue the path that leads to it; and this path is virtue, uprightness, and faithfulness, holiness, and keeping all the commandments of God, but we cannot keep all the commandments without first knowing them. . . .

Whatever God requires is right, no matter what it is, although we may not see the reason thereof till long after the events transpire. If we seek first the kingdom of God, all good things will be added. So with Solomon: first he asked wisdom, and God gave it him, and with it every desire of his heart; even things which might be considered abominable to all who understand the order of Heaven only in part, but which in reality were right because God sanctioned by special revelation. . . .

This letter was perhaps the first forthright argument for polygamy that Joseph ever put to paper.* Nancy showed it to

* Nancy gave this letter to Francis Higbee, who turned it over to Bennett, who

her father, who until now had apparently been completely ignorant of polygamy, and told him of Joseph's advances. Wild with fury, Rigdon sent for him at once. George Robinson, who was present when he arrived, wrote to a friend that Joseph at first denied everything, but when Rigdon thrust the letter in his face, he broke down and admitted the truth, lamely excusing himself by saying that he had merely been testing Nancy's virtue.*

"The story got out," Nancy's brother John commented in later years, "and it became the talk of the town that Joseph had made a proposition to Nancy Rigdon to become his wife, and that she refused him." †

The prophet could ill afford a new scandal following so close upon the heels of Martha Brotherton's. Blaming Bennett for the whole imbroglio, he decided to put an end to his insolence, and on May 11, 1842 he drew up a bull of excommunication.‡ But he knew that Bennett could be the most deadly enemy the church had ever faced. Seeking a way to stop his mouth, he called in several women whose names had been linked with that of the celebrated doctor and questioned them sharply. Now, apparently for the first time, he learned the full measure of Bennett's debauchery.

Bennett had seduced innumerable women in Joseph's name quite without benefit of ceremony. Even worse, he had promised abortion to those who became pregnant. Zeruiah N. Goddard, repeating the gossip of Sarah Pratt, reported that "Dr. Bennett told her he could cause abortion with perfect safety to the mother at any stage of pregnancy, and that he had frequently destroyed and removed infants before their time to

---

in turn published it in his *History of the Saints*, pp. 243–5. It was unsigned, and in the handwriting of Willard Richards. The Utah Church published it as an essay on "Happiness" ostensibly written by Joseph Smith, in the *History of the Church*, Vol. V, pp. 134–6, with the cryptic editorial comment: "It is not positively known what occasioned the writing of this essay."

* See Robinson's letter to James Arlington Bennett (also spelled Bennet), of Long Island, dated Nauvoo, July 27, 1842. This Bennett admitted in the *New York Herald*, November 4, 1842, that he gave the letter to John Cook Bennett, who published it in his *History of the Saints*, p. 246.

† John W. Rigdon's affidavit is published in Joseph F. Smith, Jr.: *Blood Atonement and the Origin of Plural Marriage*, pp. 81–4.

‡ *History of the Church*, Vol. V, p. 74.

prevent exposure of the parties and that he had instruments for that purpose." *

Joseph wrote nothing in his journal of the scene in which he faced Bennett with the affidavits he had collected, but Bennett later described the interview with his own carefully selected detail. When he entered the prophet's office, he wrote, Joseph locked the door, put the key in his pocket, drew a pistol, and said without preamble: "The peace of my family requires that you should sign an affidavit, and make a statement before the next City Council, exonerating me from all participation whatever, whether directly or indirectly, in word or deed, in the spiritual wife doctrine, or private intercourse with females in general, and if you do not do it with apparent cheerfulness, I will make catfish bait of you, or deliver you to the Danites for execution tonight — for my dignity and purity must and shall be maintained before the public." †

Whatever the prophet actually said, no doubt there was a bitter verbal battle. Against the sworn testimonies of the women he had betrayed Bennett had only the ambiguous, unsigned letter to Nancy Rigdon to place in the scales. But he knew several of Joseph's wives and doubtless threatened to drag them with Joseph through a dung-heap.

Joseph won out, but was forced to concede Bennett the privilege of an amicable withdrawal and a public vote of thanks for his services as mayor of Nauvoo. On May 19 Bennett appeared before the city council and began with a twisted smile: "I know what I am about, and the heads of the Church know what they are about, I expect; I have no difficulty with the heads of the Church. I publicly avow that any one who has said that I have stated that General Joseph Smith has given me authority

* See the testimony of Hyrum Smith, *Wasp* extra, July 27, 1842, republished in *History of the Church*, Vol. V, pp. 71–2; and the statement of Zeruiah N. Goddard, with whom Sarah Pratt boarded for several months, published in *Affidavits and Certificates Disproving the Statements and Affidavits Contained in John C. Bennett's Letters* (Nauvoo, August 31, 1842). There can be no doubt that Bennett was an abortionist. Sarah Pratt told W. Wyl many years later that Bennett had showed her one of his instruments and indicated that he had performed illegal operations in the city. *Mormon Portraits*, p. 61.

† Letter from Bennett to the *Sangamo Journal*, dated July 2, 1842, published July 15, 1842.

to hold illicit intercourse with women is a liar in the face of God." *

Joseph had hoped that Bennett would slip out of Nauvoo into oblivion, but he had not reckoned with the man's tenacity. Bennett prevailed on Brigham Young and Wilson Law to plead for him and did his best to placate Rigdon. Now Joseph was faced with a dismaying dilemma. Stories of Bennett's depravity had seeped through the city, and if he was now restored to favor the prophet would be accused of countenancing abortion and prostitution. An outraged High Council was grilling Bennett's closest friends, Chauncey and Francis Higbee, who justified their incontinence in the prophet's name.† Denial and counter-denial only spread the flood of slanderous rumor that now ran wild through the city.

For a time Joseph clung to the hope that Bennett would be less dangerous in the church than out and, despite the fact that the apostles and High Council had excommunicated him on May 25, agreed to keep him in fellowship if he would make a public confession. In a dramatic session before one hundred brethren in the Masonic Hall on May 26, Bennett, weeping like a child, told a goodly portion of his misdeeds. Then to the astonishment and indignation of many present, Joseph pleaded mercy for him.

This stand he had to justify not only to the brethren but also to an irate Relief Society. "A little tale will set the world on fire," he said. "At this time, the truth on the guilty should not be told openly, strange as this may seem, yet this is policy. . . . It is necessary to hold an influence in the world, and thus spare ourselves an extermination. . . . I am advised by some of the heads of the Church to tell the Relief Society to be virtuous, but to save the Church from desolation and the sword; beware, be still, be prudent, repent, reform, but do it in a way not to destroy all around you." ‡

For four weeks more Bennett remained a sore on the church, foul-smelling and insistent on attention. Finally Joseph became convinced that it was better to cut him off and let him do his

---

* *History of the Church*, Vol. V, p. 13.
† Ibid., Vol. V, p. 18.
‡ Ibid., Vol. V, p. 20.

worst than to nurture the corruption he was breeding in Nauvoo. Bennett would damn him if he used the knife, but his own people would if he did not. On June 23, 1842 he publicly exposed him and issued the bull of excommunication which had been held in reserve since the 11th of May.

On July 8, 1842 the *Sangamo Journal* in Springfield published the most sensational extra of its career. John C. Bennett, next to the prophet the most celebrated figure in Nauvoo, had been excommunicated from the Mormon Church and was writing the editor a series of letters the like of which the latter, in all his years of sifting scandal, libel, and election hoaxes, had never seen before.

"I write you now from the Mormon Zion, the city of the Saints," Bennett began the first letter, "where I am threatened with death by the Holy Joe, and his Danite band of murderers." Calling the prophet everything from an outrageous libertine to a foul and polluted murderer, Bennett heaped story upon story until he made Nauvoo a name to rank with Sodom and Gomorrah. His subsequent letters were published at irregular intervals up to the end of September, when they appeared, collected and revised, in a book called *The History of the Saints: or, An Exposé of Joe Smith and Mormonism.*

The long catalogue of Bennett's accusations was republished in the leading American newspapers. "The whole thing," said the *New York Herald* on July 24, "is full of philosophy, fun, roguery, religion, truth, falsehood, fanaticism, and philosophy. Read the following extracts, put your trust in the Lord, and learn how to restrain your passions."

Bennett accused Joseph of setting up a despotism on the frontier which aimed to overthrow the Western states and establish an empire with himself as king. This was to be accomplished through the Legion, which, Bennett said (skirting his own peculiar responsibility in the matter), had secured thirty cannon and immense quantities of small arms from the state of Illinois.*

Practically every member of the Legion, he continued, had taken the Danite oath, swearing to defend the prophet whether

* Thomas Ford, who followed Carlin as Governor of Illinois, pointed out that actually only three cannon and 350 stand of small arms had been turned over to the Mormon militia. *History of Illinois*, p. 267.

right or wrong. Twelve of the most ruthless Danites had been set apart as Destroying Angels, whose business it was to spy out the prophet's enemies and assassinate them at midnight, garbed in white robes, and wearing a wide red sash about their waists.*

Bennett's tales of Danites and "Angels" were as nothing compared with his account of the moral decadence in Nauvoo. Joseph, he declared, had set up an elaborate system of prostitution for the special benefit of the church hierarchy. The Mormon women inducted into this system were divided into three classes:

The lowest, called the Cyprian Saints, consisted of those warmhearted, carelessly generous females who had been betrayed into an indiscretion and forced to confess and who thereafter were designated as harridans for the church leaders.

The second class, the Chambered Sisters of Charity, or Saints of the Green Veil, was composed of women somewhat less disposed to a free distribution of their charms, but still sufficiently prodigal to bestow them on occasion without benefit of a marriage ceremony. If a church official wished to win a Chambered Sister of Charity, Bennett explained, he asked Joseph, who looked in his peepstone and there inquired the will of Heaven. If he desired the woman for himself, the answer was no.

Most honored among the Nauvoo women, said Bennett, were the Cloistered Saints, or Saints of the Black Veil, who went through a marriage ritual and became secret or "spiritual" wives. Joseph, he reported, had at least seven, but out of deference to their reputations he listed them by initial only.†

Joseph's affections, he continued, ranged from the handsome gentile whore who lived down by the steamboat landing up through the scale of Nauvoo society to the fiery, vivacious Nancy Rigdon. Even married women were not immune to Joseph's

* There is no reliable evidence that the Danite organization was continued in Illinois except among Joseph's personal bodyguard. White uniforms (not robes) were a part of their military attire. John D. Lee, one of Joseph's bodyguard, proudly wore his red sash in later years when he went to dances in southern Utah.

† See p. 302n. It is impossible to judge the accuracy of Bennett's stories except where they are supplemented by more reliable data. There is no other reference to Cyprian Saints, Chambered Sisters of Charity, or Cloistered Saints in any available document. Yet the Cloistered Saints roughly corresponded to the system of plural wives Joseph had set up. Whether the others were Bennett's own secret ramifications of the plural-wife system or whether he simply made them up out of whole cloth to make his exposé as lurid as possible cannot be ascertained.

importunities. There was Mrs. Sarah Pratt, wife of the apostle Orson Pratt, then on a mission to England. Bennett said that he knew her well, having boarded at her house for some months, and he described her as "one of the most elegant, graceful, amiable, and accomplished women in the place."

Mrs. Pratt, he said, told him the full details of Joseph's conversation with her. After the appropriate preliminaries the prophet said: "Sister Pratt, the Lord has given you to me as one of my *spiritual wives*. I have the blessings of Jacob granted me, as God granted holy men of old; and as I have long looked upon you with favor, and an earnest desire of connubial bliss, I hope you will not repulse or deny me."

Sarah is supposed to have replied in the following dignified language: "Am I called upon to break the marriage covenant, and prove recreant to my lawful husband? *I never will*. My sex shall not be disgraced, nor my honor sullied. I care not for the blessings of Jacob, and I believe in no such revelations, neither will I consent, under any circumstances whatever. I have one good husband, and that is enough for me."

Joseph then threatened her, Bennett said, for he was fearful lest she spread the story. "If you should tell, I will ruin your reputation; remember that. . . ." *

Bennett bolstered his accusations with several bawdy affidavits from Nauvoo prostitutes and two letters allegedly dictated by the prophet, one of these the letter to Nancy Rigdon. He held Joseph to be the most consummate charlatan in the country, so steeped in trickery that he had become scornful of God and man alike. As evidence he cited a request that Joseph supposedly made of him after they had become intimate friends:

Joe proposed to me to go to New York, and get some plates engraved, and bring them to him, so that he could exhibit them as the genuine plates of the Book of Mormon, which he pretended had been

---

* Mrs. Pratt never published a statement of her own, but in later years two men obtained interviews with her. One, Joseph Smith's eldest son, quoted her as saying: "No Joseph, your father never said an improper word to me in his life. He knew better. . . . There is no truth in the reports that have been circulated about him in this regard. He was always the Christian gentleman and a noble man." ("Memoirs of President Joseph Smith," *Saints Herald*, January 22, 1935, p. 109.) W. Wyl, on the other hand, in *Mormon Portraits*, quoted her as mentioning Joseph's "dastardly attempt on me." And there was serious trouble between the prophet and Orson Pratt after the latter's return from England. Mrs. Pratt was subjected to an intensive smear campaign, and the couple nearly left the church.

taken from him, and "hid up" by an angel, and which he would profess to have recovered. He calculated upon making considerable
money by this trick, as there would be great anxiety to see the plates,
which he intended to exhibit at 25 cents a sight. I mentioned this
proposition to Mrs. Sarah M. Pratt on the day the Prophet made it,
and requested her to keep it in memory as it might be of much
importance.*

Realizing that his own position was equivocal, Bennett prefaced his book with the statement that he had joined the Mormons only to expose them, and that he had pretended to great
friendship with the prophet in order to lay bare his perfidy. The
first fifty pages of his book were devoted to statements attest-
ing the integrity of his own character. When the historian H. H.
Bancroft read these, he commented with a nice irony: "When a
man thrusts in your face three-score certificates of his good
character by from one to a dozen persons, you may know that
he is a very great rascal."

To any discerning reader Bennett revealed himself in his own
book to be a base and ignoble opportunist. The *New York Herald,* after getting the full news value of the letters by republish-
ing them as they appeared in the *Sangamo Journal,* loftily
scorned Bennett's own collection, *The History of the Saints,* as
"obscene and licentious in the highest degree."

Even the Whig press in Illinois, while exploiting the letters
and book to the hilt as unexpected political capital, felt obliged
to make reservations about the author's character. "We can
hardly put reliance upon the statements of Bennett," said the
Quincy Whig on July 16, 1842, "they disclose so much wickedness."

The Democratic press refused to publish any of Bennett's
stories, scored the opposition for descending to political pornog-
raphy, and called the whole scandal a Whig plot. The *Illinois
State Register* on July 15 accused the Whig candidate for governor, Joseph Duncan, of publishing at his own expense thousands of copies of Bennett's "obscene, vulgar, and immoral
statements" and cried shame upon such "panderers of licentiousness and moral depravity." Nevertheless, the Democrats were

---

* When Mrs. Pratt was asked about this years later, she confirmed Bennett's story,
but it may be that Bennett concocted it himself in order to slander the prophet at his
most vulnerable point. See W. Wyl: *Mormon Portraits,* p. 21.

terribly shaken, and feared that Bennett had cost them the election.

At this point the Democrats ran into an unexpected piece of good luck. The sudden death of their candidate for governor, Adam Snyder, left the post open for a man who could stand completely aloof from the Mormon question. Since practically every leading political figure in the state had voted for the Mormon charters, this candidate was not easy to find. The party finally selected a sober, innocuous lawyer named Thomas Ford, then serving as a justice of the state Supreme Court.

Though ostensibly no politician, Ford conducted a very shrewd campaign. "I have no means of knowing," he said in his speeches in regard to the Mormons, "whether, in point of fact, they intend to vote for me or Governor Duncan. . . . I am so entirely ignorant of the Mormons that I do not know anything about them either in a religious, political, or moral point of view, and therefore I can neither defend nor condemn them. . . . I neither seek nor reject them, but leave them free, like other people, to choose between my competitor and myself." *

The Whigs tried desperately to prove that Ford had sold out to the prophet, but without success, since Ford even advocated repeal of the extraordinary powers granted in the Nauvoo charters. By election time the initial horror at Bennett's exposé had spent itself, and the campaign of counter-accusation that Joseph Smith had energetically set in motion was beginning to take effect. Ford was elected, the Whig papers ceased their fulminations, and the state settled back into its old routine.

But there was no return to routine in Nauvoo. Bennett had opened Pandora's box, and the most frantic efforts could not recapture all the furies that he loosed.

It was the prophet's good fortune, however, that Bennett so egregiously overstated his case that it was possible to discredit him in the eyes of the Mormon people. Before many weeks Joseph had made Bennett's name synonymous with licentiousness and betrayal. A *Wasp* extra published on July 27, 1842 declared him "a spoiler of character and virtue, and a living pestilence, walking in darkness to fester in his own infamy." And a special pamphlet, *Affidavits and Certificates Disproving the Statements*

* *Illinois State Register*, July 1, 1842.

and Affidavits Contained in John C. Bennett's Letters, denounced him for seduction, pandering, and abortion. Sarah Pratt and Nancy Rigdon here were publicly accused of being his mistresses.

Non-Mormons were inclined to believe both Bennett's and Joseph's collections of affidavits. But within Nauvoo no one dared accuse Joseph of polygamy since it meant identifying him with Bennett. Rigdon was so outraged at the slander against his daughter that he published a statement calling Stephen Markham, who had linked Nancy's name with Bennett, a notorious liar. Yet he was so appalled at the proof of Bennett's degeneracy that he added his own denunciation of Bennett to those of the other church leaders and kept silent about Joseph's importunities to Nancy.*

Bennett had fully expected the Pratts and Rigdon to follow him out of the church, but in both instances he was disappointed. Pratt, who had some time since returned from England to teach mathematics at the University of Nauvoo, wandered about Nauvoo like a man bereft of sense, proclaiming the innocence of his wife to every passer-by. When William Law called upon the Saints in a public meeting to acknowledge Joseph as a "good, moral, virtuous, peaceable and patriotic man," Pratt stood up, pale and lonely-looking among the thousands, to register the only negative vote.†

One morning he disappeared, and the whole of Nauvoo went out in search of him, for he was generally liked and admired. He was finally discovered miles below the town, sitting hatless on the bank of the Mississippi. Shorn of his apostleship, suspicious of friend and enemy alike, and tormented by doubts of Sarah's own denials, he had come very near suicide. But he stayed in Nauvoo, wrestling with his furies for five months, after which he was rebaptized with his wife in the Mississippi River.‡

In the seclusion of his home Sidney Rigdon alternately sulked

---

Rigdon's statement against Markham, dated September 3, 1842, was published in the *Sangamo Journal,* September 23, 1842. His denunciation of Bennett appeared in the *Wasp* extra, July 27, 1842.

† The *Wasp* extra, July 27, 1842.

‡ *History of the Church,* Vol. V, pp. 138, 256; and *The Return,* Vol. II (November 1890), p. 362. Pratt eventually became the husband of ten wives and the father of forty-five children.

and prayed for many weeks. Then one day, pale and shaken, he mounted the platform in the grove to describe a miracle. His daughter Eliza, he reported, after a brief illness had fallen into a coma and died. The doctor had pronounced her dead and left the house, and the family had given way to its grief. But Eliza had risen from her bed, called the family around her, and lashed at Nancy with a message from heaven: "It is in your heart to deny this work; and if you do, the Lord says it will be the damnation of your soul!" Bennett was a wicked man, she insisted, and the Lord was about to trample him underfoot. But if Nancy continued in the faith, she would be showered with divine blessings.

After delivering this admonition, Rigdon continued, Eliza had swooned away. For hours she had hovered between life and death, while he had knelt at her bedside praying in anguish and repentance. Finally the Lord had healed her, and now he had come to testify that Joseph was a true and not a fallen prophet, and that he was truly chosen to build up the kingdom of God.*

Eliza Rigdon's sensational experience, whatever it was, may have had psychological roots in a consuming jealousy of Nancy. At any rate, it saved the prophet a defection that might have been grave indeed. For if Bennett can be believed, Rigdon was at one time on the point of writing a book against his leader. Once again Joseph had been saved by a miracle not of his making.

For Joseph one of the worst aspects of the Bennett scandal was that instead of preaching the new marriage order more and more openly, as he had hoped to do, he was forced to ever greater secrecy. When he published the Udney Jacob pamphlet in an effort to stem the tide of revulsion against anything that hinted of matrimonial experimentation, it roused such a storm of indignation that he was obliged hastily to renounce it in *Times and Seasons* as an "unmeaning rigmarole of nonsense, folly, and trash." †

This and other public denials of spiritual wifism put a peculiar burden on his own wives and also on the leading Mormon men who were beginning to practice polygamy. Joseph per-

* *History of the Church,* Vol. V, pp. 121-2.
† Vol. IV (December 1, 1842), p. 32.

suaded a dozen prominent elders to swear that none but the conventional marriage order existed in Nauvoo, and that Bennett's system was "a creature of his own make." A similar statement was signed by a dozen important Mormon women, with Emma's name proudly at their head. But while Emma signed the affidavit in good faith, others unhappily perjured themselves. Among the signatories were Newel and Elizabeth Whitney, who but three months earlier had stood witness at the marriage of their seventeen-year-old daughter Sarah Ann to the prophet.*

Eliza Snow swore along with the rest, although she had been the prophet's wife since June 29, 1842. A sensitive and high-minded woman, she must have been pained at this denial. She was living in Joseph's home, tutoring his children as well as conducting a school, and was, next to Emma, the most beloved woman in Nauvoo. Children memorized her long didactic poems, which appeared regularly in *Times, and Seasons,* and sang her hymns on the streets. Joseph had married her in the week of Bennett's expulsion, and gossip later had it that Emma had set her to spying on the prophet and he had married her to keep her quiet.

But Eliza Snow was the last woman in Nauvoo to stoop to spying on the man she revered as a god, and her autobiography makes it clear that she had been taught the principle of polygamy for some time before she entered it, although she hoped — and believed — that years would pass before it was actually practiced. Although she was as old as Emma, the years had dealt gently with her austere beauty. It is quite likely that Joseph had admired her for a long time but because of her initial revulsion to the concept of plural marriage had not pressed his suit until Bennett's disclosures made it imperative that he take her into his full confidence.

The denials of polygamy uttered by the Mormon leaders between 1835 and 1852, when it was finally admitted, are a remarkable series of evasions and circumlocutions involving all sorts of verbal gymnastics. When the brethren attacked spiritual wifism or polygamy, it was with the mental reservation that

---

* The sworn statements were published in *Times and Seasons,* Vol. III (October 21, 1842), pp. 939–40. Sarah Ann Whitney was married to Joseph on July 27, 1842. See Appendix C.

"the patriarchal order of marriage" or "celestial order of plurality of wives" was immeasurably different.

The prophet's denials of polygamy were never as direct as
those of his leading polygamist brethren. "There is a great noise
in the city," he said in one address, "and many are saying there
cannot be so much smoke without some fire. Well, be it so. If
the stories about Joe Smith are true, then the stories of John C.
Bennett are true about the ladies of Nauvoo; and he says that
the Ladies' Relief Society are all organized of those who are to
be the wives of Joe Smith. Ladies, you know whether this is true
or not. It is no use living among hogs without a snout. This
biting and devouring each other I cannot endure. Away with
it. For God's sake, stop it." *

* February 21, 1843. *History of the Church,* Vol. V, p. 286.

CHAPTER XXIII
Into Hiding

IN THE SPRING of 1841, when Joseph was harassed by the threat of extradition to Missouri, he had said some bitter things. No scribe had recorded the speech in which he called down curses upon his persecutors, but the rumor got about that he had predicted that the hated Boggs would meet a violent death within a year and that Governor Carlin would die in a ditch.*

When, therefore, in May 1842 word came to Nauvoo that Boggs had been shot by an unknown assailant, "it went through the city as if a great prophecy had been fulfilled." † A writer in the *Wasp* who signed himself Vortex commented indiscreetly on May 28: "Boggs is undoubtedly killed according to report; but who did the noble deed remains to be found out." Certain observers in Nauvoo noted that Joseph's sinister bodyguard Porter Rockwell, who had been absent for some weeks, returned to the city just two days after the news of the shooting. He admitted to friends that he had just come from Missouri.

The Whig press, knowing the zeal of some of Joseph's men for making his prophecies come true, was quick to point the finger of suspicion and insinuated that Joseph was behind the assault. "The Mormon prophet," said the *Quincy Whig* on May 21, "as we understand, prophesied a year or so ago, his death by violent means. Hence there is plenty of foundation for rumor." Joseph replied indignantly in the *Wasp* on May 28: "Boggs was a candidate for the state senate, and, I presume, fell by the hands of a political opponent, with 'his hands and face yet dripping with the blood of murder'; but he died not through my instrumentality. My hands are clean and my heart pure from the blood of all men."

John C. Bennett wrote that he had heard the prophet offer a

---

* Carlin reported this rumor back to Joseph in a letter dated June 30, 1842. See *History of the Church*, Vol. V, p. 50.

† According to Oliver Olney, who was then in Nauvoo. See his *Absurdities of Mormonism Portrayed*, p. 19.

five-hundred-dollar reward to any Destroying Angel who would kill Boggs. At first, Bennett said, he had been certain that Porter Rockwell had been the assailant, for before his trip to Missouri he had been abjectly poor, and after his return he had "an elegant carriage and horses at his disposal, and his pockets were filled with gold." But Joseph had insisted, Bennett continued, that the carriage and gold were furnished Rockwell to haul tourists to and from the steamboat to the temple. "The Destroying Angel has done the work as I predicted," the prophet said, "but Rockwell was not the man who shot. The Angel did it!"

Bennett was not content with accusing the prophet in print. Boggs had obstinately refused to die, though he had been hit three times in the head. As soon as he had sufficiently recovered, Bennett went to him with all that he knew and more that he imagined about the attempted assassination. Boggs promptly swore to an affidavit charging Joseph with being "an accessory before the fact of the intended murder," and persuaded Governor Reynolds to ask for his extradition on the ground that he was a fugitive from justice.

When the sheriffs arrived in Nauvoo on August 8, 1842, armed with the writ and a warrant from Governor Carlin, both Joseph and Porter Rockwell submitted to arrest, but were released under a writ of habeas corpus issued by the Nauvoo municipal court. The city council then passed an ordinance giving the Nauvoo court power to inquire into the validity and legality of every writ or process served upon a Nauvoo citizen, and the right to dismiss it if the writ or process was found to have been issued "either through private pique, malicious intent, or religious persecution, falsehood or misrepresentation." *

Faced with this ordinance, which was an obvious infringement upon the powers of the state courts, the Missouri sheriffs went back to Governor Carlin for further instructions. Joseph had a thousand witnesses to prove that he had been in Nauvoo on the day of the shooting, but he was certain that extradition to Missouri meant death. That he had no faith in the legality of the ordinance and used it only as a ruse to escape arrest, the sheriffs discovered upon their return. For Rockwell had secretly

* Printed in the *Wasp,* August 13, 1842.

departed for Philadelphia and Joseph had gone into hiding close to Nauvoo.

For four months the prophet lived the uncertain, nerve-shattering existence of a fugitive from justice with a handsome price upon his head. He hid in many places, from the secret bricked-in vault under the cellar steps of his home to the farm of a friend two days' journey north of Nauvoo. He usually traveled by skiff up and down the river at night, often landing for a time on an island to baffle possible pursuers. His friends launched rumors that he had gone to Washington, to Wisconsin, and even to Europe; but the sheriffs nevertheless made repeated visits to the city hoping to catch him in one of his rare visits home.

When he first went into hiding, Joseph sank into a pit of depression that threatened to suffocate him. He thought much about death in that half-pleasant, half-grisly imagery that a young man associates with the grave, and planned an elaborate tomb on the river bank, which, he wrote in his journal, must be called "the tomb of Joseph, a descendant of Jacob."

Solitude and foreboding did not turn him to introspection, however. Although he submerged himself in his letters and journal, there was no self-communing, only rhetorical lament:

O Lord, God, my heavenly Father, shall it be vain, that Thy servant must needs be exiled from the midst of his friends, or be dragged from their bosoms, to clank in cold and iron chains; to be thrust within the dreary prison walls; to spend days of sorrow, and of grief, and misery there, by the hands of an infuriated, incensed, and infatuated foe; to glut their infernal and insatiable desire upon innocent blood; and for no other cause on the part of Thy servant, than for the defense of innocence; and Thou a just God will not hear his cry? Oh, No; Thou wilt hear me — a child of woe . . . mine enemies shall not prevail; they all shalt melt like wax before Thy face. . . .*

Emma's first visit was a great comfort to him. The Bennett exposé had been a paralyzing shock to her, and he had not been sure what she would turn to in his absence. "How glorious were my feelings," he wrote in his journal, "when I met that faithful and friendly band, on the night of the eleventh, on Thursday, on the island at the mouth of the slough, between Zarahemla

* *History of the Church*, Vol. V, p. 128.

and Nauvoo: with what unspeakable delight, and what transports of joy swelled my bosom, when I took by the hand, on that night, my beloved Emma — she that was my wife, even the wife of my youth, and the choice of my heart. Many were the reverberations of my mind when I contemplated for a moment the many scenes we had been called to pass through, the fatigues and the toils, the sorrows and sufferings, and the joys and consolations, from time to time, which had strewed our paths and crowned our board. Oh what a commingling of thought filled my mind for the moment, again she is here, even in the seventh trouble — undaunted, firm, and unwavering — unchangeable, affectionate Emma!" *

Emma was always first with Joseph, a steady, monumental presence against which all the other wives were but lights and shadows. He accorded her what he believed to be all the rights of her position — complete domination of the children and the home — and even trusted her to transact considerable business for him. Occasionally he deferred to her in matters of decorum and propriety. But his affection now was largely nostalgic. It was the "wife of his youth" to whom he paid his own special kind of devotion.

As an intellectual companion she did not exist for him, nor did any woman. One of Joseph's rare references to Emma in his journal is as revealing of this as it is of the prophet's vanity. When she was serving dinner to him and Parley Pratt one day, he complained jocularly that she always loaded the table with too much good food. When Pratt suggested that he eat by himself like Napoleon, seated at a table with just the victuals he needed, Emma spoke up quickly: "But Mr. Smith is a bigger man than Bonaparte; he can never eat without his friends." Joseph looked up at her in pleased surprise. "That," he said, "is the wisest thing I ever heard you say."

Exactly what happened between them when Bennett's letters first appeared one cannot know, but it is clear that she set herself determinedly against any intimation of her husband's disloyalty. She demanded denials — and got them. To these she clung with a desperate tenacity. For Emma was ridden with the helpless jealousy that comes to a woman growing unlovely with illness and childbearing while her husband remains madden-

ingly young. And she was proud. The thought of her sons growing up to discover one day that their father, for all his strange
genius and spiritual insight, was a common libertine — for she
never could see a polygamist as anything else — was so nause-
ating that she thrust it from her and for a long time closed her
eyes to what she dared not see.

While Joseph was in hiding she must have found some measure of content despite her terror lest he be captured, for their
visits were frequent and he wrote her tender and affectionate
letters. She could not know that during the weeks he stayed in
hiding at the farm of Edward Sayers he persuaded Mrs. Sayers
to join his circle of wives.*

With the approach of winter Joseph's maneuvering in and out
of Nauvoo became increasingly difficult. He toyed with the idea
of going to Wisconsin, but dismissed it after the inauguration of
Thomas Ford as Governor on December 8, 1842. Ford believed
that the Missouri writ for Joseph's extradition was illegal and
agreed to test it formally in an Illinois court if Joseph would
give himself up for trial.

Emma was now desperately ill, about to give birth to her
eighth child, and the prophet was willing to risk anything for
a little security. As soon as the baby came and he knew that
Emma would recover, he said that he would give himself up
to the law.

The boy was born the day after Christmas, 1842, and died
almost immediately. Since Emma had never really ceased griev-
ing after the bright-eyed little Don Carlos, and Joseph had
prayed that the new baby would still her lament, the death was
doubly bitter. Of her eight children only three had lived, and
Emma felt cheated in her motherhood.

Before leaving for Springfield Joseph called at a neighbor's
house where there were twin baby girls and said to the mother:
"Sister McIntire, I have come to borrow one of your babies. I
want her for my wife to comfort her for a time." The baby was
taken to Joseph's home by day, and at night was returned to her
mother, and in nursing this child Emma was freed of some of
her desolation.

Joseph meanwhile submitted to arrest and set forth for Spring-

* See Appendix C.

field with a retinue of forty of his best soldiers armed to the hilt with bright muskets and brighter bayonets. They stopped for the night in the village of Paris, only to be denied lodging at every inn they visited. Joseph argued good-naturedly at first and then pleaded in deadly earnest, for a prairie gale was whipping through the streets, chilling his men to the marrow and biting their fingers and faces with frost. Suspecting finally that the tavern-owners had leagued together in an agreement to bar them, he insisted harshly, his face livid: "We must and will stay, let the consequence be what it might, for we must stay or perish."

The landlord replied sullenly: "We have heard the Mormons are very bad people; and the inhabitants of Paris have combined not to have anything to do with them."

"We will stay," the prophet repeated in a tone that made the man turn pale, "but no thanks to you. I have men enough to take the town, and if we must freeze, we will freeze by the burning of these houses." The taverns were promptly opened.*

The company marched into Springfield the next day in a slow and solemn parade that caused a sensation among the citizens. "All were astounded at the course of the Prophet in giving himself up," said one newspaper man, "knowing full well that if the Missourians got hold of him he would be gibbeted."

"The prophet is a large, portly, and fine looking man," the writer continued, "six feet without shoes, looks about forty or forty-two, and weighs 220 pounds, eyes light blue, approaching to grey, light brown hair, peaked nose, large head. I think a very little self esteem, but more of the intellectual than the animal — dressed in box coat, black, blue dress coat and pants, black silk velvet vest, white cravat, a large gold ring on the finger next to the little one of his left hand, black cane, and wears a continual smile on his countenance." †

Although technically under arrest, Joseph had complete freedom in the city and met the leading figures in the Illinois state government. His youth, affability, and distinguished appearance won the grudging admiration even of the Whig party leaders, and the trial was rapidly transformed into a personal

* *History of the Church*, Vol. V, p. 211.
† A dispatch from Springfield dated January 4, *New York Herald*, January 18, 1843. Actually Joseph had just turned thirty-seven.

triumph. On New Year's Day the House of Representatives was thrown open to Orson Hyde for a sermon on Mormonism, and Joseph was showered with invitations.

James Adams, judge of the probate court of Sangamon County, who had long had an affection for Joseph and eventually was baptized into the church, insisted on his staying in his own home, though he had no other bed to offer than the living-room sofa. He liked questioning this astonishing young man on everything from his principles of marriage to the state of the millennium, and applauded warmly when Joseph prophesied in the name of the Lord that he would not go to Missouri, dead or alive.

When the decision was read on January 5, 1843, the court-room was crowded to the eaves. Judge Pope entered from the rear, accompanied by a half-dozen ladies whom he smilingly permitted to sit on the stand beside him. This good-humored mockery of the defendant was not lost on the crowd, which was as interested in the prophet's marital history as in his legal embarrassment.

"This case," the judge began after some preliminaries, "presents the important question arising under the Constitution and laws of the United States, whether a citizen of the state of Illinois can be transported from his own state to the state of Missouri, to be there tried for a crime, which, if he ever committed, was committed in the state of Illinois; whether he can be transported to Missouri, as a fugitive from justice, when he has never fled from that state." After a lengthy recital of the arguments, which revolved chiefly around the Boggs affidavit, the judge held the writ invalid and ordered Joseph discharged. The decision surprised no one.

The prophet and his men went back to Nauvoo jubilant. John "Skunk" Bennett, as he was now popularly called, had done his worst, and Joseph had come off triumphant. In a great thanksgiving celebration he served a feast to fifty of his choicest friends. As a gesture of loyalty and humility Emma and Joseph served the guests themselves, and the men and women accepted the food and drink as if it were a sacrament.

When the meal was over, Joseph announced that he and Emma had been married fifteen years to the day, whereupon there descended upon the couple such a hail of good wishes that they stood speechless with emotion. Emma must have felt vindicated at last from the aspersions of John Bennett, although, had she been in a mood for suspicion, the presence of Eliza Snow and Hannah Ells might very well have robbed her of some of the sweetness of this moment.

IF Joseph was cleared from involvement in the Boggs shooting, Porter Rockwell was not. He remained all winter in Philadelphia lonely and penniless. Finally he decided to risk a return to Nauvoo, and with brazen insouciance got off the steamboat at St. Louis for a look around the city. He was recognized, caught, and taken to prison in Independence.

The most damaging evidence against him was Bennett's charge that Rockwell had said to him on July 5, 1842: "If I shot Boggs they have got to prove it — I never done an act in my life that I was ashamed of, and I do not fear to go anywhere that I have ever been, for I have done nothing criminal." * This was flimsy evidence upon which to hang a man, and let it be said to the credit of the Missouri courts that they found it wanting. Although Rockwell was kept in prison nine months, part of the time in irons, he was eventually released.†

However, Rockwell may well have been guilty, for he later boasted of the Boggs shooting, and his subsequent career as henchman for Brigham Young did not exactly establish a reputation for innocuousness.‡ But whether Joseph ordered the deed will always be debatable. Certainly he had nothing to gain by it but trouble. Since Boggs was no longer in power, there could have been no serious motive but revenge, and Joseph was not a

---

* Bennett's account of his interview with Rockwell was printed widely, and was republished in the *Wasp*, July 23, 1842.

† The grand jury never indicted him, no doubt for lack of evidence. He escaped from jail, was recaptured, and was indicted for breaking jail. Tried on this charge in November, he was found guilty and sentenced to "Five minutes confinement in the County Jail." See Heman C. Smith: "The Mormon Troubles in Missouri," *Missouri Historical Review*, Vol. IV (July 1910), pp. 238–51, which prints the court record.

‡ William Hall, who was a Mormon during the Nauvoo years, later wrote: "I heard him afterward boast of his exploits in shooting Boggs." *The Abominations of Mormonism Exposed* (Cincinnati, 1852), p. 30. W. Wyl interviewed General Connor, who had employed Rockwell one winter in Utah. Connor reported that Rockwell admitted the Boggs shooting: "'I shot through the window,' said he, 'and thought I had killed him, but I had only wounded him; I was damned sorry that I had not killed the son of a b—'" *Mormon Portraits*, p. 255. See Charles Kelly: *Holy Murder* (New York, 1934), for Rockwell's later exploits.

vengeful man. If he dispatched Rockwell to fulfill his own prophecy, he must then likewise have planned the murder of Thomas Carlin, and the twin deeds would have been an invitation to the destruction of his whole people. But Joseph seemed content to christen one of his horses Tom Carlin and joke about "riding the Governor" whenever he wanted to provoke a grin.

Yet it should be noted that Joseph H. Jackson, one of the less savory characters Joseph Smith had in his employ for a time, confessed that the prophet in 1843 had offered him $3,000 to "release Porter, and kill old Boggs." And William Law, Second Counselor to Joseph in the Nauvoo years, in his old age swore to an affidavit that said in part: "Joseph told me that he sent a man to kill Governor Boggs of Missouri. The fellow shot the governor in his own house." This he later repeated in an interview with W. Wyl: "Let me tell you that Joe Smith told me the fact himself. The words were substantially like this: 'I sent Rockwell to kill Boggs, but he missed him, it was a failure; he wounded him instead of sending him to Hell.' " *

Bennett and Jackson are unreliable witnesses, to say the least, but Law was a man of integrity. Still it is odd that he waited forty years to accuse Joseph of inciting the Boggs shooting, since he laid many other crimes at the prophet's door when he left the church in 1844.

It is possible, of course, that Bennett's and Jackson's accusations were pure fabrication, and Law's two statements merely a distortion of memory built up through years of bitter feeling against the church. If so, it is still not difficult to understand Rockwell's motivation for the crime. As literal-minded as Brigham Young, he might easily have reasoned that fulfilling Joseph's prophecies should be the business of the Saints, since the Lord could not always be depended upon to hurl thunderbolts with the necessary precision. Or he may simply have taken it upon himself to avenge the Mormon wrongs, regarding it as a public service. Perhaps he was out of favor

* Law's affidavit, sworn July 17, 1885, remained unpublished and in the possession of Zenas H. Gurley, a founder of the Reorganized Church, until 1914. Then it was published by Charles A. Shook in *True Origin of Mormon Polygamy*, pp. 125–9. Wyl's interview was published in the *Salt Lake Tribune* and reprinted in Thomas Gregg: *The Prophet of Palmyra* (New York, 1890), p. 505. For Jackson's statement see *Narrative of the Adventures and Experiences of Joseph H. Jackson* (Warsaw, Illinois, 1844), p. 7.

and hoped thus to reinstate himself. At any rate, he received no censure.

When he returned to Nauvoo in December 1843, Rockwell was a frightening apparition. His hair hung down to his shoulders, black and stringy like a witch's; his clothes were filthy and tattered, his shoes in shreds. It was night when he rowed across the river, and he went directly to Joseph's sumptuous new home, the Mansion House, where a dancing party was in progress.

With a keen relish for practical jokes, Rockwell pushed his way past the guard with an oath and made for the prophet, muttering imprecations and pretending to be drunk. Taking him for a Missourian, Joseph began to scuffle with him and was ready to pitch him headlong out into the night when he got a good look at the man's face.

"It's Porter!" he shouted, and began thumping him on the back with joy. The women stopped screaming, the guards put away their bowie knives, and Rockwell became the lion of the evening. Laughing at his long hair, Joseph promised him that if he kept it long like Samson and lived faithful to the church, his enemies should have no power over him. Accepting this promise as the Lord's word, Porter heeded it to the end of his life.*

Joseph had not been long in the Mansion House before he transformed it into a hotel, for he was weary of entertaining at his own expense a never ending stream of curiosity-seekers. His own family occupied spacious upstairs quarters, and the huge living-room below was turned into a lobby and dining-hall. Some weeks after Rockwell's return Emma went to St. Louis to purchase furnishings. She returned to find in one corner of the lobby a well-equipped bar, with Rockwell, his hair neatly braided and tied with a ribbon, polishing glasses and dispensing whiskey.

"Joseph, what is the meaning of that bar in this house?" she cried with a passion that startled her oldest son, who had never heard his parents quarrel. Joseph was ready with arguments.

* See *History of the Church*, Vol. VI, p. 134, and James Jepson, Jr.: "Memories and Experiences," MS., a copy of which is in the Utah State Historical Society Library. Jepson's parents were at this party. See also Harold Schindler's excellent biography, *Porter Rockwell, Man of God, Son of Thunder* (Salt Lake City, 1966).

Porter was penniless; he deserved much consideration for his nine months in a Missouri jail; his acquittal was of immeasurable aid to them all. Moreover, the bar was temporary and would be transferred to the barber shop then under construction across the street.

"How does it look," she asked witheringly, "for the spiritual head of a religious body to be keeping a hotel which has a room fitted out as a liquor-selling establishment?"

He reminded her that all taverns had bars, and while it was true that no grog shops were permitted in Nauvoo, there must be some place where distinguished travelers could be permitted the refreshment to which they were accustomed. The Nauvoo city council had passed an ordinance giving him the sole right to dispense liquor in his hotel, and who better could be trusted with such a monopoly?

"Well, Joseph," Emma said quietly when she had heard him through, "the furniture and other goods I have purchased for the house will come, and you can have some other person look after things here. As for me, I will take my children and go across to the old house and stay there, for I will not have them raised up under such conditions as this arrangement imposes upon us, nor have them mingle with the kind of men who frequent such a place. You are at liberty to make your choice; either that bar goes out of the house, or we will!"

"Very well, Emma," Joseph answered immediately, "I will have it removed at once." And he did. *

* This dialogue is related in the son's narrative, "Memoirs of President Joseph Smith," *Saints Herald*, January 22, 1935, p. 110. See also *History of the Church*, Vol. VI, pp. 111, 429.

CHAPTER XXIV
The Wives of the Prophet

PROBABLY NO ONE will ever know exactly how many women Joseph Smith married. Brigham Young said quite frankly to William Hepworth Dixon in 1866: "I myself sealed dozens of women to Joseph." One Mormon historian drew up a list of twenty-seven wives, but it is clear from all the available published and manuscript records that the number may have reached or even exceeded fifty.*

In January 1846, eighteen months after his death, thirty women were sealed to the prophet "for eternity" in the Nauvoo temple, and to various other men "for time." Since it is clear from other records that more than two thirds of these women had already been married to Joseph during his lifetime, it can be assumed that for all thirty women the sealing was simply a new solemnization of an earlier ceremony. It was felt that a marriage "for eternity" was not truly binding unless sanctified within the temple, which had not been completed in Joseph's lifetime.

In later years in Utah, scores of women were sealed to the prophet posthumously, but since it is impossible to determine how many of these had been married to him during his lifetime, they are not included here. The following list, therefore, is possibly incomplete. It contains, however, the names of several women whose relationship to the prophet is admittedly little more than presumable.

The first thirty-six wives listed here are arranged in the approximate chronological order of their marriage to Joseph

* See William Hepworth Dixon: *New America* (Philadelphia, 1867), p. 225. Andrew Jenson, formerly assistant historian of the Utah Mormon Church, listed twenty-seven wives in the *Historical Record,* Vol. VI, May 1887, but he gave only the barest details, usually listing them by their maiden names and seldom providing documentation. It is clear that he did not even canvass all the Mormon sources, for he omitted several wives mentioned later by Orson F. Whitney in his *Life of Heber C. Kimball* and many other wives listed in the Nauvoo Temple Record. In the accompanying list question marks indicate where the data are doubtful. For complete documentation on every wife see Appendix C.

Smith. The remainder, where no marriage date can even be guessed at, are listed alphabetically. Since for most of these latter the date of birth is available, and since Joseph married most of his wives during 1843 and 1844, it is possible to suggest the approximate age of each woman when married.

Name	Age When Married	Date of Marriage
1. Emma Hale	22	January 18, 1827
2. Fannie Alger	17 ?	1836
3. Lucinda Pendleton Morgan Harris, wife of G. W. Harris	37 ?	1838 ?
4. Prescindia Huntington Buell, wife of Norman Buell	29 ?	1839 ?
5. Nancy Marinda Johnson Hyde, wife of Orson Hyde	24 ?	1839 ?
6. Clarissa Reed Hancock, wife of Levi W. Hancock	35 ?	1840 ?
7. Louisa Beaman	26	April 5, 1841
8. Zina Diantha Huntington Jacobs, wife of Henry B. Jacobs	20	October 27, 1841
9. Mary Elizabeth Rollins Lightner, wife of Adam Lightner	24	February 1842
10. Patty Bartlett Sessions, wife of David Sessions	47	March 9, 1842
11. Delcena Johnson Sherman, widow of Lyman R. Sherman	36 ?	Before June 1842
12. Mrs. Durfee	?	Before June 1842
13. Sally Ann Fuller Gulley, wife of Samuel Gulley	26 ?	Before June 1842
14. Mrs. A**** S****	?	Before June 1842
15. Miss B****	?	Before June 1842
16. Eliza Roxey Snow	38	June 29, 1842
17. Sarah Ann Whitney	17	July 27, 1842
18. Sarah M. Kinsley Cleveland, wife of John Cleveland	54 ?	1842 ?
19. Elvira A. Cowles	29 ?	Before December 1842
20. Martha McBride	38	Summer 1842
21. Ruth D. Vose Sayers, wife of Edward Sayers	34 ?	August 1842 ?
22. Desdemona Wadsworth Fullmer	33	1842
23. Emily Dow Partridge	19	March 4, 1843

24. Eliza M. Partridge	23	March 1843
25. Almera Woodward Johnson	31	April 1843
26. Lucy Walker	17	May 1, 1843
27. Helen Mar Kimball	15	May 1843
28. Maria Lawrence	19	Spring 1843
29. Sarah Lawrence	17	Spring 1843
30. Flora Ann Woodworth	16	Spring 1843
31. Rhoda Richards	59	June 12, 1843
32. Hannah Ells	30 ?	Summer 1843 ?
33. Melissa Lott	19	September 20, 1843
34. Fanny Young Murray, wife of Roswell Murray	56	November 2, 1843
35. Olive Grey Frost	27–8 ?	After April 1843
36. Mary Ann Frost Pratt, wife of Parley P. Pratt	34–5 ?	After April 1843
37. Olive Andrews	25–6 ?	1843–4 ?
38. Mrs. Blossom, wife of Edward Blossom	?	?
39. Elizabeth Davis	52–3 ?	1843–4 ?
40. Mary Huston	25–6 ?	1843–4 ?
41. Vienna Jacques	55–6 ?	1843–4 ?
42. Cordelia Calista Morley	20–1 ?	1843–4 ?
43. Sarah Scott	?	?
44. Sylvia Sessions	25–6 ?	1843–4 ?
45. Nancy Maria Smith	?	?
46. Jane Tibbets	39–40 ?	1843–4 ?
47. Phebe Watrous	38–9 ?	1843–4 ?
48. Nancy Maria Winchester	15–16 ?	1843–4 ?
49. Sophia Woodman	48–9 ?	1843–4 ?

It will be seen that at least twelve were married women (with living husbands), although the evidence for Mrs. Levi Hancock is only word-of-mouth tradition in the Hancock family. The ages of Joseph's wives varied all the way from the fifteen years of Helen Mar Kimball, daughter of Heber C. Kimball, to the fifty-nine years of Rhoda Richards, spinster sister of Joseph's secretary Willard Richards. The prophet married five pairs of sisters: Delcena and Almera Johnson, Eliza and Emily Partridge, Sarah and Maria Lawrence, Mary Ann and Olive Grey Frost, and Prescindia and Zina Huntington. Patty and Sylvia Sessions were mother and daughter.

The majority of the prophet's wives fall into three general

categories: first, the group of married women to whom Joseph was sealed between 1838 and the expulsion of Bennett in June 1842; and second, the leading women in the Nauvoo Relief Society, who were married to the prophet during the furor that followed Bennett's departure. The third group consists of the dozen or more unmarried women whom he married in the spring and summer of 1843. Most of them were quite young. Helen Mar Kimball was fifteen; Nancy Mariah Winchester (who may be identical with Nancy Maria Smith) was fifteen or sixteen; Lucy Walker, Sarah Lawrence and Flora Ann Woodworth were seventeen. Maria Lawrence and Melissa Lott were nineteen.

Six of the girls Joseph took as wives lived at various times as wards in his own home. These were the Partridge sisters, the Lawrence sisters, Eliza R. Snow, and Lucy Walker. One of these, the seventeen-year-old Lucy Walker, who had moved into the prophet's home after the death of her mother, described Joseph's whirlwind courtship. She thereby revealed not only her own ingenuousness but also Joseph's sophistication. Late in April 1843 Emma Smith went to St. Louis to make purchases for the Mansion House, accompanied by Lucy's brother, Lorin Walker, who was one of Joseph's business aides. During their absence Joseph asked Lucy to become his wife.

"I have no flattering words to offer," he told her after the usual preliminaries. "It is a command of God to you. I will give you until tomorrow to decide this matter. If you reject this message the gate will be closed forever against you."

"This," she said, "aroused every drop of Scotch in my veins. For a few moments I stood fearless before him, and looked him in the eye. I felt at this moment that I was called to place myself upon the altar a living sacrifice — perhaps to brook the world in disgrace and incur the displeasure and contempt of my youthful companions."

"Although you are a Prophet of God," she told him, "you could not induce me to take a step of so great importance, unless I knew that God approved my course. I would rather die."

He walked across the room, returned, and stood before her with what she described as "the most beautiful expression of countenance," and said: "God Almighty bless you. You shall have a manifestation of the will of God concerning you; a testimony that you can never deny. I will tell you what it shall be. It shall be that joy and peace that you never knew."

"Oh how earnestly I prayed for these words to be fulfilled," Lucy said. "It was near dawn after another sleepless night when my room was lighted up by a heavenly influence. To me it was, in comparison, like the brilliant sun bursting through the darkest cloud. My soul was filled with a calm, sweet peace that 'I never knew.' Supreme happiness took possession of me, and I received a powerful and irresistible testimony of the truth of plural marriage."

Emma Smith and Lorin Walker returned from St. Louis on May 2; Lucy and Joseph had been married on May 1.

Many Mormons have believed that Joseph's marriages were entirely spiritual, with consummation left to the eternal state. And with some of his wives this was no doubt the case. Vienna Jacques, Rhoda Richards, Mrs. Sarah Cleveland, and Mrs. Fanny Young Murray (sister of Brigham Young) were all over fifty. Some of the leaders of the Relief Society, whom he seems to have married chiefly for reasons of security, were probably married only "for eternity." Elvira Cowles, treasurer of the Relief Society, who was sealed to Joseph probably early in 1842, was publicly married to Jonathan H. Holmes the following December, with the prophet performing the ceremony.

But with most of his wives plural marriage meant for Joseph exactly what it meant later for all the polygamists in Utah — marriage for "time [that is, life] and eternity" — with all connubial privileges. This is clearly indicated by many of the sworn statements of the wives and especially by an unpublished manuscript by Joseph's friend Benjamin F. Johnson. Johnson described the prophet's courtship of his sister Almera in some detail, concluding with these words: "She stood by the Prophet's side and was sealed to him as a wife, by Brother William Clayton; after which the Prophet asked me to take my sister to occupy number '10,' in his Mansion Home, during her stay in the city. But as I could not be long absent from my home and business, we soon returned to Ramus, where, on the 15th day of May, some three weeks later, the Prophet again came and at my house occupied the same room and bed with my sister,

JOSEPH SMITH'S HOMESTEAD, NAUVOO

THE MANSION HOUSE, NAUVOO

ZINA D. HUNTINGTON JACOBS

Plural wife of Joseph Smith

ELIZA R. SNOW

Plural wife of Joseph Smith

that the month previous he had occupied with the daughter of the late Bishop Partridge, as his wife." *

Some time during the spring of 1843 Joseph succeeded in convincing Emma of the inevitability of the new marriage system. Like many a Mormon wife after her, she agreed reluctantly to let her husband have more wives if she could do the choosing. There were four young girls living with them at the time under Joseph's guardianship. The Partridge sisters, Eliza and Emily, he had taken in after the death of their father, and after their legacy had been considerably reduced by his borrowing ten thousand dollars from the estate.† The other two, Sarah and Maria Lawrence, were young Canadian orphans, seventeen and nineteen, who had brought to Nauvoo an inheritance of eight thousand dollars in English gold.

After much bitter hesitation Emma selected Emily and Eliza Partridge, now respectively nineteen and twenty-three, and the ceremony was performed on May 11, 1843. Emma had no idea that these girls had already been married to Joseph some two months earlier. "To save family trouble," Emily wrote ingenuously, "Brother Joseph thought it best to have another ceremony performed."

Joseph's entry in his journal for the date of these marriages indicates that he bought Emma a new carriage. But it was small solace to her. "From that very hour, however," Emily later wrote, "Emma was our bitter enemy. We remained in the family until several months after this, but things went from bad to worse until we were obliged to leave the house and find another home. Emma desired us to leave the city. . . ."

Apparently Emma consented also to Joseph's marriage to the Lawrence sisters, but this was the limit of her sacrifice. She set herself stubbornly against any additions, and though she may have feared that there were others, she could not have dreamed how many.

Since she was too discreet to voice her bitterness openly, the prophet's home seemed to the casual visitor to be harmony itself. Travelers who stayed at the Mansion House universally

* For Johnson's statement see Appendix C. Joseph's journal entry for May 15, 1843 reports a visit to Ramus and his spending the night with the family of Benjamin F. Johnson. *History of the Church*, Vol. V, pp. 391–2.

† See footnote, p. 266 above.

acclaimed her serenity and poise. "Sister Emma," Charlotte Haven wrote back to New England, ". . . is very plain in her personal appearance, though we hear she is very intelligent and benevolent, has great influence with her husband, and is generally beloved. She said very little to us, her whole attention being absorbed in what Joseph was saying." Joseph, she added, "talked incessantly about himself, what he had done and could do more than other mortals, and remarked that he was a giant, physically and mentally." *

Only Joseph's intimates knew that Emma nagged at him incessantly to be done with plural marriage. As the months went by, the group of friends in whom she could confide narrowed to none as one by one they turned cold and deaf to her complaints. Occasionally she expressed her bitterness to Joseph's "Second Counselor" William Law, whom she knew to be unalterably opposed to polygamy. He could do little to comfort her, knowing too well the sensual delight Joseph took in some of his younger wives.†

Hyrum Smith, who had several wives himself and did not have his brother's difficulties with the first, urged Joseph repeatedly to write down the revelation on celestial marriage. "I will take it and read it to Emma," he said one day in renewing the argument, "and I believe I can convince her of its truth, and you will hereafter have peace."

Joseph replied with a wry smile: "You do not know Emma as well as I do." Before the afternoon was spent, however, he sat down and dictated to his secretary William Clayton the last and most epoch-making revelation of his life. All that he had been thinking and dreaming over the past years, everything that he had conceived about heaven and hell and sex, which he had never before dared commit to paper, he now dictated in a great rush.

After a long justification of polygamy on Biblical grounds, he went to the heart of the matter in a special commandment to Emma to "receive all those that have been given unto my servant Joseph" and to "cleave unto my servant Joseph, and to

* "A Girl's Letters from Nauvoo," *Overland Monthly*, December 1890, p. 623.

† See William Law's affidavit, formerly in the possession of Zenas H. Gurley, and published by Charles A. Shook in *True Origin of Mormon Polygamy*, pp. 126–7. See also W. Wyl's interview with William Law published in Gregg: *Prophet of Palmyra*, p. 508.

none else." The penalty for her disobedience was savage: "But if she will not abide this commandment she shall be destroyed, saith the Lord; for I am the Lord thy God, and will destroy her if she abide not in my law. But if she will abide this commandment, then shall my servant Joseph do all things for her, even as he hath said; and I will bless him and multiply him and give him an hundred-fold in this world, of fathers and mothers, brothers and sisters, houses and lands, wives and children, and crowns of eternal lives in the eternal worlds."

Then followed a concise statement of the new law: "If any man espouse a virgin, and desire to espouse another, and the first give her consent, and if he espouse the second, and they are virgins, and have vowed to no other man, then he is justified; he cannot commit adultery. . . . and if he have ten virgins given unto him by this law, he cannot commit adultery, for they belong to him. . . ." *

Hyrum took the revelation to Emma and returned some time later angry and crestfallen. In all his life, he said, he had never been so abused by a woman. When Joseph had heard him through, he remarked quietly: "I told you you didn't know Emma as well as I did." †

Although she stormed at Hyrum, Emma was terribly shaken by the sight of the manuscript. Sorrowfully she said to William Law: "The revelation says I must submit or be destroyed. Well, I guess I'll have to submit." ‡ But with the passing days she grew more courageous. However inspired the revelations of the past may have been, she felt in her heart that this was a concoction of John C. Bennett and the devil.

---

* *Doctrine and Covenants*, Section 132.

† The story of the writing of the revelation was told by William Clayton in a sworn statement in 1874. See *Historical Record*, Vol. VI, pp. 224–6. Joseph gave the revelation to Newel K. Whitney, who turned it over to Joseph C. Kingsbury with orders to make a copy. Brigham Young obtained this copy from Whitney in 1846. It was first published in a *Deseret News* extra, September 14, 1852. The Reorganized Church believes that the revelation was modified by Brigham Young, who is said to have introduced all the polygamous arguments. Quite aside from the testimonies of numerous Utah Mormons who heard it read in Nauvoo and later swore that it was published unchanged, there are statements made by men who did not follow Brigham Young that should be sufficient to remove any doubt on this point. See the affidavit of Leonard Soby, November 14, 1883, published in D. H. Bays: *Doctrines and Dogmas of Mormonism*, p. 381, and that of William Law in his interview with W. Wyl, in Thomas Gregg: *The Prophet of Palmyra*, p. 510.

‡ As reported by Law to W. Wyl. See Gregg: *The Prophet of Palmyra*, p. 510.

According to Heber Kimball, Emma now threatened to leave her husband altogether.* Joseph's mother, who came to live with them about this time, apparently took Emma's part. "I have never seen a woman in my life," Lucy wrote in 1845, "who would endure every species of fatigue and hardship, from month to month, and from year to year, with that unflinching courage, zeal and patience, which she has ever done; for I know that which she has had to endure — she has been tossed upon the ocean of uncertainty — she has breasted the storms of persecution, and buffeted the rage of men and devils, which would have borne down almost any other woman." †

There was a hard core of resistance in Emma that Joseph simply could not wear down. She pleaded with him and badgered him, threatening and weeping, until finally he brought the revelation home and gave it to her. She dropped it in the fireplace, put a candle to it, and watched with grim satisfaction the long foolscap pages turn to curling, fragile bits of ash.

The burning was a purely symbolic victory. Joseph had had a copy made, which he had every intention of showing about freely to his friends. But this at least was an end to argument on his part, and to tears on hers. Never again would he humiliate her by asking her to stand witness to a ceremony of wifetaking. Nor would he even discuss plural marriage in her presence. She, on the other hand, would never acknowledge one of her husband's wives though they reached the hundredfold suggested by the revelation. Although she could no longer hope to restore the core of a normal family relationship, at least the shell would be preserved intact.

Since the polygamy revelation had threatened destruction to any wife who refused to accept the new law, the more literal-minded of the brethren, knowing Emma's attitude, fully expected her to be blasted by the Lord. Brigham Young, who had never been comfortable in Emma's presence, swore that "she will be damned as sure as she is a living woman." But to this kind of talk Joseph replied with a warmth that stopped

* The Journal History in the Mormon Church library in Salt Lake City states that Kimball asserted this in a speech in Salt Lake, July 12, 1857.

† *Biographical Sketches*, p. 169.

the critics' mouths: "I will have her in the hereafter if I have to go to hell for her!" *

THE NEWS that a revelation on plural marriage had finally been put into writing whipped through the chain of underground gossip in Nauvoo. On August 12, 1843 Joseph asked Hyrum to read the text of it to the members of the High Council. William Marks, the president, Austin Cowles (whose daughter was one of Joseph's wives), and Leonard Soby were the only men among the twelve present who opposed it, but they fought with such vigor that they put the whole council in confusion. Gradually the church hierarchy became divided into a polygamist and anti-polygamist faction, with William Law championing the minority. Emma worked quietly against polygamy among the women. "Your husbands are going to take more wives," she warned, "and unless you consent to it, you must put your foot down and keep it there." †

Incredible as it may seem, the bulk of the Mormon colony, which now numbered more than fifteen thousand in and about the city, knew little or nothing of polygamy. In particular the English converts, now numbering over four thousand in Nauvoo, were kept in ignorance. No one could have been insulated from the gossip about spiritual wifism, but the majority accepted the word of the church leaders that this system had disappeared with the expulsion of John C. Bennett. Charlotte Haven wrote home in girlish horror on September 8, 1843 that "Apostle Adams" had returned from a mission to England with a new wife and child and had persuaded his first wife to accept her. "I cannot believe," she concluded, "that Joseph will ever sanction such a doctrine." ‡

Joseph added to the bewilderment and disbelief within Nauvoo by summarily excommunicating anyone caught preaching or practicing polygamy without his sanction. "There is never

---

* See Brigham Young's sermon of August 9, 1874, *Journal of Discourses*, Vol. XVII (1875), p. 159. Young here described also the scene where Emma burned the revelation.

† As reported in a sworn statement by Bathsheba W. Smith, wife of George A. Smith. See Joseph F. Smith, Jr.: *Blood Atonement and the Origin of Plural Marriage*, p. 88.

‡ "A Girl's Letters from Nauvoo," *Overland Monthly*, December 1890, p. 635.

but one on earth at a time on whom the power and its keys are conferred," he wrote, *"and I have constantly said no man shall have but one wife at a time, unless the Lord directs otherwise."* *

While there was confusion and doubting within Nauvoo, the anti-Mormons in neighboring Warsaw were universally convinced that polygamous marriages honeycombed the church. On February 7, 1844 the *Warsaw Message* published a thirteen-stanza poem called "Buckeye's Lamentation for Want of More Wives," which showed that the contents of the revelation were practically public property:

> I once thought I had knowledge great,
>   But now I find 'tis small.
> I once thought I'd religion too,
>   But now I find I've none at all —
> For I have but ONE LONE WIFE,
>   And can obtain no more;
> And the doctrine is I can't be saved,
>   Unless I've HALF A SCORE.
>
> ***
>
> A TENFOLD glory — that's the prize!
>   Without it you're undone!
> But with it you will shine as bright
>   As the bright shining sun.
> There you may shine like mighty Gods,
>   Creating worlds so fair
> At least a WORLD for every WIFE
>   That you take with you there.

NONE of Joseph's plural wives ever publicly acknowledged having conceived a child by him, which is not surprising in view of the natural delicacy of the subject and the overwhelming secrecy that has clouded the vital statistics of polygamous marriages throughout the whole of Mormon history. Very little information about the wives would now be available for publication were it not for the fact that it was solicited by Utah Church leaders in later years to answer the stubborn argument of Jo-

---

* *History of the Church*, Vol. VI, p. 46. Harrison Sagers was brought to trial on April 13, 1844 "for preaching spiritual wife doctrine," and Hiram Brown was cut off from the church "for preaching polygamy and other false and corrupt doctrines." See *Times and Seasons*, February 1, 1844, and *History of the Church*, Vol. VI, p. 333.

seph's eldest son, who founded a separatist church based largely on the contention that his father had no wife but Emma.

There is some evidence that Fannie Alger bore Joseph a child in Kirtland. And as we have seen, young Oliver Buell, born in 1839 or 1840 to Prescindia Huntington Buell, may well have been his son. One writer claimed that Prescindia's sister, Zina, conceived a child by the prophet while her husband, Henry B. Jacobs, was on a mission to England. If so, the child must have died in infancy.

Legend among the descendants of Levi W. Hancock points to another son of the prophet. If the legend is true, the child was probably John Reed Hancock, born April 19, 1841 in Nauvoo. Oddly, the next Hancock child, born considerably after Joseph Smith's death, was named Levison, as if to satisfy any doubt that Levi Hancock was in truth the father. Mrs. Mary Rollins Lightner, who was married to Joseph in February 1842, bore a son in 1843 who may as easily have been the prophet's son as that of Adam Lightner. Lightner carried his wife away from Nauvoo several months after her marriage to Joseph. He never joined the church. Mrs. Orson Hyde bore two sons in Nauvoo — Orson Washington on November 9, 1843, and Frank Henry on January 23, 1845. These boys could have been Joseph's sons. Moroni Pratt, son of Mrs. Parley P. Pratt, born December 7, 1844, might also be added to this list.*

Of the six wives who lived for long periods in the Mansion House, apparently only the thirty-nine-year-old poetess Eliza Snow conceived a child. She as well as Emma, it seems, was pregnant in the spring of 1844. Eliza must have been torn between dread of the consequences and exaltation at the prospect of facing the world the mother of a prophet's son.

It so happened that her bedroom in the Mansion House was to the left of Joseph's, Emma's being on the right. According to tradition in the Snow family, Eliza emerged one morning at the same moment as Joseph, and he caught her to him in a quick embrace. At this instant Emma opened her own door and in a sudden terrible rage — for apparently she had trusted Eliza above all other women — seized a broomstick and began beating her. Eliza tried to flee, stumbled, and fell down the full flight of stairs. Still not content, Emma pursued her in a frenzy

* For complete documentation on all of these children see Appendix C.

that Joseph was powerless to stop, and drove her out of the
house in her nightdress. By this time the whole Mansion House
was awake, young Joseph and Alexander weeping and frightened at their mother's hysteria and begging her to be kind to the
"Aunt Eliza" they adored.

Joseph finally calmed his wife and indignantly ordered her
to restore Eliza to her room and rights in the household. The
fall, it is said, resulted in a miscarriage. After Joseph's death
Eliza married Brigham Young, but bore him no children.

Considering that, of the fifty or more women Joseph married, all except four or five were young enough to bear children
and at least eighteen were in their teens or twenties — many of
whom later bore large families — it is astonishing that evidence
of other children than these has never come to light. The fact
that after the Fannie Alger scandal Joseph for a long time deliberately and almost exclusively selected married women
would indicate an overwhelming desire to avoid a repetition of
that kind of trouble at least. Even the faithful Jedediah Grant
felt the necessity of excusing the fact that Joseph took so many
married women. "Did the Prophet Joseph want every man's
wife he asked for? He did not . . . the grand object in view
was to try the people of God to see what was in them." *

But once Joseph started in earnest marrying the virgins prescribed by the revelation, it would seem that he flung caution
to the winds. Perhaps he had learned some primitive method
of birth control from the sophisticated Bennett, who had been
a professor of midwifery as well as an abortionist. Robert Dale
Owen and Charles Knowlton, the first great exponents in
America of birth control, had published in the early thirties
their famous tracts, *Moral Physiology* and *Fruits of Philosophy,
or The Private Companion of Young Married People.* Thousands of copies had been sold. While the methods these tracts
detailed were by no means infallible, they were based on respectable medical science and not witchcraft.† Bennett must
certainly have been familiar with these publications.

Or Joseph might simply have taken advantage of the frank
advertisements in the *New York Herald* and other papers for
such items as Portuguese Female Pills, "the wonder and admira-

* *Journal of Discourses,* Vol. II (1855), p. 14.
† See Norman E. Himes: *Medical History of Contraception* (Baltimore, 1936).

tion of the world, which, however, must not be used during pregnancy as they are certain to produce miscarriage during that period," Dr. Convers Minerva Box, "sent without exposure," or Madame Restell's Preventive Powders, "the only mild, safe and efficacious remedy for married ladies whose health forbids a too rapid increase of family."

It may be that evidence of other children born to Joseph lies buried among the manuscripts in the church library in Salt Lake City, which the Mormon authorities originally were unwilling to publish out of deference to the women themselves, who would naturally resent having their intimate secrets exposed to gentile mockery. And now that polygamy among the majority of the Mormons is dead, the leaders are not anxious to re-emphasize the fact that their prophet practiced it. Certainly they are eager to forget the magnificent immoderation with which he fulfilled the new marriage covenant. For once Joseph had succeeded to his own satisfaction in revolutionizing the Puritan concept of sin, there was no stopping him.

CHAPTER XXV
Candidate for President

"EXCITEMENT HAS BECOME almost the essence of my life," Joseph Smith declared in a sermon in May 1843. "When that dies away I feel almost lost. When a man is reined up continually by excitement, he becomes strong and gains power and knowledge." If life during these weeks had been barren of adventure — despite the fact that he was marrying wives at a faster rate than ever before — his inertia and placidity were to be shortlived.

For John C. Bennett, who had continued to hound the prophet, was plotting with Lilburn Boggs in Missouri to extradite Joseph with a writ which no Illinois court could touch. In June 1843 he persuaded Governor Reynolds to issue a writ on the now four-year-old treason charge from which Joseph had fled in 1839. Once the prophet was safely jailed in Missouri, Reynolds planned to try him for the Boggs shooting as well.

The Missouri sheriffs, hand-picked for the delicate task of capturing the prophet, waited until he went unescorted on a preaching tour. Disguising themselves and pretending to be Mormon elders, they learned that he was staying near Dixon, Illinois. They caught him alone, forced him at gun point into a wagon, and without bothering with the formality of serving a process whipped their horses toward Dixon. Stephen Markham, who happened to witness the kidnaping, sprang to his horse and galloped for help.

Joseph was locked in an upper room in a tavern in Dixon and was refused permission to talk with anyone. But he would not be silenced. Shouting out of the window with a voice that could carry to an open-air congregation of ten thousand people, he proclaimed the tyranny of his captors till the whole village swarmed to hear him. The tavern-keeper, backed now by the indignation of the citizens, vowed that justice should be done and insisted that the prophet be granted a lawyer.

When the sheriffs tried to disperse the crowd, angry warnings against the "damned Pukes" and "nigger-drivers" dissuaded them. There were shouts to let the Mormon be heard and good-humored calls for a sermon on marriage. "I addressed the assembly for an hour-and-a-half on the subject of marriage," Joseph said. "My freedom commenced from that hour."

It so happened that Cyrus Walker, head of the Whig Party and the greatest criminal lawyer in Illinois, was in Dixon at the time campaigning for election to Congress. Joseph at once requested his services. Walker drove a hard bargain, demanding not only a ten-thousand-dollar fee but also Joseph's vote in the next election.* Once Joseph had agreed to these terms, the wheels of Illinois justice began grinding furiously on his behalf. The Missouri sheriffs were themselves sued for assault and false imprisonment and held in ten thousand dollars' bail.

It was agreed that the whole case should be unraveled before Judge Stephen A. Douglas, who was holding court in Quincy. When the party set forth, Joseph was still in the custody of the Missouri sheriffs and they in turn in the custody of the Dixon sheriff. Joseph was obsessed with the fear that a conspiracy existed to kidnap him near Quincy and whisk him across the Mississippi. To forestall this he sent word ahead for the Legion to meet him at Monmouth.

Meanwhile news of his arrest sent Nauvoo wild with apprehension. The city council declared virtual martial law, requiring every stranger entering the city to give his name, residence, and business to the local police and enforcing a strict nine o'clock curfew.† Two companies of the Legion were sent out to intercept the prophet, and Joseph's own steamboat, the *Maid of Iowa*, sailed to the mouth of the Illinois River where its men could intercept every steamboat entering the Mississippi.

Shortly after crossing the Fox River, Joseph saw two foaming horses charging up to the carriage. Convinced for a moment that his worst fears had come true, he was preparing to spring out for a fight when he recognized the men. He sank back with a half sob of joy: "I am not going to Missouri this time. These are my boys!"

---

* See sermon of George A. Smith, October 1868, *Journal of Discourses*, Vol. XIII, p. 109, and *History of the Church*, Vol. V, p. 444.

† See the *Nauvoo Neighbor*, Vol. I, no. 10, July 5, 1843.

Before long the carriage had an escort of one hundred and forty armed men. Many had ruined their horses with running and had forced whiskey down their throats to keep them going the last few miles; men and horses alike were utterly exhausted. But they had saved their prophet, and every man was a hero.

Walker was so anxious to give the rescue of Joseph Smith the appearance of a Whig victory that he let himself be persuaded to argue the case in Nauvoo instead of Quincy, where he suspected the political tactics of Stephen A. Douglas. The whole party, therefore, turned toward Nauvoo, over the protests of the white-faced Missouri sheriffs, who feared they would never emerge from the Mormon city alive.

As they came within view of the half-built temple, rising like a grotesque monument on the high ground to the northwest, they saw a long procession winding down the road. The citizens of Nauvoo, mustering every vehicle in the city, had turned out *en masse* to welcome the prophet home. A strange solemnity pervaded their greeting, as if Joseph had returned from the grave. Walker noted with astonishment that these men did not shout, but wept with thankfulness.

Joseph took his place at the head of the procession with Emma, who was superbly dressed in a fine riding habit, her hat a glory of nodding white plumes. The Nauvoo brass band struck up *Hail, Columbia,* and the procession wound its way slowly back to the city, where those who had been unable to find a place in a carriage lined the streets.

Crowds milled around the prophet's home after he arrived, unwilling to depart and calling for a sermon. At last he came out, leaped agilely to the top of the rail fence, and shouted: "I am out of the hands of the Missourians again, thank God. I bless you all in the name of Jesus Christ. Amen. I shall address you at the Grove near the Temple, at four o'clock this afternoon."

He gave a feast for fifty of his friends and with an ironic gesture placed the two Missouri sheriffs in the places of honor. Later he petitioned the Nauvoo municipal court for a writ of habeas corpus which would render the Missouri writ void. In this petition he argued that his name was not Joseph Smith, Jr., as the writ indicated, but Joseph Smith, Sr. He claimed also that he was not a fugitive from justice, that he had never committed treason against Missouri, and that he had already been tried for the same offense and acquitted in Warren County in June 1841.

The true issue involved here, however, was not the validity of the Missouri writ but the right of the Nauvoo municipal court to issue a writ of habeas corpus in a case ordinarily left to the state courts. Walker, with his eye fixed on a seat in the United States Senate, assured Joseph that under the special provisions of the Nauvoo charter the court did have such a right. "Thus," wrote Governor Ford in reviewing this episode, "the Mormons were deluded and deceived by men who ought to have known and did know better." *

Joseph went to the grove triumphant. "I meet you with a heart full of gratitude to the Almighty God," he began. "I hardly know how to express my feelings. I feel as strong as a giant." Then he went to the heart of the problem. "Relative to our city charter, courts, right of habeas corpus, etc., I wish you to know and publish that we have all power; and if any man from this time forth says anything to the contrary, cast it into his teeth. . . . All the power there was in Illinois she gave to Nauvoo; and any man that says to the contrary is a fool. . . . This city has all the power that the state courts have. . . . I wish the lawyer who says we have no powers in Nauvoo may be choked to death with his own words. Don't employ lawyers, or pay them money for their knowledge, for I have learned that they don't know anything. I know more than they all."

Pointing toward Walker, he said bluntly: "I have converted this candidate for congress that the right of habeas corpus is included in our charter. If he continues converted, I will vote for him."

Then he told the story of his arrest and rescue with a dramatic intensity that held ten thousand spectators breathless. "The time has come," he cried, "when forbearance is no longer a virtue; and if you or I are again taken unlawfully, you are at liberty to give loose to blood and thunder . . . before I will bear this unhallowed persecution any longer — before I will be dragged away again among my enemies for trial, I will spill the last drop of blood in my veins, and will see all my enemies in hell!

---

* Hoge, Walker's Democratic opponent, anxious not to be outdone, soon came to Nauvoo and concurred in Walker's interpretation.

"Shall we bear it any longer?" he demanded. "No!" the vast assembly roared.

"I will lead you to battle; and if you are not afraid to die, and feel disposed to spill your blood in your own defense, you will not offend me. Be not the aggressor: bear until they strike you on the one cheek; then offer the other, and they will be sure to strike that; then defend yourselves, and God will bear you off, and you shall stand forth clear before his tribunal. . . . If mobs come upon you any more here, dung your gardens with them!" *

GOVERNOR REYNOLDS of Missouri, infuriated by what he deemed the insolence of Illinois politicians, issued another writ and demanded that Governor Ford call out the militia to capture the prophet. Walker raced to Springfield to persuade Ford to deny the demand. But Ford was naturally unwilling to throw so juicy a plum into Walker's outstretched hands just before election, and told him that the decision would first require careful investigation. Actually Ford had no intention of calling out the militia merely to reverse the order of a court that had exceeded its jurisdiction. He disapproved of the Mormon abuse of their charters, but was convinced that the only way to stop it was through legislative repeal.

He had, in fact, urged the legislature to abrogate the special Mormon privileges, but in this he had been opposed by the leaders of his own party, who were certain that repeal would cost them the Mormon vote. The prophet's brother William, elected to the state legislature from the Mormon county, had argued against repeal with savage skill and had repeatedly threatened to throw the Mormon vote to the Whigs.

Had the Democrats followed Ford's suggestion, they might have saved Illinois the sorriest chapter in its history. But unfortunately Ford had no control over his party. The Democrats played politics to the bitter end. They sustained the unhealthy charters and later fought the Mormons for misusing them.

A few days before the election, when Ford was absent in St. Louis, a prominent Democratic politician who had no faith in Ford's political judgment sent word secretly to the Mormons

* *History of the Church*, Vol. V, pp. 465–73.

that Ford would not call out the militia to arrest Joseph provided the Mormons voted the Democratic ticket.*

This put the prophet in a wretched dilemma. Had he been a wiser statesman he would have let the normal democratic process run its course and allowed the Mormon vote to be divided. He could then have answered the ire of both parties in the name of the American Constitution. But two factors betrayed him into a disastrous political trick: his consuming fear of extradition and the political ambitions of his brother Hyrum.

Hyrum had promised the Democrats the Mormon vote in return for a seat in the state legislature the following year. In the last week before election he began openly campaigning for Hoge, the Democratic candidate. William Law was outraged at what he believed was a political sellout to further Hyrum's personal ambitions, and fought him at every turn. Nauvoo was thunderstruck at the spectacle of Joseph's two closest aides at swords' points and looked eagerly to the prophet to settle the issue.

Five days before election the *Nauvoo Neighbor* swung completely over to Hoge and urged unanimity in the vote: ". . . it can answer no good purpose that half the citizens should disfranchise the other half, thus rendering Nauvoo powerless as far as politics are concerned." † Then Hyrum Smith amazed the Nauvoo electorate by announcing publicly that he had received a revelation from God that Hoge was the proper candidate to receive the Mormon vote.

The day before the election Joseph mounted the platform and broke his silence: "The Lord has not given me a revelation concerning politics. I have not asked him for one. . . . As for Mr. Walker, he is the Whig candidate, a high-minded man. . . . Before Mr. Walker came to Nauvoo, rumor came up that he might be a candidate. Said I — He is an old friend, and I'll vote for him." This, Joseph then indicated, was his intention now as then. But before concluding he added significantly: "Brother Hyrum tells me this morning that he has had a testimony to the effect it would be better for the people to vote for Hoge; and I never knew Hyrum to say he ever had a revelation and it failed. Let God speak and all men hold their peace."

* See Thomas Ford: *History of Illinois*, pp. 317–18.
† August 2, 1843, p. 2.

The next day Hoge received over 2,000 Mormon votes, which accounted for practically all of the Nauvoo electorate. The vote gave Hoge an election he would otherwise have lost, for his final majority amounted to about 700 votes. The Whigs, who had been completely certain of the Mormon vote, went wild. They never forgave Joseph for this betrayal.

WHETHER Joseph realized the blunder he had made in this election one cannot know. But he decided about this time that henceforth his political role would be commensurate with his status as a prophet anointed of the Lord. He was done, somewhat belatedly, with the local politics of Illinois. He would have no more to do with petty intrigues and truckling to corrupt politicians.

James Arlington Bennett, a New York lawyer and writer who owned property in Illinois and had ambitions to become governor of the state through Mormon influence, wrote to Joseph Smith in October 1843 detailing the political strategy he hoped to use. This letter said pointedly: "You know Mahomet had his *'right hand man.'*"

Joseph, who had just renounced local politics, replied with a burst of rhetoric that put Bennett in his place: "Shall I stoop from the sublime authority of Almighty God, to be handled as a monkey's cat-paw, and pettify myself into a clown to act the farce of political demagoguery? No — verily no! . . . I combat the errors of ages; I meet the violence of mobs; I cope with illegal proceedings from executive authority; I cut the gordian knot of powers, and I solve mathematical problems of universities, *with truth — diamond truth; and God is my 'right hand man.'* " *

Joseph was now fully intoxicated with power and drunk with visions of empire and apocalyptic glory. "One man empowered from Jehovah has more influence with the children of men," he said, "than eight hundred million led by the precepts of men." This thesis was his strength, and he set about using it to translate into reality what soberer men would have called delusions of grandeur.

Any man with absolute dominion over a people, who brooks no advice that does not further his own daydreams and who

* For this exchange of letters see *History of the Church*, Vol. VI, pp. 71-8.

UNFINISHED NAUVOO HOUSE

LAST PUBLIC ADDRESS OF LIEUTENANT-GENERAL JOSEPH SMITH

grinds out policies solely in the grist-mill of his own ambition, sets up a kind of centrifugal force within himself that — by turning always away from the normal — may one day destroy him. "Joseph would allow no arrogance or undue liberties," said one friend, "and criticisms, even by his associates, were rarely acceptable, and contradictions would rouse in him the lion at once, for by no one of his fellows would he be superseded." * Herein was his great strength and his most fatal weakness. For no man whose chief virtues were love of compromise, justice, and prudence could set himself up as a prophet. But neither could any man who trampled on these virtues survive as a political force in America.

Joseph now looked upon Nauvoo as a state within a state. "We stand in the same relation to the state as the state does to the union. . . ." he said in an address to the city council on February 25, 1843. "Shall we be such fools as to be governed by its [Illinois] laws, which are unconstitutional?" †

With the bit in his teeth he proceeded to run not only over the constitutions of Illinois and the United States but also over the ancient traditions of English common law. He had the city council pass an ordinance providing that if any officer came to Nauvoo with a writ for his arrest based on the old Missouri difficulties, he should be arrested, tried, and if found guilty sentenced to life imprisonment in the city jail. He could be pardoned by the governor only with the consent of the Nauvoo mayor — that is, Joseph himself.

Another ordinance made it a criminal offense for any officer to issue a warrant in Nauvoo without first having it signed and approved by the mayor. An earlier one, designed to prevent Joseph's creditors from exacting payment of debts in the form of property, had made gold and silver the only legal tender in Nauvoo.‡ When these ordinances were published in the *Nauvoo Neighbor,* they convinced even tolerant non-Mormon observers that the Mormon prophet held the law in complete contempt.

* Unpublished letter of Benjamin Johnson to George S. Gibbs, 1903.

† *History of the Church,* Vol. V, p. 289.

‡ The first ordinance was passed December 8, 1843, the second December 21, 1843. The ordinance on gold and silver had been passed March 4, 1843. All were repealed February 12, 1844. See *Nauvoo Neighbor,* December 13, 27, 1843, and *History of the Church,* Vol. V. p. 297; Vol. VI, pp. 105, 212.

And as if this were not enough, Joseph prepared a petition for Congress in December 1843 in which he asked that Nauvoo be made a completely independent federal territory, with the Nauvoo Legion incorporated into the United States Army and the mayor of Nauvoo given power to call out the United States troops whenever necessary. This was one of Joseph's worst political blunders. The petition was certain to be rejected in Washington, and it may well have cost the Mormons what few remaining friends they had in Illinois.

But Joseph by now had become a law unto himself. He had small faith that Congress would heed the petition, but he felt the Lord's thunderbolts heavy in his hand. "I prophesied by virtue of the holy Priesthood vested in me, and in the name of the Lord Jesus Christ, that, if Congress will not hear our petition and grant us protection, they shall be broken up as a government *and God shall damn them, and there shall be nothing left of them — not even a grease spot!"* *

Actually the hope of becoming Governor of the Federal Territory of Nauvoo was a mere detail of his ambition. Joseph's utter incapacity for contentment with a moderate success — a want that had betrayed him again and again and was in the end to ruin him — led him now into his most grandiose political maneuvers.

For many years Joseph had talked about building the Kingdom of God upon earth, and with his increasing success the idea seems to have been subtly transformed from a mere symbol to a thing of substance. As he came more and more to look upon Nauvoo as an autonomous state, the Kingdom of God assumed an unmistakably temporal nature. Finally, in the spring of 1844, Joseph began to organize a government to rule over what he hoped would eventually be a sovereign Mormon state. On March 11 he began selecting with the utmost secrecy a council of fifty "princes" to form what one of them described as "the highest court on earth." Few secrets in Mormon history have been better kept than the activities of this council, but it is clear that one of their first acts was to ordain and crown Joseph as King of the Kingdom of God.†

---

* *Millennial Star*, Vol. XXII (1860), p. 455. The words I have italicized were omitted when this passage was reprinted in the *History of the Church*, Vol. VI, p. 116.

† The only detailed account of the activities of the Council of Fifty was written

The Council of Fifty was composed of men who had been reared in a tradition of militant democracy. They never dreamed of comparing their prophet with Aaron Burr, although it was the same fabulous opportunities that drove both men to destruction. What utterly disarmed Joseph's followers was that he had brought God into his realm. And these men lived close to a Bible in which God's servants had been kings.

When Joseph in a public speech on May 10, 1844 pronounced defiantly: "I calculate to be one of the instruments of setting up the kingdom of Daniel by the word of the Lord, and I intend to lay a foundation that will revolutionize the whole world," only a handful knew that the kingdom had already been established. "It will not be by sword or gun that this kingdom will roll on," he assured them, "the power of truth is such that all nations will be under the necessity of obeying the Gospel."

But this was only partly true. The Legion now numbered almost four thousand men, and an arsenal and powder manufactory were being planned;* there was substance here for an alarmist report in the *New York Sun* that a great military despotism was growing up in the West.

JOSEPH had never been so blind to the consequences of polygamy that he did not sense that some day his people would be forced to leave the United States. And the editorials in the *Warsaw Message* and *Warsaw Signal* early in 1844 made him realize reluctantly that emigration was probably the only alternative to civil war. Thomas Gregg, who had described Joseph on January 10 as "that hoary monster who rules at Nauvoo; whose

---

by Bishop George Miller in his invaluable series of letters to the *Northern Islander* in 1855. These were reprinted in pamphlet form in Wisconsin by Wingfield Watson about 1915 and also in H. W. Mills: "De Tal Palo Tal Astilla," *Historical Society of Southern California Publications* (1917), pp. 86–172. See particularly pp. 131–2. Thomas Ford had learned something of this kingdom before the publication of his *History of Illinois* in 1854. See pp. 321–2. For other references see William Decatur Kartchner: "Expedition of the Emmett Company," MS., a copy of which is in the Utah State Historical Society Library; the address of Lyman Wight on December 17, 1851, published in the *Gospel Banner*, Vol. V, p. 23; and the statement of William Marks: "I was also witness to the introduction (secretly) of a kingly form of government, in which Joseph suffered himself to be ordained king to reign over the house of Israel forever." *Zion's Harbinger and Baneemy's Organ*, Vol. III (July 1853), p. 52. There are many veiled allusions to the Council of Fifty in Joseph's history, beginning with the entry of March 11, 1844, and more definite references in Brigham Young's diary as published in the *Millennial Star*, Vols. XXVI–XXVII.

* *History of the Church*, Vol. V, p. 430; Vol. VI, p. 233.

black heart would exult in carnage and bloodshed, rather than yield one iota of what power he has obtained by his hellish knavery," wrote in the *Warsaw Message* on January 17: "We see no use in attempting to disguise the fact that many in our midst contemplate a total extermination of that people; that the thousands of defenceless women and children, aged and infirm, who are congregated at Nauvoo, must be driven out — aye, *Driven* — *Scattered* — like the leaves before the Autumn blast! But what good citizen, let us ask, what lover of his country and his race, but contemplates such an event with horror?"

With the passing weeks Gregg's editorials became more and more apoplectic. "We claim not to be a prophet nor the son of a prophet," he wrote on February 7; "yet we tell you that your career of infamy cannot continue but a little longer! Your days are numbered!"

Joseph's notions of the geography of the vast territory lying west of Iowa were perhaps none too exact, but no man could have lived in Independence without absorbing much of the lore of the Santa Fe trail and the mountain men. In recent years Marcus Whitman had made Oregon a synonym for the promised land, and 1842 had seen the first big emigrant train under Elijah White breaking a road to the Pacific.

In an open letter to the *New York Herald* James Arlington Bennett had urged the prophet to "pull up stakes and take possession of the Oregon territory in his own right, and establish an independent empire." In one hundred years, he said, "no nation on earth could conquer such a people." This letter Joseph had reprinted in the *Wasp*, along with articles extolling Oregon.

Early in July 1843 he had sent Jonathan Dunham to explore a route to the Missouri River and by August was frankly discussing a westward migration. There is some evidence that early in the spring of 1844 he ordered a few families under James Emmett and John L. Butler to move up the Missouri River and put in crops in preparation for the wholesale migration of the church. But they were ordered to keep their intentions secret.*

* See *History of the Church,* Vol. V, pp. 86, 542–9, and William Decatur Kartchner: "Expedition of the Emmett Company," MS., p. 1. Actually the Emmett expedition did not leave until after Joseph's death.

Even at this late date Joseph was not sure where he would take his people. On February 20 he instructed the twelve apostles to send out a delegation of twenty-five men to "investigate the locations of California and Oregon, and hunt out a good location, where we can remove to after the temple is completed, and where we can build a city in a day, and have a government of our own, get up into the mountains, where the devil cannot dig us out, and live in a healthful climate, where we can live as old as we have a mind to." *

Henry Clay and Stephen A. Douglas both recommended Oregon. Joseph printed in the *Neighbor* a part of John C. Frémont's valuable report of his exploration to South Pass. Editorials in the *Neighbor* denounced British imperial interests in Oregon and echoed the cry of manifest destiny. But Joseph was troubled by the fact that Oregon was peopled largely by emigrant Missourians, and for a time turned his eye to the Southwest.

Annexation of Texas was now the hottest political issue in the nation. On the one hand were the Southerners eager to increase the power of the slave bloc in Congress and the nationalists who dreamed of a continental United States. Against them was the steady pressure of the Whig Party, led by Henry Clay, and the anti-slavery Democrats backing Van Buren. These feared that annexation would precipitate a war with Mexico and wished in any case to block an accretion of Southern power.

The bloody border warfare between Texas and Mexico in 1842 had roused a violent agitation for annexation. But with the cessation of hostilities the fever had abated, and in 1843, after Texan soldiers made an abortive attempt to intercept a gold-laden caravan from Santa Fe, the American press swung round to a denunciation of Texas that deluded many into thinking that annexation would never take place. Such was the situation when Joseph and the Council of Fifty began seriously to consider a migration to the Southwest.

Lyman Wight and George Miller were especially infected with Texas propaganda and urged moving the Wisconsin Black River Lumber Company to Texas as the first step in the migration of the church. Joseph had seen an article in the *Texas Telegraph* describing ruins of Indian temples on the Rio Puerco,

* *History of the Church*, Vol. VI, p. 222.

and traces of ruined cities and aqueducts in the Cordilleras and on the Colorado. This set his imagination rocketing. What could be more appropriate than to build an empire on the site of the remnants of the vast civilizations described in his Book of Mormon?

The Council of Fifty was carried away by the Texas fever and dispatched Lucian Woodworth as "minister to Texas" with orders to negotiate a treaty. He was told to secure "all that country north of a west line from the falls of the Colorado River [the Texas Colorado, not the great river of the Far West] to the Nueces, thence down the same to the Gulf of Mexico, and along the same to the Rio Grande, and up the same to the United States territory."

What Joseph was asking for was an enormous tract comprising about three fifths of modern Texas, the eastern half of New Mexico, the Oklahoma panhandle, a bit of Kansas, a third of Colorado, and a section of south-central Wyoming. Texas was to recognize the Mormon nation, which in return would guarantee to help defend the Texans against Mexico, "standing as a go-between between the belligerent powers." If Woodworth brought back a favorable reply, Lyman Wight and George Miller were to proceed to Texas with the Black River Lumber Company and take possession.*

Joseph was not blind to the fact that regardless of whether he took his people northwest or southwest he was asking for trouble. And out of his intense anxiety both to provide security for his people and to satisfy his now completely unleashed ambition came the most grandiloquent scheme of his whole life. This was a petition to Congress late in March 1844 that he be appointed an officer of the United States Army with power to raise a hundred thousand volunteers to patrol and police the western borders of the United States all the way from Texas to Oregon.

Specifically, he promised "to extend the arm of deliverance to Texas; to protect the inhabitants of Oregon from foreign aggressions and domestic broils . . . to open the vast regions of the unpeopled west and south . . . to supersede the necessity of a standing army on our western and southern frontiers . . . to search out the antiquities of the land . . . to break down

---

* George Miller's letters to the *Northern Islander*, 1855, tell this whole story.

tyranny and oppression and exalt the standard of universal peace." *

This request for permission from the United States government to lead a private army of a hundred thousand men seems to the twentieth-century mind the delusion of a madman, but it was accounted merely excessive ambition in the "fabulous forties." Stephen A. Douglas told Orson Hyde privately that if he could command the force at the disposal of the Mormon prophet he would resign his seat in Congress and be on the march to Oregon or California within a month.†

President Tyler in his Third Annual Message to Congress had strongly recommended the establishment of military posts along the Oregon Trail to "furnish security and protection to our hardy adventurers against hostile tribes of Indians" and to take to the Western territories the same kind of law established in the United States. It was this message, which fell into Joseph's hands late in January 1844, that more than anything else had prompted the petition. And it was the extravagance of Joseph's demands rather than their essential nature that ensured the petition's defeat. On May 25 the House of Representatives refused to allow it to be read through on the floor.

For a time it looked as if plans for a Texan empire might mature. Woodworth returned from a conference with the Texas cabinet in May 1844 with a report to the Council of Fifty which George Miller said "was altogether as we could wish it." The council at once appointed three men to meet with the Texas Congress to ratify the treaty.‡

But Joseph was not destined to be caught in the crossfire of the Mexican War, and the Mormon Church was spared certain destruction as a buffer state in the most explosive section of the continent. Nor was the prophet to face a wilderness war with the ex-Missourians in Oregon. Even the choice between alternatives was denied him. For though he possessed a disturbed prescience about the ultimate fate of his people were they to remain in the United States, and though he was bursting with his grandiose plans for a future in the West, Joseph could never believe that expulsion was close at hand. Nor could he

* *History of the Church,* Vol. VI, pp. 276–7.
† Letter from Hyde in Washington, dated April 26, 1844, ibid., Vol. VI, p. 373.
‡ Ibid., Vol. VI, p. 356.

bring himself to leave voluntarily the beautiful city on the Mississippi that was the fruit of his own genius.

AT the same time that Joseph was laying plans for a western exodus he was becoming actively involved in national politics. For four years he had tenaciously badgered Congress for redress for the Missouri persecutions. Now utterly cynical, he knew that he could win neither retribution for past suffering nor security for a future western colony until Congress could be made to see that the Mormons were a political force to be reckoned with. This he intended to prove in the 1844 presidential election.

He therefore wrote to all the leading presidential candidates and asked them bluntly what they would do to win justice for his people. When their replies were noncommittal or negative, he decided to enter the lists himself. "Send every man in the city who is able to speak in public throughout the land to electioneer and make stump speeches," he ordered. "Advocate the 'Mormon' religion, purity of elections, and call upon the people to stand by the law and put down mobocracy. . . . Tell the people we have had Whig and Democratic Presidents long enough; we want a President of the United States."

Joseph suffered from no illusions about his chances of winning the supreme political post in the nation. He entered the ring not only to win publicity for himself and his church, but most of all to shock the other candidates into some measure of respect. "We have as good a right to make a political party to gain power to defend ourselves," he said, "as for demagogues to make use of our religion to get power to destroy us." * This was his justification for what otherwise might have seemed to be preposterous megalomania. He was simply following the tactics of the abolitionist Liberty Party, which, though extremely small, was to take enough votes away from Henry Clay in New York State in the 1844 election to throw the state to Polk and thus secure him the Presidency (which incidentally resulted in what the Liberty Party feared most, the annexation of Texas).

Joseph did err, however, in his appraisal of his vote-getting capacity. Nauvoo now had a population of some 12,000 Mor-

* Ibid., Vol. VI, pp. 188, 243.

mons, and the surrounding countryside contained about a third as many more.* But there was so much optimistic talk about stupendous conversions in the States and in England that most of the citizens of Nauvoo talked in terms of 100,000 to 200,000 adherents to the faith. Joseph flung these figures about in his campaign speeches, estimating in a letter to Henry Clay that his people numbered 200,000.†

The *New York Herald* caught the spirit of the Mormon campaign at once. "They claim possession of from two hundred thousand to five hundred thousand votes in Nauvoo and throughout the Union," the editor wrote on May 23, 1844, "and with that they calculate that they can hold the balance of power and make whoever they please President. Well, if so, they may be worth looking after. . . . It seems by this movement that Joe Smith does not expect to be elected President but he still wants to have a finger in the pie, and see whether something can't be made out of it."

The reactions of the Mormons to Joseph's candidacy varied all the way from George Miller's ingenuous certainty that if the election was successful Joseph and the Council of Fifty would "at once establish dominion in the United States," to John D. Lee's despairing complaint: "It was hard enough to preach the gospel without purse or scrip; but it was as nothing compared to offering the Prophet Joseph to the people as a candidate for the highest gift of the nation. I would a thousand times rather have been shut up in jail than to have taken such a trip, but I dared not refuse."

James Arlington Bennett was first nominated for vice-president, but when it was discovered that he was of foreign birth and therefore ineligible, Sidney Rigdon was finally substituted in his place. At the nominating convention held on May 17, 1844, a platform was written around the rallying cry: "Jeffersonian democracy, free trade, sailors' rights, and the protection of person and property." Every man that could be spared, including the twelve apostles, went out campaigning, while Jo-

---

* The *Times and Seasons* of November 15, 1845 quoted the *St. Louis Evening Gazette* saying the census of Nauvoo just taken showed 11,057 within the city limits and a third as many more outside. There were some defections after Joseph's death. Three hundred Saints followed Rigdon to Pittsburgh.

† *Times and Seasons,* Vol. V (June 1, 1844), p. 547.

seph busied himself writing campaign speeches unique in the history of American politics.

His main theme, the natural fruit of his own experience, was that American liberty was on the wane and that calamity was about to destroy the peace of the people. "The world is governed too much," he wrote, "and there is not a nation or a dynasty now occupying the earth which acknowledges Almighty God as their lawgiver, and as 'crowns won by blood, by blood must be maintained,' I go emphatically, virtuously, and humanely, for a Theodemocracy, where God and the people hold the power to conduct the affairs of men in righteousness." *

The injection of God into the government of the United States was the most sensational plank in Joseph's platform. That it would have meant a repudiation of democracy in favor of a one-party state Hyrum Smith made clear when he proclaimed: "We want a President of the United States, not a party President, but a President of the whole people; for a party President disfranchises the opposite party. . . . Damn the system of splitting up the nation into opposite belligerent parties." †

Joseph further advocated: "Reduce Congress at least two thirds. Two Senators from a State and two members to a million of population will do more business than the army that now occupy the halls of the national Legislature. Pay them two dollars and their board per diem (except Sundays). That is more than the farmer gets, and he lives honestly."

With his unhappy experience in Liberty jail still vivid in his memory, he advocated a drastic reform of the American penal system. Turn the jails into seminaries of learning, he said. Make work upon roads and public works the punishment for crime, and reserve rigor and seclusion only for those guilty of murder. Abolish imprisonment for debt, and pardon every convict, saying to him in the name of the Lord: "Go thy way and sin no more."

Then in a complete reversal of his earlier stand he advocated freeing the slaves. Let the slaveholders be paid for them, he urged, out of the surplus revenue arising from the sale of public lands. "Break off the shackles from the poor black man, and

---

* *Nauvoo Neighbor*, April 17, 1844.
† *History of the Church*, Vol. VI, p. 323.

hire him to labor like other human beings, for 'an hour of virtuous liberty on earth is worth a whole eternity of bondage.' " * Here he was echoing the sentiments of the Liberty Party, which since 1839 had been trying to create a third party out of the slavery issue.

Unlike any other presidential candidate, Joseph was at the same moment anti-slavery and pro-annexation, and his compromise was ingenious. Bring Texas into the Union, he urged, but curtail the power of the slave bloc at the same time by abolishing slavery in the states bordering the Mason-Dixon line.

By now Joseph's attitude toward the Negro had become so liberal — partly as a result of his correspondence with the abolitionist C. V. Dyer — that he argued with Orson Hyde that if the roles of Negro and white were reversed the former would quickly assume the characteristics of the latter.† The demagogic Hyde was not impressed, and his conviction that the abolitionists were "trying to make void the curse of God" was never wholly erased from Mormon thinking, particularly since it could be reinforced by the unfortunate anti-Negro sentiments in Joseph's Book of Abraham.‡ The Utah Church accepted the ideological fruits of Joseph's earlier stand, which actually had been a political compromise, and rejected this more courageous about-face because it was merely an utterance in a political campaign. Today the Negro is still denied a place in the Mormon priesthood.

Joseph's campaign documents were reprinted in many of the Eastern papers and provoked a good deal of editorial jesting. "Who is this modern Knight with his magic lamp?" asked the *Boston Correspondent* on May 22. "It is the Green Mountain boy of Old Vermont — the ignorant farmer of western New York, the unlettered fool of sectarian tales; the scourge and terror of out-lawed Missouri, the favorite Military Chieftain of Illinois . . . the admired of millions . . . the dread of politicians, the revered of savages; the stumbling block of nations, and the wonder of the world; and to cap the climax, he is 'JO SMITH THE MORMON PROPHET.' "

* See "Views on the Powers and Policy of the United States Government," as published in *Times and Seasons*, Vol. V, May 15, 1844. Later reprints deleted certain portions.

† See *History of the Church*, Vol. V, p. 217.

‡ See Hyde's editorial in *Times and Seasons*, Vol. VI (April 1, 1845), p. 857.

"When I get hold of the Eastern papers, and see how popular I am," Joseph said one day in high spirits, "I am afraid myself that I shall be elected." * Despite the undertones of disaster that were rumbling in and about Nauvoo, he seemed to be riding securely astride the world. He was not only candidate for President, but also mayor of Nauvoo, judge of the municipal court, merchant of the leading store, hotel-keeper, official temple architect, real-estate agent, contractor, recorder of deeds, steamboat-owner, trustee-in-trust for all the finances of his church, lieutenant-general of the Nauvoo Legion, spiritual adviser and Lord's communicant to the true church, King of the new Kingdom of God, and husband of almost fifty wives.

"I want the liberty of thinking and believing as I please," he said. "It feels so good not to be trammelled." And for all the tarring and feathering, the arrests, the leg irons, and the threats of death, America had permitted Joseph Smith the liberty of going fast and far. "Who can wonder," wrote Josiah Quincy, "that the chair of the National Executive had its place among the visions of this self-reliant man? He had already traversed the roughest part of the way to that coveted position. Born in the lowest ranks of poverty, without book-learning and with the homeliest of all human names, he had made himself at the age of thirty-nine a power upon earth."

Almost never in these days did Joseph step outside himself and look with surprise and humility upon what he had become. But once in this spring of 1844, at the funeral of a certain King Follett, he delivered one of the most profound sermons of his whole career. For the first time he proclaimed in a unified discourse the themes that he had been inculcating in fragments and frequently in secret to his most favored Saints: the glory of knowledge, the multiplicity of gods, the eternal progression of the human soul. And when he was almost finished and the exaltation of spirit that motivates a great sermon was exhausting itself, he paused and in a wanton moment of self-searching said with a kind of wonder:

"You don't know me; you never knew my heart. No man knows my history. I cannot tell it: I shall never undertake it. I don't blame anyone for not believing my history. If I had not experienced what I have, I could not have believed it myself."

* *History of the Church*, Vol. VI, p. 243.

CHAPTER XXVI
Prelude to Destruction

To a casual observer of the Mormon scene in the spring of 1844 it must have seemed that Joseph Smith was riding higher than ever before. Except for the fulminations of the anti-Mormons at Warsaw and Carthage, there was little overt resentment against him or his people. His presidential campaign was winning him much publicity and, by lifting the Mormon vote out of party politics, seemed likely to mollify certain of the antagonisms arising from political issues.

Actually the enmity against the Mormons was widespread and dangerous. Those who took Joseph's campaign seriously saw him as an evil symbol of the union of church and state, and others suspected that he would eventually renounce his candidacy and declare for a popular candidate. The Masons, annoyed at rumors of corruption of the Masonic ritual in the Mormon lodges (which now numbered five, three in Nauvoo and two in Iowa) and furious at Joseph's refusal to send the lodge records to Springfield for inspection, were determined to revoke the dispensations and declare all the Mormon lodges clandestine.* The anti-Mormons were passing resolutions calling for Joseph's extradition and hoping for some provocation from Nauvoo that would furnish an excuse for action.

But Joseph's worst peril, as he understood perfectly, was ripening within his own kingdom. "My life is more in danger from some little dough-head of a fool in this city than from all my numerous and inveterate enemies abroad," he declared. "I am exposed to far greater danger from traitors among ourselves than from enemies without. . . . I can live as Cæsar might have lived, were it not for a right-hand Brutus. . . . *we have a Judas in our midst!*" †

---

* This was done in the 1844 meeting of the Grand Lodge. See *Proceedings of the Grand Lodge of Freemasons, Illinois, from its Organization in 1840 to 1850 Inclusive* (Freeport, Illinois, 1892).

† Address on December 29, 1843. *History of the Church*, Vol. VI, p. 152.

For many months now Joseph had been watching the progressive alienation of one of his ablest and most courageous men. William Law had been his Second Counselor for more than two years, proving as steadfast and incorruptible as John C. Bennett had been treacherous and dissolute. Law had come from Canada a wealthy man. He had invested in real estate, construction, and steam mills, fostering more than anyone else the sorely needed industrialization of the city.

In the beginning Law hid his resentment over the prophet's monopoly of the management of real estate in and about the city, though he thought it unseemly in a man of God. He had been particularly shocked when Joseph threatened to excommunicate any wealthy convert who came to Nauvoo and purchased land without his counsel. Finally he came to mistrust Joseph's business judgment and refused to invest money in the publication of the revised version of the Bible, placing his funds instead in a steam mill and hemp farm.*

The prophet was constantly pleading for money to build the temple and the Nauvoo House, which Law thought might well be delayed until the acute housing shortage in the city was alleviated. The temple was now the chief spectacle on the upper Mississippi, but the workmen who sweated over its great stones were living on parched corn.

The Nauvoo House, on the other hand, despite generous donations and liberal purchases of stock, seemed scarcely to be growing at all. Law became convinced, whether rightly or wrongly, that Joseph was using the funds donated for the hotel to buy more land, which he then sold for a generous profit to new converts.

Eventually Law and Robert Foster, who were the chief contractors in the city, began to beat against the autarchic economy that hemmed them in. They purchased part of the lumber floated down the Mississippi from Wisconsin, which had been intended exclusively for church buildings, and began to build houses and stores. Since they paid wages, while the prophet paid the workmen on the temple and the Nauvoo House in goods and city scrip, a nasty labor crisis resulted.

Joseph called upon the workmen to continue on the church projects and deplored Foster's "mammoth skeletons" rising all

* Ibid., Vol. V, pp. 272–3; Vol. VI, pp. 164–5.

over the town. "There is no flesh on them," he cried, "they are all for personal interest and aggrandizement. . . . I want the Nauvoo House built. It *must* be built. Our salvation depends upon it. . . . I will say to those who have labored on the Nauvoo House, and cannot get their pay — Be patient; and if any man takes the means which are set apart for the building of that house, and applies it to his own use, let him, for he will destroy himself. If any man is hungry, let him come to me, and I will feed him at my table. . . . I will divide with them to the last morsel; and then if the man is not satisfied, I will kick his backside!" *

The rift between William Law and the prophet thus began in a fundamental divergence of economic attitudes. The final break in their friendship, however, came from a question, not of finance, but of fidelity. With sorrow and suspicion Law watched Joseph ever enlarging his circle of wives. Then the prophet tried to approach Law's own wife, Jane.†

In a violent session with his leader, Law called for a reformation and an end to the debauchery that was corrupting the church. Joseph argued, pleaded, and quoted the Old Testament, to no avail. Law threatened that unless Joseph went before the High Council, confessed his sins, and promised repentance, he would expose his seductions before the whole world.

"I'll be damned before I do," Law later quoted Joseph as saying. "If I admitted to the charges you would heap upon me, it would prove the overthrow of the Church!"

"Is not that inevitable already?" Law demanded.

"Then we can all go to Hell together and convert it into a heaven by casting the Devil out! Hell is by no means the place

* Ibid., Vol. V, pp. 285–6.

† Denison L. Harris and Robert Scott, who spied for Joseph at the meetings held by Law and Foster, reported many years later that they had seen three veiled women, one of them William Law's wife, come to one meeting and sign affidavits to the effect that "Joseph and Hyrum Smith had endeavored to seduce them; had made the most indecent and wicked proposals to them, and wished them to become their wives." (As reported to Horace Cummings, who described their accounts in the *Contributor*, Salt Lake City, April 1884, Vol. V, p. 255.) Thomas Ford also reported that Joseph attempted to win Jane Law for his wife. (See his *History of Illinois*, p. 322.) And John D. Lee wrote that Joseph wanted the "amiable and handsome wife of William Law." (*Mormonism Unveiled*, p. 147). Joseph H. Jackson wrote in 1844 that Joseph told him he spent two months vainly trying to win Jane Law, and added that Emma Smith suggested that she be given William Law as a spiritual husband. *Narrative of the Adventures and Experiences of Joseph H. Jackson*, pp. 21–2.

this world of fools suppose it to be, but on the contrary, it is quite an agreeable place."

Outraged by the prophet's banter, Law turned on his heel, saying bitterly: "You can enjoy it then, but as for me, I will serve the Lord our God!" *

This was the beginning of Law's apostasy, but for some months an open break was avoided. Like so many other disaffected members, Law believed Joseph to be not a false but a fallen prophet, led into iniquity by the teachings of John C. Bennett and his own hot passions. He clung to Joseph's earliest revelations — to the original purity of the gospel message which had made him a convert — and hoped that something would bring the prophet to his senses.

The 1843 election had given the Saints their first inkling that Law was in disfavor, and when Joseph denounced the Judas in Nauvoo, many of them guessed whom he was accusing. Law was privately told that the Destroying Angels had orders to put him out of the way, and though Joseph elaborately denied the story before a city council, Law was not wholly reassured.† Together with his brother Wilson he began to gravitate into the camp of other disgruntled Mormons.

Here were William Marks, Austin Cowles, and Leonard Soby, bitterly opposed to polygamy. There was young Francis Higbee, who had never forgiven the prophet for publicly denouncing him as debauched and profligate during the Bennett scandal; also his brother Chauncey, whose reputation in Nauvoo was little better.

Hiram Kimball was almost ready to join their ranks. Since he owned a good portion of the land along the river and had built many of the steamboat wharves, he expected to collect the wharfage himself; but Joseph insisted that it was a city prerogative, and publicly threatened to blow up the steamboats that did not pay.‡ Kimball, like Law, was further embittered by jealousy, since Joseph had once coveted his wife, Sarah, and had tried in 1842 to win her for a spiritual wife.§

---

* As described by Law in the *Nauvoo Expositor*, June 7, 1844.
† See *History of the Church*, Vol. VI, pp. 162–5.
‡ Ibid., Vol. VI, pp. 234, 238.
§ See Sarah Kimball's sworn statement, quoted on p. 306

Chief among the dissenters was Dr. Robert D. Foster, whose own grievances strikingly paralleled those of Kimball and William Law. For a long time he had resented the prophet's opposition to his business ventures, but still looked to him for guidance in spiritual matters. Then one day in the spring of 1844 he arrived home unexpectedly from a business trip to discover the prophet dining with his wife. When Joseph left and Foster demanded to know the purpose of his coming, Mrs. Foster refused to talk. Quick to anger and inordinately jealous, he drew his pistol and threatened to shoot her if she did not divulge everything the prophet had said. Gray and terrified, the woman still was silent.

Then in a melodramatic frenzy Foster seized a double-barreled pistol, thrust it into her hand, and shouted for her to defend herself. "If you don't tell me, either you or I will shoot." Thereupon she fainted. When she recovered, she confessed that the prophet had been preaching the spiritual-wife doctrine and had endeavored to seduce her.

Foster told this story to a little knot of disaffected Mormons gathered together in a corner grocery store — the Laws, the Higbees, the ne'er-do-well Joseph H. Jackson, and several others. It was the signal for a complete confession. One by one the men cast off reserve and unburdened their souls. Chauncey Higbee vowed that some of the leading elders had as many as ten or twelve wives apiece, and described how they recorded the names of all the women they wished to marry in a large book, called the Book of the Law of the Lord, kept at the home of Hyrum Smith. After the names were inscribed, he said, the book was sealed, and the seals were broken in the presence of the unsuspecting women, who were thereby convinced that the doctrine was true and that they must submit. Jackson, who had sought unsuccessfully for the hand of Hyrum Smith's daughter and had long been plotting revenge, intimated that a conspiracy was brewing that would cost the lives of every Smith in Nauvoo within a fortnight.

Two of the men who listened to these stories scurried off to the prophet. At once he ordered them to write down everything in complete detail, including Foster's account of the attempted seduction of his wife, and on April 17 he published these sworn testimonies in the *Nauvoo Neighbor*.* He did not deign to deny the stories, letting the shock of publication suffice to convince his people that they were lies.

Foster's trial was set for April 20, 1844. But when it was learned that he had marshaled forty-one witnesses and intended to turn the trial into an indictment of the prophet, a council met secretly in advance and excommunicated him along with William, Wilson, and Jane Law.†

The schism thus created in Nauvoo was small but dangerous. Although they were pariahs within the city, the apostates did not leave. It was not alone their business holdings that kept them there. William Law had courage, tenacity, and a strange, misguided idealism. Although he was surrounded chiefly by men who believed Joseph to be a base impostor, he clung to the hope that he could effect a reformation in the church. To this end he set up a church of his own, with himself as president, following faithfully the organization of the main body.

This in itself would not have been serious, for Joseph had seen rival prophets spring out of the grass at his feet before and they had come to naught. Usually they tried to imitate him, giving out revelations that sounded stale and flat beside his own, prophesying wildly and organizing badly. But Law was cut to a different pattern. Actually he was on the road to complete and ugly disillusionment, but he was walking backwards away from the church, looking eagerly for something in the landscape to which he could cling, grasping at every tree and hedgerow.

His desperate desire to reform the church made him far more formidable than if he had set out to damn the prophet and all his works. Unlike John C. Bennett, he was willing to glove his mailed fist. And more important, he and Foster had enough money to buy a printing press. The reform church was to have a mouthpiece six weeks after it was born, in a newspaper styled the *Nauvoo Expositor*.

While they were waiting for the press to arrive, the apostates started a three-pronged attack on Joseph through the courts. Francis Higbee sued him for five thousand dollars on a charge

---

* See the statements of M. G. Eaton and A. B. Williams, *Nauvoo Neighbor*, Vol. I, No. 51. These were reprinted in *Times and Seasons*, Vol. V (May 15, 1844), p. 541.
† See the *Nauvoo Expositor*, June 7, 1844.

of slander; William Law succeeded in getting a grand jury in Carthage to issue a bill of indictment against him for adultery and polygamy; and Jackson and Foster got a similar indictment for false swearing.*

Joseph was not afraid of what the Laws might swear against him in a Carthage court, for he knew they would be hard pressed to prove him guilty. For three years his clerks had accompanied him everywhere, writing down everything he had said and done. Every day was accounted for. And all references to plural marriage had been so adroitly disguised that only the initiated would understand their true significance. Of this he had made sure.†

Francis Higbee's assault on the prophet was countered with a campaign of defamation the like of which Nauvoo had not seen since the expulsion of Bennett. Joseph charged Higbee with perjury, seduction, and adultery, giving details that the staid *Times and Seasons* admitted "were too indelicate for the public eye and ear." Brigham Young swore that Higbee consorted with prostitutes, from whom he had once contracted a venereal disease. Another witness even identified the source of infection as a French prostitute from Warsaw, and said Bennett had given him medical assistance and the prophet had even tried to heal him by prayer.‡

Chauncey Higbee was attacked with the same violent invective in the *Nauvoo Neighbor* of May 29, when the editor ransacked the secret files of testimony collected in the Bennett scandal and published the old affidavits of three women whom Higbee had seduced with the promise of marriage under the spiritual-wife code. So the mud flew back and forth.

Publication of such documents was the worst sort of defensive strategy, since Joseph could not escape being involved by implication. Those who believed staunchly in his denials of polygamy were bewildered by the prodigious perjury of the apostates, and sensitive Mormons who knew something of the truth about polygamy remembered with pain the injunction of Jesus: "He that is without sin among you, let him cast the first stone."

* See *History of the Church*, Vol. VI, pp. 403, 405.
† See Joseph's own statement on this point, ibid., Vol. VI, p. 409.
‡ See testimonies of Joseph Smith, Brigham Young, and H. J. Sherwood in *Times and Seasons*, Vol. V (May 15, 1844), pp. 537 ff.

Joseph's excesses had cost him what he needed more than anything else, a few months of peace in Nauvoo unmarred by political or personal scandal. Such a period would have seen the election over and some sort of solution for the westward migration worked out. Polygamy could have been sufficiently hidden to keep the gentiles quiet and his new converts loyal. Then in Texas or Oregon or some isolated valley in the Rocky Mountains he could have taught his people the truth.

But he was blind to his own danger and in a public sermon on May 26 pressed his savage attack against the apostates with an irresponsible gasconade: "The Lord has constituted me so curiously that I glory in persecution. . . . If oppression will make a wise man mad, much more a fool. If they want a beardless boy to whip all the world, I will get on the top of a mountain and crow like a rooster: I shall always beat them. When facts are proved, truth and innocence will prevail at last. . . . Come on! ye prosecutors! ye false swearers! All hell, boil over! Ye burning mountains, roll down your lava! for I will come out on the top at last. I have more to boast of than any man ever had. I am the only man that has ever been able to keep a whole church together since the days of Adam. . . . I boast that no man ever did such a work as I. . . . How I do love to hear the wolves howl!

"God knows, then," he concluded, "that the charges against me are false. . . . What a thing it is for a man to be accused of committing adultery, and having seven wives, when I can find only one. I am the same man, and as innocent as I was fourteen years ago; and I can prove them all perjurers." *

Had John C. Bennett been editor of the *Nauvoo Expositor* instead of William Law and Sylvester Emmons, it would have been a lurid sheet. But Law was no cheap scandalmonger and had a profound pity for the plural wives in Nauvoo. He vowed that nothing "carnal" should creep into the *Expositor,* and the first issue, which appeared on June 7, 1844, was therefore — considering the facts at the editor's disposal — an extraordinarily restrained document.

The chief editorial mentioned no names, but simply described the story of a typical English girl coming alone to Nauvoo and

* *History of the Church,* Vol. VI, pp. 408–12.

being carefully indoctrinated in the mysteries of the kingdom by the prophet. This was followed by three affidavits, signed by William Law, Jane Law, and Austin Cowles, testifying that they had all seen or heard read the revelation granting every man the privilege of marrying ten virgins and forgiving him all sins save the shedding of innocent blood.

Polygamy was only the first of a long list of practices signaled out for attack. Against Joseph's attempt to unite church and state, and his grasping for political power, the *Expositor* was most eloquent: "We do not believe that God ever raised up a Prophet to christianize a world by political schemes and intrigue. It is not the way God captivates the heart of the unbeliever; but on the contrary, by preaching truth in its own native simplicity."

"We will not," it said further in an unmistakable allusion to Joseph's kingship, "acknowledge any man as king or lawgiver to the church: for Christ is our only king and law-giver."

The editors struck at Joseph's financial maneuvering and land speculation, at his constant denunciation of Missouri, and at his misuse of the privileges granted by the Nauvoo charters. They called for repeal of the charters, disobedience to political revelations, an end of the abuses of the "unit power" centered in the prophet, and the strongest censure of his "moral imperfections."

The *Expositor* spread consternation throughout the city. Those who were practicing polygamy feared a massacre by the anti-Mormons; those who had been kept in ignorance were overwhelmed by the realization that all the surreptitious gossip might after all be true.* These waited in mixed anger and dismay for the prophet's answer.

When the prophet read the *Expositor* through, he knew that he was facing the gravest crisis of his life. The paper had put him on trial before his whole people. Perhaps if Joseph had faced them with the truth and had gone to the platform in the unfinished temple and read the revelation on plural marriage to his church with his old magnificent assurance, he might have stripped the apostates of their chief weapon and freed his loyal

---

* See the letters of Sarah and Isaac Scott to their relatives in Massachusetts, dated June 16 and July 22, 1844, published in "The Death of a Mormon Dictator: Letters of Massachusetts Mormons, 1843–1848," *New England Quarterly*, Vol. IX (1936), pp. 583–617.

followers from a burden of secrecy, evasion, and lying that was rapidly becoming intolerable. Had he bared his plans for going west, he could have given them hope and a challenge.

But he had no courage for it. In spite of the elaborate metaphysics he had created to justify polygamy, in spite of all the Old Testament prophets who had lived it and the success of his own experimentation, the crisis found him soft-willed. He was empty of conviction when he needed it most.

With a kind of desperation he turned to William Marks, who had so faithfully come to his rescue in past crises with his wisdom and liberal purse, but who in recent months had turned from him in sorrow. They walked down the street together in the bright summer sunlight, turned into a little-used lane where they could talk in private, and sat down on the grassy bank.

"We are a ruined people," Joseph began.

"How so?" Marks asked guardedly, for he had so long kept a troubled silence that he no longer knew how to talk to his leader.

"This doctrine of polygamy, or spiritual wife-system, that has been taught and practiced among us, will prove our destruction and overthrow. I have been deceived; it is a curse to mankind, and we shall have to leave the United States soon, unless it can be put down, and its practice stopped in the Church."

The older man was ready to weep with gratitude. This was what he had been hoping to hear ever since he had seen the cursed revelation on polygamy almost a year before.

"Now Brother Marks," Joseph went on, "you have not received this doctrine, and I want you to go into the high council, and I will have charges preferred against all who practice this doctrine, and I want you to try them by the laws of the Church, and cut them off, if they will not repent, and cease the practice of this doctrine, and I will go into the stand and preach against it with all my might, and in this way we will rid the Church of this damnable heresy." *

But Joseph was only striking blindly for a way out of his dilemma, and the embarrassments of this particular solution must have made him discard it by sundown. He did not know

* This interview was described by William Marks in *Zion's Harbinger and Baneemy's Organ*, Vol. III (July 1853), pp. 52–3. His account may be colored somewhat by his profound antipathy to polygamy.

what to do. Only one theme persisted in all his agitation — a conviction that the *Expositor* must be throttled. But here again he was betrayed by his utter incapacity for dealing skillfully with opposition, a weakness that his political and legal successes in Nauvoo had served only to intensify. He had become an autocrat who could think only in terms of suppression.

Calling together the city council, he ordered a trial, not of the apostates, but of the *Expositor* itself. It was a strange, high-handed proceeding. There were no jury, no lawyers, no witnesses for the defense. The councilors simply stood up, one after another, and accused the editors of seduction, pandering, counterfeiting, and thievery. The prophet went so far as to say that the apostate Joseph H. Jackson had been proved a murderer before the city council.

Then he went on to add one more to his list of denials of polygamy by declaring that the revelation on polygamy referred to in the *Expositor* "was in answer to a question concerning things which transpired in former days, *and had no reference to the present time.*" * The city council now declared that the press was libelous and must be destroyed. Joseph issued a proclamation declaring it a civic nuisance; a portion of the Legion marched to the office, wrecked the press, pied the type, and burned every issue of the hated paper that could be found.

THE *Expositor* was neither the first nor the last Illinois paper to be so destroyed. Burning abolitionist presses was something of a sport close to the Mason-Dixon line. But for a leader of a hated minority to indulge in this sport was not frontier license, but a violation of the holy Constitution. It was a greater breach of political and legal discipline than the anti-Mormons could have hoped for. Joseph could not have done better for his enemies, since he had at last given them a fighting moral issue.

The apostates fled to Warsaw and Carthage. Robert Foster wrote for the *Warsaw Signal* a detailed statement in which he not only described the destruction of the press but also accused Joseph of a long list of crimes, from the hiring of Porter Rockwell to kill Boggs to the seduction of innumerable Mormon

---

* The *Nauvoo Neighbor,* June 19, 1844, printed these proceedings of the city council. The words uttered by Joseph that I have italicized were omitted from the *History of the Church* when the proceedings were reprinted. See Vol. VI, p. 441.

women. "History affords no parallel to the iniquities and enormities of this tyrant," he concluded, "who dressed in a little brief authority, perpetrates deeds at which Heaven weeps and human nature falls back ashamed of her own depravity."

Thomas Sharp's editorial on June 12 screamed with demoniac fury: "War and extermination is inevitable! CITIZENS ARISE, ONE AND ALL!!! Can you *stand* by and suffer such INFERNAL DEVILS! to ROB men of their property and Rights, without avenging them? We have no time for comments; every man will make his own. LET it be made with POWDER AND BALLS!!!"

Joseph too late saw that he had loosed an avalanche. He wrote a long defensive letter to Governor Ford justifying the destruction of the press on legal grounds, and dispatched orders to the twelve apostles to return home at once, with powder, lead, and a rifle packed discreetly in their luggage.* Then he went to instruct the Legion in the defense of the city.

Mounting the reviewing stand, his blue and buff uniform blazoned with gilt buttons and epaulets, he stood proudly before his men, betraying nothing of the tumult and anxiety racking him within. He made a dogged defense of the legality of his position. Since the burning of the press, Law and Foster had secured warrants for his arrest on the charge of riot, which with his usual dexterity he had evaded through the habeas corpus procedure of the Nauvoo municipal court. But this he knew was little more than a postponement. Hourly scouts were bringing him word of the angry crowds that were swarming the streets of Carthage and Warsaw. Missourians and Iowans were crossing the river in droves, attracted like flies to the smell of blood. Armed bands already were threatening isolated Mormon families and driving them into Nauvoo. There was lynch talk everywhere — always in the name of justice and liberty.

Joseph read to his men the inflammatory editorial of the *Warsaw Signal* extra so that they should be under no illusions about what faced them. Then he said: "We are American citizens. We live upon a soil for the liberties of which our fathers periled their lives and spilt their blood upon the battlefield. Those rights so dearly purchased shall not be disgracefully trodden under foot by lawless marauders without at least a noble effort

* *History of the Church*, Vol. VI, p. 487.

on our part to sustain our liberties. Will you stand by me to the death?"

The thousands arrayed beneath him, stiff and serious in their well-ordered ranks, shouted in unison a thunderous "Aye!"

"It is well. If you had not done it, I would have gone out there," and he swept his arm to the west, "and would have raised up a mightier people." Then drawing his sword from the scabbard, Joseph thrust it heavenward and shouted in a voice that carried over the ranks of the army and down the city streets: "I call God and angels to witness that I have unsheathed my sword with a firm and unalterable determination that this people shall have their legal rights, and be protected from mob violence, or my blood shall be spilt upon the ground like water, and my body consigned to the silent tomb!"

CHAPTER XXVII
Carthage

O NCE MORE the Mormon women braced themselves for the shock of an uprooting. They were used to it by now, some having made all five migrations, and accepted what threatened to be expulsion from Nauvoo almost with resignation. Satan would give the children of God no rest.

Was there something intrinsically alien in Mormonism that continually invited barbarity even in the land of the free? It could not have been the theology, which, however challenging, was really a potpourri of American religious thinking spiced with the fundamental ideal of inevitable progress. Nor could it have been the economy, which had shifted from communism to free enterprise and then to autarchy. Wherever the Mormons went, the citizens resented their self-righteousness, their unwillingness to mingle with the world, their intense consciousness of superior destiny. But these were negligible factors in creating the ferocious antagonisms of Missouri and Illinois.

Actually each migration had risen out of a special set of circumstances. The move to Kirtland from New York had been opportunistic; the flight from Kirtland had been largely the result of apostate rather than non-Mormon persecution. The various Missouri expulsions had been rooted deep in the slavery and Indian issues, which did not figure at all in Illinois. In the latter state, to a far greater extent than in Missouri, the political exploitation of Mormon numbers, made doubly repugnant by the presence of immigrant converts from monarchist England, was perhaps the most volatile fuel feeding the anti-Mormon fires. Those who lived closest to the Mormon mass were desperately afraid of being crushed. They hated Joseph Smith because thousands followed him blindly and slavishly.

To them the Nauvoo theocracy was a malignant tyranny that was spreading as swiftly and dangerously as a Mississippi flood and that might eventually engulf the very government of the United States. Thomas Sharp had once published in the *War-*

saw Signal a wholly imaginary story of a massacre of 500 anti-Mormons by 10,000 Mormon Legionaries. The account ended with the enraged citizens of three states marching upon Nauvoo, sacking and burning the city, and killing all the inhabitants. This was more than vicious propaganda; it was prophecy of what Sharp expected in the future.

Anti-Mormonism in Illinois was much more dangerous than it had been in Missouri, because it had a rock-bound moral foundation in the American fear of despotism. This, and not repugnance for polygamy — which, unlike the glorification of theocracy, was not yet preached openly — was the primary source of the venom in the now swiftly mobilizing opposition.

The prophet sensed something of the magnitude of the forces rising against him and probably felt also its spiritual strength. As his old buoyancy and optimism deserted him, the once occasional intuition of imminent death became a constant, chilling presence. He began seriously to think about the problem of a successor and urged Hyrum to safety in Ohio so that if the worst befell him, there might be a leader to avenge his death.

Until now the question of a successor had never seriously troubled him. He had taken it for granted that his mantle would descend, in true dynastic fashion, upon his eldest son, Joseph, now a bright, eager twelve-year-old and a favorite in the church. Shortly after he had escaped to Nauvoo from Liberty jail, Joseph had blessed the boy and promised him the succession; but few of the Saints had knowledge of the incident. In the winter of 1843, however, during a sermon to his people in the grove, he had called his son to the stand beside him and said with emphasis: "I have often been asked who would succeed me as the prophet to the church. My son Joseph will be your next prophet." *

* The Utah Mormons deny that Joseph's son was appointed his father's heir, and hold that the right of succession lay with the apostles, but the evidence that Joseph Smith intended Young Joseph to be his successor is impressive. See the sworn statements of Sophia K. Cook, niece of Martin Harris, James Whitehead, secretary to Joseph Smith, and John H. Carter, all of whom heard this speech. *Zion's Ensign*, Vol. XII, No. 29, p. 5, and *Temple Lot Case*, pp. 28, 180. Lyman Wight said in a letter to the *Northern Islander*: "Now Mr. Editor, if you had been present when Joseph called on me shortly after we came out of jail, to lay hands with him on the head of a youth, and heard him cry aloud, you are my successor when I depart, and heard the blessings poured on his head . . . you would not have been led by blind fanaticism. . . ." Reprinted in *Saints Advocate*, Vol. VII (September 1884),

At that time trouble had seemed very remote. But now Joseph feared that an assassin would cut short his days before he saw the age of forty. On April 4, 1844, when he met with the apostles in one of their last meetings before they left on a campaign tour, he rushed through instructions which Orson Hyde described as "every ordinance of the holy priesthood." Then he said: "Now if they kill me you have got all the keys, and all the ordinances and you can confer them upon others, and the hosts of Satan will not be able to tear down the kingdom as fast as you will be able to build it up." * After Joseph's death Brigham Young, who was president of the apostles, looked back to this meeting and concluded that the prophet had placed the authority of the church and all rights of succession directly in his hands.

WHEN Thomas Ford learned of the burning of the *Expositor*, he went directly to Carthage for an investigation, determined to call out the militia if necessary to bring the offenders to justice. He was appalled to discover the militia already assembling under the orders of the local constables and openly preparing for an attack on Nauvoo. After an interview with the Laws, Fosters, and Higbees, who, it may be assumed, told him the worst, Ford wrote to the prophet demanding that he and everyone else implicated in the destruction of the *Expositor* submit immediately to the Carthage constable and come to that city for trial.

This, in fact, Joseph had already offered to do, provided that he was allowed a military escort of his own men to prevent a lynching. But Ford, though admitting that the militia was already almost "beyond legal control," feared a civil war should the Nauvoo Legion march to Carthage, and denied him this privilege. "If you," he concluded, "by refusing to submit, shall

p. 478. Joseph's son swore in later years that he remembered this incident, and added: "I was also present at a meeting in the grove near the temple, and I remember my father laying his hands on my head, and saying to the people that this was his successor, or was to be his successor." *Temple Lot Case*, p. 79. Henry Brown in his *History of Illinois* (New York, 1844) stated: "The prophet, it is said, has left a will or revelation appointing a successor; and, among other things, it is stated that his son, a lad of twelve years, is named therein as his successor. Of this, however, there is no certainty." See p. 489. John D. Lee wrote in his confessions: "It was then understood among the Saints that Young Joseph was to succeed his father." *Mormonism Unveiled*, p. 155.

* *Times and Seasons*, Vol. V (September 15, 1844), p. 651.

make it necessary to call out the militia, I have great fears that your city will be destroyed, and your people many of them exterminated. You know the excitement of the public mind. Do not tempt it too far."

When Joseph, who was hiding in the secret attic room of the Mansion House, read this letter through, he shook his head in despair. "There is no mercy — no mercy here."

"No," agreed Hyrum, "just as sure as we fall into their hands we are dead men."

They talked for a while about going to Washington and laying the case before President Tyler, but knowing his unpopularity and certain defeat in the coming election, this seemed futile.

"If Hyrum and I are ever taken again," Joseph said with conviction, "we shall be massacred, or I am not a prophet of God. I want Hyrum to live to avenge my blood, but he is determined not to leave me." *

The two brothers stared at each other wordlessly for a time, while their friends stood by dumb, miserable, and helpless to aid them. Then, his face brightening, Joseph made his decision with his old swiftness and certainty: "The way is open. It is clear to my mind what to do. All they want is Hyrum and myself; then tell everybody to go about their business, and not to collect in groups, but to scatter about. There is no doubt they will come here and search for us. Let them search; they will not harm you in person or property, and not even a hair of your head. We will cross the river tonight, and go away to the West."

Within a few hours their plans were complete. The *Maid of Iowa* was to sail up the Ohio River carrying their families east to safety, and the two brothers, with the doughty Rockwell and the devoted Willard Richards, were to cross the Mississippi in a skiff.

At midnight the men bade farewell to their weeping families and started across the river in a blinding rain. Joseph could not shake off a sense of ill omen. The Mississippi, which had been such a friendly barrier between him and Missouri, was now in flood. Weeks of rain to the north had swelled it into a hideous

* This whole conversation was later reported by Abraham C. Hodge, who was present. *History of the Church,* Vol. VI, pp. 545–6.

menacing evil. For many miles above and below Nauvoo the lowland farms were inundated, newly built cabins half buried in mud or torn loose altogether and churned into a jumble of logs, joining the uprooted trees and boulders that careened down the river. River men swore it was the worst flood they had seen in a lifetime of fighting the upper Mississippi.

Porter Rockwell, whose shoulders were as tireless as an engine, took the oars. Struck again and again by snags that could not be seen in the blackness, the skiff sprang leaks, and the men were forced to strip off their boots and bail the water out to keep from sinking. It took them until dawn to fight their way across.

But the river was only one factor in Joseph's gloom. He was landing in Iowa, where there was still a price on his head. The Governor of the Iowa Territory had never agreed not to extradite him to Missouri on the old charge of treason. Moreover, Joseph had neither equipment nor appetite for the lonely and savage western trails. And he could not stifle a sense of guilt at deserting his people. In Missouri he had been their champion and by his own dramatic surrender had ransomed them from annihilation. But where now was the miraculous confidence that had borne him through that ordeal? Emma had been weeping silently when he bade her good-by, but her great hazel eyes, the only remnant of her once haunting beauty, had been full of reproach. He knew that she thought him a coward.

When they landed and dried their drenched clothing before the fireplace of a trusted Saint, Joseph dictated a short note to Emma which reflected his pessimism and indecision: ". . . Do not despair. If God ever opens a door that is possible for me, I will see you again. I do not know where I shall go, or what I shall do, but shall if possible endeavor to get to the city of Washington. . . . May God Almighty bless you and the children and mother. My heart bleeds. No more at present. If you conclude to go to Kirtland, Cincinnati, or any other place, I wish you would contrive to inform me this evening." *

Rockwell rowed back with the message, bearing orders to get Joseph's best horses across the river. In Nauvoo he learned that a posse had arrived to arrest the prophet and, discovering him

---

* The original of this letter is in the library of the Reorganized Church in Independence, Missouri.

gone, had galloped madly back to Carthage with the news. The Mormon women were wild with apprehension; the Legion was divided between those who wanted to defend the city and those who felt, like Joseph, that the safety of everyone could best be secured by their scattering. With Joseph and Hyrum gone, with the apostles away and Rigdon in Pittsburgh, the city found itself completely leaderless.

It is said that Emma took Rockwell aside and insisted that he go back to Joseph and entreat him to return. She gave him a letter bearing her own plea and saw to it that he was accompanied by Reynolds Cahoon, who was certain that unless Joseph gave himself up Nauvoo would be ravaged.

Joseph listened in silence to Cahoon, who had brought not only the opinions of the worst alarmists in the city but also fresh assurances from Governor Ford that the prophet would be guaranteed complete protection and a fair and legal trial. "When the shepherd deserts his flock," Cahoon finished, "who is to keep the wolves from devouring them?"

All of the blithe optimism and exuberance out of which so many revelations had sprung in the past when Joseph had been confronted with a crisis had now fled. "If my life is of no value to my friends," he said dully, "it is of none to myself." Turning to Porter Rockwell he asked: "What shall I do?"

The faithful Rockwell was made to obey orders and dared not influence his leader in so hazardous a decision. "You are oldest and ought to know best; and as you make your bed, I will lie with you."

Joseph now turned to his brother. "You are the oldest, Hyrum, what shall we do?"

Hyrum, who had none of Joseph's prescience and had always believed his brother invincible, replied: "Let us go back and give ourselves up, and see the thing out."

For a long time Joseph stared fixedly into the fire at his feet. Then he raised his head and spoke with a great weariness: "If you go back, I will go with you, but we shall be butchered."

"No, no," Hyrum cried with a stubborn optimism. "Let us go back and put our trust in God, and we shall not be harmed. The Lord is in it. If we live or have to die, we will be reconciled to our fate." *

* This conversation and all the details that follow, except where noted, are taken

FROM this moment forward, if the observations of the men closest to him in these hours can be relied upon, Joseph moved and spoke like a man certain he is about to die. Tender and melancholy with his friends, and filled with a consuming hunger to see familiar faces and familiar objects once more, he climbed into the boat and looked eagerly across the expanse of water to his city. As the boat drew close to the green hills checkered with redbrick houses, the great temple, complete now except for the roof and steeple, gleaming white and ethereal in the afternoon sun, he said half to himself: "I should like to speak to the Saints once more."

"We can send out word, and have them hear you by starlight," Rockwell suggested. But under the urgency of preparations for the defense in Carthage, this plan was abandoned. Although perhaps inwardly certain of his fate, Joseph was by no means resigned to it and spent most of his precious hours securing lawyers and witnesses and mapping out his case. A stranger in the Mansion House who talked with him at this time wrote later that "he was easy in his manners, and seemed sure of an acquittal if he could get a fair hearing." *

Ford had ordered the disbanding of the Legion and the surrender of all the arms belonging to the state, which consisted of several hundred stand of rifles and three small cannon. To this Joseph now agreed, despite the protests of the Legion officers, who feared a repetition of the sacking of Far West. But to make sure this time that his men would not be disarmed completely, Joseph ordered that all personal arms should be secretly stored in a convenient warehouse, where they would be available at a moment's notice.†

At midday on June 24, 1844 Joseph started for Carthage with his brother Hyrum and the handful of men who were to stand trial with them. First he rode past the temple, staring affectionately up at its high white façade. Then his eyes swept slowly

---

from the first-hand testimonies of men who accompanied the prophet until his death. They were compiled and published in *History of the Church*, Vol. VI, pp. 547–631; Vol. VII, pp. 1–164.

    * An account by B. W. Richmond, published in the Chicago *Times*, and reprinted in the *Deseret News*, November 27, 1875.

    † Diary of Oliver B. Huntington, who went with his father to stack and hide them before dawn on the day following Joseph's departure for Carthage. See Vol. I, p. 45.

down over the neat square blocks and rows of new houses, flanked by gardens and green young orchards leading down to the swelling river. "This is the loveliest place and the best people under the heavens," he cried. "Little do they know the trials that await them."

Near the edge of the city they met a company of Saints who had marched in from Ramus to join the Legion. The men were exhausted by the all-night march. Some, whose shoes were thin, had worn through the soles, and their feet were cut and bleeding. Joseph's young cousin John Lyman Smith ran up and flung his arms about him. When Joseph saw the boy's feet he began to weep. "God bless you, God bless you my dear boy."

Turning to a shoemaker who stood near by in the door of his shop, he called out: "Let these men have some shoes."

The man shrugged helplessly. "I have no shoes."

The reply angered Joseph. "Let them have boots then!" Turning to his cousin, he said: "Johnnie, the troops will be disbanded and return home. I shall go to Carthage for trial, under the protection of the Governor. Have no fears, for you shall yet see Israel triumph and in peace." *

Joseph and Hyrum were escorted into Carthage by a well-disciplined company of militia from McDonough county, who met them en route. But once they arrived in the center of the town, they were surrounded by the troops from Warsaw and Carthage, who met them with shouts of derision and triumph:

"Stand away, you McDonough boys, and let us shoot the damned Mormons!"

"God damn you, Old Joe, we've got you now!"

"Clear the way and let us see old Joe, the prophet of God. He's seen the last of Nauvoo. We'll use him up and kill all the damned Mormons!"

It was so like the capitulation in Far West that Joseph must have felt that he was living his life over. There was a great difference, however, in the two crises. The methods of Lilburn Boggs and Thomas Ford were exactly opposite. Ford, though fearing and disliking the Mormons and believing Joseph Smith to be a consummate charlatan, was determined on a legal trial. But, paradoxically, it was this very passion for justice that was

---

* A transcript of this manuscript account by John Lyman Smith may be seen in the Utah State Historical Society Library.

to be Joseph's greatest danger. Boggs's very bloodthirstiness had been a boon because gentile champions rose up to fight it and saved the prophet's life. But in Illinois Ford was his only champion, and Ford was weak.

He had had the misfortune to inherit a multitude of evils from Thomas Carlin, one of Illinois' worst governors. The state was burdened by a $14,000,000 debt foolishly incurred for canals and railroads; the currency of the state was practically worthless, and the people were either unwilling or unable to pay taxes. All these troubles were dwarfed now by the magnitude of the Mormon problem, which was threatening to precipitate a civil war at the very moment when the worst Mississippi flood in the state's history was piling up damage of from twelve to twenty million dollars.

To meet these crises Ford brought a discriminating and sensitive intelligence and a stubborn loyalty for the law. But he was a poor orator, lacking in the support of his own party and sensitive to the constant accusation that he was pro-Mormon. "He appeared," wrote B. W. Richmond, "like a man weary of human nature and of life." In his heart, as Ford confessed later, he hoped that Joseph Smith would escape from jail and leave the state. Knowing that his followers would trail him anywhere, he believed it would be the least costly method of ridding the state of the whole sect. But he took no steps to make this possible.

At the preliminary hearing in Carthage on the charge of riot, all the cases were deferred and the men released on bail. Only Joseph and Hyrum were kept in custody. Special writs had been sworn out against them on a charge of treason, the excuse being that they had declared martial law and had called out the Legion on June 19 when the posse first appeared to arrest Joseph. Ford himself admitted that this charge was extremely flimsy.

Although there had been no preliminary hearing on the treason charge, the two brothers were unceremoniously clapped into jail. Ford was aware of the high-handed procedure of the Carthage justice of the peace, but justified his own inaction on constitutional grounds. Actually he was afraid of the militia and was willing to make minor concessions to keep it in at least a nominal state of discipline.

Carthage jail was a stout two-story stone building with a spacious cell on the upper floor. Joseph was permitted the use of several rooms, and his friends had easy access to his presence. They kept him informed of all the rumors of conspiracy against him that were circulating throughout the town.

Ford himself came to the jail and talked with the prophet for several hours. They were both young men, Ford forty-four and Joseph not yet thirty-nine. But Ford's slight figure, sharp face, and thin voice contrasted strangely with Joseph's size and booming eloquence. They argued back and forth, testing each other's sincerity and strength, and came to agreement — according to the carefully detailed reports of the prophet's companions, John Taylor and J. M. Bernhisel — on almost everything save the wrecking of the *Expositor*.

"The press in the United States is looked upon as the great bulwark of American freedom," Ford insisted, "and its destruction in Nauvoo was represented and looked upon as a high-handed measure, and manifests to the people a disposition on your part to suppress the liberty of speech and of the press."

"Could we suffer a set of worthless vagabonds to come into our city," Joseph replied hotly, "and right under our own eyes and protection, vilify and calumniate not only ourselves, but the character of our wives and daughters, as was impudently and unblushingly done in that infamous and filthy sheet? There is not a city in the United States that would have suffered such an indignity for twenty-four hours. . . . there may have been some better way, but I confess I could not see it."

When Ford remarked that he was going to Nauvoo to address the Mormons, Joseph begged to be taken along, for he was certain that the Governor's presence was the only thing keeping the militia under control. Ford promised to do so.

That night Joseph lay on a mattress on the floor between two of his friends. He could not sleep, and talked in low tones to the two men beside him, who tried vainly to rally his spirits. "I would like to see my family again," he said wistfully, and then added: "I wish to God that I could preach to the Saints in Nauvoo once more."

When everyone was asleep save Dan Jones, the man on his left, Joseph whispered to him: "Are you afraid to die?"

"Has that time come, you think?" Jones asked, and then after a moment's reflection he said with quiet courage: "Engaged in such a cause I do not think that death would have many terrors."

Joseph was deeply moved. "You will yet see Wales," he said, "and fulfill the mission appointed you before you die."

When finally he fell asleep, Joseph dreamed that he was back in Kirtland, standing on the farm that for six years had been his pride. Weeds and brambles clogged the footpaths; the barn was falling into decay, its doors ripped off and the weatherboarding gone. Everywhere were signs of neglect and vandalism. Then out of the barn rushed a band of furious men railing at him for trespassing. This he denied, claiming the farm as a gift from the church and insisting that it had never been sold. The band swelled into a rabble; the men drew their knives and rushed at him cursing.

Then somehow, in the irrational fashion of dreams, the men began to fight among themselves, and Joseph slipped away. But the mud outside the barn, ankle-deep, clung to his feet like the heavy chains of the Richmond jail. He fought against it, sweating and terrified, and then awoke.

In the morning he told this dream to Dan Jones, who then went out to gather information. As Jones left, the guard whispered to him: "We had too much trouble to bring Old Joe here to let him ever escape alive, and unless you want to die with him you had better leave before sundown; and you are not a damned bit better for taking his part, and you'll see that I can prophesy better than Old Joe, for neither he nor his brother, nor anyone who will remain with them will see the sun set today."

Jones went at once to find the Governor. As he passed the square he heard a stump speaker from Warsaw haranguing a crowd and pressed close to catch his words. "Our troops will be discharged this morning in obedience to orders, and for a sham we will leave the town; but when the Governor and the McDonough troops have left for Nauvoo this afternoon, we will return and kill those men, if we have to tear the jail down." Shouting and cheering, the men lifted their rifles high and shook them in a fierce gesture of unity.

When Jones related to the Governor everything he had heard, Ford merely shook his head in annoyance. "You are unneces-

sarily alarmed for the safety of your friends, sir; the people are
not that cruel."

Ford had, in fact, decided to go to Nauvoo without the
prophet, believing that the militia would not dare commit any
violence to the prisoners so long as he himself was within easy
reach of Mormon vengeance. He ordered all the troops disbanded save three companies, one to accompany him to Nauvoo, the remaining two to guard the jail. The company from
Warsaw, most frenzied of all, were told to go home, but the
Carthage Greys, who were only slightly less incendiary, were
detailed to remain in the town overnight.

When Jones returned to the jail to bring this alarming news
to the prophet, he was denied admittance. Joseph was in the upper room calmly dictating a letter:

Carthage Jail, June 27, 1844, 20 past 8 a.m.
Dear Emma:

The Governor continues his courtesies and permits us to see our
friends. We hear this morning that the Governor will not go down
with his troops today (to Nauvoo) as was anticipated last evening,
but if he does come down with his troops you will be protected, and
I want you to tell Brother Dunham to instruct the people to stay at
home and attend to their own business, and let there be no groups or
gathering together unless by permission of the Governor. . . .

There is no danger of any "exterminating order." Should there be
a meeting among the troops (which we do not anticipate, excitement
is abating) a part will remain loyal and stand for the defense of the
state and our rights. There is one principle which is eternal, it is the
duty of all men to protect their lives and the lives of their households
whenever necessity requires, and no power has a right to forbid it.
Should the last extreme arrive, but *I anticipate no such extreme,* but
caution is the parent of safety.

JOSEPH SMITH

P.S. [in his own handwriting] Dear Emma, I am very much resigned to my lot, knowing I am justified and have done the best that
could be done. Give my love to the children and all my friends, Mr.
Brower, and all who inquire after me; and as for treason, I know that
I have not committed any and they cannot prove one appearance of
anything of the kind. So you need not have any fears that harm can
happen to us on that score.

May God bless you all. Amen.

JOSEPH SMITH.

At this point Willard Richards, who was now the only one permitted to pass in and out of the jail, brought word to Joseph that Ford had broken his promise and was off to Nauvoo without him. The prophet realized that he was trapped almost beyond hope. There was only one lean trump left in his hand, which he now feared he had waited too long to play. Hastily he scribbled an order to Jonathan Dunham to bring the Legion, break the jail, and save him at all costs. Within seconds two messengers bearing this order and the letter to Emma were off at a frantic gallop on the fifteen-mile trip to Nauvoo.

One by one the friends who had been visiting Joseph and Hyrum were forced out of Carthage at bayonet point. Only Willard Richards and John Taylor remained in the jail. About five o'clock, when the jailer suggested that they might be safer in the cell, Joseph turned to his pink-cheeked, serious clerk: "If we go into the cell, will you go with us?"

"Brother Joseph," Richards replied, "you did not ask me to cross the river with you — you did not ask me to come to Carthage — you did not ask me to come to jail with you — and do you think I would forsake you now? But I will tell you what I will do; if you are condemned to be hung for treason, I will be hung in your stead, and you shall go free."

Joseph smiled at him tenderly. "You cannot."

"I will," he insisted, and they all knew that he spoke in deadly earnest.

Dull and heavy-spirited, the prisoners finally sent for some wine, and all except Hyrum sipped a little.* When Richards handed the bottle to the guard, he started down the stairs. At that moment there was a noise at the outer door, followed by shouts to surrender and the sound of shots.

It was not the Nauvoo Legion galloping up for a dramatic rescue. For some reason never divulged, Jonathan Dunham had pocketed the order and neglected to act upon it, and no other man in Nauvoo knew of his prophet's peril.† It was the men of the Warsaw militia, who had marched out of the town as a token to the Governor, waited until he was well on his way to

---

* According to John Taylor's account. *History of the Church*, Vol. VII, p. 101.

† This story is told by Allen J. Stout in his manuscript journal, 1815–89, a transcript of which may be seen in the Utah State Historical Society Library. See p. 13. It is confirmed by T. B. H. Stenhouse in his *Rocky Mountain Saints* (New York, 1873), p. 164n.

Nauvoo, and then come roaring back to join the Carthage Greys.

Joseph had a six-shooter and Hyrum a single-barrel pistol, which had been smuggled in by friends the previous day. The other two men had nothing to defend themselves with save two hickory canes. All four sprang against the door, but retreated when the first ball penetrated the thick panel.

As the door was forced open, three of the prisoners jumped nimbly to the left. But Hyrum was caught by fire from one of the half-dozen muzzles pointing evilly toward the doorway. The first ball struck him in the nose and he stumbled backward crying: "I am a dead man!" As he was falling, three more caught him from the door, and a fourth ball from the window shattered his left side.

Joseph now discharged all six barrels down the passageway. Three of them missed fire, but the other three found marks. One of the wounded rushed back down the stairs, his arm a mass of blood and mangled flesh. "Are you badly hurt?" someone shouted.

"Yes, my arm is all shot to pieces by Old Joe," he screamed, "but I don't care; I've got revenge; I shot Hyrum!"

A shower of balls was now pouring into the room. John Taylor was hit five times, but the only bullet that might have killed him struck his watch, which was in his vest pocket, and was deflected harmlessly away. Willard Richards, who was as big a man as Joseph, miraculously escaped being hit at all, save for a ball that slightly grazed his throat and ear lobe, although he stood close to the door beating vainly at the guns with his cane. Most of the balls coming in through the window were striking harmlessly against the ceiling, while the men in the hallway who had not been hit or frightened back by Joseph's shooting were trying to fix their aim upon him.

When his pistol was empty, Joseph flung it on the floor crying: "There, defend yourselves as well as you can," and sprang to the window. He looked out upon a hundred bayonets gleaming dully in the murky light that seeped through the heavy storm clouds. Behind every bayonet there was a hideously painted face, and it must have seemed to him as if hell itself had vomited up this apparition.

It is said by some who saw him that he gave the Masonic sig-

nal of distress and cried out: "Is there no help for the widow's
son?" * Then a ball from the door caught him in the back and
he pitched slowly forward out of the window, his hands still
gripping the sill from which he had been preparing to jump.
For an instant he hung to the sill swinging, while Levi Williams, the colonel commanding the Warsaw militia, shouted:
"Shoot him! God damn him! Shoot the damned rascal!"

But no one shot. William Daniels,† who was standing petri-
fied at the sight, heard him cry: "Oh Lord, my God!" and
watched him drop to the ground. He twisted as he fell, landing
on his right shoulder and back, and then rolled over on his
face. One of the militia, barefooted and bareheaded, grinning
through his black paint, leaped forward and dragged him
against the well-curb in the yard.

The prophet stirred a little and opened his eyes. There was
no terror in them, but whether the calmness was from resignation or unconsciousness one cannot know. Colonel Williams
now ordered four men to fire at him. As the balls struck he
cringed a little and fell forward on his face.

The militia began to scatter in panic. But the same man who
had dragged him to the well-curb now raised his bowie knife
and rushed forward to cut off the prophet's head. At that moment the storm clouds parted and the setting June sun blazed
full upon the scene. To William Daniels it seemed that a pillar
of light thrust down from heaven and rested between the dead
prophet and his murderers. "The arm of the ruffian that held
the knife fell powerless," he said, "the muskets of the four who
fired fell to the ground, and they all stood like marble statues,
not having power to move a single limb of their bodies. By this
time most of the men had fled in great disorder. I never saw so
frightened a set of men before."

The body of the prophet lay for a time quite alone, until

---

* Zina Huntington Jacobs, one of Joseph's wives, said in later years in a public
address: "I am the widow of a master mason, who, when leaping from the window
of Carthage jail, pierced with bullets, made the masonic sign of distress. . . ." *Latter-
Day Saints Biographical Encylcopædia*, Vol. I, p. 698.

† See his *Correct Account of the Murder of Generals Joseph and Hyrum Smith*
(published by John Taylor in Nauvoo in 1845). Daniels was so troubled at having
been a witness to the lynching, if not a participant, that he became a convert. The
Mormons later dropped him from fellowship.

CARTHAGE JAIL

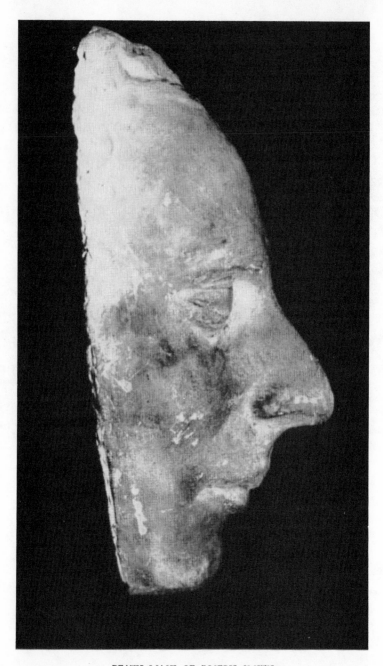

DEATH MASK OF JOSEPH SMITH

Willard Richards ventured forth to carry it back into the jail and lay it beside the body of his brother. Securing a messenger, he sent word of the murder to Ford, and a message to his own people to do nothing by way of vengeance. Only then did he give in to his shock and inner pain.

EPILOGUE

THE MURDER OF Joseph and Hyrum Smith robbed the anti-Mormons of their stomach for civil war. The worst among them had hoped that the Nauvoo Legion, upon hearing of the death of their leaders, would revenge themselves by slaying Ford. This would have given them an excuse to descend upon Nauvoo, slaughter the inhabitants, and plunder the city. Ford's death they would have counted a gain for the state in any case. But now they fled precipitately, along with their women and children, leaving Carthage forlorn and silent with its dead.

When word of the tragedy reached Nauvoo, the city was gripped in a paralysis of horror and loss. "I felt as though I could not live," Allen Stout wrote in his journal; "I knew not how to contain myself. . . . And I hope to live to avenge their blood; but if I do not, I will teach my children to never cease to try to avenge their blood and then teach their children and children's children to the fourth generation as long as there is one descendant of the murderers upon the earth."

Such passion was never translated into action, for the Mormons were a minority. The Legion followed the injunction of Willard Richards, permitted Ford to remain unmolested, and kept a rigid discipline in the city.

The bodies of the martyrs — as they were thereafter always called — were brought to Nauvoo in two wooden boxes covered with an Indian horse-blanket and prairie grass. When the wagon arrived in the city, the Nauvoo Legion formed a procession behind it, and ten thousand weeping citizens followed them to the Mansion House. When Emma was finally permitted to see her husband's body, she flung herself across it and cried in anguish: "Oh Joseph, Joseph, they have killed you at last." B. W. Richmond, a stranger and guest in the Mansion House who was watching the scene, noted a woman standing at Joseph Smith's head, her face covered and her whole frame convulsed with weeping. "She was the widow of William Morgan, of Masonic memory," he wrote. The other wives mourned the prophet less openly but no less bitterly, and it is said that Olive Grey Frost for a time went quite mad.

Before the bodies of Joseph and Hyrum were interred, twenty thousand Saints filed silently past the velvet-covered coffins in a last gesture of homage. Throngs filled the cemetery to watch the pine boxes lowered into the melancholy graves, boxes from which the bodies had been secretly removed and replaced with bags of sand. Fearing desecration of the graves, ten men buried the corpses at midnight in the basement of the Nauvoo House and heaped broken stone and rubbish over the spot.

Even in death the prophet was permitted no rest. Months later, at Emma's request, the bodies were exhumed and reburied under the summer cottage, where, despite all legend to the contrary, they remain to this day.

Five months after the murder Joseph's youngest son, David Hyrum, was born.

The *New York Herald* published an extra to announce the death of the prophet, the editor writing in a harsh obituary: "The death of the modern Mahomet will seal the fate of Mormonism. They cannot get another Joe Smith. The holy city must tumble into ruins, and the 'latter day saints' have indeed come to the latter day."

But after two days' reflection James Gordon Bennett amended this judgment, writing on July 10: "Instead of sealing the fate of Mormonism, we are now rather inclined to believe that this revolting transaction may give only additional and increased strength to that sect. Joe and his brother will be regarded as martyrs to their faith, and but little knowledge of human nature and the history of the past is necessary to inform us of the fact that violence, oppression, and bloodshed strengthen instead of subduing fanaticism."

The belated judgment was the truer one. The martyrdom gave to the story of Joseph Smith the imperishable force of tragedy. What was already a legend it converted into an epic. The martyrdom was a dramatic symbol that God had placed His seal upon the testimony of His prophet. And it was the legend of Joseph Smith, from which all evidences of deception, ambition, and financial and marital excesses were gradually obliterated, that became the great cohesive force within the church.

For a time after Joseph's death it seemed that schisms would disintegrate the church. Sidney Rigdon, after a bitter battle with Brigham Young, retired to Pittsburgh; Lyman Wight went to Texas, and Charles Thompson to St. Louis. James Jesse Strang set himself up as a king on Beaver Island, Michigan; and William Smith, claiming the succession for himself until his nephew Young Joseph should come of age, stayed in Nauvoo until expelled by Brigham Young. All of these lesser prophets followed Joseph's lead in proclaiming visions or giving forth revelations, and most of them practiced polygamy. Only Brigham Young had the sagacity to claim his authority as president of the apostles rather than as an opportunistic revelator. And it was he to whom the bulk of the Mormons turned.

When the anti-Mormons saw that Joseph's death had not destroyed the church, they began to hound it in earnest. They faithfully emulated the burning and pillaging of the Missourians until Brigham Young agreed to take his people west. The heroic epic of the trek to the Great Basin has been told over and over again, occasionally with the fidelity and the magnificence it deserves.

To say that Joseph's death enriched the church with the inspiration of a martyr's legend is not to say, however, that his murder was necessary for the survival of the Mormon movement. Historians have commonly held that his empire was crumbling from within and that only the genius of Brigham Young saved it from ruin. But there is no reason to believe that Joseph could not have survived the defection of William Law as he had that of the Book of Mormon witnesses and John C. Bennett. His own story would have lacked the moral grandeur that his death imparted to it, but this was only one factor in the survival of the church.

Had Joseph fled west, his Saints would have trailed after him, as they had followed him from Kirtland to Missouri in 1838. Open admission of polygamy would have cost him some converts, but no more than it did Brigham Young eight years later. There would probably have been less order and more suffering in the migration; and it is doubtful if Joseph would have stopped in the barren wastes of the Great Basin, for California would have been more to his taste. His empire might have been far less stable than Brigham Young's, but what it lacked in stability Joseph would have compensated for in color.

Emma did not follow Brigham Young west, but she would have followed her husband. The gentiles then would not have been able to point to her second marriage to an unbeliever, the attractive Major Lewis Bidamon, as proof that in her heart she had scorned Joseph's mission from the beginning. There is no evidence, however, that Emma scorned anything but Brigham Young, whom after Joseph's death she came to fear and despise. She clung to certain relics of her husband's memory, such as his manuscript translation of the Bible, with a superstitious reverence. "I have often thought," she wrote to her son when he took the pages away for printing, "the reason why our house did not burn down when it has been so often on fire was because of them, and I still feel a sacredness attached to them."

Polygamy, however, she always denied. "There was no revelation on either polygamy or spiritual wives," she said stubbornly. "He had no other wife but me. . . . He did not have improper relations with any woman that ever came to my knowledge." And this was her revenge and solace for all her heartache and humiliation. This was her slap at all the sly young girls in the Mansion House who had looked first so worshipfully and then so knowingly at Joseph. She had given them the lie. Whatever formal ceremony he might have gone through, Joseph had never acknowledged one of them before the world. This was her great triumph and she made the most of it. Her four sons clung grimly to their mother's word, despite the sworn testimony of women whom Joseph had loved and of the guards who had shadowed him when he paid nocturnal visits to their homes.

Young Joseph too had a score to settle with Brigham Young. Around the youth collected a little knot of disaffected, unhappy men who had tried first one and then another of the welter of sects that sprang up at Joseph's death. The legend grew among this faction that polygamy had been a monstrous fraud, conceived by John C. Bennett and developed by Brigham Young and perhaps Hyrum Smith, without Joseph's knowledge or consent. Eventually, after trying his hand at storekeeping, railroading, farming, and law, Young Joseph took over the leadership of what was called with more exactness than poetry the Re-

organized Church of Jesus Christ of Latter-day Saints. After a
time he gave forth several revelations on church government
and social behavior, modest revelations lacking all the majesty
and sweep of his father's. Eventually this church went back to
Independence, where Young Joseph and later his son Frederick did their best to recapture the magic spirit of the gathering
to Zion, fighting a bland gentile incredulity that the center of
the universe should be an old-fashioned suburb of Kansas City.

Nauvoo became almost a ghost city, its fine brick houses falling into ruin and its cabins decaying altogether. The communistic Icarians under Etienne Cabet revived it for a brief period,
but with their departure it sank into a necroscopic lethargy
which all recent Mormon attempts to make the site a shrine
have only intensified.

Before their departure the Mormons in a great burst of energy
came very near completing the temple, although they knew
that they were shortly to abandon it. Only the attic story was
dedicated, but thousands of Saints participated in the endowment mysteries, and then with a sense of release crossed the
Mississippi and headed for the Oregon Trail, while gentile
mobs prepared to sack the city. Until November 1848 the temple continued to attract tourists, though no purchaser appeared
in answer to Brigham Young's offer of sale. Then it was fired
by an arsonist, who doubtless feared that it might one day lure
the Mormons back. The gutted and partly demolished shell, described by one early traveler as the most impressive ruins in
America, was purchased by the Icarians, who hoped to remodel
it into a school. But before they could replace one stone upon
another, a capricious tornado piled the great limestone walls
into a heap of rubble, and the legend sprang up among the
Mormons that God's finger had traced the tornado's path, lest
desecration come to the holy place.

The Mormons who followed Brigham Young continued to
be temple-builders, their spires and pillars rising in Utah, Idaho,
Arizona, Canada, and Hawaii. No other portion of Joseph
Smith's religion showed the same unbroken continuity as the
temple rituals, which are even now performed, with only minor
changes, as they were in the Nauvoo Masonic Hall.

This is not surprising, since the rites were entirely extraneous
to Mormon life. But wherever the religion operated as a gen-

erative force in Mormon work and thinking, it was in turn re-
molded by its social context. Polygamy in particular underwent
an astonishing evolution. From a clandestine venture limited
to the leading elders of the church it became in the isolation
of the Great Basin an eminently respectable practice, the number of wives even symbolizing the intensity of a man's faith.
And there was no more casual marrying of married women, as
Joseph had done; every man who took a plural wife assumed
full responsibility for her honor, if not always for her support.

Under Brigham Young, what M. R. Werner has sagely called
"puritan polygamy" had none of the lush sensuality of the
harems of the Middle East; yet an aroused American public,
fed on lurid exposés of Mormon sex life, tried for three decades
to legislate polygamy out of existence in Mormon territory,
sending the leading elders to the penitentiary like common
criminals. But both the men and the women, sublimely certain
of the rightness of their cause, fought the nation with astonishing tenacity. Finally in 1890 their fourth president, Wilford
Woodruff, in a manifesto intended to win statehood and peace,
renounced the practice of plural marriage while retaining the
principle as an ideal.

Fifty years later the Mormon hierarchy in its passion for respectability had so turned against the principle as well as the
practice that it heaped upon a tiny dissenting "fundamentalist"
sect that revived polygamy all the self-righteous fury and abhorrence that the gentiles had spent upon the Mormons a generation before. Polygamy, which had always been an anomaly
in America, was not yet extinct. But for most Mormons Joseph's
last great revelation was merely a memory, and an embarrassing one.

Joseph Smith's ideal of uniting church and state, which
brought such catastrophe in Illinois, was realized under the
rigorous suzerainty of Brigham Young. But by the time of his
death the pendulum had begun to swing back. The Mormons
themselves broke up their political solidarity to aid in gaining
statehood for Utah. A generation later they even ignored the
admonitions of their leaders, now strongly Republican, to vote
in overwhelming numbers for Franklin Roosevelt. Whether
knowingly or not, they had come to reject the theocratic principle of their prophet for the American tradition of democracy.

What, then, remains of Joseph Smith in the modern Mormon Church? Most of the human qualities that endeared him to those who knew him — his jollity, kindliness, love of sport and good living, his athletic grace, and his prodigious personal charm — have been forgotten. But there remains his story, beginning with the great vision of the Father and the Son and ending with his martyrdom, a legend without parallel in American religious history.

But this legend alone is not enough to explain the vigor and tenacity of the Mormon Church. Before his death Joseph had established an evangelical socialism, in which every man worked feverishly to build the Kingdom of God upon earth. This has grown into a vast pyramidal organization, in which the workers finance the church, advertise it, and do everything but govern it. The Mormon people are still bent on building the Kingdom of God, and everyone from the twelve-year-old deacon to the eighty-year-old high priest is made to feel that upon him depends the realization of that ideal. Here as in no other church in America the people are the church and the church the people. It is not only work and sacrifice, but a sense of participation and responsibility that generates the steadfast Mormon loyalty.

The average Mormon no longer reads the holy books of Joseph Smith, and the only revelation with which he is familiar is the injunction against the use of tobacco and alcohol. Yet he believes fervently in the doctrine of eternal progression, which of all the prophet's tenets is the most endemic to America. Every Mormon, if he thinks about it at all, believes himself to be on the road to godhood. And since, according to Joseph, "a man is saved no faster than he gets knowledge," a passion for education has become one of the common denominators of Mormon culture. Joseph Smith's great zest for learning started a tradition that did not diminish with time. "The glory of God is intelligence" has become the most quoted of all his aphorisms, and there is no room for cynicism or fatalism in Mormon thinking.

Perhaps the most vigorous tradition transmitted by Joseph Smith was the identification of God with material prosperity. The practice established at Nauvoo has been continued by the church in Utah, which controls large sections of Mormon real estate and industry. Financial wizardry has come to be looked upon as equally important with spiritual excellence among the qualifications for church leadership. But the communistic ideology that pervaded the experiments of an earlier day is vehemently disavowed. Big business has become thoroughly beatified.

The religion that Joseph founded was all too well adapted to the milieu from which it sprang — the milieu of frontier America, with all its crudity as well as vigor. And the present church betrays its heritage in all its works, including the road signs which lead to its shrines. Along the lovely White River Valley of Vermont winds a highway leading to Sharon. As one approaches Joseph's birthplace, one comes upon a marker that heralds the proximity of this Bethlehem of Mormonism. Its message is too ingenuously deceptive of the true missionary spirit it embodies. *"Visit,"* it urges, *"the Joseph Smith Monument, World's Largest Polished Shaft."*

One cannot say that the prophet has been too ill served by this sign, for it only symbolizes the barrenness of his spiritual legacy. Joseph had a ranging fancy, a revolutionary vigor, and a genius for improvisation, and what he could mold with these he made well. With them he created a book and a religion, but he could not create a truly spiritual content for that religion. He could canalize aspirations formed elsewhere into a new structure and provide the ritualistic shell of new observances. But within the dogma of the church there is no new Sermon on the Mount, no new saga of redemption, nothing for which Joseph himself might stand. His martyrdom was a chance event, wholly incidental to the creed that he created.

Yet Joseph's theology — a patchwork of ideas and rituals drawn from every quarter — became in his hands a thing of color, warmth, and originality. Joseph believed in the good life upon earth, in work, laughter, and brotherhood. Tolerant of the foibles of his friends, since he could not easily forget his own, he provided a heaven where all men would be saved. And he made of that heaven a continuation of the good life of earth. Since work was a prerequisite to joy in this life, so should it be in the next. Since his wife and children were dear to him, he made the marriage covenant eternal, and allowed for its expansion. Since power was sweet to him, he gave to every convert the promise of dominion over a star.

Joseph in his own person provided a symbol of nearness to God and a finality of interpretation that made the ordinary frontier evangelist seem by comparison all sound and fury. There was a great hunger in his people, and they accepted him for what he set himself up to be. They believed the best of him and thereby caused him to give his best. Joseph's true monument is not a granite shaft in Vermont but a great inter-mountain empire in the West.

SUPPLEMENT

Oᴏɴᴇ ᴏғ the major original premises of this biography was that Joseph Smith's assumption of the role of a religious prophet was an evolutionary process, that he began as a bucolic scryer, using the primitive techniques of the folklore of magic common to his area, most of which he discarded as he evolved into a preacher-prophet. There seemed to be good evidence that when he chose to write of this evolution in his *History of the Church* he distorted the past in the interest of promoting his public image as a gifted young prophet with a substantial and growing following. There was evidence even to stimulate doubt of the authenticity of the "first vision," which Joseph Smith declared in his official history had occurred in 1820 when he was fourteen.

The original printing of this biography in 1945 stated that Joseph Smith's description of his first vision was "first published by Orson Pratt in *Remarkable Visions* in 1840, twenty years after it was supposed to have occurred," that "between 1820 and 1840 Joseph's friends were writing long panegyrics; his enemies were defaming him in an unceasing stream of affidavits and pamphlets, and Joseph himself was dictating several volumes of Bible-flavored prose. But no one in this long period even intimated that he had heard the story of the two gods. At least, no such intimation has survived in print or manuscript." And I suggested that despite Joseph Smith's protestations that his visions had caused him a great deal of persecution, particularly by the local ministers, this alleged vision actually "passed totally unnoticed in Joseph's home town," and might have been "sheer invention, created some time after 1834."

Despite dedicated searching of early newspapers and manuscripts during the past twenty-five years, no one has yet found any document written before the publication of the Book of Mormon in 1830 which mentions Joseph Smith's first vision of God and Jesus Christ, though there are indeed evidences of his claims that he had seen an angel or angels in connection with his discovery of the golden plates. Important newly released evidence from the manuscript archives of the Mormon Church in Salt Lake City does indicate that late in 1830 or early in 1831 Joseph Smith began to write and to talk with some freedom among his followers about a great vision in his youth. We now know that he dictated at least three different descriptions of the "first vision" between 1831 or 1832 and 1839, and that these descriptions differ strikingly in detail. The texts of these three versions were published in full, with scrupulous regard to accuracy in both the reproduction and the dating, by Mormon historian Dean C. Jessee in "The Early Accounts of Joseph Smith's First Vision," in the spring of 1969. *

Rumors that Joseph Smith talked of having seen God found their way into print first in the *Palmyra Reflector* of February 14, 1831. Here the local editor of Joseph Smith's home town reported that the young prophet's followers in Kirtland Ohio were saying he had "seen God frequently and personally," and that "commissions and papers were exhibited said to be *signed* by Christ himself." Sometime during 1831 or 1832 Joseph Smith began his first attempt at autobiography, dictating it to his secretary, Frederick T. Williams. It began as follows:

A History of the life of Joseph Smith Jr an account of his marvilous experience and of all the mighty acts which he doeth in the name of Jesus Christ the son of the living God of whome he beareth record and also an account of the rise of the church of Christ in the eve of time. . . .

After telling of his growing contempt for the sectarian strife of his neighborhood, Joseph Smith described his first vision in these words:

. . . I cried unto the Lord for mercy for there was none else to whom I could go and ~~to~~ obtain mercy and the Lord heard my
                                                              the
cry in the wilderness and while in~~∧~~attitude of calling upon the
             in the 16th year of my age
Lord~~∧~~a piller of ~~fire~~ light above the brightness of the sun at noon day come down from above and rested upon me and I was filled
                                          Lord
with the spirit of God and the~~∧~~opened the heavens upon me and I

my son
saw the Lord and he spake unto me saying Joseph∧thy Sins are
                                           way
forgiven thee. go thy∧walk in my statutes and keep my commandments behold I am the Lord of glory I was crucifyed for the world
                                                             behold
that all those who believe on my name may have Eternal life∧the
world lieth in sin ~~and~~ at this time and none doeth good no not one
                                                           my
they have turned asside from the Gospel and keep not∧command-
ments they draw near to me with their lips while their hearts are far
from me and mine anger is kindling against the inhabitants of the
earth to visit them according to this ungodliness and to bring to
                                          hath
pass that which∧been spoken by the mouth of the prophets and
Apostles behold and lo I come quickly as it written of me in the
          clothed
cloud∧in the glory of my Father and my soul was filled with
love and for many days I could rejoice with great joy and the Lord
was with me but could find none that would believe the hevenly
vision. . . . *

For reasons unknown to us, Joseph Smith was reluctant to
publish this first attempt at autobiography. In 1834, when he
collaborated with Oliver Cowdery in an account of the early
beginnings of his church for the *Latter-day Saints Messenger
and Advocate,* he made no mention of the first vision but simply
apologized in a defensive manner for his youthful indiscretions,
which had been amply documented in Eber D. Howe's *Mormonism Unvailed,* published earlier in the year.† The autobiography itself seems to have been abandoned.

He did, however, dictate an intermittent daily journal, and
it was from this document that Dean C. Jessee published the
second account of the "first vision." On November 9, 1835,
Joseph Smith was visited by Robert Matthias, a notorious
religious mystic calling himself Joshua, the Jewish minister, who

---

* Dean C. Jessee: "The Early Accounts of Joseph Smith's First Vision," *Brigham
Young University Studies,* IX:280, 1969, from the "Kirtland Letter Book, 1829–1835."
This document was unknown save to Mormon archivists until it was copied by
Paul Cheesman for his Brigham Young University Master's Thesis, "An Analysis of
the Accounts Relating to Joseph Smith's Early Visions," in 1965. This thesis ap-
parently stimulated the publication of Dean C. Jessee's authoritative account.

† See p. 17 of this book for the apology.

had recently been released from prison in New York, where
he had been confined on charges of contempt of court and
whipping his daughter. The Mormon prophet listened with
enormous curiosity, recorded the "Doctrines of 'Joshua the
Jewish Minister,'" in his journal and let him speak before his
people. "He made some very excellent remarks," Joseph Smith
wrote, "but his mind was evidently filled with darkness. . . . I
told him, that my God told me, that his god was the devil. . . ."*

What was not printed in the official *History of the Church*
was the fact that Joseph Smith was sufficiently stimulated by
Robert Matthias to tell him his own story of the "first vision,"
and that this account was faithfully recorded by his secretary,
Warren A. Cowdery, as part of the daily journal:

Monday Nov. 9th. . . . While sitting in his house this morning
between the hours of ten an eleven a man came in and introduced
himself to him calling himself Joshua the Jewish Minister. His
appearance was something singular, having a beard about three
inches in length which is quite grey, his hair was also long and
considerably silvered with age. He had the appearance of a man
about 50 or 55 years old. He was tall and straight, slender frame,
blue eyes, thin visage, and fair complexion. He wore a green frock
coat and pantaloons of the same color. He had on a black fur hat
with a narrow brim. When speaking he frequently shuts his eyes
and exhibits a kind of scowl upon his countenance. He (Joseph)
made some inquiry after his name, but received no definite answer.
The conversation soon turned upon the subject of Religion, and
after the subject of this narrative had made some remarks concerning the bible, he commenced giving him a relation of the circumstances, connected with the coming forth of the Book of Mormon,
which were nearly as follows. Being wrought up in my mind respecting the subject of Religion, and looking at the different systems
taught the children of men, I knew not who was right or who was
wrong, but considered it of the first importance to me that I
should be right, in matters of so much moment, matter involving
eternal consequences. Being thus perplexed in mind I retired to the
silent grove and there bowed down before the Lord, under a realizing sense (if the bible be true) ask and you shall receive, knock
and it shall be opened, seek and you shall find, and again, if any
man lack wisdom, let of God who giveth to all men liberally &

* *History of the Church*, II, 304–307. For further information on Matthias see
Gilbert Seldes: *The Stammering Century*, 1928, pp. 126–7.

upbraideth not. Information was what I most desired at this time, and with a fixed determination to obtain it, I called on the Lord for the first time in the place above stated, or in other words, I made a fruitless attempt to pray My tongue seemed to be swoolen in my mouth, so that I could not utter, I heard a noise behind me like some one walking towards me. I strove again to pray, but could not; the noise of walking seemed to draw nearer, I sprang upon my feet and looked round, but saw no person, or thing that was calculated to produce the noise of walking. I kneeled again, my mouth was opened and my tongue loosed; I called on the Lord in mighty prayer. A pillar of fire appeared above my head; which presently rested down upon me, and filled me with unspeakable joy. A personage appeared in the midst of this pillar of flame, which was spread all around and yet nothing consumed. Another personage soon appeared like unto the first: he said unto me thy sins are forgiven thee. He testified also unto me that Jesus Christ is the son of God. I saw many angels in this vision. I was about 14 years old when I received this first communication. . . .*

It will be noted that "the Lord" of the first version has become two "personages," and that Joseph Smith has pushed back his age at the time of the vision from sixteen to fourteen.

Joseph Smith dictated still a third version of his first vision in 1839. Here he implied that the "personages" are God the Father and Jesus Christ. Their directions to him are clear and precise, and the nature of his mission is spelled out. This version, published in this volume on pages 21-2, became part of the official *History of the Church,* and was the only one known to the general Mormon audience until 1965. Devout Mormon scholars have made clear that they believe the differences between the three versions are of no consequence. But to the non-devout the differences are evidence of Joseph Smith's exuberant talent for improvisation before a stimulating audience and of his lack of care about consistency of detail. They bear out my original speculation that the first vision, if not an invention, was an evolutionary fantasy beginning in "a half-remembered dream stimulated by the early revival excitement and reinforced by the rich folklore of visions circulating in his neighborhood."

* Dean C. Jessee: "The Early Accounts of Joseph Smith's First Vision," *B.Y.U. Studies,* IX, 284.

If the fantasy did begin with a dream dating back to mid-adolescence, which seems likely, Joseph Smith's carelessness about the year in which it happened would suggest that the original memory was indeed faint. The confusion of members of his family, and of Oliver Cowdery, in later years concerning the date of the great Palmyra revival and the details of the vision itself would also support this supposition. Oliver Cowdery, as we have seen, stated that the religious excitement began in Joseph's seventeenth year, not fourteenth, and his brother William put it in his eighteenth year.* Recent research by the Reverend Wesley P. Walters has demonstrated that the great Palmyra revival led by Benjamin P. Stockton and George Lane occurred in 1824 rather than 1820. Mormon historian Larry C. Porter replied to the Walters material with evidence of his own that the Reverend Lane, possibly a key figure in influencing Joseph Smith's religious bent, made trips to within fifteen miles of Palmyra several times between 1819 and 1824. † All of this underlines the continuing difficulty of reconciling devout Mormon and non-Mormon documents and of identifying conclusively which revivalist preacher kindled in Joseph Smith an enthusiasm for the religious life, and in what year.

Of greater significance is the Reverend Mr. Walters's recent discovery, in the records of the Palmyra Presbyterian Church for 1830, that Joseph Smith's mother, and his brothers Hyrum and Samuel, were active members of this church for at least eight years after 1820, the official date of the first vision. The Palmyra records point out that these three members of the Smith family began to neglect "public worship and the sacrament of the Lord's supper" about September 1828. The 1830 proceedings of this church for March 3, 10, and 29 make it clear that they were accused of this neglect and abandonment "for the last eighteen months," and that finally, at the end of March 1830, they were suspended as members of the Presbyterian Church.

This raises a question that has never been seriously studied: whether or not Joseph Smith's own family took his religious

---

* See above, pp. 24–5.

† See Wesley P. Walters: "New Light on Mormon Origins from the Palmyra Revival," in the symposium "The Question of the Palmyra Revival," *Dialogue,* IV, 59–82, 1969; also, Larry C. Porter: "Rev. George Lane," *Brigham Young University Studies,* IX, 321–40, Spring 1969.

mission seriously before his alleged discovery or unearthing of the golden plates. In this regard the last line in Joseph Smith's 1831–2 version of his first vision opens up fascinating avenues of speculation. "I could rejoice with great joy," he wrote, "and the Lord was with me but could find none that would believe the hevenly vision." Taken at face value, this would mean that his parents scoffed at him too, and, if true, this circumstance emerges as of signal importance in his evolution.

We have nowhere else to turn for information on this point save to Lucy Smith's *Biographical Sketches . . .*, which was subjected to censorship by her collaborator, Martha Coray, and her editor, Orson Pratt. Unfortunately, instead of giving her own account of her son's first vision, Lucy Smith quotes directly from his official history, adding this line, "From this time until the twenty-first of September, 1828, Joseph continued, as usual, to labour with his father, and nothing during this interval occurred of very great importance—though he suffered, as one would naturally suppose, every kind of opposition and persecution from the different orders of religionists." * Then she goes on in a remarkable passage to relate that when her son was first visited by the angel "Nephi" he was afraid to tell his father. "I was afraid my father would not believe me," he said, and gained courage enough only when the angel reassured him, saying, "He will believe every word you say to him."† Thus, when Joseph Smith wrote in 1831 or 1832 that "none would believe the hevenly vision," he was telling a quite literal truth. In his upward climb from diviner to prophet he had first of all the problem of converting his own family.

This is not to suggest that the members of his family were cynics about visionary people. On the contrary, one has only to read Lucy Smith's *Biographical Sketches . . .* to see that Joseph Smith was faced not so much with cynicism in his family as with competition. Lucy Smith herself had visions, as did her father and her sister Lovisa. Her brother Jason was a pro-

* Lucy Smith: *Biographical Sketches of Joseph Smith the Prophet and His Progenitors for Many Generations* (Liverpool, 1853), p. 78.

† Joseph Smith's earliest account of this particular vision calls the angel Nephi, and Lucy Smith repeats it. Later versions of the official history changed the name to Moroni, and Orson Pratt corrected Lucy Smith's account in a footnote. See *Biographical Sketches . . .*, pp. 79 and 82.

412]   *No Man Knows My History*

fessional faith-healer. She describes her husband's dreams as visions, and significantly, Joseph Smith has a major Book of Mormon hero, Lehi, state: "Behold, I have dreamed a dream; or, in other words, I have seen a vision."* This confusion, combined no doubt with a blurring of distinction between his own dreams and fantasies and reality, is an important aspect of Joseph Smith's character. We see the same kind of trait, though to a lesser degree, in Lucy Smith and, if her book is to be trusted, in her husband as well. Joseph Smith had no important help from his parents in reality testing; on the contrary, he grew up in a family with a prodigious appetite for the marvelous.

Lucy Smith tells us, in describing her husband's "first vision," that he was traveling with "an attendant spirit" who told him he would find "on a certain log a box, the contents of which, if you eat thereof, will make you wise, and give you wisdom and understanding." He was forced to drop it when threatened with "all manner of beasts, horned cattle, and roaring animals."† In the son's fantasy the visionary box was elaborated into the fabulous golden plates.

The discrepancies between fantasy and reality in Joseph Smith's life are nowhere more difficult to sort out than in the fiercely controversial material from the critical years before 1830. Here there are evidences not only of unbridled fantasy but also of contrivance and seeming fraud. Even if one studies minutely all the accounts of his money-digging activities as written by his neighbors and as related in the 1826 court record, and the hopelessly varying accounts of the golden plates, it is virtually impossible to determine how continuously Joseph Smith believed in his own pretensions to occult powers and communication with angels. To some friends and neighbors he seemed at times totally committed to his own mission; but to his father-in-law he could confess in tears that "he could not see in a stone now, nor never could; and that his former pretensions in that respect were all false."‡ Similarly, too, when "translating" the Book of Mormon he sometimes used what he called the sacred Urim and Thummin, sometimes the mundane

---

* I Nephi, 8:2. See also p. 84, above.
† *Biographical Sketches . . .* , p. 57.
‡ See Peter Ingersoll's account, above, p. 411.

seer stone. Often he had a curtain separating himself from his secretary, but with Cowdery he seems to have abandoned it, for the latter confesses to some mystification at watching Joseph Smith translate freely when the plates were not in sight at all.*

What converted his secretaries and no doubt his own parents was not his dubious and frequently changing mechanisms for translation but the creation itself. It was the Book of Mormon, not the magic spectacles, that captured them. The invention of the idea of the golden plates was a product of Joseph Smith's "magician" period; but the Book of Mormon itself was the creation of a newly developing and talented religious innovator.

I have already discussed in this biography the skill with which he drew upon the local Indian origin theories, the religious controversies of the day, and political anti-Masonry, weaving them with much artistry into the book that would prove him a true prophet. I did not fully describe his use of the Bible in the Book of Mormon, and I recommend now an important but slightly known study by the late Wesley M. Jones, *A Critical Study of Book of Mormon Sources,* privately printed in Detroit in 1964, for an expertly detailed analysis of the extent to which he borrowed from both the Old and New Testament.

I failed to recognize sufficiently in the original edition of this biography the extent to which the Book of Mormon provides clues not only to Joseph Smith's eclecticism but also to his inner conflicts. Like any first novel, it can be read to a limited degree as autobiography. It contains clues to his conflict with members of his own family, especially his brothers. If the book can be said to have a major theme, it is not that of parricide, as in *Hamlet* and *The Brothers Karamazov,* but of fratricide (though there are occasional hints of the former as well). One can see in Lehi and his six sons an extraordinary resemblance to Joseph Smith, Sr., and his six sons.† Two brothers even share the same names, Joseph and Samuel. The Book of Mormon begins: "I, Nephi, having been born of goodly parents." The 1831–2 version of Joseph Smith's first

---

* See above, p. 61.

† Actually, the Smith family had seven sons, but Ephraim apparently died young. Lucy Smith mentions only his birth in her *Biographical Sketches,* and states, after the death of Joseph and Hyrum, "I had reared six sons to manhood." See p. 280.

autobiography begins: "I was born in the town of Charon . . . of goodly parents."*

The amicable relationship between Lehi and his favored son Nephi is similar to that between Joseph Smith and his father, at least as implied in the official *History of the Church*. Joseph Smith, Sr., like Lehi, took his own dreams seriously, and one of them was transposed with some changes into the Book of Mormon as "The Vision of Lehi."† Both Lehi and the elder Smith lead their families "into the wilderness," searching for a promised land.

Throughout the Book of Mormon there is remarkably little dissension between fathers and sons; the murderers and threats of murders are mostly fratricidal, and the wars are between the descendants of two sets of brothers. Early in the book the evil Laman and Lemuel plan to slay both the father and the younger Nephi, and the dialogue here is remarkably suggestive of what may have been a similar conflict within Joseph Smith's own family over his veracity:

And Laman said unto Lemuel . . . Let us slay our father, and also our brother Nephi, who has taken it upon him to be our ruler and our teacher, who are his elder brethren. Now, he says that the Lord has talked with him, and also that angels have ministered unto him. But behold, we know that he lies unto us; and he tells us these things, and he worketh many things by his cunning arts; that he may deceive our eyes. . . . ‡

We do not know if Joseph Smith as a young boy was treated harshly by his older brothers. Lucy Smith tells us that when he was fourteen, "a gun was fired across his pathway, with the evident intention of shooting him." The ball lodged in the neck of a cow, but the mystery of who fired the gun was never solved.§ Since the shooting happened at the door of his own home, one cannot help wondering if young Joseph thenceforth harbored unconscious or even conscious fantasies about the would-be murderer being one of his own brothers. Certainly there is abundant evidence that he identified with Joseph of the

---

* Jessee: "Early Accounts of the First Vision," *B.Y.U. Studies*, IX, 279.

† See above, pp. 58–9n.

‡ I Nephi, 16:37–8.

§ *Biographical Sketches* . . . , p. 73.

Old Testament, who was saved from the murderous impulse of some of his brothers only to be sold into Egypt.

We know that Joseph's older brother Hyrum became a devoted follower, and in the end died at his side. One younger brother, William, was alternately friend and foe, and in later years once said in the hearing of Brigham Young: "If I had the disposing of my brother, I would have hung him years ago." *
The death on November 19, 1823, of the oldest brother, Alvin, under mysterious circumstances deserves more attention than I gave to it originally. Lucy Smith tells us that he died from an overdose of calomel prescribed by an inept doctor, though her description of the results of the autopsy is suggestive of appendicitis. Joseph Smith in his history called the death "a great affliction," and the circulation later of ugly rumors that the body had been exhumed and dissected resulted in the father's actual exhumation of the corpse almost a year after the original burial. This must have been a most harrowing family experience. It suggests also the generation of many unconscious fantasies of guilt and fear.

Alvin died only about a month after Joseph Smith told his family of the initial discovery of the golden plates, just at the time, one would guess, that the plot of the Book of Mormon was being constructed in Joseph Smith's fantasies. The constantly recurring theme in the book of brothers killing brothers would thus seem to be more than mere coincidence. Literary fantasy is an ancient therapeutic device, used by countless authors who have no understanding of how or why it brings some surcease to inner turmoil. † Certainly it is remarkable that the beginning of the Book of Mormon should consist of a story of six brothers, of whom two are so bloodthirsty and evil that they are cursed by God with a dark skin and their descendants remain "a dark, a filthy and a loathsome people." Again and again throughout the book dark brothers fight white brothers, and almost always the struggle is between white men who believe in visions and dark men who do not. Finally, in a frightful scene of genocide the Lamanites destroy altogether the "white and delightsome" Nephites.

* See above, p. 246.
† See Ernest Jones: *Hamlet and Oedipus* (New York, 1949) for material on the relationship between the death of Shakespeare's father and his writing of *Hamlet*.

Still, the triumph of the dark brothers is temporary. The white heroes, Nephi and Mormon, with whom Joseph Smith clearly identifies, have each engraved their sacred history, and their plates are buried in the Hill Cumorah, to be rescued eventually by Joseph Smith. So in the end, the whole marvelous fantasy of fratricidal strife becomes harnessed to Joseph Smith's religious ambition and to his new image of prophet. Also, a new fantasy is given expression—that of the great religious leader who will solve the mystery of the origin of the American Indians and also bring them back into the fold of Christianity.

Perhaps more importantly, the conflict between dark brother and white brother in the Book of Mormon seems also to relate to Joseph Smith's own inner conflict between the spurious world of money-digging and the hallowed world of religion. Near the end of the book we see the emergence of a new major hero, Mormon, who bears a marked similarity to the emerging young prophet, Joseph Smith. Mormon, like Joseph, is "large in stature," and he has a vision at age fifteen. "And I, being fifteen years of age and being somewhat of a sober mind, therefore I was visited of the Lord, and tasted and knew of the goodness of Jesus."* Mormon decisively rejects the "sorceries and witchcrafts, and magics; and the power of the evil one . . . upon all the face of the land," and takes up arms "against the forces of evil who practice them." † All of which suggests that in writing of the wars between the Nephites and the Lamanites Joseph Smith was wrestling with his own affection for "black" magic as opposed to the hallowed magic of Jesus Christ.

One may speculate further that on a still deeper level of consciousness Joseph Smith through his book was working out unconscious conflicts over his own identity. Was he truly blessed of the Lord, divinely ordered and destined to be a modern-day prophet? Or was he a mere pagan conjurer, a trickster and charlatan, playing with magic arts, or worse, a demonic creature who had fantasies of killing? Was he, in truth, Lamanite or Nephite?

Still another conflict that we see in the life of Joseph Smith was hinted at in his holy book. This is the theme of polygamy,

* Mormon, I, 15.
† Mormon, I, 19.

which he was to embrace with such headlong enthusiasm in his late thirties. The Book of Mormon repudiates polygamy. The good brother, Jacob, denounces it: "Hearken to the word of the Lord: For there shall not any man among you have save it be one wife; and concubines he shall have none . . . ."* In Joseph Smith's youth the impulse was condemned, though it exploded later into the remarkable plural marriage system, a system that was to serve for three generations as the identifying badge of his religious system.

The Book of Mormon thus provides tantalizing clues to the conflicts raging within Joseph Smith as to the truth or spuriousness of his magic powers and his visionary claims. But it serves only to suggest the intensity of the conflict, not to explain it. Why was this gifted young man compelled to transform his dreams into visions, to insist that his literary fantasies were authentic history engraved upon golden plates, to hold stoutly that the hieroglyphics on the Egyptian papyri he bought from Michael Chandler were actually words of the patriarch Abraham? Why did he feel compelled to resort to such obviously transparent devices as to write into both his Book of Mormon and his corrected version of the Bible prophecies of his own coming?

When he indulged in prophecy for his own followers, always a dangerous expedient, he took special risks, but he was nimble in extricating himself from failure, as when he explained the failure of his prophecy that Oliver Cowdery had raised up a church in Missouri by saying, "I see it and it will be so."† The prophecy became mere wish-fulfillment, which it had been basically from the beginning. But Joseph Smith was more than a mere predictor of the future. He had a need to cover up the spurious in himself, to prove himself a prophet by documenting his credentials in the most elaborate fashion possible.

The basic inner conflict in Joseph Smith's life was not, I believe, a conflict between his telling the truth or not telling the truth, but rather between what he really was and what he most desperately wanted to be. We can see the evidences of this struggle between his two identities all his adult life,

* Jacob, 2, 27.
† See above, p. 115.

especially on those occasions when he seemed almost deliberately to step down from the role of prophet and look at himself
with humor and candor. We see it briefly in his interview with
Josiah Quincy, in the sermon in which he said, "I don't want
you to think I am righteous for I am not," in the sermon that
gives the title to this biography, and in his comment "A prophet
is a prophet only when he is acting as such." *

It is these statements that suggest to many readers that Joseph
Smith was a mere impostor. But such readers usually use the
word as a term of derision and contempt, implying deliberate
swindling and fraud. In recent years a personality type described as "impostor" and a personality disorder described
somewhat differently under the clinical name of *pseudologia
fantastica* have been written about extensively by psychiatrists.
The eminent Dr. Phyllis Greenacre, for example, after examining the histories of several celebrated "impostors," concludes
that they were not ordinary liars but men of extraordinary conflicts. She sees in them "a struggle between two dominant identities in the individual; the temporarily focused and strongly
assertive imposturous one, and the frequently amazingly crude
and poorly knit one from which the imposter has emerged."
It is, she says, "the extraordinary and continued pressure in the
imposter to live out his fantasy that demands explanation, a
living out which has the force of a delusion, (and in the psy-
chotic may actually appear in that form), but it is ordinarily
associated with 'formal' awareness that the claims are false.
The sense of reality is characterized by a peculiarly sharp, quick
perceptiveness, extraordinarily immediate keenness and responsiveness, especially in the area of the imposture. The over-all
sense of reality is, however, impaired."

Great impostors, she holds, rely on "omnipotent fantasy," to
"the exclusion of reality testing." They are invariably good
showmen and absolutely dependent on having an audience.
"The imposture," she writes, "cannot be sustained unless there
is emotional support from someone who especially believes in
and nourishes it. . . . It is the demand for an audience in which
the (false) self is reflected that causes impostures often to become of social significance." The acting-out of the impostor role

* See above, pp. 295–6, 291, and 366.

she believes to be "largely an attempt to achieve a sense of reality and competence as a man." *

I have deliberately avoided clinical labels in describing the inner character of Joseph Smith. Dr. Greenacre's "impostor" analysis is not necessarily the decisive key to that character, but it does seem more adequate as a clinical definition than Bernard DeVoto's "paranoid," or Kimball Young's "parapath." † Nevertheless, all three words can be used to define certain aspects of Joseph Smith's behavior. My considerable discussion of this problem with several psychoanalysts has served to underline for me the difficulties of clinical diagnosis of a man long since dead, especially one who was supported by an audience with an insatiable appetite for the supernatural, an audience that included most importantly his own parents.‡

One cannot overlook the obvious evidences of pathology in Joseph Smith's life. But the clinical definitions of 1970 cannot easily be superimposed on the social and political realities of 1840. The fact that Joseph Smith at the height of his power set up a Council of Fifty to rule over his new theocracy and had himself secretly crowned King of the Kingdom of God, which he said would one day revolutionize the whole world, today seems an act of megalomania.§ Still, one can easily point out fascinating parallels between Joseph Smith's plans for a western empire with himself as king with those of Aaron Burr, who hoped to set himself up as Emperor of Mexico and most of the West. Definitely, such ideas could be somewhat more easily entertained then than now without altogether forgoing reality. The West for both Aaron Burr and Joseph Smith offered opportunities for real as well as imagined empire, a fact that the

* Phyllis Greenacre: "The Impostor," *Psychoanalytic Quarterly,* 27:359–82 (1958).

† DeVoto: "The Centennial of Mormonism," *American Mercury,* XIX, 5, 1930; Kimball Young: *Isn't One Wife Enough?* (New York, 1954), p. 82.

‡ Joseph Smith was the subject of a detailed and fruitful discussion in a seminar on leadership in Los Angeles in 1969, attended by psychoanalysts Dr. Alfred Goldberg, Dr. Robert Dorn, Dr. Ernst Levy, Dr. Ira Carson, Dr. Martha Wolfenstein, and Dr. Gerald Aronson, and by Dr. Victor Wolfenstein, Dr. Peter Loewenberg, and Dr. Arthur Slavin, of the U.C.L.A. departments of history and political science.

§ Still, historian Klaus Hansen, in writing a detailed account of this episode, developed a well-researched study of Mormon millennialism and its relation to a belief in the political Kingdom of God without anywhere suggesting that he considered Joseph Smith delusional.

canny colonizer Brigham Young demonstrated after Joseph Smith's death.

Even so, the very looseness and wildness of Joseph Smith's utterances, quite unlike the controlled rhetoric of Brigham Young, suggest the degree to which Joseph Smith was at times truly alienated from reality. In Missouri, it will be remembered, he threatened to "trample down our enemies and make it one gore of blood from the Rocky Mountains to the Atlantic Ocean," saying, "I will be to this generation a second Mohammed, whose motto in treating for peace was 'the Alcoran or the Sword.' So shall it eventually be with us — 'Joseph Smith or the Sword!'" From Liberty jail he wrote that "renegados, liars, priests, thieves, and murderers, who are all alike tenacious of their crafts and creeds, have poured down, from their spiritual wickedness in high places, and from their strongholds of the devil, a flood of dirt and mire and filthiness and vomit upon our heads." "Hell," he continued, "may pour forth its rage like the burning lava of Mount Vesuvius, or of Etna, or of the most terrible of the burning mountains; and yet shall 'Mormonism' stand. Water, fire, truth and God are all realities. Truth is 'Mormonism.' God is the author of it."

Later, in Nauvoo, he said, "Thus will I become a smooth and polished shaft in the quiver of the Almighty, who will give me dominion over all and every one of them, when their refuge of lies shall fail, and their hiding place be destroyed." And in a letter to James A. Bennett: "I cut the gordian knot of powers, and I solve mathematical problems of universities *with truth — diamond truth; and God is my 'right hand man.'*" * As we have seen, in the last year of his life he was a lieutenant-general commanding a private army, a candidate for president of the United States, a King of the Kingdom of God, and the secret husband of perhaps fifty wives.

His frantic marrying of at least two score women within two years of his death, combined with his insistent denials that he was practicing polygamy, suggests a new and ever escalating moral conflict in addition to his continuing conflict between fantasy and reality. He could be sure no one would ever find his golden plates; he could hope no one would ever challenge

* See above, pp. 230, 253, 296, and 354.

his translation of the Book of Abraham; he could confidently expect that most of his followers would continue to accept his revelations as divine. But his continuing denial of polygamy was certain to be exposed very soon as flagrant deception.

When Joseph Smith read the exposé of his polygamy in the pages of the *Nauvoo Expositor,* published by a man whom he had respected and revered, he must have felt a shattering of his own grandiose and wholly unrealistic image of himself and his role in history. He reacted with rage and destroyed the press, though he was not normally a destructive man. He was a builder of temples and cities and kingdoms — most of all, a constructor of continuing fantasy. William Law attacked this fantasy with his simple, almost gentle exposition of reality. A man called Law had called him to account, as his parents never had, and he reacted with lawlessness. It was all extraordinarily symbolic. A sense of depression, foreboding, and doom dogged the prophet thereafter, contributing inexorably to his destruction.

As WE have seen, he was destroyed only in body. His fantasies and myths lived on, and live on today as realities for many Mormons, who now number close to three million. Every generation brings several new William Laws, a new group of inquiring young intellectuals, a new phalanx of doubting scholars. But the Mormon Church continues to survive their heresy, as it has survived the growth of the science of anthropology, with scholars in every university save that named after Brigham Young holding the Book of Mormon to be a fantasy.

Long ago the Church survived the first scholarly look at the Book of Abraham, when Jules Remy in 1860 took the facsimiles of the papyri to scholars in the Louvre and was told they were ordinary funereal documents. A whole galaxy of Egyptian scholars were shown the facsimiles in 1912 by Episcopal Bishop F. S. Spalding; they agreed with Theodule Deveria of 1860.* It seems likely, too, that the Church will not seriously be shaken by the Book of Mormon anguish of the late 1960's. This began with the discovery by University of Utah Professor Aziz

* See above, p. 175.

422] No Man Knows My History

S. Atiya that the original papyri purchased by Joseph Smith had not been destroyed in the Chicago fire, as had been thought, but had found their way to the New York Metropolitan Museum of Art. Professor Atiya recognized the facsimiles that had been published with the Book of Abraham, and evidence was uncovered to trace the sale of the papyri by Emma Smith, on May 26, 1856, to A. Combs, and finally to the museum. The discovery was given much publicity in the Mormon press, and when the eleven fragments were given to the Latter-day Saints in Salt Lake City, many of the devout thought confidently that they would prove to be scientific evidence of the divine claims of their prophet.

Translation of the fragments by Egyptologists John S. Wilson and Klaus Baer of the University of Chicago Oriental Institute, and Richard A. Parker of Brown University, indicated, however, that some of the fragments were Book of the Dead scrolls belonging originally to an Egyptian woman named Ta-shere-Min, and that others were from the Egyptian Book of Breathings, specifically identified by Professor Baer as "The Breathing Permit of Hôr." The facsimiles originally reproduced in the Book of Abraham were labeled "a well-known scene from the Osiris mysteries, with Anubis, the jackal-headed god . . . ministering to the dead Osiris on the bier," and detective work uncovered evidence that Joseph Smith, or someone else involved in the original publication of the Book of Abraham, had sketched in a human head on the facsimile where a portion of the papyri had been torn away.

A remarkable compilation of the documentation on the papyri appeared in 1968 in two issues of *Dialogue, a Journal of Mormon Thought,* a scholarly Mormon publication not subject to censorship by the church leadership.* This compilation included not only the translations of the Egyptologists but also statements by official and semi-official Mormon historians. Richard P. Howard, of the Reorganized Church of Jesus Christ of Latter-day Saints, reaffirmed his church's stand that the Book

* See "The Joseph Smith Egyptian Papyri," translations and interpretations, *Dialogue,* III, No. 2, Summer 1968, pp. 66–105, and Klaus Baer: "The Breathing Permit of Hôr," *Dialogue,* III, No. 3, Autumn 1968, pp. 109–34. See also Mormon scholar Dee Jay Nelson's translation, *The Joseph Smith Papyri,* Parts I and II, and *Joseph Smith's Eye of Ra,* Modern Microfilm Co. (Salt Lake City, 1969).

of Abraham was not "a church publication," and expressed doubt about the reliability of the Book of Abraham as a translation of ancient records, counting it rather the product of a highly intuitive mind. Professor Hugh Nibley of the Brigham Young University wrote defensively: "So far everything that has appeared in print about the newly found papyri has been written either by hysterical opponents of everything Mormon or by people innocent of any bias in favor of Joseph Smith. . . . we have seen some of the papyri that were in Smith's possession, but there is no evidence that we have seen them all, and it is apparent that only one small piece among them has any direct bearing on the Book of Abraham."*

The controversy over the papyri was further heightened in 1968 by the acquisition and publication by Jerald Tanner of a filmed copy of Joseph Smith's "Egyptian Alphabet and Grammar," formerly unknown save to Mormon archivists, which proved to be at least as damaging to Joseph Smith's claims as a translator as the translations of the papyri by the Egyptologists. Tanner, together with Grant Heward, in commenting on the specific explanations Joseph Smith gave for numerous Egyptian characters, pointed out that "The characters from fewer than four lines of the papyrus make up forty-nine verses of the Book of Abraham, containing more than two thousand words."† Their study indicates that the Book of Abraham did in fact come from a portion of the papyri now under scrutiny by scholars, and that Professor Nibley's suggestion that the Book of Abraham was translated from papyri not yet found is without foundation.

What makes for an intolerable complication to the Book of Abraham controversy is the fact that several lines in the sacred book constitute the theological basis for the Mormon Church's long-standing discrimination against the Negro. In a remarkably confused passage Joseph Smith had declared that Abraham had written that the Pharaohs of Egypt were not entitled to "the priesthood," since they sprang from the loins of Ham and Egyptus:

* *Dialogue*, III, 104–5.
† See "The Source of the Book of Abraham Identified," *Dialogue*, III, No. 2, 1968, p. 95.

The land of Egypt being first discovered by a woman, who was the daughter of Ham, and the daughter of Egyptus, which in the Chaldean signifies Egypt, which signifies that which is forbidden.

When this woman discovered the land it was under water, who afterward settled her sons in it; and thus, from Ham, sprang that race which preserved the curse in the land. . . .

Now, Pharaoh being of that lineage by which he could not have the right of Priesthood, notwithstanding the Pharaohs would fain claim it from Noah, through Ham. . . .*

From this "scriptural precedent" the Mormon Church over the years developed an elaborate Jim Crow system in regard to black converts. Though all white and Oriental males were granted the right to "hold the priesthood," this right was denied to all blacks. Nor were Negroes permitted to participate in the sacred temple ceremonies. Even a small fraction of Negro blood, if discovered, was considered grounds for taking away priesthood privileges.

In recent years this discrimination has been attacked by Negroes and white civil rights advocates, including many liberals within the Church itself. The Mormon leadership now faces a dilemma of peculiar complexity. To heed the Egyptologists means repudiation of the Book of Abraham, which could make all of Joseph Smith's holy books suspect. To give the blacks the priesthood without a new revelation or "manifesto" also means implicit repudiation of the Book of Abraham. But to continue to deny blacks the full privileges or membership in the Church on the basis of a book that is manifestly suspect as history seems to an increasing number of Mormons an immoral process, alien to the ideals of the Declaration of Independence and to the fundamental injunction of Christianity about loving one's neighbor as oneself.

Every people to some extent chooses out of its own past that which it most wishes to continue to embrace. Polygamy was repudiated in 1890 partly because of outside force, but partly also because it was becoming increasingly untenable, politically, economically, and morally. The Mormons have never ceased to proselyte eagerly among American Indians, despite the fact that without miscegenation Indian converts do not become, as

* *Book of Abraham,* I, 23, 24, 27.

Joseph Smith promised in an implicitly hostile phrase, "a white and delightsome people." It is evident that modern Mormon leadership still reflects the ancient American gradation of racial prejudices, with the red man decisively above the black, a gradation that dates back at least to Thomas Jefferson and Patrick Henry, both of whom advocated intermarriage with Indians but not with Negroes.

If the Mormon Church does not modify its racist practices, it seems likely that its future converts in large part will continue to come, as they have been in recent years, from right-wing groups who are hostile to black people under any circumstances. If so, the alienation of the intellectuals from the Church will continue. This would be a pity, for many of them want to remain in the Church. They are deeply committed emotionally; they are attracted by what seem to them to be special virtues indigenous to the Mormon people.

The religious legacy of Joseph Smith can be shorn of its abracadabra of magic and still have sufficient strength to stand by itself, as Catholic scholar Thomas O'Dea demonstrated in 1957 in his perceptive study, *The Mormons*. As a social organization the Church is a dynamo of inexhaustible energy. It remains to be seen if Mormon leadership, now seriously impeded by its failure to retire before they become aged the men at the peak of the pyramid, can continue to direct this dynamo in the direction of social betterment and racial understanding.

APPENDIX A

DOCUMENTS ON THE EARLY LIFE OF JOSEPH SMITH

I

THE EARLIEST and most important account of Joseph Smith's money-digging is the following court record, first unearthed in southern New York by Daniel S. Tuttle, Episcopal Bishop of Salt Lake City, and published in the article on "Mormonism" in the *New Schaff-Herzog Encyclopedia of Religious Knowledge.** The trial was held before a justice of the peace in Bainbridge, Chenango County, New York, March 20, 1826:

People of State of New York *vs.* Joseph Smith. Warrant issued upon oath of Peter G. Bridgman, who informed that one Joseph Smith of Bainbridge was a disorderly person and an impostor. Prisoner brought into court March 20 (1826). Prisoner examined. Says that he came from town of Palmyra, and had been at the house of Josiah Stowel in Bainbridge most of time since; had small part of time been employed in looking for mines, but the major part had been employed by said Stowel on his farm, and going to school; that he had a certain stone, which he had occasionally looked at to determine where hidden treasures in the bowels of the earth were; that he professed to tell in this manner where gold-mines were a distance under ground, and had looked for Mr. Stowel several times, and informed him where he could find those treasures, and Mr. Stowel had been engaged in digging for them; that at Palmyra he pretended to tell, by looking at this stone, where coined money was buried in Pennsylvania, and while at Palmyra he had frequently ascertained in that way where lost property was, of various kinds; that he has occasionally been in the habit of looking through this stone to find lost property for three years, but of late had pretty much given it up on account its injuring his health, especially his eyes — made them sore; that he did not solicit business of this kind, and had always rather declined having anything to do with this business.

Josiah Stowel sworn. Says that prisoner had been at his house something like five months. Had been employed by him to work on farm part of time; that he pretended to have skill of telling where hidden treasures in the earth were, by means of looking through a

* (New York, 1883), Vol. II, p. 1576.

certain stone; that prisoner had looked for him sometimes, — once to tell him about money buried on Bend Mountain in Pennsylvania, once for gold on Monument Hill, and once for a salt spring, — and that he positively knew that the prisoner could tell, and professed the art of seeing those valuable treasures through the medium of said stone; that he found the digging part at Bend and Monument Hill as prisoner represented it; that prisoner had looked through said stone for Deacon Attelon, for a mine — did not exactly find it, but got a piece of ore, which resembled gold, he thinks; that prisoner had told by means of this stone where a Mr. Bacon had buried money; that he and prisoner had been in search of it; that prisoner said that it was in a certain root of a stump five feet from surface of the earth, and with it would be found a tail-feather; that said Stowel and prisoner thereupon commenced digging, found a tail-feather, but money was gone; that he supposed that money moved down; that prisoner did offer his services; that he never deceived him; that prisoner looked through stone, and described Josiah Stowel's house and out-houses while at Palmyra, at Simpson Stowel's correctly; that he had told about a painted tree with a man's hand painted upon it, by means of said stone; that he had been in company with prisoner digging for gold, and had the most implicit faith in prisoner's skill.

Horace Stowel sworn. Says he see prisoner look into hat through stone, pretending to tell where a chest of dollars were buried in Windsor, a number of miles distant; marked out size of chest in the leaves on ground.

Arad Stowel sworn. Says that he went to see whether prisoner could convince him that he possessed the skill that he professed to have, upon which prisoner laid a book upon a white cloth, and proposed looking through another stone which was white and transparent; hold the stone to the candle, turn his back to book, and read. The deception appeared so palpable, that he went off disgusted.

McMaster sworn. Says he went with Arad Stowel to be convinced of prisoner's skill, and likewise came away disgusted, finding the deception so palpable. Prisoner pretended to him that he could discern objects at a distance by holding this white stone to the sun or candle; that prisoner rather declined looking into a hat at his dark-colored stone, as he said that it hurt his eyes.

Jonathan Thompson says that prisoner was requested to look for Yeomans for chest of money; did look, and pretended to know where it was, and that prisoner, Thompson, and Yeomans went in search of it; that Smith arrived at spot first (was in night); that Smith looked in hat while there, and when very dark, and told how the chest was situated. After digging several feet, struck upon something

sounding like a board or plank. Prisoner would not look again, pretending that he was alarmed the last time that he looked, on account
of the circumstances relating to the trunk being buried came all fresh
to his mind; that the last time that he looked, he discovered distinctly
the two Indians who buried the trunk; that a quarrel ensued between
them, and that one of said Indians was killed by the other, and thrown
into the hole beside of the trunk, to guard it, as he supposed. Thompson says that he believes in the prisoner's professed skill; that the
board which he struck his spade upon was probably the chest, but, on
account of an enchantment, the trunk kept settling away from under
them while digging; that, notwithstanding they continued constantly
removing the dirt, yet the trunk kept about the same distance from
them. Says prisoner said that it appeared to him that salt might be
found at Bainbridge; and that he is certain that prisoner can divine
things by means of said stone and hat; that, as evidence of fact, prisoner looked into his hat to tell him about some money witness lost
sixteen years ago, and that he described the man that witness supposed had taken it, and disposition of money.

And thereupon the Court finds the defendant guilty.

2

BETWEEN January 6 and March 19, 1831 Obadiah Dogberry published in the Palmyra *Reflector* six articles describing the youthful Joseph Smith and his Book of Mormon.* His long introduction and digressions into the history of various religious
impostors have been omitted here:

Joseph Smith, Senior, the father of the personage of whom we are
now writing, had by misfortune or otherwise been reduced to extreme
poverty before he migrated to Western New York. His family was
large, consisting of nine or ten children, among whom Joe Junior
was the third or fourth in succession. We have never been able to
learn that any of the family were ever noted for much else than
ignorance and stupidity, to which might be added, so far as it may
respect the elder branch, a propensity to superstition and a fondness
for everything *marvelous*.

We have been credibly informed that the mother of the prophet
had connected herself with several religious societies before her present illumination: this also was the case with other branches of the
family, but how far the father of the prophet ever advanced in these
particulars we are not precisely informed. It however appears quite

* These were recently reprinted by Francis W. Kirkham in *A New Witness for
Christ in America* (Independence, Missouri, 1942), pp. 282-95.

certain that the prophet himself never made any serious pretentions to religion until his late pretended revelation.

We are not able to determine whether the elder Smith was ever concerned in money digging transactions previous to his emigration from Vermont, or not, but it is a well authenticated fact that soon after his arrival here, he evinced a firm belief in the existence of hidden treasures, and that this section of country abounded in them. He also revived, or in other words, propagated the vulgar, yet popular belief that these treasures were held in charge by some *evil* spirit, which was supposed to be either the *devil* himself, or some one of his most trusty favorites. . . . [Article Number III, February 1, 1831.]

In the commencement, the imposture of the "Book of Mormon" had no regular plan or features. At a time when the money digging ardor was somewhat abated, the elder Smith declared that his son Joe had seen the *spirit,* (which he then described as a little old man with a long beard,) and was informed that he (Jo) under certain circumstances, eventually should obtain great treasures, and that in due time he (the spirit) would furnish him (Jo) with a book, which would give an account of the ancient inhabitants (antideluvians) of this country, and where they had deposited their substance, consisting of costly furniture, etc., at the approach of the great deluge, which had ever since that time remained secure in his (the spirit's) charge, in large and spacious *chambers,* in sundry places in this vicinity, and these tidings corresponded precisely with revelations made to, and predictions made by the elder Smith a number of years before.

The time at length arrived, when young Joe was to receive the book from the hand of the spirit, and he repaired accordingly, alone, and in the night time, to the woods in the rear of his father's house . . . and met the spirit as had been appointed. This rogue of a spirit who had baffled all the united efforts of the money diggers, (although they had tried many devices to gain his favor, and at one time sacrificed a barn yard fowl,) intended it would seem to play our prophet a similar trick on this occasion, for no sooner had he delivered the book according to promise, than he made a most desperate attempt to regain its possession. Our prophet, however, like a lad of true metal, stuck to his prize. . . . Joe retained his treasure and returned to the house with his father, much fatigued and injured. This tale in substance, was told at the time the event was said to have happened by both father and son, and is well recollected by many of our citizens. It will be borne in mind that no *divine* interposition had been *dreamed* of at the period. [Article Number IV, February 14, 1831.]

. . . It is well known that Joe Smith never pretended to have any communion with angels, until a long period after the *pretended* finding of his book, and that the juggling of himself or father went no further than the pretended faculty of seeing wonders in a "peep stone," and the occasional interview with the spirit, supposed to have the custody of hidden treasures: and it is also equally well known that a vagabond fortune-teller by the name of Walters, who then resided in the town of Sodus, and was once committed to the jail of this county for juggling, was the constant companion and bosom friend of these money digging impostors.

There remains but little doubt, in the minds of those at all acquainted with these transactions, that Walters, who was sometimes called the conjurer, and was paid three dollars per day for his service by the money diggers in this neighborhood, first suggested to Smith the idea of finding a book. Walters, the better to carry on his own deception with those ignorant and deluded people who employed him, had procured an old copy of Cæsar's [Cicero's?] *Orations,* in the Latin language, out of which he read long and loud to his credulous hearers, uttering at the same time an unintelligible jargon, which he would afterwards pretend to interpret and explain, as a record of the former inhabitants of America, and a particular account of the numerous situations where they had deposited their treasures previous to their final extirpation.

So far did this impostor carry this diabolical farce that not long previous to the pretended discovery of the Book of Mormon, Walters assembled his nightly band of money diggers in the town of Manchester, at a point designated in his magical book, and drawing a circle around laborers, with the point of an old rusty sword, and using sundry other incantations, for the purpose of propitiating the spirit, absolutely sacrificed a fowl, ("Rooster") in the presence of his awestricken wealth; and after *digging* until daylight, his deluded employers retired to their several habitations fatigued and disappointed. [Article Number V, February 28, 1831.]

In June and July 1830 the Palmyra *Reflector* published a parody of the Book of Mormon called "The Book of Pukei," which said in part:

And it came to pass, that when the mantle of Walters the Magician had fallen upon Joseph, surnamed the prophet, who was the son of Joseph; that the "idle and slothful" gathered themselves together, in the presence of Joseph, and said unto him, "Lo! we will be thy servants forever, do with us, our wives, and our little ones as it may seem good in thine eyes."

And the prophet answered and said, — "Behold: hath not the

mantle of Walters the magician fallen upon me, and am I not able
to do before you my people great wonders, and shew you, at a more
proper season, where the Nephites hid their treasure? — for lo! yes
tonight stood before me in the wilderness of Manchester, the *spirit,*
who, from the beginnings had had in keeping all the treasures, hidden in the bowels of the earth.*

3

D. P. HURLBUT in 1833 collected sworn statements from more
than a hundred of the early friends and neighbors of Joseph
Smith in the vicinities of Palmyra, New York, and Harmony,
Pennsylvania. These have been largely ignored by Mormon
historians. "It was simply a matter of 'muck raking' on Hurlbut's part," wrote B. H. Roberts. "Every idle story, every dark
insinuation which at that time could be thought of and unearthed was pressed into service to gratify this man's personal
desire for revenge. . . ." † Since, however, Joseph's money-
digging is well established by the previous court record and
newspaper stories, Hurlbut's affidavits can hardly be dismissed
by the objective student, particularly since they throw considerable light on the writing of the Book of Mormon. The following are the most significant extracts: ‡

I, Peter Ingersoll, first became acquainted with the family of Joseph
Smith, Sen. in the year of our Lord, 1822. — I lived in the neighborhood of said family, until about 1830; during which time the following facts came under my observation. The general employment of
the family, was digging for money. I had frequent invitations to join
the company, but always declined . . . the said Joseph, Sen. told
me that the best time for digging money, was, in the heat of summer, when the heat of the sun caused the chests of money to rise
near the top of the ground. . . . At another time, he told me that the
ancient inhabitants of this country used camels instead of horses.
For proof of this fact, he stated that in a certain hill on the farm of
Mr. Cuyler, there was a cave containing an immense value of gold
and silver, stand of arms, also, a saddle for a camel, hanging on a
peg at one side of the cave. . . .

* *Reflector,* July 7, 1830.
† *Comprehensive History of the Church,* Vol. I (Salt Lake City, 1930), p. 41.
‡ For complete text of all the affidavits collected see Eber D. Howe: *Mormonism Unvailed* (Painesville, Ohio, 1834), pp. 232–68.

In the month of August, 1827, I was hired by Joseph Smith, Jr. to go to Pennsylvania, to move his wife's household furniture up to Manchester, where his wife then was. When we arrived at Mr. Hale's in Harmony, Pa. from which place he had taken his wife, a scene presented itself, truly affecting. His father-in-law (Mr. Hale) addressed Joseph, in a flood of tears: "You have stolen my daughter and married her. I had much rather have followed her to her grave. You spend your time in digging for money — pretend to see in a stone, and thus try to deceive people." Joseph wept, and acknowledged he could not see in a stone now, nor never could; and that his former pretensions in that respect, were all false. He then promised to give up his old habits of digging for money and looking into stones. Mr. Hale told Joseph, if he would move to Pennsylvania and work for a living, he would assist him in getting into business. Joseph acceded to this proposition. I then returned with Joseph and his wife to Manchester. . . .

Joseph told me on his return, that he intended to keep the promise which he had made to his father-in-law; but, said he, it will be hard for me, for they will all oppose, as they want me to look in the stone for them to dig money: and in fact it was as he predicted. They urged him, day after day, to resume his old practice of looking in the stone. — He seemed much perplexed as to the course he should pursue. In this dilemma, he made me his confident and told me what daily transpired in the family of Smiths. One day he came, and greeted me with a joyful countenance. — Upon asking the cause of his unusual happiness, he replied in the following language: "As I was passing, yesterday, across the woods, after a heavy shower of rain, I found, in a hollow, some beautiful white sand, that had been washed up by the water. I took off my frock, and tied up several quarts of it, and then went home. On my entering the house, I found the family at the table eating dinner. They were all anxious to know the contents of my frock. At that moment, I happened to think of what I had heard about a history found in Canada, called the golden Bible; so I very gravely told them it was the golden Bible. To my surprise, they were credulous enough to believe what I said. Accordingly I told them that I had received a commandment to let no one see it, for, says I, no man can see it with the naked eye and live. However, I offered to take out the book and show it to them, but they refused to see it, and left the room." Now, said Jo, "I have got the damned fools fixed, and will carry out the fun." Notwithstanding, he told me he had no such book, and believed there never was any such book, yet, he told me that he actually went to Willard Chase, to get him

to make a chest, in which he might deposit his golden Bible. But, as
Chase would not do it, he made a box himself, of clap-boards, and
put it into a pillow case, and allowed people only to lift it, and feel of
it through the case. . . .

PETER INGERSOLL

I, William Stafford . . . first became acquainted with Joseph, Sen.,
and his family in the year 1820. They lived, at that time, in Palmyra,
about one mile and a half from my residence. A great part of their
time was devoted to digging for money: especially in the night time,
when they said the money could be most easily obtained. I have
heard them tell marvellous tales, respecting the discoveries they had
made in their peculiar occupation of money digging. They would
say, for instance, that in such a place, in such a hill, on a certain
man's farm, there were deposited keys, barrels and hogsheads of
coined silver and gold — bars of gold, golden images, brass kettles
filled with gold and silver — gold candlesticks, swords, &c. &c. They
would say, also, that nearly all the hills in this part of New York,
were thrown up by human hands, and in them were large caves,
which Joseph, Jr., could see, by placing a stone of singular appearance in his hat, in such a manner as to exclude all light; at which
time they pretended he could see all things within and under the
earth, — that he could see within the above mentioned caves, large
gold bars and silver plates — that he could also discover the spirits
in whose charge these treasures were, clothed in ancient dress. . . .

Old Joseph and one of the boys came to me one day, and said that
Joseph Jr. had discovered some very remarkable and valuable treasures, which could be procured only in one way. That way, was as
follows: — That a black sheep should be taken on to the ground
where the treasures were concealed — that after cutting its throat, it
should be led around a circle while bleeding. This being done, the
wrath of the evil spirit would be appeased: the treasures could then
be obtained, and my share of them was to be four fold. To gratify
my curiosity, I let them have a large fat sheep. They afterwards informed me, that the sheep was killed pursuant to commandment;
but as there was some mistake in the process, it did not have the
desired effect. This, I believe, is the only time they ever made money-
digging a profitable business. . . .

WILLIAM STAFFORD

I became acquainted with the Smith family, known as the authors of
the Mormon Bible, in the year 1820. At that time, they were engaged
in the money digging business, which they followed until the latter

part of the season of 1827. In the year 1822, I was engaged in digging a well. I employed Alvin and Joseph Smith to assist me; the latter of whom is now known as the Mormon prophet. After digging about twenty feet below the surface of the earth, we discovered a singularly appearing stone, which excited my curiosity. I brought it to the top of the well, and as we were examining it, Joseph put it into his hat, and then his face into the top of his hat. . . . After obtaining the stone, he began to publish abroad what wonders he could discover by looking in it. . . .

In the month of June, 1827, Joseph Smith, Sen., related to me the following story: "That some years ago, a certain spirit had appeared to Joseph his son, in a vision, and informed him that in a certain place there was a record on plates of gold, and that he was the person that must obtain them, and this he must do in the following manner: On the 22d of September, he must repair to the place where was deposited this manuscript, dressed in black clothes, and riding a black horse with a switch tail, and demand the book in a certain name, and after obtaining it, he must go directly away, and neither lay it down nor look behind him. They accordingly fitted out Joseph with a suit of black clothes and borrowed a black horse. He repaired to the place of deposit and demanded the book, which was in a stone box, unsealed, and so near the top of the ground that he could see one end of it, and raising it up, took out the book of gold; but fearing some one might discover where he got it, he laid it down to place back the top stone, as he found it; and turning round, to his surprise there was no book in sight. He again opened the box, and in it saw the book, and attempted to take it out, but was hindered. He saw in the box something like a toad, which soon assumed the appearance of a man, and struck him on the side of his head. — Not being discouraged at trifles, he again stooped down and strove to take the book, when the spirit struck him again and knocked him three or four rods, and hurt him prodigiously. After recovering from his fright, he enquired why he could not obtain the plates; to which the spirit made reply, because you have not obeyed your orders. He then enquired when he *could* have them, and was answered thus: come one year from this day, and bring with you your oldest brother, and you shall have them. This spirit, he said was the spirit of the prophet who wrote this book, and who was sent to Joseph Smith, to make known these things to him. Before the expiration of the year, his oldest brother died; which the old man said was an *accidental providence!* . . .

In the fore part of September, (I believe,) 1827, the Prophet requested me to make him a chest, informing me that he designed to move back to Pennsylvania, and expecting soon to get his gold book, he wanted a chest to lock it up, giving me to understand at the same time, that if I would make the chest he would give me a share in the book. I told him my business was such that I could not make it. . . . A few weeks after this conversation, he came to my house, and related the following story: That on the 22d of September, he arose early in the morning, and took a one horse wagon, of some one that had stayed overnight at their house, without leave or license; and, together with his wife, repaired to the hill which contained the book. He left his wife in the wagon, by the road, and went alone to the hill, a distance of thirty or forty rods from the road; he said he then took the book out of the ground and hid it in a tree top, and returned home. . . . He said he should think it would weigh sixty pounds, and was sure it would weigh forty. . . . He then observed that if it had not been for that stone, (which he acknowledged belonged to me,) he would not have obtained the book. A few days afterwards, he told one of my neighbors that he had not got any such book, nor never had such an one; but that he had told the story to deceive the d——d fool, (meaning me,) to get him to make a chest. His neighbors having become disgusted with his foolish stories, he determined to go back to Pennsylvania, to avoid what he called persecution. . . .

WILLARD CHASE

In the early part of the winter in 1828, I made a visit to Martin Harris' and was joined in the company by Jos. Smith, sen. and his wife. . . . They told me that the report that Joseph, jun. had found golden plates, was true, and that he was in Harmony, Pa. translating them — that such plates were in existence, and that Joseph, jun. was to obtain them, was revealed to him by the spirit of one of the Saints that was on this continent, previous to its being discovered by Columbus. Old Mrs. Smith observed that she thought he must be a Quaker, as he was dressed very plain. They said that the plates he then had in possession were but an introduction to the Gold Bible — that all of them upon which the bible was written, were so heavy that it would take four stout men to load them into a cart — that Joseph had also discovered by looking through his stone, the vessel in which the gold was melted from which the plates were made, and also the machine with which they were rolled; he also discovered in the bottom of the vessel three balls of gold, each as large as his fist. The old lady said also, that after the book was translated, the plates were to be publicly exhibited — admittance 25 cents. She calculated it would bring in annually an enormous sum of money. . . .

In the second month following, Martin Harris and his wife were at my house. In conversation about Mormonites, she observed, that she wished her husband would quit them, as she believed it was all false and a delusion. To which I heard Mr. Harris reply: *"What if it is a lie; if you will let me alone I will make money out of it!"* I was both an eye and ear witness of what has been stated above, which is now fresh in my memory, and I give it to the world for the good of mankind. I speak the truth and lie not, God bearing me witness.

ABIGAIL HARRIS

. . . Martin Harris was once industrious, attentive to his domestic concerns, and thought to be worth about ten thousand dollars. He is naturally quick in his temper and in his mad-fits frequently abuses all who may dare to oppose him in his wishes. However strange it may seem, I have been a great sufferer by his unreasonable conduct. At different times while I lived with him, he has whipped, kicked, and turned me out of the house. About a year previous to the report being raised that Smith had found gold plates, he became very intimate with the Smith family, and said he believed Joseph could see in his stone anything he wished. After this he apparently became very sanguine in his belief, and frequently said he would have no one in his house that did not believe in Mormonism; and because I would not give credit to the report he made about the gold plates, he became more austere towards me. In one of his fits of rage he struck me with the but end of a whip. . . . Whether the Mormon religion be true or false, I leave the world to judge, for its effects upon Martin Harris have been to make him more cross, turbulent and abusive to me. . . .

LUCY HARRIS

I, Joseph Capron, became acquainted with Joseph Smith Sen. in the year of our Lord, 1827. They have, since then, been really a peculiar people — fond of the foolish and the marvelous — at one time addicted to vice and the grossest immoralities — at another time making the highest pretensions to piety and holy intercouse with Almighty God. The family of Smiths held Joseph Jr. in high estimation on account of some supernatural power, which he was supposed to possess. This power he pretended to have received through the medium of a stone of peculiar quality. The stone was placed in a hat, in such a manner as to exclude all light, except that which emanated from the stone itself. The light of the stone, he pretended, enabled him to see anything he wished. Accordingly he discovered ghosts, infernal spirits, mountains of gold and silver, and many other invaluable treasures deposited in the earth. He would often tell his neighbors of his wonderful discoveries, and urge them to embark in the money digging business. . . .

The sapient Joseph discovered, northwest of my house, a chest of gold watches; but, as they were in the possession of the evil spirit, it required skill and stratagem to obtain them. Accordingly, orders were given to stick a parcel of large stakes in the ground, several rods around, in a circular form. This was to be done directly over the spot where the treasures were deposited. A messenger was then sent to Palmyra to procure a polished sword: after which, Samuel F. Lawrence, with a drawn sword in his hand, marched around to guard any assault which his Satanic majesty might be disposed to make. Meantime, the rest of the company were busily employed in digging for the watches. They worked as usual till quite exhausted. But, in spite of their brave defender, Lawrence, and their bulwark of stakes, the devil came off victorious, and carried away the watches. . . .

At length, Joseph pretended to find the Gold plates. This scheme, he believed, would relieve the family from all pecuniary embarrassment. His father told me, that when the book was published, they would be enabled, from the profits of the work, to carry into successful operation the money digging business. He gave me no intimation, at that time that the book was to be of a religious character, or that it had anything to do with revelation. He declared it to be a speculation, and said he "when it is completed, my family will be placed *on a level* above the generality of mankind"!!

Joseph Capron

We, the undersigned, have been acquainted with the Smith family, for a number of years, while they resided near this place, and we have no hesitation in saying, that we consider them destitute of that moral character, which ought to entitle them to the confidence of any community. They were particularly famous for visionary projects, spent much of their time in digging for money which they pretended was hid in the earth; and to this day, large excavations may be seen in the earth, not far from their residence, where they used to spend their time in digging for hidden treasures. Joseph Smith, Senior, and his son Joseph, were in particular, considered entirely destitute of *moral character, and addicted to vicious habits*. . . .

[This statement was signed by fifty-one residents of Palmyra.]

Harmony, Pa., March 20th, 1834

I first became acquainted with Joseph Smith, Jr. in November, 1825. He was at that time in the employ of a set of men who were called "money diggers;" and his occupation was that of seeing, or pretending to see by means of a stone placed in his hat, and his hat closed over his face. In this way he pretended to discover minerals and hidden treasure. His appearance at this time, was that of a careless young man — not very well educated, and very saucy and insolent to his father. Smith, and his father, with several other "money-diggers" boarded at my house while they were employed in digging for a mine that they supposed had been opened and worked by the Spaniards, many years since. Young Smith gave the "money-diggers" great encouragement, at first, but when they had arrived in digging to near the place where he had stated an immense treasure would be found — he said the enchantment was so powerful that he could not see. They then became discouraged, and soon after dispersed. This took place about the 17th of November, 1825; and one of the company gave me his note for $12.68 for his board, which is still unpaid.

After these occurrences, young Smith made several visits at my house, and at length asked my consent to his marrying my daughter Emma. This I refused, and gave my reasons for so doing; some of which were, that he was a stranger, and followed a business that I could not approve; he then left the place. Not long after this, he returned, and while I was absent from home, carried off my daughter, into the state of New York, where they were married without my approbation or consent. After they had arrived at Palmyra N. Y., Emma wrote me enquiring whether she could take her property, consisting of clothing, furniture, cows, &c. I replied that her property was safe, and at her disposal. In a short time they returned, bringing with them a Peter Ingersol, and subsequently came to the conclusion that they would move out, and reside upon a place near my residence.

Smith stated to me, that he had given up what he called "glass-looking," and that he expected to work hard for a living, and was willing to do so. He also made arrangements with my son Alva Hale, to go to Palmyra, and move his (Smith's) furniture &c. to this place. He then returned to Palmyra, and soon after, Alva, agreeable to the arrangement, went up and returned with Smith and his family. Soon after this, I was informed they had brought a wonderful box of Plates down with them. I was shown a box in which it is said they were contained, which had to all appearances been used as a glass box of the common window glass. I was allowed to feel the weight of the box, and they gave me to understand, that the book of plates was then in the box — into which, however, I was not allowed to look.

I inquired of Joseph Smith Jr., who was to be the first who would be allowed to see the Book of Plates? He said it was a young child. After this, I became dissatisfied, and informed him that if there was anything in my house of that description, which I could not be allowed to see, he must take it away; if he did not, I was determined to see it. After that, the Plates were said to be hid in the woods. . . .

The manner in which he pretended to read and interpret, was the same as when he looked for the money-diggers, with the stone in his hat, and his hat over his face, while the Book of Plates were at the same time hid in the woods!

. . . I conscientiously believe from the facts I have detailed, and from many other circumstances, which I do not deem it necessary to relate, that the whole "Book of Mormon" (so called) is a silly fabrication of falsehood and wickedness, got up for speculation, and with a design to dupe the credulous and unwary — and in order that its fabricators may live upon the spoils of those who swallow the deception.

ISAAC HALE

ON MAY 11, 1946, the L.D.S. Church in Utah published an official review of this book in the Church Section of the *Deseret News*. It denounced the 1826 court record, published here, pp. 405–7, as "patently a fabrication of unknown authorship and never in the court records at all." Since then, thanks to the expert detective work of Mr. Stanley Ivins, Mr. Dale L. Morgan, and Miss Helen L. Fairbank, I have collected the following data, which establish the authenticity of this record beyond any doubt.

Mr. Ivins unearthed the fact that the original pages of the court record were torn out of the record book of Justice Albert Neely of Bainbridge, N.Y., who presided at the trial, by his niece Miss Emily Pearsall, who was a missionary assistant to Episcopal Bishop Daniel S. Tuttle in Salt Lake City. For Bishop Tuttle's statement on this point see the *Utah Christian Advocate*, January 1886. For biographical data on Miss Pearsall see Clarence E. Pearsall: *History and Genealogy of the Pearsall Family in England and America*, 1928.

The court record was first published by Charles Marshall in *Fraser's Magazine*, London, February 1873. Marshall had visited Salt Lake City in the spring of 1871. See also his articles on Utah in *Fraser's Magazine*, June and July 1871. Bishop Tuttle presented the original manuscript pages of the trial to the *Utah Christian Advocate*, which published them January 1886. At this point the manuscript seems to have disappeared.

There are two newspaper accounts of this trial, published independently, each by a local Bainbridge resident. Mr. Dale L. Morgan discovered the earliest, an article titled "Mormonites," in the *Evangelical Magazine and Gospel Advocate,* Utica, N.Y., April 9, 1831. This was only five years after the trial. It is signed A.W.B., and Mr. Morgan identifies him from subsequent articles as A. W. Benton. This account will be republished in Mr. Morgan's forthcoming Mormon history.

The second and more detailed description, discovered by Miss Helen L. Fairbank, of the Guernsey Memorial Library, Norwich, N.Y., was published in the *Chenango Union,* Norwich, N.Y., May 3, 1877, p. 3. It is called "Joseph Smith, the Originator of Mormonism, Historical Reminiscences of the Town of Afton," and was written by Dr. W. D. Purple, a local doctor, who had been town clerk, postmaster, and county historian. Purple was an eyewitness to the trial, and took notes. His account has been republished by Mormon historian Francis W. Kirkham in the enlarged 1947 edition of *A New Witness for Christ in America,* pp. 475ff. Kirkham faces the reality but not the implications of this document.

APPENDIX B

THE SPAULDING–RIGDON THEORY

THE SPAULDING-RIGDON theory of the authorship of the Book of Mormon is based on a heterogeneous assortment of letters and affidavits collected between 1833 and 1900. When heaped together without regard to chronology, as in Charles A. Shook's *True Origin of the Book of Mormon,* and without any consideration of the character of either Joseph Smith or Sidney Rigdon, they seem impressive. But the theory is based first of all on the untenable assumption that Joseph Smith had neither the wit nor the learning to write the Book of Mormon, and it disregards the fact that the style of the Book of Mormon is identical with that of the Mormon prophet's later writings, such as the *Doctrine and Covenants* and *Pearl of Great Price,* but is completely alien to the turgid rhetoric of Rigdon's sermons.

Protagonists of the theory do not explain why, if Rigdon wrote the Book of Mormon, he was content to let Joseph Smith found the Mormon Church and hold absolute dominion over it throughout the years, so secure in his position that he several times threatened Rigdon with excommunication when Rigdon opposed his policies. But most important, there is no good evidence to show that Rigdon and Smith ever met before Rigdon's conversion late in 1830. There is, on the contrary, abundant proof that between September 1827 and June 1829, when the Book of Mormon was being written, Rigdon was a successful Campbellite preacher in northern Ohio, who if conniving secretly with Joseph Smith, three hundred miles east, was so accomplished a deceiver that none of his intimate friends ever entertained the slightest suspicion of it.

The Spaulding theory was not born until 1833, four years after the Book of Mormon was completed. In June 1833 Philastus Hurlbut was excommunicated from the Mormon Church in Kirtland, Ohio. Shortly afterward he learned that some citizens of Conneaut, Ohio, had detected in the Book of Mormon a resemblance to an old manuscript written more than twenty years earlier by Solomon Spaulding, a Dartmouth College graduate and ex-preacher, who had hoped to publish it and solve his financial embarrassments. Hurlbut interviewed these people in August and September 1833. They told him that Spaulding, now deceased, had lived in Conneaut from 1809 to 1812, and that he had written a historical novel about the American aborigines from which he had occasionally read them extracts. Spaulding had moved to Pennsylvania, where he died in 1816.

From Solomon Spaulding's brother, John, Hurlbut obtained an affidavit, of which the significant portion read as follows:

I made him a visit [in 1813] . . . and found that he had failed, and was considerably involved in debt. He told me that he had been writing a book, which he intended to have printed, the avails of which he thought would enable him to pay all his debts. The book was entitled the "Manuscript Found," of which he read to me many passages. It was an historical romance of the first settlers of America, endeavoring to show that the American Indians are the descendants of the Jews, or the lost tribes. It gave a detailed account of their journey from Jerusalem, by land and sea, till they arrived in America, under the command of NEPHI and LEHI. They afterwards had quarrels and contentions, and separated into two distinct nations, one of which he denominated Nephites and the other Lamanites. Cruel and bloody wars ensued, in which great multitudes were slain. They buried their dead in large heaps, which caused the mounds so common in this country. Their arts, sciences and civilization were brought into view, in order to account for all the curious antiquities, found in various parts of North and South America. I have recently read the Book of Mormon, and to my great surprise I find nearly the same historical matter, names, etc. as they were in my brother's writings. I well remember that he wrote in the old style, and commenced about every other sentence with "and it came to pass" or "now it came to pass," the same as in the Book of Mormon, and according to the best of my recollection and belief, it is the same as my brother Solomon wrote, with the exception of the religious matter. By what means it has fallen into the hands of Joseph Smith, Jr. I am unable to determine.

JOHN SPAULDING

Martha, wife of John Spaulding, corroborated her husband's account:

I was personally acquainted with Solomon Spaulding, about twenty years ago. It was at his house a short time before he left Conneaut; he was then writing a historical novel founded upon the first settlers of

America. He represented them as an enlightened and warlike people. He had for many years contended that the aborigines of America were the descendants of some of the lost tribes of Israel, and this idea he carried out in the book in question. The lapse of time which has intervened, prevents my recollecting but few of the leading incidents of his writings; but the names of Nephi, and Lehi are yet fresh in my memory, as being the principal heroes of his tale. They were officers of the company which first came off from Jerusalem. He gave a particular account of their journey by land and sea, till they arrived in America, after which, disputes arose between the chiefs, which caused them to separate into different bands, one of which was called Lamanites and the other Nephites. Between these were recounted tremendous battles, which frequently covered the ground with the slain; and their being buried in large heaps was the cause of the numerous mounds in the country. Some of these people he represented as being very large. I have read the book of Mormon, which has brought fresh to my recollection the writings of Solomon Spaulding; and I have no manner of doubt that the historical part of it, is the same that I read and heard read, more than twenty years ago. The old obsolete style, and the phrases of "and it came to pass," etc., are the same.

MARTHA SPAULDING

Six of Spaulding's neighbors made additional statements, of which the most important extracts are given below:

I formed a co-partnership with Solomon Spaulding for the purpose of rebuilding a forge. . . . He very frequently read to me from a manuscript which he was writing, which was entitled the "Manuscript Found.". . . This book represented the American Indians as the descendants of the lost tribes, gave an account of their leaving Jerusalem, their contentions and wars, which were many and great. One time, when he was reading to me the tragic account of Laban, I pointed out to him what I considered an inconsistency, which he promised to correct; but by referring to the Book of Mormon, I find to my surprise that it stands there just as he read it to me then. Some months ago I borrowed the Golden Bible. . . . I was astonished to find the same passages in it that Spaulding had read to me more than twenty years before, from his "Manuscript Found." Since that time, I have more fully examined the said Golden Bible, and have no hesitation in saying that the historical part of it is principally, if not wholly taken from the "Manuscript Found." I well recollect telling Mr. Spaulding that the so frequent use of the words "And it came to pass," "Now it came to pass," rendered it ridiculous.

HENRY LAKE

I boarded and lodged in the family of said Spaulding for several months. I was soon introduced to the manuscripts of Spaulding, and perused them as often as I had leisure. He had written two or three books or pamphlets, on different subjects; but that which more particularly drew my attention, was one which he called the "Manuscript Found." From this he would frequently read some humorous passages to the company present. It purported to be the history of the first settlement of America, before discovered by Columbus. He brought them off from Jerusalem, under their leaders, detailing their travels by land and water, their manners, customs, laws, wars, etc. He said that he designed it as an historical novel. . . . I have recently examined the Book of Mormon, and find in it the writings of Solomon Spaulding, from beginning to end, but mixed up with Scripture and other religious matter, which I did not meet with in the "Manuscript Found." Many of the passages in the Mormon book are verbatim from Spaulding, and others in part. The names of Nephi, Lehi, Moroni, and in fact all the principal names are brought fresh to my recollection by the Gold Bible. When Spaulding divested his history of its fabulous names, by a verbal explanation, he landed his people near the Straits of Darien, which I am very confident he called *Zarahemla*. They were marched about the country for a length of time, in which great wars and great bloodshed ensued, he brought them across North America in a northeast direction.

JOHN N. MILLER

I first became acquainted with Solomon Spaulding in 1809 or 10, when he commenced building a forge on Conneaut Creek. When at his house, one day, he showed and read to me a history he was writing of the lost tribes of Israel, purporting that they were the first settlers of America, and that the Indians were their descendants. Upon this subject we had frequent conversations. He traced their journey from Jerusalem to America, as it is given in the Book of Mormon, excepting the religious matter. The historical part of the Book of Mormon, I know to be the same as I read and heard read from the writings of Spaulding, more than twenty years ago; the names more especially are the same without any alteration. . . . Spaulding had many other manuscripts, which I expect to see when Smith translates his other plate. In conclusion, I will observe, that the names of, and most of the historical part of the Book of Mormon, were as familiar to me before I read it as most modern history. . . .

AARON WRIGHT

All his leisure hours were occupied in writing a historical novel, founded upon the first settlers of this country. He said he intended to trace their journey from Jerusalem, by land and sea, till their arrival in America, give an account of their arts, sciences, civilization, wars and contentions. In this way, he would give a satisfactory account of all of the old mounds, so common to this country. During the time he was at my house, I read and heard read one hundred pages or more. Nephi and Lehi were by him represented as leading characters, when they first started for America. Their main object was to escape the judgments which they supposed were coming upon the old world. But no religious matter was introduced as I now recollect. . . . When I heard the historical part of it [the Book of Mormon] related, I at once said it was the writings of old Solomon Spaulding. Soon after, I obtained the book, and on reading it, found much of it the same as Spaulding had written, more than twenty years before.

OLIVER SMITH

I have lately read the Book of Mormon, and believe it to be the same as Spaulding wrote, except the religious part. He told me that he intended to get his writings published in Pittsburgh. . . .

NAHUM HOWARD

The following is from the unsigned statement of Artemus Cunningham:

Before showing me his manuscripts, he went into a verbal relation of its outlines, saying that it was a fabulous or romantic history of the first settlement of this country, and as it purported to have been a record found buried in the earth, or in a cave, he had adopted the ancient or scripture style of writing. He then presented his manuscripts, when we sat down and spent a good share of the night in reading them, and conversing upon them. I well remember the name of Nephi, which appeared to be the principal hero of the story. The frequent repetition of the phrase, "I Nephi," I recollect as distinctly as though it was but yesterday, although the general features of the story have passed from my memory, through the lapse of 22 years. He attempted to account for the numerous antiquities which are found upon this continent, and remarked that, after this generation had passed away, his account of the first inhabitants of America would be considered as authentic as any other history. The Mormon Bible I have partially examined, and am fully of the opinion that Solomon Spaulding had written its outlines before he left Conneaut.*

It can clearly be seen that the affidavits were written by Hurlbut, since the style is the same throughout. It may be noted also

---

* All these affidavits were published in Howe's *Mormonism Unvailed,* pp. 278–87.

that although five out of the eight had heard Spaulding's story only once, there was a surprising uniformity in the details they remembered after twenty-two years. Six recalled the names Nephi, Lamanite, etc.; six held that the manuscript described the Indians as descendants of the lost ten tribes; four mentioned that the great wars caused the erection of the Indian mounds; and four noted the ancient scriptural style. The very tightness with which Hurlbut here was implementing his theory rouses an immediate suspicion that he did a little judicious prompting.

However, the affidavits were arresting, and Hurlbut knew it. He visited Spaulding's widow in Massachusetts and offered her half the profits for permission to publish the manuscript. She told him that "Spaulding had a great variety of manuscripts" and recollected that one was entitled the "Manuscript Found," but of its contents she "had no distinct knowledge." During the two years she had lived in Pittsburgh, Spaulding had taken the manuscript to the office of Patterson and Lambdin, she said, but whether or not it had been returned was uncertain.*

She gave Hurlbut permission to examine Spaulding's papers in the attic of a farmhouse in Otsego County, New York; but he found there only one manuscript, which was clearly not the source for the Book of Mormon. This was a romance supposedly translated from twenty-four rolls of parchment covered with Latin, found in a cave on the banks of Conneaut Creek. It was written in modern English and was about 45,000 words long, one sixth the length of the Book of Mormon. It was an adventure story of some Romans sailing to Britain before the Christian era, who had been blown to America during a violent storm.

Hurlbut showed this manuscript to Spaulding's neighbors, who, he said, recognized it as Spaulding's, but stated that it was not the "Manuscript Found." Spaulding "had altered his first plan of writing, by going farther back with dates and writing in the Old Scripture style, in order that it might appear more ancient." This surmise may have been true, though there was no signed statement swearing to it. But it seems more likely that these witnesses had so come to identify the Book of Mormon with the Spaulding manuscript that they could not con-

* *Mormonism Unvailed,* p. 287.

cede having made an error without admitting to a case of memory substitution which they did not themselves recognize.

Hurlbut, at least, was certain that Spaulding had written a second manuscript. Eber D. Howe, Hurlbut's collaborator, now wrote to Robert Patterson, the Pittsburgh printer mentioned by Spaulding's widow. He replied "that he had no recollection of any manuscript being brought there for publication, neither would he have been likely to have seen it, as the business of printing was conducted wholly by Lambdin at that time." * The partnership of Patterson and Lambdin had not in fact been formed until January 1, 1818, two years after Spaulding's death.†

Disappointed in this source, and unable to get any confirming evidence from Joseph's neighbors in western New York, Hurlbut had to be content with insinuating that Sidney Rigdon, who had once lived in Pittsburgh, was somehow responsible for getting the Spaulding manuscript into Joseph Smith's hands.

Howe now purchased Hurlbut's affidavits for five hundred dollars and published them in his *Mormonism Unvailed*. At once the Mormons challenged Howe to produce the Spaulding manuscript, but he did not even produce the one Hurlbut had uncovered, which shortly disappeared. Some writers insinuated that Hurlbut had sold it to the Mormons for a fabulous sum; actually it lay buried in Howe's files, which were later inherited by L. L. Rice, who followed Howe as editor of the *Painesville Telegraph*. Rice eventually went to Honolulu and there discovered the manuscript among his papers. He forwarded it to Joseph H. Fairchild, president of Oberlin College, who placed it in the college library. The manuscript contained a certificate of its identity signed by Hurlbut, Wright, Miller, and others, and bore the penciled inscription "Manuscript Story" on the outside. Its discovery was jubilantly hailed by the Mormons, who held that the Spaulding theory was now proved groundless. The manuscript was first published by the Reorganized Church in Lamoni, Iowa, in 1885.

Many writers, however, still believed that a second Spaulding

* *Mormonism Unvailed*, p. 289.
† Robert Patterson, Jr.: *Who Wrote the Book of Mormon?* (Philadelphia, 1882), p. 7.

manuscript was the true source of the Book of Mormon, and labored indefatigably to prove it. Before examining their evidence, it should be noted that if, as seems most likely, there was only one Spaulding manuscript, there were certain similarities between it and the Book of Mormon which, though not sufficient to justify the thesis of common authorship, might have given rise to the conviction of Spaulding's neighbors that one was a plagiarism of the other. Both were said to have come from out of the earth; both were stories of colonists sailing from the Old World to the New; both explained the earthworks and mounds common to western New York and Ohio as the result of savage wars. John Miller had spoken of "humorous passages" in Spaulding's work, which would certainly apply to the "Manuscript Story," but not to the utterly humorless Book of Mormon.

Other features, like the scriptural style, the expression "it came to pass," and the proper names, seem too definite to be questioned. But it should be remembered, as President Fairchild pointed out in his analysis of the problem, that "the Book of Mormon was fresh in their minds, and their recollections of the 'Manuscript Found' were very remote and dim. That under the pressure and suggestion of Hurlbut and Howe, they should put the ideas at hand in place of those remote and forgotten, and imagine that they remembered what they had recently read, would be only an ordinary example of the frailty of memory." *

It is significant that five of Hurlbut's witnesses were careful to except the "religious" matter of the Book of Mormon as not contained in the Spaulding manuscript, and the others stated that "the historical parts" were derived from the Spaulding story. The narrative Hurlbut found had no religious matter whatever, but the Book of Mormon was permeated with religious ideas. It was first and foremost a religious book. The theology could not have been wrought by interpolation, since practically every historical event was motivated either by Satan or the Lord.

If, on the other hand, Hurlbut was right and there were actually two Spaulding manuscripts, one might reasonably expect

* Joseph H. Fairchild: "Solomon Spaulding and the Book of Mormon," *Western Reserve Historical Society Tract* No. 77, Vol. III (March 23, 1886), pp. 197–8.

stylistic similarities between the Book of Mormon and the extant manuscript, since the latter was full of unmistakable literary mannerisms of the kind that are more easily acquired than shed. Spaulding was heir to all the florid sentiment and grandiose rhetoric of the English Gothic romance. He used all the stereotyped patterns — villainy versus innocent maidenhood, thwarted love, and heroic valor — thickly encrusted with the tradition of the noble savage. The Book of Mormon had but one scant reference to a love affair, and its rhythmical, monotonous style bore no resemblance to the cheap clichés and purple metaphors abounding in the Spaulding story.

After the publication of Howe's book, affidavits popped up here and there, usually solicited by preachers anxious to discredit Joseph Smith. The Mormons replied with books and pamphlets of their own, such as Parley P. Pratt's *Mormonism Unveiled* in 1838 and Benjamin Winchester's *The Origin of the Spaulding Story* in 1840. Winchester quoted another of Spaulding's neighbors, one Jackson, who had read Spaulding's manuscript and maintained "that there was no agreement between them; for, said he, Mr. Spaulding's manuscript was a very small work, in the form of a novel, saying not one word about the children of Israel, but professed to give an account of a race of people who originated from the Romans, which Mr. Spaulding said he had translated from a Latin parchment that he had found."

Spaulding's widow was visited again in 1839, when she was seventy years old, by a preacher named D. R. Austin, who published her signed statement in the *Boston Recorder* on April 19 of that year. She showed an astonishing enlargement of memory over her previous statement to Hurlbut, relating that the historical romance written by her husband had been given to his "acquaintance and friend" Robert Patterson, who was "very much pleased with it" and promised to print it. She stated also that Sidney Rigdon was connected with the press at this time and had every opportunity to copy the manuscript.

Rigdon's angry denial was published in the *Boston Recorder* on May 27, 1839: "If I were to say that I ever heard of the Rev. Solomon Spaulding and his hopeful wife, until Dr. P. Hurlbut wrote his lie about me, I should be a liar like unto themselves. Why was not the testimony of Mr. Patterson obtained to give force to this shameful tale of lies? The only reason is, that he was not a fit tool for them to work with. . . ."

Two Mormons, Jesse and John Haven, now interviewed Spaulding's widow, who denied having written the letter and stated that Austin had merely asked her a few questions, taken notes, and apparently written the letter himself.* Both Spaulding's widow and daughter admitted in this interview that the manuscript they knew was an "idolatrous" not a religious story.

When Spaulding's daughter was seventy-four years old, she was interviewed, and stated that she remembered vividly hearing her father read his manuscript aloud, although she was only six years old at the time. "Some of the names that he mentioned while reading to these people I have never forgotten. They are as fresh to me as though I heard them yesterday. They were 'Mormon,' 'Maroni,' 'Lamenite,' 'Nephi.'" One is led to doubt the reliability of this memory, however, by another statement in this interview: "In that city [Pittsburgh] my father had an intimate friend named Patterson, and I frequently visited Mr. Patterson's library with him, and heard my father talk about books with him." Patterson, it will be remembered, denied knowing Spaulding at all.

Spaulding's daughter remembered seeing the manuscript in her father's trunk after his death, and stated that she had handled it and seen the names she had heard read to her at the age of six. She admitted, however, that she had not read it.†

If the evidence pointing to the existence of a second Spaulding manuscript is dubious, the affidavits trying to prove that Rigdon stole it, or copied it, are all unconvincing and frequently preposterous.

First there is no evidence that Rigdon ever lived in Pittsburgh until 1822, when he became pastor of the First Baptist Church. Robert Patterson, Jr., son of the Pittsburgh printer, conducted an exhaustive research among the old settlers of the vicinity to try to establish the truth of the Spaulding theory. This was in 1882, sixty-six years after Spaulding's death. Many

* This interview was published in the *Quincy* (Illinois) *Whig*, and later in George Reynolds: *The Myth of the Manuscript Found* (Salt Lake, 1883), pp. 21–2.

† See statement of Mrs. M. S. McKinstry (Matilda Spaulding) in Ellen E. Dickinson: "The Book of Mormon," *Scribner's Monthly*, August 1880.

were familiar with the theory and believed it, he said, but few could give first-hand information. Rigdon's brother-in-law, not a Mormon, and Isaac King, an old neighbor, swore to him that Rigdon did not go to Pittsburgh before 1822. Mrs. Lambdin, widow of Patterson's partner, denied any knowledge of Rigdon, as did Robert P. DuBois, who had worked in the printing shop between 1818 and 1820.

One woman, who had worked as mail clerk in Patterson's office between 1811 and 1816, stated that she knew Rigdon and that he was an intimate friend of Lambdin's, but that this was clearly untrue is evidenced by the statement of Lambdin's widow that she had never heard of Rigdon. Another old settler claimed that Spaulding told him the manuscript had been spirited away and that Rigdon was suspect, but this statement is in conflict not only with the facts of Rigdon's life, but also with the accounts of Spaulding's wife and daughter, who made no mention of a lost manuscript and held that the "Manuscript Found" had been carefully preserved in the trunk.*

Patterson senior never left any statement that incriminated Rigdon, although the two men knew each other casually in Pittsburgh after 1822. In the 1870's and 1880's, when anti-Mormonism was most bitter in the United States, there was a great outcropping of affidavits such as those solicited by the younger Patterson. All were from citizens who vaguely remembered meeting Spaulding or Rigdon some fifty, sixty, or seventy years earlier. All are suspect because they corroborate only the details of the first handful of documents collected by Hurlbut and frequently use the very same language. Some are outright perjury.

James Jeffries wrote on January 20, 1884: "Forty years ago I was in business in St. Louis. . . . I knew Sidney Rigdon. He told me several times that there was in the office with which he was connected, in Ohio, a manuscript of the Reverend Spaulding, tracing the origin of the Indians from the lost tribes of Israel. The manuscript was in the office several years. He was familiar with it. Spaulding wanted it published, but had not the means to pay for the printing. He (Rigdon) said Joe (Joseph) Smith used to look over the manuscript and read it

---

* For texts of all these statements see Robert Patterson: *Who Wrote the Book of Mormon?*

on Sundays. Rigdon said Smith took the manuscript and said,
'I'll print it,' and went off to Palmyra, New York." * Forty
years previous to 1884 would have been the year of Smith's
assassination. Rigdon never lived in St. Louis, nor did Joseph
Smith ever visit Ohio before 1831.

The tenuous chain of evidence accumulated to support the
Spaulding-Rigdon theory breaks altogether when it tries to
prove that Rigdon met Joseph Smith before 1830. There are
ambiguous references to a "mysterious stranger" said to have
visited the Smiths between 1827 and 1830. But only two men
ever claimed that this was actually Rigdon. Abel Chase on
May 2, 1879 (fifty-two years after the event) stated that in 1827
— "as near as I can recollect" — when he was a boy of twelve
or thirteen, he saw a stranger at the Smith home who was said
to be Rigdon.† And Lorenzo Saunders on January 28, 1885
(fifty-eight years after the event) stated that he had seen him
in the spring of 1827 and again in the summer of 1828.‡ Yet
Saunders himself admitted his recollection came only after
thirty years of puzzling over the matter and hunting for evidence.§ And it is highly probable that both men were actually
remembering Rigdon's first appearance in Palmyra in late
1830. No other of Joseph's neighbors ever made any effort to
connect the Ohio preacher with the Book of Mormon events.
And an early historian of western New York, writing in 1851,
said: "It is believed by all those best acquainted with the Smith
family and most conversant with all the Gold Bible movements,
that there is no foundation for the statement that the original
manuscript was written by a Mr. Spaulding of Ohio." ‖

Rigdon's life between 1826 and 1829 has been carefully documented from non-Mormon sources. It is clear from the following chronology that he was a busy and successful preacher and
one of the leading figures in the Campbellite movement in
Ohio. Until August 1830, when he broke with Alexander Campbell over the question of introducing communism into the

* Wyl: *Mormon Portraits*, p. 241.
† Ibid., p. 230.
‡ Shook: *True Origin of the Book of Mormon*, p. 132.
§ See his unpublished affidavit in the library of the Reorganized Church.
‖ Turner: *History of the Pioneer Settlement of Phelps and Gorham's Purchase*,
p. 214.

Campbellite Church, he was one of the four key men of that church. It cannot be held that Rigdon rewrote the Spaulding manuscript before 1827, since the anti-Masonry permeating the book clearly stemmed from the Morgan excitement beginning late in 1826.

ACTIVITIES OF RIGDON, NOVEMBER 2, 1826–NOVEMBER 14, 1830

1826	November 2	Marriage of Smith and Giles (performed by Rigdon).
	December 13	Above marriage recorded.
1827	January	Held meeting at Mantua, Ohio.
	February	Funeral of Hannah Tanner, Chester, Ohio.
	March	Held meeting at Mentor, Ohio.
	April	Held meeting at Mentor, Ohio.
	(gap of possibly one month and a half)	
	June 5	Marriage of Freeman and Waterman.
	June 7	Above marriage recorded.
	June 15	Baptized Thomas Clapp at Mentor, Ohio.
	July 3	Marriage of Gray and Kerr.
	July 12	Above marriage recorded.
	July 19	Marriage of Snow and Parker.
	August 10	Above marriage recorded.
	August 23	Met with Mahoning Association, New Lisbon, Ohio.
	(gap of one month and a half)	
	October 9	Marriage of Sherman and Mathews.
	October 20	At Ministerial Council, Warren, Ohio.
	October 27	Marriage of Sherman and Mathews recorded.
	November	Held meeting at New Lisbon, Ohio.
	December 6	Marriage of Wait and Gunn.
	December 12	Above marriage recorded.
	December 13	Marriage of Cottrell and Olds.
1828	January 8	Above marriage recorded.
	February 14	Marriage of Herrington and Corning.
	March 31	Above marriage recorded.
	March	Instructed theological class, Mentor, Ohio.
	March	Visited Walter Scott at Warren, Ohio.
	April	Conducted revival at Kirtland, Ohio.
	May	Met Campbell at Shalersville, Ohio.
	June	Baptized H. H. Clapp, Mentor, Ohio.
	(gap of possibly two months)	

	August	At Association, Warren, Ohio.
	September 7	Marriage of Dille and Kent.
	September 18	Marriage of Corning and Wilson.
	October 13	Above marriages recorded.
	(gap of possibly two months and a half)	
1829	January 1	Marriage of Churchill and Fosdick.
	February 1	Marriage of Root and Tuttle.
	February 12	Above marriages recorded.
	March	Meeting at Mentor, Ohio.
	April 12	Meeting at Kirtland, Ohio.
	May	Baptized Lyman Wight.
	(gap of possibly one month and a half)	
	July 1	Organized church at Perry, Ohio.
	August	Baptized Mrs. Lyman Wight.
	August 7	Met with church in Perry, Ohio.
	August 13	Marriage of Strong and More.
	September 14	Above marriage recorded.
	September 14	Marriage of Atwater and Clapp.
	September	Held meeting at Mentor, Ohio.
	October 1	Marriage of Roberts and Bates.
	October 7	Last two marriages recorded.
	October	At Perry, Ohio.
	November	Held meeting at Waite Hill, Ohio.
	December 31	Marriage of Chandler and Johnson.
1830	January 12	Above marriage recorded.
	(gap of possible two months)	
	March	At Mentor, Ohio.
	(gap of two months)	
	June	At Mentor, Ohio.
	July	Held meeting at Pleasant Valley, Ohio.
	August	Met Campbell at Austintown, Ohio.
	(gap of two and one half months)	
	November 4	Marriage of Wood and Cleaveland.
	November 11	Above marriage recorded.
	November 14	Rigdon baptized by Oliver Cowdery.*

Alexander Campbell, who knew Rigdon intimately, described his conversion to Mormonism with great regret in the *Millennial Harbinger,* attributing it to his nervous spasms and swoonings and to his passionate belief in the imminent gather-

* The above chronology is a rearrangement of one compiled by the Reorganized Church and appearing in the *Journal of History,* Vol. III, pp. 16–20, with additional information from Hayden: *Early History of the Disciples in the Western Reserve.*

ing of Israel. But of the authorship of the Book of Mormon he wrote bluntly: "It is as certainly Smith's fabrication as Satan is the father of lies or darkness is the offspring of night." *

Rigdon denied the Spaulding story throughout his life. When his son John questioned him shortly before his death, he replied: "My son, I can swear before high heaven that what I have told you about the origin of that book is true. Your mother and sister, Mrs. Athalia Robinson, were present when that book was handed to me in Mentor, Ohio, and all I ever knew about the origin of that book was that Parley P. Pratt, Oliver Cowdery, Joseph Smith and the witnesses who claimed they saw the plates have told me, and in all my intimacy with Joseph Smith he never told me but one story, and that was that he found it engraved upon gold plates in a hill near Palmyra, New York, and that an angel had appeared to him and directed him where to find it. . . ." †

* Vol. II (1831), pp. 95, 100.
† Life of Sidney Rigdon by his son John W. Rigdon, MS., as quoted in B. H. Roberts: *Comprehensive History of the Church,* Vol. I, pp. 234–5.

APPENDIX C

THE PLURAL WIVES OF JOSEPH SMITH

In 1887 the Utah Church historian, Andrew Jenson, drawing upon the enormous file of secret manuscript material in the church library in Salt Lake City, compiled a list of twenty-seven wives of Joseph Smith. I have added to this list another twenty-one and have collected much additional material about Jenson's twenty-seven. The Genealogical Archives in Salt Lake City and the files of the *Utah Genealogical and Historical Magazine* were consulted to make the demographic data as accurate as possible.

One source of information for wives other than those listed by Jenson was the Nauvoo Temple Record for 1846. This lists thirty women who were sealed to the prophet "for eternity" and to various other men "for time." Since it is clear from other sources that twenty-two of the thirty women had been married to the prophet during his lifetime, it can be assumed that the remaining eight had also been.

These "proxy sealings," as they were called, were simply a repetition or solemnization of an earlier ceremony. It was felt that only within the temple could marriages "for eternity" truly be sanctified, but the temple had not been completed in Joseph Smith's lifetime.

The Nauvoo Temple Record list does not represent all of Joseph's wives, since several — like Nancy Marinda Hyde and Patty Bartlett Sessions — waited until the building of a temple in Utah before having their marriages to the prophet again solemnized. Others apparently never went through a second ceremony.

In later years in Utah, scores of women were sealed to Joseph Smith "for eternity" who had had no association whatever with him during his lifetime. No attempt has been made to include them here.

This list is probably not complete and includes several whose relationship to Joseph is admittedly little more than presumptive. The thorough documentation provided below is necessitated by the stand of the Reorganized Church, which has always held the evidence that Joseph Smith ever practiced or sanctioned polygamy to be inconclusive. The first thirty-six wives are arranged in the approximate chronological order of their marriages to the prophet, and the remainder are listed alphabetically.

1. FANNIE ALGER

This was the first woman other than Emma Hale whose name was linked with Joseph Smith. The most detailed account of her is in an unpublished letter written to George S. Gibbs in 1903 by Benjamin F. Johnson, patriarch in the Utah Church and brother of two of Joseph's wives. Johnson was then eighty-five. It says in part:

In 1835, at Kirtland, I learned from my sister's husband, Lyman R. Sherman, who was close to the Prophet, and received it from him, "that the ancient order of Plural Marriage was again to be practiced by the Church." This, at the time did not impress my mind deeply, although there lived then with his family (the Prophet's) a neighbor's daughter, Fannie Alger, a very nice and comely young woman about my own age [Johnson was then seventeen], toward whom not only myself, but everyone, seemed partial, for the amiability of her character; and it was whispered even then that Joseph loved her. . . . And there was some trouble with Oliver Cowdery, and whisper said it was relating to a girl then living in his (the Prophet's) family; and I was afterwards told by Warren Parrish, that he himself and Oliver Cowdery did know that Joseph had Fannie Alger as wife, for they were spied upon and found together. . . .

Soon after the Prophet's flight in the winter of 1837 and 1838, the Alger family left for the West, and stopping in Indiana for a time Fannie soon moved to one of the cities there, and although she never left the state, she did not turn from the Church nor from her friendship for the Prophet while she lived. . . . Without doubt in my mind, Fannie Alger was, at Kirtland, the Prophet's first plural wife. . . . Fannie Alger, when asked by her brother and others, even after the Prophet's death, regarding her relations to him, replied: "That is all a matter of my own, and I have nothing to communicate." . . . her brother John, who resided and died in Southern Utah, to my knowledge, was by President Kimball in the temple at St. George introduced as the "brother of the Prophet Joseph's first plural wife."

A letter from Oliver Cowdery to his brother Warren A. Cowdery, dated Far West, Missouri, January 21, 1838, neatly corroborates the Johnson letter: "When he [Joseph Smith] was there we had some conversation in which in every instance I did not fail to affirm that what I had said was strictly true. A dirty, nasty, filthy affair of his and Fanny Alger's was talked over in which I strictly declared that I had never deserted from the truth in the matter, and as I supposed was admitted by himself." *

Andrew Jenson listed Fannie Alger as "one of the first" of Joseph's wives and stated that after his death she "married again in Indiana, and became the mother of a large family." † C. G. Webb, Joseph's grammar teacher in Kirtland, told W. Wyl in the 1880's that "Joseph's dissolute life began already in the first times of the church, in Kirtland. He was sealed there secretly to Fanny Alger. Emma was furious, and drove the girl, who was unable to conceal the consequences of her celestial relation with the prophet, out of her house." ‡

Fanny Brewer, who had gone to Kirtland in the spring of 1837, signed an affidavit in Boston on September 13, 1842 that said in part: "There was much excitement against the prophet on another account, an unlawful intercourse between himself and *a young orphan girl* residing in his family, and under his protection!" §

2. LUCINDA PENDLETON MORGAN HARRIS, wife of George W. Harris

Lucinda Harris, described by John C. Bennett in his *History of the Saints* as "a very pretty and intelligent woman," was born on September 27, 1801 in Virginia, a daughter of Joseph Pendleton. Her first husband was the famous anti-Masonic martyr William Morgan. Her second marriage, to George Washington Harris, had been noted in the *Arkansas Gazette* of January 12, 1831, which mistakenly described her new husband as a Mason. Andrew Jenson listed her as "one of the first" of the prophet's wives, and it seems likely that Joseph married her in

* This letter is in the Huntington Library, San Marino, California.
† *Historical Record,* Vols. V–VIII, pp. 233, 942.
‡ *Mormon Portraits,* p. 57.
§ John C. Bennett: *History of the Saints,* pp. 85–6.

1838 (when she was thirty-seven), for he was living at that time at the Harris home in Far West.* This circumstance would seem to corroborate the story of Mrs. Sarah Pratt, who said in an interview with W. Wyl: "Mrs. Harris was a married lady, a very great friend of mine. When Joseph had made his dastardly attempt on me [in 1842], I went to Mrs. Harris to unbosom my grief to her. To my utter astonishment, she said, laughing heartily: 'How foolish you are! Why, I am his mistress since four years.'" †

When the Harris family moved to Nauvoo, they were given a lot directly across from the prophet and next door to that of Sarah Cleveland, another of Joseph's wives.‡ B. W. Richmond, a stranger and guest in the Mansion House at the time of Joseph's death, noted "a lady standing at the head of Joseph Smith's body, her face covered, and her whole frame convulsed with weeping. She was the widow of William Morgan, of Masonic memory. . . . She is a short person, with light hair and very bright blue eyes, and a pleasant countenance." § George Harris either knew at the time — or learned later — of the relationship between his wife and the prophet, for he stood as proxy in the Nauvoo temple in January 1846 when Lucinda was sealed to Joseph Smith "for eternity."

3. PRESCINDIA HUNTINGTON BUELL, wife of Norman Buell, later the wife of Heber C. Kimball

Evidence of children born to Joseph Smith by women other than Emma is extremely scant except in the case of Prescindia Huntington Buell. Prescindia once stated to Mrs. Ettie V. Smith that "she did not know whether Mr. Buel or the Prophet was the father of her son." ‖ This statement I regarded with due reserve until I discovered a photograph of the son, Oliver Buell, which showed an unmistakable likeness to other sons of Joseph, borne by Emma Smith.¶

* *History of the Church*, Vol. III, p. 9.
† *Mormon Portraits*, p. 60.
‡ *History of the Church*, Vol. III, p. 362.
§ From an account based on Richmond's manuscript, which appeared in the Chicago *Times* and was reprinted in the *Deseret News*, November 27, 1875.
‖ *Fifteen Years among the Mormons: being the narrative of Mrs. Mary Ettie V. Smith* (New York, 2nd ed. 1859), p. 34.
¶ See p. 301 and illustration.

Prescindia Huntington, said to have been "large, tall, grand and majestic in figure, dignified in manner," was born on September 7, 1810, and married Norman Buell at the age of seventeen. Before her baptism into the church on June 1, 1836, she had borne Buell two sons, George and Silas. Silas died very young, and a daughter, born on April 24, 1838 at Fishing River, Missouri, died in infancy.

Although there is some confusion about the birth date of Oliver, it is not significant in determining his parentage. Mrs. Buell told Augusta Crocheron, editor of *Representative Women of Deseret,* that Oliver was born in the spring of 1839 in Far West, Missouri. Joseph had lived in Far West through 1838 until his arrest on October 31. Norman Buell apostatized in the spring of 1839, and if Oliver was born at that time, it is at least conjectural that he left the church because he suspected the paternity of his son.

The Genealogical Archives in Salt Lake City list Oliver's birth as having taken place on January 31, 1840 in Clay County, New York, an error in place if not in date, since Clay County is in Missouri, not New York. Even if Oliver was born at this later date, however, Joseph might still have been the father, since he escaped from the Missouri sheriff near Far West on April 15, 1839.* Prescindia was still in Missouri at this time. She had visited Joseph twice when he was in Liberty jail. The second time, March 15, 1839, she had been forbidden to see him, and the prophet at once had written her a warm letter recommending that Buell go to Illinois "if he keep the faith," and making vague but meaningful allusions to coming revelations of great significance.†

The Huntington family left Far West on April 18, but Prescindia remained with Buell. "I felt alone on the earth," she later wrote of this period, "with no one to comfort me excepting my little son George, for my husband had become a bitter apostate, and I could not speak in favor of the church in his presence." ‡ Since Joseph's journal entries make it clear that after his escape he was mingling with the last Mormon group

---

* See Hyrum Smith's account, *History of the Church,* Vol. III, p. 321n.

† Ibid., Vol. III, pp. 285–6.

‡ *The Women of Mormondom* (ed. by Edward W. Tullidge, New York, 1877), p. 213.

to leave Far West, which included the Huntington family, it is quite possible that he spent some time with Prescindia.

Prescindia remained in Missouri until the fall of 1840. By this time Buell had become reconciled to the church, and the couple moved to Lima, Illinois. It was not until December 11, 1841 that the actual plural-marriage ceremony between Joseph and Mrs. Buell was performed. According to the Utah Church historian, Andrew Jenson, who provides this date, the ceremony was performed by Prescindia's brother, Dimick.

That the Huntington family looked upon young Oliver as the prophet's son is suggested by Oliver Huntington's diary entry of November 14, 1884: "Then I stood Proxy for the Prophet Joseph Smith in having sealed or adopted to him a child of my sister Presenda, *had while living with Norman Buell*." * The ambiguous wording of the phrase I have italicized is significant, especially since there is no similar entry for any other of her children.

John C. Bennett knew of Mrs. Buell's marriage to Joseph, for he listed a Mrs. B**** as one of the prophet's spiritual wives. (Each asterisk stands for a letter.) Prescindia left Buell in 1846 to become one of the numerous plural wives of Heber C. Kimball,† to whom she bore two children.

4. NANCY MARINDA JOHNSON HYDE, wife of Orson Hyde

The stories linking Nancy Marinda Hyde's name to that of Joseph Smith disagree widely as to the date of the marriage or liaison. Born in Pomfret, Windsor County, Vermont, on June 28, 1815, Nancy later moved to Ohio, where she married Orson Hyde on September 4, 1834. The prophet lived for a time at the home of her father, John Johnson, in Hiram in 1832. According to Clark Braden, Nancy's brother Eli led the mob against Joseph in Hiram because he had been "too intimate with his sister Marinda, who afterwards married Orson Hyde. Brigham Young, in after years, twitted Hyde with this fact, and Hyde, on

---

* Vol. III, p. 236. For other references to Prescindia and Norman Buell in this diary see Vol. I, pp. 39, 44, 44a; Vol. II, pp. 16, 25, 46. A transcript of this diary is in the Utah State Historical Society Library.

† See the Nauvoo Temple Record. Prescindia was married to Joseph Smith "for eternity" and to Kimball "for time."

learning its truth, put away his wife, although they had several children." *

The Genealogical Archives in Salt Lake City show that Hyde did in fact take Nancy on July 31, 1857 and have her sealed "for eternity" to Joseph Smith. But this throws no light on when Nancy was actually married to Joseph Smith, if indeed a ceremony was performed at all during his lifetime.

John D. Lee, bodyguard to Joseph in Nauvoo, wrote in his autobiography: "Report said that Hyde's wife, with his consent, was sealed to Joseph for an eternal state, but I do not assert the fact." † William Hall, a Mormon convert between 1840 and 1847, wrote that Hyde was anxious to re-enter the church after his apostasy in 1839. "He returned and desired Joe Smith to reinstate him in his former office as one of the Twelve Apostles. The conditions imposed by Joe Smith some of us would consider a little tough. They were these: All the money he had so hardly earned had to be given up to Joe, and, also, his wife, as a ransom for his transgression, to obtain his former standing. Many jokes were cracked at his expense, and he was despised throughout the camp for his ficklemindedness." ‡

Hall's account, if true, would indicate that Nancy Marinda Hyde became Joseph Smith's plural wife in April 1839, when Hyde was reinstated as an apostle. She was then twenty-four. It may be, however, that she was not taught polygamy until December 1841, when Hyde was on a mission to Palestine, and she was favored with a personal revelation ordering her to move into the rooms above the printing shop and to "hearken to the counsel of my servant Joseph in all things." § Ebenezer Robinson, who lived above the printing shop, was forced to leave his quarters. "That evening," he later wrote, "Willard Richards nailed down the windows and fired off his revolver in the street after dark, and commenced living with Mrs. Nancy Marinda Hyde, in rooms we had vacated in the printing office building, where they lived through the winter. His family was residing at the time in Massachusetts, and Elder Orson Hyde was absent on his mission to Palestine." ‖

* *Public Discussion of the Issues between the Reorganized Church . . . , p. 202.*
† *Mormonism Unveiled,* p. 147.
‡ *The Abominations of Mormonism Exposed,* p. 113.
§ *History of the Church,* Vol. IV, p. 467.
‖ *The Return,* Vol. II (October 1890), p. 346.

The fact that Robinson's account links Nancy's name with Richards' is confusing. But that she was involved in polygamy as early as 1842 is undeniable. Between 1835 and 1858 Nancy bore ten children. Two sons were born in Nauvoo who might possibly have had the prophet for a father: Orson Washington, born November 9, 1843, and Frank Henry, born January 23, 1845.

5. CLARISSA REED HANCOCK, wife of Levi W. Hancock

There is a tradition among some of the descendants of Levi Hancock that Mrs. Hancock was sealed to Joseph Smith in Nauvoo and that one of her sons may have been his child. Since there seems to be no printed or manuscript evidence to support this story, however, it must be taken with considerable reserve. It is of some interest, however, to note that one of Levi Hancock's sons, born on June 9, 1845 in Nauvoo, was named Levison, as though to distinguish his parentage from that of a preceding son, born on April 19, 1841 and named John Reed Hancock.* The latter might have been the child in question. Mrs. Hancock was born on December 18, 1814 in New Hampshire.

6. LOUISA BEAMAN, later the wife of Brigham Young

One of the best proofs that John C. Bennett had accurate information about Joseph's earliest wives is his statement that Miss L***** B***** was married to the prophet by Elder Joseph Bates Noble.† This is clearly Louisa Beaman, popularly believed to be Joseph's first plural wife, who was married to him on April 5, 1841. Noble himself later swore to an affidavit stating that he performed the ceremony on this date.‡ Erastus Snow also wrote: "My wife's sister, Louisa Beman, was his first plural wife, she being sealed to him by my brother-in-law, Joseph B. Noble, April 5, 1841." §

Louisa was born on February 7, 1815 in Livonia, New York, and was twenty-six on her marriage day. She became Brigham

* Genealogical Archives, Salt Lake City.

† *History of the Saints*, p. 256.

‡ For text see Joseph F. Smith, Jr.: *Blood Atonement and the Origin of Plural Marriage*, p. 75.

§ *Historical Record*, Vol. VI, p. 232.

Young's plural wife on January 14, 1846 * and bore him two sets of twins. All four children died in infancy. She died on May 16, 1850 in Salt Lake City.

7. ZINA DIANTHA HUNTINGTON JACOBS, wife of Henry B. Jacobs, later the wife of Brigham Young

Zina Huntington has perhaps the most complicated record of all Joseph Smith's wives. She was born in Watertown, New York, January 31, 1821, and was married to Henry Bailey Jacobs on March 7, 1841.† Seven and one half months later, on October 27, 1841, she was married to Joseph Smith, with her brother Dimick officiating and her sister Fanny acting as a witness.‡ She was then twenty. Since her first child, Zebulon Jacobs, was born on January 2, 1842,§ she was therefore about seven months pregnant with Jacobs's child at the time of her marriage to the prophet. This was an awkward fact for Zina to face after her public admission in 1878 that she had been a plural wife of Joseph Smith.‖ When interviewed by members of the Reorganized Church, she refused to tell the month or year of her marriage to Joseph. She admitted that Dimick had officiated at the ceremony and stated that Brigham Young repeated it on his return from England,¶ an odd assertion in view of the fact that Brigham Young had actually returned from England in June 1841, several months before the ceremony in October.

That there was a good deal of gossip about Zina Jacobs in Nauvoo is evidenced by the statements of John D. Lee and William Hall. The former wrote: "I then took a tour down through Illinois [winter of 1842]. H. B. Jacobs accompanied me as a fellow companion on the way. Jacobs was bragging about his wife, what a true, virtuous, lovely woman she was. He almost worshipped her. Little did he think that in his absence she was

* The Nauvoo Temple Record for this date states that she was married to Young "for time" and to Joseph Smith "for eternity."

† Record of Marriages, Hancock County, Book A, p. 40.

‡ *Historical Record*, Vol. VI, p. 233.

§ According to the *Latter-Day Saints Biographical Encyclopædia*.

‖ See her quoted statement in *Latter-Day Saints Biographical Encyclopædia*, Vol. I, p. 698.

¶ Interview of John W. Wright with Zina D. H. Young, October 1, 1898, *Saints Herald*, Vol. LII, pp. 28–30.

sealed to the Prophet Joseph." * Hall wrote as follows: "A Mr. Henry Jacobs had his wife seduced by Joe Smith, in his time, during a mission to England. She was a very beautiful woman, but when Jacobs returned, he found her pregnant by Smith. Jacobs put up with the insult, and still lived with her." † There is no record other than this bald statement that Zina ever bore Joseph a child. If true, it must have died in infancy, for Zina's other two children were born long after Joseph's death.‡

Zina left Jacobs in 1846 to marry Brigham Young. William Hall asserted that he had heard Young say publicly to Jacobs: "The woman you claim for a wife does not belong to you. She is the spiritual wife of brother Joseph, sealed to him. I am his proxy, and she, in this behalf, with her children, are my property. You can go where you please, and get another, but be sure to get one of your own kindred spirits." § Jacobs apparently accepted Young's decision as the word of the Lord, for he stood as witness in the Nauvoo temple in January 1846 when Zina was sealed to Brigham Young "for time" and to Joseph Smith "for eternity."

8. MARY ELIZABETH ROLLINS LIGHTNER, wife of Adam Lightner

Mary E. Rollins, born on April 9, 1818, a daughter of John Rollins, was thirteen years old when she first saw Joseph Smith, in Kirtland. "When I entered the room," she wrote in her autobiography, "he looked at me so earnestly I felt afraid and thought, 'He can read my every thought, and I thought how blue his eyes were.' After a moment he came and put his hands on my head and gave me a great blessing."

Mary went to Independence in 1831 and remained in Missouri, marrying a non-Mormon, Adam Lightner, August 11, 1835. They moved to Nauvoo in 1840 or 1841 and purchased a lot just below the prophet's home. Here she taught painting to Joseph's adopted daughter, Julia. She was then the mother of three children. Curiously, she makes no mention of her mar-

* *Mormonism Unveiled*, p. 132.
† *The Abominations of Mormonism Exposed*, pp. 43–4.
‡ Henry Chariton Jacobs, son of Henry Jacobs, was born on March 22, 1846. Later Zina bore Brigham Young a daughter.
§ *Abominations of Mormonism Exposed*, pp. 43–4. This is confirmed by T. B. H. Stenhouse in his *Rocky Mountain Saints*, pp. 185–6.

riage to Joseph in her autobiography (although such references
may have been edited out), but on February 8, 1902, when
eighty-four years old, she swore to an affidavit that said in part:
"I was sealed to Joseph Smith, the Prophet, by commandment.
In the spring of 1831, the Savior appeared and commanded him
to seal me up to everlasting life, gave me to Joseph to be with
him in his Kingdom, even as he is in the Father's Kingdom.
In 1834 he was commanded to take me for a wife. I was a thousand miles from him. He got afraid. The angel came to him
three times, the last time with a drawn sword and threatened
his life. I did not believe. If God told him so, why did he not
come and tell me? The angel told him I should have a witness.
An angel came to me — it went through me like lightning —
I was afraid. Joseph said he came with more revelation and
knowledge than Joseph ever dare reveal. Joseph said I was his
before I came here and he said all the Devils in Hell should
never get me from him. I was sealed to him in the Masonic
Hall, over the old brick store by Brigham Young in February
1842 and then again in the Nauvoo Temple by Heber C. Kimball. . . ." *

Adam Lightner refused to be baptized although he was
friendly to the church. Some time after July 4, 1842 the Light-
ners moved to Pontusac. "The prophet felt very sad when he
knew we were going to leave," Mary wrote, "and with tears
running down his cheeks, he prophesied that if we left the
Church we would have plenty of sorrow." It is possible that
Mary's fourth son, born in 1843, was Joseph's child and that
Adam Lightner's desire to move from Nauvoo came from suspicion or actual knowledge of the relationship between Joseph
and his wife. He never joined the church, and did not take his
wife to Utah until 1863, but Mary remained a faithful Mormon. She bore ten children, and died on December 17, 1913,
at the age of ninety-five.

* The original of this statement is owned by Mrs. Nell Osborne of Salt Lake
City. Extracts from Mrs. Lightner's autobiography appeared in the *Utah Genealogical
and Historical Magazine,* Vol. XVII (1926), pp. 193 ff. I have fortunately obtained
a complete copy. The Nauvoo Temple Record shows not only that Mary was sealed
to Joseph Smith "for eternity" in 1846, but also that she was sealed to Brigham Young
"for time." Her autobiography makes clear, however, that she remained with Lightner.

9. PATTY BARTLETT SESSIONS, wife of David Sessions

Patty Sessions, famous midwife in Nauvoo and Utah, was born on February 4, 1795 and was married to David Sessions on June 28, 1812. According to her private journal she was sealed to Joseph Smith on March 9, 1842, when forty-seven years old. "I was sealed to Joseph Smith by Willard Richards March 9, 1842, in Newel K. Whitney's chamber, Nauvoo, for time and all eternity. . . . Sylvia, my daughter, was present when I was sealed to Joseph Smith. I was after Mr. Sessions' death [about 1850] sealed to John Parry for time on the 27th of March 1852, Great Salt Lake City."

Joseph Smith's diary entry for March 9, 1842 confirms at least the fact that he spent part of the day with Willard Richards, whom Patty names as performing the ceremony and who was "temple recorder" at the time: ". . . in the afternoon continued the translation of the Book of Abraham, called at Bishop Knight's and Mr. Davis's, with the recorder, and continued translating and revising, and reading letters in the evening, Sister Emma being present in the office." * It is significant that John C. Bennett knew about Joseph's marriage to Mrs. Sessions. He lists Mrs. S******* as one of the prophet's spiritual wives in his *History of the Saints*. Mrs. Sessions lived to be almost ninety-nine, dying on December 14, 1893.

10. DELCENA JOHNSON SHERMAN, widow of Lyman R. Sherman

Delcena Johnson, sister of Almera and Benjamin Johnson, was born on November 19, 1806 in Westford, Vermont. Apparently she was married to Joseph Smith before June 1842. The unpublished letter of Benjamin Johnson to George S. Gibbs says in part: ". . . in visiting [June 1842] my sister, the widow of Lyman R. Sherman, who died a martyr to conditions of Far West, I found her with a former acquaintance, Sister Louisa Beeman, and I saw from appearances that they were both in his (the prophet's) care, and that he provided for their comfort. . . . The marriage of my eldest sister . . . to the Prophet was before my return to Nauvoo, and it being tacitly admitted, I asked no questions."

* *History of the Church*, Vol. IV, p. 548.

11. MRS. DURFEE

Sarah Pratt told W. Wyl in 1885 the following story: "There was an old woman called Durfee. She knew a good deal about the prophet's amorous adventures and, to keep her quiet, he admitted her to the secret blessings of celestial bliss. I don't think that she was ever sealed to him, although it may have been the case after Joseph's death, when the temple was finished. At all events, she boasted here in Salt Lake of having been one of Joseph's wives." * Since John C. Bennett listed a Mrs. D***** as one of Joseph's wives, it is highly probable that she was sealed to the prophet before June 1842, when Bennett was expelled. Joseph H. Jackson listed both Mrs. Durfee and Mrs. Sessions as "Mothers in Israel," whose duty it was to initiate younger women into the mysteries of plural marriage.†

12. SALLY ANN FULLER GULLEY, wife of Samuel Gulley

Sally Ann Fuller was born at Saratoga, New York, on October 24, 1815. The date of her marriage to Samuel Gulley is not known, but the Nauvoo Temple Record states that on January 29, 1846 she was sealed to Joseph Smith, Jr., "for eternity" and to Gulley "for time." Since John C. Bennett listed a Mrs. G**** as one of Joseph's wives, it is possible that he was referring to Mrs. Gulley. If so, it would seem that her marriage to Joseph Smith took place before Bennett's expulsion in 1842.

13. MRS. A**** S****, married to Joseph by Brigham Young.
14. MISS B***** [possibly Sarah Bapson]

These women, listed by John C. Bennett in his *History of the Saints,* remain as yet unidentified.

15. ELIZA ROXEY SNOW

Of all Joseph's wives, none testified to the fact of her marriage more frequently and with greater pride than the poetess Eliza R. Snow. Born on January 21, 1804, daughter of the well-to-do Campbellite Oliver Snow, she joined the Mormons in 1835. In the spring of 1836 she taught a girls' school in Kirtland and

* *Mormon Portraits*, p. 54.
† *Narrative of the Adventures and Experiences of Joseph H. Jackson* (Warsaw Illinois. 1844), p. 14.

lived at Joseph's home. Later in Nauvoo she again moved into his home, and on June 29, 1842, at thirty-eight, she became his wife. Her detailed autobiography remained unpublished in the Bancroft Library until 1944, when it appeared serially in the *Relief Society Magazine* in Salt Lake City. Of her marriage she wrote:

In Nauvoo I first understood that the practice of plurality was to be introduced into the church. The subject was very repugnant to my feelings — so directly was it in opposition to my educated feelings, that it seemed as though all the prejudices of my ancestors for generations past congregated around me. But when I reflected that I was living in the Dispensation of the fulness of times, embracing all other Dispensations, surely Plural Marriage must necessarily be included, and I consoled myself with the idea that it was far in the distance, and beyond the period of my mortal existence. It was not long, however, after I received the first intimation, before the announcement reached me that the "set time" had come. . . . I was sealed to the Prophet Joseph Smith for time and eternity in accordance with the *Celestial Law of Marriage* which God has revealed — the ceremony being performed by a servant of the Most High. . . .*

Brigham Young had performed the ceremony, and the fact of the marriage is neatly borne out by Joseph's diary entry for the date of the marriage, June 29, 1842: "Heard the recorder read in the Law of the Lord [the mysterious book that was said to have listed all the plural wives in Nauvoo]; paid taxes; rode out in the city on business with Brigham Young." †

There is a persistent tradition that Eliza conceived a child by Joseph in Nauvoo, and that Emma one day discovered her husband embracing Eliza in the hall outside their bedrooms and in a rage flung her downstairs and drove her out into the street. The fall is said to have resulted in a miscarriage. (This tradition was stated to me as fact by Eliza's nephew, LeRoi C. Snow, in the Church Historian's Office, Salt Lake City.) Solon Foster, coachman for the prophet, was present in the Mansion House when the incident occurred. Years later he met Emma's sons, who were then publicly denouncing polygamy in Utah, and reproached them for their attitude: "Joseph, the night your mother

* See also her statement in the biography of her brother. Eliza R. Snow Smith: *Biography and Family Record of Lorenzo Snow*, p. 68.
† *History of the Church*, Vol. V, p. 49.

turned Eliza R. Snow into the street in her night clothes you
and all the family stood crying. I led you back into the house
and took you to bed with me. You said, 'I wish mother wouldn't
be so cruel to Aunt Eliza.' You called her aunt, because you
knew she was your father's wife. He did not deny it." *

C. G. Webb further corroborated the story in an interview
with W. Wyl:

> Eliza Snow . . . used to be much at the prophet's house and "Sister
> Emma" treated her as a confidential friend. Very much interested in
> Joseph's errands, Emma used to send Eliza after him as a spy. Joseph
> found it out and, to win over the gifted young poetess, he made her
> one of his celestial brides. There is scarcely a Mormon unacquainted
> with the fact, that Sister Emma, on the other side, soon found out
> the little compromise arranged between Joseph and Eliza. Feeling
> outraged as a wife and betrayed as a friend, Emma is currently re-
> ported as having had recourse to a vulgar broomstick as an instru-
> ment of revenge; and the harsh treatment received at Emma's hand
> is said to have destroyed Eliza's hopes of becoming the mother of a
> prophet's son.†

After Joseph's death Eliza in 1846 was sealed to Brigham
Young in the Nauvoo temple. She bore him no children. In
later years she became one of the leading women in the West,
and died on December 5, 1887.

16. SARAH ANN WHITNEY, later the wife of Heber C. Kimball

Sarah Whitney, daughter of Newel K. Whitney, was born on
March 22, 1825, and was married to Joseph at seventeen. Her
own sworn statement, giving the date as July 27, 1842, was published along with a confirming affidavit sworn by her mother,
in Joseph F. Smith, Jr.: *Blood Atonement and the Origin of
Plural Marriage*. It is said that she was the first woman given in
plural marriage "by and with the consent of both parents." Apparently it took a special revelation, however, to win their consent. "The revelation commanding and consecrating this union
is in existence," wrote Orson F. Whitney, "though it has never

---

* Foster recounted this in a sermon in southern Utah that was heard by John R.
Young. Young described it in a letter to Mrs. Vesta P. Crawford, who kindly consented to let me quote it here.

† *Mormon Portraits*, p. 58.

been published. It bears the date July 27, 1842, and was given through the Prophet to the writer's grandfather, Newel K. Whitney." * William Clayton and Joseph C. Kingsbury both knew of the marriage of Sarah Whitney to Joseph, and swore to this fact in separate affidavits.† Sarah in 1846 was sealed to Joseph Smith "for eternity" and to Heber C. Kimball "for time," in the Nauvoo temple. She bore Kimball several children.

17. SARAH M. KINSLEY CLEVELAND, wife of John Cleveland

Sarah Cleveland befriended Joseph and Emma Smith after the expulsion of the Mormons from Far West. Emma lived at the Cleveland home in Quincy, Illinois, while Joseph was in Liberty jail. After Nauvoo was settled, Joseph wrote to the Clevelands: "We have selected a lot for you, just across the street from our own, beside Mrs. Harris." ‡ Since Mrs. Cleveland was first counselor in the Relief Society, it seems probable that her marriage to Joseph took place shortly after the expulsion of Bennett in 1842, when Joseph married most of the leaders in that Society. She was then fifty-four years old.§

Andrew Jenson listed her as one of the prophet's wives, but gave no details. Sarah Pratt told W. Wyl that "Sarah Cleveland kept a kind of assignation house for the prophet and Eliza R. Snow." ‖ When the Clevelands left Nauvoo, in May 1843, Mrs. Cleveland wrote a farewell letter to the *Times and Seasons* on May 1, thanking her friends and explaining that her husband had not succeeded in business as had been anticipated.

The Nauvoo Temple Record states that Sarah M. Kinsley was sealed to Joseph Smith "for eternity" and to John Smith "for time," in January 1846, but whether this means that Sarah left Cleveland and remained with John Smith I have been unable to discover.

* *Latter-Day Saints Biographical Encyclopædia*, Vol. I, p. 226.

† *Historical Record*, Vol. VI, pp. 225–6.

‡ *History of the Church*, Vol. III, p. 362.

§ According to the Genealogical Archives in Salt Lake City, she was born on October 20, 1788 in Massachusetts, daughter of Ebenezer and Sarah Kinsley.

‖ *Mormon Portraits*, p. 90.

18. ELVIRA A. COWLES, later the wife of Jonathan H. Holmes

Andrew Jenson listed Elvira Cowles as one of Joseph's wives, saying that she was "afterwards the wife of Jonathan H. Holmes." Now, it happened that her marriage to Holmes, one of Joseph's bodyguard, took place in Nauvoo on December 1, 1842, with Joseph himself performing the ceremony.* If Jenson is correct, then Elvira must have been married to the prophet at an earlier date. Since she was treasurer of the Nauvoo Relief Society, it seems likely that this marriage occurred shortly after the Bennett expulsion in June 1842. Hers seems to be the only case where the prophet married a woman for "time and eternity" and then relinquished her "for time" to another man.

Austin Cowles, Elvira's father, and member of the High Council, bitterly opposed polygamy and joined the apostates who followed William Law out of the church in May 1844. He may have been embittered by Joseph's involvement with his daughter. Elvira was born in Massachusetts on November 23, 1813, and was probably twenty-nine at the time of her marriage to the prophet.

Holmes apparently knew of her relationship with Joseph, and willingly stood as proxy in January 1846 when Elvira's marriage to the prophet "for eternity" was solemnized in the newly completed Nauvoo temple.

19. MARTHA McBRIDE, later the wife of Heber C. Kimball

Martha McBride was born in Chester, New York, March 17, 1805. In 1869 she swore to an affidavit saying that she had been married to Joseph Smith in the summer of 1842.† She was then thirty-eight. The Nauvoo Temple Record states that in January 1846 she was married to Joseph Smith "for eternity" and to Heber C. Kimball "for time." She bore Kimball no children.

20. RUTH D. VOSE SAYERS, wife of Edward Sayers

Ruth Vose, daughter of Mark and Sally Vose, was born on February 26, 1808 in Boston. Andrew Jenson listed her as a

* The *Wasp*, December 10, 1842.
† For text of the affidavit see Joseph Smith, Jr.: *Blood Atonement and the Origin of Plural Marriage*, p. 72. See also O. F. Whitney: *Life of Heber C. Kimball*, p. 432.

wife of Joseph Smith, but stated erroneously that she was married to Sayers "after the death of the Prophet." * According to the Genealogical Archives in Salt Lake City, she married Edward Sayers in St. Louis on January 23, 1841. When Joseph went into hiding on August 10, 1842, he lived for several weeks at the home of Edward Sayers outside Nauvoo,† and it seems probable that he married Mrs. Sayers at this time. She was then thirty-four. She died on August 18, 1884 in Salt Lake City.

21. DESDEMONA WADSWORTH FULLMER, later the wife of Ezra T. Benson

Desdemona W. Fullmer, daughter of Peter and Susanna Fullmer, was born in Pennsylvania on October 6, 1809. She was married to Joseph Smith some time during 1842, when thirty-three years old. She was known as a "quiet, unassuming, faithful woman." William Clayton, secretary to Joseph Smith, on February 16, 1874 swore to an affidavit asserting that in February 1843 Joseph "gave me to understand that Eliza R. Snow, Louisa Beman, Desdemona W. Fullmer and others were his lawful wives in the sight of heaven." ‡ Desdemona was officially sealed to the prophet in the Nauvoo temple in January 1846. In the same ceremony she married Ezra T. Benson "for time." She went to Utah in 1848 and died in Salt Lake City on February 9, 1886.

22. EMILY DOW PARTRIDGE, later the wife of Brigham Young
23. ELIZA M. PARTRIDGE, later the wife of Amasa Lyman

Emily and Eliza Partridge, daughters of the prosperous Mormon bishop Edward Partridge, lived in the home of Joseph Smith in Nauvoo after their father's death. In 1843, when they were married to the prophet, Emily was nineteen and Eliza twenty-three, the former having been born on February 28, 1824 and the latter on April 20, 1820, in Painesville, Ohio. Emily wrote the story of their marriages in 1887:

. . . the Prophet Joseph and his wife Emma offered us a home in their family, and they treated us with great kindness. We had been

* *Historical Record*, Vols. V–VIII, p. 1004.
† *History of the Church*, Vol. V, p. 90.
‡ *Historical Record*, Vol. VI, pp. 225, 234.

there about a year when the principle of plural marriage was made known to us, and I was married to Joseph Smith on the 4th of March, 1843, Elder Heber C. Kimball performing the ceremony. My sister Eliza was also married to Joseph a few days later. This was done without the knowledge of Emma Smith. Two months afterwards she consented to give her husband two wives, provided he would give her the privilege of choosing them. She accordingly chose my sister Eliza and myself, and to save family trouble Brother Joseph thought it best to have another ceremony performed. Accordingly on the 11th of May, 1843, we were sealed to Joseph Smith a second time, in Emma's presence, she giving her free and full consent thereto. From that very hour, however, Emma was our bitter enemy. We remained in the family several months after this, but things went from bad to worse until we were obliged to leave the house and find another home. Emma desired us to leave the city, but after considering the matter over, we decided to remain with our friends.*

In this connection Joseph's journal entry for May 11, 1843 is a curiosity: "Thursday. 11 — At six a.m. baptized Louisa Beeman, Sarah Alley, and others. Eight a.m. went to see the new carriage made by Thomas Moore, which was ready for traveling. Emma went to Quincy in the new carriage. I rode out as far as the prairie." † Perhaps the carriage was intended as balm for Emma's outraged pride.

That Emma gave her consent was further sworn to by Lovina Smith Walker, daughter of Hyrum Smith, who stated in 1869: "I Lovina Walker . . . hereby certify, that while I was living with Aunt Emma Smith, in Fulton City, Fulton County, Illinois, in the year 1846, she told me that she, Emma Smith, was present and witnessed the marrying or sealing of Eliza Partridge, Emily Partridge, Maria and Sarah Lawrence to her husband, Joseph Smith, and that she gave her consent thereto." ‡ Eliza married Amasa Lyman after Joseph's death and bore him five children. Emily married Brigham Young in September 1844, at the age of twenty, and bore him seven children. She was Young's ninth wife. In January 1846, in the Nauvoo temple, the sisters were officially sealed to the prophet "for eternity" and to Lyman and Young "for time."

* Ibid., Vol. VI, p. 240.
† *History of the Church*, Vol. V, pp. 385–6.
‡ *Historical Record*, Vol. VI, p. 223.

24. ALMERA WOODWARD JOHNSON, later the wife of Reuben Barton

Few of Joseph's wives have had the fact of their marriage so thoroughly documented as Almera Johnson. Daughter of Ezekiel Johnson, she was born in Vermont on October 12, 1812, and was thirty-one at the time of her marriage. Her own sworn statement says in part:

On a certain occasion in the spring of the year 1843, the exact date of which I do not now recollect, I went from Macedonia to Nauvoo to visit another of my sisters . . . at which time I was sealed to the Prophet Joseph Smith. . . . After this time I lived with the Prophet Joseph as his wife, and he visited me at the home of my brother Benjamin F. at Macedonia.*

Almera's brother Benjamin described the courtship of his sister in his letter to George S. Gibbs:

It was Sunday morning, April 3 or 4, 1843, that the Prophet proceeded to open to me the subject of plural marriage and eternal marriage, and he said that years ago in Kirtland the Lord revealed to him the ancient order of plural marriage, and the necessity for its practice, and did command that he take another wife, and that among his first thoughts was to come to my mother for some of her daughters. And as he was again required of the Lord to take more wives, he came now to ask me for my sister Almera. His words astonished me and almost took my breath. I sat for a time amazed, and finally, almost ready to burst with emotion, I looked him straight in the face and said: "Brother Joseph, this is something I did not expect, and I do not understand it. You know whether it is right, I do not. I want to do just as you tell me, and I will try to, but if I ever should know that you do this to dishonor and debauch my sister, I will kill you as sure as the Lord lives." And while his eyes did not move from mine, he said with a smile, in a soft tone: "But Benjamin, you will never know that, but you will know the principle in time, and will rejoice in what it will bring you."

. . . the Prophet, with Louisa Beeman and my sister Delcena, had it agreeably arranged with sister Almera, and after a little instruction she stood by the Prophet's side and was sealed to him as a wife, by Brother William Clayton; after which the Prophet asked me to take my sister to occupy room number "10," in his Mansion Home,

* Joseph F. Smith, Jr.: *Blood Atonement and the Origin of Plural Marriage*, pp. 70–1.

during her stay in the city. But as I could not long be absent from my home and business, we soon returned to Ramus, where, on the 15th day of May, some three weeks later, the Prophet again came and at my house occupied the same room and bed with my sister, that the month previous he had occupied with the daughter of the late Bishop Partridge, as his wife. And at that time he sealed me to my first wife for eternity, and gave me my first plural wife, Mary Ann Hale, an orphan girl raised by my mother then living with us, who is still with me. . . .

Benjamin also signed an affidavit on March 4, 1870 giving the same facts, but more briefly and formally.* The fact of Joseph's visit to Almera is neatly corroborated by his own journal entry of May 16, 1843:

. . . started for Ramus . . . went to Benjamin F. Johnson's with William Clayton to sleep. Before retiring, I gave Brother and Sister Johnson some instructions on the priesthood. . . . Except a man and his wife enter into an everlasting covenant and be married for eternity, while in this probation, by the power and authority of the Holy Priesthood, they will cease to increase when they die; that is, they will not have any children after the resurrection. . . .†

After Joseph's death Almera married Reuben Barton and bore him five daughters, all of whom died young. Barton apostatized and Almera joined her brother in Utah in 1861. She lived to be eighty-four.‡

25. LUCY WALKER, later the wife of Heber C. Kimball

None of Joseph's wives described her courtship with such ingenuous detail as Lucy Walker. She was born in Vermont on April 30, 1826, daughter of John and Lydia Walker. After the death of her mother she came in January 1842 to live at the prophet's home. "In the year 1842," she wrote later,

President Joseph Smith sought an interview with me and said, "I have a message for you. I have been commanded of God to take another wife, and you are the woman." My astonishment knew no bounds. This announcement was indeed a thunderbolt to me. He asked me if I believed him to be the Prophet of God. "Most assuredly

    * See *Historical Record,* Vol. VI, p. 221.
    † *History of the Church,* Vol. V, pp. 391–2.
    ‡ See her obituary, *Deseret News,* March 26, 1896.

I do," I replied. He fully explained to me the principle of plural or celestial marriage. Said this principle was again to be restored for the benefit of the human family. That it would prove an everlasting blessing to my father's house, and form a chain that could never be broken, worlds without end. "What have you to say," he asked. "Nothing." How could I speak or what could I say? He said, "If you pray sincerely for light and understanding in relation thereto, you shall receive a testimony of the correctness of this principle."

I thought I prayed sincerely, but was so unwilling to consider the matter favorably that I fear I did not ask in faith for light. . . . I was tempted and tortured beyond endurance until life was not desirable. . . . The Prophet discerned my sorrow. He saw how unhappy I was, and sought an opportunity of again speaking to me on that subject, and said, "Although I can not under existing circumstances, acknowledge you as my wife, the time is near when we will go beyond the Rocky Mountains and then you will be acknowledged and honored as my wife." He also said this principle will yet be believed and practiced by the righteous. "I have no flattering words to offer. It is a command of God to you. I will give you until tomorrow to decide this matter. If you reject this message the gate will be closed forever against you."

This aroused every drop of Scotch in my veins. For a few moments I stood fearless before him, and looked him in the eye. I felt at this moment that I was called to place myself upon the altar a living sacrifice — perhaps to brook the world in disgrace and incur the displeasure and contempt of my youthful companions. . . . I had been speechless, but at last found utterance and said: Although you are a Prophet of God you could not induce me to take a step of so great importance, unless I knew that God approved my course. I would rather die. . . ." He walked across the room, returned and stood before me with the most beautiful expression of countenance, and said "God Almighty bless you. You shall have a manifestation of the will of God concerning you; a testimony that you can never deny. I will tell you what it shall be. It shall be that joy and peace that you never knew."

Oh how earnestly I prayed for these words to be fulfilled. It was near dawn after another sleepless night when my room was lighted up by a heavenly influence. To me it was, in comparison, like the brilliant sun bursting through the darkest cloud. My soul was filled with a calm, sweet peace that "I never knew." Supreme happiness took possession of me, and I received a powerful and irresistible testimony of the truth of plural marriage, which has been like an anchor to the soul through all the trials of life. I felt that I must go out into the morning air and give vent to the joy and gratitude that filled my soul. As I descended the stairs, President Smith opened the door below, took me by the hand and said: "Thank God, you have the testimony. I too have prayed." He led me to the chair, placed his hands upon my head, and blessed me with every blessing my heart could possibly desire. The first day of May 1843, I consented to become the Prophet's wife, and was sealed to him for time and all eternity, at his own house by Elder William Clayton.*

Lucy had just turned seventeen. Emma was absent on a shopping trip to St. Louis and was due to return on May 2, which may have explained Joseph's haste to have Lucy married to him by May 1.† Lucy admitted before a court in 1892 that Emma knew nothing of her marriage.‡ An entry in William Clayton's private journal, dated May 1, 1843, confirmed Lucy's story: "At the Temple. At 10 married Joseph to Lucy Walker." §

In 1845 Lucy married Heber C. Kimball. She bore him nine children. She always talked freely about her marriage to Joseph and once swore to an affidavit that told substantially the same story as the one detailed above. Here she said also that Emma "gave her consent to the marriage of at least four other girls to her husband, and . . . she was well aware that he associated with them as wives within all the meaning of all that word implies. This is proved by the fact that she herself, on several occasions, kept guard at the door to prevent disinterested persons from intruding, when these ladies were in the house." ‖

26. HELEN MAR KIMBALL, later the wife of Horace K. Whitney

Helen Kimball was born on August 22, 1828 in Mendon, New York. Her father, Heber C. Kimball, gave her to Joseph Smith for a wife when she was fifteen years old.¶ Although in later

* Lyman O. Littlefield: *Reminiscences of the Latter-Day Saints* (Logan, Utah), 1888.

† *History of the Church*, Vol. V, p. 379.

‡ *Temple Lot Case*, pp. 371–5.

§ Quoted in Joseph F. Smith, Jr.: *Blood Atonement and the Origin of Plural Marriage*, p. 55.

‖ *Historical Record*, Vol. VI, p. 230. See also the Nauvoo Temple Record, January 1846. In the Nauvoo temple Lucy was sealed to Joseph Smith "for eternity" and to Kimball "for time."

¶ William Clayton swore in 1874 that Joseph took Helen Kimball for a wife in the spring of 1843. *Historical Record*, Vol. VI, p. 225.

years she wrote vigorously in defense of polygamy, she never mentioned her marriage to Joseph, and a revealing autobiographical sketch shows her early abhorrence of polygamy. "I had, in hours of temptation," she wrote, "when seeing the trials of my mother, felt to rebel. I hated polygamy in my heart." *
Yet when she married Horace K. Whitney in the Nauvoo temple in February 1846 she allowed herself to be sealed to Joseph Smith "for eternity." She bore Whitney eleven children.

27. MARIA LAWRENCE, later the wife of Brigham Young

28. SARAH LAWRENCE, later the wife of Heber C. Kimball

Maria and Sarah Lawrence, daughters of Edward Lawrence, were born in Canada, Maria on December 18, 1823 and Sarah on May 13, 1826. Canadian-born William Law told W. Wyl in 1887:

Soon after my arrival in Nauvoo the two L—— girls came to the holy city, two very young girls, fifteen to seventeen years of age. They had been converted in Canada, were orphans worth about $8,000 in English gold. Joseph got to be appointed their guardian. . . . Emma complained about Joseph's living with the L—— girls, but not very violently . . . she used to complain to me about Joseph's escapades whenever she met me on the street.†

The tradition was strong among Joseph's wives that the Lawrence sisters had been married with Emma's consent. Emily Partridge, who like Maria Lawrence lived at the prophet's home and also married Brigham Young, once wrote: "Emma about this time [spring of 1843] gave her husband two other wives — Maria and Sarah Lawrence." ‡
According to the Nauvoo Temple Record, Maria in January 1846 was officially sealed to Joseph Smith "for eternity" and to Almon W. Babbitt "for time." Apparently the marriage to Babbitt was dissolved almost at once, for in the same month she became the wife of Brigham Young. She bore him no children and died in Nauvoo. Sarah Lawrence's marriage to Joseph

* *Representative Women of Deseret*, p. 112.

† This interview appeared in the *Salt Lake Tribune* and was reprinted in Thomas Gregg: *The Prophet of Palmyra*, p. 508.

‡ *Woman's Exponent*, Vol. XIV, p. 38. See also the court testimony of Lucy Walker, *Temple Lot Case*, p. 371, and the affidavit of Lovina Walker, *Historical Record*, Vol. VI, p. 223.

Smith "for eternity" was solemnized in the Nauvoo temple in January 1846. In the same ceremony she was married to Heber C. Kimball "for time." She divorced Kimball in Salt Lake City on June 18, 1851, married again, and went to California.*

29. FLORA ANN WOODWORTH

Flora Woodworth, daughter of Lucian Woodworth, architect of the Nauvoo House, was born on November 17, 1826 in New York State. According to William Clayton, Joseph's secretary, she was married to the prophet in the spring of 1843.† She was then sixteen. Joseph once referred to her in his journal: "May 14, 1844. Prayed for Elder Woodworth's daughter, who was sick."‡ Andrew Jenson stated that "after the death of the Prophet she married again, but this union proved unhappy. She died in the wilderness on the journey westward at the time of the Exodus from Nauvoo." §

According to Julia Murdock Farnsworth, niece of the Julia Murdock adopted by Joseph Smith, the prophet had a plural wife named Flora Gove,‖ and it is possible that this was the married name of Flora Woodworth, since she is not mentioned elsewhere.

30. RHODA RICHARDS, later the wife of Brigham Young

Rhoda Richards, eldest sister of Willard Richards, was born on August 8, 1784. "In my young days," she wrote, "I buried my first and only love, and true to that affiance, I have passed companionless through life; but am sure of having my proper place and standing in the resurrection, having been sealed to the Prophet Joseph, according to the celestial law, by his own request, under the inspiration of divine revelation." ¶ She also signed an affidavit affirming that she was married to Joseph in Nauvoo by her brother Willard on June 12, 1843.** She was then fifty-nine. The ceremony was clearly a favor by Joseph to

* *Historical Record*, Vols. V–VIII, p. 976, and Journal History, MS., June 18, 1851.
† *Historical Record*, Vol. VI, p. 225.
‡ *History of the Church*, Vol. VI, p. 377.
§ *Historical Record*, Vols. V–VIII, p. 1009.
‖ Mrs. Farnsworth before her death gave this information to Mrs. Vesta P. Crawford of Salt Lake City.
¶ *The Women of Mormondon*, pp. 421–2.
** See Joseph F. Smith, Jr.: *Blood Atonement and the Origin of Plural Marriage*, p. 75.

her brother, who was doubtless concerned over his sister's fate in the celestial kingdom. In the Nauvoo temple in January 1846 she was sealed to Joseph Smith "for eternity" and to Brigham Young "for time." She lived to be ninety-five.

31. HANNAH ELLS

Hannah Ells, daughter of Thomas and Hannah Ells, was born in New Castle, Northumberland, England, on March 4, 1813. According to Andrew Jenson, she was "a lady of culture and refinement, somewhat tall in stature." Jenson printed an affidavit by John Benbow that said in part:

Be it remembered that this 28th day of August, 1869, personally appeared before me, James Jack, a Notary Public . . . John Benbow . . . and upon his oath said that in the summer of 1843, at his home four miles from Nauvoo . . . President Joseph Smith taught him and his wife, Jane Benbow, the doctrine of celestial marriage, or plurality of wives. . . . And further that Hannah Ells Smith, a wife of the Prophet, boarded at his home two months during the summer of the same year. . . . And further, that President Smith frequently visited his wife Hannah at his house.*

Hannah Ells died in Nauvoo in 1844.

32. MELISSA LOTT, later the wife of Ira Jones Willes

Melissa Lott, daughter of Cornelius P. Lott, foreman of Joseph's farm, was born on January 9, 1824, and was nineteen when married to the prophet. Joseph's son wrote that she was a "tall, fine-looking woman with a dark complexion, dark hair and eyes — a good singer, quite celebrated in a local way." †
Melissa swore to an affidavit stating that she was married to Joseph Smith on September 20, 1843 by Hyrum Smith in the presence of her parents. This marriage and the date were recorded in the family Bible, which is now in the Church Historian's Office in Salt Lake City.‡ Joseph Smith's diary entry for September 20, 1843 clearly indicates that he spent the day

* *Historical Record*, Vols. V–VIII, pp. 222, 234, 961.

† "Memoirs of President Joseph Smith," *Saints Herald*, December 18, 1934, p. 1614.

‡ Joseph F. Smith, Jr.: *Blood Atonement and the Origin of Plural Marriage* pp. 72, 55.

with the Lotts: "Wednesday, 20. Visited my farm, accompanied by my brother Hyrum." *

When testifying in the Temple Lot case, Melissa said: "I was married to Joseph Smith September 27, 1843. As nearly as I can remember or understand it the marriage ceremony was as follows, 'You both mutually agree to be each other's companion, husband, and wife, observing the legal rights belonging to this condition, that is, keeping yourselves wholly for each other, and from all others during your lives.' I married him under that ceremony, knowing at the time he had a wife living, his wife, Emma Smith." When asked by the prosecution: "Did he agree in that marriage ceremony to keep himself from his wife Emma, for you?" she replied: "I cannot tell you. You will have to ask him that question. . . . I don't think he made any promise of that kind. . . . There were no children born as a fruit of that marriage. I married Mr. Willis in the year 1849. There have been children as the fruit of that marriage." †

Melissa never referred to the fact that in February 1846 when she was officially sealed to Joseph Smith "for eternity" in the Nauvoo temple, she was also sealed to John M. Bernhisel "for time."

33. FANNY YOUNG MURRAY, wife of Roswell Murray

Fanny Young, sister of Brigham Young, was born on November 8, 1787. She married Robert Carr in 1803. After his death she married Roswell Murray in 1832. The story of her sealing to the prophet was told by Brigham Young:

I recollect a sister conversing with Joseph Smith on this subject: "Now, don't talk to me; when I get into the celestial kingdom, if I ever do get there, I shall request the privilege of being a ministering angel; that is the labor that I wish to perform. I don't want any companion in that world; and if the Lord will make me a ministering angel, it is all I want." Joseph said, "Sister, you talk very foolishly, you do not know what you will want." He then said to me: "Here, Brother Brigham, you seal this lady to me." I sealed her to him. This was my own sister according to the flesh.‡

* *History of the Church*, Vol. VI, p. 35.
† *Temple Lot Case*, p. 314.
‡ *Journal of Discourses*, Vol. XVI, pp. 166–7.

Andrew Jenson stated that the ceremony occurred on November 2, 1843. Fanny was then fifty-six. She died on June 11, 1859.

34. OLIVE GREY FROST, later the wife of Brigham Young

Olive Grey Frost, daughter of Aaron Frost and Susan Grey, was born in Maine on July 24, 1816. Jenson, who includes her in his list of Joseph's wives, does not mention the date of her marriage, but it was probably after April 12, 1843, since she was a missionary to England with her sister and brother-in-law, Parley P. Pratt, between the fall of 1840 and that date. She was then twenty-seven. Although happy and genial in disposition, she suffered from ill health, and died in Nauvoo on October 6, 1845. She had become the eleventh wife of Brigham Young in February 1845.* Mrs. Mary Ettie V. Smith stated that when the dead bodies of Joseph and Hyrum arrived in Nauvoo from Carthage, "Olive Frost went entirely mad." †

35. MARY ANN FROST, wife of Parley P. Pratt

The Nauvoo Temple Record states that in February 1846 Mary Ann Frost was sealed to Joseph Smith "for eternity," her husband, Parley P. Pratt, standing as proxy. This is the only reference I have found linking Mrs. Parley Pratt's name to that of the prophet, but since nearly all of the wives sealed to Joseph Smith in the Nauvoo temple had clearly been married to him during his lifetime, it may be assumed that Mrs. Pratt had also been.

Mary Ann Frost was born on January 11, 1809 at Groton, Vermont, and was married to Pratt on May 9, 1837. Since she was in England with Pratt from the fall of 1840 to April 1843, it is unlikely that she became a plural wife of Joseph Smith before the latter date. Her son, Moroni, born on December 7, 1844, may be added to the list of boys who might possibly have been sons of Joseph Smith.

[The remaining names are listed alphabetically rather than chronologically.]

* See the biography written by her sister, Mary Ann Pratt, *Historical Record*, Vol. VI, p. 235.

† *Fifteen Years among the Mormons*, p. 36.

36. OLIVE ANDREWS, later the wife of Brigham Young

Olive Andrews was born on September 24, 1818, in Livermore, Maine. According to the Nauvoo Temple Record, she was married to Joseph Smith "for eternity" and to Brigham Young "for time" in January 1846.

37. MRS. EDWARD BLOSSOM

Richard Rushton, former steward in the Mansion House, told W. Wyl the following story:

"Emma started for St. Louis. The going, purchasing and return occupied about a week. At night, after the departure of the 'elect lady,' the steward gave the keys to the prophet, and in the morning he as usual stepped lightly and rapped at the door of the bed-room. A voice, strange to his ear, yet of feminine softness, rather startled him in response with the words 'Come in.' He entered timidly, when lo and behold! there lay in Emma's bed and stead the beautiful and attractive young wife of Elder Edward Blossom, a high councilor of Zion, (afterwards exalted to the apostleship by Brigham Young). With a pair of laughing, glistening eyes and with a smile of happy sweetness, she spoke in soft and pleading accents: *'I suppose, Brother Rushton, I shall have to be Sister Emma to you this morning,'* as she gracefully handed the keys to him." Astonished and blushing, the faithful steward left the room to resume his duties, leaving the adulterous prophet and his charmer to themselves. The same thing was repeated each morning during the week Emma was away purchasing supplies for the prophet's hotel.*

It should be noted, however, that, contrary to Wyl's statement, no one by the name of Blossom was ever made an apostle. I have thus far been unable to find any other reference to either Edward Blossom or his wife.

38. ELIZABETH DAVIS, later the wife of Cornelius P. Lott

Elizabeth Davis was born on March 11, 1791, in Suffolk, England. According to the Nauvoo Temple Record, she was married to Joseph Smith "for eternity" and to Cornelius P. Lott "for time" in January 1846.

* *Mormon Portraits*, pp. 65–6

39. MARY HUSTON, later the wife of Heber C. Kimball

Mary Huston was born on September 11, 1818 in Jackson, Ohio. According to the Nauvoo Temple Record, in January 1846 she was married to Joseph Smith "for eternity" and to Heber C. Kimball "for time." She was later listed by Orson F. Whitney as one of the wives of Joseph Smith who married Kimball. She bore no children.*

40. VIENNA JACQUES

Vienna Jacques was born near Boston in 1788. She came to Kirtland in 1833, and Joseph Smith in a revelation on March 8 directed her to consecrate her property to the church and receive an inheritance in Missouri.† According to the Genealogical Archives in Salt Lake City, Vienna was sealed to Joseph Smith on March 28, 1858. Descendants of her neighbors in Salt Lake City hold, however, that the marriage took place while the prophet was alive. Miss Jacques, who apparently never married anyone else, lived to be over ninety.

41. CORDELIA CALISTA MORLEY, later the wife of Frederick W. Cox

Cordelia Morley, a daughter of Isaac and Hannah Morley, was born on November 28, 1823 in Kirtland, Ohio. According to the Nauvoo Temple Record, in January 1846 she was married to Joseph Smith "for eternity" and to Frederick W. Cox "for time." She was Cox's second wife, and bore him seven children.

42. SARAH SCOTT, later the wife of Heber C. Kimball

Sarah Scott was listed by O. F. Whitney as a wife of Joseph Smith who later married Heber C. Kimball. She had no children.‡

43. SYLVIA SESSIONS, later the wife of Heber C. Kimball

Sylvia Sessions, daughter of David and Patty Sessions, was born on July 31, 1818, and was probably about twenty-five or

---

* *Life of Heber C. Kimball*, pp. 430–2.
† *Doctrine and Covenants*, Section 90.
‡ *Life of Heber C. Kimball*, pp. 430–2.

six at the time of her marriage to Joseph Smith. Since the diary of her mother makes no mention of this marriage, it is possible that Patty was unaware of it. Andrew Jenson listed Sylvia as one of the prophet's wives, and Orson F. Whitney listed her as one of Joseph's wives who later married Heber C. Kimball.* Her marriage to Kimball is noted in the Nauvoo Temple Record for January 1846. There she was sealed to Joseph Smith "for eternity" and to Kimball "for time." Sylvia was married also to Ezekiel Clark, by whom she had one daughter, Martha Sylvia, and there is some evidence that she married a Windsor P. Lyon. She died April 13, 1882.

44. NANCY MARIA SMITH, later the wife of Heber C. Kimball

Orson F. Whitney listed Nancy Maria Smith as one of the wives of Joseph Smith who later married Heber C. Kimball. He listed also Nancy Maria Winchester as a former wife of the prophet who married Kimball. It is possible that they were one and the same person, but Whitney was in a position to know the truth and would not have been likely to have made such an error.‡

45. JANE TIBBETS, later the wife of Elam Luddington

Jane Tibbets was born on August 27, 1804 at Gorham, Maine. According to the Nauvoo Temple Record, on January 17, 1846 she was sealed to Joseph Smith "for eternity" and to E. Luddington "for time."

46. PHEBE WATROUS, later the wife of Lucian Woodworth

Phebe Watrous was born on October 1, 1805 in Sharron, New York. According to the Nauvoo Temple Record, on January 19, 1846 she was sealed to Joseph Smith "for eternity" and to Lucian Woodworth "for time."

* See *Historical Record*, Vol. VI, p. 234, and *Life of Heber C. Kimball*, p. 432.
† See Frank Esshom: *Pioneers and Prominent Men of Utah*, p. 1153, and *Salt Lake Telegram*, March 3, 1952, the obituary of her daughter.
‡ *Life of Heber C. Kimball*, pp. 430–2.

47. NANCY MARIAH WINCHESTER, later the wife of Heber C. Kimball

Nancy Mariah Winchester, according to the Genealogical Archives in Salt Lake City, was born on August 10, 1828 in Erie County, New York, a daughter of Stephen and Nancy Case Winchester. But Andrew Jenson, in listing her among the prophet's wives, states that her father was Benjamin Winchester. The date of her marriage to Joseph Smith has not been published, but if it took place in 1843 or 1844, she could not have been more than fifteen or sixteen. O. F. Whitney listed her among Kimball's wives,* and the Nauvoo Temple Record states that this latter marriage took place in January 1846, when she was sealed to Kimball "for time" and to Joseph Smith "for eternity."

48. SOPHIA WOODMAN, later the wife of Gad Yale

Sophia Woodman was born on August 25, 1795 in Sanburn, New Hampshire. According to the Nauvoo Temple Record, on January 27, 1846 she was sealed to Joseph Smith "for eternity" and to Gad Yale "for time."

Since the first printing of this book, students of Mormon polygamy have continued to uncover information about Joseph Smith's wives. Mrs. Mary B. Powell was shown a significant unpublished letter in the L.D.S. Church Historian's Office in Salt Lake City, written by Joseph Smith when in hiding in 1842. This was a request, in his own handwriting, to Newel K. Whitney to bring his daughter Sarah Ann to the cornfield to spend the night with him. A copy of Mrs. Powell's manuscript is in the Huntington Library. Stanley Ivins informed me that his researches indicated that Joseph Smith was "sealed" to 66 or 67 living women, and that after his death 149 dead women were sealed to him in temple ceremonies.

* See *Historical Record*, Vol. VI, p. 234, and *Life of Heber C. Kimball*, pp. 430–2.

BIBLIOGRAPHY

THERE is a stupendous literature on Mormonism, almost all of which is valueless as source material for the study of Joseph Smith. On the other hand, county histories, antiquarian monographs, and old newspaper files are very significant, although they deal only obliquely, if at all, with the Mormon phenomenon. A useful bibliography is, therefore, difficult to compile, and I have severely restricted this list to the true "source" books to which one must go for first-hand accounts of Joseph Smith's activities, omitting all secondary histories and biographies except those few which must be taken into account by any objective student of Mormon history.

Joseph Smith's own writings, particularly the seven-volume *History of the Church* elaborated chiefly from his own journals, are by all odds the most important. The court records, few of which have hitherto been used in studies of Joseph Smith, are also basic. The great wealth of manuscript material now in the Utah State Historical Society was made available by the W. P. A. Federal Writers Project and Historical Records Survey, which made a significant contribution to Western history by copying scores of pioneer diaries and memoirs that had been buried in trunks and attics over the state. Other manuscripts, particularly the invaluable Oliver Huntington diary, were made available through the tireless activity of the Brigham Young University. Additional manuscript material was generously furnished me by friends in Utah.

My research among newspapers was greatly shortened by the painstaking scholarship of Cecil Snyder, who collected and made copies of a great many newspaper articles on Mormonism appearing in Missouri and Illinois between 1830 and 1847. Copies of the Snyder collection are now at the New York Public Library, Harvard University, Brigham Young University, and the Utah State Historical Society. I examined, in addition, the files of the Palmyra newspapers between 1820 and 1830, most of which are in the New York State Library at Albany;

the files of the *Painesville Republican,* 1837–8, and *Painesville Telegraph,* 1831–8, now in the Western Reserve Historical Society Library, and the files of the *New York Herald,* 1840–4.

The legion of secondary source books that furnished background for the life and times of Joseph Smith are not listed here, although many are mentioned in the footnotes. A history of Mormonism can, of course, be written without recourse to "anti-Mormon" accounts, but it would perforce be incomplete, for many of these provide flesh and blood for the skeletal narratives in the official histories. All such documents have been used with care, but they have not been ignored.

I

THE WRITINGS OF JOSEPH SMITH

The Book of Mormon. Palmyra, New York: Egbert B. Grandin; 1830. (Rare.)

A Book of Commandments for the Government of the Church of Christ, organized according to law, on the 6th of April, 1830. Zion [Independence, Missouri]: W. W. Phelps and Co.; 1833. (Very rare.) Reprinted by the *Salt Lake Tribune* in 1884.

Doctrine and Covenants of the Church of the Latter Day Saints, Carefully selected from the Revelations of God, and compiled by Joseph Smith, Jr., Oliver Cowdery, Sidney Rigdon, Frederick G. Williams. Kirtland, 1835. The 1921 edition, printed in Salt Lake City, is quoted throughout the book. It differs somewhat from the collection used by the Reorganized Church.

General Joseph Smith's Appeal to the Green Mountain Boys, December 1843. Nauvoo, Illinois, 1843.

Correspondence between Joseph Smith, the Prophet, and Col. John Wentworth . . . Gen. James Arlington Bennet . . . and the Hon. John C. Calhoun. . . . In which is given a Sketch of the Life of Joseph Smith, The Rise and Progress of the Church of Latter Day Saints, . . . New York: Published by John E. Page and L. R. Foster; 1844.

The Voice of Truth, containing Joseph Smith's correspondence with Gen. James Arlington Bennett; appeal to the Green Mountain boys; correspondence with John C. Calhoun,

MORMON COUNTRY
1830—1844

WISCONSIN

IOWA

TERRITORY

TERRITORY

MISSISSIPPI RIVER

Chicago

ILLINOIS

Monmouth

Montrose Nauvoo
Adam-ondi-Ahman Carthage
GRAND R. Warsaw
Gallatin
Far West Quincy Springfield
TO OREGON
Liberty DeWitt
TO SANTA FE Independence

MISSOURI RIVER

Alton

INDIAN Jefferson City St.Louis

TER.

MISSOURI

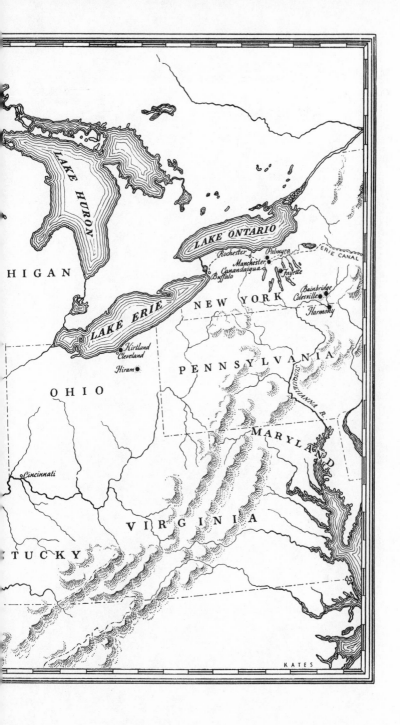

*Esq.; views of the powers and policy of the government of
the United States; pacific inuendo, and Gov. Ford's letters;
A friendly hint to Missouri, and a few words of consola-
tion for the "Globe"; also, correspondence with the Hon.
Henry Clay.* Nauvoo, Illinois: Printed by John Taylor;
1844. Most of these items were also published as separate
pamphlets in 1844.

*The Pearl of Great Price, being a choice selection from the rev-
elations, translations, and narrations of Joseph Smith.* Liverpool: Published by F. D. Richards; 1851.

*History of the Church of Jesus Christ of Latter-Day Saints.
Period I. History of Joseph Smith, the Prophet, by Him-
self.* 6 vols. Introduction and notes by B. H. Roberts. Salt
Lake City: Deseret News; 1902–12.

*The Holy Scriptures, translated and corrected by the spirit of
revelation.* Reorganized Church of Jesus Christ of Latter
Day Saints: Plano, Illinois; 1867.

II

COURT RECORDS

1. Record of the trial of Joseph Smith for disorderly conduct,
   Bainbridge, New York, March 20, 1826. Published in the
   New Schaff-Herzog Encyclopedia of Religious Knowledge.
   New York, 1883. Vol. II, p. 1576.
2. Unpublished records of the lawsuits brought against Joseph
   Smith and others to collect debts incurred in Kirtland, Ohio.
   These are in the Chardon, Ohio, courthouse. See the volumes
   for 1837–8.
3. Record of the trial of Joseph Smith for assault and battery
   against Calvin W. Stoddard, Court of Common Pleas,
   County of Geauga, Ohio, June 16, 1835. The library of the
   Reorganized Church has a copy of this record.
4. Testimony given in November, 1838, before the judge of the
   5th judicial circuit of the State of Missouri, on the trial of
   Joseph Smith jr., and others, for high treason, and other
   crimes against that state. Published in *Correspondence,
   Orders, etc., in relation to the disturbances with the Mormons. . . .* Fayette, Missouri, 1841. Published separately as
   Senate Document No. 189, 26th Congress, 2nd Session; 1841.

5. Proceedings before Judge Thomas C. Burch in the house of Elisha B. Creekmore, Daviess County, Missouri, April 8, 1839. A copy of this record is in the library of the Reorganized Church.

6. Decision in the case of Joseph Smith before Judge Pope at Springfield, January, 1843. See *Federal Cases,* Vol. XXII, p. 773.

7. *United States Circuit Court (8th Circuit) . . . The Reorganized Church of Jesus Christ of Latter Day Saints, complainant, vs. the Church of Christ at Independence, Missouri . . . Complainant's abstract of pleading and evidence.* Lamoni, Iowa, 1893. This is referred to throughout the book as the *Temple Lot Case.*

III

MANUSCRIPTS

CHASE, DARYL: Sidney Rigdon — Early Mormon. M.A. thesis, University of Chicago, 1931.

COWDERY, OLIVER: Letters to Warren A. Cowdery. (Now in the Huntington Library, San Marino, California.)

GUNN, STANLEY R.: Oliver Cowdery, Second Elder of the Church of Jesus Christ of Latter-day Saints. M.S. thesis, Brigham Young University, 1942.

HUNTINGTON, OLIVER BOARDMAN: Journal. 3 vols.*

JEPSON, JAMES: Memories and Experiences.*

JOHNSON, BENJAMIN F.: Letter to Elder George S. Gibbs, 1903.

Journal History. L.D.S. Church Historian's Office, Salt Lake City. This incorporates the printed *History of the Church* by Joseph Smith, to which are appended unpublished letters, journals, memoirs, minutes of meetings, discourses, and editorial notations.

KARTCHNER, WILLIAM D.: Expedition of the Emmett Company.*

LIGHTNER, MARY ELIZABETH ROLLINS: Autobiography.

Nauvoo Temple Record, 1846.

PANCOAST, EVA L.: The Mormons at Kirtland. M.A. thesis, Western Reserve University, Cleveland, 1929.

PECK, REED: Mormons So Called. This manuscript, dated

* Asterisk indicates a typewritten transcript in the Utah State Historical Society Library.

Quincy, Adams County, Illinois, September 18, 1839, is in my possession. It was purchased from Peck's grand-daughters, Mabel Peck Myer and Hazel Peck Cass, in 1942. It had been published in L. B. Cake: *Old Mormon Manuscript Found: Peepstone Joe Exposed,* New York, 1899.

PULSIPHER, JOHN: Journal, 1835–1874.*

Record of the First Quorum of Elders Belonging to the Church of Christ in Kirtland, Geauga County, Ohio. This is in the library of the Reorganized Church of Jesus Christ of Latter-day Saints.

ROBERTS, BRIGHAM H.: Parallel between Ethan Smith's *View of the Hebrews* and *The Book of Mormon.*

SHURTLIFF, LUMAN ANDROS: Journal.*

SMITH, JOHN LYMAN: Manuscript.*

STEVENSON, EDWARD: Life and History of Elder Edward Stevenson. 1891.

STOUT, ALLEN J.: Journal.*

STOUT, HOSEA: Journal.*

WHITMER, JOHN: History of the Church. The Reorganized Church, which owns this manuscript, published all except the last and most revealing portion, part of chapter xix, chapters xx and xxii, in its *Journal of History,* Vol. I, 1908.

IV

BOOKS AND PAMPHLETS

ADAMS, G. J.: *Plain Facts, shewing the wickedness . . . of the Rev. T. R. Matthews; with a sketch of the Rise, Faith, and Doctrine of the Latter Day Saints.* Bedford, England, 1841.

Affidavits and Certificates Disproving the Statements and Affidavits Contained in John C. Bennett's Letters. Nauvoo, Illinois, August 31, 1842. (Very rare.)

ANDERSON, MARY A.: *Ancestry and Posterity of Joseph Smith and Emma Hale.* Independence, Missouri, 1929.

ARBAUGH, GEORGE B.: *Revelation in Mormonism.* Chicago, 1932.

BENNETT, JOHN C.: *The History of the Saints; or an Exposé of Joe Smith and Mormonism.* Boston, 1842.

BRADEN, CLARK, and KELLY, E. L.: *Public Discussion of the Is-*

sues between the Reorganized Church of Jesus Christ of
Latter-day Saints and the Church of Christ, Disciples, held
in Kirtland, Ohio. St. Louis, 1884.

BOUDINOT, ELIAS: A Star in the West; or a Humble Attempt to
Discover the Long Lost Tribes of Israel. Trenton, 1816.

BROWN, HENRY: History of Illinois. New York, 1844.

BURNETT, PETER H.: Recollections and Opinions of an Old Pioneer. New York, 1880.

CAKE, L. B.: Old Mormon Manuscript Found: Peepstone Joe
Exposed. New York, 1899.

CALL, LAMONI: 2000 Changes in the Book of Mormon. Bounti-
ful, Utah, 1898.

——: Mormon Inspiration. Salt Lake City, 1928.

CAMPBELL, ALEXANDER: Delusions: An Analysis of the Book of
Mormon. New York, 1832. First published in the Millennial Harbinger, Vol. II, February 1831.

CASWALL, HENRY: The City of the Mormons, or Three Days at
Nauvoo, in 1842. London, 1842.

CLARK, JOHN ALONZO: Gleanings by the Way. Philadelphia,
1842.

Correspondence, Orders, etc., in relation to the disturbances
with the Mormons; and the evidence given before the Hon.
Austin A. King, Judge of the Fifth Judicial Circuit of the
State of Missouri, at the Court-house in Richmond, in a
criminal court of inquiry, begun November 12, 1838, on the
trial of Joseph Smith, Jr., and others, for high treason and
other crimes against the state. Published by order of the
General Assembly. Fayette, Missouri, 1841. (Rare.)

CORRILL, JOHN: A Brief History of the Church of the Latter-day
Saints (commonly called Mormons), including an account
of their doctrine and discipline, with the reasons of the
author for leaving the Church. 1839. (Rare.)

COWDERY, OLIVER: Defence in a Rehearsal of My Grounds for
Separating Myself from the Latter Day Saints. Norton,
Ohio: Pressley's Job Office; 1839. Apparently there are no
copies of the original extant. For reprints see Saints Herald, March 20, 1907, and Anti-Mormon Tract No. 9, Ash-
land Independent Publishing Co., 1909.

COWLEY, MATTHIAS F.: Wilford Woodruff; History of his Life
and Labors. Salt Lake City, 1909.

CRARY, CHRISTOPHER G.: *Pioneer and Personal Reminiscences.* Marshalltown, Iowa, 1893.

CROCHERON, AUGUSTA J.: *Representative Women of Deseret.* Salt Lake City, 1883.

DANIELS, WILLIAM M.: *A Correct Account of the Murder of Generals Joseph and Hyrum Smith.* Nauvoo: John Taylor; 1845.

"Death of a Mormon Dictator: Letters of Massachusetts Mormons, 1843–1848," *New England Quarterly,* Vol. IX (1936), pp. 583–617.

DICK, THOMAS: *The Philosophy of a Future State.* 2nd edition. Brookfield, Massachusetts, 1830.

ESSHOM, FRANK: *Pioneers and Prominent Men of Utah.* Salt Lake City, 1913.

FORD, THOMAS: *History of Illinois.* Chicago, 1854.

GOODWIN, S. H.: *Mormonism and Masonry.* Salt Lake City (7th printing), 1938.

——: *Additional Studies in Mormonism and Masonry.* Salt Lake City, 1932.

GREGG, THOMAS: *The Prophet of Palmyra.* New York, 1890.

HALL, WILLIAM: *The Abominations of Mormonism Exposed, containing many facts and doctrines concerning that singular people, during seven years membership with them; from 1840 to 1847.* Cincinnati, 1852.

HARRIS, WILLIAM: *Mormonism Portrayed.* Warsaw, Illinois, 1841.

HOWE, EBER D.: *Mormonism Unvailed, or a faithful account of that singular imposition and delusion, from its rise to the present time.* Painesville, Ohio, 1834. (Rare.) Reprinted in 1840 as *History of the Mormons.*

HYDE, ORSON: *Speech of Elder Orson Hyde delivered before the High Priests at Nauvoo, April 27, 1845.* Liverpool, July, 1845.

JACKSON, JOSEPH H.: *A Narrative of the Adventures and Experiences of Joseph H. Jackson in Nauvoo, Disclosing the Depths of Mormon Villainy.* Warsaw, Illinois, 1844. (Rare.)

JACOB, UDNEY HAY: *An Israelite, and a Shepherd of Israel. An Extract from a Manuscript entitled The Peacemaker, or the Doctrines of the Millennium, being a treatise on religion and jurisprudence, or a new system of religion and politicks.* Nauvoo: J. Smith, Printer; 1842. (Extremely rare.)

JENSON, ANDREW: *Latter-Day Saints Biographical Encyclopædia.* 4 vols. Salt Lake City, 1901.

——: "Plural Marriage," *Historical Record,* Vol. VI, May 1887.

Journal of Discourses, by Brigham Young and others, 1854–86.

KENNEDY, JAMES H.: *Early Days of Mormonism.* New York, 1888.

KIRKHAM, FRANCIS W.: *A New Witness for Christ in America.* Independence, Missouri, 1942.

KNIGHT, NEWEL: "Journal," *Scraps of Biography.* Salt Lake City, 1883.

LANG, WILLIAM: *History of Seneca County, Ohio.* Springfield, 1880.

LEE, E. G.: *The Mormons, or Knavery Exposed.* Philadelphia, 1841. (Rare.)

LEE, JOHN D.: *Mormonism Unveiled; including the remarkable life and confessions of the late Mormon Bishop, John D. Lee, written by himself.* St. Louis, 1877.

LINN, WILLIAM A.: *The Story of the Mormons.* New York, 1902.

LITTLEFIELD, LYMAN O.: *Reminiscences of the Latter Day Saints.* Logan, Utah, 1888.

LIVESEY, RICHARD: *An Exposure of Mormonism.* Wrexham, 1838.

MACGREGOR, DANIEL: *Changing of the Revelations.* Milwaukee, Wisconsin, 1927 [?].

MILLER, GEORGE: Letters to the *Northern Islander,* 1855, reprinted by Wingfield Watson, 1915 (?) in Wisconsin and printed in large part by H. W. Mills in "De Tal Palo Tal Astilla," *Historical Society of Southern California Annual Publications,* 1917.

OLNEY, OLIVER H.: *The Absurdities of Mormonism Portrayed, a brief sketch.* Hancock, Illinois, March 3, 1843. (Rare.)

PADEN, W. M.: *Temple Mormonism, its evolution, ritual and meaning.* New York, 1931.

PATTERSON, ROBERT, JR.: *Who Wrote the Book of Mormon?* (Reprinted from *The Illustrated History of Washington County.* Philadelphia, 1882.)

PRATT, ORSON: *Interesting Account of several remarkable visions and of the late discovery of Ancient American Records.* Edinburgh, 1840.

PRATT, PARLEY PARKER: *Autobiography.* Chicago, 1888.

——: *Mormonism Unveiled.* New York, 1838. (Rare.)

——: *Voice of Warning.* New York, 1837.

Proceedings of the Grand Lodge of Freemasons, Illinois, from its Organization in 1840 to 1850 Inclusive. Freeport, Illinois, 1892.

QUINCY, JOSIAH: *Figures of the Past, from the leaves of old journals.* Boston, 1883.

REMY, JULES: *A Journey to Great-Salt-Lake City.* 2 vols. London, 1861.

RICH, BEN E.: *Scrapbook of Mormon Literature.* 2 vols., Chicago, 190–?

RILEY, I. WOODBRIDGE: *The Founder of Mormonism, a psychological study of Joseph Smith, Jr.* New York, 1902.

ROBERTS, BRIGHAM H.: *A Comprehensive History of the Church of Jesus Christ of Latter Day Saints.* 6 vols. Salt Lake City, 1930.

ROBINSON, EBENEZER: "Items of Personal History of the Editor," *The Return,* Davis City, Iowa, 1889–90.

SHOOK, CHARLES A.: *Cumorah Revisited, or "The Book of Mormon" and the claims of the Mormons re-examined from the viewpoint of American archæology and ethnology.* Cincinnati, 1910.

——: *The True Origin of the Book of Mormon.* Cincinnati, 1914.

——: *The True Origin of Mormon Polygamy.* Cincinnati, 1914.

SMITH, ELIZA R. SNOW: *Biography and Family Record of Lorenzo Snow.* Salt Lake City, 1884.

SMITH, ETHAN: *View of the Hebrews; or the ten tribes of Israel in America.* Poultney, Vermont, 1823; 2nd edition, 1825.

SMITH, JOSEPH, and SMITH, HEMAN C.: *History of the Church of Jesus Christ of Latter Day Saints.* 3 vols. Lamoni, Iowa, 1897–1908.

SMITH, JOSEPH: "Memoirs of President Joseph Smith, 1832–1914," edited by Mary A. Smith Anderson, *Saints Herald,* 1934–5.

SMITH, JOSEPH F., JR.: *Blood Atonement and the Origin of Plural Marriage.* Independence, Missouri, 1905.

SMITH, LUCY MACK: *Biographical Sketches of Joseph Smith the Prophet and His Progenitors for Many Generations.* Liverpool, England, 1853. Brigham Young ordered this edition suppressed. There have been several reprints.

SMITH, MARY ETTIE V.: *Fifteen Years among the Mormons;* edited by Nelson Winch Green. New York, 1857.

SPALDING, REV. F. S.: *Joseph Smith Jr. as a Translator.* Salt Lake City, 1912.

SPAULDING, SOLOMON: *The Manuscript Found or the Manuscript Story of the Late Rev. Solomon Spaulding.* Lamoni, Iowa, 1885.

STENHOUSE, T. B. H.: *The Rocky Mountain Saints.* New York, 1873.

SWARTZELL, WILLIAM: *Mormonism Exposed, being a journal of a residence in Missouri from 28th of May to 20th of August 1838.* Pekin, Ohio, 1840. (Very rare.)

TULLIDGE, EDWARD W., ed.: *The Women of Mormondom.* New York, 1877.

VAN DUSEN, I. McGEE: *The Sublime and Ridiculous Blended; called the Endowment.* New York, 1848.

WEST, WILLIAM: *A Few Interesting Facts Respecting the Rise, Progress and Pretensions of the Mormons.* Warren, Ohio [?], 1837.

WHITMER, DAVID: *An Address to All Believers in Christ.* Richmond, Missouri, 1887.

——: *An Address to Believers in the Book of Mormon.* Richmond, Missouri, 1887.

WHITNEY, ORSON F.: *Life of Heber C. Kimball.* Salt Lake City, 1888.

WINCHESTER, BENJAMIN F.: *The Origin of the Spaulding Story.* Philadelphia, 1840. (Rare.)

WYL, WILHELM: *Mormon Portraits, Joseph Smith the Prophet, His Family and His Friends.* Salt Lake City, 1886.

YOUNG, BRIGHAM: "History of Brigham Young," *Millennial Star,* Vols. XXV-VI, 1863-4, *passim.*

V

MORMON NEWSPAPERS

Evening and Morning Star. Independence, Missouri, and Kirtland, Ohio. June 1832–September 1834. The issues from June 1832 to July 1833 were reprinted in Kirtland in January 1835 with several significant revisions.

Latter-Day Saints Messenger and Advocate. Kirtland, Ohio. October 1834–September 1837.

Northern Times. Kirtland, Ohio. February ?, 1835–October 9?, 1835.

Elders' Journal. Nos. 1 and 2 issued at Kirtland, Ohio, October and November 1837; Nos. 3 and 4 at Far West, Missouri, July and August 1838.

Times and Seasons. Nauvoo, Illinois. Vols. I–VI, July 1839–February 15, 1846.

Latter-day Saints Millennial Star. Liverpool, England. May 1840–present.

Gospel Reflector. Edited by Benjamin Winchester. Philadelphia. January 1–June 15, 1841.

The Wasp. Nauvoo, Illinois. April 16, 1842–April 26, 1843.

Nauvoo Neighbor. Nauvoo, Illinois. May 3, 1843–October 29, 1845.

The Prophet. Edited for a time by William Smith. New York City. May 18, 1844–May 24, 1845.

Nauvoo Expositor. (Apostate). June 7, 1844. One issue only.

Index

Index

[xv